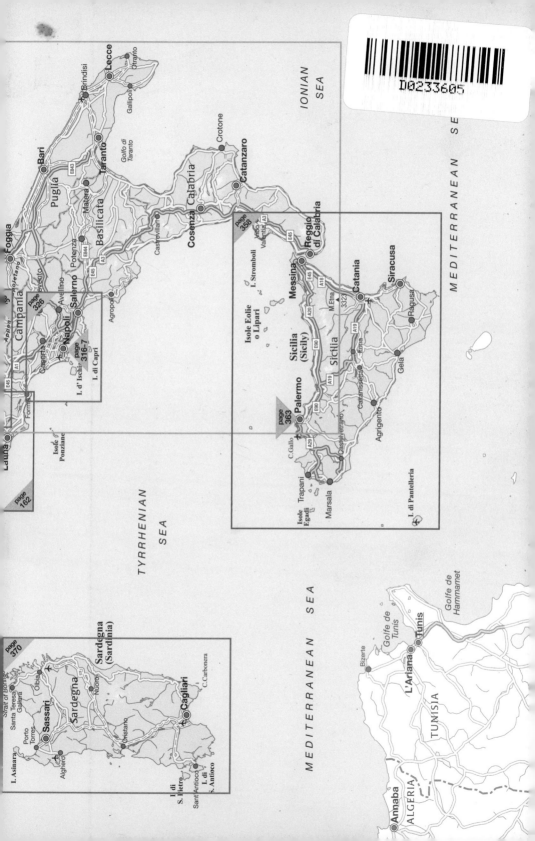

ITALY

000000484147

2

INSIGHT GUIDE
ITALY

Editorial
Project Editor
Siân Lezard
Series Manager
Rachel Lawernce
Publishing Manager
Rachel Fox
Art Director
Steven Lawrence
Senior Picture Researcher
Tom Smyth

Distribution

UK & Ireland
GeoCenter International Ltd
Meridian House, Churchill Way West
Basingstoke, Hampshire RG21 6YR
sales@geocenter.co.uk
United States
Ingram Publisher Services
1 Ingram Boulevard, PO Box 3006
La Vergne, TN 37086-1986
customer.service@ingrampublisher
services.com
Australia
Universal Publishers
PO Box 307
St Leonards NSW 1590
sales@universalpublishers.com.au
New Zealand
Hema Maps New Zealand Ltd (HNZ)
Unit 2, 10 Cryers Road
East Tamaki, Auckland 2013
sales.hema@clear.net.nz
Worldwide
**Apa Publications GmbH & Co.
Verlag KG (Singapore branch)**
7030 Ang Mo Kio Avenue 5
08-65 Northstar @ AMK
Singapore 569880
apasin@signet.com.sg

Printing

CTPS-China

©2011 Apa Publications UK Ltd
All Rights Reserved

First Edition 1985
Sixth Edition 2011

CONTACTING THE EDITORS
We would appreciate it if readers
would alert us to errors or outdated information by writing to:
**Insight Guides, PO Box 7910,
London SE1 1WE, England.
insight@apaguide.co.uk**

ABOUT THIS BOOK

The first Insight Guide pioneered the use of creative full-colour photography in travel guides in 1970. Since then, we have expanded our range to cater for our readers' need not only for reliable information about their chosen des-tination but also for a real under-standing of the culture and workings of that destination. Now, when the internet can supply inexhaustible (but not always reliable) facts, our books marry text and pictures to provide those much more elusive qualities: knowledge and discern-ment. To achieve this, they rely heavily on the authority of locally based writers and photographers.

Insight Guide: Italy is structured to convey an understanding of the country, its regions and its people as well as to guide readers through its attractions:

◆ The **Best of Italy** section at the start of the book gives you a snap-shot of the country's highlights, helping you prioritise what you want to do.
◆ The **Features** section, indicated by a pink bar at the top of each page, is a series of illuminating essays that cover Italy's rich history and contemporary culture; topics fea-tured include the Mafia, cinema, fashion, music and opera and, of course, food and wine.
◆ The main **Places** section, indi-cated by a blue bar, is a complete guide to all the sights and areas worth visiting. Places of special interest are coordinated by number with the maps.
◆ The **Travel Tips** listings section, topped with a yellow bar, provides full information on transport, hotels, restaurants, activities from culture to shopping to hiking and

LEFT: gondolas at sunrise in Venice.

RAI TV in Rome, Lisa is London correspondent to Italian *Vogue* and a contributor to *The Times* and *The Telegraph*. Her partner, previously head of the Italian tourist board, claims he knows the country better than he does.

While researching this book, Lisa was particularly struck by the emergence of unsung regions, such as Emilia Romagna, Liguria and Puglia. But she was equally delighted to find Florence, Rome and Turin enjoying a renaissance, with restored art museums, revamped districts, better restaurants and, in some cases, more eco-friendly transport, from tram tours in Turin to segway and bicycle tours in Florence and Rome.

This current edition builds on the work of other contributors to recent editions. In addition to Lisa Gerard-Sharp, these include all-round Italian experts **Christopher Catling** and **Susie Boulton**, and **Adele Evans**, **Bruce Johnston**, **Fred Mawer** and **Marc Zakian**, as well as wine writers **James Ainsworth** and **Margaret Rand**.

Like all Insight Guides, this book also owes a lot to its photography, and special mention should be made of **John Heseltine**, **Bill Wassman**, **Anna Mockford** and **Nick Bonetti**.

Insight Guide Italy was proofread by **Neil Titman** and indexed by **Helen Peters**.

skiing, an A–Z section of essential practical information, and a handy phrasebook with Italian words and expressions and a menu reader. An easy-to-find contents list for the Travel Tips is printed on the back flap, which also serves as a bookmark.

The contributors

This is the sixth edition of Insight Guide Italy; it was commissioned and edited by **Siân Lezard** at Insight Guides' London office, and builds on the work of former Insight editor **Cathy Muscat**.

Siân enlisted the expertise of Italy specialist and Insight regular **Lisa Gerard-Sharp** who revised and updated the text, including her original features on Contemporary Italy, The Italians, The Italian Look, Design, Venice Carnival, and Rome's Colosseum. Formerly an editor for

Map Legend

▬ ▬ ▬	International Boundary
▬ ▬ ▬	Regional Boundary
▬ ● ▬	National Park/Reserve
▬ ▬ ▬	Ferry Route
⊖	Border Crossing
✈ ✈	Airport: International/Regional
Ⓜ	Metro
🚌	Bus Station
❶	Tourist Information
† ✝	Church/Ruins
†	Monastery
∴	Archaeological Site
🏰	Castle/Ruins
☾	Mosque
✡	Synagogue
∩	Cave
⅃	Statue/Monument
★	Place of Interest
⸙	Beach

The main places of interest in the Places section are coordinated by number with a full-colour map (eg ❶), and a symbol at the top of every right-hand page tells you where to find the map.

Contents

LEFT: flying the flag in Naples.

THE BEST OF ITALY: TOP ATTRACTIONS

From Roman ruins to Renaissance masterpieces, Italy offers scenery of equal magnitude; mountains, volcanic islands, vineyards and beaches – there's something for everyone

△ **Explore the Dolomites:** walk or cycle through Europe's loveliest peaks, now a Unesco World Heritage site. Scenic trails may end at an Alpine inn, ideally with a concert in the meadows. *See page 206.*

◁ **Lap up Lake Como**: arguably Italy's loveliest lake, Como promises gorgeous villas and gardens, charming ports of call, fish dinners – and possible sightings of local resident George Clooney. *See page 228.*

▽ **Relish Ancient Rome:** the majestic ruins of the Colosseum, the Forum and the Palatine Hill speak to us all as potent symbols of the power centre that was Ancient Rome. *See page 127.*

△ **Wallow in Tuscan spas:** whether simple or luxurious, the spas command seductive settings, which provide a pretext for lapping up a landscape of olive groves, vineyards and cypress-clad hills. *See page 286.*

△**Go island-hopping off Sicily:** the Aeolians, seven volcanic specks off Sicily, offer sheer escapism, from barefoot luxury in boutique hotels to a back-to-nature experience. *See page 365.*

◁ **Eat white truffles in Alba:** Italy abounds in foodie feasts, but finely grated truffles transform the simplest dish into a sensation that some Piedmontese say is better than sex. *See page 237.*

△**Explore the Cinque Terre**: ramble your way through a cluster of five fishing villages which cling to the rocky coast. Byron praised this pocket of Liguria as "paradise on earth". *See page 243.*

△ **Relive the Renaissance in Florence:** no other city boasts such a concentration of Renaissance art. But beyond the Uffizi Gallery, the city itself is a Renaissance masterpiece of piazzas and palaces. *See page 261.*

▽ **See Venice from the water:** sweep down the Grand Canal on a number one vaporetto; smooch in a gondola or shun romance for an island ferry – or even a lagoon kayaking adventure. *See page 177.*

△ **Drive the Amalfi Coast:** even without a vintage Alfa Romeo, this is the drive of a lifetime. Vertiginous views await on the winding, cliff-top coastal road linking Positano, Amalfi and Ravello. *See page 329.*

THE BEST OF ITALY: EDITOR'S CHOICE

Unique attractions, festivals and events, piazzas and parks, art and culture... here, at a glance, are our recommendations, plus some tips that even Italians won't always know

BEST LANDSCAPES

● **The Abruzzo** One of Italy's last untamed wilderness, where bears and wolves still roam. *See page 303.*

● **The Maremma** A mixture of marshland, mountains and virgin coast, with trails and riding opportunities in the Parco della Maremma. *See page 283.*

● **Chianti country** and the **Val d'Orcia** The landscape of gentle hills, stately cypresses, vineyards and olive groves is the Tuscany of

postcards. *See page 275 and 290.*

● **Parco Nazionale del Gran Paradiso** An area of outstanding natural beauty, this Alpine park is fabulous trekking country. *See page 238.*

● **Parco Nazionale del Pollino** Italy's largest national park straddles Basilicata and Calabria. *See page 355.*

● **Monti Sibillini** and the **Nera Valley** A wild Umbrian landscape of gorges, mountains and vertiginous views. *See page 297.*

BEST ANCIENT SITES

● **Pompeii and Herculaneum** Remains of two thriving Roman towns set against the backdrop of Vesuvius, their slayer. *See pages 325–7.*

San Vitale, Ravenna Mosaics that are the crowning glory of Byzantine art – started under a Roman emperor, and finished

under the Byzantines. *See page 256.*

Paestum Magnificent standing temples of an ancient Greek settlement. *See page 331.*

● **Selinunte** The scattered remains of a once powerful and rich Greek colony in Sicily. *See page 362.*

● **Valle dei Templi** Classical temples and tombs in Agrigento, Sicily. *See page 362.*

● **Ostia Antica** Once the commercial port of Rome, two-thirds of the excavated Roman town can now be seen. *See page 162.*

TOP: classic Tuscan landscape. **ABOVE:** frecoes at Pompeii. **LEFT:** sheep graze by the remains of a Greek temple at Selinunte, Sicily.

GREATEST PIAZZAS

● **Piazza Navona, Rome**
A Baroque extravaganza of fountains and churches. *See page 146.*

● **Piazza San Marco, Venice** The city's ceremonial stage-set of a square. *See page 174.*

● **Piazza della Signoria, Florence** Outdoor sculpture gallery,

dominated by *David*. *See page 264.*

● **Campo dei Miracoli, Pisa** The aptly named "Field of Miracles" is home to the iconic Leaning Tower of Pisa. *See page 285.*

● **Piazza del Campo, Siena** Fan-shaped medieval square, the stage for a thrilling annual bareback race. *See page 277.*

● **Piazza Pretoria, Palermo** Its centrepiece is a legendary fountain with a sensuous abundance of near-naked nymphs, tritons and gods. *See page 364.*

● **Piazza IV Novembre, Perugia** The hub of Umbria's dynamic capital. *See page 293.*

ABOVE: sculpture of Neptune on Piazza Navona, Rome.
LEFT: Piazza Navona. **BELOW:** views from the island of Capri.

MOST SEDUCTIVE ISLANDS

● **Capri** A capsule of Mediterranean beauty, with legendary status. *See page 327.*

● **Ischia** The volcanic "green island" is renowned for its spas. *See page 328.*

● **Procida** The unique charm of Procida is a magnet to filmmakers. *See page 329.*

● **Giglio** Popular with weekending Romans and day-trippers alike. *See page 282.*

● **Elba** Dramatic scenery and lots of small beaches make this ideal for families. *See page 282.*

● **Sicily** Italy's most enigmatic island is a kaleidoscope of

ancient civilisations. *See page 357.*

Aeolian Islands Seven volcanic islands off Sicily; some offer luxury, others a back-to-nature experience. *See page 365.*

● **Sardinia** For a sun-worshipper's beach holiday. *See page 368.*

GOURMET ITALY

● From an early-morning coffee to an after-dinner grappa, eating and drinking in Italy is always a memorable experience, if not an art form.

● **Emilia Romagna** The culinary region par excellence produces balsamic vinegar from Modena, Parma ham and Parmesan cheese.

● **Pizza in Naples** Birthplace of the authentic thin-crust pizza

cooked in a wood-fired oven.

● **Piedmont** For Barolo wine, rice, gorgonzola, chocolates and white truffles.

● **Tuscany** For wine, olive oil, tagliatelle and Chianina cattle that provide meat for the classic *bistecca alla fiorentina*.

● **Milan** Risotto, osso bucco (stewed veal shank), polenta and salami are all local specialities.

BEST FESTIVALS

● **Il Palio, Siena** A climactic bareback horse race round the Campo.
● **Carnevale, Venice** A 10-day extravaganza of masked balls, pantomime and music.
● **Arena di Verona, Verona** The magnificent open-air summer opera festival in the Roman Arena.
● **Easter, Sicily** Celebrations include "The Mysteries" at Trapani and the "Easter Devils" at Prizzi.
● **Suoni dei Dolomiti, Trentino** The Sounds of the Dolomites is a summer music festival in the peaks.
● **Torre del Lago, Tuscany**, A celebration of Puccini's operas by his lakeside home.
For all festivals, See pages 424–5.

ABOVE: Portovenere on the Ligurian Coast.

COASTAL ITALY

● **Po Delta, Emilia-Romagna** The Italian Camargue, a mosaic of marshes, dunes and mudflats, with cycle tracks along raised banks. *See page 256.*
● **Portofino Promontory, Liguria** This coastal reserve embraces a chic resort, a marine reserve, and pine and olive groves on rugged slopes. *See page 243.*
● **Costa Smeralda, Sardinia** Beautiful emerald waters that draw a moneyed crowd. *See page 368.*
● **Cefalù, Sicily** Clean, picturesque and an ideal family-friendly resort. *See page 365.*
● **The Gargano promontory, Puglia** The most attractive stretch of coastline on Italy's eastern seaboard. *See page 335.*
● **The Calabrian Coast**. Tropea, known as "the Capri of Calabria", is the most picturesque of a string of resorts with some fine beaches. *See page 346.*

GREATEST CATHEDRALS

● **Duomo, Siena** Perched on a hill, Siena's Duomo is a dazzling mix of styles. *See page 277.*
● **Duomo, Milan** This is the most grandiose of Italy's Gothic cathedrals. *See page 211.*
● **Basilica di San Marco, Venice** The onion-domed and mosaic-covered cathedral dominates the square. *See page 174.*
● **Basilica di San Pietro, Rome** Its giant cupola is a Roman landmark. *See page 156.*
● **Duomo, Monreale** Glittering mosaics adorn Sicily's finest cathedral. *See page 363.*
● **Duomo, Orvieto** Hilltop cathedral with a stunning facade. *See page 298.*

LEFT: dramatic rock formation, Capri. **BELOW:** Basilica di San Marco, Venice.

TOP HILL TOWNS

● **Assisi** Birthplace of St Francis, whose life is portrayed in Giotto's frescoes that decorate the great Basilica. *See page 294.*

● **Bergamo** Rising out of the plain of the Po Valley on a steep hill, not far from Milan. *See page 225.*

● **Gubbio** The best preserved of Umbria's many medieval hill towns. *See page 299.*

● **Matera** Hill town in deepest Basilicata, famous for its cave dwellings or Sassi. *See page 351.*

● **Montalcino** and **Montepulciano** Quintessential Tuscan hill towns, both famed for their wines. *See pages 279 and 281.*

● **Ostuni** Whitewashed Puglian town with a distinctly Middle Eastern feel. *See page 340.*

● **Urbino** A remarkably well-preserved Renaissance town set amid spectacular mountains. *See page 300.*

● **San Gimignano** Medieval Manhattan in Tuscany. *See page 284.*

● **San Marino and San Leo** Medieval citadels in Rimini's rugged hinterland. *See page 301.*

● **Santo Stefano** An ancient hamlet in the wilds of Abruzzo, transformed into a model for rural tourism. *See page 307.*

ABOVE: the medieval towers of San Gimignano.

BEST BUYS

● **Murano glass** Exquisite glass made on a Venetian island. *See page 185.*

● **Designer clothes** Milan is the ultimate shopping heaven. *See page 216.*

● **Ceramics** Important centres of majolica production are Faenza, Tuscany and Umbria.

● **Leather goods** From beautiful handmade bags and shoes to the cheap and cheerful.

● **Textiles** Umbria for fine, hand-woven fabrics and lace. Como for luxury silk.

● **Marbled paper** Fine patterned paper made in Florence. *See page 429.*

CULTURAL ITALY

● **Accademia, Florence** Originally the world's first school of art, the gallery is now home to Michelangelo's most famous work, *David. See page 270.*

● **Cenacolo Vinciano, Milan** Make an advance booking to see Leonardo da Vinci's *Last Supper. See page 214.*

● **Uffizi, Florence** Countless rooms and corridors in this palace hold Italy's highest concentration of Renaissance masterpieces. *See page 265.*

● **Capitoline Museums, Rome** A rich collection of ancient sculpture. The Etruscan statue of the she-wolf nursing Romulus and Remus can be seen here. *See page 134.*

● **Guggenheim (Palazzo Venier), Venice** A superb modern art collection representing most major art movements, housed in a palazzo along the Grand Canal. *See page 178.*

● **Vatican Museums, Rome** The glorious Sistine Chapel is the inner sanctum of the papal treasure house. *See page 157.*

● **Archaeological Museum, Naples** Rich repository of Roman and Greek antiquities, including treasures from Pompeii and Herculaneum and the colossal Farnese sculptures. *See page 318.*

● **Santa Giulia Museo della Città, Brescia** Over 3,000 years of history covered in a Benedictine monastery, itself a major monument. *See page 231.*

● **Cinema Museum, Turin** Star-studded museum set in a cavernous former synagogue. *See page 235.*

● **Etruscan Museum, Volterra** Some of the best Etruscan art to be found outside Rome, housed in a papal villa. *See page 284.*

● **Archaeological Museum, Palermo** Great classical finds excavated from all over Sicily and displayed in a late-Renaissance monastery. *See page 365.*

● **Pinacoteca di Brera, Milan** Contained within a handsome 17th-century Jesuit palace, the Pinacoteca di Brera houses one of Italy's finest art collections, with works by Mantegna, Raphael and Piero della Francesca. *See page 213.*

● **Venaria Reale, Turin** Dubbed Italy's Versailles, this sumptuous, superbly restored royal residence was created in 1658 for the Savoy dynasty. *See page 237.*

THE ETERNAL SEDUCTRESS

Italy, with her unrivalled beauty and baffling
contradictions, continues to seduce and enchant
those who are drawn to her

Italy, like the sorceress Circe, tantalisingly beautiful and at the same time treacherous, has attracted kings, scholars, saints, poets and curious travellers for centuries. This is the spell of the "Eternal Seductress".

Italy has always seemed somewhat removed from the rest of Europe: physically by mountains and sea, spiritually by virtue of the Pope. In the eyes of outsiders, the Italians themselves are characterised by extremes: at one end of the spectrum, the gentle unworldliness of St Francis, and, at the other, the amoral brilliance of Machiavelli; on the one hand, the curiosity of Galileo or the genius of Michelangelo, on the other, the repressive dogmatism of Counter-Reformation Jesuits.

This book explores the land and its people, from Calabrian villagers to Milanese sophisticates, and delves into their treasures, from Etruscan statues to Botticelli's radiant *Birth of Venus*. Special features celebrate Italian passions – films, fashion, opera and food – while the history section threads its way through a tumultuous past, from the legendary founding of Rome by Romulus and Remus to the Renaissance, reunification, Mussolini and the Mafia.

In Italy the past is always present: ultra-modern museums display pre-Roman artefacts; old people in tiny mountain villages preserve customs which are centuries old while their grandchildren roar into the future on shiny new Vespas.

This is the country that inspires imagination in the dull, passion in the cold-hearted, rebellion in the conventional. Whether you spend your sojourn in Italy under a brightly coloured beach umbrella on the Riviera, shopping in Milan or diligently examining churches and museums, you cannot be unchanged by Italy. At the very least, you will receive a highly pleasurable lesson in living. Whether you are struck by the beauty of a church facade rising from a perfectly proportioned piazza, the aroma of freshly carved *prosciutto*, or the sight of a stylish passer-by, there is the same superb sensation: nowhere else on earth does just living seem so extraordinary. ❏

PRECEDING PAGES: the town of Limone on the banks of Lake Garda, Italian Lakes; Giuseppe Momo's helicoidal staircase, Vatican Museum, Rome; sailing in Sardinia. **LEFT:** St Mark's Basilica in Venice. **ABOVE:** sculpture on the Fontana di Nettuno, Piazza Navona, Rome; getting around on a Vespa, Rome.

WILD PLACES

Italy is more than a glorified art museum.
Exploring its diverse landscapes can be
as rewarding as the Renaissance art

Italy is full of Leonardo da Vinci landscapes and Piero della Francesca views. The secret is to choose an area that is off the beaten track, but well mapped, well marked and not too remote. If this sounds obvious, bear in mind that Italian maps are notoriously unreliable outside the most popular walking areas, meaning the Dolomites, Lombardy and parts of Tuscany and Umbria, with the south uncharted. The majority of Italy is mapped with old Military Institute maps, designed for aligning an artillery bombardment rather than lining up a pretty view. If footpaths are marked, there is no indication as to whether they are private or public. With this in mind, companies that organise walking holidays tend to produce their own maps or take their own guides.

On the upside, there is little risk of being outnumbered by Italians on most trails. Curiously, as far as independent walking is concerned, serious hikers are better served than "Sunday walkers":

> The locals generally only see walking as an adjunct to eating, with family expeditions focused on finding the best funghi porcini rather than the best view. The countryside is a larder rather than a living landscape.

long-distance trails in the Dolomites are generally better marked and mapped than meanders around Tuscany's hilltop hamlets. By the same token, Italian hikers, where they exist, tend to be found in "sporty" regions, especially in the north.

LEFT: olive trees dot the Tuscan landscape.
RIGHT: Lago Toblino in the Italian Lakes.

The rest can be found following the local *strada dei sapori*, the food and wine trail – by car.

Charting the country

Before heading for the hills, lakes or coastal marshes, get to grips with the geography. The boot-shaped Italian peninsula spans 1,000km (620 miles) from the Alps to the Mediterranean and is bordered by the Ligurian and Tyrrhenian seas to the west, the Ionian to the south and the Adriatic to the east. If the Alps represent the top of the boot, the jagged seam is formed by the Apennines, while the toe, heel and spur are represented by the Calabrian, Salento and Gargano peninsulas. Much of Italy is covered by peaks, notably the Dolomites, which form part of the Alps, the country's northern boundary. These Alpine borders are shared with France, Austria, Switzerland and Slovenia, with Mont Blanc (4,810 metres/15,780ft) marking the highest point in Italy. The Dolomites are the defining feature of Italy's Tyrolean Trentino-Alto Adige region, and neighbouring Veneto, with the peaks forming part of the world's largest integrated ski network, the Dolomiti Superski. Instead, the Apennines, the spine of Italy, stretch from north to south, dividing the east and west coasts, and bring a rugged climate to part of central Italy.

For lovers of seductive scenery, Italy dazzles: the north's national parks, true Alpine wilderness areas, give way to Piedmont's undulating farmland and patchwork of wine estates. The glittering lake district, framed by the jagged pinkish peaks of the Dolomites, creates the illusion of the Mediterranean meeting the mountains. Emilia's mundane farmland, coastal wetland and mountains lose out to Tuscany's Chiantishire, a gentle vision of olive groves, cypresses, vineyards and Medicean villa gardens. The rolling slopes are planted with olive groves that shimmer dark green and dusty silver. Domesticated Tuscany melds with the hazy

THE SAN REMO COASTAL TRAIL

A spectacular new cycle-pedestrian path hugs the picturesque Ligurian Coast close to the French Riviera. The first 24km (17-mile) stretch, from Ospedaletti via San Remo to San Lorenzo al Mare, offers an exhilarating Riviera route. Divided into five sections, the coastal path follows a disued railway line and wends its way through former fishing villages. The path provides access to previously unreachable beaches and a marine park, which acts as a whale sanctuary. With the Mediterranean on one side and the Alps on the other, the cycle path is one of the loveliest in Europe, and the first on the Italian coast (www.area24spa.it).

spirituality of Umbria's green hills, the serenity only frayed at the edges by wild stretches of the Apennines where wolves still roam.

Further south, Campania's natural wonders are as wild as Italy gets, from a smouldering volcano to belching, sulphurous springs and eerie lakes that myths refer to as the gateway to Hades.

The north

The Valle d'Aosta, concertinaed against the French border, is a patchwork of towering peaks and valleys in the northwestern corridor. Abutting it, Piedmont's craggy peaks loom over the region, which mellows into fertile foothills and feasts of truffles, nuts, fruit and powerful Barolo and Barbaresco wines. South of Turin, the Po Valley rises into the rolling Langhe and Roero hills, creating a carpet of vineyards and orchards. Further north lies metropolitan Milan, the gateway to Lombardy's lake district, watched over by the peaks and Alpine resorts beyond. Close to Lake Iseo, Franciacorta represents a chequerboard of prestigious vineyards while, to the south, Lombardy's fertile farmland comes into its own.

Bounded by Lombardy and the Veneto, Trentino-Alto Adige is serrated by soaring mountain ranges. The towering peaks of the Alps and the Dolomites preside over forested wilderness, Alpine pastures, meadows carpeted with wild

region, which is noted for sparkling Prosecco, Valpolicella and Merlot. The bucolic Brenta Canal winds languidly through the noble countryside, with Palladian villas lining the banks.

Framed by the Alps, and stretching from Piedmont across northern Lombardy to the

> *Italy's easternmost region, Friuli-Venezia Giulia, is a sliver of coastline across the Adriatic Sea from Venice. Were it not for the border-juggling that followed World War I, the region would probably be part of Slovenia today.*

flowers, vineyards in the foothills and orchards in the valleys. Alto Adige, the northernmost province, is Italy's South Tyrol, which belonged to Austria until the end of World War I. The area still resembles the Austrian Tyrol, while Trentino, the southern province, prides itself on looking more Italian.

East of Trentino, the Veneto stretches up into the apricot-tinged Dolomites and Cortina d'Ampezzo, the country's premier ski resort, but is bordered by the Adriatic to the east, Lake Garda to the west and the River Po to the south. Orchards, river valleys and vineyards dot the

LEFT: Odle Mountains and Val di Funes, South Tyrol.
ABOVE: Riva del Garda on Lake Garda.

Veneto, the lake district offers stunning scenery. West of Bergamo, the most appealing lakes are Como, Maggiore and Orta, matched by Iseo and Garda to the east. In terms of scenery, cognoscenti consider Como the most beguiling lake, Maggiore the most stately and Orta the most mystical. With its snow-clad peaks, romantic scenery and sluggish steamers, Como still stirs visitors, while on the Borromean Islands, Lake Maggiore boasts the grandest gardens. Pocket-sized Iseo possesses the biggest lake island in Europe but is Alpine in character, with olives and horse chestnuts rather than lemon groves and palm trees. Lake Garda remains a Mediterranean hothouse in northern climes. The old charm lingers on in the avenues lined by palms, oleanders and camellias, as well as in the profusion of lemon groves, vineyards and Italy's most northerly olive groves.

Protected by the Alps and perched on a crescent-shaped sliver of coast, Ligurian resorts enjoy balmy weather, with the Riviera di Levante, east of Genoa, the rockier, wilder stretch, especially around Le Cinque Terre.

The centre

Just east, Emilia-Romagna embraces the Po Valley, from coastal marshes to vineyards, as well as farmland dedicated to the production of Parmesan cheese and Parma ham. Its neighbour,

dernesses, Lazio is less homogeneous, from the Apennine peaks in the north to marshland in the south, via volcanic lakes, vineyards and misty, undulating hills reminiscent of Umbria, which it borders.

> *Italy's wildlife has been decimated by hunting, but this trend is being fought fiercely in Abruzzo. In the Parco d'Abruzzo bears have been successfully reintroduced, as have chamois in Gran Sasso, while wolves are protected in the Majella park.*

Tuscany, has been landscaped since time immemorial, with the Val d'Orcia, south of Siena, representing quintessential Tuscany: clusters of cypresses, ribbons of plane trees, vineyards on the slopes, farms perched on limestone ridges. Towards the Emilian border, Tuscany becomes more rugged, dramatised by deep forests, Michelangelo's marble quarries and the Apuan Alps around Garfagnana.

Umbria, "the green heart of Italy" (and the only landlocked region of the Italian peninsula) lives up to its name in densely forested slopes, misty valleys, tufa-stone outcrops and its sense of remoteness.

Compared with the brooding, dramatic landscape of Abruzzo, one of Italy's last wil-

The south

In Campania, south of Rome, the crescent-shaped Bay of Naples contains unspoilt Capri and volcanic Ischia, two of Italy's loveliest islands. On the Amalfi Coast, buildings are cantilevered above rock-studded cliffs and overlook the country's most romantic coastal drive. Campania's Cilento national park is a patchwork of wheatfields and olive groves, though wolves and wild cats survive in remote corners.

Further east, Puglia, the "heel" of the Italian boot, is the gateway to Greece, and is washed by both the Ionian and Adriatic Seas. Puglia produces more wine and olive oil than any other region yet is also a riot of carob trees and rosemary, with marine grottoes and turquoise seas framed by sun-bleached beaches and wind-twisted pines.

Forming the toe of the Italian peninsula, sparsely populated Calabria is crushed between the mountains and the sea, and significant for the Pollino park, the richest repository of wildlife in the south, all in a wilderness setting ranging from canyons to rivers, high plains to soaring peaks.

Just over the Straits awaits Sicily, as mountainous as it is mysterious. Partly thanks to its volcanic soil, the island is a major wine producer, including around Mount Etna.

The Mount Etna volcanic park presents myriad safe and accessible options for exploring this most haunting of sites. Volcanic activity is the earth's indigestion, with deep rumblings producing sudden eruptions, emitting sulphurous gases and scalding vapours through cracks in the earth's surface. Further along the Tyrrhenian Coast, the compact Zingaro reserve, west of Palermo, is a gentle introduction to Sicily's charms.

Hitting the trail

Foremost among Italy's long-distance trails is the Via Alpina, which links Trieste and the Adriatic to the Mediterranean. This great transalpine trail crosses eight countries but, in the Italian Dolomites, touches upon Europe's shared Alpine heritage. It runs through the legendary landscape of the Fassa Dolomites, linked to the Ladin people, who speak an archaic version of Latin. Beyond is the land of Oetzi the Iceman, taking us back to prehistoric times, a reminder that this path traces a common Alpine heritage. Just north of Canazei, the trail crosses Passo Pordoi, the majestic Alpine pass that marks Trentino's borders with the Veneto, revealing vestiges of World War I fortifications and views over the Sella group. Rewards come in the form of rosy-hued sunsets, the striking Marmolada glacier and the lunar landscape of the Catinaccio group. Fortunately, this Alpine area is blessed with exceptional lodges and cable-car networks – the answer to your prayers when your bed is at the top of the next peak.

In Liguria, the best-known trails lie in the rugged Cinque Terre, the Unesco-protected stretch of coast that encompasses olive-growing terraces and quaint fishing villages. The "Blue Trail" (Sentiero Azzurro) clings to the coast for 13km (8 miles) from Riomaggiore to Monterosso. Its popularity means that it is best not undertaken in the height of the summer.

Further down the coast, in Tuscany, the drained marshes of the Maremma include an unspoilt coastal park with deep Etruscan roots, and white cattle watched over by the *butteri*, Tuscan cowboys. Umbria's Sibillini park, which marks the watershed between the Adriatic and the Tyrrhenian, is home to wild boar, wolves and peregrine falcons, though botanists are keener on the orchids and Alpine anemone. Both parks have waymarked trails.

LEFT: Umbrian shepherd and his flock.
RIGHT: hiking in the Dolomites.

On the Adriatic Coast, the Po Delta coastal wetlands, studded with nature reserves and abbeys, form a Unesco heritage site and one of the wildest areas in central Italy. This mosaic of marshes, dunes, mudflats and islands is dubbed the Italian Camargue: sturdy white ponies share the marshes with migratory birds and waterfowl. Birdlife abounds on the mudflats, from cormorants, coots and reed warblers to white egrets and purple herons. Scenic trails crisscross the park between Ferrara and Comacchio, from locks and flood plains to the raised canal banks which serve as cycle trails. The salt pans are flanked by windmills, a reminder of the time

age route, the wilder parts of the peninsula have a timeless quality, from the pine groves to the coastline of cliffs, rocks and caves.

In the south, the best trail is the Sentiero Italia, which begins in Montalto, in Calabria's Parco dell'Aspromonte, and runs along the

> In terms of gentle walks though coastal scenery, chic Capri is, paradoxically, one of the wildest trails, embracing macchia mediterranea shrubland, as well as ocean views, glimpsed through exotic agave and bougainvillea.

before pumpkins, peaches and strawberries took over. Since this is farming and wine-growing country, walkers will spot asparagus beds, rice paddies, hemp-growing and even vineyards.

The peaks, forests and lakes of the Parco d'Abruzzo, dominated by the Apennines and laced with trails, are home to 40 species of mammal and 300 types of bird, from Apennine wolves to golden eagles.

Further south, in Puglia's Gargano promontory, the northern salt lakes provide a haven for wildfowl. The Gargano – a thickly wooded peninsula that juts out into the Adriatic to form the spur of Italy's boot – was an island until river sediment formed a "bridge" linking it to the mainland. Reached via an old pilgrim-

spine of the Apennines until Umbria and even as far as Trieste.

Volcano-watching

Italy's volcanic parks make fascinating places to explore, from the eerie lunar landscape of Etna to the mud baths on the gorgeous Aeolian archipelago. Although Vulcano is set in one of the most beautiful archipelagos in the Mediterranean, visitors are assailed by a sulphurous, rotten-egg stench. Ignoring the limpid seas, bathers squat in a stinking mud hole and smear foul-smelling gloop over their bodies. This yel-

ABOVE: the impossibly blue Tyrrhenian Sea.
RIGHT: steaming Mount Etna.

low volcanic soup and foul-smelling mud are common to many volcanic areas. As for Naples, Vesuvius may be an active volcano, but you can still visit the rim of the crater's mouth and gaze down into its smoldering core. The approach is dramatic, passing vineyards that produce the amber-hued Lacrimae Christi (Tears of Christ), a wine favoured by the ancient Etruscans. The puce-tinged summit induces a feeling of fore-boding, but when gazing into the volcano's core, spare a thought for Spartacus, who, a century before the eruption that buried Pompeii, hid in the hollow of the crater, which was then covered with vines.

Set off the north coast of Sicily, the seven Aeolian Islands have a stark volcanic allure and a striking natural beauty. The archipelago's appeal lies in the marine life and underwater lava formations, as well as sulphurous Vulcano and Stromboli, "the lighthouse of the Mediter-ranean", which glows incandescently at night and shoots fireballs. Locals refer to Stromboli as "Iddu, a good friend with a volcanic temper; he sleeps just like us, he lives just like us." Iddu's intoxicating explosions have occurred every 15 minutes for the past 2,500 years.

• For more information on walking, hiking and cycling through Italy, see page 426. ❑

TOP HIKING TRAILS AND BIKE RIDES

The Giro d'Italia, Italy's version of the Tour de France, is proof of the country's passion for cycling. This now translates into thrilling new trails and cyclist-friendly schemes, particularly in the Dolomites, which abound in hotels and holidays designed with cyclists in mind. In central Italy, Emilia-Romagna is blazing a trail with cycle routes between "cities of art", such as Ravenna and Faenza. It is also home to Italy's most cycle-mad cities, Ferrara and Modena, and offers easily downloadable routes (www.cycle-r.it). The south is less well-served, but is developing the long-distance Bourbon Cycle Route, linking Bari and Naples via Matera.

Liguria is superb cycling country but also has hiking trails of the stature of the Cinque Terre paths *(see page 25).*

The celebrated Poets' Trail, in the footsteps of Byron and Shelley, runs from Porto Venere to Lerici, through vineyards and olive groves, overlooking coastal cliffs and islands. Neighbouring Tuscany, Emilia and Umbria offer some of the country's most beguiling hikes, ranging from the Via Fran-cigena pilgrimage route to foodie rambles between medi-eval abbeys and homely inns. Further south, Puglia is emerging as a seductive cycling and hiking destination, embracing whitewashed villages, Adriatic seascapes and stays in the conical "beehive" homes known as *trulli.* Whether opting for a guided or self-guided break, for peace of mind and sheer choice, book through a specialist oper-ator, such as Headwater or Inntravel.

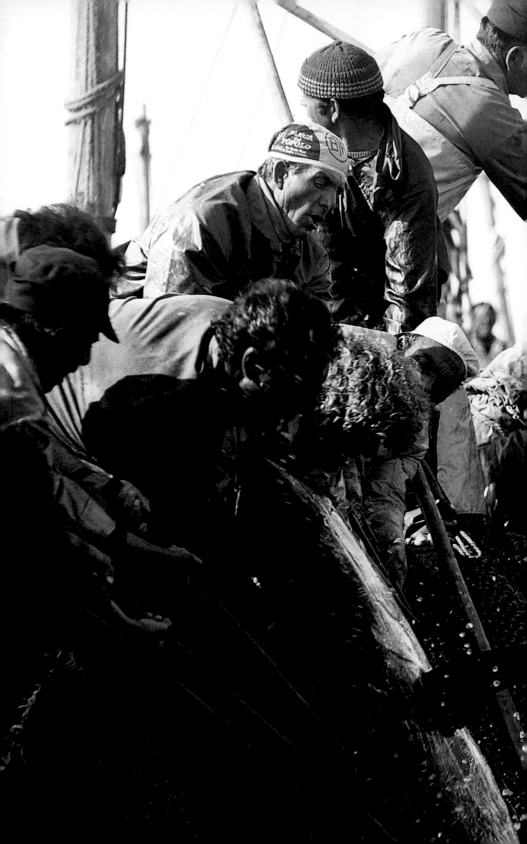

DECISIVE DATES

ORIGINS TO THE ROMAN EMPIRE

2000–1200 BC
Tribes from Central Europe and Asia, the Villanovans, settle in northern Italy.

c.800 BC
Etruscans arrive in Italy.

753 BC
Legendary date of Rome's founding.

750 BC
Greeks start to colonise southern Italy.

509 BC
Rome becomes a republic.

390 BC
Gauls sack Rome, but are expelled.

343–264 BC
Rome gains ascendancy in Italy.

264–146 BC
Punic Wars; Rome extends conquests abroad.

58–48 BC
Caesar conquers Gaul, crosses the Rubicon, made dictator but assassinated in 44 BC.

AD 96–180
Pax Romana, golden century of peace; apogee of empire.

303
Persecution of Christians under Diocletian.

306–337
Constantine makes Christianity the state religion and Constantinople the capital.

393
The empire is divided into Eastern and Western halves.

410
Invasions, notably the sack of Rome by Alaric the Goth.

476
End of the Western Roman Empire.

MEDIEVAL ITALY

535–53
Justinian brings all Italy within rule of Eastern emperor.

568
Lombards overrun much of Italy; peninsula divided into Lombard state ruled from Pavia and Byzantine province at Ravenna.

800
Charlemagne crowned Holy Roman Emperor and founds Carolingian Empire.

827
Saracens capture Sicily.

9th century
Carolingian Empire disbands, leaving behind rival Italian states.

11th century
Normans colonise Sicily and southern Italy.

1076
Pope Gregory VII and Emperor Henry IV become embroiled in a power struggle that marks the start of a 200-year conflict.

1155
Guelphs, supporting the Pope, clash with the Ghibellines, who follow the emperor.

1167
Lombard League of cities formed to oppose the emperor.

1227–50
The papacy is the victor.

LATE MIDDLE AGES AND RENAISSANCE

1265
Charles of Anjou becomes King of Sicily.

1302
Anjou dynasty established in Naples.

1309–77
Papacy established at Avignon then returns to Rome.

1442
Alfonso V, King of Aragon, is crowned King of the "Two Sicilies"(Naples and Sicily).

1469–92
Lorenzo de' Medici leads Florence; apogee of Renaissance.

1495
Wars of Italy begin when French King Charles VII invades; Medici driven from Florence.

CENTURIES OF FOREIGN DESPOTISM
1503–13
Julius II is pope; Rome is centre of the Renaissance.

1525
Battle of Pavia. Spain captures French king.

1527
Rome sacked by Charles V's imperial troops; Venice is the centre of artistic activity.

1559
Treaty confirms Spanish control of Italy.

1700–13
Austria becomes main foreign power on peninsula.

1796–1814
Napoleon invades Italy and founds several republics.

.
1814
Overthrow of French rule.

TOWARDS ITALIAN UNITY
1815
Congress of Vienna; Venice given to Austria.

PRECEDING PAGES: tuna fishing, Trapani, Sicily. FAR LEFT: Francesco Petrarch. LEFT: equestrian statue of Charlemagne, c.860–70. ABOVE: Garibaldi at Caprera by Vincenzo Cabianca.

1848
Uprisings against Austria led by Charles Albert of Savoy.

1852
Cavour is made prime minister of Piedmont.

1859–60
With the help of France, Savoy annexes most of northern Italy. Garibaldi's "Thousand" conquer Sicily and Naples.

1861
Victor Emmanuel II of Savoy proclaimed King of Italy.

1870
Unification completed; Rome becomes capital.

MODERN ITALY
1882
Triple Alliance agreed between Italy, Germany and Austria.

1915
Italy joins Allies in World War I.

1919
Rise of Fascism.

1940
Italy joins Nazis in World War II.

1943
Allies land in Sicily. Mussolini deposed, rescued by Germans to found puppet government.

1944
Liberation of Rome; abdication of King Victor Emmanuel III.

1946
Italy declared a republic.

1957
Treaty of Rome: Italy joins the Common Market.

1950s–60s
Italy's "economic miracle".

1966
Floods in Venice and Florence.

1978
Period of political instability.

1980
Earthquake strikes Campania.

1990s
Rise of the Northern League and corruption scandals.

2000
Millions flock to Rome for Holy Year.

2001
Silvio Berlusconi elected prime minister.

2005
Pope John Paul II dies and is succeeded by Benedict XVI.

2009
Earthquake strikes L'Aquila.

2010
Pompeii's House of the Gladiators collapses. State neglect is blamed.

2011
Colosseum to be restored with private funds. The discredited Berlusconi government teeters on through corruption scandals and economic austerity.

BEGINNINGS

Many primitive tribes settled in Italy, but under the Greeks and the Etruscans it became the centre of the ancient world

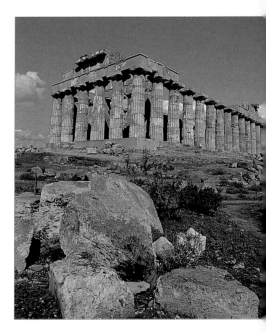

As schoolchildren often observe, Italy looks like a boot. The long, narrow peninsula sticking out of Europe's underbelly is perpetually poised to kick Sicily westward. This peculiar shape made Italy a natural site for settlement. The Alps, which cut across the only land link with the rest of Europe, protected the peninsula from the barbarians who roamed northern Europe, while the Mediterranean, which surrounds the three remaining sides, served as a highway, first to bring civilisation to the peninsula and later to export it.

The Apennine range, the so-called backbone of Italy, dominates the peninsula. These mountains zigzag down from the French Alps and Ligurian Coast in the northwest, through northern Tuscany and southeast to the Adriatic Coast, and veer west again to the Straits of Messina, between Sicily and the toe of the boot. In the central Abruzzo region, the peaks of the Gran Sasso soar as high as 2,912 metres (9,700ft).

It is no coincidence that the early inhabitants of Italy flourished in the west, on the lowland plains north and south of Rome. Here there are a few natural harbours and long rivers.

The Tiber, Arno, Livi and Volturno are easily navigated by small craft, and their valleys provide easy communication between the coast and the interior. What is more, the plains of Tuscany, Latium and Campania comprise fertile farmland, thanks to rich deposits of volcanic ash.

LEFT: an Etruscan statue of Apollo.
RIGHT: Greek temple at Selinunte in Sicily.

Villanovan civilisation

Around 200,000 years before the founding of Rome, only cave-dwelling hunter-gatherers lived on the Italian peninsula. However, with the Indo-European migrations (2000–1200 BC), tribes of primitive peoples poured into Italy from Central Europe and Asia. The Villanovan tribes were farmers who lived in round huts clustered in small villages in central Italy. These Italic, Iron Age settlers worked tools and cremated their dead, placing the ashes in tall, clay or bronze urns.

Villanovan culture spread from its original centre around Bologna south to Tuscany and Latium. Nowhere, however, did settlements grow to the size of towns, and Villanovans are not known for any great artistic achievements.

The Greeks and the Etruscans established communities on the peninsula in the early 8th century BC. Greek colonists settled in Sicily and on the west coast near modern-day Naples. Most

> *The transformation of Italy from a primitive backwater to the centre of the ancient world was due to the Greeks and the Etruscans. Both sailed across the sea in search of rich new land and sowed the first seeds of civilisation.*

farming the land around their cities, and trading with mainland Greece.

During the 5th century, both Syracuse and Athens tried to establish rival empires out of the Greek colonies in Italy. Numerous battles were fought and many Italian natives were drafted as soldiers. But after years of inconclusive fighting the Greek leaders gave up the struggle.

The colonists still argued among themselves, and therefore failed to become a dominant political power in Italy. They did, however, become the major cultural and artistic force. Italian natives were eager to trade for Greek luxury goods, the like of which they had never

came in search of land to farm, for Greece had insufficient arable land to feed its entire population. Others were political refugees: whenever a Greek king was overthrown, all his followers were forced to flee.

On arriving in Italy, Greek settlers formed independent cities, each loosely linked to their city of origin on the Greek mainland. One of the earliest colonies was at Cumae, by the Bay of Naples. Greeks from Euboea, an island northeast of Athens, settled there in about 770 BC. Other Euboeans founded Rhegion (modern Reggio di Calabria), at the tip of the boot, a few years later. The Corinthian city of Syracuse on Sicily ultimately became the most powerful of the Greek colonies. The colonists prospered,

seen. Soon Greek bronze and ceramic ware became widely available in Italy and provided the natives with sophisticated new art forms to imitate; the architecture and sculpture in the Greek cities also served as models. The civilising influence of the Greeks went beyond the visual arts. The natives adapted the Greek alphabet for their own Indo-European tongues and each native group soon had its own letters. Through example, the Greeks also taught the Italian natives about modern warfare, lessons

ABOVE: an ancient Greek dives gracefully into the unknown in a fresco from a tomb at Paestum.
RIGHT: remains of an Etruscan necropolis in Sutri, Lazio.

that they later used against their Greek teachers. The Italians learnt how to fortify towns with high walls of smooth masonry, and discovered the value of shock-troop tactics with armoured spearmen.

But exceptional wealth and knowledge did not enable the Greeks to control Italy, and failure to unify the natives under Greek leadership left great political opportunities wide open.

In about 800 BC, Etruscans settled on the west coast where Tuscany (Etruria) and Lazio are today. The origins of the Etruscans still puzzle scholars. The Greek historian Herodotus claimed that they came from Asia Minor, driven by revolution and famine at home to seek new lands. More recent research, backed by DNA analysis on Etruscan bones, suggests Middle Eastern origins. But wherever the migrants came from, it was the intermingling with the Italic tribes that created the uniquely Etruscan civilisation.

Vital trade routes

Each Etruscan city supported itself by trade. Eager to obtain luxury goods from the Greek colonists, the Etruscans developed overland routes to reach the Greek cities. These cut straight through Latium, the plain south of the

THE ETRUSCANS

The Etruscans were skilled craftsmen, metal workers, seafarers and merchants who traded with the Greeks and later the Romans, who assimilated them. Etruria, the Etruscan civilisation, flourished as a confederation of 12 city-states, tribes which gathered together to celebrate sacred rites. Divination, human and animal sacrifice were used to stave off divine retribution. Spirituality was balanced by a hearty appetite for life. Hundreds of Etruscan tombs have survived, with wall paintings depicting dancing, banquets, music-making, battle and hunting scenes. The Etruscans exerted a dynamic influence on Roman art and were praised as "founders of cities".

Tiber occupied by Italian natives called Latins.

One of their trading posts on the route south was a Latin village called Rome, originally only a cluster of mud huts. Under the influence of the Etruscans, the settlement flourished. They drained the swamp that became the Roman Forum and built grand palaces and roads.

For 300 years from the late 8th century BC, Etruscan kings ruled Rome. But, by the 5th century BC, their power was fading. In the north, Gauls overran Etruscan settlements in the Po Valley. Next, Italic tribesmen from Abruzzo threatened the main Etruscan cities. Then, in the south, the Etruscans went to war against the Greeks. The Romans chose this moment to rebel against their Etruscan masters. ❑

ROME RULES THE WORLD

Between its legendary founding by Romulus and its sacking by barbarians, Rome presided over one of our greatest civilisations

The historians of Ancient Rome wrote their own version of events leading to the overthrow of the Etruscan kings. They drew upon legends of Rome's past and claimed that the city had only temporarily fallen under Etruscan rule. According to legend, Rome was founded by the descendants of gods and heroes.

In his epic, the *Aeneid*, Virgil tells how Aeneas, a hero of Homeric Troy, journeyed west after the sack of Troy to live and rule in Latium. In the 8th century one of his descendants, the Latin princess Rhea Silvia, bore twin sons, Romulus and Remus, fathered by the god Mars. Her uncle, King Amulius, angry because the princess had broken her vow of chastity as a Vestal Virgin, locked her up and abandoned the boys on the riverbank to die. They were found there by a she-wolf which raised them. As young men, the brothers led a band of rebel Latin youths to find a new home. As they approached the hills of Rome, a flight of eagles passed overhead – a sign from the gods that this was an auspicious site for their new city.

Rape and revolt

Rome was ruled by Etruscan kings until 509 BC when the son of King Tarquinius Superbus raped a Roman noblewoman, Lucretia. She killed herself in shame and Roman noblemen rose in revolt against the Etruscans.

The leader of the Roman revolt, Lucius Junius Brutus, may have been an actual historical figure. In Roman legend he is the founder of

a republic, a vigorous leader, and a puritanical ruler. The historian Tacitus wrote that he was so loyal to Rome that he watched without flinching as his two sons were executed for treason.

In the war against the Etruscans, Rome was also aided by Cincinnatus, a simple Roman farmer who left his plough to help his city. He was so able that he rose quickly to the rank of general. But once the fight was won, he surrendered his position of power and returned to his life as an ordinary citizen.

These stories of Rome's early heroes reveal a lot about the Roman character. For the Romans, *pietas* – dutiful respect to one's gods, city, parents and comrades – was all-important. Because

LEFT: the *Augustus of Prima Porta* shows a youthful emperor looking to Rome's future of *imperium sine fine* (rule without end). **RIGHT:** Hannibal's Carthaginian forces cross the Alps during the Second Punic War.

of this, the heroes of legend were very useful propaganda tools within the empire.

Upon the overthrow of the Etruscans, Rome's leaders founded a republic based on the Greek model, and the Senate took control of the city.

Roman conquests

During the next 200 years Rome conquered most of the Italian peninsula. But Carthage, a city in North Africa founded by the Phoenicians, controlled the western Mediterranean. If Rome was to expand, Carthage had to be defeated.

The initial clash between the two cities, the First Punic War (264 BC), began as a struggle for

the Greek city of Messina on Sicily. By the time it was over, in 241 BC, the Romans had driven the Carthaginians out of Sicily completely. The island became Rome's first province. Three years later Rome annexed Sardinia and Corsica, and further military triumphs followed. When Rome conquered Cisalpine Gaul (northern Italy) and extended its borders to the Alps, it alleviated the threat of invasion by the Gauls.

War broke out again in 218 BC when the brilliant Carthaginian general Hannibal embarked on an ambitious plan to attack Rome from the north via Spain, the Pyrenees and the Alps. Rome eventually counterattacked Carthage, and Hannibal was forced to return and defend his homeland. He was defeated in 202 BC.

Final defeat of Carthage

The Third Punic War was almost an afterthought. Carthage, stripped of many of its possessions 50 years earlier, had regained its commercial power. When the Carthaginians challenged Rome indirectly, the Romans razed the city of Carthage and ploughed salt into the soil. The Carthaginians were sold into slavery.

Rome was now more prosperous than ever before, but only the middle class and the rich benefited. For the common people, many of whom had served their city faithfully during the wars, peace meant greater poverty as the menial jobs on which they had depended were now filled by slaves. Independent farmers, who traditionally formed the backbone of the Roman state, sold their land to the owners of great estates, who used slaves to work it. These displaced farmers joined the Roman mob or wandered through Italy seeking work.

The Senate's usual way of dealing with potentially explosive situations was to feed the masses bread and entertain them with circuses. But eventually a patrician, Tiberius Gracchus, challenged the exploitative system. Elected tribune in 133 BC, he campaigned to reintroduce a law limiting the size of the great estates, and proposed redistributing state-owned farm-

> *Carthage represented Rome's most formidable opponent, and took the Romans to the brink of defeat. The battles between the two powers helped forge the Roman legions and navies into the Mediterranean's supreme fighting force.*

ing and grazing land among the poor. The Senators, many of them wealthy landowners, blocked Gracchus' plan, and when he persisted and ran for re-election as tribune they engaged assassins to murder him and his supporters.

Gaius the populist

Gracchus' spirit did not die with him. Eleven years later, his brother Gaius was elected tribune. An effective speaker, he was popular with the Roman masses. Once in office, he called for sweeping land reform. Again the Senate struck back viciously. The Roman people were incited to riot, and Gaius was blamed. He was killed or forced to kill himself (the records are not clear), and his followers were imprisoned.

The power of the army commanders now became the determining factor in Roman politics. The general Gaius Marius, son of a farmer, returned to Rome from triumphant campaigns in Africa determined to smash the power of the despised Senate. To the Roman people, Gaius Marius was a god-like figure who had transformed the Roman citizen legions into a professional army. He and his supporters butchered the senatorial leaders and thousands of aristocratic Romans.

This fateful action, taken in the name of liberty, opened the way to dictatorship. The Senate turned to Sulla, a rival general and a patrician by birth, who answered Marius' violence with a

Gnaeus Pompeius, called Pompey the Great. He restored many liberties suspended by Sulla, but failed to go far enough for the rioting masses.

Pompey's solution was to join forces with two other military men, Crassus and Julius Caesar, and form Triumvirate, an unofficial agreement aimed at preserving their power. This arrangement was successful until Crassus died in 53 BC, and the two remaining leaders quarrelled. For several years Pompey and Caesar eyed each other warily. Then, in 49 BC, Caesar, after his successful campaign in Gaul, led his army across the flooded Rubicon river (the border between Cisalpine Gaul and Italy), against the

bloodbath of his own. Sulla returned to Rome and ruled as absolute dictator. The Senate could put no check on him for it had opened the door for him to take power. The Republic was effectively dead, the victim of three centuries of empire building.

Enter Pompey the Great

For two years the streets of Rome ran with blood. But in 79 BC Sulla grew tired of ruling and retired to his estate near Naples. Civil war broke out again. Sulla's successor was another general,

LEFT: Julius Caesar was not the first to put his face on a coin, but he is the most famous. **ABOVE:** Emperor Augustus built the *Ara Pacis* to celebrate peace.

BEWARE THE IDES OF MARCH

An Etruscan soothsayer had warned Caesar to beware of misfortune that would strike no later than 15 March 44 BC. On that day – the Ides of March – Caesar was scheduled to address the Senate. On his way to the Senate chamber he passed the soothsayer. Caesar remarked that the Ides had come safely. The Etruscan replied that the day was not yet over. In the chamber, Caesar was surrounded by conspirators and stabbed 23 times. When he saw that Marcus Junius Brutus, a patrician he had treated like a son, was among his murderers, he murmured *"Et tu, Brute?"* ("You too, Brutus?") and died.

orders of the Senate. With Caesar heading for Rome, Pompey left for Greece, taking his own army and most of the Senate with him. But Caesar moved first. He attacked Pompey's allies in Spain, then in Greece, forcing Pompey to flee to Egypt, where he was eventually killed in 48 BC.

Caesar returned to Rome in triumph. The masses thought his victories proved he was divinely appointed to rule Rome. For the first time in decades there were no riots in the capital. But the upper classes were wary of Caesar's autocratic tendencies. A conspiracy formed against him.

After Caesar's death, Mark Antony, Caesar's co-consul, and Octavian, his grand-nephew, simply "Augustus", meaning "the revered one", but in fact he was the first emperor of Rome. Unlike his grand-uncle before him, he took care not to offend the republican sentiments of the Romans, and therein lay the key to his success. He allowed the Senate the outward trappings of power and influence, but little of the reality. Uninterested in status symbols or ostentation, he lived and dressed simply. The competence and sensitivity with which Augustus reigned made for an unprecedented period of peace, order and prosperity; for some 200 years after Augustan reform, the Mediterranean world basked in a *Pax Romana*, a Roman peace.

joined forces to pursue and kill the conspirators. Despite their cooperation, the two were never good friends. Initially they collaborated with a Caesarian patrician, Lepidus, to form a formal but uneasy Second Triumvirate, but the arrangement faltered when Antony fell in love with the Egyptian queen Cleopatra and rejected his wife, Octavian's sister, to marry her. In revenge, Octavian turned the Senate against Mark Antony, then declared war on his former partner. When defeat was imminent, Antony and Cleopatra committed suicide.

Augustus and the *Pax Romana*

Octavian's triumphant return to Rome marked the beginning of a new era. He called himself

> *Augustus, first emperor of Rome, outlawed prostitution and drunkenness and strengthened divorce laws. He also built a vast civil service to administer his harmonious realm.*

Before Augustus assumed power, the republican institutions had been unable to administer the vast territories Rome now controlled. Military dictatorship had been the result. To meet this challenge Augustus created a personal bureaucracy within his household. In addition to footmen and maids, he also had tax collectors, governors, census takers and administrators as his "servants". He allowed this personal civil service to grow to a size sufficient to run the empire, but kept it under tight control.

With peace, art and literature flourished. The poet Virgil, who had lived through the civil wars and military dictatorships, paid tribute to Augustus' achievements in the *Aeneid*; the poet

> "Within a short time you forget everything, and everything forgets you," declared Marcus Aurelius. But the glories of Rome have survived as the finest memorial to the imperial builders.

Horace likened the emperor to a helmsman who had steered the ship of state into a safe port. Augustus himself took part in the artistic resurgence and set about rebuilding the capital. He claimed that he had found Rome a city of brick and left it a city of marble.

Augustus reigned for 41 years and set the tone of Roman leadership for the next 150. None of his successors had his ability, but his institutional and personal legacy did much to preserve peace in the flourishing Roman world.

The mad and the bad

The Emperor Tiberius had none of his stepfather's sense of proportion, nor his steadiness. He began his reign with good intentions, but he mismanaged many early problems. He spent the last 11 years of his reign at his villa on Capri, from where he issued a volley of execution orders. The historian Suetonius wrote (in the translation by Robert Graves), "Not a day, however holy, passed without an execution; he even desecrated New Year's Day. Many of his victims were accused and punished with their children – some actually by their children – and the relatives forbidden to go into mourning."

Rome was relieved when Tiberius died, only to find that there was worse to come. Caligula, his successor, ruled ably for three years, then ran wild. He insisted that he was a god, formed his own priesthood and erected a temple to himself. He proposed his horse be made consul. Finally a group of his own officers assassinated Caligula, and Rome was rid of its most hated ruler.

The officers took it upon themselves to name the next emperor. Their choice was Claudius,

LEFT: a reconstruction of the Colosseum.
RIGHT: Emperor Nero with his tigress, Phoebe.

grandson of Augustus, whom they found hiding behind a curtain in the palace after the assassination. Many thought Claudius a fool, for he stuttered and was slightly crippled, but he proved a good and steady ruler. He oversaw the reform of the civil service, and the expansion of the Roman Empire to include Britain.

Claudius was poisoned by his ambitious wife Agrippina, who pushed Nero, her son by a previous marriage, onto the throne. Like Tiberius before him, Nero started out with good intentions. He was well educated, an accomplished musician, and showed respect for the advice of others, especially senators. But the violent side

of his nature soon became apparent. He poisoned Britannicus, Claudius' natural son, and tried to do the same to his mother, but she had taken the precaution of building up an immunity to the poison. In the end Nero accused her of plotting against him, and had her executed.

Nero's excesses caused alarm among Rome's citizens. When a fire destroyed the city in AD 64, he was accused of starting it. In fact, he was away from the city at the time and stories of him fiddling while Rome burned are probably untrue.

Nero lost his throne after the Roman commanders in Gaul, Africa and Spain rebelled. With no hope left, Nero killed himself in AD 68. His suicide threw the empire into greater turmoil. He left no heir and therefore the rebellious commanders fought amongst themselves for a year until a legion commander, Flavius Vespasian, emerged as emperor.

Vespasian proved a wise emperor, and his rule ushered in a period of peace. There was a short time of troubles when his son, Domitian, became emperor but, by the time he died, the Senate was powerful enough to appoint its own emperor, Nerva, a respected lawyer from Rome.

Nerva was the first of the "five good emperors" who reigned from AD 96 to 180. He was followed by Trajan, Hadrian, Antoninus Pius and Marcus Aurelius – all educated men, interested in philosophy and devoted to their duties. They

were loved by the people of Rome for administering their vast empire well and successfully defending its borders.

Decline and fall

During the period between the death of Marcus Aurelius and the sack of Rome in the 5th century, it became increasingly difficult to defend the empire from barbarians. Between AD 180 and 285, Rome was threatened in both the east and the west by barbarian tribes. The empire doubled the size of the army. The drain on manpower and resources caused an economic crisis, and the powerful army could place emperors on the throne and remove them at will. Most of these "barracks emperors" served for less than

three years and never even lived in the capital. Plague also struck Rome, which weakened the empire and made it more vulnerable to enemy attack. On all sides wars raged. In the east, the revived Persian Empire threatened Syria, Egypt and all of Asia Minor. In the west, Franks invaded France and Spain.

Major political reform was undertaken by Emperor Diocletian in 286. He believed the empire could no longer be ruled by one man, so he divided it into eastern and western region. He chose Nicomedia in Asia Minor as his capital and appointed a soldier named Maximinus to rule the west from Milan.

Unfortunately this arrangement did not end quarrels about the succession. Constantine marched on Rome in 311 to assert his right to the throne. While on the road, however, he claimed he had a vision. The sign of the cross appeared in the sky with the words: "By this sign win your victory." As a result, when Constantine defeated his rival, Maxentius, and emerged as the sole emperor, he ruled as a Christian and granted religious freedom to existing Christians.

In 324, Constantine confirmed Christianity as the state religion. Not all citizens followed the new faith; some notable families remained true to their pagan beliefs. Under his auspices, and in

Constantine's conversion established Christianity, which had been spreading through the empire since the time of Nero, as the religion of the Roman state and thus of the Western world.

the decades which followed, the first Christian churches of Rome were built. These included the earliest constructions of the five patriarchal churches of which the Pope himself was the priest: San Pietro (St Peter's), San Giovanni in Laterano, San Paolo fuori le Mura, San Lorenzo fuori le Mura and Santa Maria Maggiore.

Despite the conversion to Christianity, the empire continued to decline. In 330, Constantine decided to move the capital east, and make a fresh start in his new city of Constantinople. Back in Italy, the barbarians gradually moved closer. The city of Rome was sacked in 410. ❏

LEFT: fragments of an enormous statue of Constantine in the Musei Capitolini.

Life in the Empire

Ancient Rome was a codified, class-conscious society, but beneath the veneer lay a devotion to pleasure and property – like Rome today

In more than 60 treatises on morality, Plutarch (AD 46–126) laid down what was expected of a Roman gentleman. It was a damnable luxury to strain wine or to use snow to cool drinks. It was "democratic and polite" to be punctual for dinner; "oligarchical and offensive" to be late. Conversation over dinner ought to be philosophical, like debating which came first, the chicken or the egg.

It would be naive to think that all Romans obeyed Plutarch's strictures. Life was as diverse as in any modern capital, with an elegant high society at one end of the scale, more unruly elements at the other. The one common factor was probably a passion for bathing. With underground furnaces heating the water, the baths got bigger and bigger. The well-preserved Baths of Caracalla could disgorge 1,600 glowing Romans per day.

In the early days, relations between patricians and plebeians were codified, as were family matters. Patricians were the source of "tranquillity", mainly by lending an ear to plebeians' problems and dispensing advice. In return, plebeians had to stump up money when the patrician was held to ransom or could not settle his debts. Money made available in such circumstances was not a loan but a plebeian's privilege, for which he was supposed to be grateful. Yet plebeians were not enslaved and could switch allegiance to more suitable patricians.

Divorce was introduced relatively late. At first, marriage was permanent and wives automatically acquired half the conjugal property. However, husbands exercised the ultimate sanction in that they were legally entitled to murder wives for serious offences, such as poisoning the children or making duplicates of their private keys. Fathers were prevented from selling sons into slavery once the boys had married.

Citizens bombarded bureaucrats with complaints about the quality of life in Rome: disgraceful traffic congestion and refuse collection; escalating inflation; homosexuals getting too big for their boots; the filthy habit of smoking dried cow dung. The

most castigated men in Rome were unscrupulous property developers who set fire to a building they wanted and then, as the flames went up, offered the uninsured owner a pittance. As soon as the deal was struck, the developer summoned a private fire brigade parked around the corner.

In a spiritual context, the lives of the Romans were wrapped up in astrology and mysticism. The spread of Bacchic rites in republican Rome alarmed the government, which called them "this pestilential evil... this contagious disease". Senators "were seized by a panic of fear, both for the public safety,

PLVTARQVE HISTORIEN
Grec.   Chap. 42.

lest these secret conspiracies and nocturnal gatherings contain some hidden harm or danger, and for themselves individually, lest some relatives be involved in this vice".

The social decadence supposedly behind the downfall of Rome had its own decorum. Petronius Arbiter, author of the *Satyricon*, orchestrated Nero's orgies. He later fell out with Nero and was ordered to take his own life. Petronius invited friends to a farewell banquet where he sat with bandages wrapped around wrists which he discreetly slashed as the evening progressed. The controlled bleeding enabled him to sustain repartee up to the moment his head slumped. It is not known whether he expressed a parting thought on the interesting question of the chicken and the egg. ❑

RIGHT: Plutarch, Greek biographer and historian.

THE MIDDLE AGES

A period that saw Lombard, Saracen and Norman
invasions and clashes between emperor and Pope

For four centuries after the sack of Rome
in AD 410, barbarian invaders, including
the Goths and the Lombards, battled
with local military leaders and the Byzantine
emperors for control of Italy. Under these conditions, the culture and prosperity that had
characterised ancient times faded. The Roman
Empire had unified Italy and made it the
centre of the world, but after its demise Italy
became a provincial battlefield. Since none of
the rival powers could control the whole of
Italy, the land was divided, and it remained so
until the 19th century.

The Dark Ages began with a series of Visig-
othic invasions from northern and eastern
Europe. The emperors in Constantinople were
still in theory the rulers of Italy, but for decades
they accepted first the Visigoth and later the
Ostrogoth leaders as de facto kings. Justinian I,
who became emperor in Constantinople in 527,
longed to revive the splendour of the empire
and sent the brilliant general Belisarius to regain
direct control of Italy. But, although he met with
initial success – he captured Ravenna from the
Goths in 540 – a new group of barbarians soon
appeared on Italy's borders: the Lombards.

Invaders from the north

The Lombards were German tribesmen from
the Danube Valley. They swiftly conquered
most of what is now Lombardy, the Veneto
and Tuscany, causing the inhabitants of the
northern Italian cities to flee to eastern coastal
regions where they were protected by the Byzantines, who still controlled the seas. Many settled around the lagoon of Venice.

Meanwhile, the Lombards altered the system
of government. They replaced the centralised

Roman political system with local administrative units called "duchies", after the Lombard
army generals who were known as *duces*. Within
each duchy a *dux* ruled as king. The land was
distributed to groups of related Lombard families, each headed by a free warrior, who owed
limited feudal allegiance to his king but had a
free hand on his own land. This, along with the
Byzantines' continuing control of many provinces, meant Italy was effectively divided.

The radical changes that the Lombards
brought to Italy's administration did not affect
the Church. Indeed, in Rome the bishopric rose
to new prominence because the emperors in
Constantinople were too distant to exert any
temporal or spiritual authority.

Greatest among the early popes was Gregory I (589–603), a Roman by birth, a scholar by instinct and training, and a great statesman. He persuaded the Lombards to abandon the siege of Rome, and helped achieve peace in Italy.

He sent missionaries to northern Europe to spread the word of God and the influence of

> The great Pope Gregory, who made peace with the Lombards to save Rome, also gave his name to the Gregorian chant, and sent the Benedictine monk Augustine to England.

Rome should have the final say on all spiritual matters, and organised an Italian revolt against the emperor. The Lombards joined the revolt on the side of the popes and used the opportunity to chase the Byzantines out of Italy.

After the imperial capital, Ravenna, fell to the Lombard army in 751, the popes, feeling more directly threatened by the powerful Lombards than by an absent emperor, sought a new ally and turned to the Franks for help.

Pepin, king of the Franks, invaded Italy in 754. He reconquered the imperial lands but ceded control to the Pope. Twenty years later, Pepin's son, Charlemagne, finished his father's work

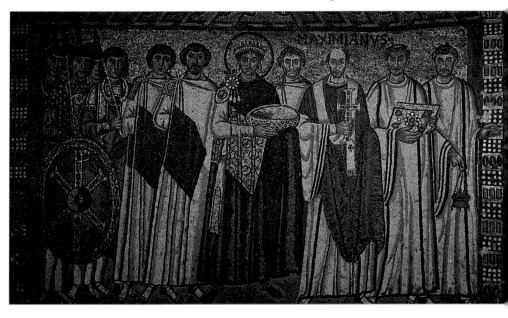

Rome, and sent the first missionaries to the British Isles.

Gregory's successors reorganised the municipal government of Rome, and effectively became rulers of the city. It was inevitable that the popes would eventually clash with the emperor in Constantinople. In 726, Emperor Leo decreed that veneration of images of Christ and the saints was forbidden and that all images were to be destroyed. The Pope opposed his decree on the grounds that the Church in

by defeating and capturing the Lombard king, confirming his father's grant to the papacy, and assuming the crown of the Lombards.

Charlemagne then returned to the north and campaigned against the Saxons, Bavarians and Avars, making himself ruler of much of western Europe. To unify his vast territories under Christian auspices, he had Pope Leo crown him Holy Roman Emperor at St Peter's in Rome on Christmas Day 800.

Charlemagne lived only 14 years after his coronation, and none of his successors matched him in ability; authority fell into the hands of Frankish counts, Charlemagne's vassals who had accompanied him south and been granted land of their own.

LEFT: Gregory I, c.540–604, later canonised. ABOVE: mosaics, such as this one of the Emperor Justinian, are glittering reminders that Ravenna was once the capital of the Western Roman empire.

A period of ensuing feudal anarchy was also marked by invasions. In the south the Saracens invaded Sicily in 827, and for the next 250 years Sicily was an Arab state. Sicily also became a base for raids on the Italian mainland, and Charlemagne's great-grandson, Louis II, who was emperor for 25 years, failed to raise an organised defence against them. The Lombard dukes in the south allied themselves with these invaders against the Carolingian emperor.

The Normans in the south

In the early 11th century, small groups of Normans arrived in southern Italy. As adventurers and skilled mercenaries, they fought for Greek, Lombard and Saracen alike, in return for land.

Soon landless men from Normandy arrived to fight, settle and conquer for themselves. The papacy lost no time in allying itself with this powerful group of Christians. In the 1050s, the Norman chief, Robert Guiscard, conquered Calabria. Pope Nicholas II "legitimised" Norman rule of the area by calling it a papal fief. Guiscard was invested as king, a role that passed to Roger II in 1130 (see panel below).

During the 9th and 10th centuries, the papacy was controlled by Roman nobles, who were often corrupt. After Emperor Otto I arrived in

THE NORMAN CONQUEST

On his accession in 1130, the Norman Roger II became the richest king in Christendom. Centred on Sicily, his realm stretched to southern Italy and North Africa. As a tolerant ruler, Roger acted as an oriental sultan, indulging his love of Arab culture (including a harem) as well as welcoming Jewish, Greek and Arab scholars. The court included Koranic astronomers, French balladeers and Sicilian poets. Arab-Norman architecture flourished under his rule, in a fusion of oriental and Western styles. Moorish masterpieces can be seen in Palermo and in the cathedrals of Monreale and Cefalù. Norman control of southern Italy only came to an end with the death of William II in 1189.

Rome in 962, he insisted that no pope could be elected until the emperor had named a candidate. But, by reforming the papacy, the emperors started a trend that would have far-reaching consequences.

In the 11th century, the popes strove to reform the Church further by imposing a strict clerical hierarchy. Throughout the Holy Roman Empire, bishops were to be answerable to the Pope, and priests to bishops. A single legal and administrative system would bind all members of the clergy together. These reforms immediately angered all lay rulers from the emperor down.

The struggle reached a climax when Emperor Henry IV invested an anti-reform candidate as archbishop of Milan in 1072. As a result, Pope

Gregory VII decreed that an investiture by a non-cleric was forbidden and excommunicated Henry. The emperor was forgiven but failed to keep his promise to recognise the claims of the papacy, and a new civil war broke out. Gregory's supporters were defeated initially and he was carried off to Salerno and death, but his suc-

> *The Lombard League, founded in 1167, an alliance of northern Italian cities, has been used as a rallying cry by secessionist movements in modern times.*

cessors ensured the triumph of Gregory's cause, and the emperors were forced to concede their rights of investiture in 1122.

During the years of the investiture controversy and the ensuing civil wars, the cities of northern and central Italy grew rich and powerful. The emperors were too distracted to administer them directly. Around the same time, Mediterranean commerce was revived. With new wealth at their disposal, the cities forced the nobles in the countryside to acknowledge their supremacy. The Italian city-states were born. The strong and separate identity of the city-states is one of the leitmotifs of Italian history, influencing the pattern of future political affiliations, fostering separate schools of art, architecture and music, and largely determining regional attitudes today.

The maritime republics of Venice, Genoa and Pisa were foremost among the Italian cities, but inland cities that were situated on rich trade routes also prospered. Milan and Verona lay at the entrance to the Alpine passes, Bologna was the chief city on the Via Emilia, and Florence had sea access via the River Arno and controlled two roads to Rome.

The growing political power of the city-states was an important factor in renewed conflict between emperor and Pope during the 13th century. Emperor Frederick II (1197–1250) tried to build a strong, centralised state in Italy. The cities that opposed him, wanting complete political autonomy, found an ally in Pope Gregory IX, who harboured imperial designs of his own.

Northern Italy became a battlefield for civil war between the Guelphs, supporters of the Pope, and the Ghibellines, allies of the emperor.

By the time Frederick died in 1250, without instituting his reforms, the Guelf cause had won. The alliance of Pope and the city-states had ruined imperial plans for a unified Italy.

The age of Dante

The Guelphs beat the Ghibellines decisively, but a feud broke out between two Guelph factions: the Blacks and the Whites. This split was especially severe in Florence, where the Blacks defended the nobles' feudal tradition against

the Whites, rich magnates who were willing to give merchants a voice in government.

Pope Boniface VIII sided with the Blacks and worked to have all prominent Whites exiled from Florence in 1302. Among the exiles was Dante Alighieri, who went on to write *La Divina Commedia (The Divine Comedy)*, a literary masterpiece that promoted Tuscan Italian to the status of a national tongue and also reveals much about the politics of the period.

When Henry VII became Holy Roman Emperor in 1308, he wanted to revive imperial power in Italy and set up a government that was neither Guelph nor Ghibelline. But the cities refused to support him. Dante's home town, Florence, was the centre of the resistance to his plans. ❏

LEFT: *Effects of Good Government*, fresco by Lorenzetti 1338–40, in the Palazzo Pubblico, Siena.
RIGHT: Dante Alighieri, by Andrea del Castagno.

THE RENAISSANCE

Free from foreign interference, the city-states flourished and witnessed an unprecedented cultural awakening

The constant fighting in northern Italy subsided in the early 14th century when both the popes and the emperors withdrew from Italian affairs. After Henry VII's demise, the emperors turned their attention to Germany. Meanwhile, the influence of the papacy declined after a quarrel between Pope Boniface and King Philip of France in 1302. The Pope insisted that Philip had no right to tax the French clergy; the king's response was to send his troops to capture the pope. French pressure ensured that the next pope was a Frenchman, Clement V, and he moved the papacy from Rome to Avignon, where it stayed until 1377.

Macchiavelli was inspired by Lorenzo de' Medici when he wrote in The Prince*: "A ruler must emulate the fox and the lion, for the lion cannot avoid traps and the fox cannot fight wolves."*

The people of Italy were thus free from outside interference during the 14th century and the Italian cities grew stronger, richer and bigger than any in Europe. Against the political background of the supremacy of the city-state, a new culture bloomed and new ideas flourished. Rulers tried new methods of administration. Scholars were allowed to rediscover the pagan past. Wealthy merchants became lavish patrons of the arts. Through their commissions, artists experimented with a new, more realistic style.

LEFT: Titian's portrait of Pope Julius II, a great patron of the arts. **RIGHT:** detail of Raphael's *School of Athens* in the Stanza della Segnatura, Vatican Museum.

Plague and depression

Not even the Black Death – the terrible outbreak of bubonic plague that ravaged Europe in the 14th century – could smother the new cultural awakening. The merchants' solution to the declining profits of the period was to change the way they did business. Their innovations included marine insurance, credit transfers, double-entry book-keeping and holding companies – all of which eventually became standard business practice.

To be a good businessman in the early Renaissance required a basic education: reading, writing and arithmetic. But the more complicated business became, the more knowledge was needed, including an understanding of law and diplomacy, and of the ways of the world. Thus the traditional theological studies of the Middle Ages were replaced by the study of ancient authors and of grammar, rhetoric, history and moral philosophy. This education became known as *studia humanitatis*, or the humanities.

Humanism grew partly out of the need for greater legal expertise in the expanding world of Mediterranean commerce. To learn how to administer their new, complex societies, lawyers looked back at the great tenets of Roman law. As they studied the codes of the ancients, they grew to appreciate the cultural riches of that long-buried civilisation. All aspects of Italian life were re-examined in the light of this new humanism. One way of life was thought to be ideal – that of the all-round man based on classical models. The Renaissance man was in fact a reincarnation of rich, talented Roman philosophers.

Despots and republics

Italians of the 14th century were citizens of particular cities, not members of a national unit. Rulers encouraged artists and writers to glorify their towns. There were a few experiences and conditions that many cities shared.

BUILDING BOOM

The leading merchant guilds of Florence spent their wealth on art, helping to turn the city into a showcase of Renaissance sculpture, painting and architecture. Clarity, rigour and geometry were the watchwords of Florentine architecture. In the second half of the 13th century construction began on the Bargello, the Franciscan church of Santa Croce and the Dominican church of Santa Maria Novella. Arnolfo di Cambio designed the cathedral and the Palazzo Vecchio, the emblem of Florentine power. The wool guild funded the construction of the cathedral. The city also hired Giotto to design the cathedral bell tower, and in 1434 chose Brunelleschi to finish the great dome.

As the authority of the popes and emperors declined, life in the cities became increasingly violent and leading families fought each other constantly. The remedy to this bloody civil strife was the rule of one strong man. The pattern was repeated over and over again in northern Italy. Traditional republican rule which could not keep order was replaced by a dictatorship. The future despot was often originally a *capitano del popolo* – the head of the local police force and citizens' army. Over time, this captain would extend his powers until he controlled the entire city and eventually made his office hereditary. This was how the della Scala (Scaligeri) family in Verona, the Gonzaga in Mantua and the Visconti in Milan came to power.

Some cities, including Venice, Florence, Siena, Lucca and Pisa, did not succumb to despotism until quite late in their history: the merchants were so powerful that rulers such as the Medici only survived by winning their support. In these cities republicanism flourished briefly, but even so the merchants dominated the organs of the republican government.

> The eminent Renaissance historian Jacob Burckhardt admired the "strict rationalism" of Visconti's Milan and called its government a work of art.

During the 14th and 15th centuries, northern and central Italy changed from an area speckled with tiny political units to one dominated by a few large states. The most successful and the most powerful was Milan. During the 14th century, the authoritarian Visconti family dominated Milan, and led the city to innumerable military and political victories until it was the largest state in northern Italy.

The Visconti regime may have been, in its efficiency, unlike anything Europe had seen for centuries, but for the Milanese people it had great drawbacks. The personal brutality of the Visconti controlled Milan. The regime could not rely on the loyalty of the populace for its survival. When the Visconti line died out in 1447, the Milanese declared a republic, but it was not strong enough to rule over all the restive towns Milan now controlled. When, in 1450, Francesco Sforza, a famous general who had served the Visconti, overthrew the republic and became the new duke, ruling with his wife Bianca Visconti, many Milanese were relieved.

The Republic of Florence

The spectacular transformation of Florence from a small town in the 1100s to the commercial and financial centre it had become by the end of the 14th century was based on the profitable wool trade. The wool guild of Florence, the Arte della Lana, imported wool from northern Europe and dyes from the Middle East. Using the city's secret weaving and colouring techniques, guild

members produced a heavy red cloth that was sold all over the Mediterranean area. Wool trade profits had provided the initial capital for the banking industry of Florence. Since the 13th century, Florentine merchants had lent money to their allies, the Pope and powerful Guelph nobles. This early experience led to the founding of formal banking houses, and made Florence the financial capital of Europe.

The rich men of Florence controlled the city government through the Parte Guelfa. With membership came the right to find and persecute anyone with "Ghibellistic tendencies". Other political non-conformities were also

MEDICI MIDAS TOUCH

Wherever you look in Florence, you encounter the Medici – not just their busts and coat of arms but the magnificent churches, palaces and works of art they commissioned. The Medici also promoted art and culture. When the humanist Niccolò Niccoli died, Cosimo de' Medici acquired his book collection and attached it to the monastery of San Marco, creating the first public library in Florence. Cosimo also created a new Platonic Academy and made Florence a centre of Platonic studies. He supplied Donatello with classical works that inspired his sculpture. Lorenzo de' Medici, patron of the arts, singled out a young Michelangelo, whose statues still adorn the city.

LEFT: *The Battle of San Romano* by Paolo Uccello, showing the victory of Florence over Siena in 1432.
RIGHT: Cosimo de' Medici in the Uffizi, Florence.

not tolerated. Members of lesser guilds who demanded a greater share of power, or joined with the lower classes to fight the Parte Guelfa, were annihilated. However, in the early 15th century the violence of class war escalated. The disenfranchised artisans struck back repeatedly. At this point the rich merchants allowed Cosimo de' Medici to rise to the leadership of Florence.

The 15th century was the golden age of the Renaissance. The stage was set for a period of unprecedented artistic and intellectual achievement. To live in Italy at this time was to live in a new world of cultural and commercial riches. Italy was truly the centre of the world.

The political history of the century divides into two parts. Until 1454 the five chief states of Italy were busy expanding their borders, or strengthening their hold on territories, which meant fighting many small wars. The soldiers who fought them were mostly *condottieri* (mercenaries). After 1454 came a period of relative peace, when the states pursued their interests through alliances. These years saw the greatest artistic achievement, when Italian states of all sizes became cultural centres.

Italian wars of the Late Middle Ages and Early Renaissance had traditionally been fought by foreign mercenaries, but by the 15th century the mercenaries were more likely to be Italian. Men of all classes and from all parts of Italy joined the ranks of the purely Italian companies to fight northern wars for rival nobles. The *condottieri* looked upon war as a professional, technical skill. The countryside, however, suffered heavily as village after village was plundered. The *condottieri* were bound by no patriotic ties, only by a

> The historian Guicciardini extolled life under the Medici: "Talented men were assisted in their careers by the recognition given to arts and letters... tranquillity reigned within her walls, and externally the city enjoyed high honours."

monetary arrangement, so an important captain could always be bought by the enemy.

One of the greatest *condottieri* was Francesco Sforza, who had inherited the command of an army upon his father's death in 1424. He fought first for Milan and then for Venice until Filippo Visconti sought to attach him permanently to Milan by marrying him to his illegitimate daughter, Bianca.

Visconti died in 1447 leaving no heir, and Milan declared itself a republic. But when the republican government proved incompetent, Sforza turned his forces on the city and starved Milan into surrender. The chief assembly of the republic invited him to be the duke of the city.

Peace and the Italian League

Sforza, the great soldier, was key to bringing peace to northern Italy. He signed, and encouraged others to sign, the Treaty of Lodi, which led to the Italian League of 1455. This was a defensive league between Milan, Florence and Venice that the King of Naples and the Pope also respected. It was set up to prevent any one of the great states from increasing its powers at the expense of its weaker neighbours, and to present a common national front against attack. The smaller states benefited most from the new league.

During the decades of peace in Italy, Florence experienced its own golden age under the rule of the Medici family. The historian Guicciardini described the Florence of Lorenzo de' Medici as follows: "The city was in perfect peace, the leading citizens were united, and their authority was so great that none dared to oppose them. The people were entertained daily with pageants

LEFT: portrait of a *condottiere* by Andrea del Castagno.

and festivals; the food supply was abundant and all trades flourished."

In part, the success of the Medici was a public relations coup. They allowed the Florentines to believe that the city government was still a great democracy. Only after Lorenzo's death, when Florence was briefly ruled by his arrogant son, did the citizens realise that their state, for all its republican forms, had drifted into the control of one family. They then quickly exiled the Medici and drafted a new constitution. Until then, both Cosimo and Lorenzo de' Medici had dominated Florence while shrewdly never appearing to be more than prominent citizens.

The internal disarray in Italy at the time was so great that the French troops faced no organised resistance. The new leader of Florence, a Dominican friar named Girolamo Savonarola, preached that Charles was sent by God to regenerate the Church and purify spiritual life. Other Italians also welcomed the French. They believed that the invaders would rid Italy of decadence and set up governments with natives in key posts. Only when these ideas proved illusory could Italian patriots recruit an army and challenge the French.

The French and Italians met near the village of Fornovo on 6 July 1495. The Italians, led by

An end to the peace

When Lorenzo de' Medici died in 1492, the fragile Italian League that had kept Italy at peace and safe from any foreign attacks died with him. Ludovico il Moro, the lord of Milan, immediately quarrelled with the Neapolitan king and proposed to the King of France that he, Charles VIII, conquer Naples and the surrounding states. Ludovico offered finance and safe passage through the north of Italy. Charles readily accepted and so began a truly demoralising chapter of Italian history.

ABOVE: Francesco Sforza married Bianca (**RIGHT**), natural daughter of the last of the Visconti rulers, to become despot of Milan.

General Francesco Gonzaga, looked certain of victory: they outnumbered the French two to one, and they could launch a surprise attack against their enemy. But the Italian strategy fell apart. When the battle ended, four thousand men had died – the majority of them Italian.

"If the Italians had won at Fornovo, they would probably have discovered then the pride of being a united people... Italy would have emerged as a respectable nation... a country which adventurous foreigners would think twice before attacking," wrote Luigi Barzini in *The Italians*. Instead, the defeat at Fornovo broke the Italian spirit and led to 30 years of foreign interventions, bloody conflicts, civil wars and revolts. ❏

RENAISSANCE ART

The revolution in art and architecture which began in
Florence in the 15th century gave us our greatest treasures
and transformed the way we see the world

I talian art shone brightest during the Renaissance when, as in most disciplines, a revolution took place. The Early Renaissance (1400–1500), the *Quattrocento*, introduced new themes that altered the future of art. Ancient Greece and Rome were rediscovered and with them the importance of man in the here and now. The human body surfaced as a new focal point in painting and sculpture. The discovery of perspective changed architecture.

The Early Renaissance centred on Florence. The city wanted to be seen as "the new Rome", and public works flourished.

First in Florence was Lorenzo Ghiberti's commission for sculpting the gilded bronze north doors (1403–24) of the Baptistery, won in a competition with Filippo Brunelleschi in 1401. Ghiberti's more famous east doors (1424–52) are so dazzling that Michelangelo called them "the Gates of Paradise".

Classical architecture

It was Filippo Brunelleschi (1377–1466) who championed the new classically inspired architecture. After losing the Baptistery door competition, he went to Rome to study the proportions of ancient buildings.

His studies led him to design such masterpieces as the dome of Florence cathedral, the arcade fronting the Innocenti orphanage, the church of San Lorenzo (1421–69), the Pazzi Chapel of Santa Croce (begun 1430–33) and Santo Spirito, all in Florence. You need no yardstick to appreciate the use of mathemati-

cal proportions. The overriding impression is of harmony, balance and calm.

If Brunelleschi was the most noted architect, Donatello (1386–1466) excelled in sculpture. His work expresses a new attitude to the human body. The figure of St George, made for the church of Orsanmichele and now in the Museo del Bargello, is not only a realistic depiction of the human form, but also a work of psychological insight. His *Gattamelata* (1445–50) in Padua was the first equestrian statue cast in bronze since Roman times, and his bronze *David* (1430–32), in the Bargello, was the first freestanding nude statue since antiquity.

The groundwork for the revolution in painting was laid a century earlier by Giotto (1267–

1337). His frescoes – in Florence's Santa Croce, Padua's Cappella degli Scrovegni and Assisi's Basilica di San Francesco – depart from the flat Byzantine style and invest the human form with solidity and volume, and the setting with a sense of space and depth. His breakthrough was carried further by the Early Renaissance's most noted painter, Masaccio (1401–28). His Florentine frescoes of *The Holy Trinity with Virgin and St John* in Santa Maria Novella (1425), and his frescoes in the Brancacci Chapel (1427) display all the traits characteristic of the Renaissance: attention to the human form, emotion and the use of perspective.

the tracing of classic motifs (columns, arches) on the exteriors of buildings, such as on the Malatesta Temple in Rimini (1450). Giovanni Bellini (1430/1–1516) triumphed in Venice. In his *Madonna and Saints* in San Zaccaria (1505), the grandeur of Masaccio's influence is tempered by Flemish detail. Detail most delicately expressed is the hallmark of Sandro Botticelli (1444/5–1510). The Uffizi Gallery houses the allegorical *Primavera* (1480) and the lovely *Birth of Venus* (1489).

The High Renaissance

The High Renaissance (1500–1600) was the heyday of some of the most celebrated artists

Domenico Veneziano moved to Florence in 1439 and introduced pastel greens and pinks awash with cool light. The palette was picked up by his assistant, Piero della Francesca (1416–92), for his frescoes at San Francesco in Arezzo (1466), marvels of pale tone as well as mathematics – heads and limbs as geometric shapes: spheres, cones and cylinders.

The artistic revolution in Florence soon spread to other parts of Italy. Leon Battista Alberti (1404–72), an author of treatises on sculpture, painting and architecture, introduced

LEFT: the anguish of Adam and Eve, from Masaccio's *Expulsion from Paradise*.
ABOVE: Botticelli's *Primavera* in the Uffizi in Florence.

in the entire history of art: Leonardo da Vinci, Michelangelo, Bramante, Raphael and Titian. Unlike their predecessors, who were thought of as craftsmen, they were considered to be creative geniuses capable of works of superhuman scale, grandeur and effort. Their extravaganzas were made possible by a new source of patronage – the papacy.

Having returned to Rome from exile in Avignon, the popes turned the Eternal City into a centre of culture. The art of the High Renaissance is marked by a move beyond rules of mathematical ratios or anatomical geometrics to a new emphasis on emotional impact. The increasing use of oil paints, introduced to the Italians in the late 1400s, began to replace egg tempera and opened new possibilities for richness of colour and delicacy of light.

Leonardo da Vinci (1452–1519) was born near Florence but left the city to work for the Duke of Milan, primarily as an engineer and only secondarily as a sculptor, architect and painter. In Milan, Leonardo painted the *Last Supper* (1495–98), in Santa Maria delle Grazie. The mural – an unsuccessful experiment in oil tempera, which accounts for its poor condition – is a masterpiece of psychological drama.

Leonardo also exploited new techniques in painting. Chiaroscuro (literally, light and dark) – the use of light to bring out and high-light three-dimensional bodies – is vividly seen in the whirl of bodies in the *Adoration of the Magi* (1481–2) in the Uffizi. Another invention was *sfumato*, a fine haze that lends a dreamy quality to paintings, enhancing their poetic potential.

In 1503, Pope Julius II, a great patron of the arts, commissioned the most prominent architect of the day, Donato Bramante (1444–1514), to design the new St Peter's. Bramante had earlier made his mark with the classically inspired gem *The Tempietto* (1502), in the courtyard of Rome's San Pietro in Montorio. The Pope's directive for the new project was to cre-

THE MANNERISTS

The drama of Leonardo, the theatricality of Michelangelo, the poetic moodiness of Giorgione: all set the stage for the Mannerist phase of High Renaissance art, when the serenity and calm classicism that characterised the works of Raphael were abandoned. In Mannerism the human form is paramount, yet it is depicted in strained, disturbing poses and violent colours.

This unnatural look grew out of the work of artists such as Michelangelo, whose exaggeration of human features create drama in the overlarge head and hands of *David*.

Expression of an "inner vision" at the expense of reality was vital to Mannerism. In Fiorentino's *The Descent from the Cross* (1521) in Volterra's Pinacoteca, the angular figures bathed in an unreal light stir feelings of anxiety. His friend Pontormo (1494–1557) also favours works of unexpected colour, unnaturally elongated figures and disquieting mood.

Bronzino (1503–72) epitomises Mannerism's achievements in his psychological portraits of Cosimo I. Parmigianino (1503–40) used distortion merely for effect, despite being inspired by Raphael's fluid grace. In Venice, Tintoretto (1518–94) combined the bold style, rich colours and glowing light inspired by Titian with a mystical inclination. His depiction of the transubstantiation of bread into the body of Christ results in the haunting *Last Supper* (1592–94) in San Giorgio Maggiore, Venice, with its swirling angels created out of vapours.

ate a monument which would surpass any of Ancient Rome. Working with a stock of classical forms (domes, colonnades, pediments) Bramante revolutionised architecture with his revival of another classical technique, concrete, which enables greater flexibility and monumental size.

Bramante died before his design was realised. In 1546, Michelangelo was put in charge of the project, and St Peter's gained its present form.

Michelangelo and Raphael

Michelangelo Buonarroti (1475–1564) first astounded the world with his sculpture:

human figures with a dignity, volume and beauty inspired by Hellenistic precedents, yet given new emotional impact. It has been said that Michelangelo sought to liberate the form of the human body from a prison of marble: an allegory for the struggle of the soul, imprisoned in an earthly body, and a condition ripe for themes of triumph and tragedy. The tension imbues his best-known works: *David* (1501–04) in Florence's Accademia, *Moses* (1513–15) in Rome's San Pietro in Vincoli, and the beloved *Pietà* in St Peter's.

LEFT: Raphael's *Entombment*, in the Borghese Gallery, Rome. **ABOVE:** detail of Raphael's *School of Athens* in the Vatican Museum.

Julius II commissioned Michelangelo to paint the Sistine Chapel ceiling. The result, which was completed in only four years (1508–12), is a triumph of emotions unleashed by the human condition: man's creation, his fall, and his reconciliation with the Lord. Michelangelo returned to the Sistine Chapel in 1534 to paint

> *In architecture, Andrea Palladio (1518–80) designed classically inspired churches, villas and palaces, including Villa Rotonda, Vicenza (1567–70), and San Giorgio Maggiore, Venice (1565).*

the spectacular *Last Judgement*. In the intervening years he went to Florence to complete the Medici Chapel of San Lorenzo (1524–34) and the Laurentian Library (begun 1524), where the drama of the design outweighs many functional considerations. Michelangelo's architectural genius culminates in his redesign of Rome's Campidoglio (1537–39). This open piazza, flanked by three facades, became the model for modern civic centres.

While Michelangelo was busy on the Sistine Chapel ceiling, a young artist from Urbino was working nearby, decorating rooms in the Vatican Palace. This artist, soon to be known as the foremost painter of the High Renaissance, was Raffaello Sanzio, or Raphael (1483–1520). His masterpiece here is the *School of Athens* (1510–11), where the dramatic grouping of philosophers suggests the influence of Michelangelo, yet the individualised intention of each recalls Leonardo's *Last Supper*.

Venetian masters

In Venice, the paintings of Giorgione da Castelfranco (1476/8–1510) have all the charm and delicacy of Bellini's; they also favour poetic mood over subject matter (*The Tempest* of 1505 in Venice's Galleria dell'Accademia is a perfect example), prefiguring the Romantic movement.

Also looking ahead to the freer brushwork and shimmering colours of the Impressionists is the Venetian Titian (1488/90–1576). He mastered the technique of oil painting, and left a legacy of richly coloured, joyously spirited religious and mythological pictures as well as masterful portraits. ❏

BIRTH OF A NATION

After centuries of foreign domination and a prolonged struggle, Italy emerged in 1870 as a united independent kingdom

The seeds of Italian patriotism, crushed by the battle of Fornovo in 1495, lay virtually dormant for three centuries. After Fornovo, all the armies of Europe came to Italy and fought among themselves for a share of the spoils. Spain, the most powerful nation in Europe at the time, eventually emerged as the clear master of Italy. The country was burdened by heavy taxation, and under Spanish influence liberty and native energy and initiative declined. The papacy was no less oppressive; the rules of the Inquisition, the Index and the Jesuit Orders forced many Italians to flee.

The Pope crowned King Charles I of Spain Holy Roman Emperor in 1530, and Charles and his descendants ruled Italy for more than 150 years.

Under the Spaniards and later (after the 1713 Treaty of Utrecht) under the equally oppressive Austrians, Italy lost its reputation as a cultural centre. But the 1789 French Revolution inspired many Italians, and patriots dreamt of an independent Italian republic modelled on France.

When Napoleon invaded Italy in 1796, the people rose against the Austrians and a series of republics was founded. For three years the whole peninsula was republican and under French rule. But in March 1799, an Austro-Russian army expelled the French from northern Italy and restored many local princes.

LEFT: Giuseppe Garibaldi, a prominent leader of the Risorgimento. **RIGHT:** Camillo Benso, Count of Cavour, Italy's first great statesman.

To work against the foreign oppressors, Italian patriots joined secret societies, such as the Carbonari. In their love of ritual they resembled the Freemasons, but they had a serious goal: to liberate Italy.

The Risorgimento

In 1800 Napoleon won back most of Italy. The kingdom that he founded lasted only briefly but, by proving that the country could be a single unit, it gave Italian patriots new inspiration. From the Congress of Vienna in 1815, which reinstated Italian political divisions, until Rome was taken in 1870 by the troops of King Victor Emmanuel II of Savoy (who also ruled over

Piedmont and Sardinia), the history of Italy was one continuous struggle for reunification.

The period is a complex one. Many northern and southern Italians wanted the peninsula to become one nation, but there was no agreement as to how it should be achieved. Some, like Giuseppe Mazzini, wanted to revive the Roman Republic. Others were for a kingdom of Italy under the House of Savoy.

In 1848, a year of revolt all over Europe, the first Italian war for independence was fought. First, rebellions in Sicily, Tuscany and the Papal States forced local rulers to grant constitutions to their citizens. In Milan, news of Parisian and

governed the city with a true democratic spirit despite the siege conditions. The commander of the city's armed forces was Giuseppe Garibaldi, a lifelong Italian patriot who had honed his fighting skills as a mercenary in the revolutions of South America, where he had fled after being

> *Giuseppe Mazzini (1805–72) was a great patriot and, with Cavour and Garibaldi, one of the founders of Italian independence. As a true republican, he never accepted the monarchical unification of Italy.*

Viennese uprisings sparked the famous "five days" when the occupying Austrian army was driven from the city. A few days later, Charles Albert of Savoy sent his army to pursue the Austrians, and the revolution began in earnest.

Charles Albert was soon supported by troops from other Italian states; however, the tide turned when the Pope refused to declare war on Catholic Austria. The newly confident Austrians drove Charles Albert's army back into Piedmont. He abdicated months later, and the House of Savoy signed a peace treaty.

Garibaldi and Cavour

Venice and the Roman Republic continued the fight. In Rome, Mazzini led a triumvirate that

convicted of subversion in Piedmont. Now he and his men faced the combined strength of the Neapolitans, the Austrians and the French. It was French forces that entered the city on 3 July 1849, the day after Garibaldi escaped into the mountains. The following month the Venetians succumbed to an Austrian siege.

The treaty the Austrians had signed with the House of Savoy kept them out of that region, so it was now the only Italian state with a free press, an elected parliament and a liberal constitution. Piedmont-Savoy was also blessed, from 1852, with a brilliant prime minister, Count Camillo di Cavour, who was devoted to the cause of Italian unity. Cavour went to England and France to raise support for the Italian cause. He contributed Piedmontese troops to the Crimean War, and thus won a seat at the peace conference, where he raised the Italian question. Although Cavour made no tangible gains at this meeting, he won moral support.

Europe was thus not surprised when France and Piedmont went to war with Austria three years later. The French emperor, Napoleon III, and Cavour had agreed that, after the expected victory, an Italian kingdom would be formed for the Piedmontese king, Victor Emmanuel, and Nice and French Savoy would be returned to France. The people of the Italian dukedoms proclaimed their allegiance to Victor Emmanuel.

arrival was a signal for the overthrow of Bourbon rule on the island. Garibaldi declared himself dictator in the name of Victor Emmanuel. After fierce fighting, with the aid of Sicilian rebels Garibaldi entered Palermo in triumph. Men from all over Italy now came to help him and, on 7 September, Naples fell to the patriots.

Meanwhile, Victor Emmanuel gathered troops and marched south to link up with Garibaldi and his men. The two groups met at Teano, and the Kingdom of Italy was declared. The new kingdom excluded Rome: the Pope preached against the patriots, and French garrisons protected the city.

Unfortunately, the French tired of fighting and made peace with Austria. The Austrians agreed to let Lombardy become part of an Italian Federation, but the Veneto region went back to Austria and the dukes of Modena and Tuscany were reinstated.

In Italy, there was outrage. Cavour resigned in protest, but first arranged plebiscites in Tuscany and Modena. Citizens refused to have their dukes back and voted to become part of Piedmont.

Garibaldi and 1,000 red-shirted volunteers sailed for Sicily from Genoa on 5 May 1860. His

Finally, in 1870, Italian troops fought their way into Rome. The Pope barricaded himself in the Vatican. For half a century, no pope emerged to participate in the life of the new Italy.

The new government of all Italy was a parliamentary democracy with the king as executive. The most powerful men in the early days of the Italian state were the loyal Piedmontese parliamentarians who were largely responsible for its creation and for designing the administration of the whole peninsula.

However, once the government moved down to Rome, this group began to splinter. This was the start of the breakdown of the party system in Italy, the effects of which are discernible even today. ❑

LEFT: Garibaldi and Victor Emmanuel II of Savoy join forces at Teano.
ABOVE: celebration of Italian unity in Turin.

THE MAKING OF MODERN ITALY

Wars, Fascism, corruption scandals... with remarkable
resilience, Italy survived every challenge
the 20th century presented to it

As governments so often do during times
of rapid change and relative instability at
home, Italy's began to look abroad for
confirmation of its hard-won independence.
Relations with France had cooled during the
final fight for unification; when France occupied Tunisia, a traditional area of Italian influence, they became positively chilly. Italy's
response was to sign the Triple Alliance with
Germany and Austro-Hungary, providing
mutual defence in the event of war.

Under the Conservative governments of
Francesco Crispi (1887–91, 1893–6), Italy also
joined the scramble for colonies in North
Africa. Crispi successfully colonised Eritrea, but
when he tried to subdue Ethiopia (Abyssinia),
the Italian army suffered a humiliating defeat at
Adwa which led to Crispi's resignation. A later
colonising attempt during the Italo-Turkish War
(1911–12) ended in victory and the Italian occupation of Libya and the Dodecanese Islands.

North–south divide

At home, the years leading up to World War I
were marked by the division that still plagues
the country today: relative wealth in the north
and extreme poverty in the south. The economy was overwhelmingly agricultural, and the
government's protectionist policies left Italy
increasingly isolated from other European
markets. The industrial boom of the late 1800s,
mostly in textiles and refining, was confined to
the north. The crushing economic conditions
in the south fuelled a wave of emigration. In the
last years of the 19th century, nearly half a mil-

LEFT: Benito Mussolini in 1928.
RIGHT: statue of Victor Emmanuel II in Venice.

lion people a year set out for the New World.

When World War I began with Austria's
attack on Serbia in July 1914, Italy had not
been consulted, in breach of the terms of the
Triple Alliance. In consequence, on 2 August,
Prime Minister Antonio Salandra declared Italy's neutrality. Public opinion began to swing
in the direction of the Allies. To help win Italy
over, the Allied governments dangled the possibility of territorial gains: Rome was offered
the chance to gain the "unrecovered" provinces of Trieste and Trentino, long held by the
Austro-Hungarian Habsburg Empire. In addition, Italy would receive the Alto Adige, plus
North African and Turkish enclaves. Finally

swayed, in April 1915 Italy signed the secret Treaty of London and, a month later, broke the Triple Alliance and entered the war on the Allied side.

Seldom had a country been so ill-prepared for war. Italy's army was poorly equipped, and Austrian troops had already dug into defensive positions in Alpine strongholds along the 480km (300-mile) shared border. For Italy the war was a costly stalemate; of the 5.5 million men mobilised, 39 percent were killed or wounded.

At the post-war conference table, the Treaty of St Germain (10 September 1919) gave Italy Trentino, the Alto Adige (South Tyrol) and

Trieste. But Fiume, Dalmatia and the other promised territories were negotiated away by the Allies.

Disappointment in the peace talks, combined with the social and economic toll of the war, produced chaotic domestic conditions. Soon there was talk that Italy had won only a "mutilated victory", despite its wartime sacrifice. Inflation soared. Factory workers took to the streets, and peasants clamoured for land reform.

Into this power vacuum marched Benito Mussolini and his Fascist Party. When he founded the party in 1919, Mussolini played on the worst fears of all Italians. To placate the rich he denounced Bolshevism. To the middle classes he pledged a return to law and order,

and a corporate state in which workers and management would pull together for the good of the country.

By mid-1922, Fascism had become a major political force. When workers called for a general strike, Mussolini made his move. On 28 October, 50,000 members of the Fascist mili-

> *After World War II, Italian politicians focused on the negative elements of the peace treaties, and so the myth of the "mutilated victory" spread, fuelling Fascist propaganda and helping Mussolini seize power.*

tia converged on Rome. Although Mussolini's supporters held only a small minority in parliament, the sight of thousands of menacing Fascists flooding the streets of the capital was enough to topple the tottering government of Prime Minister Luigi Facta. Refusing to sanction a state of siege, King Victor Emmanuel III instead handed the reins of government to Benito Mussolini.

Once in control, Mussolini quickly pushed through an act assuring the Fascists a permanent majority in the parliament. After questionable elections in 1924, he dropped all pretence of collaborative government. Italy was now a dictatorship. In Christmas of that year, he declared himself head of the government, answerable only to the king. Within two years all parties except the Fascists were banned, and opposition activists were jailed or forced into exile or underground.

Fascist rule

Despite its ugly underbelly, on the surface Fascism seemed to work. Weary of inflation, strikes and street disturbances, Italians eagerly embraced their severe new government and its charismatic *Duce*, or leader. This spontaneous response to Fascist rule was reinforced by a strong propaganda campaign. Mussolini promised to restore to Italy the glories of Ancient Rome, and for a time promises were enough. Soon, however, the government could show results. The economy stabilised, huge public works projects were launched, and Mussolini even made peace with the Vatican, hammering out the Lateran Treaty (1929), which ended the 50-year rift between Rome and the Catholic

Church. He also set out on an imperial campaign, restoring control over Libya, which had been ignored during and after World War I. In October 1935, Italian troops crossed the border of Eritrea and headed for the Ethiopian capital of Addis Ababa. The League of Nations protested, but took no action. Six months later, *Il Duce* announced to a hysterical Piazza Venezia crowd that, finally, Rome had begun to reclaim its empire.

The international outcry over the Ethiopian occupation left Rome isolated. The one government willing to overlook Mussolini's expansionism was in Berlin, where Adolf Hit-

case, most Italians opposed intervention, and the army was ill-prepared for war. But as Hitler claimed victory after victory – in Denmark, Norway and Belgium, and with France on the verge of collapse – the lure of sharing the spoils of war proved irresistible. On 10 June 1940, Italy entered the war, just before the fall of France.

Eager to pull off his own battlefield coup, in the autumn of 1940 Mussolini set his sights on taking Greece. But the Greeks fought back fiercely. The Italians suffered many casualties, and only Nazi intervention prevented a likely Italian defeat. The war was also going badly for the Axis Powers in North Africa, and eventually

ler's Nazis had held power since January 1933. Both Germany and Italy had supported General Francisco Franco's nationalist troops in the Spanish Civil War (1936–9), and this cooperation led eventually to the signing of the Pact of Steel between Berlin and Rome in May 1939.

Three months later, Hitler invaded Poland. Within days, Britain and France declared war on Germany. At first the Rome government remained neutral, as it had in 1914, arguing that Berlin's surprise attack on Poland did not require an automatic military response. In any

even the Nazi General Rommel could not prevent the collapse. In 1943 US and British troops captured Sicily.

The beginning of the end was in sight. From their base in Sicily, the Allied forces began to bomb the Italian mainland, and Italian public morale sank to a new low. On 25 July 1943, the Grand Council of Fascism voted to strip *Il Duce* of his powers. Mussolini refused to step down, but the next day, King Victor Emmanuel ordered his arrest. Mussolini was detained in the Abruzzo Mountains, but in September, German air commandos airlifted him to Munich.

Chaos broke out in the final days of the war. To placate the Germans, who would otherwise have occupied the entire country, Prime Minis-

LEFT: the Palazzo della Civiltà del Lavoro in Rome's EUR district, a prime example of Fascist architecture.
ABOVE: Axis allies – Mussolini and Hitler.

ter Marshal Badoglio publicly declared that Italy would fight on. In secret, however, he entered negotiations with the Allies, who by then had fought their way as far north as Naples. Above that line was the hastily organised *Repubblica Sociale Italiana*, headed by the liberated *Duce*. Better known as the Republic of Salo, based on Lake Garda, this was a puppet regime of Berlin, and Mussolini spent most of his time brooding on the judgement history would pass on him.

As the Allies fought northwards, the Italian Resistance felt safe enough to begin widespread activities. Combined, the forces managed to liberate Rome on 4 June 1944; the liberation of

Florence followed not long after, on 12 August. The Germans and Mussolini lasted out the winter behind the so-called "Gothic line" in the Apennines, but by spring 1945 that effort, too, had collapsed.

Mussolini tried to escape into Switzerland disguised as a German soldier, but Italian partisans found him, and he was shot. His body was hauled into Milan and hung by a rope for the public to see.

Recovery and resiliency

In the immediate post-war period, Italy suffered greatly. The Italian colonies were taken

A MARXIST PARTY WITHOUT MARX

A distinctive feature of Italian politics has been the influence of the Italian Communist Party (PCI). In the post-war years, the party cleaved to the Soviet Union's political line, and Rome's centrist government kept the communists at arm's length.

Under Enrico Berlinguer, PCI secretary 1972–84, the party's orientation changed. It often led the Eurocommunism movement, favouring more independence from Moscow; it scolded the Soviets for human rights abuses and the Russian invasion of Afghanistan. On economic issues it grew ever more centrist, prompting some to dub it a "Marxist party without Marx". By 1981 the PCI attracted a third of the popular vote, and it was second only to the Christian

Democrats (DC) in size. Catholicism and communism were the two dominant political cultures of the post-war years. The collapse of communism in Eastern Europe led to the PCI splitting into the mainstream Democratic Party of the Left (DS) and a hard-line splinter group.

After the upheavals of the 1990s, the DC was dissolved while the DS has seemingly lost its way and succumbed to infighting. Today's political scene is awash with new parties, even if many old faces remain. Tuscany and Emilia-Romagna remain left-leaning and liberal – but sleekly consumerist. This "Red Belt", once the communist heartland of central Italy, is nowadays more "pretty-in-pink" than radically red.

away and reparations paid to the Soviet Union and Ethiopia. The political system needed a complete overhaul. In the 1946 elections, voters opted for a republic, thus formally ending the days of the monarchy. The economy was in disarray, but US aid in the form of the Marshall Plan helped to ease the burden.

For over a decade after the war, centrist coalitions ran the country. Then, in the early 1960s, the Christian Democrats, Socialists, Social Democrats and Republicans formed a coalition and ruled, in various combinations, until 1968.

Fuelled by cheap labour, the economy developed rapidly. The 1950s witnessed a steady migration from rural areas to the cities and from south to north. Heavy industry such as chemicals, iron, steel and cars took off. In 1957, Italy became a founding member of the European Community. By the mid-1960s, manufacturing overtook agriculture, and observers hailed Italy's "economic miracle".

Terrorism and scandals

A few years later, however, the boom had gone bust, Italy was dubbed the "sick man of Europe", and terrorism reared its ugly head. From the late 1970s, kidnappings, knee-cappings and murders were a fact of life. The murder, in 1978, of former Christian Democrat prime minister Aldo Moro by the left-wing *Brigate Rosse* (Red Brigades) spurred new anti-terrorist measures, and eventually 32 Red Brigade members were imprisoned for the deaths of Moro and 16 others. Neo-Fascist terrorism also plagued the country, culminating, in 1980, in a bomb blast at Bologna station, killing 84 people.

In the 1980s the economy grew, and Italy briefly overtook France and Britain in the economic league. Troubles were in store, however. In the 1990s a wave of corruption scandals rocked the state. In 1992, it was alleged that some £67 million (US$100 million) had been shared out among the leaders of the five coalition parties governing Italy in 1990. Two former premiers were convicted of being chief recipients, while veteran prime minister Giulio Andreotti was charged with Mafia links *(see page 70)*, as were other leading figures, from fashion designers to industrialists. The short-lived first

premiership of media magnate Silvio Berlusconi, in 1994, also stumbled over accusations of corruption. These scandals unleashed a volley of reforms spearheaded by the first left-wing government in Italy's post-war history. In order to create stronger, more durable governments, the system of proportional representation was changed to a largely first-past-the-post system.

Into the new millennium

In a landslide victory in 2001, Silvio Berlusconi's centre-right government came to power on a tide of populism, nationalism and reforming zeal. Perceived as a free-marketeer, the media

mogul was elected to slash red tape and reform the tax system. However, by 2006, when he left office, he had singularly failed to resolve the conflict of interest between his public and business roles, and, as a convicted fraudster, evoked the tainted world of the Italian kickback culture. Commentator John Carlin likened the Milanese mogul to a megalomaniac Roman ruler: "The Roman emperors knew that the secret to exercising peaceful rule over the people was to provide them with bread and circuses. Berlusconi owns the circuses, pretty much all of it – the TV, the football, the magazines, the books. And as a head of government, who also happens to own Italy's biggest supermarket chain, he also controls, in the widest sense of the word, the bread."

LEFT: the liberation of Rome. **RIGHT:** 10.25am, on the day in 1980 when a terrorist bomb ripped through Bologna train station.

After a left-wing coalition under Romano Prodi collapsed in disarray, Berlusconi was re-elected in 2008 for his third term. Formerly known as Forza Italia, his People of Freedom party (PdL), a centre-right coalition, embraces the heirs of the newly respectable post-Fascist movement. It also relies on the support of the Northern League, the secessionist-leaning party. The League, with its power base in Lombardy, the Veneto and Piedmont, strives for greater autonomy for the wealthy, industrialised north, and resents supporting the poorer south.

The premiership is tainted by allegations of sex and sleaze scandals; in 2011 Berlusconi was being investigated for paying for sex with one of his guests (aged 17), and for "charitably" housing young female escorts in return for performances at his so-called "bunga bunga" parties.

As yet the numerous charges have not stuck. Berlusconi's critics claim that he sees himself as above the law, introducing laws to favour his business interests. The premier has appealed against charges of fraud, false accounting and corruption, and although censured, has escaped conviction. Despite a suspended sentence for fraud in 1997, Berlusconi maintains his media empire, high political profile and chairmanship of AC Milan football club.

GRAND DESIGNS

During his first premiership, Berlusconi was drawn to "grand projects" which would leave a mark and solve intractable problems with a flourish. Saving Venice for posterity should be a big enough project for any vainglorious megalomaniac. The first stage of MOSE, the controversial mobile flood barrier, was met with a mixed reception. The project won qualified support from the trusted Venice in Peril, but critics, including some environmentalists, fear that the barrier is not reversible and could affect the delicate ecological balance in the lagoon, turning it into a stagnant pond. From 2014, when the mobile barriers start operating, flooding should become a thing of the past. But the barriers can do nothing to counteract the chronically raised water level, the city's next great challenge.

One of the most pharaonic of *"grandi progetti"* is the planned Messina Bridge, the world's longest single-span suspension bridge, linking Sicily with the mainland across the Straits of Messina. Work begins on the €1.3bn 4km (2½-mile) bridge in late 2010 despite its unpopularity with environmentalists and the centre-left. Critics consider it costly, pointless, prone to high winds and rich pickings for contractors, corrupt politicians and the Mafia. The Greens note that the Calabrian motorway remains unfinished after decades of construction and sleaze. Since the south is a graveyard of grand ideas, this might, indeed, be a bridge too far.

Even so, testimony gathered by crime prosecutors in 2010 attests that the billionaire prime minister met a leading Mafia godfather in 1974 to ask for protection and safeguard his business interests. This was allegedly arranged by dell'Utri, co-founder of the Forza Italia party. There have also been

> The much-derided Northern League recently came up with a crazy proposal to increase the speed limit on Italian motorways from 130 to 150 km/h (93 mph) – but only if applied to big cars, and on motorways with speed traps.

allegations by informants that the Mafia backed Forza Italia. Berlusconi rejects allegations of Mafia links and claims to be the victim of a conspiracy orchestrated by left-wing judges. He insists that no Italian government has done more than his to combat the Mafia. Instead, investigative reporter Marco Travaglio claims that Dell'Utri put Berlusconi in the hands of the Mafia: "Cosa Nostra is not like a taxi where you jump on, pay for the trip, get off and say goodbye. Once you are on you can no longer get off. Berlusconi is terrified that his past will catch up with him."

Controversy also reigns over planned legislation to make wire taps illegal, despite (or perhaps because of) the fact that it seems designed to shield top politicians from further embarrassing revelations. Moreover, Antonio Ingroia, a leading anti-Mafia prosecutor, warns that neither the last "boss of bosses" nor his predecessor would be behind bars were it not for evidence obtained through bugging calls.

An uncertain legacy

It is too early to assess Berlusconi's legacy, particularly when his status as Italy's richest man still makes him a player in most political scenarios. Detractors point to Berlusconi's ruthless pursuit of self-interest, his lack of probity and unstatesmanlike behaviour. However, while Berlusconi's gaffes regularly made him a laughing stock on the world stage, fans claim that he has proved a loyal ally to the United

States and Britain, and tried to liberalise the economy and reform the fossilised state of Italian bureaucracy.

Italy is facing an even more unstable future than usual, with towering national debt and reduced industrial output. Economically, Italy is highly exposed to the challenges of globalisation as a disproportionate share of its manufacturing is concentrated in clothing, footwear and white goods, where it cannot compete with the Asian Tiger economies. The challenge is to liberalise the economy and weaken the straitjacket of guild-like rules that have their origins in the Middle Ages.

But Italy's greatest task is to reduce the public deficit, which is the highest in the EU: Italy owes more than the economy produces annually. In 2010, new austerity measures sought to cut public spending by €24 billion. Italians were faced with health and education cuts, pay freezes for civil servants and a crackdown on tax evasion. Luca di Montezemolo, chairman of Ferrari, put it bluntly: "We did not need the crisis in Greece to discover tax evasion in Italy, where one out of every two taxpayers claims to earn under €15,000 a year." The belt-tightening measures produced a wave of strikes and unrest. Italy finds itself in uncharted waters once more – but without a Marco Polo or Christopher Columbus in sight. ❏

LEFT: a demonstrator in Rome during the closing electoral rally of the "Olive tree" coalition.
RIGHT: peacekeepers in Lebanon.

The Mafia

With its tradition of brutal private justice and its code of silence, or *omertà*, the Mafia remains Italy's biggest blight

The Mafia still colours Sicilian life, but local attitudes are changing. Not that the Mafia is a unified entity confined to Sicily, where it is known as the "Cosa Nostra"; in Naples it mutates into the "Camorra", and in Calabria the "'Ndrangheta".

The revulsion of Sicilians to the 1992 murders of the anti-Mafia judges Giovanni Falcone and Paolo Borsellino weakened the Mafia's grip on public opinion, its greatest weapon, and dented the age-old code of silence, or *omertà*. *Pentiti* ("the penitents"), as Mafia turncoats are called, grew from a handful in 1992, when Falcone was killed, to 500 a year later. As a result dozens of Dons, including "Toto" Riina, the Godfather of Corleone, were jailed, and the Sicilian Mafia has gone underground.

The new generation of gangster is as ruthless on the stock exchange as on the streets of Palermo, and is adept at money-laundering via the web, along with arms-dealing, drugs-dealing, extortion and property speculation. The Mafia also exploits the phenomenon of *pentitismo,* infiltrating bogus

turncoats, and weaving in false evidence to discredit witnesses and sow uncertainty.

As the old Mafia guard languishes in jail, the women have stepped into the breach, acting as messengers or enforcing extortion rackets. The last Mafia taboo has been broken. But some have turned state's evidence too. In 2009 the wife of a Sicilian gangster betrayed her husband at their daughters' request, and appealed to mob women to leave their men. Carmela Luculano's evidence sent her husband, Pino Rizzo, to jail, but is relatively rare in an organisation that expects submission and respect of the code of silence.

The good old days

The Mafia emerged in the early 19th century, in the guise of brotherhoods formed to protect Sicilians from corruption, foreign oppression and feudalism, but which thrived on human misery. Between 1872 and World War I, poverty forced 1.5 million Sicilians to emigrate to the Americas, where many joined brotherhoods, and the foundations of Cosa Nostra were laid. During Prohibition, US bootlegging marked the Mafia's graduation from rural bands to urban gangsterism. In 1925, Mussolini tried to crush the Mafia but it won a reprieve in 1943, when the Allied invasion essentially reinstated the Mob, in exchange for help in paving the way for the invasion.

Naples became a fiefdom of Cosa Nostra, and was chosen by US gangsters as the site of Italy's first heroin refinery. Sicily's "Americanised" Mafia achieved its quantum leap in the late 1950s with the emerging drugs trade. In 1957, after a US crime crackdown, American bosses entrusted their Sicilian counterparts with the importation of heroin, linked to Lucky Luciano and Luciano Liggio.

Clan warfare

Liggio, a wartime marketeer, elevated his Corleonese family to the pinnacle of the Cosa Nostra. After being jailed in 1974, he was eclipsed by "Wild Beast" Toto Riina. The Corleonesi tactics were simple: the removal of mafiosi who coveted power or caused trouble. The 1980 clan wars left Palermo's streets bathed in blood, the Corleonesi undisputed victors, and Riina linked to 1,000 murders. The list of "illustrious corpses" included Palermo's prefect, dalla Chiesa, thought to have stumbled on the "Third Level", a top politician who protected the Mafia. Supergrass Tommaso Buscetta claimed that former premier Giulio Andreotti ordered the Mob to kill dalla Chiesa and a journalist, because they knew too much. His evidence led to "maxi-trials" in the 1980s, where hundreds of mafiosi sat in the dock, and launched magistrate Falcone's fight against the Mafia.

In 1992, the murder of Salvo Lima, the Sicilian leader of a faction led by Andreotti, provoked a terror campaign that saw the assassination of the public prosecutors, Falcone and Borsellino. Even if their "heroic" deaths marked a turning point, the terror continued in 1993 with bombs in Milan and Rome which killed bystanders and devastated churches, and an explosion at Florence's Uffizi Gallery. The assassinations and attempt to destroy the nation's cultural treasures strengthened Italian resolve against the Mafia.

arrested in 2007. This left the way clear for ruthless rival boss Messina Denaro from Trapani to take over and reform the "Mafia Commission" or "Cupola", which instructs the clans and acts as arbiter in turf wars.

After the Sicilian Mafia dropped the baton in the 1990s, the Neapolitan Camorra and the Ndrangheta from Reggio Calabria picked it up. Unlike the more centrally controlled Sicilian Mafia, the Camorra, with its 20 rival clans, has always been volatile. Since 2004, hundreds have died in turf wars related to an annual £11 billion (US$20 billion) drugs trade. Naples' poverty-stricken northern suburbs have become a battleground, with protec-

In 2006, the fugitive Mafia Godfather, Bernardo Provenzano, was captured after 43 years on the run. The capture of the "Phantom of Corleone", also nicknamed "The Tractor" due to his propensity for mowing people down, provoked celebrations, even if cynics suspected the mobster had long been protected in his Corleone power base. After the arrest of Godfather Toto Riina in 1993, Provenzano led the Mafia underground, consolidating the crime syndicate and abandoning overt violence. He allegedly passed the leadership to Salvatore Lo Piccolo, a Palermitan Mafia boss, who was himself

LEFT: a threatening gesture is made during one of the maxi-trials. **ABOVE:** after years in hiding, Mafia godfather Bernardo Provenzano is arrested in Corleone.

tion rackets endemic, drug dealers executed and businesses torched.

As for the Ndrangheta, in 2004 Italy's biggest anti-Mafia operation for a decade discovered that a drug-running clan had built an underground village below Plati. A year later, the vice-president of Calabria's regional council was gunned down.

Criminal practices remain entrenched, from illegal building in beauty spots to protection rackets. Francesco Messineo, Palermo's chief prosecutor, sounds resigned: "The Mafia remains true to itself. Its structures, methods and projects in the end are always the same." Still, the tide is turning in Sicily, with the redistribution of Mafia assets, the emergence of anti-racketeering associations – and even "Mafia-free" holidays (see page 361). ❏

THE CONTEMPORARY SCENE

Tradition and rebellion, conformity and
individuality, chaos and over-regulation...
Italian life is riddled with paradoxes

According to Sergio Romano, a political journalist on *La Stampa*, "Italy is a constellation of large families, whether ideological, political, professional or criminal – the Church, the business community, the trade unions, the professions, state bureaucracies and the Mafia." He observes that "each family strives for sovereignty", acting as a fierce lobby group and dooming most national reforms to failure.

At the simplest level, Italians create a cosy little world of "their" baker, dressmaker and picture-framer, conveying the social status of a patron rather than of a mere consumer. Personal recommendation is everything. And beyond lies the arbitrary world of bureaucracy, in which citizens feel powerless in the face of state indifference. Many commentators conclude that Italy would be a paradise if it could only reinvent the relationship between citizen and state. Yet without political chaos and conflicting social groups, the Italians would cease to be Italians and become Swiss.

> "It is not impossible to govern Italians, it is pointless." Mussolini's judgement has been borne out by the country's perpetual sense of teetering on the edge.

The political picture

The Italian mindset precludes a modern democracy, seeming to favour an abyss between the state and its citizens. The people swing between political disaffection and an obsession with politics. Fortunately, however, they also have an innate talent for brinkmanship, coupled with an ability to conjure compromise out of conflict. But if Italy totters along in an amiable state of chaos, it may be because Italians like it that way. "Controllers and controlled have an unspoken agreement," notes columnist Beppe Severgnini. "You don't change, we don't change, and Italy doesn't change, but we all complain that we can't go on like this."

The country positions itself as the new Italy, turning its back on a baroque political structure steeped in *clientelismo* (nepotism). Even so, one in three people finds a job through a relative. Italy remains deeply old-fashioned, despite

LEFT: a performance of *Madame Butterfly* at Verona's Arena. **RIGHT:** keeping up with the news.

its faddism. Italians pride themselves on their free spirit, yet society remains static, while protectionism has preserved many monopolies, including limiting the growth of super-pharmacies, even if shopping malls are slowly moving in. Despite their sense of tradition, Italians have a mania for modernity, novelty and new-fangled gadgetry, from the latest mobile phones to shopping malls.

Milan is the business capital, a sophisticated metropolis dedicated to moneymaking and pleasure. Most wealth is still created in northern and central regions, such as Lombardy, the Veneto and Emilia-Romagna. However, although the Ferrari, Prada and Armani fiefdoms are well known abroad, most Italian companies are small, family-run firms. These provide more than two-thirds of industrial employment, from textiles in Tuscany to designer sunglasses in the Veneto or bathroom taps in Piedmont. Even so, high unemployment and low consumer demand mask a thriving black economy. In the workplace, industrial action is commonplace.

The recession and the country's uncompetitiveness are major concerns. Privatisation of the public utilities did not end state interference. Given the traditional monopoly of top jobs in state companies by the political parties, politicians remain reluctant to give up their power. By the same token, the family dynasties who dominate the economy still hold sway. With his patrician charm and playboy reputation, the late Gianni Agnelli epitomised the closed, dynastic style of Italian capitalism. After his death in 2003, the Turin football stadium was renamed in his honour, and the Fiat family empire survives.

> *Pope Benedict has paved the way for the beatification of the wartime Pope Pius XII, despite claims he did little to prevent the Holocaust. Jewish leaders have requested a delay until files are released in 2015.*

A complex but coherent society

The social system is a rich landscape, not calibrated on class, success or wealth but on subtle distinctions. In conventional terms, a class system exists but has different connotations. The aristocracy thrives, thanks to its adaptability. Many *marchesi* (marquesses) are entrepreneurs, carving niches in the fashion, art, wine and food industries. The Strozzi are big in banking, the Tuscan Frescobaldi and Sicilian Tasca are wine dynasties, while the Ferragamo fashion and hotel empires thrive in Florence.

While class-consciousness and accent are essentially immaterial, the *borghesi* (middle classes) form a cohesive group, as do the *agricoltori* (encompassing peasants and farmers). The ranks of the middle classes are swelling, even among the criminal caste. A recent Mafia round-up revealed that many new-generation Dons are doctors or lawyers, in sharp contrast to the

IN GOOD FAITH?

Curiously, the phrase often used to bemoan declining standards is: "There's no religion left any more." Jonathan Keates describes the Italian attitude to religion as "a lackadaisical Catholicism taken out of mothballs at christenings, first communions, weddings and funerals". Increasingly, Italy's practising Catholics prefer to take their cue not from the Pope but from personal conscience or the liberal wing of the Church. Civic culture, regional pride and fierce individualism form the real Italian faith today. Even so, the death of the beloved Pope John Paul II in 2005 entwined several strands of Italian life: the sense of occasion and spectacle, softened by a poignant sense of solidarity.

Cosa Nostra's agrarian roots, and even to recent Godfathers, who were barely literate. Whatever one's profession, honorific titles count, especially in the south: an engineer is addressed as "*ingegnere*"; *dottore* (doctor) is a mark of respect bestowed on anyone with gravitas.

Apart from the north–south divide, the key distinction is between *statali*, civil servants, and

> Politics rarely impinge on social divisions: a member of the DS, the former Communist Party, may be a Catholic, wear Armani and have a Romanian maid.

non-*statali*, the rest. Civil servants are seen as cosseted, with a protected pension and a job for life. Ranged against them are the *dipendenti* (company employees), *autonomi* (self-employed), *imprenditori* (entrepreneurs) and, lastly, the *liberi professionisti* (professionals). The employees claim the moral high ground, charging civil servants with exploiting the system and accusing the self-employed and professionals of tax evasion. This is a strange Italian stalemate in which private-sector workers (non-*statali*) justify tax evasion on the grounds that their taxes would only perpetuate the bloated state bureaucracy and southern incompetence. Tax evasion is a sport and a duty. If he were to cheat on his taxes in Italy, remarks Beppe Severgnini, "Two neighbours would come round to ask me how I did it, and two more would loathe me in silence."

A new pressure group are the *precari*, workers on temporary contracts who crave security. Around 3 million people, mostly young, fall into this category, from language teachers to hotel workers. Without holiday pay, overtime or job security, many resort to "cocooning", concentrating on their private lives and opting out of the rat race. Sometimes dubbed the "IKEA generation", this group are "constrained" to buy flat-pack Swedish furniture – implying limited aspirations and prospects.

Popular culture and the arts

Both in the art world and in the broader cultural arena, Italian genius thrives on dissension, diversity and unbridled rivalry. However, music

LEFT: commercial artist at work in Trastevere, Rome.
RIGHT: Pope Benedict XVI.

and the performing arts are more dynamic than the literary scene: Italy has always been a musical, visual and verbal culture more than a literary one. Contemporary fiction is an acquired taste, one that few acquire. A recent survey reports that a third of Italians never read, and that a mere 8 percent can be considered regular readers. This is either confirmation that Italy is a predominantly visual culture, or linked to the fact that pleasure lies elsewhere – on the beach or on "the box". Italians watch more (bad) television than any other nationality in Europe.

The classical music scene is thriving and not restricted to the great opera houses: Italy boasts

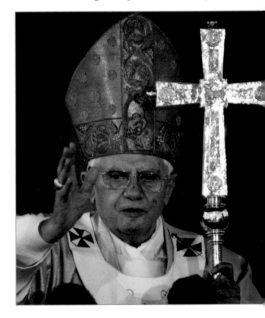

some of the best musical festivals in Europe, from the operatic masterpieces performed in Verona's lovely Roman amphitheatre, the Arena di Verona, to the Puccini Festival at the composer's lakeside home in Tuscany's Torre del Lago.

Italian high culture tends to be buffeted by perennial funding crises. The Berlusconi government urged citizens to take responsibility for their heritage. A shock advertising campaign showed images of mutilated artistic icons, such as Leonardo da Vinci's *Last Supper* with the Disciples scratched out. The provocative slogan was: "Without your help, Italy could lose something," which singularly failed to elicit mass donations to save the country's treasures. Fortunately, local businesses and banks see

Heritage Industry

Italy has more Unesco World Heritage sites than any other country – the challenge is to maintain them, without selling off the family silver

There is a price to pay for Italy's historic cultural riches. Air pollution, illegal building and sewage-laden water are endangering a third of Italy's Unesco sites, including such treasures as Pompeii's ancient ruins.

Burdened by its costly heritage, towns in Italy often resemble a cultural building site, with many buildings and monuments under wraps. That's without considering the cost of natural disasters, such as the L'Aquila earthquake in 2009 *(see page 309)*.

Vandalism is another problem, with Italy's sculptural treasures particularly vulnerable. As the despairing head of the Carabinieri's art-theft unit says: "Italy is an open-air museum, with many of its most celebrated works of art standing on streets and squares, and nowhere is this truer than in Florence."

The state is also under pressure to "sell the family silver" to the highest bidder. State assets, ranging from palaces to prisons, monasteries to islands, have already been auctioned. In the case of Venice, this Unesco gem has already "lost" numerous islands to hotel developers, while the council is currently selling Grand Canal palaces to fill depleted city coffers. At the other end of the scale, Rome is creating a theme park of Ancient Rome, as if the ruins of Ancient Rome weren't glorious enough.

Despite the threats to the nation's heritage, unqualified success stories abound. Amid the frantic fire-and-ice effects of the 2006 Winter Olympics, Turin was rebranded as a cinematic capital, Baroque stage and cutting-edge design centre. Key sites underwent makeovers, from the Egyptian Museum to the star-studded Cinema Museum. Turin's renaissance continues, marked by the restoration of the Unesco-listed Venaria Reale, Italy's Versailles, and projects celebrating the Unification of Italy in 2011.

In the meantime, the country continues to open major museums and stage dazzling art extravaganzas. All over Italy, seemingly mundane restoration work ensures that masterpieces survive, such as Caravaggio's *Adoration of the Shepherds* in Messina or the restoration of Baroque Noto, also in Sicily. Elsewhere, archaeologists are constantly unearthing Etruscan or Roman treasures, most recently in Lombardy, Tuscany and Rome. In Brescia, the discovery of frescoed Pompeian-style villas confirm that the city boasts the greatest concentration of Roman remains north of the Rome.

Given the heavyweight nature of Italian heritage, stately homes tend to be treated as a burden, with little incentive for owners to turn their properties into public attractions. Italy may lag behind its French and British counterparts in the heritage industry but local landowners are increasingly taking the initiative. In Tuscany, country seats have been reborn as wine estates or rural resorts, but even the Sicilians are showing enterprise: princesses in Palermo are staging cookery courses and masked balls to save the ancestral seats.

Near Trieste, Duino Castle, home of the princes Torre and Tasso, inventors of the modern postal service, is a model of entrepreneurial flair. The family, who trace their lineage back to Bonaparte, still live in the medieval castle yet welcome visitors, happily throwing their towers open to wedding banquets or corporate retreats. Few can resist celebrating an event on Roman ruins, overlooking a Druidic site dedicated to the sun god, or on a medieval terrace overlooking the Gulf of Trieste. The Italian heritage industry looks safe for some time to come. ❑

LEFT: view of the Grand Canal, Venice, during a regatta.

themselves as stakeholders in their city's cultural identity, so pride and political pressure usually prompt a rescue bid. Banks, such as Monte dei Paschi in Siena, can sometimes single-handedly fund "their" city's cultural life, from sponsoring blockbuster Renaissance art exhibitions to saving small museums from ruin.

The media moguls

Popular culture is dominated by television and by the power of monopolies. American-style anti-trust laws do not exist in Italy: telecommunications, publishing and the mass media are aces held in a few family hands. Berlusconi

portrayed on television. Yet sexism on television simply reflects the tawdry realities of political life, where the premier can be seen to promote beautiful babes as political candidates, irrespective of ability. Despite the setting up of an anti-sexism watchdog, and the creation of the La5 women's channel, the temple of TV sexism looks safe for now. "Taking away the sexy girls would be like trying to stop us from eating pizza," declared one (male) comic.

Tobias Jones, author of the polemical *The Dark Heart of Italy*, is acutely aware of the country's Faustian pact: "When the medium became the message, the mogul became the

dominates the airwaves by owning the three most popular channels and influences Rai TV's three "public" channels. Mediaset, his media arm, controls channels that draw 60 percent of the audience share to "trashy TV". With a few exceptions, the output is devoted to propaganda, poor-quality American imports and platitudinous game shows, although standards on Rai 3 are distinctly higher.

"Arriverderci to cleavage" were the headlines on a recent crusade to clean up sexism on state-funded television. This was in reponse to a shift in public mood to the way women are

prime minister." Having a head of state linked to the lowest form of culture epitomises the paradoxical nature of the country. In a society where aesthetics takes precedence over ethics, style triumphs over content, and stylish corruption triumphs over lacklustre probity. At best, it is partisan broadcasting; at worst it is a "videocracy", in which citizens wake up to a Berlusconi-designed world of vulgar television, political propaganda and venal advertising. The premier controls 60 percent of television advertising revenue, owns a national daily and the Mondadori publishing empire – as well as having huge interests in new media.

The turbulent state of the game reflects the cynical ethos in which a top player sees his premier

ABOVE: the annual Miss Italy contest, broadcast on Berlusconi-owned Rai Uno, draws millions of viewers.

engineer a law under which false accounting is no longer a crime. Still, if in doubt, the Italians would rather look good than be good. The country enjoys a flexible moral code, except when it comes to drugs. Italy operates a zero-

> After a bitter court battle with his cousin, Prince Victor Emmanuel has been recognised as the rightful heir to the throne of Italy. The Savoy title can now only be used by himself and his son, the winner of the reality TV show Dancing with the Stars.

tolerance policy, with anyone found in possession of hard or soft drugs open to prosecution for dealing.

Nonetheless, Italy appears in robust health. The World Health Organization rates the Italian national health service highly, even if there can be huge disparities between the north and south in terms of facilities and care.

The successful smoking ban has seen smoking decline by a further 2 million people, down to a current 11 million smokers. Surveys also show that Italians are models of moderation, the most sensible drinkers in Europe. Ninety percent claim never to consume more than two alcoholic drinks in one session. Coffee is the real vice: the Italians are reportedly the keenest consumers in Europe.

Even so, health scandals abound, with clinics, particularly in Sicily and Calabria, often linked to crime syndicates and substandard services. Second only to drug-trafficking, the control of public and private contracting is the most lucrative activity for organised crime, with a turnover of £11.8 billion (US$23 billion). Fortunately, the Mafia also cares about its own members' health and happiness: criminal gangs have resorted to cheese raids, hijacking lorries containing wheels of Parmesan cheese. The love of the good life is not restricted to the virtuous.

Not that the *dolce vita* is dead in society at large. The latest Quality of Life Index ranks the Italians in tenth place, well above the British, but below the French. An Italian version of the survey, by the respected *Il Sole 24 Ore* newspaper, rates northern Italian cities as being home to the smuggest citizens. The Alpine arc of Trieste, Belluno and Sondrio score highest for quality of life, but medium-sized towns in Tuscany and Emilia-Romagna also score highly on the happiness scale. Curiously, the sunnier the place, the less contented the population, so the south fares badly, apart from Sardinia. Facile conclusions suggest that happiness means mountain air or medium-sized, medieval towns, aided by copious amounts of coffee.

The notion of happiness is inextricably linked to *allegria*, fun, second cousin to festivity. Foremost among the reassuring rituals of Italian life is the love of spectacle. During the opera season, La Scala's marbled and mirrored lobby is awash with Milanese matrons in furs, a spectacle matched by operatic Sicilians in Palermo's Teatro Massimo. The love of display cuts across regional and social divides, from the chic Venice Carnival to the smallest Umbrian truffle festival.

Tellingly, there is no Italian term for privacy. The emphasis is on the everyday values of sociability, simplicity and pleasure. The essence of Italian sociability is the *passeggiata*, the evening parade, with pauses for preening, flirting and gossiping. Social life is neatly ordered, even underpinned by excessive planning. Commenting on the cloying social packaging of Italian life, novelist and long-term Italian resident Tim Parks says: "Cappuccino until ten, then espresso; aperitivo after twelve; your pasta, your meat, your dolce in bright packaging; light white wine, strong red wine, prosecco; baptism, first communion, marriage, funeral." ❑

Football Fever

Football is huge in Italy. Although they crashed out of the 2010 World Cup, the Italians have won the trophy four times

Football, like fashion, is at the heart of Italian life. Dolce & Gabbana declare: "We have always been football fans and footballers are, for us, the new male icons." The design duo have dressed the World Cup national team and featured the stars in steamy locker-room scenes for their collections. Dolce supports (and dresses) AC Milan, even if Gabbana favours rivals Inter Milan, the current Champions League winners.

Italy has a fine World Cup record, even if there was no jumping into fountains after the 2010 tournament. Italy won the 2006 World Cup but victory came during the Calciopoli ("Footballgate") match-fixing furore, one of the biggest scandals in sporting history. Phone taps revealed sporting fraud perpetrated by managers and referees, leaving Juventus stripped of its Championship titles and relegated to Serie B, while AC Milan and other teams were docked points. Despite the sacking of managers and the prosecution of match officials, probity has not dribbled down the wings of the Italian game. Referees face a struggle to regain their credibility. Still, recalling the notorious Rolex scandal, when the watches found their way onto the wrists of key referees, courtesy of AST Roma, lavish gifts are now considered bribes, a first for Italian football.

Subversively, football often lobs an own goal at its political masters, unsurprising in a country where the beautiful game is a metaphor for political success. Berlusconi rose to prominence on the back of his ownership of AC Milan, and named his party after a football chant. Italy's top teams have always been the ultimate boy's toys for the country's power-brokers. While AC Milan belongs to media mogul Berlusconi, Juventus remains a plaything for the Agnelli car dynasty.

At home, Italian football is not the success story it once was, even if Buffon (Juventus) is rated the world's best goalkeeper. In the 1980s these stadia drew Europe's largest crowds, with averages of

LEFT: Sardinian farmer.
RIGHT: devoted Italian fans.

nearly 40,000 a match. Since then, attendance has fallen, possibly linked to the predictability of certain fixtures rather than to the Calciopoli scandal. It is a different story abroad, where Italian coaches are greatly prized, especially in England, where Fabio Capello coaches the English side.

Controversy is never far from Italian football, especially in home derbies. Given the sectarian nature of society, rival teams in the same city are commonplace. In the case of bitter rivals Roma and Lazio, the clash is underscored by a polarised fan base: Roma supporters see themselves as liberal-minded urbanites and, unfairly, dismiss Lazio fans as country bumpkins or Fascistic thugs.

The jury is still out on whether endemic corruption is being tackled, but football violence seems to be on the wane. In 2007, the death of a policeman during violent clashes following a Sicilian derby led to the temporary closure of stadiums, and probably cost the country the chance to stage Euro 2012. The Italians pay lip-service to the lessons learnt by the British experience of hooliganism, Even so, weapons searches, harsher penalties for hooliganism, and the introduction of all-seater stadiums have been accepted.

On the pitch, a new law forbids swearing at opponents: perpetrators are sent off. With their renewed commitment to "the beautiful game", Italians were disappointed to lose the bid for Euro 2016 to France. ❏

THE ITALIANS

Individualism, a sense of survival and natural ebullience are qualities almost all Italians share – but there the similarities end

I t has been said that Italians do not exist, that those who are thought of as Italian regard themselves as Piedmontese, Tuscan, Venetian, Sicilian, Calabrian and so on. No one has ever classified the Italians convincingly: to be born in Palermo, Sicily, or in Turin, Piedmont, is a classification in itself. Sometimes even fellow-countrymen feel like foreigners. In Pietro Germi's film *Il Cammino della Speranza (The Path of Hope)*, a peasant says: "There's bad people in Milan, they eat rice."

Generations have learned the art of *arrangiarsi*, of getting along in difficult situations. Adjusting to political change and foreign conquest has generated a flexible mentality and a detached attitude towards political regimes, all of which are considered ephemeral. The forest of rules, statutes, norms and regulations has engendered distrust of the state.

> The popular saying, fatta la legge trovato l'inganno *(a law is passed, a way past it is found)* is almost a national motto.

North versus south

"Southerners tend to make money in order to rule, northerners to rule in order to make money," declared the writer Luigi Barzini. The conflicting values of north and south reflect different cultures and history. Compared with the industrialised, progressive north, the agrarian, conservative south experienced feudalism, oppression, corruption, poverty and neglect. Known as the Mezzogiorno, the region has suffered grandiose white elephants, called "cathedrals in the desert": steelworks sited in remote

places with no proper infrastructure. Cut off from the progress and markets of northern Europe, southerners left for their own survival. Before 1914, more than 5 million emigrated to North America alone.

Although emigration is on the wane, the south still suffers from depopulation, perceived backwardness and a great gap between rich and poor. Southerners, known as *meridionali*, often encounter prejudice, with northerners resenting "subsidising" the south through taxation. Indeed, some northerners see such aid as pour-

ABOVE: the beach in Sorrento near Naples – a love of *il mare* is a strong Italian trait.
RIGHT: market day in Dogliani, Piedmont.

ing their hard-earned money into the pockets of the Camorra in Naples or the Mafia in Sicily. The north–south divide, in all its tragicomic aspects, remains at the heart of Italian life.

Navel-gazing about what it means to be Italian is not a common pastime. However, the marking of the 150th anniversary of Italian Unification in 2011 put the issue of *Italianita* (Italian-ness) on the agenda. The conclusions suggest that in an intensely parochial nation, regional differences are, in themselves, a defining feature of being Italian. As for unity and shared values, all the natives will agree on is a devotion to Italian cuisine, in all its forms, and feverish support for *gli azzuri*, "the boys in blue" in international football matches.

Politics and individualism

The average person in the street expresses a revulsion for politics: *la politica è una cosa sporca* (politics are a dirty thing) is a typical view. This is based on a belief that all parties are the same, and that politics work only for politicians. The Italians remain sceptical of the state, and cannot conceive of abstract solutions or trust in ideologies. Behind such opinions lurks an unrestrained individualism that denies civic responsibility. Yet hand in hand

BIG BABIES

Italy is full of "big babies", a social phenomenom steeped in significance for family-minded Italians. Known as *bamboccioni*, these "big babies" live at home until they marry – and then move next door, to a flat bought by their parents. The concept of *mammoni*, sons who cling to apron strings, is common, with boys over-indulged into adulthood. But girls can also be "big babies", reluctant to flee the nest.

The government recently proposed a law to oblige children to leave home at 18, a ploy designed to stimulate debate about the fact that three-quarters of Italians in the 18–35 age group still live at home. Renato Brunetta, Minister of Public Administration, didn't mince his words: "All these young people think they're living in a free hotel but their parents keep control of them, emotionally, socially and financially – and deny them their freedom and the chance to stand on their own two feet."

In their defence, some "big babies" claim that their studies or finances preclude them from renting a flat. They might even be *precari*, part-timers, seasonal workers or freelancers, with no job security. This in a country where job security is traditionally seen as one's birthright. There is still no social stigma in being supported by the family. In 2010 a 32-year-old student from Bergamo won a court case against her father after he had decided to stop funding her tuition – after eight years and no degree in the offing.

with individualistic entrepreneurship, there is a nostalgic yearning for "the strong man" whose power and will is stamped on his face, whose voice captures the nation's mood. It was a wave of such nostalgia for authoritarian answers that swept Alessandra Mussolini, grand-daughter of Benito, into parliament in 1992, and, more recently, helped Silvio Berlusconi to his third term as premier.

The strong sense that Italians have of their own self-importance is evident in their dislike of queuing or of respecting rules. "We think it's an insult to our intelligence to comply with a regulation," writes commentator Beppe Sev-

ergnini. "Obedience is boring. We want to think about it. We want to decide whether a particular law applies to our specific case. In that place, at that time." Hence red traffic lights rarely mean stop. A pedestrian crossing at 6am might count as a "negotiable red", a "weak orange" at a busy traffic junction might be a *rosso pieno*, a full red. It all depends. Only a cappuccino after 10am is non-negotiable.

Italians are far more conformist than they would wish, whether with regard to drinking coffee at set times, obeying non-smoking laws or wearing orange, if deemed the season's colour. Self-regard is reflected in the way Italians dress. Shoes, ties, lovely fabrics and liberty of the imagination all contribute to the *costume*.

Fastidious care is lavished on cars, seen as extensions of their owners' personalities. Yet beyond the surface gloss, there is a sense of humanity that transcends differences. As Severgnini wrily points out, Italian air hostesses are hopeless at serving you coffee but good at cleaning it up and sympathising when you spill it. Giulio

> During Lent, the Vatican has encouraged Italy's faithful to give up texting rather than more traditional treats. Italians send an average of 50 texts a month, second only to the British.

Andreotti, the machiavellian seven-times premier, also singles out this sense of common humanity: "In Italy there are no angels nor devils, only average sinners." This tolerant Roman Catholic society is nurtured on the concept of original sin, universal temptation and redemption, so penitence can erase sins, even crimes.

Despite an authoritarian pope, abortion and divorce are legal, while contraception is widely accepted. Indeed, much to the chagrin of the Vatican, Italy has the lowest birth rate in Europe. Catholicism has a stronger hold in the south and in the Veneto than in the former "red belt" of Emilia-Romagna, Umbria and Tuscany. According to a recent survey, more than 85 percent of Italians claim to be Catholics, but only a quarter attend Mass regularly. Nonetheless, Catholicism still plays an important role in rituals, from first holy communion to the marriage ceremony and Christian burial.

Sex and the family

While the family remains the bedrock of traditional Italian society, *mammismo*, the cult of the mother, is its cornerstone. The iconic image of the mother pervades the male approach to courtship and his choice of bride. Once married, however, male infidelity is often quietly condoned, provided that the family is supported and appearances preserved.

A recent report reveals that divorce happens every four minutes in a country once regarded as a bastion of marriage. Tellingly, three out of 10 marriages fail because of the unhealthily close

---

LEFT: garrulous Italians are the biggest mobile phone-users in Europe. **RIGHT:** children are cosseted and *la famiglia* remains sacred.

attachment of Italian men to their mothers. An intrusive mother-in-law may expect her adult offspring to eat with her every Sunday, or may deal with her married son's domestic chores. Moreover, disillusioned daughters-in-law help account for the popularity of the therapist's couch, a trend exacerbated by the "super-woman" syndrome, which is, in turn, linked to the low birth rate, the lowest in Europe: if so much is now expected of working women, having one child is challenging enough.

In terms of morality, a north–south divide prevails, with southern values more traditional and northern mores similar to those of north-ern Europe. Even here, appearances are more important than reality. A slick young Milanese banker attaches as much importance to family ties as does the humblest Calabrian peasant, and neither would dare miss Sunday lunch with their parents.

As for sex, discretion counts for much, and provided premarital relationships are not flaunted, honour is maintained. Since students tend to live at home, and offspring are reluctant to flee the nest, romantic assignments can take on the complexity of a Pirandello farce. Male offspring may also rely on a doting mother to act as a domestic drudge.

THE ITALIAN LANGUAGE

Of the Romance languages, Italian is one of the closest to Latin. Modern Italian owes much to writers such as Dante and Manzoni, who assumed as their standard the educated language of Tuscany. Today the finest form of speech is said to be *la lingua toscana in bocca romana* ("the Tuscan tongue in the Roman mouth").

Italian is considered the most musical language in the world: in the 16th century, the Holy Roman Emperor, Charles V, is said to have spoken Spanish with God, French with men, German with his horse, but Italian with women since it was capable of expressing such subtleties of thought and feeling. Italian can be as precise as any other language, yet the style of newspaper editorials, art criticism and political speeches, in particular, is often pretentious and wilfully obscure.

Until recently, more than 1,500 dialects existed alongside Italian, most virtually incomprehensible beyond their own village. The advent of television has done much to further the cause of "standard" Italian but has not dealt a death blow to dialects. Although on the decline, dialects are still spoken by the elderly in the countryside, and in some cities and regions. Many dialects contain foreign terms introduced by past occupiers, including borrowings from Arabic in Sicilian dialects, or French influences in the Piedmontese dialect. All dialects are a way of staying in touch with one's roots, and there is little stigma attached to regional accents either.

A style of life

The Italian style of life is beset by intractable problems, from officialdom to a barely functioning legal system and dysfunctional governments. In the workplace, fear of failure stymies innovation, as does the Italians' reluctance to relocate, should a better job beckon. At the deepest level, Italians seem unable to believe in the possibility of constructive change. But merely listing the ills is missing the point. Italian life is not about work and progress, but about survival and individualism, family and friends, roots and relaxation. Italian life sparkles with a brilliance unmatched anywhere else in

Europe. The Italians have perfected a lifestyle that may be short on efficiency but is long on enjoyment. Simple things, such as eating a meal, taking a walk, having an ice cream, watching the world go by, become special in Italy. Life is enjoyed to the fullest, with a flair gained over centuries of practice.

The new Italians

For a country with its roots in so many races, Italy is far from being a multiracial society, and Italian culture predominates. Settlers linked to Carthage, Constantinople, Normandy, North Africa and Moorish Spain have all made their mark in Italy, whether as colonisers or plunderers. But given Italy's lack of significant empire

since Roman times, the colonial lessons have been lost. Italians have been slow to accept that someone can be visibly non-European yet fully assimilated, or even an Italian citizen.

> *In a classic Berlusconi gaffe that passes for immigration policy among his devoted fans, the premier recently told his Albanian counterpart: "We will only accept the pretty girls from Albania".*

In the last decade or so, the influx of newcomers has made an impact, both in the northern cities and in the southern countryside. Cosy assumptions have been shattered by the existence of ethnic-looking children, born in Italy, who speak Italian with a Roman accent, or by Romanian therapists who have taken Italian citizenship and integrated perfectly. More usually, the different ethnic groups lead parallel lives in their own communities, and there are few mixed marriages and little assimilation.

Italy's historic ethnic groups comprise the Greek, Jewish, Armenian and Albanian communities who have had footholds in Italian towns since medieval times. In many cases, local traditions are retained, as happens with the Greeks and Albanians in Sicily and Calabria.

Officially, foreigners make up less than 5 percent of the population. Albanians, Romanians, Moroccans, Ukrainians and Chinese are the biggest ethnic minority groups, along with the French and South Americans, but recent waves of migrants have been from Africa and Eastern Europe. Most immigrants remain second-class citizens, unable to vote and unlikely to gain Italian citizenship. Moreover, immigrants do the jobs that Italians shun, whether on factory production lines or in the tomato fields of the south. The latest scandal was the discovery of North Africans literally used as slave labour to pick oranges in Calabria. Racist incidents occur sporadically in immigrant "hotspots", including street battles between North African and South American immigrants in a deprived Milanese suburb.

As the back door to Europe, Italy struggled to cope with the influx of boat people, especially from Albania and Africa. First it was Puglia, caught in the eye of the "Albanian Hurricane". Then it was Sicily's turn in 2006, with thousands washed up on the remote island of Lampedusa, sandwiched between Sicily and Libya. Even if the European Union was the goal, many stayed in Italy nonetheless, particularly given the magnetic pull of the wealthy northern cities, including Milan and Brescia.

Integration and segregation

In 2009 Italy cracked down on illegal immigration, declaring it a crime for the first time. Immigrants caught without a permit can now be expelled immediately, as well as being heavily fined. Certain categories, such as doctors, are to be treated more leniently. Other measures include tough fines for landlords who rent to

With little recent history of empire, the Italians veer between demonising and fetishising foreigners, particularly non-EU citizens. The typical professional workplace is still closed to ethnic minorities, but to dub the Italian majority racist misses the point: Italians are most scathing about their fellow-countrymen from "rival" regions. A *straniero* can be a foreigner or someone from the next village, so ingrained is the sense of belonging to one's own village, town or region. Moreover, the political agenda of separatist groups has exploited the resentment of the wealthy north towards the impoverished south.

illegal immigrants, and a longer waiting period for foreigners seeking citizenship through marriage. The wearing of a *burqa* can incur a fine, which happened for the first time in Piedmont recently. All these measures followed equally controversial policies to repatriate "boat people" to Libya, which critics say violated their rights. Those not granted asylum can now be held in detention centres for up to six months prior to deportation. After an initial outcry from the Catholic Church and human rights groups, the controversy has died down, and the waves of "boat people" fallen dramatically.

LEFT: demonstration against racism, Pianura, Naples.
ABOVE: a Chinese stoneworker at the Luserna caves.

However, there is implicit racism in the word *extracomunitari*, common parlance for non-white immigrants, and the *vu compra*, the pejorative term for African street vendors, who traipse tourist haunts, selling fake designer bags. People-trafficking, prostitution and gangsterism are attributed to "foreigners", even if the natives have proved perfectly competent at drug-running and Mafia murder themselves.

On a positive note, even in cities where racial tensions are most felt, such as Brescia and Milan, there is nothing resembling a ghetto, and none of the race riots that have scarred France. Ethnic restaurants and bohemian bars have been slow in coming, but Italians have finally acquired a taste for them. ❑

THE ITALIAN LOOK

Supreme visual sense, a feeling for fashion
and a creative twist on classic lines form
the essence of the Italian look

Only an Italian fashion editor could be so sweeping: "The Versaces and Armanis are our modern-day Michelangelos, helping dress our dreams. Anything else isn't *moda* – it simply serves to cover us." In other words, from the Renaissance to Romeo Gigli is but a small step, preferably taken in Ferragamo footwear, La Perla lingerie and Prada sunglasses. On Planet Fashion, you don't so much name-check the designer brands as breathe them, eat them, sleep them, and even live their dreams. Milan is at the cutting edge of consumerism and bombards us with beguiling messages. Brand brainwashing has fashionistas going to bed with Bulgari, waking up with Armani, and breakfasting with Gucci. The designers are getting in on the lifestyle act, beguiling us with branded bars, spas, bars and galleries.

Secret conformists

Italians may pride themselves on their individuality and exhibitionism but are often bound to brands or conventions. Dressing appropriately for the occasion is more important than dressing to please one's mood. To be accidentally overdressed for a visit to a park or pizzeria can be a cardinal sin; equally, a mere "stroll" can be code for parading in one's finery. If in doubt, the look of de luxe anonymity is the safe sartorial badge.

In a country that worships visual display, style is an emblem of high seriousness, with great attention accorded to the simple purchase of a picture or a place mat. The world remains in awe of Italian taste, inviting native talent to style American furniture, Japanese cameras, German limousines and French family cars. As a result, *la linea italiana*, Italian style, has a continuing impact on international design.

Milan: fashion mecca

The contribution of fashion to Italy's balance of payments is second only to tourism. Commercially, the industry is more successful than its French counterpart, with the Milan collections considered more wearable.

Italian fashion thrives on a long craft tradition, a ready supply of home-grown talent and a contemporary feel, essentially a creative twist on classic lines. Its deep design roots lie in medieval craftsmanship, traditional skills which are prized in haute couture (*alta moda*) as well as in the making of quality fabrics, jewellery, bags and shoes. Native designers also have a highly developed aesthetic sense dating back to the Renaissance.

Florence was Italy's original fashion capital but, for cognoscenti, Milan now has a monopoly on "the Italian look". Milan's fashion and design status has developed not by chance but by design. An innovative industrial culture and sound mass-production techniques set the city

> The fashion and design showrooms are located between the Brera and Piazza San Babila in the Quadrilatero, Milan's chicest shopping district. Here, the Japanese buy swathes of Gucci belts or 10 Prada bags apiece to take home.

Cutting-edge Turin

Yet Turin also sees itself as a vibrant, visionary city, proud of its cutting-edge culture and museums of contemporary art. As the centre of the car industry and Capital of Design in 2008, Turin is currently Italy's leading city of contemporary art and design. The Luci d'Artista art festival and Artissima art fair appeal to the general public as well as to art buffs. The 2006 Winter Olympics put the city on the design map, including showcasing Pininfarina, the greatest car-design studios on the planet. During the opening ceremony, the sight of a red Ferrari doing tight spins on the ice reminded the world

on its successful course, particularly after World War II, when the design industry came into its own. The Triennale, the Italian "temple of design", is now in the 1940s premises that pioneered mass production of household objects; it also boasts an exhibition of Italian design, from vintage scooters to early Olivetti computers.

As the country's design capital, Milan remains a well-tailored, cosmopolitan city that knows how to put on a show, whether during Fashion Weeks or at the equally celebrated Furniture Fair.

LEFT: Dolce & Gabbana celebrate Naomi Campbell's 25 years in the fashion industry in a store in New York. ABOVE: the Prada look.

that the Italian car industry was born here. Futurism thrived in Turin, and at its core was the cult of speed. "Italian design has become a universal language of car design," says Lorenzo Ramaciotti, general manager of Pininfarina: "An American car is expected to be solid and a little flamboyant. An Italian car is expected to be aggressive, sporty and very sexy."

A sense of style

A sense of style and design is in the Italian genes. In 1946, the Italian architect Ernesto Nathan Rogers stated that design should be all-embracing, "from the spoon to the city". Italian designers dutifully filled our world with high-tech telephones and computers, office furniture in fluid shapes, sleek chrome kitchen appliances and twirly pasta quills. Giandomenico Belotti's Spaghetti Chair was literally inspired by pasta.

Italian design encompasses the austere, the provocative, the restrained and the kitsch. The roll-call of honour includes the Olivetti type-writer and the Artemide lamp, as well as the Ferrari, a symbol of national pride. Italy has a reputation for inspired car and motorbike design, from chic Maseratis to cheap Vespa scooters *(see panel opposite)*. In reply, the fashion world fields designers with the aspirations of Renaissance princelings: Armani's fluid lines clash with Roberto Cavalli's camp eroticism

and favoured practical, perfect forms such as his Superleggera, the consummate chair, a sculpted lightweight piece. Ponti designed Milan's Pirelli Tower (1956) as well as creating the espresso machine.

The highlights of Italian design history reveal both its readiness to innovate and its essential classicism. In the 1950s, the Modern-ists abhorred meretricious designs, but eclectic designers were eager to experiment. The 1960s avant-garde relished visual disorder and inflat-able fantasies. Yet even during the Pop Art period and Swinging Sixties, designers did not abandon their love of craftsmanship or use of

and Dolce & Gabbana's Sicilian kitsch.

Aesthetically, Italy is known for its smooth, streamlined objects, from washing machines to motorbikes and coffee machines – designed in 1938, the Gaggia was the first modern steamless coffee machine, and swiftly became recognised as a design icon thanks to its sleek lines and sheer functionality.

Design diversity

The design field has traditionally cultivated cross-fertilisation between the craftsman and architect, designer and artist. Giò Ponti, the 20th century's greatest Modernist, believed that Italy had been created half by God and half by architects. He detested the superfluous

high-quality materials such as leather. The 1970s represented the high point of Italian minimal-ism, with austere tubular steel chairs. Even so, minimalism remains a Milanese default mecha-nism, even in the new millennium.

The belief in *bellezza,* beauty for its own sake, means that even high-tech must be aes-thetically pleasing. High-tech in the home has a distinguished pedigree, with cult objects by Aldo Rossi, Ettore Sottsass and Robert Ven-turi, including coffee pots, chairs and trays in severe metallic designs. Particularly prized are stainless-steel kettles by Alessi, or Achille Cas-

ABOVE: designers Dolce & Gabbana pose with Kylie after their show. **RIGHT:** Ferrari, the ultimate in style.

tiglioni cutlery and lamps. The Italians broke the mould of lighting design: "Light does not simply illuminate, it tells a story," says Sottsass. The modern lighting heyday was the 1970s, but certain lamps, from 18th-century Murano chandeliers to Pietro Chiesa's Art Deco funnel lamps, stand the test of time.

Temples of consumerism

Milan may be the design showcase, but most cities are citadels of good taste, with smart shops and shiny people. If the authentic article is too costly, then dedicated shoppers will settle for a fake: appearances are everything. Naples is the capital of counterfeit culture, where painted marzipan fruit looks finer than real peaches.

It is invidious to single out the most prestigious designers, but Armani, the master of deconstruction, wins accolades for his sleek, sophisticated look and minimalist colours. Armani's polar opposite is Versace, which opted for vulgarity, glamour and sex appeal. The coolly intellectual approach of Prada chimes with jaded fashionistas, while supremely sexy designers such as Dolce & Gabbana are currently enamoured of red-carpet glamour. As always, Italians are beguiled by *la bella figura*, a fatal weakness for beauty and surface gloss. ❏

VESPA VERSUS LAMBRETTA

The Vespa, the most celebrated scooter on the planet, was created after World War II by the Italian manufacturer Piaggio, which turned its back on warplane production after its factory was destroyed by American bombers. Amid the wreckage, the workers found a German scooter that had been used by paratroopers, and it became the prototype Vespa. The thinking behind the brand was to create a form of transport that was practical, cheap, easy to handle and simple to repair. The Vespa ("Wasp") was a runaway success from its first launch and is now the height of retro-chic.

The Lambretta, another design classic, was the rival to the Vespa, and produced in 1947, a year before the Vespa. The wartime engineer Pierluigi Torre was commissioned to design a scooter boasting a tubular steel frame construction. The Lambretta A 125cc scooter came with a three-speed gear box and foot-operated gear changer, but had no body panels to cover the frame or engine. The brand returned to Grand Prix racing in 2010 with its new 125cc bike and catchphrase, "Lambretta – it's an Italian thing."

Lambrettas and Vespas are as popular as ever, whether in car-clogged cities or with hobbyists – there are owners' clubs worldwide and 17 million users. Vespas have featured in many films, including *Roman Holiday*, *American Graffiti* and *The Talented Mr Ripley*.

Who's Who in Italian Design

With its supreme grace, craftsmanship and lovely lines, Italian design leads the world in lifestyle – here we highlight its biggest names

Alberta Ferretti

The designer champions ultra-feminine styles. With its love of floaty fabrics, the label attracts romantics rather than adventurous fashionistas.

Alessi

Based by Lake Orta, this family-run design house is known for its playful products, ranging from quirky cutlery to colourful kettles and corkscrews. Alessi has always drawn on the skills of top designers of the calibre of Castiglione, Sottsass and Philippe Starck.

Armani

With its sleek yet understated look, Armani is the epitome of Italian chic. Giorgio Armani's alluring womenswear transcends boring beige. The look works for rock royalty and real royalty. "Women want to be more grown up," claims Giorgio. The designer has fully embraced lifestyle, with his own bars, restaurants and hotels.

B&B Italia

The market leader in luxury furniture design was founded in 1966 on the innovative principle of streamlining research, manufacture and marketing into a seamless whole. The company attracts leading designers, from Gaetano Pesce to Patricia Urquiola and designs hotels, stores and even cruise ships.

Benetton

Luciano Benetton is dubbed "the prince of pullovers" yet the company's real success was to introduce mass production to the sleepy Italian textile industry. This close-knit Treviso-based firm is a global casual-clothing brand, but remains innovative, sponsoring Fabrica, its creative think-tank.

Bottega Veneta

Once a moribund Venetian family accessories firm, the luxury brand is now part of the Gucci Group. Classic rather than trend-driven, it offers pared-down clothes that sell on fabric and cut alone. Menswear favours the Milanese gentleman look, while womenswear is timelessly elegant.

Dolce & Gabbana

Sicilian Domenico Dolce and Venetian Stefano Gabbana may no longer be a couple, but the creative partnership survives. Arguably the glitziest of Italian fashion labels, its strengths are sharp tailoring, cutting-edge styling and a Latino sensibility, part peasant, part Sicilian gigolo. *"Molto sexy"* is the only instruction to the D&G catwalk models.

Ermenegildo Zegna

Steeped in history, this family firm are the fashion designers with the deepest roots in fabric production and design. Based in Biella's "textile valley," Zegna is both *the* luxury menswear brand and a supplier of fabrics to its rivals. Heirs to old-fashioned Piedmontese paternalism, the family puts a lot back into the local community.

Fendi

Under Karl Lagerfeld, Fendi has had a resurgence and produces chic collections for city sophisticates. Fendi's legendary love of fur can make the label controversial abroad, but to Italians, the Fendi femme fatale is still a seductive fashion icon.

Ferragamo

This Florence-based fashion dynasty started with Salvatore, a Neapolitan shoemaker to the stars, who invented the wedge. Leatherware and accessories are no longer the essence of the brand: glamour-puss cocktail dresses feature, along with hotels, boat companies and wine estates.

Gucci

Gucci began as humble Florentine saddle-makers but its leather range, made from honey-cured hides, was a stepping stone to stardom. Family feuds led to the collapse of the dynasty, and the firm is now a mega-brand, with a glam-rock style that appeals to footballers' wives and celebrities.

Lagostina

For generations of Italian mammas, Lagostina is synonymous with the best stainless-steel Italian kitchenware. Known as the "Michelangelo of stock-pots", it is still on most Italians' wedding lists.

Marcolin

This Veneto-based firm is one of the major producers of eyewear, both spectacles and sunglasses, and is owned by both the family and the Florentine designers behind Tods, Diego and Andrea della Valle.

Missoni

Missoni are the knitwear masters, and produce intricate, imaginative and eye-catching designs, with clothing and homeware collections. This family-run firm is now headed by Angela Missoni, who has reworked her parents' hippy-chick knit-wear by creating equally vibrant, swirly designs.

Moschino

Noted for its visual tricks and bold spirit rather than its tailoring, Moschino boasts a sexy yet daring look and bucks many fashion trends. Moschino's big-gest fan is the burlesque striptease artiste, Dita Von Teese, who embodies the label's Forties silhou-ette and retro glamour.

Pininfarina

The world's pre-eminent car design firm dates back to the 1930s, when car chassis and bodywork were assembled separately. "Pinin" Farina (succeeded by his son) created car concepts for Alfa Romeo, Lancia and Ferrari (including the Testarossa in 1984), as well as branching out into the design of coffee machines, aircraft and even the Olympic Torch.

Prada

Husband and wife team Miuccia Prada and Patrizio Bertelli have propelled the brand to fame. Prada is an intellectual yet classless brand with a "less is more" ethos. Arguably the coolest, most sought-after brand of recent years, Prada prides itself on its contemporary styling and well-cut, fuss-free designs, with the focus on crisp, demure shapes.

LEFT: sofa by B&B Italia. **RIGHT:** a Matthew Williamson design in the Pucci spirit.

Pucci

Founded by the eccentric Florentine aristocrat Emilio Pucci, the brand revels in swirling, Sixties-inspired silk prints, a spirited hippy-de luxe style. It remains true to its fun-loving founder, who said: "The aim of fashion is to produce happiness."

Roberto Cavalli

The Cavalli attitude evokes man-eating sexiness and red-carpet glamour. The Cavalli dress is a red-carpet show-stopper, but the Florentine fashion house is shifting away from thigh-high splits and animal prints. Cavalli also brands his own wine and bars, including funky Café Giacosa in Florence.

Valentino

The Rome-based couturier caters for a sleekly sophisticated and ultra-groomed clientele. Rarely a trendsetter, the label excels at romantic evening-wear, from prom dresses to crimson gowns and wedding dresses for the Hollywood set. Despite selling the company, Valentino's brand survives.

Versace

Founded by Gianni Versace, the flamboyant fashion house has been run by his sister Donatella since his death. The label's glitzy vulgarity has been toned down to create elegant, wearable, well-cut collec-tions. Even so, menswear remains the sexiest and most figure-hugging of top Italian brands. Now also designs hotels, jewellery and a home collection. ❏

DESIGN CLASSICS

Furniture, clothes, cars, typewriters, even kitchen appliances – the influence of Italian design has permeated the way we live and work today

Italian designers bask in their reputation for refinement, innate good taste and eye for colour and line. "Quite simply, we are the best," boasts architect Luigi Caccia. "We have more imagination, more culture, and are better mediators between the past and the future." The distinction between architect and industrial designer is blurred, with practitioners dabbling in factory building and furniture design, office lighting and graphics. In the words of Ettore Sottsass, one of the most influential designers: "Design should be a discussion of life, society, politics, food and the design itself."

MODERNISM TO POP ART

Since the beginning of the 20th century, Milan has led industrial design, reaching its apogee in the 1970s and 1980s. The Italians produced seminal designs for cars and lamps in the 1930s, matched by radios and motorbikes in the 1940s. Milan also pioneered innovative design in the 1950s, with the mass production of household appliances, from cookers and washing machines to kitchen utensils. Italian modernism supplanted the post-war European taste for the safe, handcrafted homeliness of Scandinavian design. Stylish kettles and coffee percolators became cult objects in the 1960s, followed by quirky Pop Art furniture and the fashion-designer chic of subsequent decades, from cool Armani to pared-down Prada. The inimitable character of *la linea italiana*, Italian style, sets the standard for international design values.

ABOVE: the Ferrari Spider (1993 model) is in a long line of fabulous cars from the most admired Italian manufacturer. Enzo Ferrari (1898–1988), the firm's founder, was also a racing-car designer.

BELOW: a Prada suit in Milan's fashion district. Prada is the fashion company that best captures the *Zeitgeist* of the new millennium. Its designs have made it the most copied label on the city streets.

LEFT: Zanussi's rigorous designs, streamlined look and user-friendly features have long made it a European market leader in the field of white goods.

CLASSIC CAR STYLE

Ever since the 1930s, Italian car design has been characterised by stylistic restraint, versatility and timeless elegance. At one end of the scale, the Italians still produce some of the greatest status symbols in the world. In the 1950s, the beautiful Alfa Romeo convertibles spelt playboy raffishness; Ferrari's Spider, the ultimate in glamour, was produced from 1966 to 1992, making it the only sports car to have a longer production run than Germany's Porsche 911.

Yet the Italians have also had great success with Fiat's bland but eminently practical models. Topolino ("the little mouse") was launched to great acclaim in 1939, and continued into the 1950s. The late Giovanni Agnelli studied North American mass-production techniques and from the 1950s the family dynasty had a captive market, with customers eager for Fiat 500, which has recently been relaunched with great success. The car industry is based in the north, with Fiat in Turin, Alfa Romeo in Milan and Ferrari in Modena. The huge Fiat Lingotto plant was set up near Turin in the 1920s, and today, the city's fortunes are still inextricably linked to Fiat.

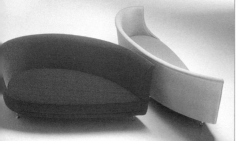

ABOVE: Italian design often takes ideas to their extreme, as in these eye-catching New Tone sculptural sofas by Atrium. This is subversive, unconventional, avant-garde living.

RIGHT: Postmodernist bookcase in laminated plastic, a bold design for the Memphis studio by Sottsass (1981). Memphis was the design event of the 1980s, inspired by Bob Dylan's song, *Memphis Blues*.

BELOW: the Piaggio Vespa ("wasp"), first produced in 1946, became the symbol of freedom for the post-war generation.

ITALIAN CUISINE

Each region is a culinary adventure, from velvety pasta in Emilia-Romagna to earthy Tuscan soups or the spicy flavours of Sicily

For Italians, a meal is a celebration of life itself – less of man's art than of nature's wondrously bountiful providence. A deep respect and admiration for ingredients is found throughout the country, although both history and geography have played their part in making the cooking of Italy so strongly regional.

One of the secrets of Italian cuisine, impossible to replicate elsewhere, lies in Italy's soil. After making pulp of Mexico, the Spanish conquistador Hernando Cortés returned to the Old World laden with strange new fruits and vegetables, among them a humble, fleshy yellow sphere smaller than a ping-pong ball which, in 1554, the Italians dubbed the *pomo d'oro* (golden apple). Two hundred years on, thanks to the rich Italian soil, these jaundiced cherries had become huge, lush tomatoes in deep ruby hues.

These days, as well as being a key ingredient in many more elaborate Italian dishes, tomatoes are stuffed with beans or rice, offered as an antipasto with alternating slices of fresh mozzarella cheese, or simply served lightly dressed in olive oil and topped with sprigs of basil.

Certain regions are intrinsically dedicated to healthy eating – including Tuscany, whose staples are inspired by peasant cuisine and hearty bean soups, or Liguria, which depends on pesto, vegetables and fresh fish.

LEFT: a wide selection of salami for sale at Nemi, in Castelli Romani near Rome.
RIGHT: preparing *bistecca alla fiorentina* – steak Florentine made from Tuscany's Chianina cattle.

A savoury past

Until the Renaissance, the history of Italian cooking largely corresponded with Italy's military fortunes. In the 9th century, the Arabs invaded Italy, introducing Eastern sherbets and sorbets, originally served between courses to refresh the palate. Sicily, where Arab influence was most entrenched, is still noted for its sorbets and sumptuous sweets, including *cassata siciliana*, sweet sponge filled with ricotta cheese or pistachio cream and decorated with candied fruit. Two hundred years after the Arabs left mainland Italy, the Italians set off on their own holy wars. Their return was sweetened by the presentation of sugar cane which they had discovered in Tripoli.

Sometime in the late Middle Ages, pasta appeared. Nobody knows exactly how or where it was invented, but the legend of Marco Polo bringing it back from Cathay (as China was called) is firmly refuted by Italians.

As for pasta, the Roman gastronome Apicius, writing in the 1st century AD, describes a *timballo* (a sweet or savoury pie made with pasta). Later, in the Middle Ages, Boccaccio recommended the combination of macaroni and cheese.

It was during the Renaissance that cooking became a fine art and evolved along the lines familiar to us today. Bartolomeo Sacchi, a Vatican librarian also known as Platina, composed a highly sophisticated cookbook entitled *De Honesta Voluptate ac Valetudine* (Concerning Honest Pleasures and Well-Being); within three decades the volume had seen six editions. Florentine merchants spent huge sums on establishing schools for the promotion of culinary knowledge.

Consolidation of the Venetian Spice Route led to fragrant innovations. New pastry cooks invented macaroons, *frangipane* (filled with cream and flavoured with almonds) and *panettone* (a spicy celebration brioche incorporating sultanas). Conquistadors bombarded the Old World with its first potatoes, pimentos and, of course, tomatoes. When Catherine de' Medici, a keen gourmet, married Henry II of France, she took with her to France her Italian cooks, thus laying the foundations for French cuisine. Until then, France had no cuisine of its own. Even *Larousse Gastronomique* honours Italy as the "mother" cuisine.

Regional divides

The concept of an Italian national cuisine is highly treacherous. Italy offers the world 20 regional cuisines, a diversity reflecting the country's pre-unification history and the importance of locally available produce (for example, beans, boar, rabbit and chestnuts in Tuscany; pork and truffles in Umbria; buffalo mozzarella, squid and *polpo* – octopus – in Naples). Distinctive culinary identities evolved as naturally as particular painting styles. Even more influential than political boundaries were natural variations in soil type, climate and proximity to the sea.

Although there are territorial distinctions between the north and the south, the distinctions between individual regions are even more marked. Compared with the olive oil-loving south, there is a preference for butter in certain northern and central regions, notably in Emilia-Romagna, but not, for instance, in Tuscany or Liguria. As for pasta, in the Austrian-influenced Alpine regions of Trentino-Alto Adige, polenta takes the place of pasta, while in French-influenced Piedmont, rice is favoured. Traditionally, northerners tend to eat more flat, ribbon-shaped pasta, while southerners prefer more tubular-shaped pasta. By the same token, much northern pasta is prepared at home with eggs and eaten immediately, while southerners are more associated with 'dried' pasta, made without eggs, a tradition stemming

from the days when pasta was dried in the warm sea breezes around Naples. Not that one should generalise about pasta in a country where most regions boasts a full complement of local styles and sauces.

A feast of fish

Situated between the Adriatic and the Tyrrhenian seas, Italy hauls in well over 320 million kg (700 million lbs) of fish a year. Alpine streams make the Adriatic significantly less salty than most oceans, and it is therefore an ideal habitat

ABOVE: fresh pasta and fresh pesto.
RIGHT: *The Fruit Vendor*, a 16th-century still life by Vicenzo Campi.

for turbot *(rombo)*, sea bass *(spigola)*, sea bream *(orata)* and grouper *(cernia)*. Seafood dishes, whether linked to grills, pasta or soups, will often include clams, mussels, lobster, octopus, cuttlefish and, in the south, swordfish.

Zuppa di pesce, which is more of a stew than a soup, is a stalwart of many menus and usually served in an enormous tureen. Luxurious versions include *buridda alla Genovese*, incorporating octopus, squid, mussels, shrimps and clams.

Anchovies and sardines are classic Mediterranean fish. *Pasta con sarde*, a speciality of Palermo, is pasta with a sauce of wild fennel, pine nuts, raisins and fried sardines. A more intricate dish,

often found as an antipasto, is sardines stuffed with capers, pine nuts, Sardinian pecorino cheese, bread and eggs.

Meat and game

Italy also produces some of the finest meats in the world, which may explain why the Italians don't find it necessary to add sauce to their national specialities. Tuscany's Chianina cattle are alabaster in colour and grow to weigh 1,800kg (4,000lbs). Chianina beef is used to best advantage in *bistecca alla fiorentina* – a recipe in which the steak is marinated in a little olive oil, wine vinegar and garlic, then rapidly grilled.

SLOW FOOD

Founded in Piedmont in 1986, the Slow Food movement has conquered the world with its crusade against junk-food culture. Its manifesto declared: "Let us rediscover the flavours and savours of regional cooking and banish the degrading effects of fast movement." The movement now has more than 60,000 members spread across five continents. Carlo Petrini, the founder, explains: "The goal of this movement is the propogation of leisurely, more epicurean eating habits, and a more enlightened and patient approach to life." Publisher Alastair Sawday champions its ethical dimension in *Go Slow Italy:* "While globalisation creates inconceivable wealth for a few, a Slow economy acknowledges the need for local solutions and restraint."

Italy remains one of the leaders in food and wine tourism, with hundreds of *strade dei sapori* (food trails) and *strade del vino* (wine trails). The bewildering choice runs from Parmesan cheese and Parma ham trails to routes dedicated to Calabrian leeks, Puglian olive oil, Barolo wine or Asti truffles. Whether it's Tuscany's Chianti country, the Amalfi Coast wine route or Treviso's radicchio trail, there is ample fodder for gastronomes. Depending on the region, the trails may be nothing more than a clutch of inns, growers and wine estates, or a well-trodden path through gorgeous scenery, with welcoming food and wine outlets en route. As celebrity chef Giorgio Locatelli enthuses, "the Slow Movement is connecting people with their regional culture."

Lamb and kid are popular in hilly regions, including Sardinia.

Game birds are also used extensively (Italians are said to eat anything which flies, however small), and warbler, bunting, lark, quail and pheasant are favourites on regional menus. However, even more prized is wild boar *(cinghiale)* which features on many autumnal menus, including in Tuscany, and venison, which is favoured in regions such as Trentino.

Regional differences

Rome's cuisine comes nearest to that associated with feasting. Suckling pigs and suckling lambs

LEARNING TO COOK ITALIAN

Attending a cookery course is about getting to know the underbelly of Italy and coming home with a new skill. In Piedmont, chef and sommelier Carlo Zarri can guide you through truffle and Barolo country and teach you the secrets of a silky risotto. In Florence, Silvia Maccari of Camilla in Cucina can take you through the food markets to taste oils, wines and cheeses before conjuring up stuffed pasta and Tuscan biscuits with your help. In medieval Certaldo, Cucina Giuseppina, assisted by her son, passes down her Tuscan family recipes, from pasta to truffle dishes, with wine appreciation and truffle-hunting experiences optional *(see page 425)*.

are mouth-watering specialities. The justly famous *saltimbocca alla romana* (a thin slice of veal wrapped around a slice of *prosciutto* and a sage leaf, browned in butter and simmered in white wine) lives up to its name – "jump into the mouth". Romans also thrive on gnocchi – feathery dumplings incorporating butter, eggs, nutmeg and Parmesan – while their poor relation, polenta, made from yellow maize flour, is popular in the Veneto and Trentino.

Emilia-Romagna, long celebrated for its gastronomy, is home to the country's most opulent cuisine. Bologna, the capital of Italian cuisine, relishes its reputation as "the fat" *(la grassa)*, but

> The only authentic Parmesan cheese is Parmigiano-Reggiano, produced around Parma, Reggio nell'Emilia and Modena. It is sold as young (under 18 months), medium (18–24 months) or mature (24–36 months).

foodies regard the stuffed pasta as supremely rich rather than fattening. *Prosciutto* is synonymous with Parma, while Bologna claims *mortadella*, a classic cold cut, as well as meaty *ragu*, the true Bolognese sauce, rather than the bastardised versions served abroad. Parma has also patented Parmesan cheese while neighbouring Modena guards the secrets of its renowned artisanal vinegar, *aceto balsamico*.

Bologna is also the home of tortellini, rosebud-shaped pasta filled with spinach and ricotta cheese. "If the first father of the human race was lost for an apple, what would he not have done for a plate of tortellini?" goes a local saying. Legends as to tortellini's origins abound. One version gives credit to a young cook of a wealthy Bolognese merchant who modelled the curiously shaped pasta on the navel of his master's wife, whom he had seen sleeping naked.

Lombardy produces more rice than any other European region, and the famous *risotto alla milanese*, seasoned with saffron, does justice to the native grain, which is ideally suited to slow cooking. Variations on risotto include *risotto nero*, in which the rice is coloured black by cuttlefish ink. Another way to transform a risotto is to shave a little truffle over the top. The best white truffles are found in the Alba area of Piedmont, where they are sniffed out by specially trained dogs; white and black truffles are also found in Tuscany, while black truffles are associated with Umbria.

Bread and pizza

Naples is the place to eat pizza baked over wood in a brick-lined oven – traditionally, *pizza napoletana* (tomatoes, mozzarella, anchovies and oregano), *pizza Margherita* (topped with mozzarella, tomatoes and basil leaves) and *pizza marinara* (topped with tomatoes, garlic, clams, mussels and oregano).

Bread, eaten without butter, accompanies most meals, and comes in myriad varieties. Speciality breads include focaccia, a flat bread driz-

lar order. The first course *(il primo)* invariably consists of a pasta or rice dish (especially in the north) or soup. (Antipasti, such as toasted bread with olive oil and garlic, seafood salad or grilled vegetables, are generally served only in restaurants or at banquets.)

The second course *(il secondo)*, comprising meat or sometimes (especially on Friday) fish, complements or elaborates the theme begun by the first. For example, if the first course was tortellini filled with parsley and ricotta, the second would probably be something light – such as a sautéed chicken dish with lemon and a little more parsley, echoing the first course. The

zled with olive oil and sprinkled with salt, or topped with olives or onions. Sardinia is noted for its *carta da musica* (music-paper bread), a wafer-thin unleavened bread, which is crunchy and long-lasting. Shepherds traditionally took it with them on long expeditions into the hills with their flocks.

The ritual of the feast

Wherever you are in Italy, the rituals surrounding food and eating remain the same. Though their specialities differ greatly, all regions eat their particular dishes in a remarkably simi-

second course is usually enhanced by at least one, often two or three vegetable dishes, such as *funghi trifolati* (mushrooms sautéed with garlic and parsley), *fave in salsa di limone* (broad beans in lemon sauce) and *cicoria all'aglio* (chicory with garlic sauce).

Afterwards comes the grand finale: the desserts *(dolci)*, not forgetting an array of Italian cheeses *(formaggi)*, perhaps served with pear. While *tiramisu* and ice cream are now widespread, many desserts still remain intensely regional. Depending where you are, tuck into Tuscan *cantuccini* biscuits dipped in Vin Santo, or sample sweet Sicilian *cassata* or *cannoli*. Needless to say, each course is washed down with copious quantities of wine. ❑

LEFT: bakery and cake shop, Turin.
ABOVE: making pizza in Naples, where it all started.

WINE IN ITALY

In Italy wine is intensely regional – and a compelling
social ritual that transforms any occasion into
a pleasurable celebration of life itself

Just as there is hardly any such thing as Italian cuisine, so the wines of Italy, too, are distinctly regional. Vine-growing echoes the north–south divide, largely for climatic reasons; as one travels south, the grape varieties become increasingly exotic, even if unusual grape varieties are not the preserve of the south.

> Italy grows over 2,000 grape varieties, more than any other country, so the wine map is a challenge – but an infinitely rewarding one.

Light but quaffable

The Veneto region – from Venice to Lake Garda – is a major wine producer of DOC wine *(see page 102)*. Soave, the country's biggest-selling dry white DOC, can be bland, so choose a *Soave Classico* instead, made by first-rate producers. The same broad range is true of *Valpolicella*, where one billed as *Ripasso* will have more character.

To the north and east of Venice, Friuli-Venezia Giulia produces some of the country's finest crisp, white wines, including in the Collio area, near the Slovenian border, where Marco Felluga is a noted producer.

Up above Lake Garda, in mountainous Trentino-Alto Adige, the vineyards cling to precipitous slopes under peaks that are snow-covered until well into the spring. The Alto Adige, or South Tyrol, was once part of Austria, and many growers have distinctly un-Italian names. Reds from here can be chewy and plummy, or

strawberry-fresh; whites are as crisp as the mountain air, light and refreshing.

Trentino is also a major wine region, producing almost a third of Italian sparkling wines *(Spumante)*, including some which rival champagne. Other distinctive wines include ruby-red *Marzemino*, Mozart's favourite tipple, purplish *Teroldego*, as well as aromatic white *Muller-Thurgau* and elegant *Pinot Grigio*.

In Lombardy, Franciacorta, the area near Lake Iseo, produces the country's most prestigious sparkling wines, a world away from supermarket *Spumante*, and a genuine alternative to French bubbles. Piedmont is prestigious wine country and a wonderful place to visit

---

LEFT: grapes in the Marches.
RIGHT: Tuscan vineyards.

in autumn, when the early morning fog that hangs over the vineyards clears slowly, and the streets of Alba smell of white truffles. The main red grape variety, *Nebbiolo*, ripens very late, so it can cope with the humid climate that would threaten thinner-skinned varieties; it is also

> The fog (nebbia) in the wine-growing region of Piedmont gives its name to the main red grape variety, Nebbiolo, which ripens very late. The thick skin enables it to survive the humidity and avoid rot.

responsible for the wine's deep colour, and for mouth-puckering tannins that make *Barolo* and *Barbaresco* such big, powerful wines. These are perfect for a leisurely dinner, leaving a less full-bodied red, such as *Nebbiolo d'Alba*, better for a lighter lunch.

Chianti country

Tuscany challenges Piedmont as producer of the country's most aristocratic wines. Some of the noble families in the business today (Antinori and Frescobaldi, for example) have been making wine since before the Renaissance. *Chianti* is the staple, Italy's best-known red wine, made mostly from the *Sangiovese* grape. The "blood of Jove" manifests itself in varying forms, from light and fruity to capable of ageing in the bottle. Standards of winemaking have improved dramatically, so that most *Chianti* is gratifyingly good.

Brunello di Montalcino and *Vino Nobile di Montepulciano*, both *Sangiovese*-based wines, have traditionally represented the heights to which Tuscan reds could aspire. *Morellino di Scansano* is a fruity, juicy red made from Sangiovese grapes. But Super-Tuscans, a loose-knit family of brilliant wines that burgeoned in the 1980s, also represent some of Tuscany's greatest stars. Each has its individual style: they sprang from the desire of certain winemakers to produce their dream wine outside the stultifying conventions of the time. They have snappy names like *Sassicaia* or *Solaia*, and are pricey, but with inimitable richness and complexity. Dry white wines from Tuscany are less exalted. *Galestro* is a brave attempt to show that Italy's

HOW TO READ AN ITALIAN WINE LABEL

Given a mixture of individuality, marked regionalism and outdated demarcations, Italian wines are notoriously difficult to classify. That's before facing the fact that the country boasts over 2,000 varietals. *Denominazione di Origine Controllata* (DOC) is a delimited wine region, the equivalent of the French *Appellation Contrôlée*. Not all DOC wines are very good, and some top wines are in fact not DOC; the producer's name is often a surer guide. DOCG (the G standing for *e garantita*) is meant to be a better wine than a straight DOC. *Indicazione Geografica Tipica* (IGT) is a classification between DOC and *vino da tavola*, which embraces the two ends of the scale – cheap everyday wine and some high-quality, expensive wines made by producers dissatisfied with DOC restric-

tions. *Classico* refers to the heartland of a wine region, often producing the best wine. Other words to look for are *abboccato* (semi-sweet), *amabile* (sweet, usually in reference to sparkling wine), *secco* (dry), *frizzante (pétillant)* and *spumante* (sparkling), which may be made by the *metodo classico* (champagne method). *Passito* is sweet wine made from semi-dried grapes to concentrate the flavours, *recioto* a sweet or dry wine made from dried grapes, and *ripasso* a rich red wine fermented in the barrels previously used for a *recioto*. In Valpolicella, *amarone* is a dry wine of great character made from dried grapes. It is fermented for a longer period to produce a full-bodied wine. *Riserva* is wine given extra ageing in the barrel.

high-yielding Trebbiano grape can turn into something tasty, especially when blended with *Sauvignon blanc*, *Chardonnay* and others. *Vernaccia*, from the medieval town of San Gimignano, is made in more traditional style.

In Emilia-Romagna, where dishes are gloriously rich and sticky, *Lambrusco*, an acquired taste, can be a natural partner, especially the dry, red version, with the best vastly superior to its reputation as cheap fizz. Look out for *Lambrusco di Sorbara* to get a taste of the real thing. Although not exported widely, the regional wines can be eccentric or distinctive, not just made from *Sangiovese*.

Further south

Most of the best wines of central and southern Italy are red, although regions such as Sardinia and Sicily also produce notable whites. The centre and south are associated with quaffable wines, such as *Montepulciano d'Abruzzo*, with southern wines historically cheaper. But don't be fooled: a winemaking revolution has taken place in these sun-baked villages, including in Sicily and Sardinia, with a shift away from high yields. Sicilian wine was once synonymous with insipid blending but now native grape varieties are appreciated by discerning drinkers. Full-bodied red *Nero d'Avola* is one of the stars, but good whites and blends are prospering, including at such reputable estates as Planeta and Regaleali.

The whites generally don't live up to the reputation of the reds but tend to be clean, fresh, well made, perfect for a summer's day, with *Frascati* a typical example. More notable are *Orvieto Classico*, from Umbria, which can have good nutty fruit, and *Vermentino* in Sardinia, with Sella & Mosca one of the best names in general. Much white wine is Trebbiano-based and quaffable, but the better producers often use *Malvasia*.

Sweet wines

Southern Italy abounds in sweet or fortified wines, especially Sicily and the Aeolian Islands – although calling them whites seems perverse when most age to a rich tawny colour. Look for the names of the *Malvasia* or *Moscato* grapes on the label. *Marsala*, a Sicilian fortified wine, has

made a resurgence, either served as a sweet dessert wine or chilled as an aperitif.

In Tuscany, try the *Vin Santo* ("holy wine") made from grapes which have been hung to dry for months or even years. Traditionally, this was offered to favoured guests as refreshment, along with *Cantuccini* almond biscuits.

One of the pleasures of Italy is to follow local drinking rituals. Traditionally, Italians drink an *aperitivo* (such as *Prosecco* or *Spritz* in the Veneto) before a meal and might follow a heavy dinner with a *digestivo*, such as *Vin Santo* in Tuscany, *Limoncello* on the Amalfi Coast, or *grappa* in the Dolomites. *Cin cin!* ❏

TOP WINE TRAILS

Italy abounds in appealing wine trails, which are increasingly linked to foodie routes and charming inns. Enquire about the local *Strada del Vino* (wine route) wherever you happen to be. In Tuscany, the Chianti Trail is the best known, and is a way of combining wine-tastings with Renaissance scenery. Lake Garda offers Valpolicella, Bardolino and Soave trails, but the Valtenesi wine and olive oil route north of Desenzano is the most engaging. Sometimes, as in Franciacorta, near Lake Iseo, the wine trail combines culture, food and wine. Here, the rolling countryside is dotted with wine estates centred on castles, villas and manor houses.

LEFT: traditional winemaker Giampiero Bea.
RIGHT: *Chianti* is stored in oak barrels.

ITALIAN CINEMA

As windows of the nation's soul, Italian films
showed veracity and vitality once freed
from the fictions of Fascism

Italian cinema runs the gamut from gritty realism to epic drama, often tinged with satire or sentimentality. From the outset, the Italians blazed their own trail. In Britain, the United States and France, the early directors were steeped in vaudeville or music hall, and their output was generally classed as lowbrow entertainment. By contrast, Italy's first filmmakers were from the aristocracy or intelligentsia, intent on creating highbrow epics or art-house cinema. At a time when most countries saw film as an amusing novelty, Italy was using it to express the meaning of life.

Directors soon had a sense of themselves as *"auteurs"*, as masters of the medium, not that Italian cinema is a story of unqualified success. The heyday of Italian cinema, in the 1960s and 1970s, coincided with Federico Fellini working at the height of his powers. Since then, Italian cinema has been more a case of light and shade, although the annual Venice Film Festival is as glamorous as ever.

Founded as a showcase for Fascist Italy in 1932, the Venice Film Festival is the world's oldest, and rivals Cannes in terms of prestige and glamour.

Early extravaganzas

When the Alberini-Santoni production company released *La Presa di Roma* in 1905, the Italian feature film was born. The subject is the 1870 rout of the Pope by Garibaldi's troops.

LEFT: Marcello Mastroianni, Italy's most sophisticated leading man. **RIGHT:** Maciste, an earlier heart-throb.

In its most famous scene, Bersaglieri rallies his forces to breach the wall at Rome's Porta Pia. Because so much of it was shot on location, the film anticipates two dominant themes in Italian cinema: realism and historical spectacle.

Early in the 20th century, two directors, Enrico Guazzoni and Piero Fosca, revolutionised Italian films. Both directors' melodramatic tastes were in tune with Italy's burgeoning nationalism, and both glorified the martial exploits of Ancient Rome. Guazzoni's significance was as much for his business acumen as for his cinematic talent. *Quo Vadis?* (1913), which established his reputation, used the world's first gargantuan sets. Guazzoni limited distribution to art-house theatres, and in New York *Quo Vadis?* received its first star-studded première. Shrewd marketing set a precedent for producers to raise huge financial backing for future films.

Piero Fosca's contribution was more aesthetic. His major opus, *Cabiria* (1913), depicts the adventures of virtuous maidens, villains and heroes during the legendary wars between Rome and Carthage. Fosca was one of the first to pan cameras across vast scenes, and introduced live orchestras at screenings. More importantly, *Cabiria* introduced subtle characterisation to the epic genre.

architects to design full-scale sets. Furnishings in period dramas were often borrowed from the private collections of the dynasties depicted in the movies; and if a film included aristocrats, authentic aristocrats were invited to make guest appearances.

This first golden age of Italian cinema barely had time to blossom before the Fascists came to power. Mussolini "regulated" the film industry, so convinced was he of the power of the medium. Directors deemed ideologically sound were eligible for state financing, with particularly patriotic endeavours, such as *Scipione l'Africano*, often fully funded.

After the success of *Quo Vadis?* and *Cabiria*, Italy woke up to cinema as a medium. Industrialists realised the moneymaking potential of movie-making. Equally intrigued were the aristocracy, the natural milieu of many of Italy's filmmakers and patrons. Luchino Visconti, a first generation neo-realist, was from an aristocratic Sicilian background. Roberto Rosselini, instead, was bankrolled by a Roman countess, enabling him to make the celebrated *Roma, Città Aperta*.

The aristocratic influence is one explanation for the high production standards of early Italian cinema. While directors in France and the United States were still pinning up painted backdrops, Italians hired the nation's finest

Neo-realism

In 1944, while the Germans were still retreating from Rome, Roberto Rossellini made *Roma, Città Aperta*, a film whose unflinching truthfulness unnerves audiences to this day. The film, co-written by Federico Fellini, is about a Resistance leader tracked down by the Nazis. Every scene, except those set in the Gestapo headquarters, was shot on location. *Roma, Città Aperta* has a rough, visceral feel that was ground-breaking for the times, with sequences that resemble documentary footage.

ABOVE: Federico Fellini, the godfather of Italian cinema. **RIGHT:** still from *Cinema Paradiso* (1988), Giuseppe Tornatore's nostalgic tribute to cinema.

> ❝ *We discovered our own country… we could look freely around us now, and the reality appeared so extraordinary that we couldn't resist watching it and photographing it with fresh eyes.*
> Federico Fellini describes the post-war spirit that gave birth to neo-realism ❞

Despite its sense of immediacy, *Roma, Città Aperta* has a hidden meaning. The film elevates drug addicts, priests, German lesbians and Austrian deserters without sacrificing their unique personalities. Pina (Anna Magnani), an anguished matriarch, is both utterly convincing and representative of the desperate plight of Italian housewives during the war.

Rossellini, along with Visconti and Vittorio de Sica, developed a new kind of cinema. Neo-realism remains the core of what is considered modern in film. The movement arose from the remarkable homogeneity Italy achieved just after World War II, with the widespread conviction that Fascism was wrong. Neo-realist directors spoke from – and for – an Italy which could admit to contradictions.

Golden age

During the 1960s and early 1970s, prosperity helped to usher in a new wave of Italian film-making. The leading lights were Federico Fellini, Michelangelo Antonioni and Francesco Rosi. This was also the era of Luchino Visconti's *The Damned*, Bernardo Bertolucci's The

Conformist and Paolo Pasolini's The *Decameron*. Rosi was born in Naples, and southern Italy is a dominant theme in his films. Antonioni's exploration of existential angst and individual crises reached a climax with *Blow Up* (1967). Another Antonioni masterpiece, *Identification of a Woman* (1982) shows Venice as a magical yet murky world. However, the undisputed Venetian masterpiece is Visconti's *Death in Venice* (1970), based on Thomas Mann's classic novella. Visconti wanted "the light of the sirocco, the pale, still pearl light" and, with his artistic decision to use dawn and night shoots, forced his stars into sleeplessness.

ITALY IN THE MOVIES

Rome, Tuscany, Venice and Sicily provide seductive backdrops to the cinematic illusion of Italy. Of non-Italian directors, Peter Greenaway's *Belly of an Architect* (1987) arguably best captures the elusive character of the Eternal City. Instead, *Eat, Pray, Love* (2010), starring Julia Roberts, delights in the sexiness of the *dolce vita* capital, as does a Daniel Day Lewis harem in the bitter-sweet film musical *Nine* (2010). Tuscany evokes the Merchant-Ivory *Room with a View* (1985), both a classic and a cliché, shot in Florentine villas. Quirkier are Jane Campion's *Portrait of a Lady* (1996), set near Lucca, and Tarkovsky's *Nostalgia* (1983), filmed in Bagno Vignone's moody Roman baths south of Siena. Anthony Minghella's *The English Patient* (1996) and *The Talented Mr Ripley* (1999) are

paeons to Tuscany and Ischia, while Ridley Scott's *Gladiator* (2000) lingers on Tuscany's Val d'Orcia.

Venice is at home with costume drama, art-house or action flick. *Don't Look Now* (1973) by Nicolas Roeg brings a couple to an eerily deserted Venice shortly after the death of their child. Al Pacino is an aggrieved Shylock in Michael Radford's *The Merchant of Venice* (2004), while 007 Daniel Craig survives drowning in the lagoon in *Casino Royale* (2006). Venice is also the decadent backdrop for *Casanova* (2006), directed by Lasse Hallström and starring Heath Ledger.

Sicily is not just *The Godfather* but Rossellini's *Stromboli* (1950) set on a volcanic outpost, and *The Leopard* (1968) Visconti's hymn to princely grandeur and Sicilian pathos.

The incomparable Fellini, arguably the greatest Italian director of all time, produced a string of classics. His characters are torn between self-realisation and conformity. Fellini said that his films were a "marriage of innocence and experience", but they were also about fantasy and loss, tinged with irony, fun and sadness. In *Amarcord* (1975), Fellini's surreal flights of fancy turned Rimini, his home town, into a virtual-reality world. It was sweet revenge on the "inert, provincial, opaque, dull" Adriatic seaside resort he left for Roman chic. In his 1954 masterpiece *La Strada*, he based the central character on the lost innocence of his actress wife, Giulietta Masina, who starred in the film.

Fellini, who had a virtual monopoly on Roman sensibility, loved to satirise his fellow citizens on film. In *La Dolce Vita* (1960) and *Roma* (1972), he held a distorting mirror to Roman reality. *La Dolce Vita* (1960) was the first time Fellini worked with his male muse, Marcello Mastroianni, who was chosen for his simplicity and "normal face, a face with no personality". The filmic frolicking in Rome's Trevi Fountain turned Anita Ekberg into an international sex symbol.

In 1967, with *A Fistful of Dollars* and *The Good, the Bad and the Ugly*, Sergio Leone gave world cinema a new genre: the Spaghetti Western. These witty and stylised films, made on surprisingly low budgets, became the Italian movie industry's most successful exports since Sophia Loren, Gina Lollobrigida and Claudia Cardinale, sirens matched by Monica Bellucci today.

In the 1980s the generation of angry young Marxists and Sixties radicals gave way to commercial producers eager to create pale imitations of Hollywood action pictures. Bernardo Bertolucci is an exception in his ability to command Hollywood budgets for international blockbusters or to concentrate on more low-key work. Although best-known for *The Last Emperor* (1987), Bertolucci returned to Tuscany to shoot *Stealing Beauty* (1996), set in a rustic villa and idyllic wine estates.

The next generation

A new wave of actors and directors are slowly putting Italian cinema back on the world map. Italian cinema needed a boost. Competition

CINEMA IN THE SOUTH

Southern Italy is a self-conscious movie in the making. Cinematically, the two poles of attraction remain Sicily and Naples, confirming their cultural superiority. As well as being intensely visual, the south is seen as a place of extremes, of exquisite morality and cold-blooded Mafia murder. Movie fans have long been enthralled by a mob mythology of sharp-suited Dons wearing fedoras and carrying machine-guns in violin cases. The sun-bleached image of Sicily is the land of *The Godfather*. Mafia-infested Corleone lends its jagged rocks and sullen populace to the trilogy. But Hollywood's infatuation with the glamour of gangsterland is matched by the nostalgic, whimsical appeal of such films as *Cinema Paradiso* and *Il Postino*. Giuseppe Tornatore is the best-known Sicilian director, thanks to the Oscar-winning *Cinema Paradiso* (1990). This nostalgic slice of history, which shows the arrival of the Talkies in a benighted backwater, celebrates Sicilian exuberance with a bitter-sweet humour that mocks the grinding poverty. In the United States, the film broke box-office records for a foreign film.

In Naples, director Francesco Rosi served his apprenticeship with De Sica in the heyday of Italian neo-realism and dwells on the underbelly of southern society. *La Sfida* (*The Challenge*, 1957), tackles the Camorra's corrupt control of the city markets. The story is revisited for our times in Matteo Garrone's *Gomorrah* (2008), which is a far more brutal exposé of the same Neapolitan Mafia today.

from Italian television networks has had a detrimental effect on feature films, as did the privatisation of Cinecittà, the Roman film studios and former hothouse for Italian directors. Yet, after years in the wilderness, Cinecittà is making a comeback. Although the main focus is television, rather than feature films, the state-of-the-art studios are attracting foreign producers. In 2002, Martin Scorsese reconstructed blocks of New York slums in the studios for *Gangs of New York* – but the extras were all Romans. The array of international productions includes Mel Gibson's *The Passion of the Christ* (2004), Steven Soderbergh's *Ocean's*

fostering new movie-making, particularly in the south. Southern Italy has long been a source of inspiration for film makers, with turbulent settings presented on a plate *(see panel opposite)*.

It is invidious to single out stars, but Roberto Benigni is arguably the most popular comic actor since the legendary Totò. Benigni shot

> The 2010 Venice Film Festival saw film director Quentin Tarantino, who led the jury, accused of nepotism as he presented awards to some of his friends.

Twelve (2004) and the BBC television epic, *Rome* (2005). The life-size stage sets of Roman monuments have been left in place in the hope of enticing other producers to embark on epics. More recently, the musical *Nine* (2010), starring Daniel Day Lewis, was filmed in Cinecitta and is a tribute to the studios as well as to Fellini's *Eight and a Half.*

Regional film commissions, including those in Campania, Ischia and Tuscany, are instrumental in attracting foreign filmmakers and

LEFT: Nanni Moretti, scootering around Rome in the film *Caro Diario (Dear Diary)*. **ABOVE:** a break between takes on the set of the epic drama *Rome*, in the Cinecittà studios.

to fame with his Oscar-winning performance in *La Vita è Bella* (*Life is Beautiful*, 1997). Italy's most consistently acclaimed director is witty maverick Nanni Moretti, Rome's left-wing Woody Allen. The capital's changing moods are confronted by Moretti in his magical comedy *Caro Diario* (*Dear Diary*, 1994). Another film, *The Son's Room*, was awarded the Palme d'Or at Cannes in 2001.

As for putting on the glitz, Venice Film Festival never fails. Whatever the failings of the films, the city shines. The Lido is awash with sleek movie stars scurrying from screenings to private yachts. Stephen Spielberg laps it up: "More than anything, we are in show-business – this is the show." ❑

Music and Opera

Italy's contribution to music is unparalleled.
And where better to enjoy the art of opera
than where it began and flourished?

"**B**ewildering plots, exotic locations, spectacular music and temperamental singers and conductors: this is the world of opera," claims Antonio Pappano, director of London's Royal Opera. Italy is rightly known as the home of music, and Milan's image is inextricably bound up with La Scala, Italy's principal opera house and a symphony of red, cream and gold. When opera houses burn down, people cry in public and the country grieves. Fortunately, the country still has an abundance of major opera houses. However, Italy's contribution to Western music goes beyond operatic rococo interiors and impassioned outpourings of Verdi.

> Before the fire which destroyed Venice's La Fenice, diva Joan Sutherland dubbed it "the most beautiful opera house in the world, like being inside a diamond". Critics complain that the "reborn" theatre is too brash.

It was an Italian monk, Guido d'Arezzo, who devised the musical scale, while a Venetian printer, Ottavino Petrucci, invented a method of printing music with movable type. The language of music remains resolutely Italian, including such terms as *soprano, drammatico* and *soprano lirico*.

Italy also gave us the piano, the accordion and the fabulous Stradivarius and Guarneri violins and cellos. Cremona has been the capital of violin masters since the 16th century. Indeed, it is not too fanciful to see the curves of violins echoed in the elaborate spiral cornices of city palaces.

The food of love

Without the Italian sensibility, the world of music would be without the nobility and intensity of Verdi or the seductive strains of Vivaldi. The lush strings of Albinoni perfectly chime with the public's taste for haunting Baroque music, while opera-lovers are rewarded with Rossini's *Il Barbiere di Siviglia (The Barber of Seville)*, a comic masterpiece, Bellini's ravishing melodies, and the dramatic flow of Puccini's *Tosca* and *Turandot*. Other musical keynotes are *bel canto*, the traditional Italian art of singing, and Neapolitan love songs, as much part of the passionate city as pizza and Mount Vesuvius.

Opera was Italy's greatest musical achievement, a rousing art form which came into being in 14th-century Florence and was perfected by Monteverdi. In his opera *Orfeo*, the title role was taken by a *castrato*, a male soprano or contralto with an unbroken voice. *Castrati* were in great demand during the 17th and 18th centuries, thanks to their strong, flexible yet voluptuous voices. Farinelli (1705–82) was the most famous, a soprano whose singing and stage presence caused women to faint with excitement. Italian divas have also graced the stages of the great *teatri lirici* (opera houses), including Cecilia Bartoli in the present day, the mezzo-soprano acclaimed for her interpretations of Mozart. Italy, which gave the world

since Toscanini, whose first public performance at the age of 19 was *Aida*, conducted from memory after stepping in at short notice. After Toscanini, Claudio Abbado is arguably the greatest Italian conductor of the 20th century. Formerly at La Scala, he is currently musical director of the Mozart Orchestra of Bologna and the Lucerne Festival Orchestra. Riccardo Muti currently conducts at the Chicago Symphony Orchestra as well as at Rome's Teatro dell'Opera, and runs the Ravenna Music Festival, close to his home. Conductors Daniele Gatti, Riccardo Chailly and Giuseppe Sinopoli have also found fame abroad.

Enrico Caruso and Beniamino Gigli, has also boasted a clutch of talented tenors, from Luciano Pavarotti to Andrea Bocelli, as well as the romantic Roberto d'Alagna, raised in Paris by Sicilian parents.

The world's their stage

Gian Carlo Menotti (1911–2007) was acclaimed as the founder of the Spoleto Festival in Umbria, which continues to be a highbrow celebration of music, theatre and ballet. It is currently led by film and theatre director Giorgio Ferrara. As for conductors, this has been an Italian forte

LEFT: Verdi, great opera composer and Italian patriot.
ABOVE: Greek theatre in Taormina, Sicily.

THE LEGEND OF "BIG LUCY"

In his lifetime, Luciano Pavarotti (1935–2007) was the world's most recognised tenor. "Big Lucy" began singing for sweets aged five, and his career was launched with the winning of a Welsh choral competition. Throughout his long and prolific career, he was as happy singing Neapolitan love duets and Puccini arias as crooning with international rock stars such as Sting and U2. He achieved legendary status in the 1990s singing with Carreras and Domingo as the "Three Tenors". His last performance was in 2006 at Turin's Winter Olympics opening ceremony. Pavarotti, who died at home in Modena, will be remembered as one of the greatest tenors of the 20th century.

Conductors working abroad are probably relieved to escape their knowledgeable but critical audiences back home. Italian audiences are hard taskmasters, with applause led by the official clapping societies that are present in the major houses. Yet if the opera falls short of perfection, the *loggionisti*, those in the gods, are ready to rain down abuse on fallen divas, with

> Brave visitors who wish to show their appreciation at the end of an operatic performance can shout "*bravo*" for tenors, "*brava*" for sopranos and "*bravi*" for all.

booing and hissing commonplace. Ultimately, as long as the opera provides a spectacle, of people-watching or, perish the thought, of mellifluous music, then an Italian audience usually goes home happy, whether the fat lady sings or not.

Opera's golden age

Giacomo Puccini once said of himself, "I have more heart than mind." In these characteristics lies the key to Italian opera. It is essentially sensual and lush, appealing more to the emotions than the intellect.

The bookends of Italian opera's golden age stand clear: on the one side, the 1815 production of Rossini's classic *opera buffa* (comic opera), *Il Barbiere di Siviglia*; on the other, the posthumous 1926 opening of Puccini's last and unfinished opus, *Turandot*. Between the two lies more than a century of operatic triumphs.

During the 19th century, when Giocchino

Rossini, Gaetano Donizetti and Vincenzo Bellini dominated the scene, Italian opera became infused with vitality, and Europe once again looked towards Italy for operatic innovation. All three composers, born within a decade of one another, shared much in style, and their careers followed similar paths and detours.

Rossini is probably most celebrated for his productions of *Il Barbiere di Siviglia* and *Guillaume Tell*, while Donizetti's masterpieces are *Lucia di Lammermoor* and *La Fille du Régiment*. Bellini is celebrated for his *semi seria* works, *La Sonnambula*, *Norma* and *I Puritani*. These operas are part of standard repertoires which

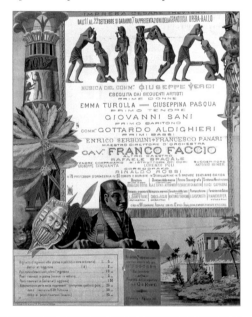

ITALY'S OPERA HOUSES

Beyond their gilt-and-stucco interiors, Italy's glittering opera houses *(teatri lirici)* are mostly neoclassical affairs. Historically, the rivalry of noble courts gave birth to private opera houses, which gradually opened their doors to the public – beginning with Venice in 1637. The fashion for opera spread, and by the 18th century there were 20 in Venice alone. Most opera houses are in Lombardy and Emilia-Romagna, linked to great courts such as Cremona, Parma and Mantua.

Milan's La Scala is the premier opera house. Opened in 1778, it has been radically refurbished. All the great Italian composers have written for La Scala, notably Rossini, Donizetti, Bellini, Puccini and Verdi. Its heyday coincided with Verdi's patriotic works, but glory returned under Toscanini's direction in the early 20th century.

Naples's Teatro San Carlo enjoys a reputation second only to La Scala, followed by Venice, Florence and Rome. Rebuilt in 1816, San Carlo won a name as a "singer's theatre", where vocal gymnastics and artistic rivalry were pre-eminent. Venice's La Fenice (The Phoenix) was devastated by fires in 1836 and 1996 but rose from the ashes in 2003, a red-and-gold rococo confection rebuilt exactly as before.

Other theatres include Parma, Genoa, Bergamo, Modena and Turin. Palermo's Teatro Massimo reopened in 1998 with a glittering production of Verdi's *Aida*, after a scandalous 25-year closure, during which it had opened its doors only once – to allow the filming of *The Godfather: Part III*.

are performed throughout the world.

The three composers shared a small-town background, and all enjoyed great success at an early age, although Bellini was already 22 years old when he made his operatic debut. Not surprisingly, there was a fierce and jealous rivalry between them. Upon hearing that Rossini had composed *Il Barbiere di Siviglia* in 13 days, Donizetti shrugged proudly and concluded, "No wonder – he is so lazy."

They acquired gold and glory all over Europe, but, tragically, all three burnt themselves out. Bellini and Donizetti died young, the latter a crazed syphilitic, and Rossini's last triumph was

productions, *Oberto* (1839) and *Un Giorno di Regno* (1840), met with lacklustre receptions at La Scala premières, rave notices for the epic *Nabucco* (1842) marked the beginning of a long and distinguished career. From then on, Verdi saw success after success, highlighted by *Rigoletto* (1851), *Il Trovatore* (1853), *La Traviata* (1853), *La Forza del Destino* (1862), *Don Carlo* (1867), *Aida* (1871) and *Otello* (1887). With premières in London, Paris, St Petersburg and Cairo, along with those in the theatres of Italy, Verdi was a composer of true international stature.

Verdi's sharp, almost brutal dynamism freed Italian opera from the lingering vestiges of

achieved before he reached 40. They were followed by the brightest light in Italian opera.

The brightest star

Giuseppe Verdi was born in 1813 (the same year as Richard Wagner) in Le Roncole, a small village near Parma. Verdi came from a poor, unmusical background but young Giuseppe made a mark as the local church organist. In 1832, he was denied admission to the prestigious Milan Conservatory. But the young Verdi was persistent, and, although his first two

LEFT: poster for a performance of Verdi's *Aida* in La Fenice (1881). ABOVE: an animated 19th-century audience in the Teatro San Carlo in Naples.

empty convention. Verdi also refused to tailor his works to the whims of individual singers, something that no composer had dared do in the past. His independence extended to his personal life. In a very conservative and religious society, he openly lived with his mistress, the soprano Giuseppina Strepponi, for more than a decade before taking her to the altar in 1859.

If Verdi was permitted artistic and personal freedom, he was still constrained by the political realities of his day. Censorship was a constant impediment in an Italy dominated by foreign powers. Verdi was himself an ardent nationalist. His historical works were charged with analogies of the Italians' plight – allusions that were not lost upon native audiences. From 1848, his name became a rallying cry for his countrymen in the fight for freedom from Austrian domination. The acronym V(ittorio) E(manuele) R(e) D'I(talia) was used as a reference to the first king of Italy, eventually crowned in 1861. A dear friend of Count Cavour, Verdi briefly served in the new chamber of deputies after unification. On his death in 1901, Verdi was mourned not only as a composer but also as a patriot.

The best-loved tunes

Although operas of fine quality continue to be composed today, the golden age of Italian opera drew to a close with the career of Giacomo Puccini, who was inspired by Verdi's *Aida* to become an operatic composer. Others contended for the mantle of Verdi, but Puccini had the advantage of the blessing of the old man himself. "Now there are dynasties, also in art," lamented rival Alfredo Catalani, "and I know that Puccini 'has to be' the successor of Verdi… who, like a good king, often invites the 'crown prince' to dinner!" A dynasty it may have been, but one clearly based on merit. Puccini's success lay as much in his great gift for melody as in his unerring sense of theatre. *La Bohème* (1896), *Tosca* (1900) and *Madama Butterfly* (1904) are today among the best-loved works of opera. ❑

FESTIVE SPIRITS

The best-known opera festival is the Arena di Verona, with operas performed outdoors, in Verona's magnificent Roman amphitheatre. Florence's Maggio Musicale, the oldest music festival in Italy, is matched by Umbria's Spoleto's Festival dei Due Mondi, which embraces classical, jazz and world music. The Stresa Festival, centred on Lake Maggiore, combines world-famous orchestras with smaller concerts in churches around the lake, including concerts on the islands of Isola Bella and Isola Madre, and in the mysterious Hermitage of Santa Caterina del Sasso. On the Adriatic, the Ravenna Festival focuses on Italian opera. Parma, for ever associated with Verdi, has an annual festival in his honour, with a similar festival dedicated to Rossini in Pesaro. Loveli-

est of all, Torre del Lago in Tuscany celebrates its illustrious son, Puccini, every summer with opera by the lake.

Most festivals share spellbinding settings, from the Ravello Festival, overlooking the Amalfi Coast, to Sicily, where Taormina's summer showcase presents theatre, ballet, rock and opera in its Greek theatre. The Roma Opera Festival benefits from its setting in the ancient Baths of Caracalla. Summer in the Dolomites ushers in music festivals in the South Tyrol (Alto Adige) and Trentino. South Tyrol's concert cycle, The Sound of Music, means that, even without Julie Andrews, the hills are alive with concerts. Equally magical is Trentino's Sounds of the Dolomites, when summer concerts are staged in glorious scenery, often reached by cable car.

Sounds of Success

In the last 60 years Italy has developed a successful home-grown music scene to compete with British and American pop imports

Italy's pop singers have sometimes found success beyond national boundaries. This was particularly true in the 1950s when Italian-American singers like Sinatra, Perry Como and Tony Bennett were defining the easy-listening sound. Dean Martin crooned Domenico Modugno's *Volare* to international fame, and his version of *Arriverderci Roma* was a nostalgic hit for people remembering their Italian holidays.

During the 1960s, a group of young pop stars emerged to dominate the domestic market. These included Mina, Rita Pavone, Adriano Celentano, Lucio Battisti and Gianni Morandi. In his 40-year career Celentano sold 70 million records, while Battisti's classics, such as *La Canzone del Sole, Mare Nero* and *Aqua Azzurra Acqua Chiara* were the soundtrack for a generation of 1970s adolescents.

As the political dissent and liberation movement of the late 1960s took hold, a group of engaged singer-songwriters emerged. Known as *cantautori*, they created some of the most innovative Italian contemporary music, though their lyric-rich compositions were never going to translate abroad.

Italy's Bob Dylan is considered to be the late Fabrizio De Andre, with compositions such as *La Canzone di Marinella* and *La Guerra di Piero*. Singer-songwriter Francesco De Gregori's album Rimmel is vintage '70s, while Ivano Fossati peerlessly mined Italy's melancholic soul with compositions like *I Treni a Vapore*. His *La Canzone Popolare* remains an election anthem for the centre-left.

Rome's local *cantautore* Antonello Venditti immortalised his city in *Roma Capoccia*, and his albums of well-crafted, if sometimes disposable, pop still chart. Neapolitan musical tradition continues with Eduardo Bennato's politically tinged rock. But the city's musical statesman is Pino Daniele. Singing in his local dialect, Daniele fuses rock, blues and jazz. His hometown anthem, *Napule E'*, encapsulates the city's melancholic spirit.

Bolognese songwriter Lucio Dalla emerged in the '70s with a lyrical blend of humour, politics and profanity. From the satirical peace anthem *Se lo Fossi Angelo* to the domestic reality of *Anna e Marco*, Dalla chronicles all aspects of Italian life.

Italian rock music has flourished in recent decades, even if it is often mocked abroad, with the most dated aspects showcased in the annual San Remo song contest, which is still considered the country's major musical event.

Although the English-speaking world has been more resistant to Italian pop, the rest of the world has embraced two of the nation's singers. Laura Pausini has racked up global sales of 28 million records, and in 2006 she became the first Italian

female to win a Grammy, taking Best Latin Pop Album with *Escucha*. Roman-born popster Eros Ramazzotti has found fame beyond Italian shores, with his catchy singer-songwriting talents. Megastar Zucchero scored a rare success in the British market when he re-versioned the classic hit *Senza una Donna*, duetting with Paul Young.

One Italian singer who has become a household name at home and abroad is Andrea Bocelli, who offers a mellifluous blend of classical music, traditional song and pop. He has performed on international opera stages and even sang at the White House. The legacy of popular legends from Caruso to Pavarotti would weigh heavy on any tenor, but Bocelli, it seems, is more than capable of picking up the baton. ❑

LEFT: opera in Rome. **RIGHT:** Grammy award-winner Laura Pausini.

PLACES

A detailed guide to the entire country,
with principal sights cross-referenced
by number to the maps

Negotiating the tangle of one-way streets in an Italian city takes years of experience. Often a helpful native will point the way, or even take you there personally. But if no one materialises, simply follow the signs for *Centro Storico* (historic centre) and *Duomo* (cathedral), and remember that *senso unico* means "one way". Then find the first *parcheggio* (car park), for most Italian cities are best explored on foot and increasingly pedestrianised. If you arrive by train, the station will invariably be in the seedier part of town, so leave it behind for the better-preserved *Centro Storico*.

Modern life has stamped even small villages with a bar and a large population of moped-riding youths. Every town has its Duomo, but how different is the austere Romanesque cathedral of Puglia from the lavish Baroque one in Turin. Every town has at least one piazza: in the south they might be crowded with men smoking and playing cards; in the north, the men are still there, but so are the women and the tourists.

Our favourite places in Italy include many spots less frequented than the tried and true trio of Rome, Florence and Venice. We suggest that, after visiting Rome, you take an excursion east into Abruzzo or Molise, those hitherto remote regions whose architecture, parks, mountains and beaches rank among the most refreshing vacation spots in the country. Or, if you happen to be exploring the Bay of Naples, rent a car and continue down to Italy's heel and toe – Puglia, Basilicata and Calabria – even taking the ferry across to Sicily. Puglia (also known as Apulia) is increasingly popular, while Basilicata is an emerging destination.

The north has Venice, of course, but also Milan and Turin, two utterly contemporary cities packed with art and history. You could follow the path of generations of travellers who, with Dante and Ariosto in hand, toured the cities of Lombardy, the Veneto, Emilia-Romagna and Tuscany. If you want to catch your breath and relax, retreat into the green hills of Umbria, home of Italy's beloved St Francis of Assisi.   ❏

PRECEDING PAGES: the Trevi fountain in Rome; Roman *ragazzi* playing in the street; the village of Poggio in the mountains near Genoa. **LEFT:** terraced landscape in Liguria. **ABOVE:** remains of a Greek temple near the town of Agrigento, Sicily; golden lion, symbol of Venice, on the Palazzo Vecchio.

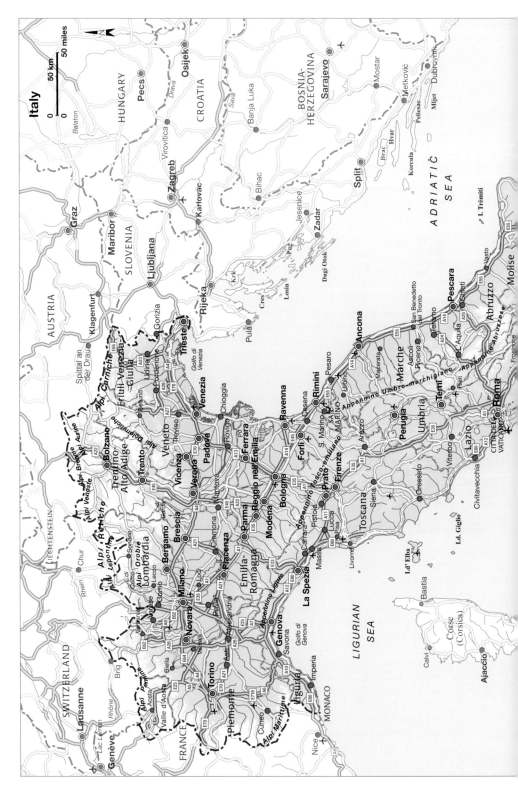

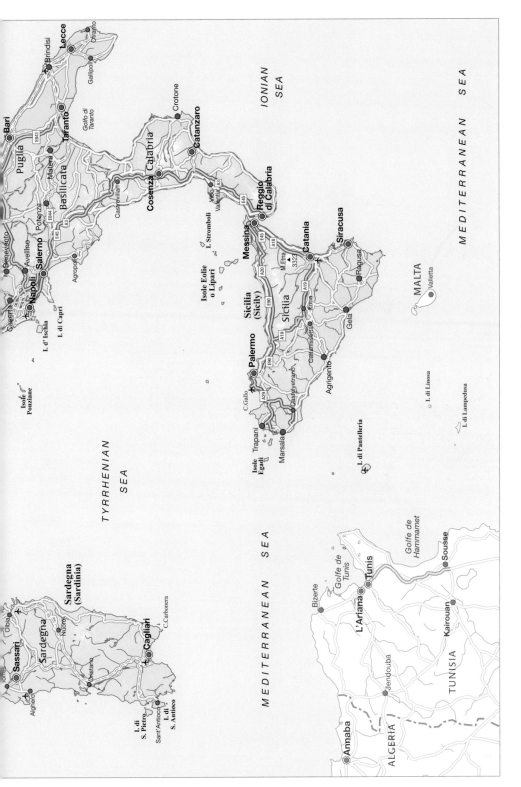

ROME

Follow in the footsteps of emperors and saints, discovering the monuments and churches that define Rome as the capital of Italy and the ancient world

Since its millennial revamp for Holy Year, Rome has rarely looked lovelier. The Eternal City has shaken off its dusty toga and slipped into contemporary clothes. The facelift to its ancient sites has been matched by subtle plastic surgery to its arts scene. Revamped galleries, new contemporary art museums and the creation of a superb music complex have helped turn the city's face towards the future. While not a new *dolce vita*, there is a cinematic gloss to the emerging city: eclectic festivals, a funky club scene, sleek cafés, boutique hotels and a more cosmopolitan air. As the Mayor says: "Rome dares to dream again." Cynics retort: but this is not why we flock to Rome. True, but to remain "Ancient Rome" and still be a contemporary city is the cleverest trick of all.

The Palatine Hill

The best introduction to Rome is not Piazza Venezia, the terrifying roundabout at the centre of the modern city, but the more pastoral **Palatino** ❶ (Palatine Hill; daily 8.30am–7.15pm in summer, until 4.30pm in winter, last entry one hour before closing; charge – ticket also valid for the Colosseum and Forum). The Palatine is traditionally associated with Romulus, the legendary founder of Rome. Remarkably, his presumed cave dwelling has recently been identified. Decorated with seashells, mosaics and pumice stones, the grotto was discovered near the ruins of the palace of Emperor Augustus.

Nearby are the remains of the **Tempio di Cibele**, picturesquely planted with an ilex grove. The cult of the Eastern goddess of fertility was introduced to Italy during the Second Punic War (218–201 BC). Though its mystical rites – involving throngs of frenzied female worshippers, priests committing self-mutilation, and bull sacrifices – were distasteful to old-fashioned Romans,

Main attractions
PALATINE HILL
ROMAN FORUM
CAPITOLINE MUSEUMS
TRAJAN'S MARKETS
THE COLOSSEUM
SAN GIOVANNI IN LATERANO
PALAZZO DORIA PAMPHILI
TREVI FOUNTAIN
ARA PACIS AUGUSTAE
PIAZZA DEL POPOLO
PALAZZO BARBERINI
GALLERIA BORGHESE
VILLA GIULIA
MUSEO NAZIONALE ROMANO
THE PANTHEON
PIAZZA NAVONA
THE MAXXI (MUSEUM OF 21ST-CENTURY ARTS)

LEFT: Piazza della Repubblica.
RIGHT: buzzing around on a Vespa.

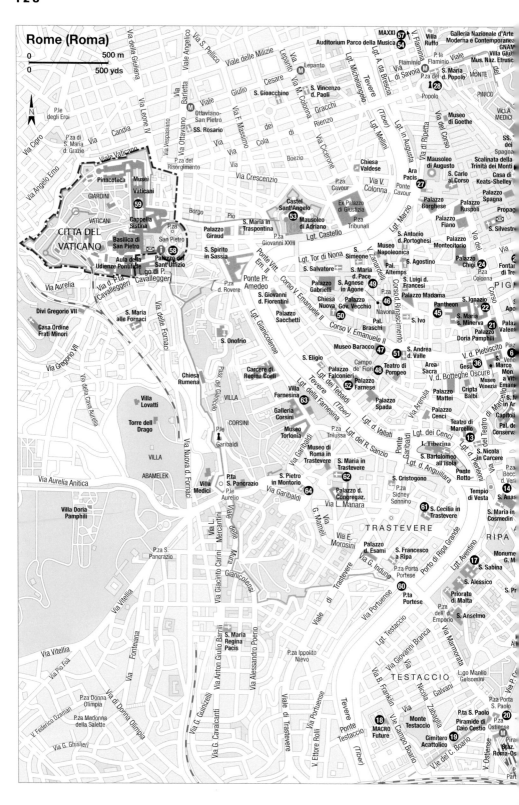

Rome (Roma)

0 ————— 500 m
0 ————— 500 yds

N

Via della Giuliana

Via Cipro

Via Angelo Emo

P.le degli Eroi

P.za di S. Maria d. Grazie

Via Leone IV

Candia

Via Ottaviano

Via Vespasiano

Via Barletta

Via S. Pellico

Viale Angelico

Viale delle Milizie

Via M. Colonna

Giulio Cesare

Via F. Massimo

Cola di Rienzo

Via

Via Crescenzio

Boezio

Lepanto M

S. Gioacchino

Ottaviano-San Pietro M

SS. Rosario

P.za del Risorgimento

Borgo

Pio

S. Vincenzo d. Paoli

Gracchi

Via Cicerone

Chiesa Valdese

Via Michelangelo

Tevere

Lgt. di Brescia

Lgt. in Augusta

Lgt. Marzio

Lgt. in Ripetta

P.le Flaminio

P.za del Popolo

Popolo

S. Maria d. Popolo M

MONTE

PINICO

MAXXI 57 V. Flaminio 54

Auditorium Parco della Musica

Villa Ruffo

Galleria Nazionale d'Arte Moderna e Contemporanea GNAM

GNAM
Villa Giulia
Mus. Naz. Etrusc.

VILLA MEDICI

Museo di Goethe

SS. dei Spagna

Scalinata della Trinità dei Monti

S. Carlo al Corso

Casa di Keats-Shelley

Mausoleo di Augusto

Ara Pacis 27

Ponte Cavour

P.za Cavour

Palazzo Borghese

Palazzo Ruspoli

Palazzo Spagna

Propag

S. Silvestro

Pinacoteca

Musei Vaticani

GIARDINI VATICANI

CITTA DEL VATICANO

Cappella Sistina 59

Cappella Sistina

Basilica di San Pietro

Aula delle Udienze Pontificie

L.go di P. Cavalleggeri

Via d. P.ta Cavalleggeri

Via Aurelia

P.za San Pietro

58

Palazzo del Sant'Uffizio

S. Spirito in Sassia

Castel Sant'Angelo 53

S. Maria in Traspontina

Mausoleo di Adriano

Ex Palazzo di Giustizia

S.ta Tribunali

Ponte Vitt. Em. II

Palazzo Giraud

P.za Pia

Borgo

Via Aurelia

Divi Gregorio VII

Casa Ordine Frati Minori

Via Gregorio VII

Via della Cava Aurelia

S. Maria alle Fornaci

Via delle Fornaci

S. Onofrio

Carcere di Regina Coeli

Chiesa Rumena

Passeggiata del Gianicolo

VILLA

CORSINI

Villa Lovatti

Torre dell Drago

VILLA

ABAMELEK

Via Nuova d. Fornaci

Via Aurelia Antica

P.le Garibaldi

P.za S. Pancrazio

Villa Doria Pamphili

Villa Medici

P.ta S. Pancrazio

P.le Aurelio

Via L. Mercantini

Viale delle Mura Gianicolensi

Via Giacinto Carini

Via Anton Giulio Barrili

Via G. Guinzelli

Via Vitellia

Via Vitellia

Via Pio Foà

V. Federico Ozanam

P.za Donna Olimpia

P.za Madonna della Salette

V. G. Ghisleri

Via di Donna Olimpia

Via G. Cavalcanti

S. Maria Regina Pacis

Via Alessandro Poerio

P.za Ippolito Nievo

Palazzo Giraud

S. Spirito in Sassia

P.za S. Giovanni XXIII

Ponte Pr. Amedeo

S. Giovanni d. Fiorentini

Palazzo Sacchetti

Lgt. Gianicolense

S. Eligio

Villa Farnesina

Galleria Corsini

Museo Torlonia

P.le Trilussa

Museo di Roma in Trastevere

S. Pietro in Montorio 64

Via Garibaldi

Via G. Mameli

Via E. Morosini

Palazzo d. Esami

S. Maria in Traspontina

Corso Vitt. Emanuele II

Palazzo Gabrielli

Chiesa Nuova 50

Pal. Braschi

Museo Baracco 47

Palazzo Falconieri

Palazzo Farnese 52

Palazzo Spada

Campo de' Fiori

Teatro di Pompeo 48

Palazzo Cenci

Lgt. del Tebaldi

Lgt. della Farnesina

Lgt. dei Tebaldi

Lgt. del R. Sanzio

Lgt. d. Vallati

Lgt. dei Cenci

63

Via della Lungara

S. Maria in Trastevere 62

S. Egidio

Palazzo d. Congregaz.

60

P.ta Portese

Via di Trastevere

Viale di Trastevere

Via Portuense

P.za Porta Portese

P.za dell' d. Emporio

Tevere

Ponte Testaccio

V. Ettore Rolli

Via Campo Boario

V. di Ostiense

18 MACRO Future

Cimitero Acattolico 19

TESTACCIO

Lgt. Testaccio

Via B. Franklin

Via Giovanni Branca

Via Marmorata

Via Nicola Zabaglia

Galvani

L.go Manlio Gelsomini

P.za Porta S. Paolo

P.ta S. Paolo 20

Piramide di Caio Cestio

Braz. Staz. Roma-Lido

Via Ostiense

Via del C. Boario

RIPA

Lgt. Aventino

17 S. Sabina

S. Alessico

Priorato di Malta

S. Anselmo

Monume G. M.

S. Pr

S. Maria in Cosmedin

Tempio di Vesta 14

Ponte Rotto

S. Bartolomeo all'Isola

I. Tiberina

Ponte Garibaldi

Lgt. d. Anguillara

S. Cristogono

61 S. Cecilia in Trastevere

TRASTEVERE

P.za Sidney Sonnino

Teatro di Marcello

13

S. Nicola in Carcere

Lgt. dei Pierleoni

Capitoli

Pal. dei Conserva

Teatro di Marcello

Cripta Balbi

Palazzo Mattei

Palazzo Cenci

V.d. Botteghe Oscure

Area Sacra

Gesù 36

Palazzo Venezia

Museo Venezia

S. Marco Mon a Vit

V. Venez

Piaz

6 V. Vene

Pantheon

Palazzo Madama 46

S. Agnese in Agone 49

Palazzo Gov. Vecchio

P.za Navona

S. Ivo

S. Andrea d. Valle 51

45 S. Ignazio

S. Maria s. Minerva 21

Palazzo Doria Pamphili

Palazzo Valen

22

Palazzo Chigi 24

Fontar di Tre

PIG

Apo

6

Piaz

Palazzo Madama

S. Luigi d. Francesi

Palazzo Montecitorio

Palazzo Fiano

S. Antonio d. Portoghesi

Museo Napoleonico

Pal. Altemps

S. Salvatore

S. Simeone

Lgt. Tor di Nona

S. Maria d. Pace

V. Zanardelli

S. Agostino

P.za Colonna

Via

S. Maria in Traspontina

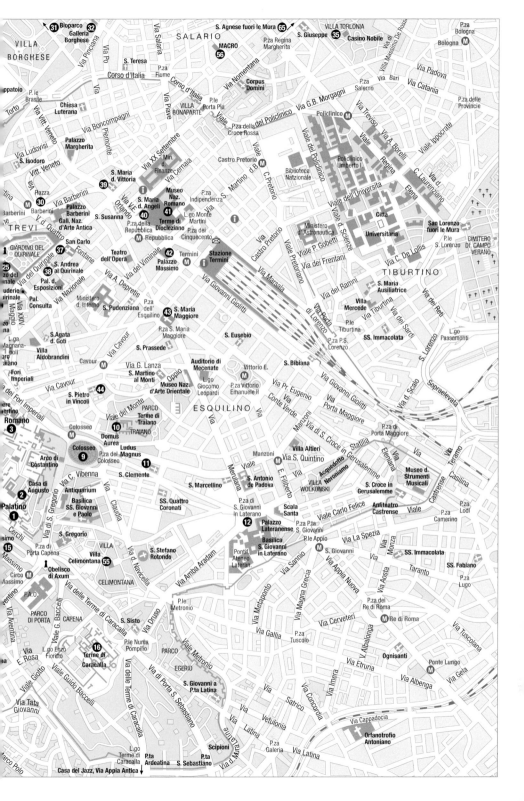

Letters in stone in the Forum.

BELOW: friendly Roman welcome.

the cult spread widely during the imperial era.

In Roman times the Palatine Hill was celebrated for the splendour of its palatial dwellings, the preferred home of the emperors. The earliest was the Domus Augustana. A portion of it, known as the **Casa di Livia** (Livia was Augustus' second wife), is renowned for its wall paintings and floor mosaics. Best of all is the newly opened section, known as the **Casa di Augusto** ❷ (Mon, Wed, Sat 11am–3.30pm; to book tel: 06-0608; ticket also valid for the Forum and Colosseum). The emblematic ruins reveal colonnaded gardens and the emperor's frescoed quarters, including his study.

To the north, alongside the Palazzo di Tiberio (now mostly covered by the Farnese Gardens) runs the **Criptoporticus**, a vaulted underground passage built by Nero to connect the palaces of Augustus, Tiberius and Caligula to his own sumptuous 'Golden House' (Domus Aurea) on the Esquiline Hill. To the southeast of this passage extend the remains of the **Domus Flavia**, built at the end of the 1st century AD by the Emperor Domitian. An infamous sadist who took pleasure in torturing everything from flies to senators, Domitian suffered from an obsessive fear of assassination. According to the ancient historian Suetonius, author of *Lives of the Caesars*, an entertaining if not entirely trustworthy source, the emperor covered the walls of the peristyle (the section with an octagonal maze) with reflective moonstone so that no assassin could creep up on him unobserved. Next to the peristyle lie the remains of a splendid banqueting hall, hailed by contemporaries as "the dining room of Jove".

Following the fortunes of the city, the imperial palaces fell into disuse during the Middle Ages, when monks made their home among the ruins. During the Renaissance building boom, Cardinal Alessandro Farnese bought a large part of the Palatine and in 1625 laid out the world's first botanical gardens on the slope overlooking the Forum. The lush **Orti Farnesiani** are delightful, with their formal landscaping, the sounds of fountains and birds, and views over Rome.

For lovers of the picturesque, the ruins of the Palatine are hard to beat. It is the last place in Rome where you can find a pastoral scene as it might have been drawn by Piranesi or Claude Lorraine. Roses, moss and poppies growing amid the crumbling bricks and shattered marble give it a romantic rather than an imperial splendour. It is the perfect place in which to wander, dream, sketch or picnic.

The Roman Forum

The Clivus Palatinus leads from the domestic extravagances of the emperors down into the **Foro Romano** ❸ (Roman Forum; daily 8.30am–one hour before sunset; charge), the civic centre of Ancient Rome. This area, once a swamp between the Capitoline and Palatine hills, used as a burial ground by the original inhabitants of the surrounding hills, was drained by an Etruscan king in the 6th century BC. Until excavations began in the 19th century, the Forum – buried under 8 metres (25ft) of debris – was known as the "Campo Vaccino" (Cow Field) because smallholders tended their herds among the ruins. Today it reveals a stupendous array of ruined temples, public buildings, arches and shops.

At the bottom of the Clivus Palatinus, the **Arco di Tito** (Arch of Titus) commemorates that emperor's destruction of Jerusalem and its sacred Temple in AD 70. This event marked the beginning of the Diaspora and the shift from the Temple in Jerusalem to local synagogues as the focus of Jewish worship. Until Israel was founded in 1948 and the return to Palestine became possible, pious Jews refused to walk under this arch.

The Via Sacra leads past the three remaining arches of the **Basilica di Costantino**, a source of inspiration for Renaissance architects. Bramante said of his design for St Peter's: "I shall place the Pantheon on top of the Basilica of Constantine." The **Tempio di Antonino e Faustina**, also known as San Lorenzo in Miranda, is a superb example of Rome's architectural layering. Originally a temple erected in AD 141 by the Emperor Antoninus Pius, it was converted into a church in the Middle Ages. During the 17th century

TIP

The Roma Pass (tel: 06-0608; www.06 0608.it/www.romapass. it) is a 3-day combined museum, monument and transport pass that includes two free museum entrances, further discounted entrances and free public transport as well as discounts on guided tours.

BELOW: view over the Forum.

a Baroque facade was added, as was the case with so many Roman churches.

Across the Via Sacra is the lovely, round **Tempio di Vesta** (Vesta was the goddess of the hearth), where the six Vestal Virgins took turns tending the sacred fire. The punishment for allowing the fire to die down was a whipping by the priest. Service was for 30 years and chastity was the rule. Few patricians were eager to offer their daughters, and the Emperor Augustus had to pick girls by lot. Laxity about vows was common, and the Emperor Domitian resorted to the traditional punishment of burying errant virgins alive and stoning their lovers to death. Living in the lovely **Casa delle Vestali** was some compensation for this demanding life. The ruins remain a rose-scented haven.

The ancient Romans were keen litigants. Walk past the three elegant columns of the Temple of Castor and Pollux to the **Basilica Julia** (on the left of the Via Sacra), where trials were held, as many as four at a time. The acoustics were terrible, and on one occasion the booming speech of a particularly loud lawyer was applauded by audiences in all four chambers. The Senate met across the way in the Curia, the best-preserved building in the Forum. Its sombre, solid appearance befits the seriousness of its purpose.

At the western end of the Forum rises the famed **Rostra,** where the orator Cicero declaimed to the Roman masses. After his death, during the second Triumvirate's anti-Republican edicts, Cicero's hands and head were displayed here. Opposite the Rostra is the single **Colonna di Foca** (Column of Phocas). For centuries the symbol of the Forum, it was described by Byron as the "eloquent and nameless column with the buried base". Unburied and named, it is still, as the Italians say, *suggestivo* (atmospheric). To the right is the **Arco di Settimio Severo**.

At the end of the Via Sacra, in the shadow of the Capitoline Hill, rise the eight Ionic columns of the **Tempio di Saturno**. Saturn's festival, the Saturnalia, marked the merriest occasion in the Roman calendar, when gifts were exchanged and distinctions between master and slave reversed. Occurring

in the middle of winter, this was the feast that Christians later transformed into Christmas. Behind the temple are, from left to right, the Temple of Vespasian and Titus, and the Temple of the Concordia.

Outside the Forum excavations, across from Pietro da Cortona's Chiesa di Santi Luca e Martina, is the **Carcere Mamertino** ❹ (Mamertine Prison; daily 9am–12.30pm, 2.30–6.30pm; donation), home to some famous prisoners. According to legend, this dank, gloomy dungeon was where St Peter converted his pagan guards. Miraculously, a fountain sprang up so that he could baptise the new Christians.

The Capitoline Hill

From the **Capitolino** ❺ (Capitoline Hill) the Temple of Jupiter Capitolinus (509 BC) watched over the city. It was here also that modern Italians raised their tribute to Italy's unification. The **Vittoriano** (Victor Emmanuel Monument; daily 9.30am–5.30pm, until 4.30pm in winter; free), completed in 1911 and dedicated to Italy's first king, captures the neoclassical bad taste of

the 19th century. The monument is famously despised by locals, who call it the "typewriter" or "wedding cake".

Throughout Rome's history hopes for Italy's future have centred on this hill. In 1300, the poet Petrarch was crowned laureate here; in 1347 Cola di Rienzo roused the Roman populace to support his short-lived attempt to revive the Roman Republic; in the 16th century Michelangelo planned the elegant Campidoglio, thus restoring the Capitoline's status as the architectural focal point of the city.

If you are feeling energetic, climb the 124 steps to the 7th-century **Santa Maria in Aracoeli** (if you happen to be here at Christmas, come for the Midnight Mass). The weak-kneed will probably prefer Michelangelo's regal staircase (known as the *cordonata*), flanked at the top by monumental statues of Castor and Pollux. In the back of the Campidoglio, Palazzo Senatorio surmounts the ancient Tabularium, dating from Republican times. On the right of Palazzo Senatorio rises **Palazzo dei Conservatori**, and on the left, the **Palazzo Nuovo**. Together

The quintessentially cool Fiat 500 in Via del Corso.

BELOW: the *Dying Gaul* in the Musei Capitolini.

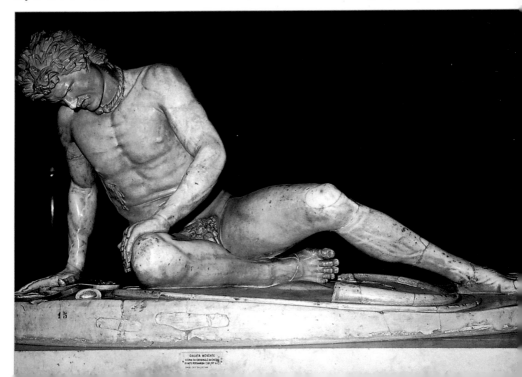

Controversially, the Colosseum could be festooned with advertising hoardings if current plans come to fruition: this is the price of a £20-million sponsorship deal needed to restore the landmark.

they make up the revamped **Capitoline Museums** (Tues–Sun 9am–8pm; entry is via the Palazzo dei Conservatori; charge; book online at www. pierreci.it), an imposing collection of classical art and statuary. Highlights include the Etruscan bronze she-wolf nursing Romulus and Remus and, in the new wing, a bronze of Hercules and a monumental statue of Marcus Aurelius. Escape to the café-terrace for panoramic views and time to ponder on the world-weary physiognomies of the later Roman emperors.

Mussolini's remodelling of Ancient Rome

Piazza Venezia ➏, at the foot of the Vittoriano, marks the centre of modern-day Rome. Brave the traffic to reach the Palazzo di Venezia. Rome's first great Renaissance palace (built in 1455), dominates one side. This was Mussolini's headquarters from 1929, and his most famous speeches were delivered from the balcony. The light burning in his bedroom at all hours reassured the Italians that the "sleepless one" was busy solving the nation's problems

(though according to Luigi Barzini the light was often left on when Mussolini was not there). Now the palace contains the **Museo di Palazzo Venezia** (Tues–Sun 8.30am–7.30pm, charge; book on www.ticketieria.it), with a collection of medieval and Renaissance paintings, sculptures and tapestries.

"Ten years from now, comrades, no one will recognise Italy," proclaimed *Il Duce* in 1926. One of the most dramatic changes the Fascists wrought on Rome was the Via dei Fori Imperiali. Mussolini demolished old neighbourhoods (reminders of Rome's decadent period) in order to excavate the fora and build the road. Such brutal means were intended to create a symbolic connection between Rome's glorious past and his own regime.

The Forum and Colosseum

North of the Imperial Fora is **Foro Traiano ➐** (Trajan's Forum), dominated by the famous **Trajan's Column**, sculpted with his victories over the Dacians. Behind are the recently restored **Mercati di Traiano** (Trajan's Markets; Tues–Sun 9am–7pm; charge). The engaging, well-conceived museum complex aims to explain the function and design of all the main Roman fora, as well as putting the impressive five-storey market into context.

Adjoining the Forum but reached along Via IV Novembre is **Palazzo Valentini ➑** (Mon–Fri 8.30am–6pm; tel: 06-67661), headquarters of the provincial administration, but also a wonderful new Roman site. The unearthing of several patrician villas prompted the restoration project of 2nd–4th-century mosaics which were discovered amid the debris of a World War II air-raid shelter. The site is illuminated by a virtual reality presentation by Piero Angelo, Italy's finest popular historian. The palazzo, and the remains of these senatorial villas, connect with the majestic open-air museum in the heart of Ancient Rome, which remains the haunt of the city's ubiquitous *gatti* (cats).

BELOW: Trajan's Column.

At the end of all this ruined splendour rises the **Colosseo** ➒ (Colosseum; daily 8.30am–one hour before sunset; Aug–Oct Sat late-night opening until midnight; ticket also valid for the Palatine and Forum). Stripped of its picturesque wild flowers and weeds and encircled by a swirling moat of traffic, the site currently looks rather forlorn. Even if this symbol of the Eternal City is less splendid than it was in its marble-clad, imperial days, new underground sections have been opened and a full restoration is promised.

The Colosseum was begun in AD 79 when the Emperor Vespasian drained the lake of Emperor Nero's **Domus Aurea** ➓ (Golden House; partially closed for restoration; tel: 06-3996 7700; booking essential). The message was clear: where Nero had been profligate, emptying the imperial coffers to construct his own pleasure palace, the Colosseum's creator built a public monument. Also nearby is the **Arco di Costantino** (Arch of Constantine).

From the Colosseum, Via di San Giovanni in Laterano leads to **San Clemente** ⓫ (Mon–Sat 9am–12.30pm and 3–6pm, Sun noon–6pm; free), an intriguing puzzle of a church. A 12th-century basilica descends to a 4th-century basilica, which, in turn, leads to a 1st-century Roman apartment building containing, in its courtyard, a Mithraic temple honouring the most-popular cult of imperial Rome.

Further along, Via di San Giovanni opens up into **Piazza di San Giovanni in Laterano** ⓬, containing some of the most important buildings in Christendom. The **Obelisk** is the tallest and oldest in Rome and a suitable marker for the Church of Rome, **San Giovanni in Laterano** (daily 7am–6.30pm; free), founded by Constantine the Great. The **Palazzo Laterano** was the home of the popes until the Avignon exile in 1309. The pious may want to ascend the 28 steps of the nearby **Scala Santa** (on their knees of course – daily 6.15am–noon and 3–6.30pm), said to be the 'holy steps' Christ descended after being condemned by Pontius Pilate. Constantine's mother, St Helena, retrieved them from Jerusalem.

TIP

North of the Colosseum lies the traditional *rione* (neighbourhood) of Monti. In parts, particularly in the hilly, leafy streets between Via Panisperna and Via Cavour, it has retained interesting traces of its medieval past, as well as an intimate village atmosphere.

BELOW: inside the Colosseum.

Detail of a mosaic in the Baths of Caracalla.

The Ghetto

Rome's former Ghetto lies on the western side of the Capitoline Hill, near the ruins of the **Teatro di Marcello,** , an ancient theatre. The city has had a substantial Jewish community since the Republican era, but its isolation dates from the Counter-Reformation and the papacy of Paul IV (1555–9). From then on, the gates to the Ghetto were locked from sunset to sunrise, Jewish men had to wear a yellow hat, the women a yellow scarf, and most professions were closed to Jews.

A plaque on Via Portico d'Ottavia is a reminder that more than 2,000 Roman Jews were deported to a Nazi concentration camp. Next to the synagogue on Lungotevere Cenci, the **Museo Ebraico** (Jewish Museum; Sun–Thur 10am–7pm, until 5pm in winter, Fri 10am–4pm, until 2pm in winter; charge) sensitively documents the history of Rome's Jewish population. To lift your spirits, taste Jewish Rome in **Da Giggetto** (Via del Portico d'Ottavia; tel: 06-686 1105), including fried artichokes and salted cod.

The Via del Teatro di Marcello leads south to **Piazza Bocca della Verità** ⑭, which yokes together two Roman temples, a Baroque fountain and the medieval church of Santa Maria in Cosmedin. In the portico of this church is the **Bocca della Verità** (daily 9.30am–5.50pm), a marble slab resembling a human face and considered to be one of the world's oldest lie detectors. If a perjurer puts his hand in the mouth, so the legend goes, it will be bitten off. In fact, the slab's origin is sadly prosaic: it once covered a drain.

The oldest and largest of the famed Roman racetracks, the **Circo Massimo** ⑮ (Circus Maximus) is nestled between the Aventine and the Palatine hills. It once seated 250,000 people. In addition to the main event, vendors, fortune tellers and prostitutes plied their trades beneath the arcades.

The ancient Romans are probably best known for their love of bathing, and their public baths inspired great praise. In addition to three pools (hot, warm and cold), the **Terme di Caracalla** ⑯ (Baths of Caracalla, Tues–Sun 9am–sunset, Mon 9am–2pm; charge) offered gyms, libraries and lecture

Room with a Ruin

A resurgent Rome is now awash with cool hotels and old-school splendour. Diehard design junkies will find achingly arty beds behind conventional facades. Fashionistas flock to Ferragamo's **Portrait Suites**. **Aleph** is a spirited design hotel that strikes a chord with the fashion crowd, thanks to a courtyard resembling a backgammon board.

Despite its museum of Roman ruins, the slick **Radisson SAS** hotel is an essay in minimalism, while the Hotel Art is futurism run riot, with avant-garde furniture clashing with the frescoed lobby. Rock-and-roll couples can lay their woozy heads in the **Ripa**, in the heart of Testaccio clubland, while arty **Capo d'Africa** attracts a hip crowd, including gay fans attracted to Rome's burgeoning gay scene, centred on Viale San Giovanni Laterano.

Wine-lovers can snooze in **Il Palazzetto**, a Wine Academy (with beds) by the Spanish Steps. **Exedra** is an unschmaltzy hideaway that blends Italianate charm with individuality, including photographic homage to Fellini. For sleepier souls not on an imperial budget, the Monteverde district on Gianicolo Hill is dotted with turn-of-the-century villas, converted into guesthouses.

The peeling *pensioni* of old have been supplanted by eclectic guesthouses, such as **Casa Howard** *(pictured)*, with intimate spaces enlivened by ethnic objets d'art. At the grander end of the scale, **Hotel de Russie** remains the most gracious, timeless Roman hotel, with its unfussy decor, lush terraced gardens, Roman ruins, butterfly reserve and soothing tea rooms. In Rome, expect much more than a room with a view.

halls, for the improvement of mind and body. But less salubrious activities also went on, especially when mixed bathing was permitted. Some took cleanliness to extremes: Emperor Commodus supposedly bathed eight times a day. But essentially the baths represent a triumph of the Roman public spirit, demonstrating that cleanliness was a right, not a privilege for the rich. At night, the baths are illuminated and become a stage-set for opera in summer.

The Aventine and Testaccio

Escape the dusty ruins by visiting the Aventine, one of modern Rome's most desirable residential neighbourhoods. As you climb the Clivo dei Pubblici, the smell of roses wafts down from the pretty garden at the top of the hill. Via Santa Sabina leads to **Santa Sabina**, ⓱, a perfectly preserved 5th-century basilica. Inside, shafts of sunlight illuminate the antique columns of the nave. Outside, in the portico, are some of the oldest wooden doors in existence (5th century).

Bordered by Via Marmorata to the east is **Testaccio**, the former meat-packing district centred on an artificial mound – essentially an ancient landfill site formed by shards of amphorae. Testaccio retains its gritty neighbourhood charge despite pockets of gentrification and its notoriety as the pulsating heart of clubland. A reliable food market on Piazza Testaccio is now complemented by trendy boutiques and bars fanning out from its new cultural hub: the cutting-edge contemporary art museum known as the **MACRO Future** ⓲ (Piazza Orazio Giustiniani 4; Tues–Sun 4pm–midnight; www.macro.roma.museum). Set in the Mattatoio complex, formerly Rome's slaughterhouse, it accommodates large-scale exhibitions that wouldn't work in the MACRO, its sister museum (see page 149).

South of Testaccio, in the shadow of the Piramide Cestio, lies the **Cimitero Acattolico** ⓳ (Protestant Cemetery; Mon–Sat 9am–4.30pm, Sun 9am–12.30pm; donation), one of the most picturesque spots in Rome. Scores of unfortunate travellers who fell fatally ill on a Grand Tour are buried here. In the old section lies Keats's tomb, graced

TIP

The so-called Protestant Cemetery covers all religions except Catholicism and is divided into two parts: the older section, containing the tomb of Keats, lies to the left of the entrance. Keats fans can also visit the poet's home in Rome (see page 140).

BELOW:
Testaccio Market.

The earliest known portraits of the four Apostles – St Peter, St Paul, St John and St Andrew – have recently been brought to light in 4th-century catacombs near the basilica of San Paolo fuori le Mura. Pope Benedict XVI is apparently convinced of their authenticity.

BELOW RIGHT:
Trevi Fountain.

by the epitaph: "Here lies one whose name was writ in water." In accordance with the poet's wishes, the tombstone does not mention Keats by name. The modern part of the cemetery contains Shelley's heart – his body was burnt on the shore near Pisa. As Keats's close friend Lord Byron put it: "All of Shelley was consumed, except his heart, which could not take the flame and is now preserved in spirits of wine."

Outside the **Porta San Paolo** ❷⓿ is the basilica of **San Paolo fuori le Mura** (daily 7am–7pm), one of the major basilicas of Rome, which is built on the supposed site of St Paul's tomb. A fire in 1823 means that much of what you see now dates from the 19th century, but it is impressive nonetheless. The bronze aisle doors are original, dating from 1070, as is the cloister.

The Corso, a corridor through time

Back in the city centre, **Via del Corso** ("the Corso") provides a delightful amble through Roman history, taking in Baroque churches and fountains, patrician palaces, classical remains, and

the ancient gateway to the city. The Corso stretches from Piazza Venezia to **Piazza del Popolo** *(see page 140)*. Lined with elegant *palazzi*, this bustling shopping street has always been a place for taking the pulse of the city.

At the Piazza Venezia end of the Corso is **Palazzo Doria Pamphili** ❷❶ (daily 10am–5pm; free audioguide; charge), home of the Galleria Doria Pamphili. The collection is superb and a rarity, housed in a palace inhabited by the same family for centuries. The grand apartments and ornate galleries make an atmospheric backdrop to paintings by Titian, Caravaggio and Raphael. The star of the collection is Velázquez's portrait of Pope Innocent X. Do check whether a concert of Baroque music happens to be on.

Further along stands the Jesuit church of **Sant'Ignazio** ❷❷ , with a ceiling by Andrea dal Pozzo. To appreciate its fantastic Baroque perspectives, stand in the middle of the nave and look heavenwards: the vault seems to disappear as an ecstatic St Ignatius receives the light he will disperse to the four corners of the earth. Pozzo also painted

Baroque Rome

The Baroque art movement (1600–1750) was born in Rome and was nurtured by a papal campaign to make the city one of unparalleled beauty "for the greater glory of God and the Church".

One of the first artists to answer the call was Michelangelo Merisi da Caravaggio (1573–1610), whose early secular portraits of sybaritic youths revealed him to be a painfully realistic artist. His later monumental religious painting entitled *The Calling of St Matthew*, in San Luigi dei Francesi, shocked the city by setting a holy act in a contemporary tavern.

The decoration of St Peter's by Gianlorenzo Bernini (1598–1680) was more acceptable to the Romans: a bronze tabernacle with spiralling columns at the main altar, a magnificent throne with angels clustered around a burst of sacred light at the end of the church and, for the exterior, the classically simple colonnade embracing the piazza (1657).

Bernini's rival was Francesco Borromini (1599–1667), whose eccentric designs were the opposite of Bernini's classics. Many of Borromini's most famous designs hinge on a complex interplay of concave and convex surfaces, which can be seen in the undulating facades of San Carlo alle Quattro Fontane, Sant'Ivo and Sant'Agnese in Piazza Navona (1653–63).

a fake dome, since the Jesuit fathers were unable to afford a real one.

Via delle Muratte, to the right off the Corso, leads to the most grandiose of Rome's Baroque fountains: the **Fontana di Trevi ㉓** (Trevi Fountain), where the voluptuous Anita Ekberg frolicked in Fellini's film *La Dolce Vita* (1960). Tossing a coin into the pool is supposed to ensure your return to Rome.

But the ancient city rears its head even in a seemingly contemporary shopping district. **Piazza Colonna ㉔**, about halfway down the Corso, displays the Column of Marcus Aurelius (AD 180–93). Sixtus V (1585–90) crowned this column with a statue of St Paul and Trajan's Column with one of St Peter. (Sixtus was always eager to appropriate Roman triumphal symbols for Christianity: he placed many fallen, forgotten obelisks in front of churches.)

From the Trevi Fountain, consider strolling to the **Piazza del Quirinale,** dominated by colossal statues of Castor and Pollux, originally from Constantine's Baths, complemented by the obelisk taken from the Mausoleum

of Augustus. Facing the square is the imposing **Palazzo del Quirinale ㉕**, once the summer palace of the popes but now the residence of the Italian president. On the far side are the former papal stables, **Le Scuderie del Quirinale ㉖** (Sun–Thur 10am–8pm, Fri–Sat 10am-10.30pm; www.scuderie-quirinale.it). The monumental Quirinale Stables, constructed over the remains of a Roman temple and baths, represent a dramatic space for major art exhibitions. The Quirinale is also a convenient stepping stone to Rome's greatest Baroque churches *(see panel opposite)*.

Off the northern end of the Corso lie impressive relics of the Augustan era, restored and reassembled during the Fascist era: the **Mausoleo di Augusto** and the **Ara Pacis Augustae ㉗** (Tues–Sun 9am–7pm; charge).

For centuries the Ara Pacis, built from 13–8 BC to celebrate peace throughout the empire, was in pieces. Fragments were found in the Louvre in Paris and the Uffizi in Florence. Finally, in 1983, the Ara Pacis altar was reconstructed but remains the most

When the new metro line is complete, in 2014, Romans can be assured that the 30 new stations will become mired in controversy connected to the hundreds of archaeological sites unearthed in the process.

BELOW: non-stop shopping on Via del Corso.

The Trinità dei Monti at the top of the Spanish Steps is a familiar Roman landmark.

controversial of revitalised Roman sites, especially in a city where novelty is often conceived as an affront to the natural order. This steel, glass and travertine structure was designed to house a 2,000 year-old Altar of Peace that, ironically, was used for sacrifices. Created by Richard Meier, this is the first new public monument erected in the historic centre since Mussolini's day. Art critic Vittorio Sgarbi called it "an indecent cesspit", while others have praised it as an airy, accessible building that lets citizens see into the mindset of Emperor Augustus and Ancient Rome.

Marking the end of the Corso, the **Piazza del Popolo** ㉘ remains one of Rome's loveliest squares, with views southwards into the city's heart. Everyone – from triumphant emperors to footsore pilgrims – has entered Rome through the **Porta del Popolo** (Porta Flaminia). To the east rises the lush green of the Pincian Hill, reputedly haunted by Emperor Nero's ghost. **Santa Maria del Popolo**, the landmark church on the square, contains splendidly decorated chapels adorned with art by Pinturicchio, Raphael (the Chigi Chapel) and Caravaggio, notably his masterly *Conversion of St Paul* and *The Crucifixion of St Peter*. The church was allegedly erected over the burial place of Nero in an attempt to sanctify the site.

Rome's drawing room

From Piazza del Popolo, take Via del Babuino to **Piazza di Spagna**, named after the seat of the Spanish embassy to the Vatican. Essentially Rome's drawing room, the square's daily parade revolves around the famous Spanish Steps, the **Scalinata della Trinità dei Monti** ㉙. Caricaturists sketch tourists; old crones sell roasted chestnuts; sightseers rinse their hands in Bernini's fountain; students sunbathe on the steps; buskers strum guitars, and the moneyed set joins Roman matrons in ogling the elegant shop-windows. Off this piazza stretch the most fashionable shopping streets in Rome: Via dei Condotti, Via Frattina and Via Borgognona. Underneath the Pincian Hill, the quiet Via Margutta is the place to buy art.

Since the Romantic era, this quarter has been the haunt of British and American expatriates. John Keats died in the house overlooking the steps, which now contains literary memorabilia. The **Keats-Shelley House** (Mon–Fri 10am–1pm and 2–6pm, Sat 11am–2pm and 3–6pm; tel: 06-678 4235; www.keats-shelley-house.org; charge) is essential viewing for romantic ghost-seekers. Muse some more over high tea in **Babingtons** (Piazza di Spagna), where expat writers and Roman high society have taken tea since 1893.

The street between Trinità dei Monti and Santa Maria Maggiore was carved out by Sixtus V, a pope bent on improving Rome and glorifying his own name. The view down the length of the road is dramatic – culminating in the obelisk which Sixtus raised in front of Santa Maria Maggiore. Once called Strada Felice, the road now changes

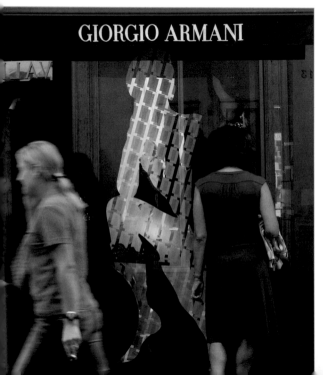

GIORGIO ARMANI

name three times as it cuts through the tangled streets.

The first leg, Via Sistina, leads down to **Piazza Barberini** ㉚, in the centre of which is Bernini's sensual **Fontana del Tritone**, featuring a sea deity blowing fiercely on a conch shell. In the base is the unmistakable coat of arms of the Barberini family: three bees. Designed by Bernini and Borromini, the neighbouring **Palazzo Barberini** houses the **Galleria Nazionale d'Arte Antica** (Tues–Sun 8.30am–7.30pm; charge; book online at www.ticketeria. it). Don't miss Pietro da Cortona's *The Triumph of Divine Providence*, a celebration of the Barberini Pope Urban VIII – a pope who quarried the ruins of Ancient Rome so extensively that he inspired the witticism: "What the barbarians didn't do, the Barberini did."

Via Veneto swoops off the Piazza Barberini. Before strolling along its wide streets or retiring to one of its cafés, stop at the **Chiesa dei Cappuccini**, also known as Santa Maria della Concezione (church daily 7am–noon and 3–7pm; free; crypt Fri–Wed 9am–noon and 3–7pm; donation) to see its macabre crypt. According to legend, a group of artistically and ghoulishly inclined friars decided to put the dead brothers' bones (4,000 monks in all) to a cautionary use. Four rooms of rococo sculptures contain a playful filigree of hip bones, a garland of spines and an array of skulls stacked as neatly as oranges and apples on a fruit vendor's stall.

The **Via Veneto** became famous after World War II as the centre of Rome's *dolce vita*. Although no longer the hub of glamorous Roman nightlife, Via Veneto is still an excuse for donning your shades and sipping a glass of Frascati at an outdoor café before collapsing in the gorgeous Villa Borghese gardens to the north.

Villa Borgese and gardens

The **Villa Borghese**, which encompasses the 17th-century grounds of Cardinal Scipione Borghese's fabulous villa, serves as a repository for some of Rome's finest treasures. Paradoxically, it is also the city's loveliest park and a bucolic retreat when the weight of history proves overwhelming. Children

BELOW: Spanish Steps.

might be tempted by the **Bioparco** ㉛ (9.30am–7pm), the small-scale zoo, but the park itself has infinite family appeal, whether for picnicking, boating or kite-flying. For adults, the Villa Borghese's Orangery now houses the **Carlo Bilotti Museum** (Tues–Sun 9am–7pm; charge), a quirky collection including works by de Chirico and Warhol.

Close to the Via Veneto entrance awaits one of Rome's heart-stopping collections, the **Galleria Borghese** ㉜ (Tues–Sun 8.30am–7.30pm; visits by reservation only; tel: 06-32810 or book online at www.ticketeria.it). Created by the cultured Cardinal Borghese, the world-class collection is housed in the cardinal's palatial summer residence, a frescoed affair studded with masterpieces by Bernini, Caravaggio, Raphael, Titian, Rubens and Canova.

Instead, if drawn by Italy's more recent artistic achievements, visit the **Galleria Nazionale d'Arte Moderna e Contemporanea** ㉝ (Tues–Sun 8.30am–7.30pm; charge). Although Italian artists feature prominently, so too do international artists of the stat-

ure of Henry Moore, Pollock, Cézanne and Kandinsky, and many more dating from the 1800s to the present.

To the north of the Villa Borghese is another aristocratic palace, built for Julius III. The **Villa Giulia** ㉞ has a beautiful Renaissance garden and, inside, the fascinating **Museo Nazionale Etrusco di Villa Giulia** (Tues–Sun 8.30am–7.30pm; charge; tel: 06-32810 or book online at www.ticketeria.it) full of pre-Roman art. The Etruscan terracotta sculptures are masterly, as is a statue of Apollo and a touching, Volterra-style sarcophagus of a husband and wife with enigmatic smiles.

East of Villa Borghese lies **Villa Torlonia** ㉟, another patrician park dotted with intriguing villas and follies. The centrepiece is the **Casino Nobile** (summer Tues–Sun 7am–7pm, winter times vary; www.museivillatorlonia.it), the last grand villa to grace Rome's skyline. Now a museum, the neoclassical affair was Mussolini's ostentatious residence between 1925 until 1943 and is linked to his stark bunker. Less overweening is the neighbouring **Casina delle Civette** *(times as above)*, a patrician folly

BELOW: temple and entertainment in Villa Borghese park.

built for Prince Torlonia which combines a Swiss chalet-style facade with a faux-medieval interior.

Back to Baroque: Bernini and Borromini

Baroque is a Roman art form par excellence *(panel page 138)*. Exuberant, awe-inspiring and outrageous, Baroque architecture offers such a profusion of decorative detail, gilt and marble statuary that it often overwhelms. But what pleasure there is in discovering a particularly winning *putto* winking at you from an architrave, in craning to see a fantastic ceiling by Pietro da Cortona or Andrea dal Pozzo, and in seeing saints and biblical figures made flesh by Bernini. In terms of art, the most prodigious talent was Caravaggio, whose works adorn the city churches. Rome's Baroque churches are also the setting for classical recitals.

Roman Baroque can best be grasped in the **Gesù** ❸❻ (Mon–Sat 7am–12.30, 4–7.45pm), near Piazza Venezia on the Via del Plebiscito. This was the headquarters of the Jesuit Order, champions of the Counter-Reformation. The Council of Trent (1545–63) laid down the rigorous principles for strengthening the Catholic Church against the Protestant heretics. Originally, the Gesù was meant to be austere; its Baroque makeover took place in the late 17th century when the Counter-Reformers used the art to illuminate the biblical message and impress their fervent flock with the immense power of the Church. Andrea dal Pozzo's altar to St Ignatius is particularly sumptuous. But the glory is the ceiling, with Il Baciccia's painting *The Triumph of the Name of Jesus*. Statues cling to the gilded vaults, some supporting the central painting which spills out of its frame.

In Via Botteghe Oscure, near the Gesù, make time for the **Crypta Balbi** *(see panel page 145)*, which is a key to understanding Roman history long before Baroque existed.

From here head east towards the **Palazzo del Quirinale** *(see page 139)*. The route then fans east to the Esquilino district, and takes in some of the wonders of both Baroque and Ancient Rome in the area around the railway station.

Sculptural detail on the Villa Medici in Villa Borghese.

BELOW: the Baths of Diocletian.

From the intersection of **Via delle Quattro Fontane** and Via XX Settembre admire the drama of Roman urban planning, where obelisks scrape the sky in three directions. The Via XX Settembre contains several splendid Baroque churches, notably **San Carlo alle Quattro Fontane** ❸. Also known as San Carlino, this tiny church was designed by Francesco Borromini (1599–1667). The undulating facade is a hallmark of this eccentric architect's style, as is the fantastic game of ovals inside. The astute monks who commissioned the church were impressed by Borromini's ability to economise – by using delicate stucco-work rather than marble or gilding – but without detracting from the beauty of the interior.

Along Via del Quirinale, off the other side of Via delle Quattro Fontane, is another oval gem by Borromini's arch rival, Gianlorenzo Bernini (1598–1680). **Sant'Andrea al Quirinale** ❸ offers quite a contrast to its neighbour. Every inch of this church is covered with gilt and marble. *Putti* ascend the wall as if in a cloud of smoke. Yet the architect's masterful,

classical handling of space creates a marvellous sense of simplicity.

For another masterpiece, head to **Santa Maria della Vittoria**, ❸ in Largo Santa Susanna (off Via XX Settembre), home to Bernini's sculpture of the 17th-century Spanish mystic St Teresa of Avila. The artist captures her at the moment when she was being struck by the arrow of divine love.

Return to Ancient Rome

Amid all the Baroque, Ancient Rome still rears its head again. Across Via XX Settembre, on the north side of Piazza della Repubblica, is **Santa Maria degli Angeli** ❹, a church Michelangelo created from the *tepidarium* of the **Terme di Diocleziano** (Baths of Diocletian; Tues–Sun 9am–7.45pm; charge), the most extensive baths in Rome, built between AD 298 and 306. The *esedra*, the open space surrounded by porticoes and seats where the Romans would chat, gave its form to Piazza della Repubblica. The **Fontana delle Naiadi** (Fountain of the Naiads) in the centre of the square, dating from around 1900, caused a scandal when it was unveiled, because of the "obscene" postures of the nymphs. The baths were also once the principal venue of the **Museo Nazionale Romano** ❹, but this great collection of ancient art is now dotted among four significant sites, notably in the neighbouring **Palazzo Massimo** ❹ (Tues–Sun 9am–7.45pm; charge), just across from Santa Maria degli Angeli. This is undoubtedly the most impressive section of the Museo Nazionale Romano, with its superb collection of statuary, frescoes and mosaics (*see panel opposite*).

Rome has more churches dedicated to the Virgin Mary than to any other saint. The largest and most splendid is **Santa Maria Maggiore** ❹ (daily 7am–7pm), one of the four patriarchal churches of Rome. Here the mixture of architectural styles is surprisingly harmonious: early Christianity is represented in the basilican form and in the 5th-century mosaics in the

nave. Medieval remodelling includes the campanile (the largest in Rome), the Cosmati floor and the mosaics in the apse. The coffered ceiling was supposedly gilded with gold Columbus brought from America. But the overwhelming effect is Baroque, so the church represents a fitting resting place for Bernini, the master of the genre.

If your head is spinning with a surfeit of gilt and marble, head down the Via Cavour to **San Pietro in Vincoli ⓲** (daily 7am–12.30pm and 3.30–7pm) to discover Michelangelo's massive and dignified *Moses*, the incarnation of the powerful law-giver. The statue was intended to form part of an enormous freestanding tomb for Pope Julius II. Giorgio Vasari, the first historian of art, waxed lyrical over the work: "No modern work will ever approach it in beauty." The church also displays the chains that bound St Peter in his prison cells in Rome and Judaea, hence the name of the church (St Peter in Chains).

For a dramatic shift eastwards in global terms, visit Palazzo Brancaccio, near Santa Maria Maggiore, to see the most important collection of oriental art in Italy, the **Museo Nazionale d'Arte Orientale** (Via Merulana 248, on the Esquiline Hill; Tues, Wed, Fri 9am–2pm, Thur, Sat, Sun 9am–7-.30pm; charge).

Around the Pantheon

During the Middle Ages, most of Rome's population was concentrated between Via del Corso and the Tiber (Campus Martius to the ancients) or crowded into **Trastevere** (*see page 158*) across the river. Trastevere is best reached on a walk across the charming island the **Isola Tiberina**. Now, the Pantheon quarter, sandwiched between the Corso and the Tiber, remains one of the most engaging districts and, despite the hordes of tourists, offers a flavour of real Roman life. While buzzing at night, early morning holds its own appeal, when you can admire palatial facades in peace, enter churches with only the faithful as companions, and watch the Romans starting their day.

Have a *cornetto* (an Italian croissant) and a cappuccino in **Piazza della Rotonda** and admire the exterior of

Inside the Pantheon dome.

BELOW LEFT: a stone vessel outside the Baths of Diocletian.

Museo Nazionale Romano

The Museo Nazionale Romano is one of the most important archaeological collections in the world. It is split up into four main sites. The vast **Terme di Diocleziano** (Baths of Diocletian; Via Enrico de Nicola 78 – *see page 144* was the original home of the museum. The Aula Ottagona (Octagonal Hall, Via Romita 8), an integral part of the baths, still contains some important sculptures. But the bulk of the collection is at the **Palazzo Massimo alle Terme** (Largo di Villa Peretti 1). Highlights include splendid floor mosaics and wall paintings from the villas of wealthy Romans, seen at their best in the delicate frescoes from Villa Livia. The **Palazzo Altemps** (Piazza Sant'Apollinare 44) is a Renaissance palace off Piazza Navona, with a beautiful courtyard which houses a fine collection of ancient sculptures. The **Crypta Balbi** (Via delle Botteghe Oscure 31) – the remains of the theatre built by Balbus in 13 BC – traces the city's development from the pre-imperial era to early Christian and medieval times.

All sites are open Tues–Sun 9am–7.45pm. A ticket is valid for all the sites of the museums for a period of three days. An Archeologia Card includes the four museum sites, the Colosseum, the Palatine, the Baths of Caracalla, the Tomb of Cecilia Metella and the Villa of the Quintili. Book online at www.pierreci.it or tel: 06-3996 7700.

Shop in the Jewish quarter.

BELOW RIGHT: a lively market is held in Campo de' Fiori.

the **Pantheon** ㊺ (Mon–Sat 8.30am–7.30pm, Sun 9am–6pm, holidays 9am–1pm; free) – the best preserved of all ancient Roman buildings. For those who question the greatness of Roman architecture and dismiss it as inferior to Greek, the Pantheon is an eloquent answer. This perfectly proportioned round temple proves how adept the Romans were in shaping interior space. Rebuilt by the Emperor Hadrian, its architectural antecedents are not the Republican round temples – such as the one in the Forum Boarium – but the round chambers used in the baths.

Western architecture owes the Romans an enormous debt for their skilful work with vaults and domes. The only light is provided by a large hole set in the centre of the dome – the *oculus* – and this means that the building has been open to the elements for nearly 2,000 years.

Facing the Pantheon is the **Caffe San Eustachio**, which supposedly serves the best coffee in town, with *gran caffe*, a sweet, frothy double espresso, its signature drink.

Near the Pantheon, in front of **Santa Maria Sopra Minerva** (daily 7am–7pm), Bernini's much-loved elephant carries the smallest of Rome's obelisks. Inside the church, the only Gothic church in Rome, are a chapel decorated by Fra Filippo Lippi and Michelangelo's statue of *Christ Bearing the Cross*. Caravaggio masterpieces adorn neighbouring churches. **San Luigi dei Francesi** (10am–noon, 4–7pm) features *The Calling of St Matthew, St Matthew and the Angel* and *The Martyrdom of St Matthew*. Another Caravaggio work, *The Madonna of the Pilgrims,* is displayed in Sant'Agostino. Borromini's **Sant'Ivo,** tucked into the courtyard of Palazzo Sapienza, boasts a dazzling interior and a spiralling campanile.

Around Piazza Navona

Although the chariot races are no more, nothing can mask the vibrancy of **Piazza Navona** ㊻, from the milling crowds of mime artists, caricaturists and ice-cream eaters to the preening girls and patrolling Roman youths. This space was once the Stadium of

Campo de' Fiori

South of Piazza Navona is the equally vibrant Campo de' Fiori. It has been the site of a raffish market for centuries, and was one of the liveliest areas of medieval and Renaissance Rome, when cardinals and pilgrims would rub shoulders with fishmongers, vegetable sellers and prostitutes.

The Campo de' Fiori is the most secular of Roman squares, for although it is as old as Rome itself, it has never been dedicated to any cult, and to this day is free of churches. Its present aspect dates from the end of the 15th century, when the whole area was reshaped. It was surrounded by inns for pilgrims and travellers. In the Renaissance, some of these hotels were the homes of successful courtesans, Vannozza Catanei, mistress of the Borgia Pope Alexander VI, among them. On the corner of the square and Via del Pellegrino you can see her shield, which she had decorated with her own coat of arms and those of her husband and lover.

With its reputation for being a carnal, pagan place, the square must have seemed a natural spot to hold executions. Of all the unfortunate victims, Giordano Bruno was the most important figure to be burnt at the stake here, in 1600. A priest and philosopher, he was accused of heresy and found guilty of freethinking.

Domitian, parts of which can still be seen off the northern end. On Piazza Sant'Apollinare, just across the street, stands the **Palazzo Altemps** *(see panel page 145)*, a Renaissance palace housing a fine collection of classical statuary.

Between Piazza Navona and the Campo de' Fiori is the **Museo Barracco** ❹ (Tues–Sun 9am–7pm), which showcases Egyptian, Etruscan and Roman sculpture in an intimate setting. At any time of day, the neighbouring **Campo de' Fiori** ❹ *(see panel opposite)* makes a perfect stop for the footsore.

Nearby, the church of **Sant'Agnese in Agone** boasts a curvaceous Borromini facade. In one version of the saint's martyrdom, Agnes, who had vowed to be a virgin bride of Christ, was banished to a brothel where her chastity was miraculously preserved; a subsequent attempt to burn her was also unsuccessful; finally, she was beheaded.

Borromini's rival Bernini designed the **Fontana dei Quattro Fiumi** (Fountain of the Four Rivers) in the centre of the piazza. A popular tale claims that the statue of the Nile facing Sant'Agnese is covering its eyes for fear it will collapse. However, the fountain was completed in 1651, before Borromini had even started work on the church.

Close by, **Piazza di Pasquino** contains a battered statue that once functioned as the underground newspaper of Rome. The papal censors allowed so little criticism that irrepressible commentators attached their writings to statues in the city. The most famous satirist was Pasquino.

Near the piazza is the elegant church of **Santa Maria della Pace** ❹ (Mon–Sat 10am–noon and 4–6pm, Sun 10am–noon). Inside are frescoes by Raphael and beautiful cloisters by Bramante which often display contemporary art. If the front door is locked, enter through the Bramante cloister. To the north, Via dei Coronari is lit with torches every night.

At the end of Via dei Cornari, turn left to reach the **Chiesa Nuova** ❺ (daily 7.30am–noon and 4.30–7.30pm), dedicated to St Filippo Neri, one of Rome's patron saints, who lies buried here. The apse contains three fine

Monti is a district popular with artists and students drawn by the reasonable rents.

BELOW:
Piazza Navona.

works by Rubens, who lived in Rome from 1606 to 1608. The Oratorio dei Filippini was built between 1637 and 1662 by Borromini as a place of worship for the fraternity of St Philip Neri, who instituted the musical gatherings that later became known as oratorios.

But the district's show-stopping Baroque church is the ornate **Sant'Andrea della Valle ⑤**, which Puccini chose as a setting for the opening act of *Tosca*. Act II takes place at the nearby **Palazzo Farnese ⑥**, the most splendid of Renaissance palaces and suitably intimidating as headquarters for the villainous Scarpia. The palace is now the French embassy and, alas for the visitor who would like to see Annibale Carracci's frescoes, it is closed to the public.

Act III of Puccini's *Tosca* takes place on the west bank of the Tiber, in the notorious **Castel Sant'Angelo ⑥** prison (Tues–Sun 9am–7pm, in summer also Fri–Sat 8pm–midnight; charge). Visiting this fortress takes us from Rome into **the Vatican City,** the world's smallest state *(see page 153 for both sights)*.

Roman resurgence

For all its history, Rome is no longer mired in the past: its partying reputation is slowly being matched by a new contemporary art, music and theatre scene that is dragging the city into the 21st century. This being Rome, there is often a retro touch or some tacit recycling involved.

In the Villa Borghese gardens, **Globe Theatre Roma** (June–Sept; tel: 06-8082058; www.globetheatreroma.com) is a case in point. This replica of London's Elizabethan theatre of the same name stages Shakespearean and contemporary drama. The open-air theatre is a reminder that summer is when Rome comes alive, with a riot of outdoor events held in villas, gardens and squares, from open-air concerts to parties in the park.

The music scene has been revitalised by the Renzo Piano-designed **Auditorium Parco della Musica ⑥** (tel: 06-8082058; www.auditorium.com). Set north of the Borghese gardens, this is Rome's pre-eminent music venue. Beetle-like pods create perfect acoustics in settings just right for recitals, rock

and Latin music, from symphonies to soul, or from Rachmaninov to Lou Reed. The Academy of Santa Cecilia, one of the oldest musical institutions in the world, founded in 1585, is now based here. The orchestra is led by Antonio Pappano, the Italian, London-born but American-educated conductor.

The **Casa del Jazz** (tel: 06-704731; www.casadeljazz.it), set in the gardens of Villa Osio, a property confiscated from a Mafia boss, has grown into the city's major dedicated jazz venue, although the biggest names tend to perform at the Auditorium. Lovely alternatives include **Villa Celimontana** ⑤ (www.villacelimontanajazz.com) for jazz and the **Baths of Caracalla** for opera *(see page 136)*.

The arts scene has been revitalised with bold showcases for contemporary art, a sign that the city has regained its radicalism. Not far from the Auditorium is the **MACRO** ⑤, the Museo d'Arte Contemporanea Roma (Tues–Sun 9am–7pm; tel: 06-6710 70400; www.macro.roma.museum). Set in a converted brewery on Via Reggio Emilia, Rome's primary contemporary art museum has been remodelled by French architect Odile Decq, with a new gallery and rooftop restaurant. The permanent collection explores trend-setting Italian artwork since the 1960s that has represented cutting-edge approaches to contemporary art. The museum is complemented by **MACRO Future** in Testaccio *(see page 137)*.

Architecturally, the most radical arts museum is the **MAXXI** ⑤ (Tues–Sun 11am–7pm, until 10pm Thur; www.fondazionemaxxi.it; charge). Set on Via Guido Reni, this grand project sees a former army barracks reborn as the Museum of 21st-Century Arts. Designed by Anglo-Iraqi architect Zaha Hadid, the gallery, ribboned with walkways and a curving staircase, eclipses the work but is gradually acquiring worthy collections of art and photography. Pippo Ciorra, MAXXI'S senior curator, heralds the project as a breakthrough in a city where young Romans are crying out for modernity: "The city has been a battleground for modern architecture," he laments. But given the glories of Ancient Rome, few visitors care too deeply. ❏

Coat of arms on Sant' Andrea della Valle.

BELOW: sleek interior of MAXXI.

THE COLOSSEUM: BREAD AND CIRCUSES

"While the Colosseum stands, Rome shall stand; when the Colosseum falls, Rome shall fall; when Rome falls, the world shall fall"

The Venerable Bede's 8th-century prophecy has been taken to heart and the Colosseum shored up ever since. The ancient amphitheatre is a stirring sight, a place of stupendous size and spatial harmony. Begun by Vespasian, it was inaugurated by his son Titus in AD 80, and completed by Domitian (AD 81–96). Titus used Jewish captives as masons. The Colosseum had 80 entrances, allowing over 50,000 spectators to be seated. "Bread and circuses" was how Juvenal, the 2nd-century satirist, mocked the Romans who sold their souls for free food and entertainment.

FALL AND RUIN
With the fall of the empire, the Colosseum fell into disuse. During the Renaissance, the ruins were plundered to create churches and palaces, including the Palazzo Farnese, now the French embassy. The Colosseum was still neglected on the German writer Goethe's visit in 1787, with a hermit and beggars "at home in the crumbling vaults". In 1817 Lord Byron was enthralled by this "noble wreck in ruinous perfection", while Edgar Allan Poe celebrated its "grandeur, gloom and glory".

Mussolini, attracted to the power that the Colosseum represented, demolished a line of buildings to create a clear view of it from his balcony on the Palazzo di Venezia. To celebrate Holy Year (2000) the Colosseum was restored and reopened for more "bread and circuses".

ABOVE: Renaissance historians believed that Roman arenas were sometimes flooded to stage mock naval battles, but there is scant evidence to suggest such a display ever took place in the Colosseum.

LEFT: this coin depicts Emperor Vespasian, who consolidated Roman rule in Britain and Germany. As the founder of the Flavian dynasty and emperor between AD 69 and 79, he began the arena.

RIGHT: the Colosseum illuminated at night.

ENTERTAINMENT FOR THE MASSES

The Roman appetite for bloodshed was legendary, with barbaric blood sports introduced as a corrupt version of Greek games. The animals, mostly imported from Africa, included lions, elephants, giraffes, hyenas, hippos and zebras. The contests also served to eliminate slaves and proscribed sects, Christians and criminals, political agitators and prisoners of war. Variants included battles involving mock hunts and freak shows with panthers pulling chariots or cripples pitted against clowns. Seneca, Nero's tutor, came expecting "fun, wit and some relaxation", but was dumbfounded by the butchery and cries of "Kill him! Lash him! Why does he meet the sword so timidly?"

In AD 248, the millennium of the founding of Rome was celebrated by contests involving 2,000 gladiators and the slaying of giraffes and hippos as well as big cats. Although convicted criminals were fed to the lions, Christian martyrdom here is less well documented. St Ignatius of Antioch, who described himself as "the wheat of Christ", was dutifully devoured by lions in AD 107. Gladiatorial combat was banned in AD 404, while animal fights ended in the following century.

RIGHT: this 18th-century view by Giovanni Volpato reflects the nostalgic sensibility of the Romantic era. Visitors on the Grand Tour were beguiled by the ruins bathed in moonlight or haunted by the sense of a lost civilisation.

TOP: gladiatorial combat was a favourite form of entertainment for all strata of society.

ABOVE: a movable wooden floor covered in sand (to soak up the blood) concealed the animal cages and sophisticated technical apparatus, from winches and mechanical lifts to ramps and trapdoors.

BELOW: the Gate of Life was reserved for victorious gladiators, while vanquished gladiators were doomed to the Gate of Death.

THE VATICAN AND TRASTEVERE

From the spirituality of St Peter's, with its extensive museums and magnificent art treasures, to the earthiness of Rome's medieval quarter

The west bank of the Tiber offers contrasting experiences. Cheek by jowl with the Vatican, with all its papal pomp, is the intimate district of Trastevere, with its narrow streets and lively nightlife.

As you cross the Tiber using Ponte Sant'Angelo, it is not the domed heart of the Vatican you see first, but the almost windowless walls of the medieval citadel, the Castel Sant'Angelo (Tues–Sun 9am–7pm, in summer also Fri–Sat 8pm–midnight; essential booking on 06-32810 or online www.ticketeria.it; charge).

Back in AD 139, this was the site of the mausoleum of the Emperor Hadrian. Later it became a fortress and prison, then a residence to which the popes could flee in times of turbulence. Today it reveals intriguing shifts between the Roman mausoleum, cisterns and oil stores to the medieval prisons, princely fortress and frescoed papal apartments. The new night tours take in the prisons, as well as Clement VII's frescoed bathroom, complete with underfloor heating.

Puccini's heroine, Tosca, plunged to her death from the parapet where visitors now come to admire the views across Rome. Towering over the battlements is a gigantic statue of St Michael, the warlike archangel after whom the castle is named.

Vatican City

For centuries the Vatican was the unchallenged centre of the Western world. Its symbolic significance and its enduring international role, as both a religious and a diplomatic force, have put this tiny city-state on the map.

Covering a total area of slightly more than 40 hectares (100 acres), the Vatican City is by far the world's smallest independent sovereign entity, crossed at a leisurely pace in under half an hour. Yet the Vatican serves as an exception to the rule that tiny nations

Main attractions
CASTEL SANT'ANGELO
PIAZZA SAN PIETRO
BASILICA DI SAN PIETRO
 (ST PETER'S)
VATICAN MUSEUMS
SISTINE CHAPEL
TRASTEVERE
SANTA MARIA IN TRASTEVERE
TEMPIETTO
VIA APPIA ANTICA
CATACOMBS

LEFT: view over the Vatican.
RIGHT: Castel Sant'Angelo.

What other nation is as small as New York's Central Park? What other nation can lock its gates at midnight, as the Vatican's doorkeepers do each night, opening them only at the ring of a bell?

are famous for little more than their postage stamps.

In imperial Roman days, the lower part of what is now the Vatican City was an unhealthy bog, known for its snakes and diseases. In the 1st century AD, the dowager empress Agrippina had the Vatican Valley drained and planted with imperial gardens. Under Caligula and Nero, chariot racing and executions – including that of St Peter – were regular events on what was to become St Peter's Square.

Aside from an impressive array of palaces and office buildings, there is also a Vatican prison, a supermarket and a printing press, which publishes the daily *L'Osservatore Romano* and scripts in a wide range of languages, from Coptic to Ecclesiastical Georgian to Tamil.

Novelist Alberto Moravia used to say: "Rome is an administrative city dominated by two institutions: the State and the Church." While an over-simplification, Rome *is* the meeting place of temporal and spiritual powers and, as the capital, lives and breathes politics. As for piety, the Vatican has

traditionally been treated as a temporal power, as the corporate arm of the papacy. "Faith is made here but believed elsewhere," is the local dictum. Essentially, the Romans are more ritualistic than religious, even if the death of John Paul II saw an outpouring of emotion that surprised cynical Rome-watchers.

Piazza San Pietro

From Castel Sant'Angelo, Via della Conciliazione leads to St Peter's, at the heart of the Vatican City. Bernini's spectacular, colonnaded **Piazza San Pietro** ❺❽ is, according to one's viewpoint, either the welcoming embrace of the Mother Church or her grasping claws.

The Via della Conciliazione, constructed in 1937 to commemorate the reconciliation between Mussolini and Pope Pius XI, changed the original impact of the space. Before this thoroughfare provided a monumental approach to St Peter's, the entrance was by way of smaller streets, winding through the old Borgo and arriving, finally, in the enclosed open space, with the biggest church in the world

BELOW: inside St Peter's Basilica.

Subjects of the Holy See

The papal ranks have included patrons of the arts, great persuaders and profligate princes, not to mention numerous political players

To be one of the 800 or so citizens with a Vatican passport is to belong to one of the world's most exclusive clubs – the privilege of citizenship hinges on a direct and continuous relationship with the Holy See. The Pope himself carries passport No. 1, and he rules absolutely over the Vatican City.

The word "pope" comes from the Greek *pappas*, meaning "father". Despite two millennia having passed since St Peter first assumed the mantle, the Pope's role remains paternal, alternating between concern for humanity and stern warnings against theological or spiritual deviation. John Paul II (1978–2005) asserted his moral authority vigorously. His 1993 encyclical denounced contraception, homosexuality and other infringements of the faith as "intrinsically evil". His successor, Benedict XVI, is cast in the same ethical mould.

There have been 263 popes. The shortest reign of a pope was that of Stephen II, who died four days after his election in March 752. At the other extreme, the 19th century's Pius IX, famous for his practical jokes and his love of billiards, headed the Holy See for 32 years. The youngest pope on record, John XI, was just 16 when he took the helm in 931; the oldest, Gregory IX, managed to survive 14 years after his election in 1227 at the age of 86.

While the great majority have been of either Roman or Italian extraction, Spain, Greece, Syria, France and Germany have all been represented, and there has been at least one of African birth (Miltiades, 311–14), and one hailing from England (Hadrian IV, 1154–9). John Paul II was the first Pole to lead the Catholic Church. At least 14 popes abdicated or were deposed from office. Ten popes met violent deaths, including a record three in a row in the 10th century.

The process of electing a new pope is necessarily unique, as the papacy is the world's only elective monarchy. Members of the Sacred College of Cardinals, a largely titular body of 120 bishops and archbishops, are sealed into the Sistine Chapel soon after the death knell tolls in the Vatican Palace. They cannot leave until a new successor has been chosen. Voting can proceed by acclamation, whereby the cardinals all shout the same name at the same time; by scrutiny, in which four ballots are cast daily until one candidate has captured a two-thirds majority plus one; or, as a last resort, by compromise.

All modern popes have been selected by the second method. Paper ballots are burnt after each tally, and onlookers watch the chapel's chimney for dark smoke, which indicates an inconclusive vote, or white plumes, which denote a winner (electors are provided with special chemicals so that there can be no mistake). Finally the cardinal dean announces *"Habemus Papam"* (We have a pope) to the faithful, and the chosen cardinal appears in one of three robes (sized small, medium and large) kept on hand for the occasion. The coronation takes place on the following day. In the words of the Medici Pope Leo X: "God has given us the papacy – let us enjoy it." ❏

ABOVE: in St Peter's Square.
RIGHT: Swiss Guard at the Vatican.

Pinturicchio's painting of Renaissance Pope Alexander VI.

BELOW: *The Creation of Adam, the most famous scene from Michelangelo's Sistine Chapel ceiling.*

at one end and an enormous Egyptian obelisk in the centre.

Church, museum, mausoleum: the Basilica di San Pietro, **St Peter's** (daily 7am–7pm, until 6pm in winter, dome 8am–6pm, until 5pm in winter; modest dress code; free except for visits to the dome) is all three. No other temple surpasses it in terms of historical significance or architectural splendour. The immensity of the interior might seem at odds with the intimate act of prayer, but the architects and patrons of St Peter's intended the building to symbolise worldly power as much as spiritual piety. Just about every important Renaissance and Baroque architect from Bramante onwards had a hand in the design of St Peter's. The idea for rebuilding the original 4th-century basilica only became a reality when Julius II became pope. Bramante was succeeded by Raphael, Michelangelo and Bernini, to name but three masters.

The interior is vast – 186 metres (610ft) long, with a capacity for around 60,000 people. On the right, as you walk in, is Michelangelo's *Pietà*, an inspiration to beholders ever since

the sculptor finished it in 1500, at the age of 25. At the end of the nave is the bronze statue of *St Peter*, its toe worn away by the kisses of pilgrims.

Over the high altar, which is directly above the tomb of St Peter, rises Bernini's garish bronze baldachin, resembling the canopy of an imperial bed; Pope Urban VIII stripped the bronze from the Pantheon. But Bernini outdid himself in the design for the Cathedra Petri (the Chair of St Peter) in the apse. Four gilt bronze figures of the Church Fathers hold up the chair. Above, light streams through the golden glass of a window crowned by a dove (symbol of the Holy Ghost). The chair bears a relief of Christ's command to Peter to "charge his sheep". Thus the position of the Pope is explained and bolstered by Christ's words and the teachings of the Church Fathers, and blessed by the Holy Ghost.

Further confirmation of the Pope's sacred trust is found in Christ's words inscribed on the dome: "You are Peter and on this rock I will build my Church and I will give you the keys to the kingdom of heaven."

The Vatican Museums

The **Musei Vaticani** 59 (Mon–Sat 9am–6pm, last entry two hours before closing, last Sun of the month 9am–2pm, also Sept–Oct Fri 7–11pm; charge; to avoid queues book online at www.vatican.va; tel: 06-6988 4341) merit a lifetime's study. But for those who have only a few hours, some sights should not be missed. If you have time, select the additional gardens or the necropolis tours (email: scavi@fsp.va). If hurried, head for the **Museo Pio-Clementino**, which contains the Pope's collection of antiquities.

Be sure to visit the Belvedere Courtyard, home of the cerebral *Apollo Belvedere* and the contrasting muscle-bound, sensual *Laocoön*. The Gabinetto delle Maschere (Mask Room) displays mosaics of theatrical masks from Hadrian's Villa in Tivoli. The Vatican **Pinacoteca** contains superb paintings, including Raphael's *Madonna of Foligno* and *Transfiguration*. **The Raphael Rooms** (the Stanze di Raffaello) comprise four rooms painted by Raphael, the Sala di Costantino, Stanza di Eliodoro, Stanza della Segnatura and Stanza dell'Incendio di Borgo. Downstairs, colourful frescoes by Pinturicchio decorate the Borgia Apartments.

But the world's most sublime frescoes await in the **Cappella Sistina (Sistine Chapel)**. The chapel has always served as both the Pope's private chapel and the setting for the conclaves by which new popes are elected *(see page 155)*. The walls are covered in paintings by the Renaissance masters Botticelli, Pinturicchio and Ghirlandaio, but the star of the show is Michelangelo's ceiling, begun in 1508 and completed by 1512. The shallow barrel vault is divided into panels tracing the story of the Creation.

No reproduction can ever do justice to the interplay of painting and architecture, to the drama of the whole chapel, alive with colour (considerably brighter since the controversial cleaning of the frescoes was unveiled in 1994) and human emotion. "All the world hastened to behold this marvel and was overwhelmed, speechless with astonishment," Vasari wrote. The astonishment is no less today than it was in the Renaissance.

Miracle of the Mass at Bolsena, *one of the Vatican's many works by Raphael.*

BELOW: Giuseppe Momo's helicoidal staircase.

One of the gems of the Renaissance is Bramante's Tempietto.

Trastevere

The heart of medieval Trastevere, literally "across the Tiber", is southeast of the Vatican City. This is home to a popular restaurant and nightlife district as well as to a sprawling Sunday flea market, the **Porta Portese** ❻❶ (5am–2pm). Once fiercely working-class, Trastevere is now largely gentrified but retains its engagingly bohemian air, despite the touristy restaurants and boisterous wine bars. The winding streets are the perfect place to seek out an original gift from the area's many artisanal workshops.

South of Viale di Trastevere are two churches worth visiting. **Santa Cecilia** ❻❶ (daily 9.30am–1pm and 4–6.30pm; charge for crypt) was built on top of the house of a Christian martyr whom the Roman authorities attempted to scald to death in her own *caldarium* (hot bath). When this failed, she was sentenced to decapitation, but three blows failed to sever her head and she lived for a further three days (enough time to consecrate her house as a church). Carlo Maderno's touching statue of the saint curled in a foetal position was inspired by his observations when her tomb was opened in 1599.

A contrastingly sublime statue of a woman in her death throes is Bernini's *Blessed Luisa Albertoni* in nearby **San Francesco a Ripa**. This late work of the master captures even more powerfully than his *St Teresa* the conflict between joy and sorrow felt by a woman who is between this world and the next.

In the piazza of the same name, **Santa Maria in Trastevere** ❻❷ (daily 7.30am–8pm) is one of the oldest churches in Rome, built on a site where a fountain of oil is said to have sprung on the day of Christ's birth. Most of the structure you see today dates from 1140. The church has some beautiful Byzantine mosaics, and it is worth taking a pair of binoculars to enjoy their details. *The Life of the Virgin* series is by Cavallini (1291).

After these sobering places of worship, preoccupied with the horrors of this world and the glories of the next, it is a relief to come to the **Villa Farnesina** ❻❸ (Mon–Sat 9am–1pm; charge), a jewel of the Renaissance, worldly and pagan. A ceiling fresco by Raphael details the love of Cupid and Psyche. In the next room, Raphael's *Galatea* captures the moment when the nymph, safe from the clutches of the cyclops, looks round. Upstairs, Baldassare Peruzzi, who designed the villa, devised a fantastic *trompe l'œil* of bucolic life. In the bedroom is Sodoma's erotic painting *The Wedding of Alexander and Roxanne*.

To reach another important Renaissance monument, climb the steps up the Gianicolo to the church of **San Pietro in Montorio** ❻❹ (Mon–Sat 8.30am–noon and 3–4pm; free). In the courtyard is **Bramante's Tempietto** (Tues–Sun 9.30am–12.30pm and 4–6pm, 9.30am–12.30pm and 2–4pm in winter), a circular church that marks what was once mistakenly believed to be the site of St Peter's martyrdom. It is a homage to antiquity and the first monument in High Renaissance style.

Climb a little further to the Fontana Paola, and the shady **Passeggiata del Gianicolo** (meaning "a stroll up Janiculum Hill") leads to panoramic views over the city. The flat dome of the Pantheon, the twin domes of Santa Maria Maggiore and the Victor Emmanuel Monument are all easy to spot from up here.

Into the bowels of the earth

Do make time for the basilicas and catacombs from the early Christian era. The secretive beginnings of Christianity are recalled in **Sant'Agnese fuori le Mura** ⑥ (daily 8am–noon and 4–7pm; charge) beyond Michelangelo's Porta Pia on the Via Nomentana. Beneath the church run extensive catacombs (Tues–Sat 9am–noon and 4–6pm; charge), where the martyred Roman maiden St Agnes was buried.

Also in the complex is the incomparable **Santa Costanza**, the mausoleum of Constantine's daughter, which is encrusted with some of Rome's most beautiful mosaics. For those not averse to tortuous tunnels winding endlessly past burial niches, there are countless catacombs outside the walls of Rome, along the picturesque **Via Appia Antica** (Appian Way; visit on the handy Archeobus or by bike, especially on Sunday when it's closed to cars; www.parcoappiaantica.it). You can picnic amid the remains of the **Villa of the Quintili** (Tues–Sun 9am–4.30pm; charge), an area overrun with wild flowers and lizards. Above ground sits what Byron called the "stern round tower" of the **Tomba di Cecilia Metella**. Below spread the **Catacombs of St Callixtus** (San Callisto), the most famous in Rome (Thur–Tues 8.30am–noon and 2.30–5.30pm, until 5pm in winter, closed Feb; charge) and those of saints Sebastian and Domitilla.

Return to **Trastevere** for some light relief. Clubland is centred on Testaccio and Via Ostiense, but Trastevere's arty ambience is more low-key and mellow, offering an evening spent listening to the blues, followed by an *affogato* ice cream, drenched in liqueur. Roman life is too Latin for a Protestant work ethic. ❏

The Catacombs of St Sebastian (San Sebastiano) are perhaps the most significant of those on the Appian Way (Via Appia Antica). The basilica (tel: 06-785 0350) contains a large fragment of stone which is said to bear Christ's footprints.

BELOW LEFT: instrument-restorer in Trastevere.

A Roman Easter

Easter is the most heartfelt Roman festival, when history and tradition merge with common piety and cheerful consumerism. At Easter, the Eternal City is at ease with its Roman and Christian heritage, from St Peter's relics to the Scala Santa, the marble staircase that Christ supposedly ascended to meet Pontius Pilate. In San Giovanni in Laterano, the faithful climb to the top on their knees. On Good Friday, the Pope retraces Christ's Via Crucis on a moving candlelit procession, ending in a huge open-air Mass on St Peter's Square on Easter Sunday. On becoming pope, Benedict XVI opened up the Porta Santa Rosa entrance to the Vatican, as a gesture of openness. The Easter procession winds from the Colosseum to Monte Palatino, re-enacting the 14 Stations of the Cross, from Christ's death sentence to his entombment, with the Pope uttering prayers at each station. Pilgrims gather with torches to follow this solemn procession, which coincides with concerts in city churches. Rome's pastry shops display Easter eggs stuffed with tiny silver picture frames or costume jewellery. Wealthier Romans even instruct their chocolatiers to encase treasured gifts in the eggs, ranging from engagement rings to symbolic crosses. Despite their sophistication, Romans love the chocolate-wrapped trappings of piety, and tangible symbols of truth, a reminder that even Christian Rome was founded on relics.

ROME'S ENVIRONS

Escape to the Castelli Romani, Rome's hills, villas and gardens, a playground first popularised by the Roman emperors, before visiting Etruscan settlements for an insight into a vanished world

During the sweltering summers, Romans head for the hills, the lakes and the beach. The Pope is not alone in choosing the gentle, wine-growing Castelli Romani hills for his annual retreat. Tivoli's Villa d'Este, with its pleasure palace and water gardens, has been a favoured spot since Roman times, while Ostia Antica draws romantics to its ruined amphitheatre.

Curiously, Ancient Rome and Fascism are inextricably entwined in **Lazio** (former Latium). The Fascists boasted that they represented the continuation of Ancient Rome; the official art of the regime appropriated forms of Roman grandeur. Mosaics inspired by ancient Roman floors decorate the walls of the **Foro Italico ❶**, the ambitious sports centre created in 1931 northwest of the capital. Sixty colossal statues of athletes set the scene, even if the sheer scale of the modern Olympic Stadium overpowers Mussolini's legacy.

There is similar bombastic homage in **EUR ❷** (**Esposizione Universale di Roma**), the city's strangest suburb, and Mussolini's attempt to showcase imperial Rome and Fascist achievements. In 1938 Mussolini aspired to build a magnificent Third Rome, the natural successor to imperial Rome and the Rome of the Renaissance. Plans for an exhibition in 1942 to commemorate 20 years of Fascism were overtaken by

World War II, and the overall design was left uncompleted. In the 1950s, expansion saw government offices and museums move here, and EUR evolved into a sought-after residential quarter.

Among the showpieces is the **Palazzo della Civiltà del Lavoro** – commonly called the "Square Colosseum". Equally compelling is the **Museo della Civiltà Romana** (Tues–Sat 9am–2pm, Sun 9am–1.30pm; charge), devoted to the history of Ancient Rome. The museum contains bizarre scale models of Roman sites, as well as a cast of

Main attractions

Main attractions
EUR
MUSEO DELLA CIVILTÀ ROMANA
OSTIA ANTICÀ
CASTELLI ROMANI
VILLA ADRIANA
VILLA D'ESTE
VILLA GREGORIANA
SUBIACO
MONTECASSINO
CERVETERI
TARQUINIA

LEFT: sculpture at Hadrian's Villa, Tivoli.
RIGHT: rustic sign in Tarquinia.

The Roman Temple of Vesta at the Villa Gregoriana.

Trajan's Column and a model of the city under Constantine.

Ancient apartment dwellers

Ostia Antica ❸ (Tues–Sun 8.30am–6pm in summer, until 5pm in winter; charge) was founded around the end of the 4th century BC as a fortified city to guard the mouth of the Tiber. Later it developed into the commercial port of Rome as well as its naval base.

It was from here that the Romans set out to establish their empire. By the time of Constantine, Ostia had turned into a residential town for middle- and lower-class Romans. The legacy is a city whose ruins are second only to Pompeii in their legibility: the stratified nature of an ancient Italian city is laid bare. Ostia's innovations included social housing and a surprisingly modern resort-style complex with communal gardens. In the case of the early apartment block, the inner courtyard has remained a feature of Italian housing ever since. The *domus*, the typical Pompeiian residence built for the very rich, and restricted to one floor, was very rare in Ostia.

The **Piazzale delle Corporazioni** merchant quarter includes mosaics that denote the traders' wares, from the sign of a flotilla, indicating shipping services, to an elephant used to signify the importation of exotic circus animals. Flanking one side of the square, the **Teatro** was enlarged by Septimius Severus at the end of the 2nd century to seat 4,000 spectators. Today, this theatre is used as a summer venue for concerts, drama, dance and cabaret (www.ostiaantica.net).

If heading to the beach, spurn the overcrowded **Lido di Ostia** ❹ in favour of Fregene, a northern resort with pine groves and cachet, or, to the south, choose charming Sperlonga, Gaeta, and the island of Ponza.

The Castelli Romani

The Alban hills, clustered around the capital, have long represented a summer retreat for Romans. Known as the **Castelli Romani**, in ancient times these hills were scattered with villas and pleasure gardens, a tradition followed by the Renaissance popes. **Castel Gandolfo** ❺, overlooking Lake

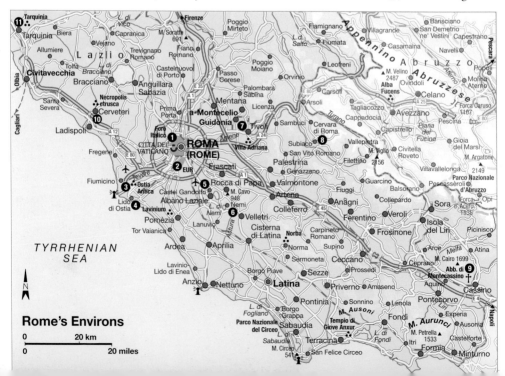

Rome's Environs

0   20 km

0   20 miles

Albano, remains the retreat of the papacy. When in residence, the Pope addresses the crowds from the balcony of the papal palace. On summer weekends, this cluster of hill towns is still a popular pretext for Roman recreation, with the appeal lying in hilltop views and gentle walks, especially if linked to lunch in a local inn, or wine-tasting around **Frascati**, famed for its villas and crisp white wine.

Volcanic **Nemi** ❻, 10 miles (6km) southeast, is another popular weekend excursion, with its early medieval castle and compelling views over the dark-blue waters of Lake Nemi.

Tivoli

At the height of the Roman Empire, **Tibur** ❼ (Tivoli), on the lower slopes of the Sabine hills, was a retreat for the ruling elite, and eulogised by Roman poets. The lavish villas scattered around sacred woods and scenic waterfalls entertained visitors of the stature of Horace, Catullus and the Emperor Trajan. In AD 117 the Emperor Hadrian commissioned his luxurious retirement home on the gently sloping plain below Tivoli. **Villa Adriana** (Hadrian's Villa; daily 9am–7pm summer (later if dance and music events), 9am–6pm winter; charge) was the largest and richest residence in the Roman Empire, inspired by the monuments which had most impressed Hadrian on his extensive travels. Yet these soothing, romantic ruins go beyond mere imitation. The succession of terraces, water basins and baths seems a joyful reaction against functionality, but the design doesn't resort to extravagant artifice. Instead, it is a rigorous, geometrical, classical controlling of nature.

By contrast, a spirit of glorious frivolity pervades Tivoli's **Villa d'Este** (Tues–Sun 8.30am–one hour before sunset, July–Sept additionally 8.30pm–midnight; www.villadestetivoli.info; charge), the sumptuous residence commissioned by Cardinal Ippolito d'Este, son of Lucrezia Borgia. The frescoed Renaissance mansion has a faded grandeur,

but the glory lies in the water gardens, steeply raked on terraces. Pools and elegiac cypresses extend into the distance; water spouts from obelisks, gurgles from the mouths of mythological monsters, springs from the nipples of a sphinx or from the multiple-breasted Artemis of Ephesus. Dedicated purely to pleasure, the gardens display triumphant theatricality, signalling the beginnings of Baroque.

Nearby, **Villa Gregoriana** (Tues–Sun 10am–6.30pm, until 2.30pm in winter; charge), an oasis of waterfalls, ravines and grottoes, is wilder than Villa d'Este. The park has been revitalised, with walks from the main waterfall, which plunges into a rocky gorge, to the Temple of Vesta, an elegant structure dating back to the 1st century BC.

Monastic foundations

Picturesque **Subiaco** ❽, a summer playground in Emperor Nero's day, is better known as the birthplace of Western monasticism. The future St Benedict spent several years here as a hermit in a rock-hewn cave. His legacy remains in several surviving monasteries. The

BELOW: fountains at the Villa d'Este.

BELOW: part of the Etruscan necropolis at Cerveteri.

Abbazia di Santa Scolastica has three delightful cloisters and pillars recycled from Nero's villa. The **Abbazia di San Benedetto**, however, perched on a craggy peak, displays Perugian and Sienese frescoes and, in the depths, Benedict's original grotto, hewn out of the mountainside. A staircase leads to a portrait of St Francis, believed to have been painted from life.

Around AD 529 Benedict and his faithful monks moved to **Montecassino** ❾ and founded a monastery which followed the Benedictine Rule, thereby setting the model for monastic orders ever since. By St Benedict's death in AD 547, the abbey was one of the richest in the world (daily 8.30am–12.30pm and 3.30–6pm, until 5pm in winter). The illuminated manuscripts, frescoes and mosaics were so skilfully executed that they became the inspiration for others throughout medieval Europe.

During World War II, Montecassino rose to prominence once more. After US forces entered Naples, Montecassino became the Germans' front line (the so-called Gustav Line), designed to defend Rome. When repeated attacks by the Allies failed to penetrate the powerfully strengthened bulwark, a decision was made to bomb. It resulted in the total destruction of Montecassino. The ancient abbey was swept away. What one sees today is a faithful reconstruction of what existed before the catastrophe.

Etruscan Cerveteri

Before Rome ruled supreme, central Italy had a highly refined civilisation: that of the Etruscans *(see page 34)*. Their zest for life and emphasis on physical vitality has fascinated many, including D.H. Lawrence, who saw them as a happy contrast to the puritanical Romans. Although Tuscany considers itself the soul of the Etruscan civilisation and has fine Etruscan museums, Lazio boasts the best-preserved Etruscan tombs.

The small medieval town of **Cerveteri** ❿, north of Rome on the Via Aurelia, was built on the site of the Etruscan town of Caere. In the 6th and 5th centuries BC, Caere was one of the most populated towns of the Mediterranean. Artistic and trading links with

Greece made Caere a sophisticated cultural centre. Its decline began in AD 384, when Pyrgi harbour, its main port, was devastated by a Greek incursion. Eventually the barbaric strength of Rome wiped away what had been a refined and joyous civilisation. Nothing remains today of the ancient town of Caere, bar a few walls.

Caere's necropolis occupies a hill outside the city proper, the **Necropoli della Banditaccia** (Tues–Sun 9am–one hour before sunset; charge). From here it could be seen from the ramparts of the city, gay with painted houses and temples. The oldest tombs (8th century BC) have a small circular well carved into the stone, where the urns containing the ashes of the dead were placed. (Two modes of burial, cremation and inhumation, continued side by side for centuries.) The first chamber tombs, also cut into the stone and covered with rocky blocks and mounds (*tumuli*), appeared as early as the beginning of the 7th century BC. The noble Etruscans were either enclosed in great sarcophagi with their effigies on top, or laid out on stone beds in their chamber tombs.

Excavations of the tombs not already rifled – the Romans were the first collectors of Etruscan antiquities – revealed goods of gold, silver, ivory, bronze and ceramic. The vases show strong Greek influence as well as superb Etruscan craftmanship. Much is now on display in the **Museo Nazionale Archeologico di Cerveteri** (Tues–Sun 9am–7.30pm; charge), housed here, in the medieval Castello di Ruspoli, as well as in Rome's Museo di Villa Giulia and in the Vatican Museums (*see page 157*).

Etruscan Tarquinia

The Etruscan town of **Tarquinia** ⓫ stood on a hill northwest of the picturesque medieval town bearing the same name. The town existed as early as the 9th century BC, and two centuries later was at its height. The **Museo Nazionale Tarquiniense** (Tues–Sun 8.30am–7.30pm; charge), set in a 15th-century palazzo, displays Etruscan treasures, including the famous 4th-century BC terracotta winged horses.

The **Necropolis of Tarquinia** (Tues–Sun 8.30am–one hour before sunset, until 2pm in winter, last entry 90 mins before closing; charge), together with that of Caere, is the most important Etruscan necropolis. It stands on a hill south of the original town, occupying an area 5km (3 miles) long by 1km (½ mile) wide. The frescoed tombs needed to be bright in order to stand out in the shadowy setting, lit only by faint oil lamps. Ribbons of colours frame the animated scenes below: the feasting in the Tomba dei Leopardi; the hunters in the Tomba del Cacciatore; the erotic scenes in the Tomba dei Tori; the prancing dancers, diving dolphins and soaring birds of the Tomba della Leonessa. Many of the scenes depict the distress of departing the earthly world, but there are also sombre scenes and glimpses of demonic dancing, reflecting the decline of Etruscan civilisation. Yet overwhelmingly, visitors leave these dusty houses of death full of renewed faith in life and its many mysteries. ❏

In Etruscan tombs, men were usually portrayed as red-skinned while women were painted white, with clothes depicted in bright colours made from precious mineral dyes such as lapis lazuli and ochre.

BELOW:
Etruscan sculpture at Tarquinia.

THE NORTH

"Above all the sense of going down into Italy – the delight of seeing the North melt slowly into the South – of seeing Italy gradually crop up in bits and vaguely, latently betray itself – until finally at the little frontier village of Isella, where I spent the night, it lay before me warm and living and palpable"

– HENRY JAMES (from his *Letters*, Vol. 1, ed. Leon Edel)

For centuries, most travellers arrived in Italy from the north. They crossed the mountains from Switzerland or France, and often, if physically fit and romantically minded – as was the young Henry James – made part of the journey on foot. This way Italy came into focus gradually, as they left the cold north behind and made their way south from the lakes to Milan, and the cities of the Po Valley.

This is still the best way to approach northern Italy. Rather than rush through, with your eyes on the train timetables and your mind checking off the cities, see fewer places, but see them well. Each one is awash with artistic and literary associations. After all, this is the Italy of Shakespeare – *Romeo and Juliet* (Verona), *The Taming of the Shrew* (Padua) – and of medieval city-states and Renaissance princes. The great families – the Visconti in Milan, the Gonzaga in Mantua, the della Scala in Verona – are still remembered for their artistic triumphs, as well as for the political scandals of their courts.

We pass from Byzantine Venice to the great cities of the Veneto – Padua, Verona and Vicenza – magnets for university students since the Middle Ages. From Venice to the Brenta Canal and Treviso, this is Palladio country, studded with Palladian villas designed in a harmonious architectural style that has conquered the world.

We then move to Milan, the style and shopping capital of Italy, via the magnificent glaciated landscapes of the Alps to the villas, lakes and gorgeous romantic gardens of the Italian lake district.

Northern Italians, although more aloof and self-contained than the gregarious southerners, are always pleased to share a little-known fact about their hometown with a stranger. The locals might well bear more than a fleeting resemblance to the figures in the 15th-century frescoes of the local Duomo – in these regions, the past is always present. ❑

PRECEDING PAGES: the island of San Giorgio Maggiore, dominated by the monastic church of the same name. **LEFT:** a snow-fed waterfall in the Valle d'Aosta. **ABOVE:** Riva del Garda on Lake Garda; Baptistery and Duomo in Florence; Juliet's balcony in Verona, where Shakespeare set *Romeo and Juliet*.

VENICE

"... out the wave her structures rise.
As from the stroke of the Enchanter's wand"

— LORD BYRON, *Childe Harold's Pilgrimage* (1812)

When Lord Byron arrived in Venice in 1810, the "Queen of the Adriatic" had been in decline for many years. Though nonetheless enchanted by the beauty of the city, the poet describes her palaces as "crumbling to the shore". The seeds of decline were sown at the turn of the 15th century, when the Portuguese stripped Venice of its monopoly of the spice trade. A decade later the League of Cambrai put an end to Venice's hold on crucial cities on the mainland.

But even if Venice was crumbling for years, it continued to captivate visitors. For centuries the city has inspired poets, painters and writers, including Proust, Hemingway and Henry James. Few other cities in the world have produced a more talented school of painters, from Bellini and Giorgione to Titian, Tintoretto and Tiepolo.

Built on over 100 islets, supported by millions of wooden piles and linked by 400 bridges, Venice is the only city in the world which is built entirely on water. The sense of precariousness, associated with the city for centuries, inevitably adds to the fascination. There is always a feeling that once you turn your back on all this fragile glory, the islands, once inhabited by refugees fleeing the hordes of Attila the Hun, will disappear like a mirage into the sea.

In January 1996 La Fenice, Venice's historic opera house – where Verdi's *La Traviata* and *Rigoletto* were first performed – was razed to the ground. La Fenice finally rose from the ashes in 2003 after a fire which was started by disgruntled electricians. The plush, gilt-encrusted interior has been faithfully recreated, but the city faces far greater challenges today.

MOSE, the controversial mobile flood barriers designed to protect the city from major inundation, should be functioning by 2014. However, according to

---

LEFT: gondola cruising down the canals.
RIGHT: St Mark's Square, Basilica and Campanile.

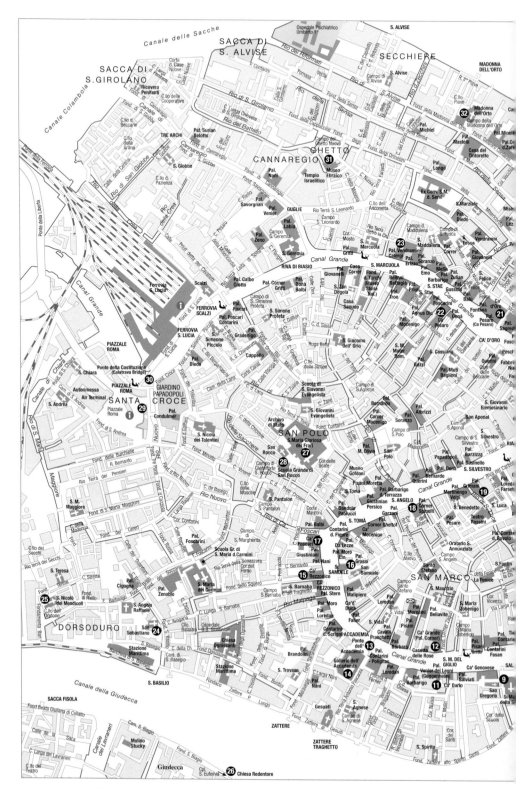

Canale delle Navi

CIMITERO
S. Michele

Venice

0   200 m
0   200 yds

N

CIMITERO
S. MICHELE

S. Michele

Canale delle Fondamente Nuove

Caterina
Fondamenta Nuove
C.llo
S. Antonio
Pal. Zen
Fond. Zen

33 Gesuiti
Oratorio
d. Crociferi

FONDAMENTE NUOVE

Campo
dei
Gesuiti

C. Venier

SS. Apostoli
Campo dei
SS. Apostoli
stole

S. Canciano

Campo d.
Madonna

Campo
S. Cancian

Rio dei Mendicanti

S. Lazzaro
Mendicanti

OSPEDALE CIVILE

S. Giovanni
Crisostomo

Pal. Boldù
Teatro
Malibran

34 S. Maria
dei Miracoli

Pal.
Sanudo

38

Colleoni

Scuola Gr. di
S. Marco

S. Maria
del Pianto

Ospedale
Civile

SS. Giovanni e
Paolo **39**

Ospedale
dei Vecchi

CELESTIA

Fond. Case Nuove

BACINI

Pal.
Amadi
Pal.
Grisandin
Carabba

Pal.
Marcello

Pal.
Pisani

Campo
SS. Giovanni
e Paolo

Ospedaletto

Campo
S. Francesco
della Vigna

S. Francesco
della Vigna

Cor. delle
Muneghe

S. Cio

Pal.
Pridli

37

Pal. Donà

Rio della Tetta

Campo della
Confraternita

Campo
della
Celestia

S. Maria
della Fava

Pal.
Faccanon

Campo
S. Maria
Formosa

Pal. Vitturi

C. Larga S. Larenzo

S. Lorenzo

S. Giustina

Pal.
Gradenigo
Salizzada S. Giustina

Convento

Canale delle Galeazze

Pal.
Zulian

S. Maria
Formosa

Pal.
Grimani

Pal.
Trevisan

Campo
S. Lorenzo

Questura

S. Giovanni
di Malta

Darsena Arsenale Vecchio

Darsena Grande

Pinacoteca
Querini
Stamp.

Pal.
Zorzi

Scuola di
S. Giorgio degli
Schiavoni **35**

Calle del Furlani

C.llo
Due Pozzi

Torre dell'
Orologio **4**

Pal.
Priuli

Mus.
dell. Inst.
Ellenico

Cor.
della Grana

Pal.
Patriarcale

Pal.
Trevisan

S. Giorgio
dei
Greci

S. Antonio

CASTELLO

Portal des
Arsenale

1 **3**
2

Basilica di
San Marco
Campanile
di S. Marco

San
Zaccaria

36

Campo
S. Martino

Il Ponte
dei Sospiri **8**

Campo
S. Zaccaria

S. Giorgio
in Bragora

S. Martino

C.llo Pescaria

Piazza di
San Marco

Museo
Correr

Museo
Archeologico

Palazzo
Reale

Procuratie Nuove

7

Palazzo
Ducale

Pal. Prigioni

Pal. Dindolo

La Pietà

Pal.
Navagero

40
Arsenale

Libreria
Sansoviniana

Riva degli Schiavoni

Riva

degli Schiavoni

Istituto
Ca' di Dio

della

Tana

Cor.
Cottrera

S. MARCO
GIARDINETTI

5
La
Zecca

GIARDINETTI
REALI

i

S. ZACCARIA

ARSENALE

Riva di Ca di Dio

Museo
Navale

S. Biagio

S. Francesco
di Paola

Campo
della
Colomba

S. MARCO
VALLARESSO

Canale   di   S. Marco

Riva   dei   Sette   Martiri

Via   G.   Garibaldi

Monumento
a Garibaldi

Punta della
Dogana

Campo
S. Giorgio

Campanile di
San Giorgio
Maggiore

S. GIORGIO

6

San Giorgio
Maggiore

Viale Trento

Biennale

GIARDINI
(BIENNALE)

Viale dei Gia Pubblici

41

Canale della Giudecca

S. Giorgio
Maggiore

Fond. S. Giovanni

I stood in Venice, on the "Bridge of Sighs"; A Palace and a prison on each hand: I saw from out the wave her structures rise/ As from the stroke of the Enchanter's wand: A thousand Years their cloudy wings expand Around me, and a dying Glory smiles O'er the far times, when many a subject land Look'd to the winged Lion's marble piles, Where Venice sat in state, throned on her hundred isles!
– LORD BYRON, *Childe Harold's Pilgrimage*

BELOW:
St Mark's Basilica.

Venice in Peril, water levels are still chronically high and damaging the building fabric. Yet even if the physical threats come from the sea, the social challenges are no less serious. Venice may be mired in its glorious past, with Gothic palaces galore, but it needs to retain its population if it is to stave off its fate as a theme park. Since the population recently fell below 60,000, the city has had a rude wake-up call. A simmering rebellion against exorbitant property prices and the creeping colonisation of mask shops and hotels reflects a local backlash against mass tourism. There is no magical solution, but pressure groups are calling for investment in culture and crafts, and a revitalised contemporary arts and events scene, to prevent *La Serenissima* from sinking into museum-dom.

St Mark's Square

The heart of Venice is the vast **Piazza di San Marco ❶**. Described by Napoleon as the most elegant drawing room in Europe, this is the great architectural showpiece of Venice. With its café bands and exotic shops under the arcades, it is also the hub of tourist Venice; only late at night does it revert to a semblance of solitude. At one end of the piazza, crouching like an enormous, amphibious reptile, the great Basilica di San Marco (St Mark's Basilica) invites visitors to explore its mysterious depths.

Basilica di San Marco

The **Basilica di San Marco ❷** (Mon–Sat 9.45am–5pm, Sun 2–5pm, daily from 7am for worshippers; online booking to avoid queues, www.venetoinside.com; charge to Sanctuary, Pala d'Oro and Treasury; all bags now need to be left in the Ateneo San Basso on Piazzetta dei Leoncini – a free left-luggage service) is named after the Evangelist St Mark, whose remains were recovered (or stolen, depending on your viewpoint) by the Venetians from Alexandria in the 9th century.

If fully visible, the square reveals its lovely Clock Tower at the landward end of the piazza, and the Basilica itself, with its sumptuous portals decorated with shimmering mosaics. (Lack of funds for renovation means that St

Mark's Square is periodically swathed in advertising hoardings – the Faustian pact undertaken by the city to bridge the deficit.) The only original mosaic – in the doorway to the far left – gives a good idea of the appearance of the basilica in the 13th century. Above the main portal are replicas of the famous bronze horses, thought to be Roman or Hellenistic works of the 3rd or 4th century AD and looted by the Venetians from Constantinople in 1204. They were taken to Paris by Napoleon in 1797 and returned in 1815, and are now kept inside the Basilica, protected from pigeons and pollution.

The Basilica's interior, in the shape of a Greek cross, is thought to have been inspired by the Church of the Apostles in Constantinople. Above the columns of the minor naves, lining the arms of the cross, are the women's galleries or *matronei*, designed in accordance with Greek Orthodox custom, which separates the sexes. The luxurious atmosphere of the interior is enhanced by the decoration of the walls: marble slabs cover the lower part, while golden mosaics adorn the vaults, arches and

domes. Following a complex iconographic plan, the mosaics cover 4,000 sq metres (43,000 sq ft), which is why St Mark's is sometimes called the Basilica d'Oro (Church of Gold).

Among the many gems housed in the church are the **Pala d'Oro**, a jewel-studded gold-and-enamel altarpiece dating from the 10th century. The **Treasury** also houses a priceless collection of gold and silver from Byzantium. The **Marciano Museum** (daily 9.45am–5pm; charge), reached by steep steps from the entrance narthex, affords fine views of the interior as a whole, while the open-air terrace beyond the museum gives a bird's-eye view of Piazza di San Marco. It was here that the doge and other dignitaries gathered to watch celebrations taking place below.

A panoramic view

A striking feature of the square is the soaring **Campanile** ❸ (daily July–Sept 9am–9pm, Apr–June and Oct 9am–7pm, Nov–Mar 9.30am–3.45pm; charge), a faithful replica of the original tower that collapsed in 1902.

Mosaic of Christ in St Mark's.

BELOW LEFT: the Rio Canonica and Bridge of Sighs.

Navigating Venice

Venice is Italy's most expensive, confusing and popular city. To keep costs down, and to avoid queuing at major attractions, it's worth pre-booking from among the myriad city museum, church and transport passes. The sites with the longest queues are St Mark's Basilica, the Doge's Palace and the Accademia. The attractions that must be pre-booked are the Clock Tower and the Secret Itineraries tour of the Doge's Palace.

Venice Connected (www.veniceconnected.com) is an integrated, online-only booking system for key museums and transport, with discounts offered in quieter periods to encourage sustainable tourism.

Hello Venezia (www.hellovenezia.com; tel: 041-2424) is most useful as a transport- and/or museum-booking system and sells the VeniceCard, which covers 12 museums and the 16 Chorus churches *(see below)*, and offers the full range of integrated transport passes for different times.

Vivaticket (www.vivaticket.it; tel: 84 808 2000, Italy-only call centre) is a booking service for opera, concerts, ballet and blockbuster exhibitions, as well as major attractions and unusual guided tours, notably the Secret Itineraries tour and the Clock Tower, both around St Mark's.

The Chorus Pass (www.chorusvenezia.org; tel: 041-275 0462) allows access to 16 Venetian churches (including the Frari), with charges going towards local church restoration projects.

Inside, a lift – or, for the energetic, a stairway – climbs 100 metres (330ft) to the top for a sweeping panorama of the city and lagoon. The piazza's other tower is Coducci's intricate **Torre dell'Orologio** ❹, the recently restored Clock Tower, designed in 1496 (English-language tours Mon–Wed 10 and 11am, Thur–Sat 2 and 3pm; for booking, tel: 84-808 2000; charge). Adjoining the piazza and extending to the waterfront is the **Piazzetta San Marco**. On the right as you face the lagoon stands the 16th-century **Biblioteca Nazionale Marciana**, which is home to the **Libreria Sansoviniana** ❺ (Apr–Oct daily 9am–7pm, Nov–Mar daily 9am–5pm; charge, also combined ticket and access via Museo Correr; tel: 041-240 5211), where classical concerts are occasionally staged. Palladio, Italy's greatest 16th-century architect, considered this structure one of the most beautiful buildings ever constructed. Today it houses the **Archaeological Museum** (daily 9am–7pm; charge, combined ticket and access via Museo Correr), the National Library of St Mark and the Venetian Old Library –

with a collection of treasures from the city's golden years.

At the lagoon end of the Piazzetta stand two large 12th-century columns, one crowned with a winged lion, the symbol of Venice, the other with a statue of St Theodore, the original patron saint of the city. The square has served as a marketplace, meeting place and execution site, with public executions once staged between the two columns.

Across the water lies one of Venice's great landmarks – the majestic church of **San Giorgio Maggiore** ❻ (daily 9.30am–12.30pm, May–Sept 2.30–6pm, Oct–Apr 2.30–4.30pm; charge for Campanile). This classical masterpiece by Andrea Palladio, the finest monastic church in the lagoon, displays works of art by Tintoretto; and the views from the Campanile extend, on a clear day, as far as the Alps.

The Doge's Palace

The **Palazzo Ducale** ❼ (daily Apr–Oct 9am–7pm, Nov–Mar 9am–5pm; charge) flanks the eastern side of the Piazzetta. This "vast and sump-

tuous pile", as Byron described it, is the grandest and most conspicuous example of Venetian Gothic in the city. The official residence of the doge and the seat of government during the republic, it stands today as eloquent evidence of the power and pomp of Venice in its heyday.

Inside, the three wings of the palace reveal a seemingly endless series of grandiose rooms and halls. The largest of these is the Sala del Maggior Consiglio (the Great Council Chamber), which could accommodate all 480 (and later 1,700) of the Venetian patricians who sat on the council. The art collection here gives a foretaste of the countless artistic treasures scattered throughout the city, and includes works by the two Venetian giants – Tintoretto and Veronese. Tintoretto's *Paradise* (1588–92) was for many years the largest painting in the world (7 metres by 22 metres/23ft by 72ft). In the same room, Veronese's *Apotheosis of Venice* is another compelling masterpiece, though his finest work in the palace is *The Rape of Europa* in the Anticollegio.

Adjoining the palace is the former prison. Once tried and convicted in the palace, prisoners were led across the slender covered bridge to their cell. Since the windowed bridge offered the captive his last glimpse of freedom, it was called **Il Ponte dei Sospiri ❽** (the Bridge of Sighs). However grim its original purpose, it has a romantic air, and is favoured today by young lovers who believe that if they kiss under the bridge (presumably in a gondola) their love will last.

A tour of the Ducal Palace is best rounded off with a coffee break in the piazza. The most famous café is **Florian,** once a fashionable high-society haunt. Henry James conjures up the atmosphere in *The Aspern Papers* (1888): "I sat in front of Florian's café, eating ices, listening to music, talking with acquaintances: the traveller will remember how the immense cluster of tables and little chairs stretches like a promontory into the smooth lake of the Piazza."

The Grand Canal

The **Canal Grande** winds for 3.5km (2 miles) through the city. This splendid

TIP

The Itinerari Segreti (Secret Itineraries) are fascinating guided tours of lesser-known parts of the Doge's Palace and prison cells (tours in English run daily Sept– June 9.55am, 10.45am and 11.35am; booking essential, tel: 041-4273 0892 or, in Italy, tel: 84 808 2000).

BELOW: a boat ride down the Grand Canal affords unparalleled views.

Patron of the arts Peggy Guggenheim's collection of modern masterpieces is not to be missed.

BELOW: Ponte dell'Accademia.

shimmering thoroughfare is flanked by pastel-coloured palaces in a mixture of Byzantine, Gothic, Renaissance and Baroque styles, built mostly between the 13th and the 18th centuries.

The best way to see the canal is from a boat. If you are feeling flush, hire a gondola from the San Marco waterfront. Thomas Mann, who commented that the gondolas of Venice were "black as nothing else on earth except a coffin", nonetheless found their seats "the softest, most luxurious, most relaxing in the world". Far cheaper, but equally engaging, is the No. 1 waterbus (*vaporetto*), which plies the length of the canal at frequent intervals. Alternatively, try the faster No. 82 service, which makes fewer stops.

Starting from San Marco, the canal is overshadowed by the great Baroque church of **Santa Maria della Salute 9**, designed by the 17th-century architect Baldassare Longhena, and erected in thanks for the city's deliverance from the plague of 1630. To the enamoured Henry James, the church was "like a great lady on the threshold of her salon… with her domes and scrolls, her

scalloped buttresses and statues forming a pompous crown, and her wide steps disposed on the ground like the train of a robe".

Beside it, commanding the point, is the **Punta della Dogana 10** (Wed–Mon, 10am–7pm; charge), the former Customs House, now a showcase for contemporary art. Restored by the Japanese architect Tadao Ando, the airy mezzanine space allows for a lovely interplay between the interior and the exterior (*see panel below*).

The Guggenheim

On the same side is **Palazzo Venier dei Leoni 11**, better known as the **Guggenheim** (Wed–Mon 10am–6pm; charge), the famous residence-museum of the late American patron of the arts, Peggy Guggenheim (1898–1979).

This is Venice's leading contemporary art museum, with a superb, eclectic collection of works representing the major avant-garde movements of the last century. Paintings by legendary names including Picasso, Braque, Kandinsky and Bacon are all on display alongside a large representation

Life in Venice

Venice is being bold again, with a sleek bridge over the Grand Canal, a mobile flood barrier in construction, a revamped Art Biennale, designer B&Bs, and a cutting-edge contemporary art museum facing St Mark's. But it's a delicate balancing act: visitors also come for the gondolas, the Gothic palaces and the sense of being marooned in a gorgeous Disney-

land for grown-ups. The sleepy Castello district is redrawing its image to attract modern art merchants of Venice. During the Biennale jamboree, an arty crowd heads to the pavilions in the Giardini gardens and to the new exhibition spaces in the Arsenale. Every two years, these historic shipyards welcome a swirling morass of contemporary art, displayed in converted ropeworks and munitions stores.

Over the water, bohemian Dorsoduro is becoming less maiden aunt and more arty trustafarian. Few would com-

plain if they had an aunt as eclectic as Peggy Guggenheim, whose legacy lingers on in the eponymous modern art collection. But a new flagship in arty Dorsoduro lies a short stroll along the waterfront. **Punta della Dogana**, designed like a ship's prow, showcases a superb new collection of contemporary art belonging to French fashion tycoon François Pinault.

Around the corner, **Linea d'Ombra** (Ponte dell'Umilta; tel: 041-241 1881) is one of numerous design-conscious restaurants that are challenging Venetian stereotypes. It is matched by design B&Bs, such as **DD694** (tel: 041-277 0262). As for chic bars, on Giudecca, **Skyline**, in Molino Stucky, is a cool rooftop haunt where Japanese raspberry-vodka cocktails are de rigueur. Suspended over the lagoon, Skyline is Venice-meets-Tokyo in a *Lost in Translation* moment. Quintessential "new Venice".

of Surrealist art, which was close to Guggenheim's heart – she was briefly married to Max Ernst, one of the movement's founders. His works, along with those of Dalí, Magritte, Jackson Pollock and de Kooning, are all here. The 18th-century palazzo was built for the noble Venier family and was nicknamed the "Nonfinito", because the building remained unfinished. It is a splendidly eccentric setting for the collection, with a lovely garden, chic café and courtyard, where chained lions were once kept, earning it the sobriquet "dei Leoni".

The Accademia

On the right bank opposite is **Ca' Grande ⑫**, a Renaissance residence by Sansovino, now the office of the city magistrate. The first bridge that spans the canal is the wooden **Ponte dell'Accademia ⑬**, built in 1932 as a temporary structure but retained through popular demand. It is named after the nearby **Gallerie dell'Accademia ⑭** (Tues–Sun 8.15am–7.15pm, Mon 8.15am–2pm; booking tel: 041-520 0345; charge)

housed in the former Scuola della Carità. This contains the world's finest collection of Venetian paintings, with works by Mantegna, Bellini, Giorgione *(The Tempest)*, Carpaccio, Titian, Tintoretto, Veronese, Tiepolo, Guardi and Canaletto, mostly arranged in chronological order.

Baroque palace

Further down the canal on the same side stands the imposing Baroque palace of **Ca' Rezzonico ⑮** (Wed–Mon, Apr–Oct 10am–6pm, Nov–Mar 10am–5pm; charge), housing a superb museum of 18th-century Venice, dedicated to the swansong of the Serene Republic – *La Serenissima*. The stately rooms are richly decorated with period paintings, furniture and frescoes. It was here that the poet Robert Browning died in 1889.

Palazzo Grassi ⑯ (Wed–Mon, 10am–7pm; charge), on the opposite bank, is an imposing patrician palace and model of neoclassical restraint. Now linked to the **Punta della Dogana,** Tadao Ando's conversion has turned the palace into another slick

> "
> *The Rialto Bridge area is one of the most vibrant and picturesque parts of Venice. I often go for a drink at Bancogiro (Campo San Giacometto, tel: 041-523 2061) or one of the bars that look over the Grand Canal there with some of my fellow gondoliers after work.*
> Danielle Morasco, gondolier
> "

BELOW: carnival masks and Veronese's *Feast in the House of Levi* (in the Accademia).

showcase for exhibitions based on the collections of the owner, French magnate François Pinault (*see panel page 178*).

Back on the left bank, **Palazzi Giustiniani** was where Richard Wagner composed the second act of *Tristan and Isolde* in 1858–9. Next door, **Ca' Foscari** ⓱ is the ancestral home of the 15th-century doge who masterminded Venetian conquests on the Italian mainland.

Beyond the Sant'Angelo landing stage, on the right bank, **Palazzo Corner Spinelli** ⓲ was designed during the early Venetian Renaissance in the Lombardic style by Coducci. Beyond the next side canal, the **Palazzo Grimani** ⓳, now the Court of Appeal, is a late Renaissance masterpiece by Sanmicheli. In front of you, Venice's most famous bridge, **Ponte di Rialto** ⓴, arches over the canal. The former wooden drawbridges built across the canal at this point all collapsed, necessitating the erection of a more weighty stone structure. Antonio da Ponte beat the greatest architects of the day, including Michaelangelo and Palladio,

Carnival costume – the disconcertingly blank mask (called a bauta), *complete with bold tricorne hat and full-length black cloak, will lend any carnival-goer an undeniably cruel charisma* (see page 186).

BELOW: the arcaded Pescheria, Venice's main fish market.

to secure the commission, and supervised its construction between 1588 and 1592. The single-span, balustraded bridge has two parallel rows of tightly packed shops selling jewellery, leather, masks, silk and souvenirs.

Ca' d'Oro

The most beautiful Gothic palace in Venice, the **Ca' d'Oro** ㉑ (Tues–Sun 8.15am–7.15pm, Mon 8.15am–2pm; charge) appears on the right at the first landing stage beyond the bridge. When built in 1420 by the wealthy patrician Marino Contarini, it was covered in gold leaf, hence the name "House of Gold". Inside, the Giorgio Franchetti art gallery displays paintings, frescoes and sculpture.

Further along, on the left bank, the enormous Baroque **Ca' Pesaro** ㉒ is another masterpiece by Longhena; this one houses the **Galleria d'Arte Moderna** and the **Museo Orientale** (Tues–Sun, Apr–Oct 10am–6pm, Nov–Mar 10am–5pm; charge). The last building of note before the railway station is **Palazzo Vendramin-Calergi** ㉓, one of the finest Renaissance palaces by Mauro Coducci (1440–1504). Wagner died here in 1883, but this is now the elegant city casino (tel: 041-529 7111), albeit one with a Wagnerian restaurant.

The six districts of Venice

The greatest experience the city can offer to the inquisitive visitor is the maze of tiny alleys, the narrow silent canals and the pretty squares and courtyards only minutes away from **San Marco**, the most central of the six districts (*sestieri*) of Venice. Leading north from the Piazza San Marco, starting at the Clock Tower, is the **Merceria dell'Orologia**. This ancient maze of alleys is still devoted to commerce, and is awash with small shops and boutiques.

Dorsoduro is the most southerly section of historic Venice – an excellent area to stay if you are looking for a sought-after small hotel within easy

access of St Mark's. To the south, the area is bounded by the **Zattere**, a long, broad and peaceful quayside whose cafés and restaurants afford splendid views across the water to the island of Giudecca. East of the Accademia, the Dorsoduro is quiet and intimate, characterised by pretty canals, galleries and chic residences.

Northwest of the Accademia, the area around San Barnaba was traditionally the quarter for impoverished Venetian nobility. Today it is the scene of cafés, artisans and one of the last surviving vegetable barges. Further west, the 16th-century church of **San Sebastiano** ❷ (Mon–Sat 10am–5pm; charge; book through Chorus: *see panel page 175*) was the parish church of Veronese and provided a classical canvas for his opulent masterpieces, painted between 1555 and 1565.

The area becomes picturesquely shabby and appealing towards San Nicolò dei Mendicoli, erstwhile home of sailors and fishermen. The charming Romanesque church of **San Nicolò dei Mendicoli** ❷ (Mon–Sat 10am–noon) was expertly restored by the British

Venice in Peril Fund in the 1970s.

The island of **Giudecca**, across the Giudecca Canal, is Venice's most diverse neighbourhood, a mixture of earthy working-class, funky designer and palatial grandeur. The main landmark on its waterfront is Andrea Palladio's **Redentore** church ❷ (Mon–Sat 10am–5pm), built in gratitude for the city's deliverance from plague in 1576. On the third Sunday in July, the city commemorates this event by building a bridge of boats from the Zattere to the Redentore, where a special Mass is held. That night, a firework display lights up the sky.

San Polo

The *sestiere* of **San Polo** lies within the large bend of the Grand Canal, northwest of San Marco. The quarter around the **Rialto**, the oldest inhabited part of mainland Venice, became the gathering place of merchants from the East and thence the commercial hub of the city. It is still a bustling area, with shops and market stalls. Fruit and vegetables are laid out under the arcades of the Fabbriche Vecchie, while the mock-

The Rialto, built in the late 16th century, is the oldest bridge across the Grand Canal.

BELOW LEFT: Venetian barman.

A Venetian Bar Crawl

The Rialto market marks the start of a Venetian bar crawl, *a giro di ombre*, in the backstreet wine and tapas bars known as *bacari*. On offer are an array of exotic Venetian snacks *(cichetti)* and glasses of wine *(ombre)* in snug, rough-and-ready bars, often dating back to the 15th century. All'Arco, in Calle Arco, serves titbits such as calamari or prawns on bread, while Bancogiro, on Campo San Giacometto, brings the *bacaro* concept up to date. On Calle delle Veste, near the Fenice opera house, Vino Vino is the place to rub shoulders with gondoliers over tasty tapas, from sweet-and-sour sardines to salt cod and polenta. Good food, gruff service and gondoliers generally go together. In Canareggio, Alla Vedova is another delightful den for gorging on meatballs and guzzling a Veneto house red *(see page 408)*.

On a wine crawl, don't forget to sample the local aperitif, *spritz* (pronounced "spriss" in dialect). The lurid-looking drink was introduced under Austrian rule (named after the introduction of *selzer*, tonic water) and soon became a firm favourite. It consists of roughly equal parts of dry white wine, tonic and an aperitif, usually Campari or Aperol. Ask for a *spritz al bitter* for a stronger, less cloying taste. The *spritz* may be an acquired taste, but once acquired, it's the clearest sign that you've fallen for Venice.

The Ghetto remains at the heart of Jewish life, with fine synagogues and workshops selling liturgical objects.

BELOW: 13th-century figure near Campo dei Mori in Cannaregio.

Gothic stone loggia of the **Pescheria** marks the site of the morning fish market. Arrive early, as the market begins to close by noon.

The Frari

The major church of San Polo is the majestic brick Gothic **Santa Maria Gloriosa dei Frari** ㉗ (Mon–Sat 9am–6pm, Sun 1–6pm; charge), usually referred to as the Frari. The interior houses some of Venice's finest masterpieces, including an exquisite *Madonna and Child* by Bellini, Titian's celebrated *Assumption* (crowning the main altar) and his *Madonna di Ca' Pesaro*. Buried in the Frari are the composer Claudio Monteverdi, the sculptor Canova (who lies in a pyramidal tomb he designed as a monument to Titian) and several doges.

Nearby, the **Scuola Grande di San Rocco** ㉘ (daily 9.30am–5.30pm; charge) is celebrated for its series of religious works by Tintoretto, painted on the walls and ceilings in 1564–87. The scenes from *The Life of Christ* culminate in *The Crucifixion*, of which Henry James wrote: "Surely no single picture in the world contains more human life; there is everything in it, including the most exquisite beauty."

Santa Croce ㉙, lying north and west of San Polo, is a relatively unexplored district. Its core is a maze of covered alleyways lined by peeling facades and criss-crossed by canals barely wide enough for the passage of a barge. Its squares are pleasingly shabby, bustling with local life. The only real concession to tourism is the **Piazzale Roma**, the arrival point for those coming by road. The area is enlivened by a striking new addition to the cityscape, **Ponte della Costituzione** ㉚, the fourth bridge over the Grand Canal, and the only one to be illuminated at night. Designed by Calatrava, the acclaimed Spanish architect and bridge fanatic, this elegant, understated sliver of a structure connects the station with the road terminal.

The origins of the Ghetto

Cannaregio is the quietest and most remote district in Venice. Its name derives from *canne* (reeds), for this area was once marshland. The *sestiere* forms the northern arc of the city, stretching

from the railway station to the Rio dei Mendicanti in the east. At its heart lies the **Ghetto ㉛**: its name originated from an iron foundry *(getto)* which once stood here. This was Europe's first ghetto, an area for the exclusive but confined occupation of Jews. Built in the early 16th century, it gave its name to isolated Jewish communities throughout the world. It remained a ghetto until Napoleonic times. Though very few Jews live here, the synagogues, tenements and kosher restaurants lend a distinctive Jewish air, and the area's history is well documented in the **Museo Ebraico** (Sun–Fri 10am–7pm, until 6pm Oct–May, and earlier closing on Fri; closed Sat and Jewish holidays; charge), a museum on the main square, and the starting point for guided walks round the Ghetto (tel: 041-715 359).

In the northern part of Cannaregio is the lovely Gothic church of the **Madonna dell'Orto ㉜** (Mon–Sat 10am–5pm; charge). Tintoretto was born round here and lived at No. 3399, near the Campo dei Mori. Forming the northern border of Cannaregio, the **Fondamente Nuove** are the main departure point for ferries to the northern islands. Across the water you can see the walled cemetery on the island of San Michele. Back from the quayside, the Baroque church of the **Gesuiti ㉝** (daily 10am–noon and 5–7pm) has an outrageously extravagant green-and-white marble interior, and contains Titian's dramatic *Martyrdom of St Lawrence*.

It is worth exploring the warren of alleys and canals to the east of Cannaregio. With luck, you will stumble upon the church of **Santa Maria dei Miracoli ㉞** (Mon–Sat 10am–5pm; charge). Designed in the 1480s by Pietro Lombardo and his workshop, it is one of the loveliest Renaissance churches in the city. Decorated inside and out with marble, it is often likened to a jewel-box.

Castello

The city's eastern section, **Castello**, varies in character from the busy southern waterfront near San Marco to the humble cheek-by-jowl residences of the north. The area behind Riva degli Schiavoni is worth exploring for its pretty canals, quaysides and elegant faded

Tiepolo's Abraham Visited by the Angels *in San Rocco.*

BELOW: Cannaregio.

Italian ice cream, the best in the world.

BELOW:
Renaissance
gateway to the
Arsenale, built in
1460 by Antonio
Gambello.

palaces. Essential viewing for those interested in art is the frieze by Carpaccio in the **Scuola di San Giorgio degli Schiavoni** ❸ (Tues–Sat 9.15am–1pm and 2.45–6pm, Sun 9.15am–1pm; charge) and Coducci's 16th-century church of **San Zaccaria** ❸ (Mon–Sat 10am–noon, 4–6pm).

The **Campo Santa Maria Formosa** ❸ (church: Mon–Sat 10am–5pm; charge) is a pleasant market square with a fine Renaissance church, which is home to Palma il Vecchio's splendid *St Barbara and Saints* of 1510. The spiritual heart of Castello is **Campo Santi Giovanni e Paolo** ❸, better known in Venetian dialect as San Zanipolo. The square is dominated by Andrea del Verrocchio's masterly bronze equestrian statue of the mercenary Bartolomeo Colleoni. Presiding over the square is the majestic Gothic church of **Santi Giovanni e Paolo** ❸ (daily 7.30am–6.30pm, Sun noon–7.30pm; charge), where 46 doges are buried. Many of their tomb monuments are magnificent, as is Paolo Veronese's *Adoration of the Shepherds* in the Cappella del Rosario.

Part of eastern Castello is occupied by the **Arsenale** ❹, the great shipyard of the republic where Venice's galleys were built and refurbished. It is now largely abandoned and inaccessible to the public, but you can explore parts of it during the Art Biennale, and there is an excellent **Naval Museum** (Mon–Fri 8.45am–1.30pm, Sat until 1pm; charge) alongside the main entrance gate. To the east of the public gardens is the site of the **Art Biennale** ❹, an international exhibition of modern art (held in odd-numbered years; *see page 424*).

Island excursions

Beyond "central Venice", yet reached on regular ferries, the scattered lagoon islands make a refreshing retreat from hardcore culture and the summer crowds. The island of **San Michele**, just north of Venice, is occupied by the cemetery (summer 7.30am–6pm, until 4pm in winter) and the early Renaissance church of San Michele in Isola, designed by Coducci. As the first church faced in white Istrian stone, San Michele was the model for similar churches throughout the Veneto.

Napoleon, who forbade burials in the historic centre, established the cemetery. Ezra Pound and Igor Stravinsky were two of the eminent visitors to Venice who are buried here. As the island closest to Venice, it is served by ferries from the Fondamente Nuove.

Further north, the island of **Murano,** which resembles a smaller-scale Venice, has been the centre of the city's glass-blowing industry since the 13th century, when factories were moved from the centre for fear of fire. The **Museo del Vetro** (Thur–Tues 10am– 6pm, until 5pm in winter; charge) is housed in the Fondamenta Giustinian, originally the seat of the bishop of Torcello, which was transferred here after the earlier settlement was abandoned. The museum has exquisite examples of glasswork.

Venice's tiny lace industry is based in **Burano,** northeast of Venice. This is a colourful island where canals are lined by brightly painted fishermen's cottages, unpretentious seafood restaurants and stalls selling lace. For a flavour of rural Venice, cross the footbridge to the island of **Mazzorbo** and visit **Venissa** (tel: 041-527 2281),

recently rescued as Venice's sole vineyard. The Veneto wines can be sampled over dinner with bed an option if you overindulge on Bisol Prosecco (*see page 410*).

Torcello, the most remote of these islands (an hour by ferry), is the least populated and, for many, the most interesting. This rural, marshy island was the site of the original settlement in the Venetian lagoon. Still standing is the magnificent Byzantine cathedral. A large striking mosaic of the Virgin, standing above a frieze of Apostles, decorates the chancel apse of the church, while the entire western wall is covered by a huge and elaborate mosaic depicting *The Last Judgement*.

To the south of Venice, on a different route, lies the **Lido,** where Thomas Mann's unhappy Aschenbach loitered too long, feasting his tired eyes on the unattainable boy Tadzio, and died of cholera. The Lido is no longer the fashionable resort depicted in *Death in Venice*, but in the hot summer months, when the city and its sights can be overwhelming, the sands and sea air provide a welcome break. ❑

The church of Santa Maria Assunta in Torcello.

BELOW: colourful houses in Torcello.

LIFE AS A MASQUERADE

Carnival in Venice is supreme self-indulgence, a giddy round of masked balls and private parties suggesting mystery and promising romance

In Venice, Carnival is a 10-day pre-Lenten extravaganza, culminating in the burning of the effigy of Carnival on Shrove Tuesday. Carnival represents rebellion without the risk of ridicule. The essence of the "feast of fools" lies in the unfolding Venetian vistas: processions of plague doctors, doges, nuns and Casanovas swan past shimmering palaces, passing surreal masqueraders tumbling out gondolas. As the revellers flock to Florian's café or pose by the waterfront, the air is sickly sweet with the scent of fritters and the sound of lush Baroque music. Carnival capers include costumed balls, bands, firework displays and historical parades. In an attempt to reclaim Carnival, the Venetians are shifting celebrations to the neighbourhoods, but the set-pieces and the crowds still congregate on St Mark's Square.

SPIRIT OF RESISTANCE

Carnival is often dismissed as crassly commercialised, but Venetian traditionalists view it differently. The leader of a venerable Carnival company sees the event as saving his city: "Life in Venice is inconvenient and costly. With the Carnival, we give a positive picture and show the pleasure of living here. Carnival is a form of resistance. By resisting the temptation to leave, we are saving the spirit of the city for future generations."

ABOVE: masks originally allowed the nobility to mingle incognito with the common people in *casini* (private clubs), but are now an excuse for all-purpose revelry.

LEFT: the painted white mask is a popular disguise. It is a modern variant on the slightly sinister *volto*, the traditional Venetian mask.

LEFT: a mask makes everyone equal. Masqueraders are addressed as *"sior maschera"* (masked gentleman) regardless of age, rank or even gender.

RIGHT: costumes can be historical, traditional or simply surreal. You can hire out noble Renaissance and rococo costumes in all their finery.

BELOW: the classic Venetian disguise of the 17th and 18th centuries was known as the *maschera nobile*, the patrician mask, and you will see many varieties of this in the city.

MASTERS OF DISGUISE

Mask-makers had their own guild in medieval times, when a *mascheraio* (mask-maker) helped a secretive, stratified society run smoothly. Venetians wore masks for about six months a year, with the *bauta*, the expressionless white mask, the most common disguise. Masks were a ploy for protecting the identity of pleasure-seeking Venetians, from secret gamblers to lascivious priests and un-virginal nuns.

Modern masqueraders can follow suit, choosing between the deathly-white *volto* mask, the gaudy harlequin, the rococo courtesan, or the sinister black-caped plague-doctor, with his white-beaked mask. *Columbina* (Columbine) is the elegant domino mask; more catlike and seductive is the *civetta* (flirt).

Traditional masks are made of leather or papier-mâché, but contemporary creations can be ceramic or silk. If seeking inspiration, study Pietro Longhi's exquisite Carnival paintings, which hang in Ca' Rezzonico. To don a stunning disguise, visit Atelier Nicolao, the most authentic costumier's (www.nicolao.com; tel: 041-520 7051). Choose a cloak and handcrafted mask or rent a full costume and slip back into Casanova's era. Nicolao designed the costumes for *Casanova* and can turn anyone into a convincing Latin lover or Venetian courtesan.

RIGHT: you will see amazing fantasy masks on display in shop windows; they are creative rather than authentic, and appeal to individual tastes.

THE VENETO

Although Venice reigns supreme, the Veneto also embraces romantic Verona, Palladian Vicenza, Giotto's Padua – and a countryside dotted with wine trails

At first sight the terra firma towns pale into insignificance before **Venice ❶** *(see pages 171–85)*, the shimmering capital. Yet in the Veneto's civilised cities and landscaped countryside, trade with the famed republic has left a legacy of impressive merchant palaces and Palladian villas. This is one of Italy's artiest regions, linked to legendary painters such as Giotto, Bellini, Tiepolo and Veronese. These were all artists of colour and light, who reflect the chameleon qualities of the shimmering lagoon city of Venice.

The Veneto stretches up into the apricot-tinged Dolomites and Cortina d'Ampezzo, but is bordered by the Adriatic in the east, Lake Garda in the west *(see page 231)*, and the River Po to the south. Orchards, river valleys and vineyards dot the region, which is noted for sparkling Prosecco, Valpolicella and Merlot. Between Venice and Padua, the bucolic **Brenta Canal** *(see page 192)* winds languidly through the noble countryside, with Palladian villas, formal gardens and farms lining the banks.

Shakespeare called **Padua ❷** (Padova) "Fair Padua, nursery of Arts", and described it as a place where Renaissance Englishmen came to "suck the sweets of sweet philosophy". Dante and Galileo both lectured here, and in the mid-17th century a learned woman earned a doctorate here, the first woman in Europe to do so. (Padua's most famous daughter is, without doubt, Katherina, Shakespeare's tameable shrew.)

Padua is Italy's second-oldest university city (after Bologna), but long before the university was established in 1222, Padua was an important Roman town, and the birthplace of the Roman historian Livy. Padua is also a magnet for the faithful. Every June, pilgrims come from all over the world to honour St Anthony of Padua, a 13th-century itinerant preacher whose spellbinding sermons packed churches.

The **Basilica di Sant'Antonio** (daily

LEFT: Basilica di Sant'Antonio, Padua.

6.20am–7pm, 7.45pm in summer), built over his remains between 1232 and 1307, celebrates his sanctity handsomely, notably with works by Donatello (who lived in Padua 1443–53). **Venice** is, of course, very close to Padua, and Venetian influence is evident in the church's design. Byzantine domes, an ornate facade and two slender bell-towers give the exterior an oriental appearance.

Padua's piazzas

In **Piazza del Santo**, to one side of the basilica, stands Donatello's famous equestrian statue *Gattamelata*. This sculpture of the great Venetian *condottiere* (mercenary) is believed to be the first great bronze cast in Italy during the Renaissance. Also in the piazza is the **Oratorio di San Giorgio** (9am–12.30pm and 2.30–7pm, closes at 5pm in winter; charge), originally a private mausoleum but best known for an oratory decorated with Giotto-esque frescoes. On the square is the **Scuola di Sant'Antonio** (daily 9am–12.30pm and 2.30–7pm in summer, until 5pm in winter; charge), with paintings by Bellini, Titian and Giorgione.

Via Belludi leads to another notable piazza, the **Prato della Valle**, centred on a small park bounded by four stone bridges and a circular moat. In the park, a circle of statues represents famous past citizens of Padua.

The lively **Piazza delle Erbe** is home to the **Palazzo della Ragione**, known as **Il Salone** (Tues–Sun 9am–7pm, until 6pm Nov–Jan; charge). Designed as law courts in 1218, this is the largest undivided medieval hall in Europe. Coats of arms adorn the facade, while the frescoed interior houses a large wooden horse copied from Donatello's bronze masterpiece.

Behind Il Salone is **Caffè Pedrocchi**, famous as a gathering place for intellectuals during the Risorgimento *(see page 59)*, and today still a popular meeting place for conversation or jazz sessions.

A short walk through **Piazza dei Signori** leads to Padua's **Duomo**. Although the cathedral was designed by Michelangelo, subsequent rebuilding and alterations make for a rather disappointing result, unlike the magnificent frescoed baptistery (Mon–Sat 7.30am–noon and 3.30–7.30pm, Sun

BELOW: Giotto's fresco cycle in the Cappella degli Scrovegni.

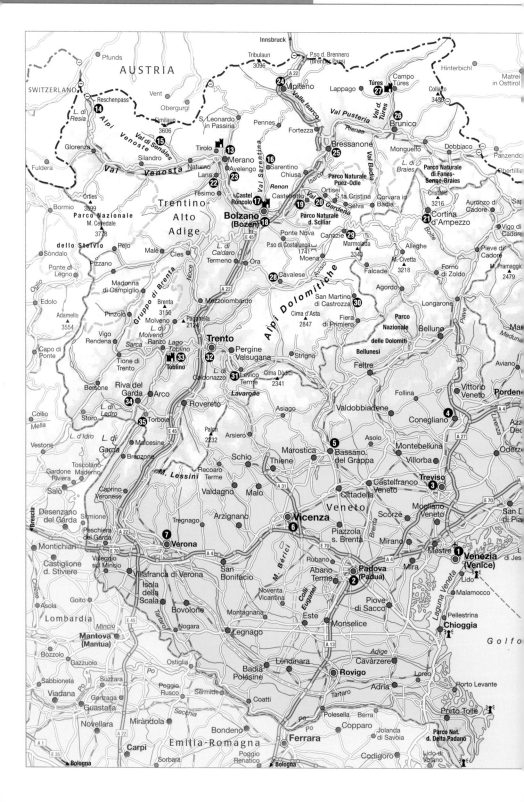

Northeastern Italy

AUSTRIA

Heiligenblut

Obervellach

Winklern

Möllbrücke

Spittal an
der Drau

Greifenburg

Oderdrauburg

Kötschach-
Mauthen

Kirchbach

Gmünd

Döbriach

Radenthein

Techendorf

Mösel
Hermagor

S. Stefan

Villach

Alpi Carniche

Paluzza

Comeglians

Pontebba

Tolmezzo

Chiusaforte

Podkoren

J.di Montasio
2754

Sella Nevea
2571

Friuli
Venezia
Giulia

Gemona
del Friuli

Tarcento

Zaga

Kobarid

Bohinjska
Bistrica

S. Daniele
d. Friuli

Spilimbergo

Cividale
del Friuli

Tolmin

Udine

SLOVENIA

Codroipo

Cormons

Gorizia

Castions
di Strada

Palmanova

Ajdovscina

Cervignano
d. Friuli

Latisana

Aquileia

Monfalcone

Castello di
Duino

Sezana

Lignano
Sabbiadoro

Grado

Castello di
Miramare

Barcola

Trieste

Kozina

Caorle

Bibione

Golfo di
Trieste

Koper

Umag

Buje

Buzet

CROATIA

Venezia

Porec

Baderna

Pazin

Vrsar

Zminj

Rovinj

ADRIATIC

SEA

Pula

0   20 km
0   20 miles

N

8am–1pm and 3.30–8.45pm; baptistery daily 10am–6pm; charge).

Miser's Madonna

To the north of the university lies the **Cappella degli Scrovegni** (daily 9am–7pm; by appointment only, every 15 minutes; tel: 049-201 0020; charge includes Eremitani Museum). Enrico Scrovegni commissioned this richly decorated chapel in 1303 to atone for his father's miserliness and usury. Inside is Giotto's masterpiece, a fresco cycle dedicated to the Virgin, the Life of Christ and the Last Judgement. The solidity and emotional depth of the figures marked a turning point in Western painting. As Giorgio Vasari noted in the 17th century: "painters owe to Giotto, the Florentine painter, exactly the same debt they owe to nature, which constantly serves them as a model and whose finest and most beautiful aspects they are always striving to imitate and reproduce."

Thankfully, the chapel escaped the fate of the nearby **Eremitani** church whose apse, covered with precious Mantegna frescoes, was bombed during World War II – Italy's greatest art loss of the war.

This bare church stands in poignant contrast to the rich collection of paintings, frescoes, bronzes and mosaics in the **Eremitani Museum** (daily 9am–7pm; charge includes Scrovegni Chapel) alongside, which displays Bellini's *Portrait of a Young Suitor* and Tintoretto's *The Crucifixion*.

Garden of Venice

Underrated **Treviso ❸**, often dubbed "the garden of Venice", makes a tranquil base from which to explore Venice and the Palladian countryside, with the lagoon city a mere 30 minutes away by train. Treviso is more a living city than a museum city so its charms are subtle, centred on picturesque canals and a self-consciously slow pace of life. The prettiest spot is the **Buranelli Canal**, which reveals pastel palaces, quaint bridges and tiny inns tucked into the backstreets – in contrast to the designer boutiques and hip bars elsewhere in town.

North of Treviso, Prosecco country beckons. **Conegliano ❹** boasts Europe's oldest wine school, while neighbouring

Cruising the Brenta Canal

Inspired by Palladian masterpieces around Padua, Vicenza and Treviso, the villas along the Brenta Canal reflect gracious country living

The Brenta Canal (36km/22 miles) is a placid showcase for Venice's rural treasures, sumptuous villas which are regularly open to visitors. This limpid area linking Venice and Padua is known as the Riviera del Brenta, reflecting its role as a summer retreat for the Venetian nobility. In echoes of the Grand Tour, visitors can take a canalboat along the Brenta to Padua, passing over 50 sumptuous villas. The route involves nine swingbridges and five locks, a reminder that there is a 10-metre (33ft) difference in water level between Venice and Padua.

The Veneto possesses the blueprint for the patrician villa, a harmonious rural retreat framed by waterside formal gardens and a working farm estate. Characterised by a classical portico, and modelled on a Graeco-Roman temple, these Palladian gems have influenced architectural styles the world over. From Renaissance times, the Venetian nobility commissioned these residences as retreats from the summer heat. The villa also represented the glorification of the dynasty and a practical investment of profits earned from maritime trade. In summer, the villa became a society haunt, originally a focus for humanist gatherings, but later a setting for lavish festivities, notably gambling, a Venetian vice. To this end, most villas have a *barchessa*, a colonnaded wing used as a summer house, banqueting hall or gambling pavilion.

From Venice, the first masterpiece is Villa Foscari, better known as **La Malcontenta** because of its troubled romantic past. This distinctive villa was designed for the Foscari family, and is still owned by their descendants. Raised on an elevated pedestal to protect it from floods, it has a temple-like facade mirrored in the Brenta and a vaulted *piano nobile* modelled on the interiors of Roman baths.

Further along, set on a scenic bend in the canal, is **Villa Widmann**, decorated in fanciful French rococo style. The galleried ballroom is adorned with Arcadian scenes. The grounds are lined with cypresses, horsechestnut and limes, and dotted with neoclassical statuary, centred on an ornamental lake. Barchessa Valmarana, which faces Villa Widmann across the water, is all that remains of a villa destroyed in the early 20th century to avoid death duties. Although reduced to its colonnaded guest wings, this glorious relic has been restored and contains frescoes rivalling its more famous neighbours.

Closer to Padua is **Villa Pisani**, a palatial masterpiece which owes much to French classicism. A ballroom frescoed by Tiepolo is matched by grandiose grounds dotted with follies, an appropriate setting for Mussolini and Hitler's first meeting in 1934. At Stra, just beyond Villa Pisani, looms **Villa Foscarini Rossi**, a testament to the ambitions of the Foscarini dynasty, including Doge Foscarini, a past owner. The Palladian-inspired villa contains Baroque *trompe l'œil* frescoes depicting allegories of war and peace, science and the arts. The heroic adventurer Lord Byron, a previous resident, must have felt at home.

The best way to explore the Brenta Canal is on a cruise from Venice or Padua, with a bus making the return trip. Several companies offer Brenta boat trips between March and October, including visits to several villas and an optional lunch included. **Il Burchiello** (www.ilburchiello.it; tel: 049-820 6910) and **I Battelli del Brenta** (www.battellidelbrenta.it; tel: 049-876 0233) are two recommended tour companies. ❏

LEFT: Villa Foscari, better known as La Malcontenta.

Valdobbiadene is awash with tastings in wine bars. Prosecco can be downed with *cicchetti*, Venetian tapas, such as marinated artichokes, meatballs in deep-fried breadcrumbs, or polenta topped with creamy salt cod. But for a serious tasting in a Palladian-style ambience, Villa Barbaro *(see page 194)* is an atmospheric villa-estate. Any sparkling Prosecco trail around Treviso swiftly turns into a Palladian parade.

Towards Vicenza, **Bassano del Grappa ❺** is a delightful old town noted for **Palladio's Bridge**, dating from 1569, but faithfully rebuilt after war damage. The bridge, supported by four trapezoidal piers and topped by a trussed roof, was designed in wood to offer more flexibility and resistance to the fast-flowing river. At the western end lies **Grapperia Nardini** (tel: 0424-227 741; www.nardini.it), the Veneto's oldest grappa distillery, and an intriguing port of call, not just for those needing something stronger than Prosecco. But between a medicinal grappa and a mellow Prosecco, Palladio could only have opted for the elegance of Prosecco.

Palladio's Vicenza

In **Vicenza ❻** Andrea Palladio *(see panel page 197)* remodelled the city, focusing on private palaces and public buildings, matched by princely villas around Vicenza and Treviso. As the most prominent architect of the Italian High Renaissance, Palladio (1508–80) was given free rein by the Vicenza gentry. As a result, there is hardly a street in central Vicenza not graced by a Palladian mansion, despite the destruction of 14 of Palladio's buildings in World War II. Palladio's glorious architecture led Unesco to declare the city a World Heritage site.

In **Piazza dei Signori**, at the city's heart, stand two of Palladio's masterpieces. The newly restored **Basilica**, his first major work, is not a church but a remodelling of a Gothic courthouse (called *basilica* in the Roman sense – a place where justice is administered). Palladio's elegant design features two open galleries, the lower one with Tuscan Doric columns and the upper one with Ionic columns. Facing the Basilica is the **Loggia del Capitaniato**, a later Palladian work commissioned in 1571

TIP

To find out about unusual tours around Treviso, from wine-tasting to villas, contact Guide Veneto (www.guideveneto.it; tel: 0422-56470) and the helpful tourist office Marca Treviso (www.marcatreviso.it; tel: 0422-541 052).

BELOW: Palladio's Villa Capa (La Rotonda), outside Vicenza.

EAT

Near Vicenza, Molin Vecio (tel: 0444-585 168; www.molinvecio.it) is a converted mill offering "authentic" Palladian feasts based on noble 16th-century fare, from sweet and sour onions to artichoke risotto, beef stewed in juniper and candied fruit tart.

to honour the victory over the Turks at Lepanto.

The rebuilt city's Gothic-style **Duomo** stands just behind the Basilica and is crowned by a Palladian cupola. North of the Duomo is **Corso Palladio**, the city's main street, lined with fine residences. Number 163 is the so-called **Casa del Palladio**, distinguished by its classic lines and precise geometric proportions. But the embodiment of the Palladian urban style is **Palazzo Chiericati**, in Piazza Matteotti, at the end of Corso Palladio. This harmonious mansion houses the **Museo Civico** (Tues–Sun 10am–7pm; charge) and an art collection including Tintoretto's *Miracle of St Augustine* and works by Flemish artists.

The **Teatro Olimpico** (Tues–Sun 9am–5pm; charge) is the city's greatest sight, a perfect example of Renaissance architecture. The still functioning theatre is a wood-and-stucco structure with a permanent stage-set of a piazza and streets in perfect perspective. Built between 1580–82, the world's oldest surviving indoor theatre was Palladio's theatrical last gasp.

The Palladian Trail

The following are just a few of the delightful villas that can be visited from Vicenza and Treviso. Set on a low hill outside Vicenza, Villa Capra is better known as **La Rotonda** (grounds: mid-Mar–mid-Oct Tues–Sun 10am–noon, 3–6pm; interior: Wed only, same hours, by appointment; tel: 0444-879 0879; charge). La Rotonda is an architectural set-piece, a stage for admiring the undulating view. Inspired by the Pantheon in Rome, the cube-shaped villa-temple is topped by a shallow dome.

At Maser, near Treviso, **Villa Barbaro** (Villa di Maser; tel: 042-392 3004; Tues–Sat 10am–6pm, Sun 11am–6pm; July–Aug Tues, Thur, Sat, Sun 10.30am–6pm) is an iconic Palladian villa which still doubles as a wine estate. Often described as the "perfect house" the villa combines grandeur with intimacy and an emotional charge.

At Fanzolo, just west of Treviso, **Villa Emo** (daily 10am–12.30pm, 2.30–5.30pm) resembles a shimmering Greek temple but is as functional as it is decorative. In typical Palladian style,

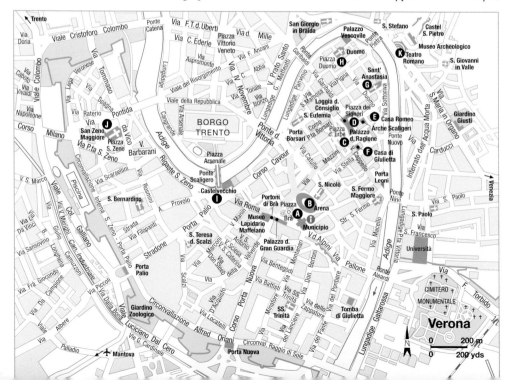

the adjoining farm outbuildings taper into dovecotes. (The carrier pigeons carried messages to Venice in under an hour.)

Inside the villa proper, the "noble floor" is sumptuously frescoed living space, with the kitchens and cellars on the floor below, and the granaries consigned to the roof space.

Between Vicenza and Bassano del Grappa, **Villa Godi Malinverni** (Tues 3–7pm, Sat 9–2pm, Sun 10–7pm) is a Palladian pile which, heretically, puts fine dining before an architectural feast. The **villa's Il Torchio Antico** (tel: 0445-860 358) serves dishes dating from Palladio's day, such as zabaglione with pine nuts, spices and candied peel. Since the Venetian Republic had a monopoly on spices, cinnamon and cloves dominated in Palladio's day, not simply to disguise the smell of suspect meat.

You can even rent **Villa Saraceno**, south of Vicenza (www.landmarktrust.org, visit by appointment Wed only). Palladio's layout has been respected, from the granary to the theatrical grand *sala*, flanked by frescoed apartments and a loggia. The villa is set in gentle countryside, in a setting of plains, poplars and canals unchanged since Palladio's day.

Verona

Built in the distinctive local pink marble, **Verona** ❼ has a rosy hue, as if the sun were constantly setting. What was once a thriving Roman settlement is today one of the most prosperous and elegant cities in Italy. Shakespeare's setting for *Romeo and Juliet* appeals to lovers of all ages. You can now even get married on "Juliet's Balcony". The celebrated Arena di Verona opera season attracts opera buffs to the Roman amphitheatre. The sophisticated centre remains a people-watching parade, from café-studded Piazza Brà to Piazza delle Erbe, once the site of the Roman forum. Verona is also a citadel of consumerism, awash with sunglasses, shoes and jewellery.

The **Piazza Brà** Ⓐ is where the Veronese gather day and night to talk, shop and drink together. They sit or stroll in the shadow of the glorious 1st-century AD Roman **Arena** Ⓑ (Aug–

The winged lion of St Mark in Piazza delle Erbe, Verona.

BELOW: Piazza Brà, Verona.

Relief in the Castelvecchio.

May Tues–Sun 8.30am–7pm, June–July same times plus Mon 8.30am–5pm, last entry one hour before closure; tel: 045-800 3204; charge), the third-largest structure of its kind in existence. The highest fragment, called the Ala, reveals the Arena's original height. It is often used for city fairs and, in summer, up to 25,000 people at a time fill it to attend performances of popular Italian opera – notably Verdi's *Aida* (if you are fortunate enough to get tickets, take a cushion and do not drink for several hours beforehand – the toilets are virtually impossible to reach). *See page 420 for booking details.*

The Roman Forum was located in what is now **Piazza delle Erbe** **C**, off the **Via Mazzini**. This large open space has a quirky beauty, due to the variety of *palazzi* and towers that line its sides. Among the most impressive is the Baroque **Palazzo Maffei**, next to the **Torre del Gardello**, the tallest Gothic structure in the square. The palace with the attractive double-arched windows on the corner of Via Palladio is the medieval guildhouse – the **Casa dei Mercanti**.

The adjoining **Piazza dei Signori** **D** is more formal than its neighbour. The **Palazzo della Ragione**, the Gothic law courts, borders the two squares. The inner courtyard has a delicate Gothic stairway. Opposite rises the **Loggia del Consiglio**, considered the finest Renaissance building in the city. Nearby are the tombs of the della Scala family (the Scaligeri), one-time rulers of Verona. The elaborately sculpted monuments stand outside the tiny church of Santa Maria Antica, surrounded by a wrought-iron fence featuring the family's staircase motif (della Scala means "of the stairs").

Verona is, of course, the city of *Romeo and Juliet*. Though the Capulet and Montague families immortalised by Shakespeare did exist, the story of the star-crossed lovers was entirely fictional. However, what is now a rather seedy bar on the Via delle Arche Scaligeri was allegedly the **Casa Romeo** **E**. Rather better maintained is **Juliet's House** **F** (Tues–Sun 8.30am–7pm, Mon 1.30–7.30pm; charge) at No. 23 Via Cappello, a medieval townhouse complete with balcony, where

BELOW: frescoes in Verona's cathedral.

lovers can now exchange their vows. It is also possible to visit a slightly tacky Juliet shrine. The "tomb" (Tues–Sun 8.30am–7.30pm, Mon 1.45–7.30pm; charge) is several miles out of the centre on Via del Pontiere, along the Lungoadige Capuleti.

If your taste runs to the Gothic, head for **Sant'Anastasia** , which houses a magnificent painting by Pisanello of St George, and frescoes by Altichiero and Turone. Verona's **Duomo** (Mar–Oct Mon–Sat 10am–5.30pm, Sun 1–5.30pm, Nov–Feb Tues–Sat 10am–1pm and 1.30–4pm, Sun 1–5pm; charge) is nearby. Inside is Titian's *Assumption of the Virgin*.

The **Castelvecchio** (Tues–Sun 8.30am–7.30pm, Mon 1.45–7.30pm; charge) on the River Adige is a reminder of one of the grimmer chapters in the history of "fair Verona". The castle was first built in 1354 by the hated tyrant Cangrande II Scaliger for protection if a rebellion occurred. But he met his end not at the hands of the mob but through the treachery and ambition of his own brother, who stabbed him. As elsewhere in Italy, this fortress is now an excellent museum, with works by Veronese and Tiepolo.

A saint and a prophet

Little is known about St Zeno, Verona's patron saint, but his basilica is one of the finest Romanesque monuments in Italy. St Zeno's most famous miracle is depicted by Nicola Pisano on the porch of the **Basilica di San Zeno Maggiore** (Mar–Oct Mon–Sat 8.30am–6pm, Sun 1–6pm, Nov–Feb Tues–Sat 10am–1pm and 1.30–5.30pm, Sun 1–5pm; charge). According to the story, the saint was out fishing when he saw a man being dragged into the Adige by crazed oxen. St Zeno made the sign of the cross and exorcised the devils. The bronze doors of the church are of splendid workmanship.

Most people are drawn to Verona because of *Romeo and Juliet* and other Shakespeare plays which are frequently performed in the **Teatro Romano** , the perfectly proportioned Roman theatre dating from the 1st century BC. The theatre is carved into the hillside in a strategic spot overlooking a bend in the river. ❏

TIP

The Palladio Card (www.palladiocard.it) allows free or discounted access to a collection of the finest Palladian villas, palaces and monuments, from the Teatro Olimpico in Vicenza to Villa Barbaro near Treviso. It can also be booked through the Vicenza tourist office (tel: 0444-994 770).

BELOW LEFT: Romeo's Juliet immortalised in bronze.

Perfect Palladianism

Andrea Palladio (1508–80) was the first modern architect, a stonecutter who changed the way we see the world. If these symmetrical, ghostly villas seem familiar, maybe they've flitted across your screen in *Casanova* or *The Merchant of Venice*. More likely they're simply part of your birthright, an imprint of an ideal home that's both familiar but timeless. The 500th anniversary of the West's most influential architect was celebrated worldwide in 2008.

From the White House to plantation piles in Southern Carolina, Palladianism proffers dignity and status – to connoisseurs or charlatans. We have Palladio to thank for the "classical homes" on executive estates and for footballers' wives' pillared and porticoed mansions. But between Venice and Vicenza, the original Palladian villas wipe the floor.

The Palladian rural retreat represented a perfect "machine for living": although a place for contemplation and noble pursuits, it was also the hub of a prosperous farm estate. In the 16th century, the craze for country living allowed the Venetian nobility to turn to their lands. They could easily believe that the ennoblement of agriculture validated the glorification of the dynasty. Palladio had even grander aspirations. Behind his blueprint for living was a desire to create harmony and set standards for civilised behaviour, values that went well beyond porticoes and pediments.

FRIULI-VENEZIA GIULIA

The influence of successive invaders has given Italy's northeastern corner a cosmopolitan feel, combining flavours of Italy, Austria and Slovenia

The region belongs to everyone and no one. If Trieste feels marooned in Mitteleuropa, Aquileia feels resolutely Roman, Udine feels resolutely Venetian, while the slumbering lagoon resort of Grado feels Byzantine. Since the 2nd century BC – when the Romans took over this corner of the Italian peninsula – Friuli-Venezia Giulia has been a victim of invasions. Attila the Hun earned his nickname "the Scourge of God" here in 452, and in 489 came Theodoric and the Ostrogoths.

Many of today's gracious modern towns began as barbarian outposts, such as **Cividale del Friuli**, which as a result has an outstanding collection of sculpture, jewellery and weapons from this period, displayed in the **Museo Archeologico** (Mon–Sun 9am–7pm; charge) and the **Museo Cristiano** in the cathedral (Mon–Sat 9am–1pm, 3–6pm). A short walk away is the **Tempietto Longobardo** (Mon–Sun 9am–12.30pm, 3–6pm; charge). This prestigious monument is an 8th-century Lombardic relic with fine 14th-century frescoes. Subsequent invaders – the Venetians and the Austrians – left their mark, adding to the cosmopolitan flavour of this region, which shares a frontier with Slovenia.

The border runs through the bilingual city of **Gorizia**, which has a fascinating castle (Tues–Sun 9.30am–1pm,

3–7.30pm; charge) and a small war museum. On the coast, the spa town of **Grado** was founded by the Habsburgs but is today a seaside resort somewhat stuck out on a limb.

Trieste

Of all Friuli's foreign "invaders", perhaps the best known is James Joyce, who arrived in **Trieste ❽** in March 1905. He may not be Trieste's favourite son – he was constantly in debt, often drunk, and given to shouting in the theatre – but the city was to become

his home for the following 10 years.

Today the city has an air of faded elegance. Once Venice's rival for trade on the Adriatic, later the maritime gateway for the Austro-Hungarian Empire, Trieste is now a port without a hinterland, a city that history left behind. In the Città Nuova, long, straight avenues flank a Grand Canal where tall ships once anchored. Southwest of the canal is the café-filled **Piazza dell'Unità d'Italia** – the largest sea-facing piazza in Italy, and a favourite promenade area. On the east side of the piazza stands the ornate **Municipio** (town hall), of 19th-century Austrian inspiration. At its foot, across the railroad tracks, stretches the long quay with its **Acquario Marino** (Tues–Sun 9am–7pm; charge) exhibiting Adriatic and tropical fish.

The Old City

Behind the Municipio are the narrow, winding streets of the **Città Vecchia**. Stairs by the **Teatro Romano** (closed to visitors) ascend steeply to the 6th-century **Duomo di San Giusto**. Two 5th-century basilicas were here com-

bined into a single four-aisled structure in the 14th century. The hill is surmounted by the 15th-century Venetian **Castello di San Giusto** (Piazza Cattedrale 3; daily Apr–Sept 9am–7pm, Oct–Mar 9am–5pm), with a sweeping view of the city and harbour. The **Museo del Castello di San Giusto** (Tues–Sun 9am–1pm; charge) displays a collection of art and weaponry. On your way back down, consider stopping at the **Civico Museo di Storia ed Arte** (Tues–Sun 9am–1pm, Wed until 7pm; charge), which features relics from the invaders and inhabitants of Friuli-Venezia Giulia. Also worth a visit is the 12th-century **Basilica of San Silvestro** on the hillside. Overlooking Piazza Venezia is the **Museo Revoltella** (Via Diaz 27; Mon and Wed–Sun 10am–6pm). This was once the grand residence of Trieste's most important merchant, but now showcases modern art.

Before leaving Trieste, embark on a café crawl; the cosmopolitan port is home to historic, literary cafés that make it the capital of Italian coffee culture. Caffe degli Specchi and Caffe San Marco are just two of the Viennese-

style literary cafés, with creamy-white decor and rich Mitteleuropean cakes.

Fairytale castles

Seven km (4 miles) west of Trieste, set in lush green gardens, is the fairytale **Castello di Miramare** ❾, near the seaside town of **Barcola**. A mock medieval fortress, it was the summer home of Archduke Maximilian. This was his dream palace, built with his wife Charlotte, daughter of Leopold I of Belgium, between 1856 and 1860. Set on a promontory overlooking the sea, with rooms resembling the interiors of ships, this is Italy's best relic of the Austro-Hungarian Empire. A museum (daily 9am–7pm, park 9am–7pm; charge) honours the ill-fated archduke, who later became Emperor of Mexico and died in front of a revolutionary firing squad.

Castello di Duino ❿ (9.30am–5.30pm Wed–Mon; charge), just along the coast, is an equally splendid castle, a medieval affair with delightful grounds, sweeping seascapes and a romantic cliff-side walk.

Only 15km (9 miles) from Trieste is the **Grotta Gigante** (Giant Cave; guided tours Tues–Sun in summer every half-hour 9am–noon and 2–6pm, in winter every hour 10am–noon and 2.30–4pm; tel: 040-327 312; charge). This vast cavern is part of an underground river system.

Roman and Venetian towns

The Romans based their Northern Adriatic fleet at **Aquileia** ⓫, which now lies several miles inland. Here is the ruin of a once-vast harbour, dating from the 1st century AD. Best of all is the **Basilica** (daily, summer 9am–7pm, winter 9am–1pm and 2–5pm), begun in AD 313. The stunning Roman mosaic floor depicts biblical tales and mythological scenes. Stretching the entire length of the nave, it was laid down in 314, but the current building was consecrated in 1031 under Patriarch Poppo, who had the mosaics covered. They did not see daylight again until 1909, and in 2000 a major restoration took place.

Udine ⓬ has an appealing style all its own. Echoes of Venetian rule are everywhere: the 16th-century **Castello** that towers over the city was built as the residence for Udine's Venetian governors and now houses the city's art and archaeology museums (Tues–Sat 10.30am–7pm). At the foot of the castle hill, the graceful Piazza della Libertà boasts a Gothic, Venetian-style loggia and graceful Renaissance porticoes. The **Galleria d'Arte Moderna di Udine** (GAMUD; Wed–Mon 10.30am–7pm) showcases both Italian and foreign 20th-century art. Tiepolo, the greatest Venetian rococo painter, painted three gold-and-pink chapels in the city's **Duomo**.

Northwest of Udine, the hillside town of **San Daniele del Friuli** produces raw *prosciutto*, and has done since the time of the Celts. Some people consider San Daniele ham to be superior even to Parma ham. San Daniele pigs are kept outside so their flesh is leaner, and their diet of acorns gives it a distinctive flavour. Produced in much smaller quantities than Parma ham, it is even more expensive.   ❏

Every October more than 2,000 sails meet in the Gulf of Trieste. The Barcolana is a 26km (16-mile) nautical route that forms Europe's biggest sailing regatta. It is the only race to set a single start line for so many yachts (www. barcolana.it).

BELOW:
Loggia di San Giovanni, Udine.

TRENTINO-ALTO ADIGE

The limestone peaks of the Dolomites frame an area of castles, lakes and Mitteleuropean-style spas, with its own distinctive mix of Italian and Germanic culture

This mountainous region, which stretches north to the Italian-Austrian border, first came to the attention of tourists in the English-speaking world in 1837 when John Murray, the London publisher, brought out a handbook for travellers. The book's description of the Dolomites sparked interest particularly among mountaineers who had conquered the Swiss Alps and were looking for new challenges: "They are unlike any other mountains, and are to be seen nowhere else among the Alps. They arrest the attention by the singularity and picturesqueness of their forms, by their sharp peaks or horns, sometimes rising up in pinnacles and obelisks, at others extending in serrated ridges, teethed like the jaw of an alligator."

Today, Trentino-Alto Adige is a popular holiday retreat for hikers, skiers and watersports enthusiasts, stretching from Lake Garda to the Dolomites. Here, it is possible to hike around a secluded Alpine lake in the morning, sample wine in an Italian vineyard at noon, stroll along the palm-lined promenade of a Continental spa in the afternoon and then slip into bed in a medieval castle at the end of the day. It is the mix of cultures, as well as the rugged scenery, that make this region so intriguing.

LEFT: paraglider in the Dolomites.
RIGHT: Germanic traditions are still flourishing in this region.

Two provinces: two cultures

Yet Trentino-Alto Adige is an anomaly, reflecting the region's chequered ethnic divide. Each is a province with the mentality of a region. Trentino is resolutely Italian, with a Latin soul, while Alto Adige is decidedly Teutonic and German-speaking, though officially bilingual. Alto Adige also prefers to be known as the Sudtirol (South Tyrol). It belonged to Austria until the end of World War I so still resembles the Austrian Tyrol and feels Tyrolean. In contrast, Trentino, the southern province,

Main attractions
BOLZANO'S "ICE MAN"
ALPE DI SIUSI
THE DOLOMITES
SKI RESORTS
BRESSANONE
HIKING IN TRENTINO
CASTELLO DEL BUONCONSIGLIO
RIVA DEL GARDA

prides itself on looking (and sounding) more Italian, though the subtle distinction is often lost on visitors.

The Germanic traditions, culture and language colour the South Tyrol, despite post-World War I efforts by Mussolini to stamp them out. In a subtle form of ethnic cleansing, the dictator Italianised the names of the towns, mountains and rivers and forbade schools to teach in German. Today the two autonomous provinces tolerate one another but cherish their separate cultural identities and go their own way.

The South Tyrol

In terms of scenery and culture, the South Tyrol resembles the Austrian Tyrol. Here, signs are bilingual, with place names written in both Italian and German, as in Bolzano (Bozen) or Merano (Meran), but German is preferred. The sleepy spa town of **Merano ⑬** (Meran), with its palm-lined promenades, exclusive shops, fine restaurants and Belle Epoque cafes, offers the visitor a taste of Old Europe. Merano has played host to the great and

BELOW: view from the Stelvio Pass, near Venosta Valley.

the gracious for well over a century. Those who can afford it come to relax and take the cure in a Mediterranean-like climate. The city owes its famously mild climate to its position in a deep basin, protected to the north by the massive Alpine peaks and opening to the Etsch Valley in the south. Merano flourished between the late 13th and early 15th centuries, when it was the capital of the Tyrol. Thereafter, it passed into relative insignificance until its value as a spa town was discovered. Merano hosts one of the biggest wine festivals in Italy in the first weekend of November. It also offers "grape cures", which involve a copious diet of grapes for the duration of the regime.

A short distance north of Merano is the romantic **Castel Tirolo** (Schloss Tirol), the ancestral home of the counts of Tyrol, and now an imaginative museum of Tyrolean history (Tues–Sun 10am–5pm). Just down the hill is **Castel Brunnenburg**, where Ezra Pound (1885–1972) spent the last years of his life.

To the west of Merano, the **Venosta** (Vinschgau) Valley extends all the way

to the Swiss–Austrian–Italian border. The route leading over the **Reschen Pass**  was first constructed during Roman times as an important link between Augsburg and the Po Valley. Vinschgauer bread, a speciality of the region which is baked in small flat loaves and flavoured with aniseed, is worth sampling.

The **Val di Senales** ⑮ (Schnals Valley), which branches to the north, just past Naturno, passes through the region of the Similaun glacier. It was here that the 5,000-year-old "Ice Man" was found in 1991. This frozen corpse is now on view in Bolzano.

In the heart of Alto Adige lies the **Val Sarentina** (Sarn Valley), a place where time seems to have stood still. Old farms perch precariously on the mountainsides, rushing brooks carve deep gorges through the mountain walls, and the people themselves, celebrating traditional festivals dressed in colourful costumes, add to the feeling of yesteryear. In **Sarentino** ⑯ (Sarnthein) you can watch the craftsmen at work embroidering leather shoes, braces, handbags and book covers.

The road leading out of the valley towards the provincial capital of Bolzano winds through numerous tunnels before emerging at **Castel Roncolo** ⑰ (Schloss Runkelstein), built on a towering cliff in 1250 and today housing a museum enlivened by Gothic frescoes (Tues–Sun 10am–6pm; charge).

Bolzano

Bolzano ⑱ (Bozen) is a testament to the coexistence of Italian and Germanic cultures in one city. The vibrant old part of the city, centred on Piazza Walther and the arcades of the Via dei Portici, is marked by patrician houses and German Gothic architecture. Adjacent to Piazza Walther is the impressive Gothic **Duomo**, and reputedly the oldest hall church in Alto Adige.

The **Museo Archeologico dell'Alto Adige** (Tues–Sun 10am–6pm, daily July–Aug; charge) has a fascinating collection including, famously, the mummified body of "Ötzi", the Iceman. Found by hikers in the Ötzaler Alps in 1991, the extraordinarily well-preserved remains, including his clothing and copper axe, are estimated to be over 5,000 years old.

The Gothic Duomo in Bolzano.

BELOW: fresco in Castel Roncolo.

Mountains and pasture

From Bolzano a cable car takes visitors on a scenic journey up to the **Renón** (Ritten) **Plateau**, a popular resort area. On a clear day, the views of the Dolomite formations are spectacular.

South of the city, **Schloss Sigmundskron** (Tues–Sun 10am–6pm) is a medieval castle that houses MMM Firnian, the centrepiece of Reinhold Messner's mountain project, spread over five castles. The Dolomites have inspired the Dalai Lama, Pope John Paul II and, of course, Reinhold Messner, the charismatic South Tyrolean mountaineer. This particular castle is dedicated to the inspiration behind mountaineering, and to the South Tyrol in particular.

Just east of Bolzano is the **Sciliar** (Schlern) massif, towering like a great stone fortress above the surrounding area. At its base is the **Alpe di Siusi** (Seiser Alm), Europe's largest expanse of mountain pastureland, comprising almost 50 sq km (20 sq miles) and offering an abundance of hiking and ski trails. Following the road from Sciliar to **Castelrotto ⓳**, one emerges in

the **Val Gardena** (Grödner Valley) ⓴, with the popular ski resorts of **Ortisei** (St-Ulrich), **Santa Cristina** and **Selva** *(see panel below)*. Ortisei is famed for its woodcarving, but many other villages have maintained their craft traditions. Linger over handcrafted lace, embroidered leather – or even a *loden*, that typical Tyrolean coat.

From **Selva**, the Sella Joch Pass winds its way between the jagged peaks of Mount Langkofel and the majestic Sella massif. Travellers through this pass enjoy a panoramic view of the Marmolada, the region's highest mountain, standing at 3,343 metres (10,965ft). This route connects with the Great Dolomite Road which leads east to **Cortina d'Ampezzo ㉑**, in the Veneto, a chic winter resort, and west over the **Costalunga** (Karer Pass) to Bolzano. The road from Bolzano passes the **Catinaccio** (Rosengarten) massif. At twilight, the rose-coloured rays of the setting sun bathe the cliffs of the Rosengarten (literally "rose garden") in red, which is known as the *enrosadira*.

Lana ㉒, located between Bolzano and Merano, is the centre of the apple-

BELOW: Mayen Castle near Lana, nestled in the hills of the South Tyrol.

Skiing in the Dolomites

Dubbed the world's loveliest winter playground, the Dolomites do not disappoint. Even the kitsch après-ski is the perfect antidote to days spent among the stark peaks and spires of the mountains. The resorts, with a few celebrity-studded exceptions, such as Cortina d'Ampezzo and Madonna di Campiglio, are stylish rather than snooty, cosy rather than blasé. The Dolomiti Superski is the world's biggest ski area, offering 1,220km (760 miles) of *pistes* in 12 ski areas, with the 26km (16-mile) Sella Ronda circuit the jewel in the crown. The resorts en route include Ortisei, Selva and ritzy Alta Badia (Corvara, Colfosco and La Villa). The Dolomites resorts offer superb food, from hearty Tyrolean feasts in Alpine inns to Michelin-starred fare in San Cassiano in the Alta Badia *(see page 389)*.

growing region. The parish church in **Niederlana** contains Alto Adige's largest late Gothic altarpiece, over 14 metres (46ft) in height. Across the valley is **Avelengo** ㉓ (Hafling), home of the famous Hafling breed of horses.

In central Alto Adige, the **Isarco** (Eisach) **Valley** has, for the past 2,000 years, served as the major route connecting the German north to the Latin south via the Brenner Pass. The former commercial importance of **Vipiteno** ㉔ (Sterzing), the northernmost town on this route, is still evident today in its patrician houses.

Bressanone

Bressanone ㉕ (Brixen), the region's oldest settlement, was a bishopric from 990 until 1964, when the bishop moved to Bolzano. Interesting sights include the prince-bishop's palace and the Baroque Duomo, which features impressive marble work and fine ceiling frescoes. A stroll through the Gothic cloisters adjacent to the Duomo is worthwhile. The frescoes here, dating from 1390 to 1509, are among the best examples of Gothic painting in the Alto Adige. The Romanesque chapel of St John at the southern end of the cloisters was built as a baptismal church.

Just north of Bressanone, stretching to the east, is the **Pusteria Valley**. The valley's chief town is **Brunico** ㉖ (Bruneck), its main street lined with medieval houses overshadowed by the castle. **Schloss Bruneck**, the site for Messner's fifth castle museum, opens in 2011. From Brunico, the **Túres Valley** leads north to **Castle Túres** ㉗ (Schloss Taufers). This frescoed and fully furnished castle is one of the finest in the South Tyrol (to book a tour tel: 0474-678 053). The Pusteria Valley is the gateway to the Sexten Dolomites, where the majestic Three Pinnacles and the Sexten Sundial formations are located. The latter was used by early astronomers as a point of orientation.

Trentino and the Dolomites

Trentino is an inspirational lakes and mountains destination, with almost 300 lakes and a foothold on Lake Garda. The majestic Dolomites tower over forests, pastures and vineyards – or the

Bilingual road signs.

BELOW: taking to the air in the Dolomites.

ski slopes *(see page 206)*. Whether grey and windswept or bathed sunset-pink, the peaks are inspirational enough to persuade mere mortals to pick up their hiking boots *(see page 426)*. In 2009 the Dolomites were added to Unesco's list of World Heritage sites.

Southeast of Bolzano awaits the rugged landscape around **Cavalese ㉘**, the chief resort for the Val di Fiemme. Both a ski resort and a delightful summer retreat, Cavalese has a sumptuously frescoed medieval town hall.

Further north is **Canazei ㉙**, the centre of the Val di Fassa, and another popular ski and summer destination. Spectacular views of the Dolomites, including the Marmolada, lie in wait at Belvedere, reached by cableway.

Legendary Trails

In the Trentino Dolomites, the scenery may be Tyrolean but the welcome is Italian. The "Legendary Trails" cover the majestic mountains in eastern Trentino and are classic high trails with superb vantage points. This 200km (125-mile) circuit covers the Val di Fiemme, Val di Fassa and Pale di San Martino peaks.

South of Canazei, **San Martino di Castrozza ㉚** basks in typical Dolomites landscape, lying at the foot of the pinnacle-crowned mountains. The **Pale di San Martino** form the main mountain group in the southern Dolomites and are a springboard for hiking excursions. Chair lifts give access to stunning views over glaciers and craggy peaks soaring over meadows and woodland. These mountains also shelter Paneveggio, the magical forest where Stradivarius selected the finest spruce to make his legendary violins.

Here, and in the vertiginous canyons of the Fassa and Fiemme valleys, walkers enjoy stunning views over glaciers and visions of craggy peaks soaring over meadows, forests and Alpine lakes. The scenery spans the lunar landscape of Sass Pordoi, the screes of Catinaccio and dramatic mountain passes. One trail connects San Martino di Castrozza, the Colbricon lakes and Mount Cauriol.

There are hikes to suit walkers of all abilities, with most allowing for easy access back to the valleys, either by cable car, bus, or by pre-arranged pick-up.

BELOW: snow in Brunico.

This allows hikers to stay in cosy, walker-friendly hotels rather than in basic Alpine huts. The Peace Path, in southern Trentino, hugs the former front line in the Great War and is an intriguing trail, running from Austro-Hungarian military fortifications to Roman ruins and vineyards (*see page 25*).

A long winding route leads south to **Levico Terme ③**, a dignified spa resort dotted with Art Nouveau villas. Nearby, **Lago di Caldonazzo** offers swimming, sailing and canoeing.

Trento to Lake Garda

Just west is **Trento ②**, the provincial capital and site of the Council of Trent (1545–63). It was during these sessions, called by the Catholic Church to discuss the rising threat of Lutheranism, that the seeds of the Counter-Reformation were sown. Noteworthy sights include streets lined with frescoed facades, the Romanesque-Gothic **Duomo**, and the **Castello del Buonconsiglio**, one of Italy's grandest castles and the residence of the prince-bishops who ruled the city for centuries. The bastion contains exquisite Gothic frescoes contrasting the noble high life with peasant labours in a cycle of the months (Tues–Sun 10am–6pm in summer, 9.30am–5pm in winter; charge).

Castel Toblino ③, west of Trento, is a romantic lakeside castle, sensitively converted into a restaurant (tel: 0461-864 036) and marks the start of a short walking trail.

Further south, **Riva del Garda ④** lies on the rugged northern tip of Lake Garda. Riva is charmingly sedate, blessed with a castle, compact medieval quarter and lush Mediterranean vegetation. As the most popular resort in the region, it makes a natural base for exploring the lake. Trentino also lays claim to being Italy's most environmentally aware region, with pristine lakes, and a ban on motor boats on its stretch of the sea-like Lake Garda.

Torbole ⑤, Riva's sister resort, is a watersports mecca, where windsurfers race in the afternoon breeze, turning the lake into a flurry of pastel-coloured sails. Yet just beyond the lake loom the jagged pinkish peaks of the ever-present Dolomites, creating the illusion of the Mediterranean meeting the mountains. ❏

TIP

The olive oil estates north of Lake Garda are the most northerly in Italy and remain a port of call for foodies heading to Latin climes.

BELOW: vineyard in Termeno.

Trentino on a Plate

When eating out, expect homely charm and Slow Food in cosy inns and *rifugi*, rustic Alpine lodges which often double as ski huts. The hearty yet refined local cuisine blends Italian and Austrian traditions. Peasant-style dishes with a Tyrolean twist include dumplings *(canederli)*, gnocchi, smoked meats and venison, *finferli* mushroom risotto, and steaming polenta oozing with cheese. The region also produces around a third of Italian sparkling wines, which rival those found in Franciacorta or even Champagne. Other major wines include Marzemino, Mozart's favourite tipple, as well as purplish Teroldego and elegant Pinot Grigio. Look out for the *Osteria Tipica Trentina* logo, which denotes a convivial atmosphere, rustic charm and regional produce, including local wine and juniper-flavoured grappa.

MILAN

For Henry James, Milan's reserved northern European flavour made it more "the last of the prose capitals than the first of the poetic". But there is poetry in Milan in spite of its modernity

Main attractions
THE DUOMO
GALLERIA VITTORIO EMANUELE
LA SCALA
PINACOTECA DI BRERA
CASTELLO SFORZESCO
LEONARDO'S LAST SUPPER
BASILICA DI SANT'AMBROGIO
MUSEO DELLA SCIENZA
QUADRILATERO SHOPPING DISTRICT
MUSEO BAGATTI VALSECCHI

Milan (Milano) is one of the world's fashion capitals, and home to both Leonardo's *Last Supper* and the world's premier opera house, La Scala. Above all, Milan is the centre of business in Italy, and it is here and in provincial Lombardy that the demand for federalism – embodied by the right-wing Northern League – is strongest. The prosperous Milanese are courteous but reserved towards visitors.

There is no better place to begin a tour of Milan than at its spiritual hub, the **Duomo** Ⓐ (daily 8.30am–6.45pm), described by Mark Twain as "a poem in marble". Recently restored, this gargantuan Gothic cathedral (the third-largest church in Europe after St Peter's in Rome and Seville's cathedral) was begun in 1386 but not finished until 1813. Decorating the exterior are 135 pinnacles and over 3,400 marble statues from all periods. The "Madonnina", a beautiful 4-metre (13ft) gilded statue, graces the top of the Duomo's highest pinnacle, soaring 109 metres (358ft) above ground. The building requires continuous restoration and can be treated as a work in progress.

Inside the Duomo

The English novelist D.H. Lawrence called the Duomo "an imitation hedgehog of a cathedral", because of its pointy intricate exterior. But inside the church is simple, majestic and vast. Five great aisles stretch from the entrance to the altar. Enormous stone pillars dominate the nave, which is big enough to accommodate some 40,000 worshippers. In the apse, three large and intricate stained-glass windows attributed to Nicolas de Bonaventura shed a soft half-light over the area behind the altar. The central window features the shield of the Visconti, Milan's ruling family during the 13th and 14th centuries. It was Duke Gian Galeazzo Visconti, the

LEFT: Galleria Vittorio Emanuele.
RIGHT: view from the roof of the Duomo.

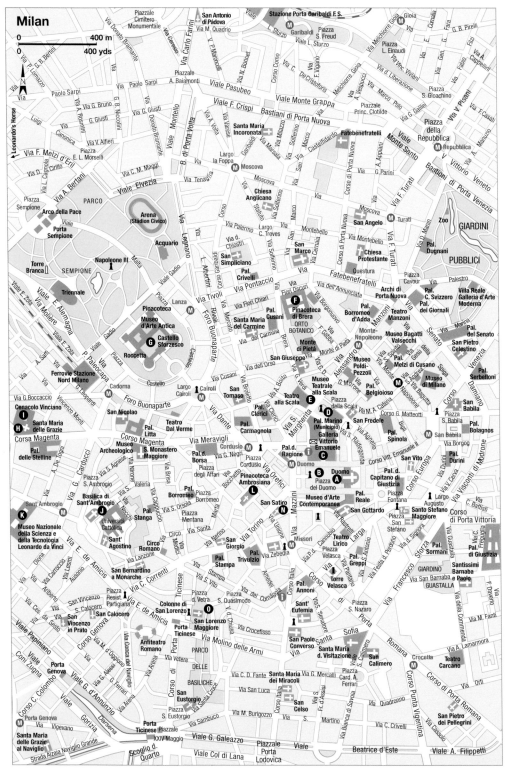

Milan

0 ⎯⎯⎯⎯⎯⎯⎯ 400 m
0 ⎯⎯⎯⎯⎯⎯⎯ 400 yds

Leonardo's Horse

Piazzale Cimitero Monumentale

San Antonio di Pádova
Via M. Quadrio

Stazione Porta Garibaldi F.S.

Gioia

Via Cereso

Via Donato Bramante

Via Carlo Farini

Garibaldi
Piazza S. Freud
Viale L. Sturzo

Piazza S. Gioachino

Piazza L. Einaudi

G. B. Pirelli

Cornalia

Via A. Cappellini

Via Canonica

Paolo Sarpi

Via P. Lomazzo

Via G. B. Bertini

Via P. Maroncelli

Corso Como

Via C. De'Cristoforis

Via d. Liberazione

Via P. L. Lomazzo

Piazzale A. Baiamonti

Viale Pasubeo

Via N. Bonnet

Via N. Vivaiani

Via V. Pisani

Via G. Bruno

Via A. Rosmini

Via G. Giusti

G. B. Niccolini

Via F. Crispi

Viale Monte Grappa

Melchiorre Gioia

Via Vasquez

Via Marco Polo

Via G. Galilei

F. Casati

Via V. Alfieri

Via G. Giusti

Montello

Via A. Volta

Bastiani di Porta Nuova

Piazza della Repubblica

Via Carlo Farini

Santa Maria Incoronata

Via Marsala

Castelfidardo

Fatebenefratelli

Viale Monte Santo

Repubblica

Vittorio Veneto

Via F. Melzi d'Eril

E. L. Morselli

Via C. M. Maggi

Largo la Foppa

Via Solferino

Corso di Porta Nuova

Via G. Parini

Bastioni di Porta Venezia

Via D.

Via L. Cagnola

Via A. Bertani

Viale Elvezia

Moscova

Moscova

Via F. Turati

Via Cirillo

Moscova

Chiesa Anglicano

Via Solferino

Via Montebello

San Angelo

Turati

Zoo

GIARDINI

PARCO

Via Statuto

Largo C. Treves

Via Palermo

Via San Marco

Montebello

Chiesa Protestante

Via F. Turati

Pal. Dugnani

Piazza Sempione

Arco della Pace

Porta Sempione

Arena (Stádion Civico)

Acquario

Via d. Chiostri

San Simpliciano

Pal. Crivelli

San Marco

Via Fatebenefratelli

Questura

Piazza Cavour

PUBBLICI

Torre Branca

SEMPIONE

Napoleone III

Via Gadio

Via L. Alberti

Via Pontaccio

Archi di Porta Nuova

Pal. C. Svizzero

Villa Reale Galleria d'Arte Moderna

Viale E. Zola

Triennale

Via Legnano

Via Tivoli

Via Fiori Chiari

Via Fiori Oscuri

Via Borgonuovo

Pal. Cusani

Pinacoteca di Brera

Borromeo d'Adda

Pal. dei Giornali

Pal. del Senato

Viale E. Alemagna

Via Moliere

Via E. Zola

Pinacoteca

Museo d'Arte Antica

Castello Sforzesco

Piazza Lanza

Foro Buonaparte

Via Mercato

Santa Maria del Carmine

ORTO BOTANICO

F. Gabba

Monte di Pietà

Monte-Napoleone

Teatro Manzoni

San Pietro Celestino

Venezia

Roccetta

Via del Carmine

Brera

San Giuseppe

Via Alessandro Manzoni

Museo Poldi-Pezzoli

Museo di Milano

Pal. Serbelloni

Ferrovie Stazione Nord Milano

Cadorna

Castello

Via Cusani

Via dell'Orso

Via A. Boito

Via Verdi

Museo Teatrale alla Scala

Pal. Belgioioso

Via S. Andrea

Via della Spiga

Corso

Via G. Boccaccio

Foro Buonaparte

Largo Cairoli

Cairoli

San Tomaso

Teatro alla Scala

Piazza della Scala

Via M. A. Colonna

San Damiano

San Babila

Cenacolo Vinciano

San Nicolao

Pal. Clérici

Teatro Dal Verme

Via Dante

Pal. Carmagnola

Via S. Margherita

Pal. Marino (Municipio)

San Fredele

Via S. Agnello

Corso G. Matteotti

Pal. Spinola

Piazza S. Babila

San Babila

Pal. Bolagnos

Santa Maria delle Grazie

Corsa Magenta

Museo delle Stelline

Corso Magenta

Via Meravigli

Via Meravigli

Cordusio

Galleria Vittorio Emanuele

Pal. d. Ragione

Corso Vitt. Emanuele II

San Vito

Pal. del Capitano di Giustizia

San Vito

Corso Europa

Pal. Durini

Via Visconti di Modrone

Pal. delle Stelline

Via A. De Togni

Via Carducci

S. Monastero Maggiore

Pal. d. Borsa

Pinacoteca Ambrosiana

Piazza degli Affari

Via G. Negri

Via Orefici

Duomo

Piazza del Duomo

Duomo

Museo d'Arte Contemporanea

Pal. Reale

San Gottardo

Piazza Fontana

Santo Stefano Maggiore

Corso di Porta Vittoria

Sant'Ambrogio

Basilica di Sant'Ambrogio

Pal. Borromeo

Piazza Borromeo

Pal. Litta

Piazza S. Ambrogio

Via Nirone

Via S. Agnese

Via Brisa

Piazza Borromeo

San Satiro

Via Mazzini

Museo d'Arte Contemporanea

Piazza S. Stefano

Largo Augusto

Pal. Sormani

Museo Nazionale della Scienza e della Tecnologia Leonardo da Vinci

Pal. Stanga

Università Cattolica

Sant'Agostino

Circo Romano

Via Santa Marta

San Giorgio

Via Torino

San Giorgio

Pal. Trivulzio

Via Zebedia

Missori

Teatro Lirico

Pal. Greppi

GIARDINO

Santissimi Barnaba e Paolo

GUASTALLA

Via Cesare Correnti

San Bernardino a Monarche

Piazza Resist. Partigiana

Via C. Correnti

Ticinese

Pal. Stampa

Via S. Vito

Via Mercato

Pal. Annoni

Torre Velasca

Sant'Eufemia

Via Festa del Perdono

Largo Francesco

Pal. di Giustizia

Via Olona

S. Calocero

San Vincenzo

San Calocero

Colonne di San Lorenzo

Piazza della Vetra

S. Quasimodo

Pal. Annoni

San Paolo Converso

Santa Maria d. Visitazione

San Calimero

Teatro Carcano

Viale Papiniano

San Vincenzo in Prato

San Lorenzo Maggiore

Porta Ticinese

Via Molino delle Armi

Anfiteatro Romano

PARCO DELLE BASILICHE

Via Crocefisso

San Celso

Santa Maria dei Miracoli

Card. A. Ferrari

San Pietro dei Pellegrini

Porta Genova

Porta Genova

Santa Maria delle Grazie al Naviglio

Porta Ticinese

San Eustorgio

Piazza S. Eustorgio

Piazzale XXIV Maggio

Darsena

Scoglio di Quarto

Strada Alzaia Naviglio Grande

Viale G. Galeazzo

Piazzale Porta Lodovica

Beatrice d'Este

Corso C. Colombo

Viale Con Zugna

Viale G. d'Annúnzio

Gorizia

Viale Col di Lana

Viale A. Filippetti

Corso di Porta Romana

Corso Punta Vigentina

most powerful member of the family, who commissioned the Duomo.

A gruesome statue of the flayed St Bartholomew, carrying his skin, stands in the left transept. In the right transept is an imposing 16th-century Michelangelo-esque marble tomb made for Giacomo di Medici. The crypt contains the tomb of the Counter-Reformation saint Charles Borromeo, the 16th-century Archbishop of Milan who epitomised the Lombard virtues of energy, efficiency and discipline.

Outside, a lift goes up to the **Duomo rooftops** (9am–noon, 1–6pm; tel: 02-7202 3375; charge) among the pinnacles and carved rosettes. The view is spectacular: on a clear day it stretches as far as the Alps.

Piazza del Duomo

Come down into the well-restored **Piazza del Duomo B**, where Milan's many worlds converge. The large equestrian statue standing at one end of the square honours Italy's first king, Victor Emmanuel (after whom major boulevards in cities throughout Italy are named). The piazza is lined on two sides with porticoes, where Milanese of all ages and styles love to gather. To the north is the entrance to the **Galleria Vittorio Emanuele C**, Italy's oldest and most elegant shopping mall. Its four-storey arcade is full of boutiques, bookshops, bars and restaurants. But, before you sit down to watch the world go by, be forewarned: the cafés here are pricey. Among the Galleria's best cafés and restaurants are the Art Nouveau Camparino at No. 78, a classic spot for an *aperitivo*, especially a Campari – Davide Campari, the inventor of the drink, was born here on the first floor. Another perfect people-watching spot is the Gucci café.

La Scala

At the other side of the Galleria is **Piazza della Scala D**, site of the famed **La Scala** opera house, which has now been opulently restored. It was built between 1776 and 1778 by Giuseppe

Piermarini, and it was here that Verdi's *Otello* and Puccini's *Madama Butterfly* were first performed. The **Museo Teatrale alla Scala E** (Opera House Museum; daily 9am–12.30pm and 1.30–5.30pm; charge) displays a rich collection of memorabilia, including original scores by Verdi, Liszt's piano and other objects connected to great musicians and composers. The visit includes a look into the theatre itself from one of the boxes – as long as there are no rehearsals under way.

Follow the Via Verdi from La Scala to the **Pinacoteca di Brera F** (Tues–Sun 8.30am–7.15pm; for bookings tel: 02-9280 0361; charge), home of one of Italy's finest art collections. Paintings of the 15th to the 18th century are especially well represented. Famous works included in the collection are Mantegna's *The Dead Christ* (viewed from the pierced soles of his feet), Caravaggio's *Supper at Emmaus*, and the restored 15th-century *Madonna and Saints* by Piero della Francesca. Raphael's beautiful *Betrothal of the Virgin (Lo Sposalizio)*, a masterpiece of his Umbrian period,

TIP

Milan's main tourist office has moved to Piazza del Duomo, on the corner of Via Silvio Pellico; tel: 02-7252 4301; www.milanoinfo tourist.com and www. turismo.comune. milano.it.

BELOW: Pinacoteca di Brera.

From 2012 Milan will be at the centre of several high-speed rail networks – the controversial TAV, crossing northern Italy, and which will also tie into new rail networks to southern and eastern Europe, as far as Lisbon and Kiev.

was his first painting to show powers of composition and draughtsmanship far in advance of his biggest stylistic influence, Perugino.

A despot's dwelling

Off the Piazza del Duomo is Via Mercanto. From there, Via Dante leads to the **Castello Sforzesco**  (daily 7am–6pm; museums Tues–Sun 9am–5.30pm), stronghold and residence of the Sforza family, the despotic rulers of Milan in the 15th century (*forza* means strength in Italian). The greatest was Francesco, a mercenary general who became the fourth duke of Milan, and commissioned this Sforza castle.

The residential part of the castle, the Corte Ducale, contains a magnificent collection of sculpture, including Michelangelo's last work, the unfinished *Pietà Rondanini*, an almost abstract work charged with emotion. Michelangelo worked on this *pietà* until within a few days of his death in 1564.

West of the castle stands the church of **Santa Maria delle Grazie**  (daily 7.30am–noon and 3–7pm), begun in

1466 but expanded in 1492 by Bramante, who also built the exquisite cloisters.

The Last Supper

Next door, the **Cenacolo Vinciano**  (Tues–Sun 8.15am–6.45pm; booking essential, visit restricted to 15 minutes; tel: 02-9280 0360; charge), once a refectory for Dominican friars, is home to Leonardo's iconic *Last Supper* (1495–7). Leonardo painted on dry plaster which would allow him more time to retouch the work, using an experimental mix of tempera and oil. However, excessive humidity combined with the faulty mixture used for binding the paint caused the fresco to deteriorate even during Leonardo's lifetime. Restoration of the work began in 1977 and took 22 years to complete.

Whatever your view of its controversial restoration, *The Last Supper* remains a powerful and moving work. It is far larger than expected – some 9 metres (30ft) wide and 4.5 metres (15ft) high. Not all the expressions on the Disciples' faces can be discerned, but the careful composition of the work

BELOW: Leonardo da Vinci's masterpiece, *The Last Supper*.

remains completely clear. On either side of Jesus sit two groups of three Apostles, linked to each other through their individual gestures and glances. It vividly captures the moment when Jesus announces that one of them is about to betray him. This painting was seminal to the perception of the artist as a creative thinker rather than just an artisan. The painting's popularity has been even further enhanced by the huge success of Dan Brown's thriller *The Da Vinci Code*, in which it played a significant role. Do not leave before seeing the equally thrilling **Sacrestia Bramante** (Bramante's Sacristy; Tues–Sun 8.30am–7pm).

From Santa Maria delle Grazie, proceed to the **Basilica di Sant'Ambrogio** ❶ (daily 8am–noon and 2.30–7pm; Via Carducci). Milan's best-loved and most beguiling church is dedicated to the city's patron saint, St Ambrose.

The church is dark and low, but compelling in its antiquity. Founded between 379 and 386 by St Ambrose, then Bishop of Milan – it was he who converted St Augustine – the basilica was enlarged first in the 9th century and again in the 11th. The brick-ribbed square vaults that support the galleries are typical of Lombardic Romanesque architecture. The **Museo della Basilica** (daily 10am–noon and 3–5pm; charge) displays illuminated manuscripts.

Leonardo in Milan

Down Via San Vittore is the **Museo della Scienza e della Tecnologia Leonardo da Vinci** ❶ (Tues–Fri 9.30am–5pm, Sat–Sun 9.30am–6.30pm; charge). The highlight is the huge gallery filled with wooden models of Leonardo da Vinci's most ingenious inventions. It remains one of the most important science and technology museums in the world. Don't miss the reconstruction of his famous flying machine.

Return in the direction of the Duomo to the **Pinacoteca Ambrosiana** ❶, an art gallery founded by Cardinal Federico Borromeo in 1618, along with a frescoed library that also displays designs by Leonardo da Vinci (Tues–Sun 9am–7pm; for bookings tel: 051-588 1589; www.ambrosiana.eu; charge). The newly restored gallery

Scooting around the city in style.

Fashion for Foodies

Visitors come to Milan as much to shop and dine as to take in Leonardo's *Last Supper*. As with the fresco, you will need to book in advance if you plan to eat at a top establishment. One is the chic but approachable **Acanto** (Principe di Savoia, Piazza della Repubblica 17; tel: 02-659 5838), where you can try the definitive *risotto alla Milanese*. It is a place for superb food and posing in style, as befits Donatella Versace's favourite haunt. Just as exclusive is the two Michelin-starred **Cracco,** at Via Victor Hugo 4, where you can enjoy gourmet creative cuisine, including asparagus ravioli with black truffles (tel: 02-876 774). **Sadler** in the Navigli district (Via Asciano Sforza 77; tel: 02-5811 2343) is another Michelin-studded temple to gastronomy, but for exceptionally good value try its stylish offshoot, **Chic' n Quick** (tel: 02-8950 3222; same address). If your budget doesn't allow for the full gastronomic blow-out, you can always shop for picnic ingredients at **Gastronomia Peck**, Via Spadari 9 (tel: 02-802 3161), choosing from the enticing selection of top-quality gourmet cheeses, meats and pastries on display. When in the *Quadrilatero*, at the junction of Montenapoleone and Sant'Andrea, seek refuge from the haughty sales staff in the Caffè Cova. *For more restaurant recommendations in Milan, see page 404.*

*Mannequin wearing
Emilio Pucci.*

(same times) houses an art collection dating from the 15th to the 17th century. Most notable among the works are Leonardo's *Portrait of a Musician*, Titian's *Adoration of the Magi* and Caravaggio's *Basket of Fruit*.

Leonardo da Vinci is inextricably linked to Milan, even if Milan is rarely linked to the Renaissance. Apart from his celebrated *Last Supper* and the ingenious inventions on display in the Museum of Science, Leonardo, with his passion for hydraulic engineering, also designed the complex locks in Milan's Navigli canals. Leonardo was the complete Renaissance Man, at home with art, astronomy, mechanics and warfare. Nowhere is this revealed better than in the Sacrestia Bramante, Bramante's Renaissance sacristy, and the Biblioteca Ambrosiana *(see page 215 for both)*, a 17th-century frescoed library, sites chosen to display the polymath's complete Codex Atlanticus folios. The Codex, the largest extant collection of Leonardo drawings and designs, has been in the Ambrosiana since 1637, but can only be displayed properly now (www.ambrosiana.eu).

Fashion avenue

For a break from culture and sightseeing, stroll down **Via Montenapoleone** Ⓜ, which extends off Corso Vittorio Emanuele between the Duomo and Piazza Santa Babila. The "Vie" Montenapoleone, Sant'Andrea, della Spiga and Manzoni are home to great designer shops. *(For more on the fashion scene, see page 218.)*

Also within Milan's designer area is the eccentric **Museo Bagatti Valsecchi** (Via Gesù; Tues–Sun 1–5.45pm; charge). The Bagatti Valsecchi brothers were avid collectors, and commissioned period-style furnishings from skilled Lombard craftsmen in order to recreate an authentic Renaissance atmosphere in their own home. The resulting museum, housed in a delightful neo-Renaissance palazzo, is a collector's paradise, where it is fun to try to distinguish authentic 16th-century pieces from the reproductions.

In this cutting-edge city, cutting-edge art is showcased at the **Padiglione d'Arte Contemporanea** (**PAC**) (Via Palestro 14; times vary depending on exhibitions; www.comune.milano.it/

pac). Large, experimental works of contemporary art feature in all their forms in this museum.

The **Museo Poldi-Pezzoli** (Via Alessandro Manzoni 12; Tues–Sun 10am–6pm; www.museopoldipezzoli. it; charge) is a treasure trove amassed by the wealthy Giacomo Poldi-Pezzoli in 1881. The interior is a testament to 19th-century patrician tastes, filled with paintings (by Botticelli, Bellini, Piero della Francesca and Mantegna), jewellery, porcelain, timepieces and sundials, tapestries, ancient armaments and period furniture.

If you have time, two more churches are worth seeking out. In the Via Torino, near the Piazza del Duomo, stands **San Satiro** ⓝ, built by Bramante in 1478–80. Inside, the architect cleverly used stucco to create an illusionistic effect, giving the impression that the church is far larger than it actually is. **San Lorenzo Maggiore** ⓞ, nearby on Corso di Porta Ticinese, attests to Milan's antiquity. The basilica was founded in the 4th century and rebuilt in 1103. Martino Bassi restored it in 1574–88, but its octagonal shape

and many beautiful 5th-century mosaics are original. The vast dome creates an awe-inspiring interior.

Milan's expansion

Much like the Duomo, Milan is a work in progress, building with more panache than anywhere else in Italy, for good or ill. Milan is doubling the reach of its metro system, creating three expressways and upgrading its railways. Dilapidated industrial areas are being transformed, and Futurist-style districts being created, including "Fashion City".

But the major redevelopment project, comparable with London's 2012 Olympic site, is EXPO 2015, designed to relaunch Milan as a model of urban renewal. Elsewhere, historical districts, such as the **Navigli canal quarter**, the bohemian entertainment centre (see margin), are also being given a facelift. Milan continues to open new galleries, including the **Triennale** design centre (see page 219). One would expect nothing less revolutionary from a city where Leonardo da Vinci made such a mark. ❑

SHOP

Navigli, the engaging canal quarter. has some excellent markets. Every Saturday the Darsena and Naviglio Grande are taken over by the Fiera di Senigallia, with stallholders displaying bric-a-brac along the canal banks. At night, the clubs and bars take over.

BELOW: the renovated Navigli quarter.

Planet Fashion

Milan has become a brand, Planet Fashion, a glitzy galaxy where you can live by fashion alone – but the designers also give something back

After waking up in Frette sheets in the **Bulgari** design hotel (Via Privata Fratelli Gabba), you can have breakfast in the glass-domed Gucci café, trim your designer stubble at the Dolce & Gabbana barber and take a dip in Giorgio Armani's new spa retreat. That's before sipping cocktails in **Just Cavalli**, attending the opera at La Scala and/or dining nearby in the fashion designers' **Trussardi alla Scala** (Piazza della Scala 5; tel: 02-8068 8201). Afterwards, dance the night away (on a beige carpet, naturally) in **Privé**, Armani's exclusive nightclub.

Not that the Milanese designers are all vapid airheads. A Milanese tradition of patronage of the arts means that many major designers boast lofty cultural foundations. **Fondazione Prada** (Via Fogazzaro 36) favours contemporary art exhibitions, as does **Trussardi** *(as above)*.

Piazza Duomo is as good a spot as any to plan a shopping campaign. Overlooking the cathedral is

Rinascente, the city's slick department store, where Giorgio Armani started his career as a window-dresser. From here, fashionistas will be drawn to the designer honey-pots of the Golden Triangle. Known as the **Quadrilatero d'Oro**, this chic (but physically square) fashion district is bounded by Via della Spiga, Via Manzoni, Via Montenapoleone, Via Sant'Andrea and Corso Venezia.

In this partly pedestrianised district, discreet courtyards and classical palaces conceal the most ostentatious of international brands. Via Montenapoleone takes in Emilio Pucci, a Prada flagship store, Versace glitz, Gucci glamour, sumptuous cashmere from Loro Piana and Alberta Ferretti. Other designers include Salvatore Ferragamo, Fratelli Rossetti, Valentino, Cartier, Etro and Louis Vuitton. Ultra-chic Via della Spiga is home to Dolce & Gabbana, Moschino, Roberto Cavalli, Agnona – the womenswear arm of Ermenegildo Zegna – as well as Krizia, Sergio Rossi, Bottega Veneta, Tod's, Prada and Bulgari.

A way of life

All the designers are getting in on the lifestyle act, adding spas or bars with gay abandon. **Dolce & Gabbana** menswear emporium (Corso Venezia 15) has a grooming salon and Martini bar. **Roberto Cavalli** (Via della Spiga), where more is always more, responds with a goldfish bowl, a fashionable bar framed by an aquarium with models parading around in the latest tactile collection. Less theatrically, **Armani Superstore** (Via Manzoni 31) pays homage to the master of minimalism and showcases his main collections, as well as his new hotel and spa. Diehard fans will salivate over Armani books, cutlery and designer chocolate in the store's Armani Café and swanky Nobu restaurant partly owned by actor Robert de Niro (tel: 02-6231 2645).

Fashionistas are easily satisfied, but the city also caters to a more conservative set. For dapper Italian politicians, the king of ties is **Angelo Fusco Cravatte Sette Pieghe** (Via Montenapoleone 25). Created as an amusing sideline by Angelo, a practising cosmetic surgeon, the firm produces intricate designer ties made of seven-times-folded jacquard silk, hand-stitched and presented in a wax-sealed box.

For couples with a wedding list, Italy between the sheets is best represented by **Frette** (Via Monte-

LEFT: a Prada shop window with the inevitable tempting display.

kitchenware. Also consider attending the world's finest **Furniture Fair**, Salone del Mobile, which coincides with arty spring events.

Not far from fashion central is the elegant **Brera district**, centred on Via Solferino, and home to upmarket yet bohemian boutiques. The funky **Navigli canal district** is a cool quarter, boasting hip shops and vibrant nightlife. **Via Tortona** is the design centre, with a Design Week in April. Antonioli (Via Pasquale Paoli 1) sells cutting-edge fashion labels in a former cinema, while Kitchen (Via E. De Amicis 45) is packed with cooking utensils and cookbooks. On the rise is the **Garibaldi station district**: its funky design outlets are no longer the wrong side of the tracks but in an old steam factory known as the Fabbrica del Vapore.

A short train ride from Milan, Como is to silk what Milan is to fashion and Venice is to glassware. The city remains the country's leading centre for luxurious silk creations, and is a lovely place to shop. **La Tessitura**, a sleek outlet run by Mantero, Como's famed silk factory, claims to be the world's sole concept store "dedicated to the art of silk". The store is housed in an old textile mill, built in 1870. Combine brunch in the store's Loom Café with live music and shopping for silk (Viale Roosevelt 2A; tel: 031-321 666). Como is a delightful interlude, but Milan's masters of merchandising will soon tempt you back to Planet Fashion.   ❏

napoleone 21). The firm is the leading creator of desirable bed linen, embracing linen sheets, baby blankets, cashmere throws and silk cushions, tempting lovers of luxury.

For those on a non-designer budget, salvation lies in the form of **Il Salvagente** (Via Fratelli Bronzetti 16), one of Milan's most reliable discount outlets for designer clothes.

At the other end of the spectrum, the most beguiling shopping experience in Milan remains the stylish **10 Corso Como** (Corso Como 10; tel: 02-2900 2674; www.10corsocomo.com), Milan's sexiest concept store. Designed by a former fashion editor, this bazaar-like emporium, café and restaurant is the haunt of style gurus and supermodels.

After celebrity-spotting over handbags or home furnishings, slip away from the designer clothes to the store's stylish design gallery or the café in the conservatory (where low-carb menus attract the waif-like models).

Design capital

Milan is as much a design mecca as it is a fashion capital. For inspiration and design history, visit the **Triennale** (Via Alemagna; Tues–Sun 10.30am– 8.30pm), Italy's major design museum.

For cutting-edge furniture and lighting, make tracks for **Via Durini**. Dominating "Design Street" are the rival showrooms of B&B Italia, Armani Casa, Cassina and Meritalia. **High Tech** (Piazza XXV Aprile 12) is an eclectic homeware store housed in a former ink factory. For seductive design icons, **Alessi** (Corso Matteotti 9) is a style guru who specialises in corkscrews and coffee pots, cutlery and

Above: designer shoes to die for.
Right: window-cleaning in style.

LOMBARDY

Beneath is spread like a green sea /
The waveless plain of Lombardy, / Bounded by
the vaporous air, / Islanded by cities fair
– PERCY BYSSHE SHELLEY

F rom the heights of the central Alps to Lake Como and the low-lying plains of the Po Valley, the province of Lombardy is remarkably diverse. The cities of art flourished in medieval and Renaissance times and still maintain their distinct identities. In fact, the land was named after the Lombards, one of the barbarian tribes who invaded Italy in the 6th century. A strong sense of a Lombard identity is still felt locally, including support for separatism in an area that is the stronghold of the Northern League's separatist movement.

Certosa di Pavia

An easy day trip from **Milan ❶**, or a stopover on a journey south, is the **Certosa di Pavia ❷** (Charterhouse of Pavia; May–Sept Tues–Sun 9–11.30am, 2.30–6pm, Oct–Mar until 4.30pm, Apr until 5.30pm). This world-famous church, mausoleum and monastery complex, founded in 1396, is a master-piece of Lombardic Renaissance archi-tecture, complete with relief sculpture and inlaid marble. The interior of the church is Gothic in plan, but highly embellished with Renaissance and Baroque details. Inside stand the tombs of Ludovico Visconti and his child-bride, Beatrice d'Este.

Behind the Certosa is the magnifi-cent Great Cloister where Carthusian monks, who had taken vows of silence, lived in individual dwellings and col-lected meals through a hatch beside the doorway.

Nowadays, Pavia is a backwater, but between the 6th and 8th centuries it was the capital city of the Lombards. Pavia's fame was augmented in 1361 when the university was founded, and to this day it remains a prestigious centre of learning.

On the Via Diacono, in the old centre of town, is the church of **San Michele**, consecrated in 1155. Here

Main attractions
CERTOSA DI PAVIA
MANTUA
PALAZZO DUCALE
ACCADEMIA CARRARA
BERGAMO ALTA
COLLEONI CHAPEL

LEFT: Limone sul Garda.
RIGHT: cloister at Certosa di Pavia.

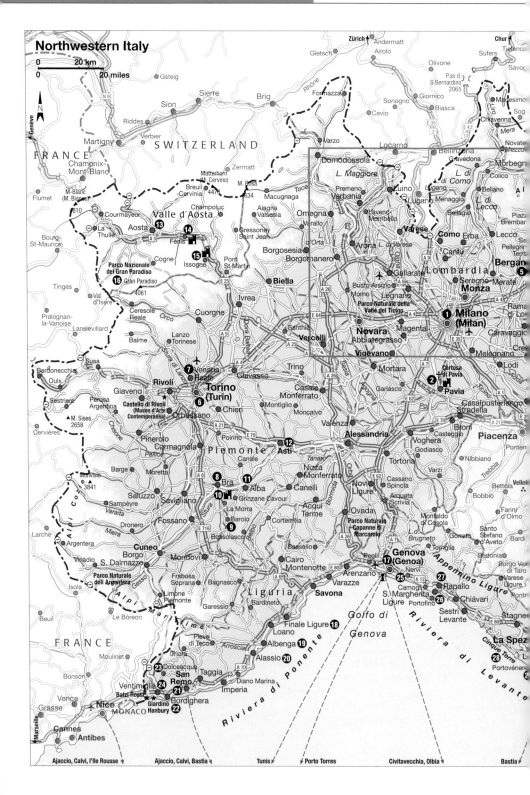

Northwestern Italy

0 _____ 20 km
0 _____ 20 miles

N

SWITZERLAND

FRANCE

Zürich
Andermatt
Airolo
Gletsch
Olivone
Chur
Tiefenca
Sufers
Savo
P.so d.
S.Bernardino
2065
Madesim
Mezzo
Novate
Sog
Mera
Chiavenna
Morbegn
L. di
Como
Colico
Bellano
L. di
Lecco
Bellagio
Menaggio
Piazz
Brémbar
Lecco
Pellegri
Bergamo
A
Terp

Gsteig
Sierre
Sión
Riddes
Verbier
Martigny
Brig
Rhône
Formazza
Sonogno
Giornico
Biasca
Cevio
Locarno
Bellinzona
Gravedona
Domodossola
L. Maggiore
Premeno
Verbania
Luino
Lugano
Laveno-
Mombello
Varese
Como
Erba
Cantù
Lombardia
Seregno
Monza
Merate

Chamonix-
Mont-Blanc
M-Blanc
(M. Bianco)
810
Courmayeur
La
Thuile
Aosta **13**
Valle d'Aosta
Matterhorn
(M. Cervino)
Zermatt
Breuil
-Cervinia 4477
M. Rosa
4634
Champoluc
Fénis **14**
15 Issogne
Pont
St Martin
Macugnaga
Alagna
Valsesia
Gressoney
Saint Jean
L.
d'Orta
Omegna
Verallo
Borgosesia
Borgomanero
Arona L. di Varese
Gallarate
Busto
Arsizio
Momo
Legnano
Parco Naturale della
Valle del Ticino
Abbiategrasso
Novara
Magenta
Milano
(Milan)
Caravaggio
Rama
di Lo
Cre

Flumet
Bourg-
St-Maurice
Cogne
Parco Nazionale
del Gran Paradiso
16 Gran Paradiso
4061
Biella
Ivrea
Santhià
Vercelli
A 25
Vigevano

Tinges
Val
d'Isère
Pralognan-
la-Vanoise
Lanslevillard
Ceresole
Reale
Orco
Cuorgné
Lanzo
Torinese
Balme
Dora Baltea
A 5
Trino
Mortara
Garlasco
Po
Cassano
Spinola
Lodi
Melegnano
Cre
Casalpusterlengo
Stradella
A 21

Bardonecchia
Oulx
Susa
7 Venaria
Reale
Chivasso
Casale
Monferrato
Montiglio
Moncalvo
Valenza
Alessandria
Tortona
Broni
Casteggio
Voghera
Godiasco
Varzi
Nibbiano
Piacenza
Ponten
Trebbia
Bettola
Vellei

Sestriere
Perosa
Argentina
M. Sises
2658
Cervières
Rivoli
Giaveno
Castello di Rivoli
(Museo d'Arte
Contemporanea)
Torino
(Turin) **6**
Chieri
Orbassano
A 21
Poirino
E 70
Carmagnola
Pinerolo
Piemonte **Asti** **12**
Canale
Nizza
Monferrato
Novi
Ligure
Cassano
Spinola
Arquata
Scrivia
Montaldo
di Cosola
Bobbio
Farini
d'Olmo

M.Viso
3841
Barge
Moretta
Saluzzo
Sampèyre
Varaita
Dronero
Maira
Bra **8**
11 Alba
10
La Morra
Ghinzane Cavour
9 Barolo
Cortemilia
Acqui
Terme
Bossolasco
Sassello
Ovada
Parco Naturale
Capanne di
Marcarolo
Pegli
Goreto
Santo
Stefano
d'Aveto
Bardi
Borgo
Val
di Taro
Varese
Ligure

Larche
Argentera
Vinadio
Savigliano
Fossano
Cuneo
Borgo
S. Dalmazzo
Parco Naturale
dell'Argentera
Isola
Mondovì
Frabosa
Soprana
Bagnasco
Cairo
Montenotte
E 80
Arenzano
Varazze
Savona
Genova
(Genoa) **17**
Nervi
25
S. Margherita
Ligure
Portofino
Camogli
26
Rapallo **27**
Chiávari
Sestri
Levante
Appennino Ligure
Stagne
E 80
La Spez **28**
Portovénere
Cinque Terre
Riviera di Levante

Beuil
Le Béreon
Limone
Piemonte
Garessio
Bardineto
Liguria
Pieve
di Teco
Arroscia
Finale Ligure **18**
Loano
Albenga **19**
Alassio **20**
Golfo di
Genova
Riviera di Ponente

Bonson
Vence
Grasse
Moulinet
Triora
Dolceacqua
23
San
Remo
Taggia
A 10
Diano Marina
Imperia
Nice
Cannes
Antibes
MONACO
Balzi Rossi
Ventimiglia **24**
21
Bordighera
Giardino
Hanbury
22

Genève
Marseille

Ajaccio, Calvi, l'Ile Rousse | Ajaccio, Calvi, Bastia | Tunis | Porto Torres | Civitavecchia, Olbia | Bastia

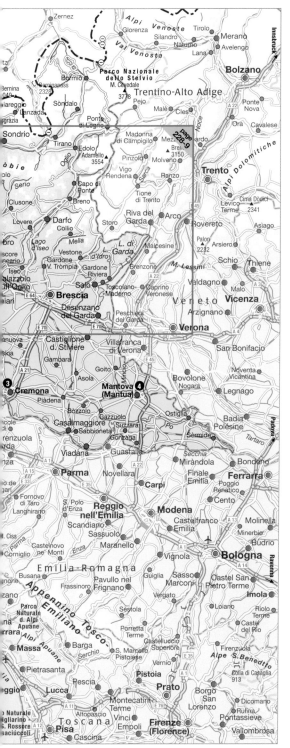

the great medieval Lombard leader, Frederick Barbarossa, was crowned King of Italy. Look for the carefully sculpted scenes of the battle between good and evil above the three doorways.

Eclectic and electric

To reach the **Duomo**, follow the Strada Nuova from San Michele. This cathedral is an eclectic mixture of four centuries of architectural styles. The basic design is Renaissance (Bramante and Leonardo worked on it), but the immense dome, the third-largest in Italy, is a late 19th-century touch, and the facade was added in 1933.

If you continue on the Strada Nuova you will arrive at the **Università**, where 17,000 students currently attend classes. One of Pavia's most famous past graduates was Alessandro Volta, the physicist who discovered and gave his name to electrical volts. His statue stands in the left-hand court of the university complex.

At the end of the Strada Nuova stands the **Castello Visconteo**, an imposing square fortress built in 1360–65. Today, the castle is the home of the **Museo Civico** (Tues–Sun 10am–6pm, July–Aug 9am–1.30pm; charge). Included in the museum's collection are many fine Lombardic Romanesque sculptures and remnants of Roman Pavia, including inscriptions, glass and pottery.

Go west from the castle to reach **San Pietro in Ciel d'Oro**, a fine Lombardic Romanesque church, smaller than San Michele, but quite similar. A richly decorated Gothic arch at the high altar is said to contain the relics of St Augustine.

Before leaving Pavia, have a bowl of the town's speciality, the hearty *zuppa alla pavese*, a recipe said to have been concocted by a peasant woman for Francis I of France. The king was about to lose the battle of Pavia (1525) to the Spanish when he stopped for a bite to eat at a nearby cottage. His hostess wanted her humble minestrone to be fit for a king, so she added toasted bread, cheese and eggs.

Cremona

About two hours' drive from Pavia lies the city of **Cremona ❸**, a world-famous centre of violin-making set on the banks of the

TIP

Try to visit Mantua on a Thursday, when Piazza delle Erbe, Piazza Mantegna and nearby streets become an enormous market.

River Po. The greatest of Cremonese violin-makers was Antonio Stradivari (1644–1737), whose secret formula for varnish may partly account for the beautiful sound of a Stradivarius violin. Some of these glorious instruments are on display in the grandiose 13th-century **Palazzo Comunale** (Tues–Sat 9am–6pm, Sun 10am–6pm), with more in the **Museo Stradivario**, the museum dedicated to Stradivarius (open same times; charge) around the corner, and the modern **International School of Violin-Making** nearby. On occasions, concerts are held in the Palazzo Comunale, using the original instruments.

The pink marble **Duomo** was built in the Lombardic Romanesque style. Although consecrated in 1190, it was not completed until much later. Inside are 17th-century tapestries representing the *Life of Samson*.

Mantua

Because **Mantua** ❹ (Mantova) lies on a peninsula in the River Mincio, surrounded by a lagoon on three sides, it is known as *Piccola Venezia* (Little Ven-

ice). But history has given the city a more resonant name: "Ducal Mantua", because from 1328–1707 the enlightened but despotic Gonzaga family ruled the city-state from their sombre fortress. Often swathed in mist, Mantua wallows in a state of melancholic introspection: the quiet cobbled streets evoke a stage set from a Shakespearean drama or a Verdi opera.

During the Renaissance, the Gonzaga court was one of the bright lights of Italian culture, especially under the influence of Isabella d'Este (1474–1539), who modelled her life on *Il Cortegione*, a textbook for courtiers and ladies written by Castiglione. She also hired Raphael, Mantegna and Giulio Romano to decorate the Reggia dei Gonzaga (**Palazzo Ducale**), once the largest palace in Europe. A selection of the palace's 450 or so rooms can be visited on a guided tour (Tues–Sun 8.15am–7.15pm; charge). Particularly worth seeing are the tapestries in the Appartamento degli Arazzi that were made in Flanders from drawings by Raphael. The Camera degli Sposi (the Matrimonial Suite) is decorated with frescoes by Mantegna depicting scenes from the lives of Ludovico Gonzaga and his wife, Barbara of Brandenburg.

Across town is the **Palazzo del Te** (Tues–Sun 9am–6pm, Mon 1–6pm; audioguides; charge), the supremely elegant Gonzaga summer retreat which doubled as a boudoir for Gonzaga mistresses. Designed by Giulio Romano in 1525, this Renaissance palace is delicate and pleasing, featuring rooms frescoed with summery scenes, and complemented by a lovely garden.

Mantua's **Duomo**, located near the Reggia, has a Baroque facade and a Renaissance interior, with stucco-work by Giulio Romano. Also worth a visit is the **Basilica di Sant'Andrea** in Piazza Mantegna. The Florentine architect Alberti designed most of Sant'Andrea, starting in 1472, but the dome was added in the 18th century. Inside, the celebrated frescoes that adorn the walls

BELOW: café break in Cremona.

were designed by the great painter Andrea Mantegna, who died in 1506, and executed by his pupils, among them Correggio.

Bergamo

If you want to escape from the hot stillness of "the waveless plain of Lombardy", **Bergamo ❺** makes a refreshing diversion. The combination of cobbled streets, cypress-clad hills and mountain air adds to its appeal. Curiously, Bergamo is, in fact, two cities: Bergamo Bassa and Bergamo Alta.

Though pleasant and spacious, the modern **Bergamo Bassa** lacks the appeal of Bergamo Alta, perched on a rough-hewn crag above. The main reason for visiting this area is the **Accademia Carrara** (Tues–Sun 10am–1pm and 2.30–5.30pm; entrance charge). Where else but in Italy can you find, in a small city, a collection of paintings that the grandest metropolis would be proud to have? In this case, it is thanks to the good taste of the 18th-century Count Giacomo Carrara. You will probably have the paintings to yourself, including an array of art by Bellini, Tiepolo, Carpaccio and Mantegna.

Opposite the Carrara, the **Galleria d'Arte Moderna e Contemporanea** (Tues–Sun 10am–1pm and 3–7pm) hosts a permanent collection featuring such artists as Sutherland and Kandinsky, as well as exhibitions by contemporary artists and sculptors.

If you enjoy mountain-climbing, take the creaking funicular to **Bergamo Alta**, a medieval town built in warm brown stone. The best spot in which to sit and admire it is the central **Piazza Vecchia** – a good place to find the local speciality *polenta con gli uccelli* (polenta with quail). The piazza is flanked by the 17th-century Palazzo Nuovo and the 12th-century Palazzo della Ragione. Beyond the medieval building's arcade is the small Piazza del Duomo, packed with ecclesiastical treasures: the Romanesque **Santa Maria Maggiore** and the Renaissance

Colleoni Chapel (daily 9am–12.30pm and 2–6.30pm, Nov–Feb Tues–Sun until 4.30pm), designed by Amadeo who contributed to the Certosa di Pavia, and with an 18th-century ceiling by Tiepolo. The chapel is dedicated to the Bergamesque *condottiere* Bartolomeo Colleoni. The mercenary fought so well for the Venetians that he was rewarded with an estate in his native province, which was then under Venetian rule.

Opera composer Gaetano Donizetti, the city's most famous son, is buried here. He died here in 1848, quite insane, having composed 75 operas, of which the best known today is *Lucia di Lammermoor*. Just behind the Citadella is the **Museo Donizettiano** (Donizetti Birthplace Museum; June–Sept Tues–Sun 9.30am–1pm and 2–5.30pm, Oct–May mornings only). Within are several of the composer's artefacts, such as his piano and portraits.

Ongoing excavations in Bergamo have unearthed traces of an Early Christian basilica below the Duomo, and part of the Roman forum near the Palazzo del Podesta. ❑

BELOW: Basilica di Santa Maria Maggiore in Bergamo.

THE LAKES

Sheltered by the Alps, most Italian Lakes benefit from a superb microclimate, allowing for that perfect combination – a Mediterranean lifestyle in a mountainous landscape

The Italian Lakes have long been a retreat for romantics. Writers drawn to their shores include Pliny the Younger, Shelley, Stendhal and D.H. Lawrence. "What can one say of Lake Maggiore, of the Borromean Islands, of Lake Como, except to pity people who do not go mad over them?" wrote Stendhal.

There are five major lakes in the Italian lake district (from west to east: Lakes Maggiore, Lugano, Como, Iseo and Garda), and each has its own character. The lakes were formed during the last Ice Age, which ended around 11,000 years ago, and are the result of glaciers thrusting down from the Alps and gouging out deep valleys wherever softer rock created an easy pathway for the ice. Later, as the ice melted, the lakes were formed in the valley bottoms. Most of the lakes enjoy sheltered microclimates that make them warm and mild in winter, with the southern shores benefiting from winter sunshine – while the northern shores tend to be overshadowed by Alpine peaks.

Lake Maggiore

The westernmost lake, **Lago Maggiore ❶**, has a special attraction: the **Isole Borromee ❷** (Borromean Islands), named after their owners, a Milanese family whose members included a cardinal, a bishop and a saint. **Isola Bella**,

the most romantic of the three islands, was a desolate rock with just a few cottages until the 16th century, when Count Charles Borromeo III decided to civilise the island in honour of his wife, Isabella. With the help of the architect Angelo Crivelli, Charles designed the splendid palace and gardens (mid-Mar–Oct daily 9am–5.30pm; charge).

Isola dei Pescatori is, as the name suggests, a fishing village. Another Borromean palace and elaborate botanical gardens decorate **Isola Madre** (same opening times as Isola Bella). All three

Main attractions
BORROMEAN ISLANDS
LAKE COMO BY BOAT
BELLAGIO
VILLA CARLOTTA
MONTE ISOLA, LAKE ISEO
VAL CAMONICA ROCK CARVINGS
SANTA GIULIA MUSEUM
IL VITTORIALE
SIRMIONE
LAKE GARDA BY BOAT

LEFT: dramatic shoreline of Lake Garda.
RIGHT: sun and sport at Torbole, Lake Garda.

Postcard-pretty Como tumbles down to the shoreline.

are served by ferries from the main lakeside towns.

The most celebrated settlement on the shores of Lake Maggiore is **Stresa** ❸ (put on the literary map by Hemingway's *A Farewell to Arms*), with its many beautiful Belle Epoque villas. Two famous villas adjoining the landing stage are the **Villa Ducale**, residence of the philosopher Antonio Rosmini (1797–1855), and the **Villa Pallavicino** (daily Mar–Oct 9am–6pm; charge) just outside town on the road to Arona, remarkable for its fine gardens. From Stresa, it's a short drive or cable-car ride from Stresa Lido to the summit of **Monte Mottarone** and a stunning view of the Alps, the lake and the town below.

Baveno ❹, northwest of Stresa, is noted for its villas, among them the **Castello Branca** where Queen Victoria spent the spring of 1879. The drive south from Stresa to **Arona** ❺ along the Lungolago is especially pretty: the road is tree-lined, the views of the lakes and islands spectacular. Arona itself is a rather unremarkable resort town, but it does contain a number of attractive 15th-century buildings.

Lake Lugano

Much of **Lago di Lugano** ❻ lies within Swiss territory; only the very eastern tip is Italian, plus the enclave of Campione d'Italia, a little lakeside town that remains proudly and typically Italian, whilst being entirely surrounded by Swiss territory (and using Swiss currency and postage stamps). Visitors come to Campione for the casino and its nightlife.

Lake Como

Lago di Como ❼, known locally as "Lario", is the most dramatic of the lakes. It is almost 50km (30 miles) long and up to 5km (3 miles) across; at 410 metres (1,345ft), it is the deepest inland lake in Europe. At many points the shore is a sheer cliff, and the Alps (providing year-round skiing on the glaciers, although they are receding) loom like a wall at the northern end of the lake.

Como ❽ itself is a historic yet thriving town. Silk-weaving, a traditional craft, is still significant, with Como supplying 70 percent of Europe's silk, including to most of the big fashion designers. The silk itself may now

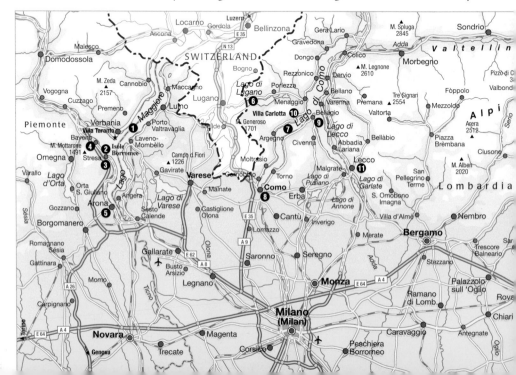

come from China but it is "finished" in Como, with the creation of sheens, pleating and veining.

Como's peaceful gardens, the **Giardini Pubblici,** are home to the Tempio Voltiano (Tue–Sun 10am–noon and 3–6pm; charge), a classic rotunda dedicated to Alessandro Volta, who gave his name to the volt. Many of the instruments he used in his electrical experiments are on display.

It's an easy walk across the town to **Santa Maria Maggiore** (daily 7am–noon and 3–7pm), Como's 14th-century marble cathedral. The intricately carved portal is flanked by a statue of the two Plinys, who were among the earliest admirers of Lake Como. "Are you given to studying, or do you prefer fishing or hunting, or do you go in for all three?" the younger Pliny asked a friend, and boasted that all three activities were possible at Lake Como.

The 11th-century church of **Sant'Abbondio** (daily 9am–noon and 3–6pm) on the outskirts of Como will transport you back to Como's pre-resort days, when it was a pious and prosperous medieval village. The

chances are that you will have this solemn Lombardic church to yourself, including the 14th-century frescoes of the *Life of Jesus* in the apse.

It can take an hour of driving on narrow, twisting roads to reach **Bellagio ⑨**, "the jewel of the lake", from Como. Going by public boat from Como's pier is a more pleasant way of getting there. Bellagio sits on the point of land that divides Lake Como into three parts, revealing a spectacular view of the Alps. "Sublimity and grace here combine to a degree which is equalled but not surpassed by the most famous site in the world, the Bay of Naples," wrote Stendhal in *The Charterhouse of Parma*. The Frenchman set part of his novel in the **Villa Carlotta ⑩** (across the lake from Bellagio) after staying here as a guest. Today the villa (Apr–Sept daily 9am–6pm, Mar and Oct 9am–noon, 2–4.30pm; charge), originally built by a Prussian princess for her daughter, and its idyllic gardens, provide the perfect setting for a picnic lunch.

Lecco ⑪, at the southeastern end of Lake Como, is famous as the setting of Alessandro Manzoni's novel *The*

After the murder of celebrity designer Gianni Versace in 1998, it was here, in the grounds of his beloved Montrasio villa, that his family chose to scatter his ashes.

BELOW: sculpture by Canova in Villa Carlotta, across the lake from Bellagio.

TIP

The lifestyle store La Tessitura is a temple to silk, awash with garments, textiles and furnishing accessories by Mantero, Como's historic silk manufacturer. Viale Roosevelt 2/a, Como; Tues–Sat 11am–7pm; tel: 031-321 666; www. latessitura.com.

Betrothed, a classic which most Italians study at school. The author, Italy's greatest 19th-century novelist, was a native of Lecco and a political activist instrumental in bringing about Italian unification. Visitors can explore his childhood home, the **Villa Manzoni** (Tues–Sun 9.30am–5.30pm; charge).

Although Lecco's scenery is more inspiring than the sights, spare a moment for the **Basilica**, with its medieval frescoes depicting *The Annunciation*, *The Deposition* and *The Life of St Anthony*. Lecco's pride and joy is the Ponte Vecchio, the reconstructed 14th-century bridge spanning the River Adda.

Lake Iseo

Lago d'Iseo ⓬ is sweeter, quieter and less self-consciously quaint than its rival lakes. Measuring 24km (15 miles) long by 5km (3 miles), the lake is dominated by the bulky form of **Monte Isola** which, at a height of 600 metres (1,970ft), makes it the highest lake island in Europe. The charm of Lake Iseo embraces the lakeside port of **Iseo**, as well as the peaceful island itself, whose shores are lined with reliable

fish restaurants. A day out in the neighbouring vineyards of **Franciacorta** is a way to combine prestigious wine estates with castles and gastro inns.

To the northeast, **Capo di Ponte** is the springboard for exploring the unpolished **Val Camonica**, renowned for its prehistoric rock carvings. In Italy's first designated Unesco World Heritage site, over 300,000 rock carvings have been found, dating as far back as 8,000 years ago. The carvings, etched into glacier-seared sandstone, are a record of the hunting, farming, social and religious rituals of the local Camuni tribes. The sites are scattered over a wide area, but the most convenient site is the **Parco Nazionale delle Incisioni Rupestri di Naquane** (National Rock Engravings Park; Tues–Sun 8.30am–7pm, until 4.30pm in winter; charge). Given the bewildering array, focus on the impressive boulders nearest the entrance.

Brescia

Southeast of the lake is Lombardy's prosperous but vastly underrated second city, **Brescia** ⓭, which has a

BELOW: on the shore of Lake Garda.
BELOW RIGHT: Santa Maria delle Neve, Iseo.

world-class museum. Indeed, **Santa Giulia Museo della Città** (Mon–Thur 9am–7pm, Fri–Sun 9am–8pm; charge) is arguably the best historical and archaeological museum complex in Italy. Santa Giulia showcases Brescia's past in monuments from the Bronze Age to Roman times and the present day. The beguiling complex incorporates an 8th-century nunnery, the Renaissance church and cloisters of Santa Giulia, the Romanesque oratory of Santa Maria, and the Lombard basilica of San Salvatore. The church alone is a major monument, with Byzantine, Lombard and Roman remains.

Also in Brescia is the Capitolium and Teatro Romano, a reminder of the city's rich Roman heritage. Surmounting the hill, a medieval castle houses the **Museo delle Armi**, Italy's finest collection of ancient weaponry (June–Sept Tues–Sun 10am–1pm, 2–5pm; entrance charge).

Lake Garda

Lago di Garda ⓮ is the cleanest and largest of the Italian lakes. It is especially popular with northern European tourists, who come to sail, windsurf and water-ski. Its equable climate is responsible for Soave and Valpolicella wines, as well as for producing the most northerly olives in Europe, close to Riva del Garda. Lemons, grown in Limone del Garda for centuries, also add to the lakes' Mediterranean air.

On the shores of this lake is a garish remnant of the Fascist era – **Il Vittoriale** ⓯ – the home of the flamboyant Italian poet and patriot Gabriele d'Annunzio, which was given to him by his greatest admirer, Benito Mussolini (park and gardens daily Apr–Sept 8.30am–8pm, Oct–Mar 9am–5pm; the house must be seen on a guided tour, which runs throughout the day; charge). Located in **Gardone Riviera**, once Lake Garda's most fashionable resort, Il Vittoriale is more than a house, it is a shrine to d'Annunzio's dreams of Italian imperialism. Included in the estate is the prow of the war-

ship *Puglia*, built into the hillside. In the auditorium, the plane d'Annunzio flew during World War I is suspended from the ceiling. The house itself is a monument to megalomania but still remains one of the most memorable sights in Italy.

From Salò and Gardone Riviera it takes no more than an hour to reach **Sirmione** ⓰, a medieval town built on a spit of land extending into the lake. The picturesque castle and self-conscious charm of the resort means that it is besieged on summer weekends.

The **Rocca Scaligera** (Mar–mid-Oct 8.30am–7pm, mid-Oct–Feb until 5pm; charge), a fairytale castle, dominates the town's entrance. It was originally the fortress of the Scaligeri family, rulers of Garda in the 13th century, and it is said that they entertained the poet Dante here. An enjoyable hour or two can be spent exploring the local shops, dipping into churches and following the footpath that leads to the tip of the peninsula, with its extensive ruins of a Roman spa, the **Grotte di Catullo** (Tues–Sun 9am–7pm, 8.30am–4.30pm in winter; charge). ❑

Lake Garda's dependable offshore winds make the lake popular with sailors and windsurfers. This is caused by temperature and air-pressure differences between the warmer water and the cooler surrounding mountains. Sunbathers on the shores can bask in warm still air, while a stiff wind blows on the lake itself.

BELOW: Villa Fiordaliso on Lake Garda.

PIEDMONT, VALLE D'AOSTA AND LIGURIA

If it is not so Italian as Italy it is at least more Italian than anything but Italy
– HENRY JAMES

BELOW: the Alps form a dramatic backdrop to Turin.

Piedmont (Piemonte) may strike today's visitors, as it did Henry James, as not very Italian. The bordering nations of France and Switzerland have greatly influenced the cultural life of this northwestern region, as have the unforgiving Alpine landscapes. But the particularly sensible Piedmontese twist on Italian life is not unappealing. No wonder that it was a Piedmontese king, Victor Emmanuel, and his Piedmontese adviser, Count Camillo Cavour, who guided Italy to independence.

Yet sensible **Turin** ❻ (Torino) is also a seductive city, with its gilt-encrusted cafés designed for dangerous liaisons, and its Baroque squares built for grand gestures. Curiously, this former industrial powerhouse, first capital of a unified Italy and historic home to the Savoy kings, has always been ambivalent about its heritage. The Piedmontese are diffident and undemonstrative by nature; they would rather let the city do the talking. Of course, it helps if the menu includes Italy's most aristocratic cuisine and finest wines – served in the capital of Slow Food. As the cradle of Italian café culture, the city also abounds in opulent coffee houses and chocolate shops.

But Turin now prefers to cast itself as a vibrant, visionary city, proud of its contemporary arts scene, its cinematic heritage and its cutting-edge design. Turin was made World Design Capital in 2008, which confirmed its status as Italy's leading city for contemporary art and design. The city has built on its industrial car design heritage to become a creative place for all designers and architects. This creative confidence is demonstated in the glut of cool city art galleries and the stylish Luci d'Artista festival, which celebrates contemporary art installations in public spaces. Turin's innate conservatism is being challenged by the city's burgeoning new districts and by the success of Lingotto, a new exhibition centre born out of the former Fiat

factory, which was the epicentre of the 2006 Winter Olympic Games.

Historic town centre

The hub of civic life in Turin is the fashionable **Via Roma**, an arcaded shopping street that connects the **Stazione Porta Nuova ⓐ** with **Piazza Castello ⓑ**, a huge rectangular Renaissance square planned in 1584. In the centre stands **Palazzo Madama**, a 15th-century castle that houses the **Museo Civico di Arte Antica** (Museum of Ancient Art). Included in this museum's collections is a copy of part of the famous *Book of Hours* of the Duc de Berry, illustrated by Jan van Eyck.

Here, too, is the Baroque church of **San Lorenzo**, once the royal chapel. The royal residence was the 17th-century **Palazzo Reale ⓒ** (Tues–Sun 8.30am–7.30pm; guided tours; charge; garden open daily). From its balcony, Prince Carlo Alberto declared war on Austria in March 1848.

Behind the Palazzo Reale, in **Piazza San Giovanni**, are the Renaissance **Duomo ⓓ** (Mon–Sat 7am–12.30pm and 3–7pm, Sun 8am–12.30pm and 3–7pm) and Baroque **Campanile**. The Duomo was damaged by fire in 1997, but fortunately the flames did not consume the **Cappella della Sacra Sindone** (Chapel of the Holy Shroud; daily 8am–noon and 3–7pm; charge). The chapel contains the Turin Shroud, for centuries believed to be the shroud in which Christ was wrapped after the Crucifixion. The cloth is imprinted with the image of a bearded man crowned with thorns. Although controversy reigns about the authenticity of the shroud, thousands of fervent believers, including Pope Benedict, prayed before it on its most recent outing in 2010.

On Via San Domenico, **the MAO** (**Museo d'Arte Orientale**) ⓔ is Turin's impressive new Museum of Oriental Art (Tues–Sun 10am–6pm, and July–Aug also Thur late opening until 11pm; book online www. maotorino.it; charge). The eclectic col-

lection is divided according to theme, but highlights include: the Japanese meditative rock gardens; the Chinese ceremonial bronzes and lacquer-ware; Buddhist statuary from Southeast Asia; and Islamic ceramics from Turkey, Iran and Iraq.

Nearby is the **Porta Palazzo** market ⓕ (Mon–Sat 8.30am–1.30pm), which sprawls around Piazza della Repubblica. The market attracts a cosmopolitan crowd and sells everything from flowers to hams, cheeses and squid. The market adjoins the intriguing **Quadrilatero Romano** ⓖ district, the so-called Roman Quarter west of Piazza Castello. Clustered around the ruins of a Roman theatre and gate, this peaceful pedestrianised area livens up at night. Nearby, sedate **Piazza San Carlo** ⓗ is dubbed Turin's drawing room, and is a place of Baroque facades and Belle Epoque coffee houses.

Around the corner is the **Museo Egizio ⓘ**, the revamped Egyptian Museum (Tues–Sun 8.30am–7.30pm; charge) housed in the Palazzo dell'Accademia delle Scienze, off Via Roma. As the greatest assemblage

Palazzo Madama.

BELOW: authentic café in Turin, for coffee and chocolates.

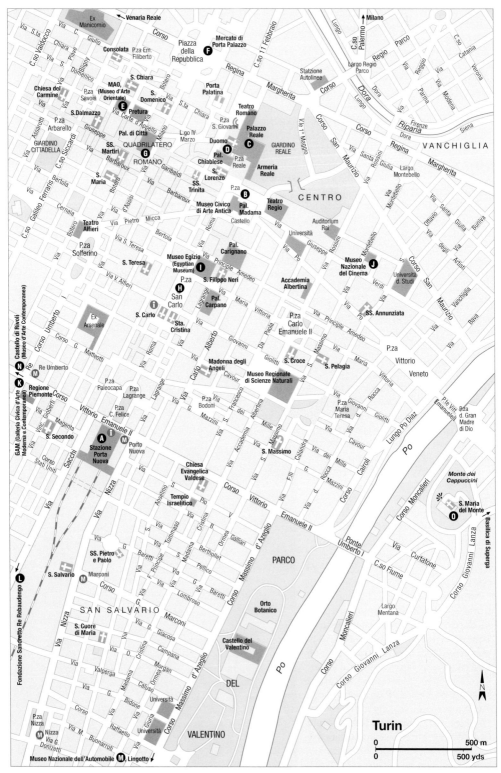

Turin

0   500 m

0   500 yds

Egyptian treasures outside Cairo, the newly revamped collection is unmissable. Its centrepiece is a statue of Rameses II, one of the masterpieces of Egyptian sculpture.

The same palazzo contains a good picture collection on the second floor in the **Galleria Sabauda** (Tues, Fri, Sat and Sun 8.30am–2pm, Wed–Thur 2–7.30pm; charge). Made up of the main art collection of the House of Savoy, this is a treasure trove of Italian Masters, and displays works by Veronese, Bellini and Mantegna. Dutch and Flemish artists, such as Van Dyck and Jan van Eyck, are well represented, as are French landscape artists such as Claude Lorrain and Poussin.

Cine scene

For sheer theatricality, the Egyptian Museum is surpassed by the star-studded **Museo Nazionale del Cinema** ❶ (Cinema Museum; Tues–Sun 9am–8pm, until 11pm on Sat; charge), set in a show-stopping, cavernous former synagogue, dissected by a panoramic, glass-walled lift. The is the iconic **Mole Antonelliana**, a local landmark. From 1906 to 1916 Turin was the world film-production capital, until overtaken by Hollywood. The story of cinema is told through myriad means, from film clips to costumes ranging from Marilyn Monroe's bodice to Fellini's scarf, coat and hat. The ride in the lift to the top (Tues–Fri 10am–8pm, Sat 10am–11pm, Sun 10am–8pm; charge) leads to spectacular views over the city and the Alps.

Modern art-lovers will be tempted by the **GAM** ❻ (Galleria Civica d'Arte Moderna e Contemporanea; Tues–Sun 10am–6pm; charge). The museum has excellent visiting exhibitions and an illustrious permanent collection featuring works by such luminaries as Picasso, Modigliani, Chagall, Renoir and Klee.

For more contemporary art, visit the **Fondazione Sandretto Re Rebaudengo** ❶ (www.fondsrr.org), where cutting-edge art is showcased in a minimalist gallery in the gritty San Paolo district.

Lingotto, car capital

It is no surprise that the car capital of Italy has a fine car museum. It can take hours to explore the **Museo Nazionale dell'Automobile** ❿ (Tues–Sun 10am–6.30pm; charge). Exhibits include the earliest Fiat, the Itala that won the world's longest automobile race (between Peking and Paris in 1907) and an elegant Rolls-Royce Silver Ghost. This area south of the city centre was the heart of Turin's car industry. The Fiat company, founded in 1899, made Turin the city of cars. The areas of Lingotto, Italia 61, Mirafiori and Millefonti, once the powerhouse of the industry, have now been transformed into a multi-million-euro "suburbs project", with many new sports and leisure facilities constructed for the 2006 Winter Olympics.

Under the skilful eye of architect Renzo Piano, the area was transformed into a multi-purpose exhibition centre. Today, it is the setting for cultural events and fairs, such as the Salone del Gusto, the showcase of the international Slow Food Movement. Lingotto also encompasses an

BELOW: inside the Museo Nazionale del Cinema.

The Slow Food Movement was born in Piedmont and urges us to "rediscover the flavours and savours of regional cooking and banish the degrading effects of fast food". Sample the delights at the October Salone del Gusto (www. salonedelgusto.it), staged in Turin's Lingotto complex.

auditorium, shopping mall, hotels and a racing track.

Turin still represents Italian passion for design and speed. In the revitalised Lingotto district, Turin's former car factory is gorgeous enough to welcome the suitably high-tech Art+Tech, an Art Deco hotel with a racing track on the roof – and emblem of Turin's prestigious design heritage. This spectacular rooftop test track was the setting for a Mini Cooper car chase in the iconic *Italian Job* but is now the preserve of hotel guests with a head for heights and a passion for jogging.

Also on the Lingotto rooftop is the **Pinacoteca Giovanni e Marella Agnelli** (Tues–Sun 10am–7pm; charge; tel: 011-006 2713). Designed by Renzo Piano and known as "Lo Scrigno" (the jewellery box), it showcases treasures from the art collection of the Agnelli family, the owners of Fiat, including works by Picasso and Renoir.

Gastronomic pleasures

Lingotto's final surprise is reserved for foodies. **Eataly** (Tues–Sun 10am–10pm, Via Nizza; tel: 011-1950 6811; www.

eatalytorino.it) claims to be the world's largest food and wine centre. Appropriately for Turin, it has a history: the factory that originally produced Vermouth has become a gastrodome in the fullest sense of the word. The aperitif was first invented here in 1786, when Carpano produced Vermouth by means of a secret blend of white wine and an infusion of herbs.

Today, reborn as a food laboratory, Eataly is dedicated to the tastes of Italy. As well as meals, curious visitors can do cookery courses, wine-tastings, ice cream-making or quiz top food producers and well-known chefs. Naturally, Eataly works with Slow Food because, in Turin, eating is always about food culture as well as flavour.

To the west of the city, at the gateway to the Valle di Susa, lies the eye-catching **Castello di Rivoli**, which houses the **Museo d'Arte Contemporanea** (Tues–Thur 10am–5pm, Fri–Sun 10am–9pm; charge). The imposing Baroque building, designed by Juvarra, contrasts with cutting-edge installations. Works by avant-garde artists such as Jeff Koons contrast dra-

BELOW: Gran Paradiso National Park, south of Aosta.

matically with the stuccoed interior. There are around 400 pieces in the permanent collection, and major temporary exhibitions are also staged. There is a good museum café and a famous gastro-haunt, the Combal.Zero.

Cross the Po to visit the **Monte dei Cappuccini ⓞ**, a small hill crowned by a Capuchin convent. From here, take a bus to the **Basilica di Superga** (Apr–Oct Mon–Fri 9am–noon and 3–6pm, Sat–Sun 9am–12.45pm and 3–6.45pm, Nov–Mar closes one hour earlier). Henry James called it a "great votive temple", as Juvarra's creation was intended to house the tombs of the kings of Sardinia and the princes of Savoy. This basilica sits on a hill overlooking the natural amphitheatre of the Alps. The circular church is dominated by its 75-metre (246ft) dome, flanked by twin 60-metre (196ft) high bell towers.

After hurtling through museums and palaces all day, you can sink into cafés all night. Piedmontese cuisine, from creamy risotto to pungent white truffles, is among the finest in Italy. Despite all its transformations, Turin stays faithful to its café culture; you'll find sophisticated *Torinesi* in the chocolate-box interior of Caffe Baratti & Milan for example, where *cioccolato* Baratti is a deliciously dark drink. Known as *"aperitivi"* time, between 6 and 8pm, the ritual remains an excuse to sample Turin's aperitifs and tapas in beguiling old-world bars.

Outside Turin

Just 10km (6 miles) to the north of the city is the stunningly restored **Venaria Reale ⓞ** (castle Tues–Fri 9am–4pm, Sat until 8.30pm, Sun until 7pm, gardens 9am–7pm summer, winter until 5pm; charge; online booking through www.lavenaria.it). Often called the Italian Versailles, this was a royal hunting lodge that became a royal palace, complete with frescoed interiors, chapels, stables, parkland and a model town.

Southeast of Turin, Piedmont turns into a region of rolling hills, faintly reminiscent of Tuscany. Like Tuscany it is an excellent wine-growing area, with the most prestigious estates in **Le Langhe,** the area around Alba. The hills are cloaked with vineyards and crowned with medieval fortresses.

From Turin head towards Alba along the *autostrada*. If you have time, make a stop at **Bra ⓞ**, birthplace of the Slow Food Movement *(see page 97)*, to see a fine Baroque church, **Sant' Andrea.** The slopes surrounding the small town of La Morra, 10km (6 miles) from Bra, represent red wine country. In particular, the charming village of **Barolo ⓞ** boasts a medieval castle, wine-tasting centre and vineyards that produce the "king" of Italian red wines. In neighbouring **Grinzane Cavour ⓞ** looms the Castello Cavour, an imposing medieval castle, the feudal home of Count Cavour, which also houses a wine museum (Wed–Mon 9.30am–7pm, last entry 6.30pm; closed Jan; charge).

As the centre of the white truffle district, prosperous **Alba ⓞ** has long been a favourite with gourmets. Truffles can be sniffed at the autumnal truffle fairs or sampled in the city's reliable res-

Some of Italy's finest wines come from Le Langhe, the hilly region south of Turin.

BELOW: medieval castle in the Valle d'Aosta.

EAT

In Valle d'Aosta, the cuisine matches robust mountain flavours with French flair. The soft fontina cheese is produced here – a vital ingredient for *fonduta* (fondue) and delicious with white truffles from Alba.

taurants during the October–January truffle season. At other times, you will have to content yourself with culture, and the late Gothic cathedral, with its noted Renaissance choir.

For more tickling of the tastebuds, head to **Asti ⑫**, famous for its production of sparkling Asti Spumante, even if Piedmontese reds, notably Barolo and Barbaresco, are vastly superior.

Valle d'Aosta

The beautiful Alpine valleys around Piedmont have much to offer. The region is noted for its glaciers, hilltop castles, clear mountain lakes and streams, pine forests and green meadows. The most striking area is the Valle d'Aosta. Here rise Europe's highest mountains: Mont Blanc, Monte Rosa and the Cervino (Matterhorn). The capital, **Aosta ⑬**, was an important city in Roman times and has many interesting Roman ruins. Roman walls surround the city, and the ruins of the **Roman Theatre** (daily 9am–8pm Apr–Aug, until 7pm Mar and Sept, until 6.30pm Feb and Oct, until 5pm Nov–Jan), in the northwest corner of Aosta, include

the well-preserved backdrop of the stage. Emperor Augustus nicknamed Aosta the "Rome of the Alps", and it is the Arch of Augustus that guards the main entrance to the city.

Dating from Aosta's medieval period are the cathedral and several smaller churches. Among the latter group, the **Church of Sant'Orso** is the most striking, a blend of Gothic and Romanesque. St Orso – who converted the first Christians in the Valle d'Aosta – is buried beneath the altar. Be sure to visit the Romanesque cloisters, noted for their sculpted pillars.

The valley southeast of Aosta abounds in fine castles, notably the fairytale fortress at **Fénis ⑭** (Mar–Sept daily 9am–6.30pm, July and Aug until 7.30pm, Oct–Feb Wed–Mon 10am–noon and 1.30–4.30pm; charge), which bristles with towers, turrets and crenellations, and **Issogne ⑮** (daily 9.30am–6.30pm in summer, 10am–4.30pm in winter; charge), which is more a chateau than a fortress.

Centred on **Cogne**, just to the west, the **Gran Paradiso park ⑯**, at 4,061 metres (13,321ft), was the royal hunting reserve of the House of Savoy but is now a paradise for ibex, chamois, marmots and ermines. Set in a landscape of meadows, valleys, glaciers, waterfalls and high Alpine beauty, the park is criss-crossed with mule-tracks and marked trails. The *rifugi* (mountain huts) welcome summer hikers.

The region of Liguria

Liguria is still an underrated destination. Centred on regenerated Genoa, this rugged region celebrates the outdoors lifestyle, with picturesque fishing villages, hidden coves and an authentic hinterland. Protected by the Alps, and perched on a crescent-shaped sliver of coast, Ligurian resorts enjoy balmy weather, with the Riviera di Levante the wilder stretch, especially around the Cinque Terre coastal reserve. Portofino is perfection, an idealised fishing village that put the Italian Riviera on the map.

BELOW: Genoa's historic streets.

Sandwiched between the mountains and the sea, **Genoa** ⑰ is a concertina of a city, with slate-topped palaces and squat skyscrapers bearing down on the old port. By turns sleekly streamlined and self-consciously restored, the ancient port is the glittering symbol of regenerated Genoa. Above is a dramatic natural amphitheatre ringed by ridge-top forts. In between are alleys burrowing under medieval palaces, funiculars reaching dizzying heights, and tunnels emerging where least expected.

Genoa is a complex yet conspiratorial city. Walk everywhere in this pedestrianised maze, stopping for coffee in time-warp cafés; stroll with your gaze focused upwards: virtually every alleyway has striking architectural details, from friezes to *trompe l'œil* frescoes.

Immediately behind the docks, the lower city begins. The ancient, winding alleys – called *carrugi* – are lined with exotic shops. The late afternoon *passeggiata* takes place on the elegant **Via Luccoli** ❹.

Not far from the docks stands the **Stazione Principe** ❺, with a striking statue of Christopher Columbus facing

the station. From here, Via Balbi leads past sombre Renaissance palaces to the centre. Stop at the 17th-century **Palazzo Reale** ❻, famous for the Galleria degli Specchi (Hall of Mirrors) and its art collection (Tues–Wed 9am–1.30pm, Thur–Sun 9am–7pm; charge).

Continue along Via Balbi until it becomes the patrician **Via Garibaldi** ❼. Once the heart of aristocratic and mercantile Genoa, this is now the museum district, with late Renaissance palaces sprouting grandiose courtyards, hanging gardens, the odd waterfall and Baroque grotto, as well as major art collections. These Unesco-listed homes of the richest families were designated ambassadorial residences, "Palazzi dei Rolli", fit for visiting kings or courtiers. **Palazzo Bianco** ❽ (Tues–Fri 9am–7pm, Sat and Sun 10am–7pm) is one of the most magnificent palaces and boasts a collection of Flemish masters. Across the street is **Palazzo Rosso** ❾ (gallery Tues–Fri 9am–7pm, Sat–Sun 10am–7pm; charge), where great art by Veronese and Guercino is outdone by the frescoed and stuccoed interior and lovely courtyard.

Door knocker in the Palazzo Ducale.

BELOW: in Genoa's aquarium.

Genoa Café Life

Sweet-toothed Genoa is serious about its pastry shops and traditional tea-rooms, where you can tuck into cakes and coffee at most times of day. **Caffe Klainguti** (Via di Soziglia 100) is a marble-and-gilt tearooms, bar and pastry shop in business since 1829. The Art Nouveau tearooms, complete with chandeliers, are a classic haunt for shoppers. **Romanengo** (Via di Soziglia 74) is the most celebrated *pasticceria* in town, a frescoed, mirrored and chandeliered setting for pyramids of cakes, chocolate and candied fruit, with secret family recipes dating back to 1780. **Pasticceria Romanego** (Via degli Orefici 31) is an offshoot, a grand, old-world chocolate-box of a café. **Pasticceria Villa** (Via del Portello 2) is noted for *pandolce*, a rich cake studded with candied fruit.

Nearby, on Piazza Pelliceria, **Palazzo Spinola G** (Tues–Sat 9am–8pm, Sun 1pm–8pm) is a gilded tribute to its ancestral owners. When the Spinola line died out in 1958, the palace was preserved in aspic, with its frescoed family chapel and gallery of mirrors, modelled on Versailles. It is the quintessential city palace, austere on the outside, gorgeous within: a portrait of the secretive Genovese aristocracy.

Further south, the Romanesque-Gothic **Duomo H** is dedicated to St Lawrence, and a Gothic portal depicts the Roman saint's gruesome martyrdom. While being burnt alive, St Lawrence said to his tormentors: "One side has been roasted, turn me over and eat it."

The Doria family, who ruled Genoa in the Middle Ages, built their residences and a private church around the **Piazza San Matteo I**, lying just behind the cathedral. Each of the buildings on this small, elegant piazza has a black-and-white facade. Between San Matteo and the port lies the most beguiling part of Old Genoa. Also near the cathedral is the 16th-century **Palazzo Ducale J**,

once the seat of government but now a cool cultural centre, which stages jazz and art exhibitions.

Towards the medieval city's eastern limits is the **Porta Soprana**, the twin-towered gateway and the **Casa Colombo de Cristoforo** (Sat–Sun 10am–6pm; charge). This is the reconstructed boyhood home of Genoa's most famous son, Christopher Columbus (1451–1506).

Genoa's port

The aromas of pesto, pasta and grilled fish mingle in the labyrinthine alleys behind the glittering waterfront and the **Porto Antico K**. As a medieval trading empire, Genoa fought with Venice and Pisa for mastery over the Mediterranean shipping channels and trade with the Orient. Today, the city is Italy's most important port, with one of the most densely packed historical centres in Europe.

Genoa's second-most famous son is the architect Renzo Piano, whose work has helped transform the city. The transformation began with the Columbus celebrations in 1992, which marked

BELOW: Camogli.

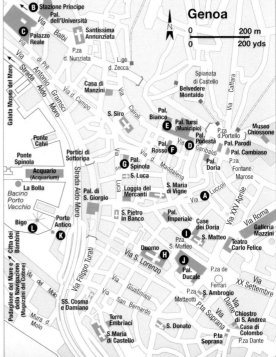

the 500th anniversary of the discovery of the Americas. Building upon Piano's work on the harbour, the Porto Antico was given a facelift for the city's celebrations as European City of Culture in 2004. In this model urban regeneration project, which covered the whole city, the port area retained its raffish charm, with rough and ready dockside cafés, at one with the sensitive conversion of shipyards and customs houses.

Styled on an ocean-going cargo ship docked in the harbour, Renzo Piano's **Acquario** (Aquarium; daily Mar–June and Sept–Oct 9am–7.30pm, Sat–Sun until 8.30pm, July–Aug 8.30am–10pm, Nov–Feb 9.30am–7.30pm, Sat–Sun until 8.30pm, last entrance 2 hours before closing; charge) is the biggest in Europe, and is one of Italy's most visited attractions. The Aquarium houses spectacular shark and dolphin tanks, and plays a vital role in monitoring the coast and rescuing beached dolphins.

Next door, Renzo Piano's **La Bolla** (daily Mar–Oct 10am–7pm, Nov–Feb until 5pm; charge) is a futuristic glass-and-steel bubble containing tropical plants and a collection of rare ferns, among which butterflies flit around freely. Inspired by sails, **Il Bigol ❶** (Tues–Sun 10am–11pm, Mon 4–11pm; times reduced in winter; charge) is an enormous crane, visible for miles, which whisks passengers 40 metres (130ft) high in a cylindrical lift for panoramic views over the city and waterfront.

The dockyards (Darsena) have also been regenerated, creating new entertainment and cultural centres. Maritime culture is showcased in the **Galata Museo del Mare** (Museum of the Sea; daily Nov–end Feb Tues–Fri 10am–6pm, until 7.30pm Sat and Sun, Mar–Oct Tues–Sun 10am–7.30pm, last entry 1½ hours before closing; charge). Housed in old cotton warehouses, the museum occupies the most ancient part of the arsenal and the boatyards where galleys were constructed. The highlight is a faithful reconstruction of a 17th-century Genoese galley, a design that conquered the world.

With the redesigned waterfront, Genoa now has a port worthy of a maritime republic. As well as welcoming new museums, Porto Antico functions as the new city piazza: it has a swimming pool that transforms into an open-air theatre in summer; and an ice rink that turns into a summer concert venue. All done with great taste and no hint of a theme park.

The Italian Rivieras

Flanking Genoa are two distinctive coasts and different moods. The western **Riviera di Ponente**, stretching from Genoa to the French border, is generally home to the larger, long-established resorts. In contrast, the eastern **Riviera di Levante** is characterised by rocky cliffs and promontories, as well as by smaller, more romantic resorts, which are mostly overgrown fishing villages.

Heading towards France from Genoa, miss the industrial port of **Savona** in favour of **Finale Ligure ⓲**, where the **church of San Biagio** is graced by an octagonal Gothic bell tower.

Albenga ⓳, the most appealing town on the Riviera di Ponente, is

San Remo's Russian Orthodox church.

BELOW: Portovenere.

a Roman town with well-preserved medieval walls, 17th-century gates and a cathedral dating from the 5th century. Even older are the Roman aqueduct and the ruins of a Roman amphitheatre. In addition to the historic monuments are opportunities for swimming and boating. The neighbouring resort of **Alassio** ⓴ has long been popular with celebrities, who are drawn to the pretty bay and long sandy beach.

The resort of **San Remo** ㉑ was once a watering hole of the European aristocracy and retains an air of sophistication, accentuated by its palm-lined promenade and popular casino. The **Chiesa Russa**, an authentic Russian Orthodox church (1913) reflects San Remo's heyday as a haunt of the Russian nobility (daily 9.30am–12.30pm and 3–6.30pm, 6pm in winter; charge). Another landmark is the Art Nouveau **Villa Nobel**, erstwhile home of philanthropist Alfred Nobel (1833–96). But the biggest boost to tourism is the exciting new coastal cycle-pedestrian path, which follows

a disused railway line and revels in stunning sea and mountain views (*see below*).

Further along the coast is the more charming **Bordighera** ㉒, where the medieval Old Town is complemented by a palm-lined promenade, which makes a delightful evening *passeggiata*, with artisanal ice cream the usual pretext. Just inland lies a rugged, more authentic Liguria, where picturesque **Dolceacqua** ㉓ surveys a ruined castle, humpbacked stone bridge and vineyards beyond.

The gateway to France is via rundown **Ventimiglia** ㉔, a centre of flower cultivation, with an excellent Friday market and a dilapidated medieval quarter. Set on the Cape about 6km (4 miles) away is the **Giardino Hanbury** (mid-June–mid-Sept daily 9.30am–7pm, until 5pm in winter; charge). Here, Sir Thomas Hanbury, an English botanist and Victorian merchant, created an atmospheric botanical paradise, widely regarded as the most evocative gardens in Liguria.

West of Ventimiglia, virtually on the French frontier, are the prehis-

BELOW: stylish San Remo.

Riviera Coastal Route

A spectacular new cycle and pedestrian path hugs the picturesque Ligurian coast en route to the French Riviera. It is the perfect way to explore quaint fishing villages and the glamorous resort of San Remo.

The first 24km (15 miles) from Ospedaletti to San Lorenzo al Mare offer an exhilarating Riviera break for cycling fans, families or walkers. When finished in 2012, this will be Europe's longest coastal cycle path, part of a regenerated coastal park. The 74km (46-mile) long path will run to Finale Ligure but already abounds in magnificent coastal views as well as links to food trails in the hills. The current path provides access to 5km (3 miles) of previously unreachable beaches and a vast marine park, which acts as a whale sanctuary.

toric caves, **Balzi Rossi** (Tues–Sun 9am–12.30pm and 2–6pm in summer, 9am–1pm and 2.30–6pm winter; charge). In addition to skeletons dating from over 100,000 years ago, there are fossils, fertility figures, weapons and tools.

Riviera di Levante

Among the eastern suburbs of Genoa is **Quarto dei Mille**, famous as the starting point of Garibaldi's valiant 1,000-man expedition that liberated Sicily and led to the unification of Italy. Nearby **Nervi** ㉕, reached by train or on a boat trip from Porto Antico, is dotted with lavish villas, including several turned into art museums. Come for the combination of low-key art in intimate villas, cliff-top strolls, swimming off the rocks, or grilled fish and a crisp white Cinque Terre wine. This life is too good to leave to the villa-owning Genovese "shipocracy".

After the beguiling former fishing village of **Camogli**, drive or take a boat to picture-postcard **Portofino** ㉖, the Riviera's calling card. Once, only fishing boats docked in the narrow, deep-green inlet, edged by high cliffs, but it is now a berth for luxury yachts.

Part of Portofino's attraction is its size. There are no beaches, and little to do except lap up the views, especially from the quaint Castello Browne at the top of the village. The pleasures of the port are visual – the watery reflection of painted facades, the ragged edges of stone heights set against the brilliant blue sky. Far more down to earth is **Rapallo** ㉗, a sedate resort, with a large beach, unpretentious hotels and a welcoming atmosphere.

"Paradise on earth" is how Lord Byron described the cluster of five little fishing villages that make up **Le Cinque Terre** ㉘. Monterosso al Mare, Vernazza, Corniglia, Manarola and Riomaggiore cling perilously to the steep rocky coast north of La Spezia, and are best reached by train (www.parconazionale5terre.it). This 16km

(10-mile) stretch of protected parkland is laced with cliffside walking trails which offer vertiginous views over terraced olive groves and jaunty villages. Hikes usually end over a plate of pesto-scented pasta and aromatic white wine.

From Dante to Shelley, the Gulf of La Spezia has been praised so often by poets that it is also known as the Golfo dei Poeti. On its western point the elongated orange-and-yellow houses of **Portovenere** ㉙ stretch up the precipitous mountain.

Anglophiles and romantics should make a pilgrimage to the grotto from where the virile Lord Byron began his famous swim across the Gulf to visit Shelley in **Casa Magni**. If you take the 20-minute boat ride to **Lerici** ㉚ you will appreciate what a powerful swimmer the poet must have been.

Shelley had less luck against the waves when his ship sank off the coast. A plaque on Casa Magni commemorates the tragedy: "Sailing on a fragile bark he was landed, by an unforeseen chance, in the silence of the Elysian Fields." ❏

Monterosso, one of the Cinque Terre, five fishing villages towering above the coastline.

BELOW: church above Portovenere.

CENTRAL ITALY

Subtle differences in art, cooking, architecture and attitude to life – even between neighbouring towns – help to form a destination that appeals to both the heart and the head

To many travellers, central Italy is the true Italy – that is, the Italy they know from Merchant-Ivory films of E.M. Forster novels, or from the pictures that adorn all the tour brochures. Ironically, the people of this region are reluctant to admit to being Italian at all. They are Tuscan, Florentine, Sienese, Bolognese or Perugian – not a semantic distinction, but a deeply held conviction based on history, culture, and even tribal and genetic differences from the pre-Roman era. And this is an area where history is not the dry stuff of academic books, but a living part of the culture – for anthropologists, central Italy has long been fertile ground for testing the belief that competition for resources leads people to emphasise their differences. If you want to see this process in action, visit any Umbrian or Tuscan town during its annual festivities – not to mention Siena during Palio, or Florence during Calcio in Costume (Football in Costume) – and feel the intense and elemental atmosphere of inter-parish rivalry.

Such rivalries are reflected in myriad ways that make exploring the region a delight for the sensitive and enquiring traveller. Food is an obvious indicator, whether it be the subtle differences between sheep's-milk cheeses, the more emphatic distinctions between a crisp Orvieto wine and a soft, fruity Chianti, or whether it be the view firmly held by every seafront restaurant along the Tuscan Riviera that theirs is the only authentic fish soup (*cacciucco*), and that it is far superior to anything the French produce.

Art and architecture is another indicator: labels, such as Florentine, Lombardic or Pisan Romanesque, at first seem designed to confuse the uninitiated, until continued exposure to some of the world's finest artistic creations helps you distinguish between the light-filled limpidity of the School of Perugino and the crisply delineated and boldly coloured frescoes of Benozzo Gozzoli – unmistakably Florentine even when encountered in the tiny Umbrian hill town of Montefalco. ❑

PRECEDING PAGES: the Duomo dominating the Florence skyline at sunset.
LEFT: *la dolce vita*: girls enjoying the nightlife. **ABOVE:** bridges across the Arno in Florence, with Ponte Vecchio in the foreground; delicious cakes; 6th-century mosaics in San Vitale Basilica, Ravenna, of Christ the Redeemer.

EMILIA-ROMAGNA

Italy's gastronomic heartland is also noted for its cities of art, smart beach resorts and the late Roman mosaics of Ravenna – these are beguiling cities, built on a human scale

BELOW: delicacies on display in a Bologna deli.

Emilia-Romagna is the land of plenty, arguably the most civilised region in Italy. Fertile plains and centuries of agricultural wealth have helped foster a well-managed economy, typified by the citizens' love of good food. It is no accident that Bologna is the country's gastronomic capital, and home to Parma ham, Parmesan cheese and the richest stuffed pasta.

The region is also home to some of Italy's greatest cities of art, including the Unesco World Heritage sites of Ferrara, Ravenna and Modena. In the Renaissance, Ferrara was the home of the d'Este dynasty, whose court was a centre of culture and learning. Ravenna was a great international centre from the 4th to the 8th centuries, originally as a centre of the Western Roman Empire, then as the capital of Byzantine Italy.

Bologna

The capital of Emilia-Romagna, **Bologna ❶** mastered the art of living in medieval times when a pink-brick town grew up around Europe's oldest university. The city is also celebrated for its cuisine, its traditional left-wing stance and its beautifully preserved medieval heart. Built in a soft reddish brick, the the city is lined with handsome porticoes, designed to shelter the population from inclement weather. The porticoes, Bologna's trademark, also add an air of conviviality to everyday life.

The Old City evolved around two adjoining squares, **Piazza Maggiore ❶** and **Piazza del Nettuno ❸**. Together these squares form the symbolic heart of the city, showcasing the political and religious institutions that define independent-minded Bologna. The space also forms a stage set for Bolognese life, from Prada-clad beauties to protesting students and pot-bellied sausage-makers.

On the south side of Piazza Maggiore stands **San Petronio ❹**, the largest church in Bologna. Originally, the Bolognese had hoped to outdo St

Peter's in Rome, but Church authorities decreed that some funds be set aside for the construction of nearby Archiginnasio. San Petronio's barn-like design is by Antonio di Vincenzo, and although construction began in 1390, the facade is still unfinished. The completed sections are of red-and-white marble and decorated with reliefs of biblical scenes. The interior is simple but elegant. Most of the bare brick walls remain unadorned. In the fifth chapel on the left is a spectacular 15th-century altarpiece of the *Martyrdom of St Sebastian* by Lorenzo Costa.

Behind San Petronio is the **Palazzo Archiginnasio D**, former seat of Europe's most ancient university, in whose 17th-century **Sala Anatomica** (Mon–Fri 9am–6.45pm, Sat 9am–1.45pm; summer hours vary, tel: 051-276 811) some of the first dissections in Europe were performed.

Stroll back to Piazza del Nettuno to appreciate the **Fontana di Nettuno E**, a 16th-century fountain with bronze sculptures by Giambologna of a muscle-bound Neptune surrounded by cherubs and mermaids. A puritanical papal edict once decreed that Neptune should be robed, but the priapic sea god is now free to frolic. (The locals take great delight in pointing out the best vantage point for viewing the god's impressive manhood.) On its west side is the majestic **Palazzo Comunale F**, the medieval town hall remodelled in the Renaissance. The bronze statue above the gateway is of Pope Gregory XIII, a native of Bologna. To the left is a beautiful terracotta Madonna by Niccolò dell'Arca. Inside are grand public rooms and the **Museo Morandi** (Tues–Sat 9am–6.30pm; free), a fine collection of works by Bolognese artist Giorgio Morandi (1890–1964), one of the greatest still-life painters of modern times.

Foodie heaven

From here, plunge into the maze of alleys known as the **Mercato di Mezzo G** (Mon–Sat 7am–1pm, 4–7pm). Here,

the mood is as boisterously authentic as it was in its medieval heyday. **Via Pescherie Vecchie** even conceals Bologna's oldest "inn", Osteria del Sole, a wine shop since 1486. This market area promises a true taste of Emilia, with open-air stalls, food shops and a covered market selling the finest regional produce, from parmesan to *charcuterie*, olive oil, pasta and wine. Gaze and graze is the mantra as eyes are drawn to: juicy peaches; sculpted pastries; belly-button shaped pasta; slivers of pink Parma ham; succulent Bolognese mortadella; Modena artisanal balsamic vinegar; single-estate virgin olive oil; jiggling, jelly-like ricotta; still-flapping fish; and wedges of superior "black rind" parmesan. Few can resist a pasta-based lunch on meaty ravioli or tortellini at **Tamburini** (Via Drapperie/Via Caprarie 1), a legendary gourmet delicatessen and self-service.

Piazza del Nettuno acts as a familiar magnet, now sending you to Bologna's leaning towers. Simply follow **Via Rizzoli**, a picturesque street lined with cafés, down to **Piazza di Porta Ravegnana H**, at the foot of the **Due**

The iconic Vespa is still the favoured means of transport for young people.

BELOW: market stalls in Via Pescherie Vecchie, Bologna.

Santo Stefano is still run by stern Benedictines, one of whom confides: "Dante often came here to meditate in 1287 but we are not fussy – at Easter even the local prostitutes come here for confession."

Torri, the "leaning towers" of Bologna. In medieval days, 180 of these towers were built by the city's leading families; now only a dozen remain. Legend has it that the two richest families in Bologna – the Asinelli and the Garisenda – competed to build the tallest and most beautiful tower in the city. However, the Torre Garisenda was built on weak foundations and was never finished. For safety's sake it was shortened between 1351 and 1360, and is now only 48 metres (157ft) high and leans more than 3 metres (10ft) to one side. The **Torre degli Asinelli** (daily 9am–6pm, until 5pm in winter; charge) is still standing at its original height of 97 metres (318ft), but it too leans more than 1 metre (3ft) out of the perpendicular. It's a stiff climb to the top up 498 steps, but worth the effort for the wonderful views.

The **Strada Maggiore** leads east from the two towers along the original line of the Via Aemilia Roman road to the **Basilica di San Bartolomeo** ❶. Inside, look for the *Annunciation* by Albani in the fourth chapel of the south aisle, and a beautiful Madonna by Guido Reni in the north transept.

Further down the porticoed, patrician Strada Maggiore (at No. 34) is the **Museo della Musica** ❿ (Tues–Fri 9.30am–4pm, Sat–Sun 10am–6.30pm; free). Portraits of musicians and instruments are displayed in a palatial setting. Even non-classical music fans will be entranced by the *trompe l'œil* courtyard and the frescoed interiors, a rare chance to see how the Bolognese nobility lived. Beyond is **Santa Maria dei Servi** ❿, a well-preserved Gothic church.

The **Abbazia di Santo Stefano** ❿ (daily 9am–12.30 and 3.30–6.30pm) – a complex of churches all dedicated to St Stephen – is further down Via Santo Stefano, just south of the Casa Isolani, a medieval warren of palaces converted into chic galleries and pleasant cafés.

Santo Stefano is seven churches in one, like a nest of Chinese boxes. Dating back to AD 392, the complex became a Lombard basilica, then a Benedictine sanctuary in the 10th century. A harmonious ensemble is created by the interlocking churches and

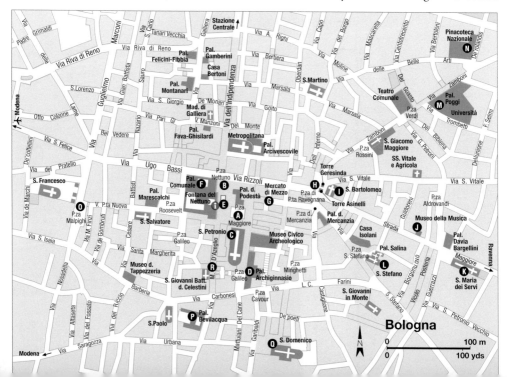

Bologna

0   100 m

0   100 yds

courtyards, including the Benedictine cloisters, graced by an elegant wellhead. Bathed in mystical light, Santi Vitale e Agricola feels the most compelling church, while Santo Sepolcro houses the tomb of St Petronius, the city patron.

Ancient university

Bologna's **University**, located on **Via Zamboni**, is the oldest in Italy and indeed Europe; it was founded in the 11th century and was famous in its early days for reviving the study of Roman law. Petrarch attended classes here, as did Copernicus. Today, although faculties are spread throughout the city, the official seat is the 16th-century **Palazzo Poggi** Ⓜ.

Past the university, on the left, is the **Pinacoteca Nazionale** Ⓝ (National Gallery; Tues–Sun 9am–7pm; charge), which showcases Bolognese and Emilian art from the Middle Ages to the 1700s, including works by Vitale da Bologna (especially the painting of *St George and the Dragon*) and Guido Reni. Other highlights are Raphael's *Ecstasy of St Cecilia* (1515) and Peru-

gino's *Madonna in Glory* (1491).

South and west of the Piazza Maggiore, Bologna has more architectural treasures. Follow the Via Ugo Bassi west to **Piazza Malpighi** Ⓞ. On the west side of this piazza rises **San Francesco,** a church constructed between 1236 and 1263, with a design of French Gothic inspiration. From San Francesco walk southeast until you reach **Palazzo Bevilacqua** Ⓟ, a medieval Tuscan-style palace where the Council of Trent met for two sessions after fleeing an epidemic in Trent. It is the boldest of Bologna's senatorial palaces and has a sandstone facade, wrought-iron balconies and a courtyard surrounded by a loggia.

Nearby, **San Domenico** Ⓠ dominates Piazza San Domenico. Dating from 1228, it was remodelled in Baroque style but incorporates Romanesque walls. The interior displays the tomb of St Dominic, founder of the Dominican Order, decorated with sculptures by Nicola Pisano and Arnolfo di Cambio of the Pisan School, as well as two by the young Michelangelo.

Parmesan, the king of Italian cheeses.

BELOW LEFT: Piazza Grande in Modena.
BELOW: stone lion outside Modena's Romanesque Duomo.

Return to Piazza Maggiore along **Via d'Azeglio ®**. This forms part of the city's *passeggiata*, or ritual evening stroll, and is a chance to see the city at its most sociable. This pedestrianised street is known as "*il salotto*", the open-air drawing room, the place for chatting over cocktails and designer shopping.

Bologna has earned a number of epithets: "*La Dotta*" (The Learned One), "*La Turritta*" (The Turreted One), "*La Rossa*" (The Red One, as much for its reddish buildings as for its politics) and finally "*La Grassa*" (The Fat One) for its rich cooking. Consider dining on mortadella (salami), tortellini or tagliatelle, said to have been invented for the marriage feast of Lucrezia Borgia and the Duke of Ferrara.

Modena

Prosperous **Modena ❷** is associated with fat tenors and sleek cars. The late Pavarotti came from Modena, as do Maserati and Ferrari. But the city is a Unesco World Heritage site in its own right. If Modena remains underrated it is partly because the smug locals have done little to attract visitors. Since the Romans conquered Modena in the 2nd century BC, the city has thrived. The success of the food, Ferrari and ceramics industries has been instrumental in making tourism a mere afterthought in this cosseted land of plenty.

Modena's massive and magnificent Romanesque **Duomo** was founded in the late 11th century by Countess Matilda of Tuscany, who engaged Lanfranco, the greatest architect of the time, to mastermind the project. The pink Verona marble structure is a mirror of the medieval mind, with friezes of saints and monsters, pilgrims and knights, griffins and doves, dragons and deer. The **Museo del Duomo** (Tues–Sun 9.30am–12.30pm and 3.30–6.30pm) contains impressive 12th-century metopes, low reliefs which once surmounted the flying buttresses.

The partly Gothic, partly Romanesque bell tower that stands to one side is the famous **Torre Ghirlandina**. It contains a bucket whose theft from Bologna in 1325 sparked off a war between the two cities.

Frequently seen strolling around Modena are the smartly dressed students of the **Accademia Militare**, Italy's military academy, housed in a 17th-century palace in the centre of Modena.

The major Modenese cultural hub, **Palazzo dei Musei**, contains several galleries, including the impressive art collection in the **Galleria Estense** (Tues–Sun 8.30am–7.30pm; charge), and the **Biblioteca Estense** (Mon–Sat 9am–1pm; charge), the library of the d'Este family, dukes of Modena as well as Ferrara. On permanent display in the library is a collection of illuminated manuscripts, a 1481 copy of Dante's *Divine Comedy*, and the stunning Borso d'Este Bible, which contains 1,200 miniatures.

Parma

Parma ❸ is a byword for fine living, from Parmesan and Parma ham to music and Mannerist art. There is no better place to become a connoisseur of *parmigiano* (Parmesan) than in Parma, where the cheese is made.

Napoleon's widow, Marie Louise, was ceded this city after her husband's death. Apart from building roads and founding public institutions, she also created the superb **Galleria Nazionale** (Tues–Sun 8.30am–1.30pm; charge). It is set in the 16th-century **Palazzo della Pilotta**, a palace which also contains the **Teatro Farnese**, a Palladian theatre with Italy's first revolving stage. Italy's noble courts gave birth to countless such theatres, but this one was the largest of its day.

However, the main attraction in Parma is the **Duomo** (daily 9am–12.30pm and 3–7pm) and adjoining Baptistery. Its nave and cupola are decorated with splendid frescoes by Correggio. Contemporaries gushed over them: Titian said that if the dome of the cathedral were turned upside down and filled with gold it would not be as valuable as Correggio's frescoes. Vasari wrote of the *Assumption*: "It seems impossible that a man could have conceived such a work as this is, and more

impossible still, that he should have done it with human hands."

The brilliantly restored **Baptistery** (daily 9am–12.30pm and 3–6.45pm; charge) is the work of Benedetto Antelami, who built this octagonal building in rich rose-pink Verona marble and then sculpted the reliefs that adorn both the interior and the exterior. Inside is a superb cycle of frescoes. Antelami's earliest known work, the *Deposizione* (1178), can be seen in the Duomo. This deeply moving sculpture was hewn from a single piece of marble.

In the dome of **San Giovanni Evangelista** another splendidly sensuous Correggio fresco (*c.*1520) can be seen. It depicts St John gazing up at heaven where the Apostles are gathered, and is matched by frescoes by Parmigiano. Nearby are Renaissance cloisters, a refectory and a Benedictine library. Of particular interest is the Benedictine Dispensary (pharmacy; Tues–Sun 8.30am–1.30pm, June and Sept Mon–Fri 8.30am–6pm, Sat–Sun until 7pm; charge), complete with 16th-century apothecary's jars.

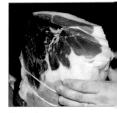

Parma ham (prosciutto di Parma) has a slightly nutty flavour, which comes from the fact that Parmesan whey is sometimes added to the pigs' diet.

Parma Ham and Parmesan

Parma ham and Parmesan cheese *(parmigiano)* are intricately linked, because it is the whey – the waste-product from Parmesan production – that is used to feed the pigs that produce Parma ham. True Parma ham is branded with the five-pointed crown of the medieval dukes of Parma, and is produced in the hills south of Parma. Here the raw hind thighs are hung in drying sheds for up to 10 months. The air that blows through the sheds is said to impart a sweet flavour to the meat – unlike cheap, mass-produced *prosciutto crudo*, which is injected with brine and artificially dried to speed up the curing process.

Try it as a starter *(antipasto)*, sliced into wafer-thin slivers for eating with bread, melon or figs; end your meal, perhaps, with slivers of superior *parmigiano-reggiano*, partnered with apples, pears or a good red wine.

Another regional speciality is *aceto balsamico* (balsamic vinegar), which, in its prized (and pricey) artisanal version, bears no resemblance to the industrial slime often found in supermarkets. It is made from sweet grape juice, boiled slowly and reduced to a syrup, mixed with vinegar and then aged in wooden casks for many years. A few drops transform a salad, but it can even be drizzled over fresh berries or ice cream.

Beyond Parma

If driving northwest on the Via Aemilia towards Piacenza, consider making a quick stop in **Fidenza ❹** to see another glorious Romanesque cathedral. Just beyond Fidenza is the turn-off for the little town of **Roncole Verdi ❺**, where you can visit the humble cottage in which Giuseppe Verdi (1813–1901) was born (Tues–Sun 9.30am–12.30pm and 3–7pm Apr–Sept, until 5pm in winter; charge).

Situated at the point where the Via Aemilia meets the Po, **Piacenza ❻** has been a lively trading post since 218 BC. Nothing remains of the Roman period, though there are many fine medieval and Renaissance buildings. At the centre of the city is the massive **Palazzo del Comune** (not open to the public), called "Il Gotico". Begun in 1280, it is a well-preserved building of brick, marble and terracotta.

In front of it loom two massive Baroque equestrian statues of Piacenza's 16th-century rulers, the Farnese dukes. At the end of Via Venti Settembre stands Piacenza's Romanesque **Duomo** (daily 7.30am–noon and 4–7pm).

Although gloomy inside, the cathedral is worth a visit for the frescoes on the columns near the entrance.

Ferrara

Set on the banks of the misty River Po, **Ferrara ❼** is both a one-dynasty town and one of most beguiling cities in the region. Its Unesco World Heritage status springs from its artistic self-sufficiency and the jewel-like appeal of its frescoed, Renaissance palaces. The mist lends an air of mystery, as do the secret gardens and city walls.

The d'Este family ruled Ferrara from the late 13th century until 1598, a time of prosperity when their court attracted poets, scholars and artists. The Renaissance, the city's golden age, is reflected in all the major monuments.

Dominating Ferrara's skyline is the restored medieval **Castello Estense** (Tues–Sun 9.30am–5.30pm; charge; café and tourist office inside), complete with moats, drawbridges and towers. Just behind the castle is Ferrara's 12th-century **Duomo**. Among the noteworthy paintings here and in the adjoining museum (Museo della

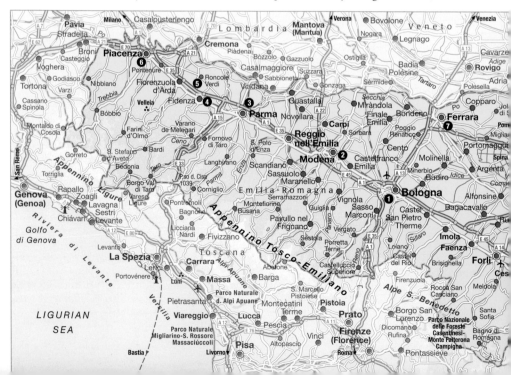

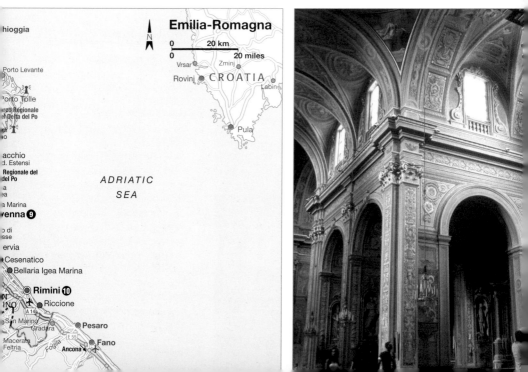

Cattedrale; Tues–Sun 9am–1pm and 3–6pm; charge) are Cosimo Tura's *St George* and his *Annunciation*, and Jacopo della Quercia's *Madonna della Melagrana* (1408).

Across from the Duomo is the **Palazzo del Comune** (not open to the public), a medieval building with a beautiful Renaissance staircase. The piazza in front of this town hall is the hub of life in modern Ferrara, and teeming with bicycles, the number-one method of transport in this very flat region of the Po Valley.

Medieval splendour

Many of the medieval streets south of the cathedral are lined with fortified mansions, and, stretching across the **Via delle Volte**, a narrow street near the Po, there are a number of elegant arches. At the beautiful **Palazzo Schifanoia** (Tues–Sun 9am–6pm; charge), one of the d'Este family's summer residences, you can climb the steep stairs to the Salone dei Mesi, a large, high room decorated with colourful frescoes of the months. However, most have deteriorated and their colours dulled. These were executed for the duke of Borgo d'Este by masters of the Ferrarese School, including Ercole de' Roberti.

Just around the corner is another d'Este palace, the **Palazzo di Ludovico il Moro**, designed by the famous Ferrarese Renaissance architect Biagio Rossetti. This houses the **Museo Archeologico Nazionale** (Via XX Settembre; Tues–Sun 9am–2pm; charge), which has a fine collection of Etruscan artefacts.

North of the Duomo, Ferrara is a city of broad avenues. Along one of the prettiest streets, Corso Ercole d'Este, is Rossetti's **Palazzo dei Diamanti**, a late Renaissance structure, characterised by a bizarre facade studded with diamond shapes created in honour of the d'Este family, whose emblem it was. The first floor is home to the **Pinacoteca Nazionale** (Tues–Sat 10am–1pm, Sun 3–6pm; charge), a permanent collection of masterpieces from the Veneto and Venice. The **Spazio Espositivo** on the ground floor is dedicated to temporary blockbuster exhibitions of modern or contemporary art (www. palazzodeidiamanti.it).

Ariosto, Petrarch, Tasso, Mantegna and Bellini were just some of the great Italian poets and painters patronised by the d'Este family of Ferrara.

BELOW: inside Ferrara's cathedral.

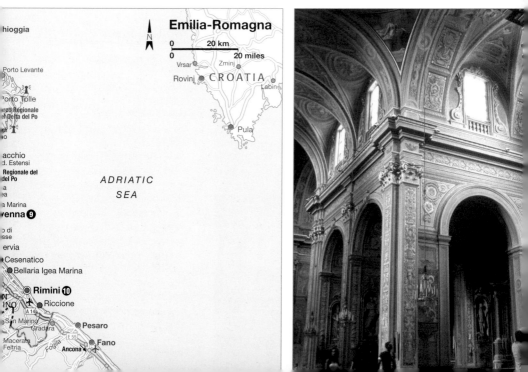

The Po Delta

From Ferrara you can explore the **Po Delta wetlands** by car, with lunch in **Comacchio ⑧**, a miniature Venice, and a visit to **Pomposa Abbey** (Abbazia di Pomposa), a Romanesque Benedictine foundation with fine frescoes.

The drive through Italy's Camargue, between Ferrara and Comacchio, passes nature reserves, water defences and drainage schemes, from locks and flood plains to the raised canal banks, which now serve as scenic roads and cycle tracks. A summer trip could end at a discreet beach. **Lido degli Estensi** is a sought-after resort set among pine groves, while the sand dunes at Lido di Pomposa are conveniently close to Pomposa Abbey.

Ravenna

When the unstoppable barbarians overran Rome in the 5th century AD, **Ravenna ⑨** benefited, gaining the honourable rank of capital of the Western Empire. This Adriatic port town continued as capital under the Ostrogoths, and the barbarian leaders Odoacer and Theodoric also ruled their vast dominions from here. Later, when the Byzantine emperor Justinian reconquered part of Italy, he too made Ravenna its capital, liking it for its imperial tradition under the barbarians and – perhaps more importantly – for its direct sea links to Byzantium.

Under Justinian's rule the Ravenna we know today began to take shape. New buildings arose all over the city, including a handful of churches that are among the wonders of Italian art and architecture. There is no preparation in their simple brick exteriors for the brilliant mosaics within. It is these mosaics that make modern Ravenna, if no longer capital of the Western world, at least a capital of the Western art world.

Amazing mosaics

Start with **San Vitale** (daily 9am–7pm; charge), the city's great 6th-century octagonal basilica, famous for the mosaics in its choir and apse. These "monuments of unageing intellect", as the Irish poet W.B. Yeats called them, immediately draw the eye with their marvellous colours and intricate detail.

BELOW: interior of Sant'Apollinaire in Classe, Ravenna.

Poetic Licence

After the death of Dante, Italy's greatest poet, the repentant Florentines wished to honour their famous son with a splendid tomb, but proud Ravenna refused to give up the poet's remains. The battle over the bones continued for hundreds of years.

In 1519, the rich and powerful Medici of Florence sent their representatives to Ravenna with a papal injunction demanding the relics. The sarcophagus was duly opened, but the bones were not inside. Someone had been warned of the Florentine scheme and had removed the bones to a secret hiding place. They were not found again until 1865, and now rest within Dante's sarcophagus in Ravenna. To this day, the city of Florence provides the oil for the lamp which burns on his tomb.

Bright ducks, bulls, lions, dolphins and a phoenix intertwine with flowers and corners of buildings to frame Old Testament scenes and portraits of Byzantine rulers with humour and exactitude.

In the dome of the apse a purple-clad and beardless Christ sits on a blue globe flanked by archangels and, at the far sides, St Vitalis and Bishop Ecclesius. Christ hands the saint (Ravenna's patron) a triumphal crown, while the bishop (who founded the church in 521) carries a model of the building as it finally appeared many years after his death. Below stretch imperial scenes of Justinian with his courtiers and Theodora, his beloved wife, with hers.

San Vitale is not the only place to see mosaics in Ravenna. Nearly every church contains a pristine example of the art. Just north, another set may be seen at the **Mausoleo di Galla Placidia** (daily 9am–7pm; charge). This interesting lady was born a Roman princess, sister to Emperor Honorius, but after she was captured by the Goths, she married their leader, Athaulf, and ruled with him. He, however, soon died, and she next married a Roman general to whom she bore a son. This son became Emperor Valentinian III. As Valentinian's regent, and a woman with connections in the highest barbarian circles, Galla Placidia played a powerful role in the world of "the decline". The building that houses her tomb has a simple exterior, but inside the walls, floors and ceiling are covered with glorious mosaics, the oldest in Ravenna. Built between 425 and 450, it is bathed in green light which becomes aquamarine higher up the walls. The mystical atmosphere is intensified by the strikingly simple style of the mosaics, including the cobalt-blue sky sprinkled with gold stars. Despite the simple Christian iconography, the realism of the figures reflects the naturalistic Roman style as much as a nascent Christian one.

Through the gate that lies between San Vitale and Galla Placidia are two Renaissance cloisters that now house the **Museo Nazionale** (Tues–Sun 8.30am–7.30pm; charge). The museum includes, as one might expect, many mosaics, as well as other relics from

The glorious mosaics depicting an ethereal blue sky sprinkled with gold stars which fill the vaulted ceiling of the Mausoleo di Galla Placidia are said to have inspired Cole Porter to write his timeless song "Night and Day".

BELOW: mosaics at the Mausoleo di Galla Placidia.

TIP

In Ravenna, take Via
Barbiani to visit the
excavated mosaic floors
known as Domus di
Tappetti di Pietra
(Carpet of Stones). This
underground mosaic
pavement was
unearthed within a
14th-century church
and reveals the dining
room of a classical
Roman villa (10am–
6pm Mon–Sat; tel:
0544-32512).

Ravenna's past. There is glass from San Vitale and also fabrics from the tomb of St Julian at Rimini.

The Baroque Duomo

A pleasant walk along Via Fanni, Via Barbiani and left onto Via d'Azeglio leads to Ravenna's **Duomo** – originally constructed in the 5th century but redone in Baroque style in the 1730s. Far more attractive than the cathedral itself is the adjoining **Battistero Neoniano** (daily 9am–7pm; charge), a 5th-century octagonal baptistery that was once a Roman bathhouse. The interior combines spectacular Byzantine mosaics with marble inlay from the original.

Across Piazza Caduti from the cathedral complex is **San Francesco**, another 5th-century church almost completely redone in the Baroque style. To the left stands the **Tomba di Dante** (closed for restoration; Tel: 0544-30252), not a remarkable building architecturally, but significant historically. Dante, the author of *The Divine Comedy*, was exiled from his home in Florence for his political outspokenness and found refuge

in Ravenna in 1317. He spent the remaining four years of his life here, putting the finishing touches to his great work (*see panel page 256*).

Down the Via di Roma is another church full of mosaics, **Sant'Apollinare Nuovo** (daily 9am–7pm; charge). Flanked by a cylindrical bell tower, it was built between 493 and 496. The scenes are of processions, one of virgins and the other of martyrs who appear to be moving towards the altar between rows of palms. Above, the decorations depict episodes from the *Life of Christ*. Opposite stands the basilica of **San Giovanni Evangelista** (daily 7.30am–noon and 3.30–6.30pm), with a sculpted marble portal. Dating from the 5th century but much altered, it was built by Galla Placidia. Legend has it that she had vowed to build the church in return for surviving a shipwreck on a voyage from Constantinople.

Rimini

As the capital of the Riviera, **Rimini** ❿ is a year-round destination, although regularly dismissed as a lacklustre

BELOW: mosaic of the three Magi in Sant'Apollinare Nuovo in Ravenna.

+SCS BALTHASSAR +SCS MELCHIOR +SCS GASPAR

beach resort. The coastal strip may be dominated by bland hotels, but the San Giuliano fishing district is quaint and the historic centre charming.

Begin in its heart, in Piazza Cavour, and admire the **Vecchia Peschiera**, the former fish market, just off the square. This area is part of Rimini's revival, confirmed by a clutch of boutique hotels, bars and design stores which are drawing more sophisticated visitors. But this is no mere makeover: the resort has been revitalised by the opening of a major new Roman site, complemented by an intriguing archaeological museum, and the transformation of the dynastic Malatesta castle into a cultural centre. Rimini's seaside sauciness remains, but the resort's reputation as a graveyard for pensioners on package tours is being put to rest.

Roman remains

From Piazza Cavour the bustling Corso leads to **Piazza Ferrari**, home to the **Rimini Domus** archaeological site, the adjoining Roman **Surgeon's House** (**Domus del Chirugo**) and the archaeological wing of the **Museo Civico** (Tues–Sat 10am–12.30pm; 4.30–7.30pm, Sun 4.30–7.30pm). The interlinked complex contains fine Roman mosaics and frescoes, which date back to the 2nd century AD. This grand home belonged to an army surgeon, whose medical instruments are on display, including mortars, scalpels and a gruesome gadget designed to extract arrowheads. The area was then abandoned until the early 5th century, with the transfer of the imperial capital to Ravenna. The new archaeological section charts the region's history from pre-Roman to Celtic times.

A stroll along the Corso leads to **Piazza Tre Martiri**, named in honour of three Italian partisans hanged here by the Nazis in 1944. Yet the square is also the site of the Roman forum, whose columns now support the porticoes of the two eastern buildings.

Around the corner is the **Tempio**

Malatestiano (Mon–Sat 8am–12.30pm and 3.30–7pm, Sun 9am–1pm and 3.30–7pm; free) a tribute to the dynastic ruler Sigismondo Malatesta, who transformed a Gothic Franciscan church into a Renaissance gem fit for his mistress Isotta. Pope Pius II threatened to excommunicate the debauched Sigismondo, calling the site "a temple of devil-worshippers".

Sigismondo had better luck with women and artists. He was patron of such luminaries as Leon Battista Alberti, who designed this temple, inspired by the Roman Arch of Augustus which still stands at the gates of Rimini. Inside the temple, on the right, is Sigismondo's tomb, decorated with his initials intertwined with Isotta's. Note the fresco of Sigismondo praying at the feet of St Sigismond, by Piero della Francesca.

For a Roman farewell to Rimini, walk along **Corso di Augusto** to the **Arco di Augusto**, dating from 27 BC. This Arch of Augustus marked the junction of the Via Aemilia and Via Flaminia, the route from Rome to the Adriatic. ❏

Film director Federico Fellini (1902–93) was born in Rimini. His Oscar-winning film Amarcord *immortalised the area in the 1970s, and the Fellini-esque atmosphere is still evident in the narrow streets and small houses around the Borgo San Giuliano. The famous "old lady" of Adriatic hotels, the Grand, stands in the park named after him.*

BELOW: the beach and Grand Hotel, Rimini.

FLORENCE

One of the world's great architectural masterpieces, packed with palaces and art galleries, Florence is an essential stop on any modern-day Grand Tour

More than any other Italian city, Florence is defined by its artistic heritage. The city is both blessed and burdened by a civic identity bound up with the Renaissance, and basks in its reflected glory. As the birthplace of the Renaissance, the city witnessed the Florentine miracle, a flowering of the human spirit that has left a lasting artistic imprint. The churches, palaces and galleries are studded with the world's greatest concentration of Renaissance art and sculpture. In 1743 Anna Maria Lodovica, the last of the Medici line, bequeathed her property to Florence, ensuring that the Medici collections remained intact for ever. As a result, Florence is still awash with many of the treasures that Vasari, the first art historian, mentions in his *Lives of the Artists* (1550).

Although Renaissance glories have given way to insatiable art tourism, the city remains the most harmonious in Italy. To counter the crowds, visit out of season, combine major and minor attractions, and book a private guide to see a secret side of Florence reflecting your own interests (Link; tel: 055-218 191; www.link firenze.it). Moreover, to avoid queues, pre-book the "blockbuster" museums, such as the Uffizi (tel: 055-294 883; www.firenzemusei.it).

LEFT: Florence's Duomo.
RIGHT: on the steps of the Duomo.

Where the Renaissance started

To see where the Renaissance began, stand in **Piazza del Duomo**. Approaching this massive square, you file through sober streets lined with buildings presenting a stern defensive face. Suddenly the **Duomo ❶** (Cathedral; Mon, Tues, Wed, Fri 10am–5pm, Thur 10am–3.30pm, Sat 10am–4.45pm, Sun 1.30–4.45pm; free) is revealed, all festive in its polychrome marble – green from Prato, white from Carrara and red from the Maremma. The design

Main attractions

DUOMO AND BATTISTERO (CATHEDRAL AND BAPTISTRY)
MUSEO DELL'OPERA DEL DUOMO
PIAZZA DELLA SIGNORIA
PALAZZO VECCHIO
UFFIZI GALLERY
CAPELLA BRANCACCI (BRANCACCI CHAPEL)
PALAZZO PITTI (PITTI PALACE)
GIARDINO DI BOBOLI (BOBOLI GARDENS)
SANTA CROCE
BARGELLO
CAPPELLE MEDICEE (MEDICI CHAPELS)
ACCADEMIA
SAN MARCO

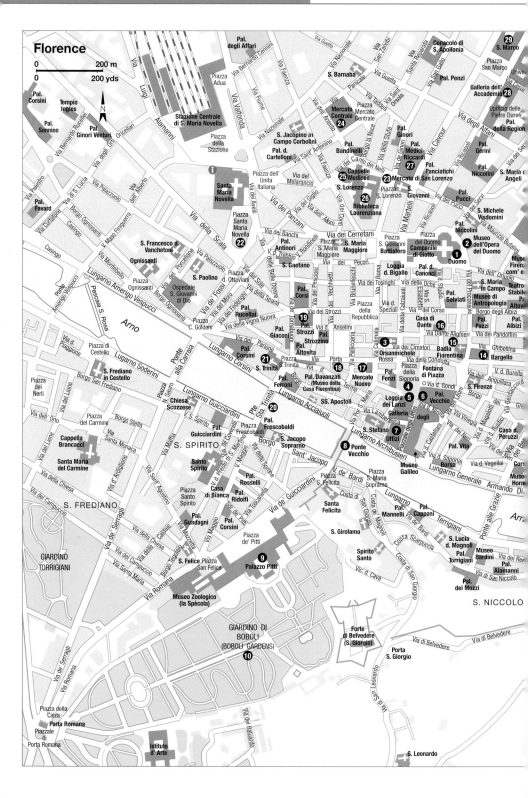

Florence

0   200 m

0   200 yds

Pal. Corsini

Tempio Ingles

Pal. Sonnino

Pal. Ginori Venturi

Stazione Centrale di S. Maria Novella

Piazza Adua

Piazza della Stazione

Piazza dell' Unita Italiana

Santa Maria Novella

Piazza Santa Maria Novella

Pal. degli Affari

Mercato Centrale

Piazza Mercato Centrale

S. Barnaba

Pal. Penzi

Cenacolo di S. Apollonia

S. Marco

Piazza San Marco

Univ

Galleria dell' Accademia

Opificio delle Pietre Dure

Pal. della Region

Pal. Gerini

S. Jacopino in Campo Corbolini

Pal. d. Cartelloni

Pal. Bandinelli

Pal. Ginori

Pal. Medici-Riccardi

Cappelle Medicee

Mercato di San Lorenzo

S. Lorenzo

Biblioteca Laurenziana

Piazza S. Lorenzo

S. Giovanni

Pal. Panciatichi

Pal. Niccolini

S. Michele Visdomini

S. Maria Maurizio Bufalini

Pal. Pucci

Pal. Niccolini

Museo dell'Opera del Duomo

Campanile di Giotto

Duomo

Piazza del Duomo

Piazza S. Giovanni

Battistero

Loggia d. Bigallo

Pal. d. Canonici

S. Maria Maggiore

S. Gaetano

Pal. Antinori

Via dei Cerretani

Pal. Corsi

Pal. Rucellai

Santa Maria d. Vanchetoni

Ognissanti

S. Francesco d.

S. Paolino

Piazza d. Ottaviani

Ospedale S. Giovanni di Dio

Piazza Ognissanti

Piazza C. Goldoni

Pal. Favard

Lungarno Amerigo Vespucci

Arno

Pal. Giacomi

Pal. Strozzi

Pal. Strozzino

Pal. Altovita

Pal. Corsini

S. Trinita

Piazza S. Trinita

Pal. Ferroni

Casa di Dante

Museo Firen. com' e

S. Maria in Campo

Museo di Antropologia

Teatro Stabil

Pal. Salviati

Pal. Pazzi

Pal. Albizi

Badia Fiorentina

Bargello

Casa d. Peruzzi

S. Firenze

Orsanmichele

Pal. Davanzati (Museo della Casa Fiorentina)

SS. Apostoli

Mercato Nuovo

Pal. Fenzi

Fontana di Piazza

Piazza della Signoria

Mercato Nuovo

Loggia dei Lanzi

Galleria degli

Palazzo Vecchio

S. Stefano

Uffizi

Museo Galileo

Borsa

Pal. Vita

Ponte Vecchio

Pal. Frescobaldi

Pal. Guicciardini

Chiesa Scozzese

S. SPIRITO

Santo Spirito

Casa di Bianca

Pal. Rosselli

Pal. Ridolfi

Pal. Corsini

Pal. Guadagni

Piazza Santo Spirito

S. Felice

Piazza de' Pitti

Piazza San Felice

Palazzo Pitti

Museo Zoologico (la Spècola)

GIARDINO TORRIGIANI

S. FREDIANO

S. Frediano in Cestello

S. Maria del Carmine

Cappella Brancacci

Piazza del Carmine

Piazza Santo Spirito

Pal. Mannelli

S. Maria Soprano

Santa Felicita

S. Girolamo

Spirito Santo

S. Lucia d. Magnoli

Museo Bardini

Pal. Torrigiani

Pal. Alamanni

Pal. dei Mozzi

S. NICCOLO

Pal. Capponi

GIARDINO DI BOBOLI (BOBOLI GARDENS)

Forte di Belvedere (S. Giorgio)

Porta S. Giorgio

Via di Belvedere

Piazza della Calza

Porta Romana

Piazzale di Porta Romana

Istituto d' Arte

S. Leonardo

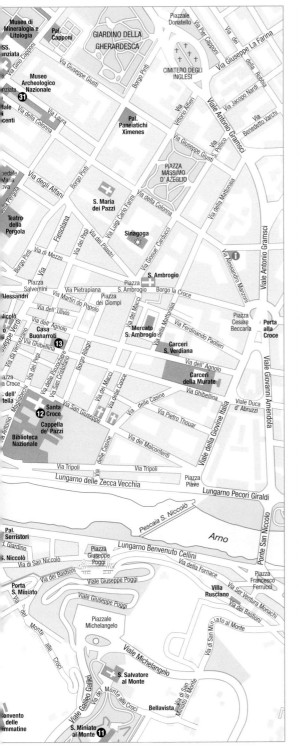

echoes that of Giotto's slender **Campanile** (daily 8.30am–7.30pm; charge), arguably Italy's loveliest bell tower. You can climb the 414 steps of the bell tower for intimate views of the cathedral dome and roofscape, or simply contemplate the bold cathedral facades from one of the cafés on the south side of the square.

The octagonal **Battistero** (Baptistery; Mon–Sat noon–7pm, Sun 8.30am–2pm; charge), to the west of the cathedral, dates from the 6th century, though the interior was redesigned and given its ceiling mosaics of the *Creation* and *Last Judgement* in 1300. The Baptistery has several sets of bronze doors, and those to the north play a seminal role in art history, often seen as marking the start of the Renaissance. In 1401 Ghiberti and Brunelleschi were adjudged joint winners of a competition to design the doors, but Brunelleschi, a fiery-tempered genius, refused to work with Ghiberti, who completed the doors in 1424. The doors show the hallmarks of Renaissance art: realism, a sense of perspective, and narrative clarity combined with dramatic tension. Ghiberti's following set of doors, for the east portal (1452), are known as the Paradise Doors after Michelangelo hailed them as fit to serve as the "gates of Paradise".

Biggest dome in the world

Brunelleschi (1377–1446) returned from studying ancient Roman architecture in Rome, confident that he could complete the cathedral by erecting the vast **dome**. In typically Florentine fashion, the city had decided to build the biggest dome in the world without knowing how to achieve it. If you enter the cathedral and climb the 436 steps to the top (Mon–Fri 8.30am–7pm, Sat 8.30am–5.40pm; charge) you can study how the problem was solved.

Brunelleschi's stroke of genius was to devise a cunning system of an inner shell and outer dome to distribute the weight of the cupola, with thick walls negating the need for further buttressing. Brunelleschi went on to create some of the purest Renaissance architecture in the city, buildings which are striking in their simplicity and pared-down loveliness. Using rigorous geometry based on classical forms, the buildings are the perfect expression of a rational use of space. Out of respect for Brunelleschi's achievement, the city forbade the construction of any building taller than the Duomo; to this day, the massive dome dominates the red rooftops, rising almost higher than the surrounding hills. Brunelleschi was also buried in the cathedral – an honour granted to him alone – and his tomb can be seen in the **crypt** (Mon–Wed and Fri 10am–5pm, Sat until 4.45pm; charge), among the excavated ruins of Santa Reparata, the city's first (4th-century) cathedral.

The cathedral's stark interior features a fine fresco on the north aisle wall, painted by Paolo Uccello in 1436, depicting Sir John Hawkwood, the English mercenary who served as captain of the Florentine army from 1377 to 1394. Otherwise, to see the cathedral treasures you must visit the underrated **Museo dell'Opera del Duomo** ❷ (Mon–Sat 9am–7.30pm, Sun 9am–1.45pm; charge) on the east side of Piazza del Duomo. On display are outstanding sculptures, from Donatello's

haggard *Mary Magdalene*, carved in wood in the 1460s, to the same artist's superb *cantoria* (choir gallery), decorated with angels and cherubs engaged in frenzied music and song. The star exhibit here is Michelangelo's *Pietà*, begun around 1550. Michelangelo intended this for his own tomb, but left it unfinished. Its magnetic hold over visitors derives from the fact that the tall hooded figure of Nicodemus is Michelangelo's self-portrait.

Showpiece of the guilds

From the cathedral square, **Via dei Calzaiuoli** leads south. This was the principal street of Roman and medieval Florence, and is lined with interesting shops. Partway down, on the right, is the church of **Orsanmichele** ❸ (Tues–Sun 10am–5pm; free), a former granary and church. The exterior niches are filled with Renaissance statues sponsored by the guilds. The finest, Donatello's *St George*, made for the Guild of Armourers, has been moved to the Bargello museum (*see page 268*) and replaced by a copy.

The same fate befell Michelangelo's *David*, which once stood in **Piazza della Signoria** ❹, just to the south. The original was moved to the Accademia (*see page 270*) in 1873, but the copy that now stands in front of the Palazzo Vecchio is faithful to the original. David's companions are *Hercules* (1534, by Bandinelli), the mythical founder of Florence, and Ammannati's licentious *Neptune Fountain* (1575). Nearby, the **Loggia dei Lanzi** ❺ (1382) shelters Cellini's *Perseus* (1554) and Giambologna's *Rape of the Sabine Women* (1583), alongside ancient Roman statues.

These statues are highly symbolic, not least *David* himself, carved by Michelangelo to represent Florentine independence. Yet Goliath, in the form of Cosimo de' Medici, triumphed, crushing republicanism and entrenching Medici power through a dukedom which remained in place until Tuscany joined the united Kingdom of Italy in 1861. The Medici administration was

BELOW:
Michelangelo's masterpiece, *David*.

based in the **Palazzo Vecchio** ❻ (daily 9am–7pm, until 2pm on Thur, until midnight in July and August; charge), which remains the town hall of Florence, and which was comprehensively redesigned during the reign of Cosimo I.

The Palazzo Vecchio, with its bold swallowtail crenellations and asymmetrical bell tower, is the most evocative of city symbols. The palace, under different guises, has been the emblem of Florentine power since the 14th century. Vasari's monumental staircase leads to the frescoed **Salone dei Cinquecento**, the Hall of the Five Hundred, where members of the Great Council held their meetings. Cosimo I set his stamp on the chamber by commissioning a series of vast frescoes, painted by Vasari, which glorified his military triumphs. Beyond the art and the style, the palace is revealing of everyday Medici court life. It is also one of the few museums in conservative Florence to have moved into the 21st century in terms of presentation. The use of multimedia, "secret itineraries" and a children's perspective on great artworks has proved a resounding success.

The Uffizi

Under Cosimo I, Tuscan bureaucracy grew to the point where new offices were required to house the burgeoning army of lawyers and notaries, the guilds and the judiciary. Thus it was that the **Uffizi** ❼ (Tues–Sun 8.15am–6.50pm, until 10pm Tues and Wed July–Sept, last entry 45 mins before closing; charge; pre-book timed tickets online, www.firenzemusei.it or tel: 055-294 883) came to be built alongside the Palazzo Vecchio – now a world-famous art gallery but originally intended to serve as utilitarian offices.

Vasari built a well-lit upper storey, using iron reinforcement to create an almost continuous wall of glass running round the long inner courtyard, a novel idea. (It was this glass wall that caused so much damage when a terrorist bomb exploded near the west wing of the Uffizi in May 1993.) Cosimo's heirs decided that the airy upper corridor would make a perfect exhibition space for the family statues, carpets and paintings, and Italy's first public gallery was born. As the world's greatest collection of Italian art, the Uffizi

A copy of Michelangelo's David in Piazza della Signoria.

BELOW: the Uffizi at night.

TIP

Queues for the Uffizi and Pitti can be achingly long, so tickets are best reserved in advance. Call Firenze Musei, tel: 055-294 883, where, for a small fee, you're given a booking number – or log on to www. firenzemusei.it or www. tickets.uffizi.com at least a day in advance (booking fee, with tickets collected at a separate entrance).

BELOW: the Ponte Vecchio, built in 1345.

is both a feast for the senses and an indigestible banquet. What you choose to be moved by will depend on your mood. Expect crowds in the Leonardo da Vinci room, which pays tribute to the greatest genius of the age, the master of the High Renaissance style. Contemplation of great works of art is still possible, at least away from the Leonardo da Vinci line, the Botticelli bottleneck and the Giotto genuflection. Fra Angelico, Perugino, Pollaiuolo and Mantegna, to name but a few of their Renaissance peers, are often left to sleepy custodians and connoisseurs.

Presented roughly chronologically, the collection's star attractions include Botticelli's *Primavera* (1480) and the *Birth of Venus* (1485). Also seek out the Medici portraits in the octagonal **Tribune**, including Bronzino's *Portrait of Bia*, illegitimate daughter of Cosimo I (1542). (The Tribune is currently being restored and the paintings moved to Room 35 until late 2011.) The Uffizi corridors are lined with ancient Roman and Greek statues, but even greater are Michelangelo's influential *Holy Family* (*Doni Tondo*, 1506–8), Raphael's tender

Madonna of the Goldfinch (1506) and Titian's erotic *Venus of Urbino* (1538).

Vasari planned the **Corridoio Vasariano** (closed for restoration until 2013), as a secret passage linking the Palazzo Vecchio to the Pitti Palace, passing through the Uffizi and along the top of the Ponte Vecchio. This overhead passageway permitted the Medici dukes to walk between their various palaces without having to mix with their subjects in the streets below.

En route to the Pitti Palace, the corridor passes over the **Ponte Vecchio** ❽, with its medieval workshops used by butchers and tanners until these noxious trades were banned by ducal ordinance in 1593. Today, the bridge has been taken over by jewellers, buskers and streams of tourists shopping for trinkets. It was the only Florentine bridge to be spared by the Germans in World War II.

Eclectic craft shops await in the Oltrarno district south of the bridge, as do the churches of **Santo Spirito**, an architectural masterpiece by Brunelleschi, and **Santa Maria del Carmine** (Wed–Sat and Mon 10am–5pm, Sun

1–5pm; charge), where the **Cappella Brancacci** contains Masaccio's moving fresco cycle, one of the great works of the early Renaissance. The Brancacci Chapel is tiny, with room for only 30 people, so expect queues and a visit limited to 15 minutes (tel: 055-238 2195 to book).

Residence of the Medici Grand Dukes

Space is not a problem at the fortress-like **Palazzo Pitti** ❾ (Pitti Palace), the "new" residence of the Medici Grand Dukes. Brunelleschi produced bold plans for the palace shortly before his death. Set on a slope to create more impact, and built on solid rock to support the weighty foundations, the Pitti was the first private palace to be built commanding its own piazza. The Medici swiftly shaped the palace in their own image, establishing summer and winter apartments, private picture galleries and libraries.

The most rewarding collection is the **Galleria Palatina** (Palatine Gallery; Tues–Sun 8.15am–6.50pm, ticket office closes 45 mins earlier; charge; book online, www.firenzemusei.it), especially the richly decorated ceiling frescoes by Pietro da Cortona. These illustrate the education of a prince under the tutorship of the gods. In Room 1, the prince is torn from the arms of Venus (love) by Minerva (knowledge), and later learns about science from Apollo, war from Mars and leadership from Jupiter. Finally the prince takes his place alongside Saturn, who, in mythology, presided over the Golden Age.

Among the paintings displayed are wonderful portraits by Titian, who turns the reformed prostitute, Mary Magdalene, into a delectable study of the delights of the female form. More disturbing is Rubens's celebrated masterpiece *The Consequences of War* (1638), an allegory of the Thirty Years War.

Behind the Palazzo Pitti lies the **Giardino di Boboli** ❿ (daily Jan–Feb and Nov–Dec 8.15am–4.30pm, Mar and Oct until 5.30pm, Apr–May and Sept until 6.30pm, June–Aug until 7.30pm; closed first and last Mon of month; summer concerts; charge). The landscaping of the Boboli Gardens, following the natural slope of the hill, perfectly complements the sumptuous palace, and became the model for Italianate gardens for centuries to come. As Florence's most beguiling late Renaissance garden, the Boboli reveal statues, fountains, ornamental pools, grottoes and even an Egyptian obelisk. At every turn, classical and Renaissance statuary gives way to whimsical Mannerist grottoes dotted with grotesque sculpture.

Jewel on the hill

On one of the hills above Florence sits **San Miniato al Monte** ⓫ (daily 8am–7.30pm), a jewel-like Romanesque church. Catch the No. 13 bus up, and meander down on foot via **Piazzale Michelangelo** for a classic Florentine vista. Set high above the city, the terrace is adorned by copies of Michelangelo's famous works, and overlooks the River Arno and the full sweep of the city below.

By 1565, the Vasari Corridor (see opposite) across the Arno was completed and, by linking the political seat of power with the private residence, symbolised the reality that, even from afar, the city was permanently and irrevocably ruled by the Medici.

BELOW: Palazzo Pitti.

The Bargello was built in 1255 and became a national museum in 1865.

Prominent in the view, to the east of the city, is the massive Gothic church of **Santa Croce** ⑫, which features in E.M. Forster's novel (and the Merchant-Ivory film) *A Room with a View* (church: Mon–Sat 9.30am–5pm, Sun 1–5pm, including Capella de' Pazzi, cloisters and museum; charge; 7.30am–7pm for services). Here you will find frescoes by Giotto and his pupils, and the tombs and monuments of famous Florentines, including Michelangelo, Machiavelli and Galileo (who was protected by the Medici after his excommunication for holding the heretical view that the earth goes round the sun, rather than the reverse).

Weaving your way back through the Santa Croce district, you pass the **Casa Buonarroti** ⑬ (Wed–Mon 9.30am–2pm; charge). Michelangelo's former home contains a juvenile work, the *Madonna della Scala*.

Sustained by an ice cream at **Bar Vivoli Gelateria** (Via Isole delle Stinche 7), continue along the art trail to the **Bargello** ⑭ (daily 8.15am–1.50pm, except closed 2nd and 4th Mon and 1st, 3rd and 5th Sun of the month;

charge). Once a prison, the Bargello is now a museum devoted to sculpture by Donatello, Michelangelo, Cellini and Giambologna. The Bargello's tantalising calling card is Donatello's coquettish *David*, a rival to Michelangelo's more virile version in the Accademia.

Dante was born in this district in 1265, and opposite the Bargello you can see the abbey church, the **Badia Fiorentina** ⑮ (Mon 3–5pm), where the poet watched his beloved Beatrice attending Mass. Round the corner is the **Casa di Dante** ⑯ (Mon and Wed–Fri 1–6pm; charge), the poet's presumed birthplace.

Further west stands the **Mercato Nuovo** ⑰ (Mon–Sat), a "New Market" that has been here since 1551. Few can resist touching the talismanic bronze boar, **Il Porcellino**, whose shiny nose attests to the good fortune bestowed on countless visitors.

From here, Via Porta Rossa leads to the newly restored **Palazzo Davanzati** ⑱, a delightful townhouse, known as the **Museo della Casa Fiorentina** (Tues–Sat 8.15am–1.50pm, and 1st, 3rd and 5th Sun of month, and 2nd and

4th Mon). A vivid picture of domestic life in late medieval Florence unfolds in the vaulted entrance hall and the staircase supported by flying buttresses. The great Gothic halls on the second and third floors are frescoed to give the semblance of fabrics and drapery. The lofty, galleried palace bridges the medieval and Renaissance eras, making Palazzo Davanzati the most authentic surviving example of a merchant dwelling from the period.

Far grander is **Palazzo Strozzi** ⓳ (daily 9am–8pm, Thur until 11pm; charge for exhibitions; tel: 055-264 5155; www.palazzostrozzi.org), a neighbouring cultural centre and the setting for blockbuster art exhibitions. This bombastic building is a testament to the overweening pride of the powerful merchant banker Filippo Strozzi, who dared to build a bigger palace than the Medici's. The monumental nature of the rusticated facade is echoed by the inner courtyard. As the quintessential 15th-century Florentine princely palace, Palazzo Strozzi was a model for centuries to come.

Straddling the **River Arno** is the **Ponte Santa Trinità** ⓴, a bridge blown up by the retreating Nazis in 1944 but dredged up from the river bed and fully restored. Beside it stands **Santa Trinità** ㉑ (Mon–Sat 8am–noon and 4pm–6pm, Sun 4–6pm), a church frescoed by Ghirlandaio.

Beyond is escapism in **Via de' Tornabuoni,** lined with chic boutiques showcasing such Florentine designers as Ferragamo and Cavalli, not to mention Gucci, who began as humble saddle-makers in the city. Call into the aristocratic **Palazzo Antinori** to sample Tuscan wines or try a Negroni cocktail in **Caffè Giacosa**, which is where it was invented. Now owned by Roberto Cavalli, who lives in the Florentine hills, the chic café is both a celebrity haunt and a place to try the designer's estate wine and chocolates.

Piazza Santa Maria Novella ㉒ is dominated by the **Basilica di Santa Maria Novella**. The Dominican complex features in Boccaccio's *Decameron*, and contains vivid frescoes by Ghirlandaio and Masaccio. In the adjoining **cloisters** (Mon–Thur and Sat 9am–5.30pm, Sun 1am–5pm; charge) you can see what remains of Paolo Uccello's masterpiece, the *Universal Deluge*, a depiction of the flood that drowned all but Noah and his entourage, and a fresco that was, ironically, badly damaged by the Florentine floods of 1966.

Florentine tripe

Heading back to the heart of town, browse in the market maze of **San Lorenzo** ㉓, which sells bags, belts and shoes. On the adjoining square awaits the more rewarding covered food market, **San Lorenzo Mercato Centrale** ㉔ (Mon–Sat 7am–2pm). Although increasingly touristy, it still offers a taste of working-class Florence and is a reliable place for Tuscan specialities. Some, such as offal, are not for the faint-hearted, but the intrepid will try a hot tripe sandwich (*lampredotto*) at Nerbone. The squeamish might prefer the myriad oils, cheeses, mushrooms, salami, cantuccini biscuits and even

BELOW: fresco by Gozzoli in the Palazzo Medici-Riccardi.

Sculpture in the Accademia.

BELOW: atrium of the Annunziata.

truffles. Kinder stallholders will let you try before buying, or you can stay for a tripe-free picnic lunch.

At the back of San Lorenzo is the entrance to the **Cappelle Medicee** ㉕ (daily 8.15am–1.50pm, also 1st, 3rd, 5th Sun and 2nd, 4th Mon of the month; charge), the mausoleum of the Medici family, for which Michelangelo carved two splendid tombs featuring the allegorical figures of *Night* and *Day*, *Dusk* and *Dawn*. The church itself represents Renaissance rationalism, all cool whites and greys and restrained classical decoration. By contrast, the two huge pulpits carved by Donatello with scenes from the *Life of Christ* are full of impassioned emotion, and Michelangelo's staircase leading to the **Biblioteca Medicea Laurenziana** ㉖ (Laurentian Library; Sun–Fri 9.30am–1.30pm; charge), off the cloisters, is even more exuberant.

Just off Piazza di San Lorenzo is the **Palazzo Medici-Riccardi** ㉗ (Thur–Tues 9am–7pm; charge), the first Medici seat, containing a frescoed chapel, state rooms and library. The palace's masterpiece is the Cappella

dei Magi, frescoed by Benozzo Gozzoli (1420–97). The *Procession of the Magi*, painted in 1459, fuses worldliness and piety in a gorgeous cavalcade. Yet if visitors smile involuntarily upon entering the room, it is because the work represents Renaissance art on an intimate, human scale.

There is no escaping Michelangelo's most famous work, *David*, in the **Galleria dell'Accademia** ㉘ (Tues–Sun 8.15am–6.50pm; charge) close by, in Via Ricasoli. Other highlights include Michelangelo's unfinished *Four Slaves*, the plaster cast of Giambologna's *Rape of the Sabines* (on display in the Loggia dei Lanzi) and Filippino Lippi's striking *Deposition from the Cross*.

The nearby monastery of **San Marco** ㉙ (church: Tues–Sun 8.15am–6pm; museum: Tues–Fri 8.15am–1.50pm, Sat until 7pm; closed 1st, 3rd, 5th Sun and 2nd and 4th Mon every month; charge) contains virtually every painting and fresco produced by the saintly artist Fra Angelico.

Return home via the **Piazza della Santissima Annunziata** ㉚, with its delicate Renaissance colonnade adorning the **Spedale degli Innocenti** orphanage, the work of Brunelleschi, and the **Museo Archeologico Nazionale** ㉛ (Mon 2–7pm, Tues and Thur 8.30am–7pm, Wed and Fri–Sun 8.30am–2pm; charge), with its ancient Etruscan and Egyptian treasures.

If the glory of Florence is that it contains the world's greatest concentration of Renaissance art and architecture, the price is responsibility. The American critic Mary McCarthy put the dilemma forcefully: "Historic Florence is an incubus on its present population. It is like a vast piece of family property whose upkeep is too much for the heirs, who nevertheless find themselves criticised by strangers for letting the old place go to rack and ruin."

Thankfully, the Florentines are respecting the trust put in them by the last of the Medici. Rack and ruin look a long way off. ❏

Florentine Firsts

From street paving and glasses to capitalism and the theory of the universe – Florence's contributions to the modern world are amazing

Old records show that street paving began in Florence in the year 1235, and by 1339 the city had paved all its streets – the first in Europe to do so. And while Florentines had little to do with the discovery of the New World, Amerigo Vespucci provided the word "America", and Leonardo da Vinci created the first world maps showing America. A tablet in Santa Maria Maggiore church documents another first: "Here Lies Salvino d'Amato degli Armata of Florence, the Inventor of Eyeglasses, May God Forgive His Sins, Year 1317."

Two developments in music are among the most solidly documented Florentine firsts. The pianoforte was invented in Florence in 1711 by Cristofori, and the origins of opera are traced to the performance, in 1600, of *Euridice*, a new form of musical drama written by Iacopo Peri in honour of the marriage in Florence of Maria de' Medici to Henry IV of France.

An earlier marriage was the impetus for modern table manners. When Catherine de' Medici wed the future Henry II and moved to France, she was apparently appalled at the French court's table manners; in contrast to Florence, no one used a fork. Before long, all of Paris society was imitating her. It is also possible that Catherine, equally appalled at French food, sent for her own chefs, and was responsible for the birth of French haute cuisine.

In the field of science, Galileo, the first astronomer to make full use of the telescope, is often called the father of modern astronomy. Not that Florentine prophets were universally lauded: Galileo was jailed by the Inquisition while Dante was exiled. Many firsts, of course, are related to the arts. Florentine-based artists produced the first Renaissance masterpieces. Donatello's *David* (1430) is regarded as the first freestanding nude statue of the Renaissance. Donatello is also credited with the first freestanding equestrian statue of the Renaissance.

RIGHT: Dante sketched by A. Bronzino.

The grandiose claim that Brunelleschi is the father of modern architecture is one of the least contested. He was the first Renaissance architect to evolve the rules of linear perspective, and he developed a new approach, detailing specifications in advance and separating design from construction.

Machiavelli, through *The Prince* and other works, is credited with inventing modern political science. Another literary great was Dante, whose Florentine language became the basis for modern Italian. Also in the literary field, Petrarch can be considered the father of vernacular Italian poetry and Boccaccio the father of modern Italian prose. Guicciardini is sometimes heralded as the father of modern history.

In the financial world, it is arguable that 13th-century Florentine banks were responsible for modern capitalism, and that the city's medieval merchants were the first of a new, and eventually dominant, social class.

But there is less doubt that those early Florentine financiers originated credit banking and double-entry bookkeeping, both of which contributed to the success of capitalism. Finally, it is well documented that in 1252 Florence became the first city to mint its own gold coin, the florin, which was widely used throughout Europe.   ❑

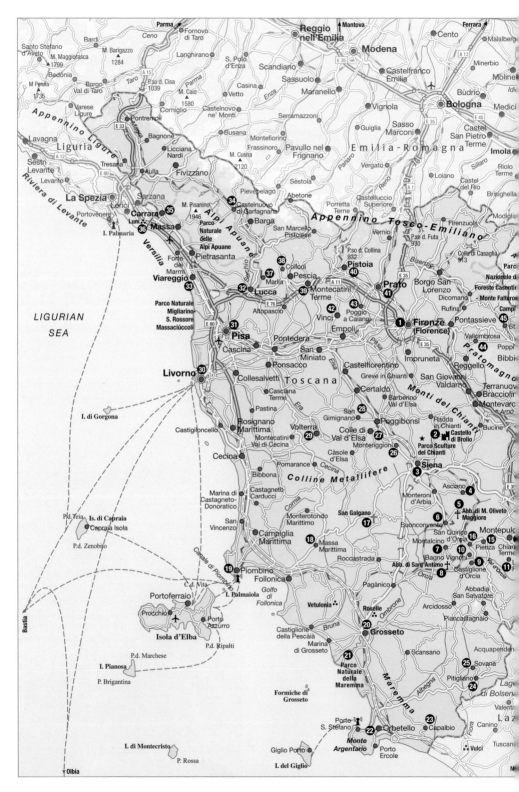

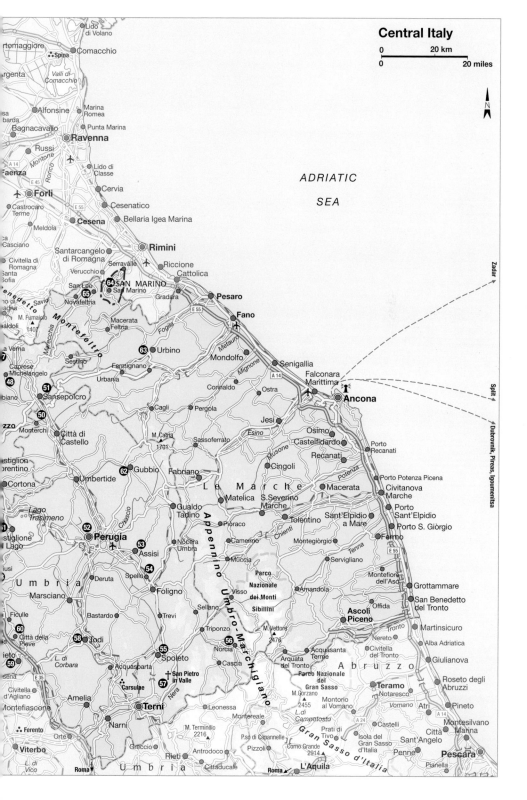

Central Italy

0   20 km
0   20 miles

N

ADRIATIC

SEA

Lido
di Volano
rtomaggiore   Comacchio
        Spina
rgenta
Valli di
Comacchio
Alfonsine   Marina
Romea
sa
barda
Bagnacavallo   Punta Marina
Russi   Ravenna
Michelangelo
Faenza   Lido di
Classe
Forlì   Cervia
Castrocaro
Terme   Cesenatico
Meldola   Bellaria Igea Marina
ca
Casciano   Cesena
Civitella di
Romagna   Santarcangelo   Rimini
di Romagna
Santa   Serravalle   Riccione
Sofia   Verucchio   Cattolica
enedetto   San Leo   64 SAN MARINO
ho di   65   San Marino   Pesaro
agna   Novafeltria   Gradara
aldoli   M. Fumaiolo   Macerata   Fano
1407   Feltria
Fogila
a Verna   63 Urbino
Caprese   Sestino   Metauro
Michelangelo   Fermignano   Mondolfo
48   Urbania   Mignone   Senigallia
biano   51 Sansepolcro   Corinaldo   A 14
Ostra   Falconara
Marittima
50   Cagli   Pergola   Ancona
zzo   Monterchi   M. Catria   Jesi
Città di   1701   Sassoferrato   Esino   Osimo
stiglion   Castello   Musone   Castelfidardo
orentino   62 Gubbio   Recanati
Cortona   Umbertide   Fabriano   Cingoli   Porto
Recanati
Le Marche   Porto Potenza Picena
Lago   Matelica   S.Severino   Macerata   Civitanova
Trasimeno   52   Gualdo   Marche   Marche
Tadino   Porto
stiglione   Perugia   Pioraco   Tolentino   Sant'Elpidio   Sant'Elpidio
Lago   53   Nocera   a Mare   Porto S. Giòrgio
Assisi   Umbra   Camerino   Montegiòrgio   Fermo
iusi   54   Muccia   Servigliano   E 55
Deruta   Spello   Parco
Umbria   Nazionale   Montefiore
Marsciano   Foligno   Visso   dei Monti   Amandola   dell'Aso   Grottammare
Ficulle   Bastardo   Sibillini   Offida   San Benedetto
60   Trevi   Sellano   del Tronto
Città della   58 Todi   Triponzo   M.Vettore   Ascoli   Martinsicuro
Pleve   2476   Piceno
ieto   55   56 Norcia   Tronto   Nereto   Alba Adriatica
59   L. di   Spoleto   Acquasanta   Civitella   Giulianova
Corbara   Cascia   Arquata   Terme   del Tronto
sena   E 35   Acquàsparta   del Tronto   A b r u z z o   Roseto degli
San Pietro   Parco Nazionale   Abruzzi
Civitella   57 in Valle   del   Teramo   Montesilvano
d'Agliano   Carsulae   M.Gorzano   Gran Sasso   Notaresco   Marina
Montefiascona   Amelia   Leonessa   2455   Castelli   Atri   Pineto
Terni   Montoro   L. di   Vomano   A 14
Ferento   Narni   M. Terminillo   Campotosto   Gran Sasso   Città   Sant'Angelo
Orte   2216   P.so di Capannelle   Prati di   d'Italia   Sant'Angelo
Viterbo   Greccio   Antrodoco   Pizzoli   Tivo   Penne
L. di   Rieti   Corno Grande   Isola del   Pescara
Vico   Roma   Umbria   Cittaducale   Roma   L'Aquila   2914   Gran Sasso   Pianella

ITALY
●Rome

TUSCANY

Compelling architecture, seductive cities of art, evocative landscapes, spas and soft red wine form an essential part of Tuscany's appeal

It's a travesty to equate Tuscany with "Chiantishire", a parody of an English country-house party transposed to Italy. It is also misleading to reduce the region to Renaissance art, Florentine architecture and the Chianti vineyards. The Tuscan landscape is as beautiful as the art. This soothing scenery, dotted with hill towns, inspired the Renaissance masters. The art and architecture of medieval Siena and Renaissance Florence may be unmissable, but spare time for compelling but less well-known cities, such as Lucca. Also lap up the Unesco-protected Val d'Orcia countryside south of Siena, mountainous Garfagnana, and the wild coastal area of the Maremma.

The Tuscan lifestyle is arguably the greatest lure, with villa-living or farm stays the ideal way of appreciating the landscape. The Tuscans seem to have found a perfect balance between country and city living. As well as pampering in olive oil treatments and wallowing in hot springs, you can enjoy pasta feasts and gorgeous views. That's in addition to visiting the cities of art, from Siena to Lucca, Pisa and Arezzo, as well as the Etruscan sites around Volterra and Chiusi.

On the Chianti wine trail

For those not fascinated by frescoes, the delights of **Florence ❶** can quickly fade,

and the desire to escape the cauldron-like atmosphere of the city in summer can prove overwhelming, as it did in the case of the English writer Laurie Lee: "I'd had my fill of Florence, lovely but indigestible city. My eyes were choked with pictures and frescoes… I began to long for the cool uplands, the country air, the dateless wild olive and the uncatalogued cuckoo."

Lee escaped to the **Chianti**, walking south along the Chiantigiana, the Chianti Way (the N222 road), which takes you to Siena via pretty towns

Main attractions
THE CHIANTI
SIENA
LE CRETE
MONTE OLIVETO MAGGIORE
VAL D'ORCIA
MONTEPULCIANO
PIENZA
MAREMMA
SAN GIMIGNANO
VOLTERRA
PISA
LUCCA
SAN FRANCESCO, AREZZO

LEFT: Pisa's Leaning Tower and Duomo.
RIGHT: classic Tuscan landscape.

A statue by the Duomo shows Remus and the she-wolf. Remus' son is said to have founded Siena.

in the Chianti Classico wine-growing region. If you are driving, the journey takes around an hour from Florence, unless you succumb to the scores of *fattorie* (wine estates) offering tastings and wine sales *(vendita diretta)*.

Florence's **Greve in Chianti** might be quintessential Chiantishire, but the Sienese Chianti is quieter, yet just as charming. A meander between wine estates acts as an introduction to the region's famous red wines.

A charming variant is to leave the N222 at **Castellina in Chianti** and drive east, stopping for a walk round the pretty town of **Radda in Chianti** before rejoining the N429 to the **Badia a Coltibuono** (gardens and cellars May–Oct daily 2–5pm), a 12th-century abbey estate set among pines, oaks, chestnuts and vines. Below the abbey are cellars filled with Chianti Classico, the abbey's traditional living. Wine, together with locally produced olive oil and chestnut honey, can be bought on the premises or savoured in the excellent abbey restaurant (tel: 0577-749 424; www.coltibuono.com). The erstwhile monastic cells (now a farm stay) await those who overindulge.

South of Gaiole in Chianti is **Cas-tello di Brolio ❷** (tel. 0577-7301; www.ricasoli.it; charge), the birthplace of the modern Chianti industry. It was in this castle in 1870 that Barone Bettino Ricasoli established the formula for making Chianti wines that has been used ever since, requiring a precise blend of white and red grape juice and the addition of dried grapes to the vat to give the wine its softness and fruit-filled flavour. This large estate is still run by the noble Ricasoli family: Tuscan aristocrats, including the Antinori and Frescobaldi families, have often been making wine since Renaissance times.

Civilised Siena

Siena ❸ is the counterpoint to Florence and is as medieval as its ancient rival is Renaissance. This compact, pink-tinged city is a delight to explore, from the shell-shaped Campo to the galleries full of soft-eyed Sienese Madonnas. Given its narrow alleys threading between tall rose-brick palaces, Siena is mostly pedestrianised. Visitors with hotel reservations are generally allowed to drive in, if only to park in a designated spot.

All roads eventually lead to the **Campo ❹**, the huge amphitheatre

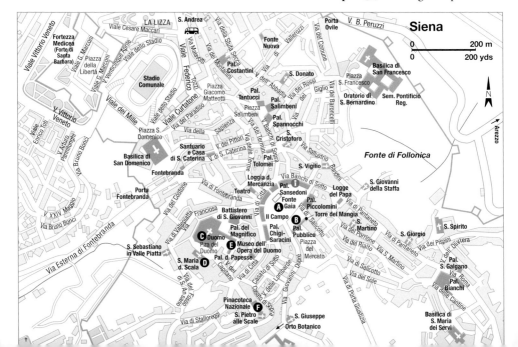

of a space – the Sienese liken it to the enveloping cloak of the Madonna, who, with St Catherine of Siena, is the city's patron saint.

From the comfort of a café on the curved side of the Campo, note the division of the paved surface into nine segments, commemorating the beneficent rule of the Council of Nine Good Men which governed Siena from the mid-13th century to the early 14th, a period of stability and prosperity when most of the city's main public monuments were built. Twice a year, on 2 July and 16 August, the Sienese recreate their medieval heritage in the Palio, a sumptuous pageant-cum-horserace around the Campo. The Palio has raced through war, famine and plague: the residents of the city's 17 *contrade*, or districts, pack the square as their representative horses and riders career around the Campo, and the rider who wins the race and the Palio, a heraldic banner, becomes an instant local hero.

At the bottom of the square stands the **Palazzo Pubblico** **Ⓑ**, with its crenellated facade and waving banners. Erected in the 14th century, it housed the offices of the city government and is framed by a slender bell tower, the **Torre del Mangia** (daily Mar–Oct 10am–7pm, Nov–Feb 10am–4pm; charge). Climb more than 500 steps for a panorama of the city.

Although bureaucrats still toil in parts of the palazzo, as they have for some seven centuries, much of the complex is now devoted to the **Museo Civico** (daily 10am–7pm in summer, until 6pm in winter; charge), which houses some of the city's greatest treasures. Siena's city council once met in the vast **Sala del Mappamondo**, although the huge globe that then graced the walls has disappeared. What remains are two frescoes attributed to the medieval master Simone Martini: the majestic mounted figure of Guidoriccio da Fogliano and, opposite, the *Maestà*. The *Maestà* is signed in Simone Martini's own hand, but in recent years doubts have been cast on

the authenticity of the Guidoriccio. A smaller fresco recently uncovered below the huge panel may be Simone Martini's original, and the Guidoriccio may have been executed long after the artist's death.

In the Sala della Pace is Ambrogio Lorenzetti's *Allegory of Good and Bad Government*. Intended as a constant moral reminder to the city fathers, it depicts the entire sweep of medieval society, from the king and his court down to the peasants working the terraced hillsides outside the city walls.

Just up the hill is the **Duomo** **Ⓒ**, a vast striped cathedral (June–Aug Mon–Sat 10.30am–8pm, Sun 1.30–6pm, otherwise Mon–Sat 10.30am–7.30pm, Sun 1.30–5.30pm; charge). The facade is a riot of green, pink and white marble, a prelude to the bold black-and-white geometric patterns of the interior.

The Duomo is at its best in August and October when the intricate marble inlaid paving is on display.

Duccio's masterpiece, the *Maestà*, the Virgin enthroned, painted for the altar, is now in the Museo dell'Opera del Duomo. The **crypt** is an extraordi-

In Siena, the Enoteca Medicea, the wine centre in the old Medici fortress, is the place to study and savour Sienese wines, from Chianti Classico to Vino Nobile di Montepulciano, Brunello di Montalcino and Vernaccia di San Gimignano.

BELOW: rooftops of Siena.

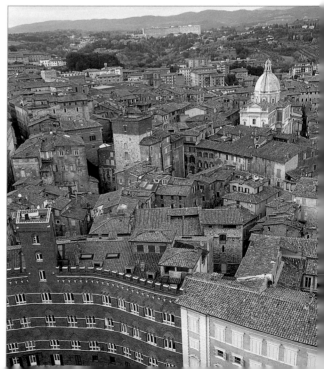

Church in the well-preserved town of Buonconvento.

BELOW: 5th-century Tomb of the Monkey, Chiusi.

nary discovery, with recently revealed frescoes attributed to Duccio or his school. Because the frescoes were perfectly concealed for so long, the intensity of the colours shines through in a vivid array of blue, gold and red. Given that the frescoes date from 1280, the "modern" expressiveness is all the more remarkable.

Opposite the cathedral, **Santa Maria della Scala** ❶ (daily 10.30am–7.30pm) is often described as a city within a city. The far-sighted foundation functioned as a hospital and pilgrims' hostel for nearly 1,000 years, but is now a magnificent museum complex, embracing frescoed churches, granaries and an archaeological museum. The Pilgrims' Hall, depicting care for the sick, is frescoed by Siena's finest 15th-century artists.

Siena has two other important museums: the **Museo dell'Opera del Duomo** ❸ (Cathedral Museum; daily 9.30am–7pm in summer, June–Aug until 8pm, Nov–Feb 10am–5pm; charge), to the right (south) of the cathedral, and the **Pinacoteca Nazionale** ❻ (Picture Gallery; Tues–

Sat 8.15am–7.15pm, Sun and Mon 8.30am–1pm; charge), in the Palazzo Buonsignori on the Via San Pietro, just south of the Campo. If the Pinacoteca is full of luminous Madonnas, the Cathedral Museum's main attraction is Duccio di Buoninsegna, especially his moving *Maestà* (1308).

Rounded hills of the Crete

All routes from Siena are lovely, especially the route southwest along the N438 to the dramatic Crete region. The N438 leads to unpromising **Asciano** ❹, passing through postcard Tuscany. The Crete is a moonscape of pale clay hummocks and treeless gullies, with sightings of stately avenues of cypresses, winding across the landscape to an isolated farm, Romanesque church or *borgo*, a fortified village.

Asciano's main street, Corso Giacomo Matteotti, is lined with stately *palazzi* and home to the Romanesque **Collegiata** and the **Museo Archeologico e d'Arte Sacra** (Tues–Sun 10am–1pm and 3–6.30pm), an illuminating collection of Sienese Gothic art, as well as minor archaeological finds.

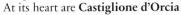

Beyond lies the spiritual remoteness of the Benedictine **Abbazia di Monte Oliveto Maggiore** ❺ (daily 9.15am–noon and 3.15–6pm, until 5pm in winter). Set among cypress groves, Tuscany's most atmospheric monastery exudes an air of aloofness. The Great Cloister is covered in quirky, memorable frescoes ostensibly depicting the *Life of St Benedict*, begun by Luca Signorelli in 1495 and completed by Sodoma from 1505. In one scene Sodoma portrays himself with his pet badgers (one wearing a scarlet collar) looking like a pair of well-trained dogs.

Bound by massive medieval walls, **Buonconvento** ❻ links the moody Crete area with the domesticated Tuscany of vineyards surveyed by hilltop towns. From a distance, **Montalcino** ❼ even looks like a *Trecento* Sienese painting. The streets are narrow and steep, and from the airy heights of the walls there are entrancing views. The highest point is the **Fortezza** (Fortress), housing a respected wine centre or *enoteca* (daily 9am–8pm in summer, 9am–6pm in winter; charge), where regional vintages can be sampled and the ramparts explored.

Few need much prompting to indulge in a leisurely lunch, washed down by full-bodied Brunello di Montalcino.

Further south is another postcard sight that is ravishingly beautiful in the flesh. The ancient abbey church of **Sant'Antimo** ❽, built of creamy travertine and set against tree-clad hills, has inspired poets and painters for years. The Romanesque church reveals capitals carved with biblical scenes, and recorded plainsong echoes around the walls as you explore. The small community of Augustinian monks who tend the church sing the Gregorian chant at Mass every Sunday afternoon throughout the year.

Val d'Orcia World Heritage

A tortuous route leads through the **Val d'Orcia**, a Unesco World Heritage landscape. This part of Tuscany has been landscaped since time immemorial, with the Val d'Orcia, south of Siena, representing quintessential Tuscany: clusters of cypresses, ribbons of plane trees, vineyards on the slopes and farms perched on limestone ridges.

At its heart are **Castiglione d'Orcia**

Fresco in Monte Oliveto Maggiore.

BELOW: Tuscan landscape.

BELOW: cycling against a backdrop of bougainvillea.

❾ and **Rocca d'Orcia.** Both hilltop villages boast medieval castles built to watch over the valley of the River Orcia, and down to the tiny spa town of **Bagno Vignoni** ❿. Where the village square ought to be, there is a large stone-lined pool: sulphurous vapours rise above the hot, bubbling waters which well up from volcanic rocks deep under the earth. Some famous bodies have bathed in this pool in times past, including St Catherine of Siena. Bathing is now forbidden, but on the main square you can sample the spa and Tuscan trattoria at Albergo Le Terme (tel: 0577-887 150).

Just north of Bagno Vignoni, a minor road leads up to **Castellúccio** and **La Foce** ⓫, from where there are spectacular views of a cypress-lined Etruscan road zigzagging up the hill. The next town is **Chianciano Terme** ⓬, a popular spa resort with the pampering **Terme Sensoriali** (tel: 0578-68480) making a delightful day spa. Although better-known for its spas, historic centre and tiny Etruscan museum, Chianciano is now on the art map. The **Museum of Art of Chianciano** (280

Viale della Liberta; tel: 0578-60732; www.museodarte.org) presents a collection of works by the Realists, Surrealists and Post-Impressionists, as well as temporary exhibitions.

Chiusi ⓭, one of the most powerful cities in the ancient Etruscan League, is more compelling for Etruscan history. Chiusi's pride is the **Museo Archeologico Nazionale** (daily 9am–8pm; charge), which has one of the finest collections in Italy – a thoughtfully arranged display of Etruscan funerary urns, canopic jars, sculptures and Greek-style vases excavated from local tombs. Arrangements can be made at the museum for a guided visit to one of the tombs in the vicinity.

The town's Romanesque church is a delight, built from recycled Roman pillars and capitals, while the **Museo della Cattedrale** (tel: 0578-226490; charge) displays a collection of Roman and Lombardic sculpture. It is also the place to book a fascinating guided visit of an underground network of galleries, dug by the Etruscans and reused as Christian catacombs. The tour passes a giant Roman cistern and ends under the bell

tower, which you can climb for views of Monte Amiata and the Val d'Orcia.

Chiusi stands almost on the border with Umbria, but our Tuscany tour continues north, up the fertile Val di Chiana, where cattle supply the raw ingredients of *bistecca alla fiorentina* (steak Florentine), then west to **Montepulciano** ⓮. This splendid hilltop town deserves leisurely exploration, with stops to sample the local Vino Nobile wines, either in rock-hewn cellars or in the elegant Caffè Poliziano (Via del Corso Voltaia 27). As the stand-in for Volterra in a popular vampire series, Montepulciano's main square now draws teenagers looking for bloodsucking romance.

The **Piazza Grande** sits at the town's highest point. On one side is the 15th-century **Palazzo Comunale** (Town Hall), a miniature version of the Palazzo Vecchio in Florence. On the other side, Sangallo's intriguing 16th-century **Palazzo Contucci** houses a hotel and wine cellars (closed 12.30–2.30pm). The Contucci family has lived in Montepulciano since the 11th century and has been making wine since the Renaissance.

Between the two palaces stands the gloomy **Duomo** (daily 9am–12.30pm and 3–6pm), which contains an altarpiece from the Siena School, the huge *Assumption* triptych (1401) by Taddeo di Bartolo. The revamped local museum complex, the **Musei di Montepulciano** (Tues–Sun 10am–1pm, 3–6pm), features Gothic art in a Gothic palace.

When leaving Montepulciano for Pienza, do not resist the **Madonna di San Biagio,** perched on a platform below the city walls. This domed church of honey-and-cream-coloured stone, a Renaissance gem begun in 1518, is an Antonio da Sangallo masterpiece.

Model Renaissance city, built for a pope

Pienza ⓯ is an exquisite Renaissance construct, a city inspired by one vision. It is also famous for its Pecorino cheese, and for the fact that the future Pope Pius II was born here in 1405. He commissioned Bernardo Rossellino to rebuild the village of his birth as a model Renaissance city. Only the papal palace and the cathedral were completed and both are now suffering from subsidence.

Some of the best producers of Vino Nobile di Montepulciano are Avignonesi, Le Casalte and Poliziano.

BELOW: characteristic café in Pienza.

Giglio is the second-largest island after Elba in the Tuscan archipelago, a chain of seven islands between the Ligurian and Tyrrhenian seas. It attracts weekending Romans, day-trippers and divers, and makes for a lovely excursion. It can be reached by ferry from Porto Santo Stefano on the rugged Argentario peninsula (accessed via Orbetello).

Despite the cracks, the listing cathedral is uplifting, flooded with light from the great windows that the Pope requested – he wanted a *domus vitrea*, a house of glass, to symbolise the enlightenment of the Humanist Age. The **Palazzo Piccolomini** (mid-Mar–mid-Oct Tues–Sun 10am–6.30pm, winter Tues–Sun until 4.30pm; closed Jan–mid-Feb; guided tours only; charge) is filled with the Pope's possessions, while the loggia was designed to frame views of Monte Amiata, the distant, cone-shaped peak of an extinct volcano. In summer, the palace opens its courtyard to classical concerts.

To complete a tour around Val d'Orcia, visit **San Quirico d'Orcia** 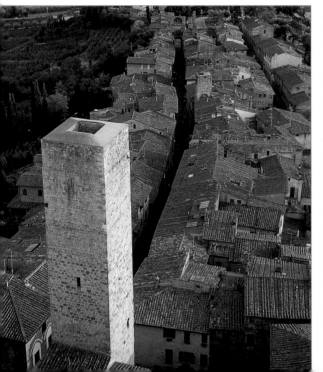 **⑯**, with its splendid Collegiata (parish church), including a Romanesque west portal carved with dragons and mermaids.

Back in Siena, the N73 winds southwestwards through the sparsely populated foothills of the Colline Metalliferre, the Metal-Bearing Hills, which have been mined for iron, copper, silver and lead ores since Etruscan times. Some 20km (12 miles) out of Siena,

make time for the ruined Cistercian abbey of **San Galgano ⑰**, with its huge and roofless abbey church, where swallows skim in and out of the glassless Gothic windows and sunlight plays on the richly carved capitals of the nave. On a hill above the church is the beehive-shaped oratory built in 1182 on the site of San Galgano's hermitage. Look out for the sword in the stone, thrust there by the saint when he renounced his military career to become a hermit.

The Maremma

The Maremma is an evocative term but confusingly embraces the hilltop villages of the Alta Maremma, such as Massa Marittima, as well as the inland Etruscan settlements, such as Pitigliano. That's in addition to the unspoilt coastline, centred on the chic Monte Argentario peninsula and the simpler Castiglione della Pescaia. The landscape ranges from metal-bearing hills to lagoons, dunes and drained marshland.

Massa Marittima ⑱ is the ancient mining capital, but there are no ugly industrial scars, just two museums devoted to the history of mining (which flourished in the 13th century) and an impressive Romanesque church, decorated with sculptures. Massa Marittima is the gateway to the south coast's sandy beaches. These enjoy a sunnier reputation, notably different from the harsher climate to the north.

From **Piombino ⑲**, ferries take visitors to the island of **Elba**, either on day trips to see the villa where Napoleon was exiled, or for a relaxing week of *cacciucco* fish soups at family-friendly resorts. Further south along the coastal Via Aurelia, the city of **Grosseto ⑳** is only worth visiting for its **Archaeology Museum** (Tues–Sat 9am–6pm, Sun 9am–1pm, 3–6pm; free). The collection sheds light on the otherwise indecipherable Etruscan ruins at **Vetulonia** (22km/13 miles northwest of Grosseto) and **Roselle** (7km/4 miles north).

BELOW: one of the medieval towers of San Gimignano.

Just south of Grosseto lie the drained marshes of the **Maremma,** including an unspoilt coastal park with deep Etruscan roots, and white cattle watched over by the *butteri,* Tuscan cowboys. The **Parco della Maremma** ㉑, also known as the Uccellina, is a protected traffic-free nature reserve, rich in wildlife, with a long stretch of unspoilt beaches. The park office in **Alberese** (Mar–Sept 8am–5pm, Oct–Mar 8.30am–1.30pm) supplies information on walking trails.

The **Monte Argentario** peninsula presents a different face of the Maremma, from the chic resort of **Porto Ercole** to the wildlife haven in the lagoon north of Orbetello, an important wintering spot for birds. **Orbetello** ㉒ was a Spanish garrison town, and the Baroque architecture reflects this, with the sea lapping the stout city walls.

Inland, tiny villages like **Capalbio** ㉓ specialise in robust Tuscan dishes, such as wild boar and even baked porcupine (both are hunted locally). For a sybaritic experience, swim beneath the stars in the hot falls just south of Saturnia or opt for a Roman treatment in the luxury spa of the same name. The other villages in this forgotten corner of Tuscany are situated above dramatic tufa-stone cliffs. These are spectacular at **Pitigliano** ㉔, where the locals have long excavated caves in the rock for storing wine and olive oil, and at **Sovana** ㉕, where the Etruscans excavated tombs in the soft rock below the town. The tiny one-street village has two outstanding proto-Romanesque churches.

Tower country – San Gimignano to Pisa

More spectacular sights await to the west of Siena. The N2 passes **Monteriggioni** ㉖, a hilltop town built in 1213 to guard the northern borders of Sienese territory, encircled by walls and 14 towers.

Next, drive through the lower, modern town of **Colle di Val d'Elsa** ㉗ and, taking the Volterra road, head for the more ancient upper town. Here the main street is lined with severe 16th-century *palazzi,* only broken by a viaduct from which there are splendid views of the surrounding landscape.

The symbol of Massa Marittima's "New Town".

BELOW: Pisa's Campo dei Miracoli.

TIP

Villa Bernardini (tel: 0583-370 327; www. villabernardini.it), outside Lucca, is one of the most engaging villas, gardens and wine estates (9.30am–noon, 3–7.30pm). The family also run an excellent restaurant and wine bar in town.

The shops here are filled with fine glassware made in the factories down in the valley.

Perhaps the most spectacular sight anywhere in Tuscany is **San Gimignano 28**, bristling with ancient towers. This "medieval Manhattan" has scarcely changed in appearance since the Middle Ages and remains richly rewarding – despite the huge number of visitors. (It is best to stay overnight here, in one of the characteristic hotels, to savour the atmosphere after the day-trippers have gone). The bustling main street is lined with speciality food shops, with the best buys being Vernaccia wines and wild-boar ham.

The tall defensive towers which dominate the two squares at the highest point of the town were built as status symbols rather than for defensive purposes. Other highlights are the *Wedding Scene* frescoes in the **Museo Civico** (daily Mar–Oct 9.30am–7pm, Nov–Feb 10am–5.30pm; charge), showing the newly-weds taking a bath together and climbing into bed. Equally engrossing are the frescoes that cover every inch of wall space in the

Collegio, the collegiate church, depicting the *Last Judgement* and stories from the Old and New Testaments.

Volterra 29 is another rewarding place, sited high on a plateau with distant views to the sea. The entrance to the city is dominated by a Medicean castle, now used as a prison, and if you wander through the park that lies beneath its walls you will come to the **Museo Etrusco Guarnacci** (daily mid-Mar–Oct 9am–7pm, Nov–mid-Mar 8.30am–1.45pm; charge) in Via Don Minzoni. This is packed with Etruscan urns excavated from cemeteries. *The Married Couple* urn is a masterpiece of realistic portraiture, and even more stunning is the bronze statuette known as *L'Ombra della Sera* (The Shadow of the Night), resembling a Giacometti sculpture but cast in the 5th century BC.

The Piazza dei Priori, the present-day town hall, was designed by Maestro Riccardo of Como in 1208. Younger fans are flocking to it as the "true" setting for the vampires' home in *Twilight*, even if the film preferred Montepulciano as a more luminous location. Volterra's handsome main square has

BELOW: San Gimignano.

some of the oldest civic buildings in Tuscany, and provides a showroom for the local alabaster-carving industry; galleries selling alabaster are located all over the town. The cathedral has a wealth of carvings from an earlier age, including a balletic *Deposition*, sculpted in wood in the 13th century.

West or north of Volterra, the landscape changes rapidly from hilly terrain to marshy coastline. You could be forgiven for missing out **Livorno** ㉚, for, although it has a gritty harbour area and a famous Renaissance statue (the *Four Moors* monument), World War II bombing and modern industry have stripped the city of its character.

Pisa ㉛, by contrast, is a must. All the main attractions lie around the well-named **Campo dei Miracoli** (the Field of Miracles). The Cathedral and Baptistery owe much to the influence of Islamic architecture, which Pisan merchants and scholars experienced through trading with Moorish Spain and North Africa. The gleaming marble facades are covered in arabesques and other ornamentation, as densely patterned as an oriental carpet.

The **Duomo** (Cathedral; Apr–Sept 10am–8pm, Mar and Oct 10am–7pm, Nov–Feb 10am–12.45pm and 2–5pm; charge), built between 1068 and 1118, is one of Italy's major monuments and contains one of its greatest sculptures, the magnificent pulpit by Giovanni Pisano.

The **Battistero** (Baptistery; June–Aug 8am–11pm, Apr and Sept 8am–8pm, Mar and Oct 9am–6.30pm, Nov–Feb 10am–5pm), built in the same Pisan Romanesque style as the cathedral, has another fine pulpit, sculpted in 1260 by Giovanni's father, Nicola. Also see the related sculpture museums and the cloisters (same times as Battistero), a lovely spot for summer concerts.

In 2001, after a decade under wraps to halt the dramatic tilt, the iconic **Leaning Tower** reopened (Torre Pendente; daily June–end Aug 8am–11pm, Apr, May and Sept 8.30am–8.30pm, Mar and Oct 9am–7pm, Nov–Feb 10am–

5pm; no entry to children under eight years; no bags; online booking on www.opapisa.it; charge). Visits are restricted to 40 people at a time, so aim to arrive for opening time if you can, or book in advance through the website. It may be possible to buy tickets on the day from the Campo dei Miracoli information office to the right of the Tower, open daily 9.30am–6.30pm. In summer, lucky visitors can attend a classical concert in the cloisters off the Field of Miracles. Equally atmospheric is **Bagni di Pisa**, just outside town: the romantic 18th-century spa resort even enjoys a view of the Leaning Tower.

Lucca, Garfagnana and the Tuscan Riviera

Lucca ㉜, a short way north, is a city of seductive charms, not least the ramparts encircling the city, which were transformed into a tree-lined promenade in the 19th century. The city has more than its fair share of splendid Pisan-Romanesque churches, with ornate facades of green, grey and white marble. The best include **San Michele** (daily 9am–noon and 3–6pm), with its

Getting the picture by Pisa's Baptistery.

BELOW: decorated columns on the facade of Lucca's Duomo.

TIP

Torre del Lago, 5km (3 miles) from Viareggio, has been staging the Puccini Festival, created by Giacomo Puccini (1858–1924), every summer since 1930. The Maestro's villa, mausoleum and outdoor theatre wallow in a suitably operatic lakeside location (www. puccinifestival.it).

tiers of arcading and hunting scenes, **San Frediano** (daily 9am–noon and 3–5pm), with its massive Romanesque font, and the splendid **Duomo di San Martino** (summer Mon–Sat 8.30am–6pm, Sun depending on services, winter Mon–Sat 9am–noon, 3–5pm). The Duomo contains one of the most famous relics of medieval Europe, the *Volto Santo* (Holy Face), conceivably carved by Nicodemus, who witnessed the Crucifixion – hence it was believed to be a true portrait of Christ (in fact, the highly stylised figure is probably a 13th-century copy of an 11th-century copy of an 8th-century "original"). Each year on 13 September, this revered relic is paraded through the candlelit streets in a huge procession that captivates the whole population.

Lucca is a classic Tuscan city on a human scale, with just enough cultural attractions to beguile but not bewilder. In summer, outdoor concerts add to Lucca's appeal, as do the discreet wine bars and cosy inns. Before leaving, browse the city's delightfully old-fashioned yet upmarket shops, including L'Erbario

Toscano, which sells Tuscan beauty products and local crafts, from silk scarves to embroidery.

Lucca is the gateway to domesticated villa country as well as to mountainous Garfagnana, and to the **Tuscan Riviera**, a string of coastal towns known as **Versilia**. The beaches have a regimented feel (you pay for access but get facilities such as sun-loungers, showers, beach cabins and a bar or restaurant). **Viareggio ㉝** is most interesting for its Art Nouveau architecture, its plentiful fish restaurants specialising in *cacciucco* (a hearty fish soup) and its atmospheric harbour area. It is the oldest of the coastal towns in Versilia and is famous for its February Carnival. Themed floats are usually spiced up with political satire and irony. Slightly further up the coast is **Forte dei Marmi**, *the* resort for socialising and being seen, while the Maremma beaches are for low-key nature-lovers.

To the north, towards the Emilian border, Tuscany becomes more rugged, dramatised by deep forests, Michelangelo's marble quarries and the Apuan Alps around the **Garfagnana**.

BELOW RIGHT: Fiat 500s in Lucca's main square.

Tuscan Spas

Tuscan spas are arguably the most beguiling in Italy. Landscape as seductive as the history plays a part: you can wallow in sybaritic spas that have been around since Etruscan or Roman times. In the 1st century AD, Emperor Augustus' physician issued a prescription to the poet Horace to visit the Tuscan spas, which is one of the first medical prescriptions on record. Lorenzo the Magnificent, ruler of Florence, who suffered from arthritis, was a notable spa enthusiast. Near Pisa, spas such as **Bagni di Pisa** and **Grotta Giusti** combine gracious 19th-century living with thermal pools and steamy grottoes dubbed "the eighth wonder of the world" by Giuseppe Verdi.

Fonteverde is a true destination spa and a favoured hideaway for anyone wishing to lap up laidback luxury among Siena's remote, rolling hills. **Saturnia**, set in the Maremma, and fed by historic springs, is a sophisticated resort at odds with the rugged Etruscan countryside beyond. In Chianciano, the **Terme Sensoriali** are both exhilarating and pampering. In Rapolano, the stylishness of **Terme di San Giovanni** contrasts with the unpretentiousness of its friendly rival, the Antica Querciolaia baths. The old-school spa, **Bagni San Filippo**, floats along on faded charm and a Fellini-esque blend of a surreal setting, cheerful improvisation and larger-than-life characters. *(For full details, see page 395.)*

This is a wild area of high mountains, seemingly perpetually covered in snow because the peaks are made of marble. Designated a nature reserve, the Garfagnana is not just a hiking paradise but a citadel of Slow Food. Information on waymarked trails is available from the main town, **Castelnuovo di Garfagnana** ❹ or plan a trail in Il Vecchio Mulino (tel: 0583-62192), both a rough-and-ready inn and a temple to Slow Food. But to meet the cheesemakers and craftsmen, weavers and wine makers, book a day's tour with Sapori + Saperi (*see margin*).

Further west, in the Apuan Alps awaits the marble town of **Carrara** ❺, with several quarries offering guided tours and workshops. Just outside Carrara is **Luni** ❻, the site of well-preserved Roman ruins.

Towards Lucca, numerous ornate villas and gardens are open to the public, including the **Villa Reale** (also known as Villa Pecci-Blunt; guided garden tours Mar–Nov Tues–Sun on the hour from 10am–noon and 2–6pm; charge) at **Marlia** ❼, whose Teatro Verde (Green Theatre), surrounded by clipped yew hedges, is the setting for concerts during Lucca's summer music festival.

Another splendid villa, with theatrical gardens spilling down the steep hillside, is the **Villa Garzoni** (garden daily 9am–sunset in summer, winter closed one hour before sunset; charge; villa closed) at **Collodi** ❽. Collodi was also the pen name of Carlo Lenzini, the author of *The Adventures of Pinocchio* (1881), who spent his childhood here. The Pinocchio theme park in the village (daily 8.30am–sunset) is a welcome distraction for children and is dotted with sculptures based on episodes from the book.

Montecatini Terme ❾ is the most elegant spa town in Tuscany, with ornate buildings surrounded by flower beds and manicured lawns. Day tickets allow you to sample the waters and admire the delightful marble-lined pools, splashing fountains and Art Nouveau tiles depicting nymphs at the **Terme Tettuccio**.

Pistoia, Prato and Arezzo

Pistoia ❿ and its neighbour Prato are both industrial towns specialising in textiles and metalworking, but with attractive historical centres. Both towns share an enthusiasm for contemporary art lacking in much of Tuscany. Pistoia's Piazza del Duomo is graced with the Romanesque **Cattedrale di San Zeno** and Baptistery. The town's churches contain a remarkable number of carved fonts and pulpits from the pre-Renaissance period; they include Giovanni Pisano's pulpit of 1301 in **Sant'Andrea** church, his masterpiece, more accomplished even than the pulpit he made for Pisa Cathedral in 1302. Instead, the Palazzo del Tau displays work by a prominent modern sculptor, Marino Marini (1901–80), now the **Museo Marino Marini** (Mon–Sat 10am–6pm, until 5pm Oct–Mar; charge), on Corso Silvano Fedi.

Prato ⓫ is a complex city, at once an ancient textile town and a city open to contemporary art and foreign

Sapori + Saperi (tel: +39 339-763 6321; *www.sapori-e-saperi.com*) specialise in Slow Travel and Slow Food in northern Tuscany. These are culinary adventures to meet Slow Food and wine producers and get a taste of their lives, far from Chiantishire stereotypes.

BELOW: Pistoia's 12th-century cathedral.

The chapterhouse of Prato's Church of San Francesco contains splendid frescoes by Niccolò Gerini.

immigration. The **Duomo** displays superb newly restored frescoes by Fra Filippo Lippi and Agnolo Gaddi. More bizarrely, on the facade, Donatello's outside pulpit also displays the Virgin's Girdle four times a year. (A local merchant had married a Palestinian woman in 1180 and discovered that her dowry included this unique relic.)

Instead, Prato's textile heritage can be seen in the excellent **Museo del Tessuto** (Mon–Fri 10am–6pm, Sat until 2pm, Sun 4–7pm; charge). Also worth visiting is the 13th-century **Castello dell'Imperatore** (9am–5.30pm, 4.30pm in winter; charge), the only one of its kind in Italy, built for the Holy Roman Emperor Frederick II of Swabia. Set in a Tuscan rationalist building, the **Luigi Pecci Centro per Arte Contemporanea** (Wed–Sun 10am–7pm; www.centropecci.it) includes a sculpture park as part of this dynamic contemporary art complex.

On the Leonardo and Piero della Francesca trails

Beyond Pistoia is the tiny hilltop village of **Vinci** ⓐ, birthplace of Leonardo da Vinci, where the castle has been turned into an entertaining **museum** (daily 9.30am–6pm; charge) dedicated to the great man and his inventions. The displays consist of wooden models of a bicycle, a submarine, a tank, a helicopter – all beautifully crafted and based on Leonardo's notebooks.

From Vinci, take a winding rural road into Florence, stopping at **Poggio a Caiano** ⓑ (daily June–Aug 8.15am–7.30pm, Apr–May and Sept until 6.30pm, Mar and Oct until 5.30pm, Nov–Feb until 4.30pm; closed 2nd and 3rd Mon each month; guided tour only).

Built for Lorenzo de' Medici, the villa became the archetype for the grand Tuscan summer residence. Skirting Florence, you can speed south to Arezzo on the A1 *autostrada*, or break the journey by leaving at the Incisa intersection and following signs for **Vallombrosa** ⓒ. The reward is the surrounding beech wood; the poet John Milton, visiting in 1638, was inspired enough to write a description of Vallombrosa's autumnal leaves in *Paradise Lost*.

More delights await if you take the N70 to **Stia** ⓓ. From here, you can

visit two sacred sites set high in spectacular woodland, cut by mountain streams and waterfalls. One is the hermitage at **Camaldoli** ⑯ (open only to male visitors), 17km (10 miles) east of Stia; the other is the monastery at **La Verna** ⑰, further south, best reached by driving east from Bibbiena. It was here that the hands and feet of St Francis were miraculously marked with the stigmata in 1224. The monastery commands panoramic views.

On the way south from here to Arezzo, seek out **Caprese Michelangelo** ⑱, which has a sculpture park in the grounds of the castle where Michelangelo was born. The views over Alpine countryside explain why Michelangelo attributed his good brains to the mountain air he breathed as a child.

Arezzo ⑲ has an **archaeological museum** in a monastery occupying the site of the Roman amphitheatre (daily 8.30am–7.30pm; charge). It is full of Arretine tableware, fashionable during the Roman period. For most visitors, though, the highlight will be Piero della Francesca's painstakingly restored fresco cycle in the church of **San Francesco** (Mon–Fri 9am–7pm, Sat 9am–6pm, Sun 1–6pm; essential to pre-book; tel: 0575-352727 or online www.pierodellafrancesca.it). The frescoes illustrate the *Legend of the True Cross*, a complex story presented in the artist's compelling, beguiling style. Fans of his work will be tempted to follow the Piero della Francesca trail, like the heroine of *A Summer's Lease*, a novel by the English writer John Mortimer. If so, the trail proceeds to **Monterchi** ⑳, 25km (15 miles) west along the N73, where a former schoolhouse displays his striking *Madonna del Parto*, the Pregnant Madonna.

From there, you should continue 12km (7 miles) north to **Sansepolcro** ㉑, where the **Museo Civico** (mid-June–mid-Sept daily 9.30am–1.30pm and 2.30–7pm, other months closes 6pm; charge) has Piero della Francesca's 1463 masterpiece, *The Resurrection*, hailed by Aldous Huxley as "the best picture in the world". To complete the trail, worship in **Urbino**, in the Marches, to see *The Flagellation of Christ* and other works in the Ducal Palace (*see page 300*). ❏

Sculpture from the Eremo di Camaldoli, a small monastery near Arezzo which, unlike some monasteries, can be visited by both men and women (tel: 0575-556 021; www.camaldoli.it).

BELOW: view from Caprese Michelangelo.

ROLLING HILLS AND CYPRESS TREES

The harmonious, cultivated Tuscan countryside has for centuries been a favourite haunt of travellers looking to escape the madding crowds

As glorious as its historic cities and artistic treasures may be, Tuscany's timeless landscape has long been a draw to visitors. After a hectic, sticky visit to Florence, Siena, Pisa or any of the other major towns, the relative coolness and freshness of a rural escape is a welcome treat. Small medieval hilltop towns overlook a rolling landscape which embraces both orderly agriculture and nature at its wildest. Terraces of vines and silvery groves of olives vie for attention with Tuscany's own peculiar landmark – tall, slender cypresses, often planted in rows as windbreaks. These elegant trees have studded the skyline here for centuries, prompting the writer D.H. Lawrence to accuse them of hiding the secrets of the Etruscans, the early settlers of these parts. He described them as "the sinuous, flame-tall cypresses/That swayed their length of darkness all around/ Etruscan-dusky, wavering men of old Etruria". These and other images of the Tuscan countryside feature strongly in the background of some of the greatest works of Renaissance art.

LEFT: the 16th-century church of Santa Maria Nuova lies just beyond the ancient Etruscan walls of Cortona. Its simple form and the colour of the local stone blend in with its surroundings.

LEFT: fruit trees are cultivated throughout the region, although more commonly you will see the silvery leaves of olive groves. Some wine estates now produce very high-quality olive oils. Badia a Coltibuono also offers cookery courses to help you appreciate its wines and oils.

BELOW: the hills around Siena are known for their reddish-brown clay, used in the construction of most of the city's buildings. The distinctive pigment in the clay is known as burnt sienna.

TOWERS OF POWER AND PRESTIGE

In the Middle Ages, towers protected the wealthiest families in times of internal and external strife; today, they mark out some of Tuscany's oldest towns, catching the traveller's eye from afar. No better example exists of this distinctive skyscape than San Gimignano *(above)*, which has 13 towers – although at one time it had more than 70.

San Gimignano's many towers date from the 12th and 13th centuries, and are mostly windowless, possibly to afford further protection; families could retreat into the many rooms inside for months at a time. Defence was not the only purpose of these lofty extensions, however: they were also status symbols. Building a tall, imperious tower was a way of flaunting your wealth and social standing.

Another theory about the towers concerns the textile trade for which San Gimignano was noted. Towers may have been built to house and protect valuable dyed fabrics, as there was little room to spread them out at ground level.

As many of Tuscany's medieval towns were built on hilltops, a climb to the top of a tower is usually rewarded with magnificent views over the town and the beautiful surrounding countryside.

BELOW: old chapel in the Orcia Valley.

ABOVE: south of Florence, the hills are dominated by rows of vines growing predominantly Sangiovese grapes, which are pressed to make Chianti wines.

BELOW: Chianina cattle, native to the region, provide the meat for *bistecca alla fiorentina,* the classic Florentine steak dish. Tuscan farmers also cultivate olives, fruit, barley, maize and tobacco.

UMBRIA AND THE MARCHES

Castles cling to ravines and woodland cloaks the wild mountains in the green heart of Italy, home to one of Christianity's best-loved saints

Umbria, the birthplace of St Benedict and Francis of Assisi, seems bathed in a mystical glow. The undulating landscape, harmonious hill towns, luminous frescoes and enigmatic churches only serve to underline its lofty otherness. **The Marches** (Le Marche) are no slouch in the spirituality stakes either, with their low-key churches counterpointed by the grandeur of the Sibillini mountainscape.

Perugia

Perugia ② is the sun around which the other towns of Umbria orbit. In Perugia's **Piazza IV Novembre** spouts the splendid **Fontana Maggiore**, a Romanesque masterpiece created by the Pisan sculptors Nicola and Giovanni Pisano. On the far side of the fountain rise the steps to the austere Gothic cathedral, where people and pigeons gather to preen and flirt. Inside, the mystic *Deposition*, painted by Barocci while under the influence of poison proffered by a rival, inspired the Rubens masterpiece known as *The Antwerp Descent*.

Sweeping down from the piazza is the bustling **Corso Vannucci**. On the right bristle the Gothic crenellations of the **Palazzo dei Priori** (Town Hall), one of the grandest public palaces in Italy. Fan-shaped steps lead to the **Sala dei Notari**, the lawyers' meeting hall, painted at the end of the 13th century.

The complex houses the **Galleria Nazionale dell'Umbria** (Tues–Sun 8.30am–7.30pm; charge), a repository of Umbrian art, displaying works by Perugino and Pinturicchio, as well as Tuscan masterpieces by Piero della Francesca and Fra Angelico. Next door is the 15th-century **Collegio del Cambio** (daily 9am–12.30pm and 2.30–5.30pm in summer, Tues–Sun 9am–2pm in winter, Sat 9am–12.30pm all year; charge). This medieval money exchange is graced by Perugino's frescoes, which fuse classical and Christian themes.

Main attractions
PERUGIA
ASSISI
SPOLETO
MONTI SIBILLINI
TODI
ORVIETO
GUBBIO
URBINO
SAN MARINO
SAN LEO

LEFT: Urbino. **RIGHT:** Madonna in the Palazzo dei Priori, Galleria Nazionale dell'Umbria.

The artist Pietro Vannucci (c.1450– 1523), better known as Perugino, was born near Perugia but found fame in Florence and Rome, where he decorated part of Rome's Sistine Chapel before returning to his homeland.

Corso Vannucci, and its early evening *passeggiata*, can best be appreciated from a café terrace, and includes a parade of locals dressed up to the nines as well as foreign students. Strolls often end in the **Giardini Carducci** and the second-best view in Perugia: the hills twinkling under the stars. No wonder Henry James called Perugia the "little city of infinite views".

South of the town is the eclectic **San Pietro**, with its superb 16th-century choir stalls, carved with a medieval bestiary featuring ducks, crocodiles and elephants. Closer is the barn-like **San Domenico**, with a melancholy interior redeemed by the striking tomb of Pope Benedict XI, who died in Perugia in 1304 after eating poisoned figs.

The adjacent cloisters are home to the **Museo Archeologico** (daily 9am–1pm and 2.30–5.30pm; charge) and a collection of Etruscan pottery and metalwork, including a bronze chariot. West of the centre stands **San Bernardino**, its facade decorated with angels and musicians in diaphanous robes, much like figures in Mucha's

Art Nouveau posters, except that these date back to 1451, not to the 1890s.

Assisi and the Vale of Spoleto

There is no place quite like **Assisi** ⑤. Despite the crowds, and despite the damage caused by the 1997 earthquakes, it remains an inspiring and spiritual city. The sight, as you approach Assisi, of the mighty arches supporting the Basilica di San Francesco, rising above the perpetual Umbrian haze, and of Monte Subasio, the great peak towering behind, is sufficient to make the rest of the world seem blissfully far away. The streets are almost too postcard-perfect: flower-bedecked balconies give way to secret gardens, and the smell of roses and wood smoke permeates the air.

The **Basilica di San Francesco** (daily Lower Church 6am–6.45pm in summer, until 5.45pm in winter, Upper Church from 8.30am; closed Sun am for services; audioguides; free) is perfectly situated for sunsets. The facade, designed by a military architect, is like the saint it commemorates, beautiful in its austerity. The main doors lead into the Upper Basilica, decorated with Giotto's famous fresco cycle on the *Life of St Francis*. The frescoes have been restored following the 1997 earthquake: several saints have been reinstated, though the cycle will never look like it used to; the restoration is fragmentary yet faithful. With this cycle, Giotto revived the art of fresco painting in Italy, and this is his most accomplished work (though it is now believed that at least three other artists contributed to the cycle, including Pietro Cavallini), admired by all the great artists of the Renaissance for the degree to which it introduced realism into Western art.

The walls of the **Basilica Inferiore** (Lower Basilica) are a jigsaw puzzle of frescoes by many hands, all inspired by the life of St Francis. They vary between scenes of uplifting sweetness by Simone Martini, where even

BELOW: Assisi's Basilica di San Francesco, Upper Church.

the horses seem to smile, to the sternly didactic vault frescoes depicting the monastic virtues of Chastity, Poverty and Obedience. Equally stern is the crypt where St Francis is buried, but the face of the little monk, painted in the transept by Cimabue and said to be a faithful portrait, tells a very different story.

Chronologically, a tour of the rest of Assisi begins with the **Roman Forum** beneath the **Piazza del Comune**. The forum's above-ground vestige is the **Tempio di Minerva** (Minerva's Temple), whose interior has been revamped in an unfortunately gaudy manner. In the northeast sector of town, the **Anfiteatro Romano** (Roman Amphitheatre), where live naval battles were staged, has been topped by homes that follow its original oval structure.

The forbidding **Rocca Maggiore**, looming above the town, was part of a string of towers guarding Assisi. The Romanesque **Duomo** (7am–noon, 2pm–sunset) is best appreciated for the its three-tiered facade and sculpted central portal, decorated with lions and griffons. Below

the Duomo stands **Santa Chiara**, dedicted to the founder of the Order of the Poor Clares, the female wing of the Franciscans. The pink-and-white exterior is supported by buttresses that are decidedly feminine in their generous curves.

For a sense of the solitude and spirituality that suffused the lives of St Francis and St Clare, visit a couple of evocative retreats on the outskirts of Assisi. **San Damiano**, just south of town, is the convent where St Clare spent most of her reclusive life, and it retains the air of a simple religious retreat. More remote still is the Franciscan hermitage of the **Eremo delle Carceri** (daily 6.45am–sunset), a tranquil spot on the wooded slopes of Monte Subasio, 3km (2 miles) east of the town.

Unrivalled views stretch from the summit of **Monte Subasio** (1,290 metres/4,230ft). For centuries the mountain was quarried for its pink stone, from which so many of the local buildings are made. The road through the Parco Regionale del Monte Subasio begins at the hermitage car park (closed at 6pm).

A selection of salami for sale, including coglioni de mulo ("mule's balls"), a speciality of the region – made from pork, not donkey.

BELOW: Assisi's Basilica di San Francesco.

Orvieto's volcanic slopes are covered in vineyards which produce its popular crisp white.

The town of Assisi sits on the rim of a dried-up lake bed called the Vale of Spoleto, which was drained in the 16th century. Several other towns of great character line the eastern shore, including **Spello ㊴**, which boasts Umbrian-style frescoes by Pinturicchio. **Spoleto ㊵**, which sits at the southernmost point of the former lake, is renowned for its summer arts jamboree, the Festival dei Due Mondi, a highbrow summer arts festival. The Upper Town has a monopoly on charm, even if the Lower Town is home to several Romanesque churches and Roman ruins.

The town's dominant building, the **Rocca Albornoziana** (times of tours and museum vary; tel: 0743-46434; charge) was built as a papal stronghold and became the home of Lucrezia Borgia. It served as a prison until 1983, including incarcerating members of the Red Brigades, but now the well-restored castle contains the Museo del Ducato, dedicated to local archaeology, art and history, including the spread of monasticism. Alongside is the striking **Ponte delle**

BELOW: Ponte delle Torri, Spoleto.

Torri, spanning the gorge that yawns between the castle and the opposite hill. The medieval bridge was built as an aqueduct in the 13th century, and you can walk across the top of the (now dry) water channel.

Spoleto's outstanding treasure is the harmonious Romanesque **Duomo** (daily 8am–12.30pm and 3–7pm in summer, until 5.30pm in winter). Its medieval porch is surmounted by a rose window, while the bell tower incorporates recycled Roman stone. The cathedral floor has an intricate herringbone and spiral Romanesque design. The chapel to the right was decorated by Pinturicchio, while the apse is ablaze with Filippo Lippi's final work, an exquisite Madonna surrounded by a rainbow and an arc of angels.

On the north side of the stairs leading to the Piazza del Duomo is the solemn Romanesque **Chiesa Sant'Eufemia** (10am–6pm); its chaste perfection contrasts with the cathedral's grandeur. Note Sant'Eufemia's massive and ancient stone throne behind the altar.

Spoleto makes a good base for exploring the **Monti Sibillini** range in the east of Umbria *(see panel below)*. An appealing drive leads, via Triponzo, to **Norcia** ⑤⑥, the birthplace of St Benedict and a major centre of the truffle and salami industries. On the return journey you can take in the pleasing 8th-century monastery at **San Pietro in Valle** ⑤⑦ (10.30am–12.30pm and 2.30–4.30pm; tel: 0744-780 129 to check; the monastic complex is now a hotel, but the church can still be visited), with its Lombardic sculpture and 12th-century frescoes.

Bewitching Todi

West of Spoleto is the hilltop town of **Todi** ⑤⑧, a beguiling medieval city of Etruscan and Roman origins. The town transcends its quiet charms, from labyrinthine alleyways to film-set main square. Unsurprisingly, Todi has become the haunt of history of art scholars and a smugly knowing expat set.

The lovely view from the **Piazza Garibaldi** is enhanced by scents from the gardens below. Nearby is the mesmerising **Piazza del Popolo**, seat of the civic and religious powers, and widely regarded as one of Italy's most magical medieval squares. Symbolically surrounding the **Duomo** are the three medieval civic powers, represented by the Gothic **Palazzo dei Priori, Palazzo del Capitano** and **Palazzo del Popolo**. The well-restored Palazzo dei Priori (1293–1337), today's town hall, commands most attention with its crenellations, battlements and mullioned windows. The grand staircase leads to a **Museo-Pinacoteca** (Museum and Gallery; Apr–Oct Tues–Sun 10.30am–1.30pm and 2.30–5 or 6.30pm, closes 5pm Nov–Mar), which spans the upper floors of both palaces. The frescoed main salon mostly overshadows the art and ceramics.

The **Duomo** dates from the early 12th century and stands on the site of a Roman Temple to Apollo. The three-tiered facade and bold rose window reveal a dusky interior, fine choir and stained-glass windows. The Gothic campanile, built 100 years later, strays from the fine Romanesque style.

A brisk walk around the hill will bring you to the church of **San Fortunato**. The seemingly squat structure was begun in 1292 but only finished in 1462. In keeping with Umbrian tradition, it is a large vaulted church, a variant on simpler, low-pitched Tuscan "barn" churches. The sculpted central portal reveals whimsical Gothic depictions of humans and beasts. The interior is light and airy, with the eggshell whiteness of the stone enhanced by the deep sable colour of the finely carved choir.

After enjoying the view from San Fortunato's bell tower, head through **Parco della Rocca** for more sweeping views, and on down the mountain to the Renaissance church of **Santa Maria della Consolazione** and the shady gardens nearby. The church, based on a Greek cross design, has mistakenly been attributed to Bramante because of the similarities

Umbria's Green Heart

Umbria's arty hill towns are often surpassed by the wild scenery to the east of the region, close to the borders with Le Marche. The rural area bounded by Spoleto, Terni and Norcia offers stunning landscapes and food trails. These wild hilltop hamlets are places to try peasant cheeses, salami and lentils, as well as local olive oil and princely black truffles.

The **Nera Valley** (Valnerina) is often called "the soul of Umbria" for its entrancing blend of narrow river gorges, fast-flowing waters and wooded slopes dotted with hermitages and fortified hamlets. The Marmore waterfall, created by the Romans, remains a magnificent sight. The Nera water park (tel: 0744-389 966) appeals to outdoor enthusiasts who can indulge in canoeing and rafting on the river. The valley flows into the far larger **Sibillini park** (tel: 0737-972 711). Spoleto is a stepping stone to the mountainous east of Umbria, where winding narrow roads climb past beech forests to the snowy peaks of the **Monti Sibillini** range, arguably the loveliest section of the Apennines. Norcia, with its tempting truffles and salami feasts, makes a good base. From Norcia, roads climb ever higher to the spectacular Piano Grande, a vast open plain that is carpeted in rare Alpine plants in summer. High pastureland and seemingly impenetrable forests make this area a hikers' paradise and the home of wolves and wild cats, peregrine falcons and golden eagles.

The interior of Santa Maria della Consolazione.

BELOW: St Patrick's Well in Orvieto, which dates back to 1527.

with St Peter's in Rome. The stark, if airy, interior comes as a disappointment after the harmonious exterior but remains one of Todi's rare disappointments.

Vine-growing Orvieto

Looming on a sheer ledge of lavastone, **Orvieto** ⑨ is a brooding Etruscan presence hewn out of dark volcanic rock. As such, the hill is porous and in danger of bringing the city down as it crumbles. More positively, the fertile volcanic slopes are covered in the vineyards that produce Orvieto's famously crisp white wines.

A climb up serpentine curves, past scaffolding-clad streets, is rewarded with the startling expanse of the **Piazza del Duomo**. With any luck, the late-afternoon sun will be glittering off the mosaics of the 14th-century cathedral's astonishing facade. The Romanesque-Gothic **Duomo** (Mon–Sat 9am–12.45, 2.30–7.15pm) was commissioned in 1290 but was only completed four centuries later. The massive undertaking required the input of legions of architects, sculptors, painters and mosaicists.

The facade is bolstered by striped horizontals of basalt and travertine.

Inside the cathedral, the black-and-white stripes point up the curvilinear arches. The apse is decorated with scenes from the *Life of the Virgin*, completed by Pinturicchio. On the left-hand side of the altar is the **Cappella del Corporale**, painted by Ugolino and his assistants and depicting *The Miracle of Bolsena*. To the right of the altar is the boldly frescoed **Cappella Nuova**, whose decoration was begun by Fra Angelico in 1447 and completed by Luca Signorelli at the turn of the next century.

Also on Piazza del Duomo, opposite the cathedral, is the **Museo Claudio Faina** (Tues–Sun 9.30am–6pm in summer, Tues–Sun 10am–5pm in winter; charge). This is home to an important archaeological collection of Etruscan and Hellenistic works. The highlights include Etruscan black *bucchero* ware, Attic vases and 4th-century pots depicting Vanth, the Etruscan winged goddess of the underworld, who has snakes wrapped around her arms.

Via Duomo and **Corso Cavour** are lined with elegant restaurants, boutiques and craft shops selling Orvietan ceramics, including reproduction Etruscan ware or carved wooden sculptures. To the right, off Corso Cavour, is the striking 12th-century **Palazzo del Popolo**, made of basalt and tufa-stone.

Straight ahead are the **Palazzo Comunale** and the church of **Sant'Andrea** in the **Piazza della Repubblica**. The dark volcanic stone lends a slightly gloomy air to the city, but the **medieval quarter** remains an engaging part of the town, tucked into ancient walls hung with pots of tumbling geraniums, and tiny cave-like workrooms of Orvietan artisans.

A fascinating **underground tour** (www.orvietounderground.it) visits the hidden city that winds its way underneath the main monuments, and reveals secret Etruscan tunnels. You can even get married in one of the Etruscan chambers, or dine in a converted well (Trattoria Sciarpa, Via della Cava; tel: 0763-342 373).

Lakeside pursuits

The road north from Orvieto will take you to **Città della Pieve ⓺**, birthplace of Perugino, father of the Umbrian School of painting. The town has several of his works, including *The Adoration of the Magi*, which features Lake Trasimeno in the background.

Today **Lake Trasimeno** (Lago di Trasimeno) is Umbria's summer playground, ringed by campsites and with opportunities for tennis, riding, swimming, sailing, boat trips and wine-tasting. **Castiglione del Lago ⓺**, strung out along a charming promontory, is the lake's engagingly touristy capital, offering splendid views from the ramparts of the 14th-century castle.

North of the lake, the road through Umbertide takes you to **Gubbio ⓺**, which lays claim to being one of the most intact medieval towns in Italy. Once known as the "city of silence" because of its desolate position in the Umbrian backwoods, today it is within easy reach of those who love good food and architecture. Gubbio clings to the side of Monte Ingino, and its major buildings are stacked on steep terraces.

At the top of Monte Ingino (take the funicular railway from the station in Via San Geraloma to the top, then walk back down) rises the **Basilica di Sant'Ubaldo**. The remains of the saint are kept here in a crystal urn above the altar. The basilica also displays the three immense candles with which the sturdy men of Gubbio race up the hill in a celebration of the saint's day every 15 May.

Returning to the town, your path should take you to the fine **cathedral** to see the great Gothic rib-vaulting and the medieval stained glass. Across a small passage from the cathedral is the **Palazzo Ducale** (Tues–Sun 8.30am–7.30pm; charge), begun in 1476 by Federico da Montefeltro, Duke of Urbino.

Gubbio's skyline is dominated by the bell tower of the restored 14th-century **Palazzo dei Consoli**, which is home to the **Museo Civico** (daily 10am–

Detail of a 13th-century mosaic in the dome of Orvieto Cathedral.

BELOW: Orvieto cathedral.

Pottery for sale in Orvieto.

BELOW: the Corso dei Ceri festival in Gubbio, which takes place in May.

1pm and 3–6pm in summer, 10am–1pm and 2–5pm in winter; charge). Its Great Hall houses a quixotic collection of medieval paraphernalia, including examples of medieval plumbing. A side room contains the **Tavole Eugubine**: seven bronze plates upon which a precise hand has translated the ancient Umbrian language into Latin.

The Marches (Le Marche)

After the stunning hill towns of Umbria, the neighbouring region of the Marches holds very few sights that can compete, with the singular exception of **Urbino ㊳**, the stronghold of the wise old warrior Duke Federico da Montefeltro. Here he constructed one of the loveliest Renaissance palaces in Italy. Urbino is an eyrie whose golden buildings are set high amid spectacular mountains. Urbino remains one of the few hill towns left in Italy not ringed by the unsavoury intrusions of modernity. The original Old City remains almost completely "unimproved", perched at the top of its two peaks.

The **Piazza del Popolo** is a tourist centre by day. By night, groups of university students recline here on the steps or in the cafés, or stand in the street and discuss politics, the latest foreign film, or last night's poetry reading. The facades are old; the faces are generally young. The contrast exemplifies the relaxed symbiosis that exists between Urbino's walls and the lives they enclose.

The duke and his humanist contemporaries felt man was the centre of the universe – a significant break with Christian philosophy. The courtyard of his **Palazzo Ducale** is paved with a hub, with radiating spokes of marble to symbolise man's central position. The building itself is part palace and part fortress: a graceful, secure nest in the rarefied mountain air for the duke to feather with marvellous works of art. The **Galleria Nazionale delle Marche** (Tues–Sun 8.30am–7.15pm, Mon 8.30am–2pm, last entry 75 mins before closing; charge; book tours online, www.palazzoducaleurbino.it), now housed in the palace, has several fine works by Piero della Francesca, including his enigmatic and disturbing *Flagellation of Christ*, and by the town's most

famous artist, Raphael. Also remarkable is the *trompe l'œil* inlay work in the duke's study.

Down the street from the ducal palace is **Casa di Raffaello** (Mon–Sat 9am–1pm and 3–7pm, Sun 10am–1pm in summer, Mon–Sat 9am–2pm, Sun 10am–1pm in winter; charge) where Raphael spent his childhood. In the courtyard is the stone upon which Raphael and his father, Giovanni, also an artist, ground their pigments.

Pocket-sized republic

Nearby awaits the **Republic of San Marino ❻❹**, a toy-town state which nevertheless commands territory larger than Monaco. The appeal of this pocket principality lies in its anomalous status: self-governing San Marino produces its own stamps and arms, allowing its 26,000-strong population to live on tourism supported by tax-haven revenues. The foundation of the republic is celebrated every 3 September with a crossbow competition and a game of bingo. Tax-free crossbows aside, the citadel also offers magnificent fortifications and breathtaking hilltop views.

Park by the cable-car entrance and ride up to the **Rocca,** a citadel bound by 16th-century walls and studded with touristy shops selling everything from bejewelled daggers to full body armour. A steep stairway affords views of massive 16th-century walls and medieval towers. San Marino's other vocation is much in evidence on the main square, with a duty-free shop proclaiming: "Booze at the right price." Surveying the scene from above is Torre di Gualta, the Citadel's boldest castle.

Just west of San Marino stands Federico da Montefeltro's hilltop fortress of **San Leo ❻❺**, a perfectly preserved citadel perched on a cliff. Resembling an aloof hermitage, San Leo commands a bold panorama stretching from the Adriatic to the Apennines. Before heading to the castle, collect your thoughts in the Romanesque **Duomo**, as well as in the parish church where St Francis preached. Known as the **Rocca** (daily 9am–7pm), the castle offers vertiginous views over a rocky spur towards San Marino. San Leo is infinitely more seductive than San Marino, with an other-worldly air that survives the patina of tourism. ❑

Materialistic San Marino, a toy-town state masquerading as an independent principality, is the place to buy postage stamps and duty-free alcohol – as well as weaponry and medieval suits of armour.

BELOW: the citadel of San Marino.

ABRUZZO AND MOLISE

Two huge national parks, Abruzzo and Gran Sasso, make this a region where the wonders of nature rule supreme

From the dramatic Alpine peaks of the Gran Sasso to the wild wolves in the national park; from craggy medieval hill towns to the sandy Adriatic coastline and Slow Food – Abruzzo offers everything an Italophile could wish for.

For years the region's wild beauty was hidden from the world by the Apennines. Then, helped by regular flights to Pescara, the growth of eco-tourism and Slow Food, this once hidden corner began to emerge from the shadows. The region received a major blow when its capital, L'Aquila, was struck by an earthquake in 2009 (see page 309) but the rest of the region remains unscathed, although desperately dependent on tourism to relaunch the shaken local economy. But at heart, Abruzzo remains as robust as its ruby-red signature wine, Montepulciano d'Abruzzo, and as earthy as Abruzzese cuisine.

Pescara

The energetic city of **Pescara ❶** has been a stepping stone to the Adriatic since Roman times. The modern-day communication links have turned the city into a bustling commercial capital. Even so, Pescara, which was heavily bombed in World War II, would win few beauty contests. Much of the local building may be mundane but, with

an eye to becoming an Adriatic Riviera hotspot, Pescara is changing. The centre has smartened itself up, with much of the action gravitating around Piazza della Rinascita. By day, stroll the pedestrianised streets with their Art Nouveau-style facades, including the birthplace of Italy's bold but bombastic poet, d'Annunzio (Corso Manthonè 116; daily 9am–2pm; charge).

In the hinterland, the hilltop towns of **Loreto Aprutino ❷** and **Penne** are a short drive away, but a world away in atmosphere. Loreto Aprutino is a

LEFT: sunflowers abound in summer.
RIGHT: the peaks of Gran Sasso.

medieval settlement clustered around a castle with a distinctive restaurant and views to match *(see page 415)*. Here, as elsewhere in Abruzzo, there is a passion for Slow Food, which can be experienced on market day (Thursday). Simple dishes include chargrilled meats, fish stews, ribbon pasta dishes, salami, wild saffron and Pecorino cheese. **Penne** ❸, another quaint village, is the province's oldest settlement, and a place for pottering from the cathedral to Corso Alessandrini, which is lined with noble facades.

Chieti to the coast

Half an hour inland from Pescara is the ancient town of **Chieti** ❹, spread over a ridge. Known since antiquity for its views across mainland Abruzzo

and the sea, it is home to the region's finest archaeological museum, **La Civitella** (Tues–Sun 9am–8pm), which itself occupies the site of the Roman amphitheatre. The highlights include temple friezes, imperial busts and the symbol of Abruzzo, the serene, 6th-century BC Capestrano Warrior, who embodies the Zen-like fighting spirit of the region. The statue was displayed in the conference hall at the G8 summit of world leaders, which took place in Abruzzo in 2009.

As you travel south down the coast from Pescara on the coast road towards **Vasto** ❺, the natural beauty of Abruzzo reveals itself. Beach umbrellas disappear as you reach the coast of the *trabocchi*. Fishermen weave tales of these fantastical stilt-like fishing

platforms, supposedly created by local farmers too timid to take a fishing boat out to sea. Vasto's resort, the **Marina di Vasto**, embraces both sand dunes and rocky inlets, while Vasto itself, perched above the coast, indulges its foodie spirit and sense of fun. Summer visitors can combine castle-visiting with a two-month Slow Food festival dedicated to fish stew, known as Il Brodetto (tel: 085-448 2301). Traditionally a poor fisherman's stew, made from leftover fish, the feast involves infinite variety and is as big a draw as the summer music festival, charming main square and 15th-century castle.

The rugged interior

Inland from the coast runs the Sangro Valley, which leads to **Lanciano** ❻, and possibly a truffle lunch when in season. Lanciano also boasts a fine cathedral and an imposing clock tower built on brick bridges which may date back to Roman times.

After World War II many farmers left to look for work, and the hill towns were often ringed with ugly apartment blocks to accommodate them. A nota-

ble exception is **Roccascalegna**, where St Peter's Church and Castle is a beacon for conservation, balancing on top of a limestone bluff. The **Castle** (10am–1pm and 3–6pm, until 8pm Aug and 5pm Dec–Jan; charge) is home to the legend of a wicked baron who was murdered when he made a local girl submit to the *droit de seigneur*.

As the River Sangro forges down the valley towards the majestic Maiella mountain, it pauses to form the lake at **Bomba**. You can go canoeing or cruise the lake on the Valsangro Boat (tel: 0872-940 484) and spot leaping fish and diving herons. Or you can simply sit by the shore and watch the sun go down to the sound of a frog chorus. Hikers can head up into Monte Palano, with its oak and chestnut-tree woods underscored by a seasonal explosion of cyclamen, wild roses, broom and rare orchids.

The nearby ruins of **Juvanum** are a reminder of ancient times, including the remains of Samnite temples and a Roman theatre. Walk in the footsteps of legionaries at this Roman settlement sitting among farmers' fields

The dramatic landscape of the national park of Gran Sasso.

BELOW: *trabocchi,* traditional wooden fishing platorms.

Park Life

Known as the "region of parks", a third of Abruzzo's territory is protected – including in the Abruzzo, Maiella and Gran Sasso-Laga national parks. The most diverse landscape is the Abruzzo national park, home to a surviving 40 or so Marsican bears. Rangers escort the public on bear-watching trips, where visitors have a reasonable chance of viewing the 227kg (500lb) Marsicans.

The park is also home to around 50 Apennine wolves, as well as lynxes, chamois, roe deer, wild boar, eagles and griffons. Although no longer endangered, the wolves are elusive but can be spotted on a wildlife tour. Ecotour (tel: 0863-912 760), based in Pescasseroli in the heart of the park, leads groups on wolf-howling sessions, with the wild wolves responding to a soundtrack of howling.

Sulmona's moving Holy Week processions evoke an encounter between the Virgin Mary and the Risen Christ. The Good Friday procession starts in the Baroque Annunziata church, while Easter Sunday's version is a procession of friars from the church of Santa Maria della Tomba.

BELOW: Santo Stefano, an example of sustainable tourism.

against the backdrop of the Maiella peaks (park open until dusk, museum 10am–1pm and 4–7pm; free).

From Lanciano, either head to Vasto and the coast or explore the rugged hinterland. The Sangro Valley opens onto Abruzzo's treasured **Parco Nazionale**. Founded in 1923, the park is home to some of Europe's rarest animals (*see panel page 305*). Medieval **Barrea** ❼ makes an inviting gateway, with its terracotta rooftops and stone-clad Old Town sitting above a deep blue lake.

Across the valley from Barrea is the hillside town **Civitella Alfedena**, known as the "village of the wolves". Sightings of wolves and lynxes living in semi-captivity are frequent. From Alfedena it's a short drive down to **Pescasseroli** ❽, a curious mixture of Alpine architecture and traditional *centro storico*. As well as being an engaging ski resort, in summer it becomes a base camp for nature-lovers. This is hiking country, with sightings of eagles, falcons and hawks, and conceivably even wolves. The rugged terrain and dense forests give way to fields of wheat, vineyards and olive groves closer to the coast.

Heading away from the national park towards L'Aquila, you reach the appealing town of **Sulmona** ❾. "*Sulmo mihi patria est*" (Sulmona is my homeland) proclaimed its most famous son, the Roman poet Ovid, whose statue takes pride of place in Piazza Settembre. Sulmona is also noted for its religiosity and heartfelt Easter festivities, which end with the flight of doves, from which the local people claim to predict the bountifulness of the harvest. It was to Sulmona that Pope Benedict made an exceptional visit in summer 2010, in an act of solidarity with Abruzzo a year after the region's devastating earthquake. Other visitors can show their solidarity by buying the local sugared almonds.

Sulmona's pride is the **Palazzo della Santissima Annunziata**, once a combination of hospital, church and granary. It wears its four centuries of architecture in style: with a Gothic portal on the left, a Renaissance doorway, and a flamboyant Baroque church next door. On the first floor of the Annunziata is a museum of local archaeology (Tues–Sun 9am–1pm and 3–7pm; charge).

The road between Sulmona and L'Aquila (Route 261) offers one of the most spectacular drives in Abruzzo, following the Aterno River Valley past medieval villages, each with its ruined castle and church. Expect the Gran Sasso mountain to dominate: this is the high point of the Apennines in every sense – 2,914 metres (9,560ft) of majestic rock, reminiscent of the limestone peaks in the Tyrol.

Santo Stefano

Just inside the Gran Sasso Park lies the delightful village of **Santo Stefano** ⑩, once an unknown *borgo* but now a model of rural living *(see panel below)*. Peering down on Santo Stefano is **Rocca Calascio**, a picturesque stony hamlet. Beyond stretch the plains of **Campo Imperatore**, a low-key winter sports resort and summer outdoor playground. This Alpine highland resonates to a soundtrack of cowbells and bleating sheep. Known as "little Tibet", in summer its dried ravines and riverbeds contrast with vivid green pastures – an ideal place for hiking and cycling.

L'Aquila's earthquake zone

Dominated by the Gran Sasso, the highest mountain in the Apennines, **L'Aquila** ⑪ was Abruzzo's loveliest city until struck by a major earthquake in April 2009 *(see page 309)*. Only voyeurs will find any solace in the scene of devastation that awaits in the historic centre, so the city is best avoided for the foreseeable future. After the capital of Abruzzo is restored, and the city centre reopened, come back to see whether this masterpiece of medieval town planning is a shadow of its former self.

Molise

Molise broke away from Abruzzo in 1963, and has been a separate entity ever since; it enjoys the lowest profile of any Italian region. Although clinging onto Abruzzo's coat-tails, Molise shares a similarly wild spirit. Molise is a place for lapping up the rural, sleepy lifestyle, rather than the sites. Foodies will appreciate the robust red wines and ricotta-filled ravioli, as well as the fish soup, truffles, mushrooms and Caciocavallo cheese. Families will

L'Aquila was put forward as a candidate for Unesco World Heritage status in 2010 in an attempt to focus the eyes of the world on the reconstruction of the devastated earthquake zone.

Village People

A decade or so ago the medieval hamlet of Santo Stefano (www.sextantio.it) was crumbling into the hills of Abruzzo, and fast becoming a ghost town. Then Daniele Kihlgren, an idealistic Milanese-Swedish entrepreneur, rode by on his motorbike. Smitten by a vista unchanged for 500 years, he bought up the abandoned buildings and hatched an idea, an "extended hotel" *(albergo diffuso)*. The idea was to build nothing new but simply make use of existing rooms located in different houses dotted throughout the village. Despite designer quirks, each bedroom is faithful to its medieval origins; ancient 15cm (6-inch) long iron keys open timeless doors; traditional bed covers are hand-woven and dyed in Santo Stefano's own craft workshop.

Santo Stefano is the flagship for Kihlgren's mission to awaken Abruzzo and draw attention to the region's neglected heritage. Given the exodus from the countryside and Italy's overabundance of ancient villages, scant attention has sometimes been paid to the importance of conserving "everyday" buildings. The rejuvenated Santo Stefano has drawn praise from its politician and writer guests, including Romano Prodi and Umberto Eco. Kihlgren, who is working on further ruined villages in Abruzzo, continues to campaign for sustainable tourism and planning regulations which will preserve the region's character. *For more information, see page 397.*

EAT

Molise is rural rather than backward, with tasty produce ranging from olive oil to truffles, mushrooms and Caciocavallo cheese. Sample Brodetto fish soup from Termoli and Calcioni ravioli filled with ricotta, pork and Provolone cheese. The full-bodied red wines include Montepulciano di Molise and Aglianico.

head to the wild coastline and the sandy beaches on the Adriatic. The cities are often disappointing but beyond those, Molise is frontier country: catch it while it lasts.

If you take the train from Termoli to Campobasso between 25 and 27 May, stop at the medieval village of **Larino** ⓬. The Sagra di San Pardo festival takes place at this time, when ox-carts are paraded through the streets. While there, visit the old cathedral, with its beautiful facade, and climb up the monumental staircase of the Palazzo Reale: Larino is little known yet deeply rewarding.

Termoli ⓭, on the Adriatic, is a popular fishing port and beach resort which boasts a lovely Blue Flag beach at Rio Vivo and a bay which is popular with yachties. The Old Town, set on a promontory, offers appealing views. Well garrisoned behind a small castle built by Frederick II are labyrinthine streets and a fine cathedral.

The gulf between old and new Molise is revealed in **Campobasso** ⓮, the dispiriting capital. Presided over by the medieval Castello Monforte, from

which tumble the steeply stepped streets of the Old Town, Campobasso's modern quarters spread out to the station below.

Ninety minutes away by train is **Isernia** ⓯, a springboard to the remote hill towns. In 1979, an ancient settlement was discovered on the outskirts, with evidence that man lived there a million years before the birth of Christ. Bones of elephants, rhinoceroses, hippos, bison and bear were also discovered, some now displayed in the archaeological museum, the **Museo Santa Maria delle Monache** (daily 9am–7.30pm; charge).

A far more worthwhile sight awaits at **Sepino**, where the rugged medieval town in the foothills of the Matese mountains is the base for exploring the Roman ruins of **Saepinum** ⓰. The site reveals the model for a surprisingly well-preserved Roman provincial town. The charm lies in the rural setting, with the mountains beyond, and the complexity of the site, complete with public baths, basilicas, battlements and a small museum (daily 9am–1.30pm, 3–6pm; free). ❏

BELOW: the fishing port of Termoli.

L'Aquila Earthquake

Italians live with the fact that most of the country is seismically active – Abruzzo, on geological fault lines, was simply the latest casualty

On 6 April 2009 a magnitude-6.3 earthquake struck L'Aquila, Abruzzo's handsome capital. Dawn revealed 308 dead, 1,500 injured and around 65,000 citizens made homeless. Italy is only too used to such natural disasters. The 1980 earthquake in Naples caused nearly 3,000 deaths, 9,000 injuries and displaced a further 30,000 people. In 1997 it was Umbria's turn, when a quake destroyed a priceless fresco cycle in Assisi and damaged cathedrals in Orvieto and Urbino. In 2002, an earthquake shook Campobasso, in Molise, and killed 55 locals, many of them schoolchildren.

Silvio Berlusconi recovered from a major gaffe – telling the homeless victims to treat the experience as a camping holiday – to marshal the aftermath well. His master stroke was to stage the G8 summit in Abruzzo, thus ensuring the attention of the world's media. In the immediate aftermath there was a groundswell of support, with mobile phone companies providing free phones, the railways offering train carriages as dormitories, and celebrities staging charity appeals. Pope Benedict XVI visited L'Aquila shortly after the tragedy and aid flooded in from around the world.

The government was credited with providing fast emergency relief and rehousing 17,000 people before the first winter after the tragedy. Since then, however, a string of sleaze scandals have tainted what was seen as an act of huge generosity by the government. The head of the civil protection agency, responsible for handling the earthquake response, is currently under investigation for hosting "megagalactic sex parties" in return for obtaining illegal building contracts.

Over a year after the tragedy, there are still over 50,000 "refugees" waiting to be rehoused, people currently living in hotels, barracks, camper vans or tents. There is still no electricity, gas or running water in the historic centre. Householders cannot return home and, in protest at the perceived inertia of the authorities, recently started clearing away

the rubble in wheelbarrows. Many fear that the city could become another Pompeii, with the symbolic monuments restored but the vast majority of minor museums and homes abandoned for ever.

Almost three-quarters of L'Aquila was damaged, with churches, palaces and homes reduced to rubble. But heritage bodies, regional banks and foreign governments were quick to "adopt" a monument. The French government is funding the restoration of the Suffragio church while the FAI, Italy's heritage body, has taken on the restoration of the monumental fountain. Santa Maria di Collemaggio lost its cupola, but papal holy relics were "miraculously" pulled out of the rubble intact. Even celebrities have shone. In *The American*, George Clooney chose the province of Aquila as a film set as his way of supporting the region. The locations included Sulmona, Castel del Monte, Castelvecchio and Calascio. Yet ultimately, the citizens must draw comfort from the past: when the 1703 earthquake nearly razed L'Aquila, it was simply rebuilt.   ❑

ABOVE AND RIGHT: images of Aquila's destruction.

THE SOUTH

To discover one of Europe's most seductive regions, venture beyond Naples and Sicily into the *Mezzogiorno*

When foreign travellers visit the remote parts of Basilicata and Calabria, they are sometimes greeted by stares. So few foreigners visit these sun-baked regions that anybody who does is looked upon as a bit of a maverick. The growing number of travellers who do come, follow the footsteps of the Greeks and Romans to Naples, Pompeii, the Amalfi Coast and Capri. They flock to Sicily and its temples or Sardinia's glitzy Costa Smeralda but skim over the rest.

Then there is northern prejudice. Northerners see themselves as enlightened, industrious and entrepreneurial. Southerners are dismissed as superstitious, fatalistic and backward. But get beyond the stereotypes and you will find that southern hospitality and hidden treasures more than compensate for poor public transport and itineraries which don't go according to plan – but are better.

Southern Italy is utterly bewitching. It is a romantic land of castles, churches and classical ruins, endless plains, and misty mountains where shepherds roam. It is increasingly a place for contemporary retreats, whether in Sicilian villas, cool cave dwellings, Positano palaces, or Puglian manor-houses *(masserie)*. Culturally, Naples, the Bay of Naples and Sicily

are the richest regions, from the classical sites to museum collections and even cuisine. In Sicily, the Hellenistic temples are matched by Arab-Norman cathedrals and a cultural resurgence in key cities. Sardinia is increasingly popular, as much for its rural lifestyle as its beaches, now rivalled by resorts on the Aeolian Islands.

Puglia is firmly on the map, helped by its Romanesque and Baroque architecture, crusader castles and conical beehive dwellings known as *trulli*. Basilicata is an emerging destination, partly thanks to its "deep south" spirit. In Calabria, rediscover the Greeks – in particular, the Greek bronzes of Riace and landscapes first described by Homer. ❏

PRECEDING PAGES: pastel-coloured houses, Naples. **LEFT:** an ancient fresco of *Spring* in Naples's Archaeological Museum. **ABOVE:** conical houses *(trulli)*, in Alberobello; *pastiera napoletana*, a traditional Neopolitan Easter cake; clusters of padlocks along Naples's seafront promenade – the modern equivalent of love knots.

NAPLES

Noisy but thrilling, Naples has it all –
Baroque churches, buzzing street life, world-class
museums and cosmopolitan verve

Naples (Napoli) remains a glorious assault on your senses, as explosive as Vesuvius, its local volcano. Naples has always been the black sheep of Italian cities, the misfit, the outcast, the messy brother that nobody knew quite what to do with. It is burdened by poverty, unemployment, bureaucratic inefficiency and organised crime, but remains, nonetheless, a triumph of the human spirit. Fortunately, Naples is one of the most beautiful Italian cities, with a friendly population and beguiling cultural heritage. Like all black sheep, troubled Naples is simply the most interesting member of its family.

The name Naples derives from Neapolis, the New City founded by settlers from Cumae in the 6th century BC. Romans flocked there, drawn by the golden climate, the sparkling bay and the political freedom which retention of the Greek constitution allowed. Virgil wrote the *Aeneid* here; emperors built gardens and bathed in this *Campania felix*, or "happy land".

Since then, the Neapolitans have survived Norman, Spanish and Bourbon rule, as well as infamous Mafia (known locally as Camorra; *see pages 70–71*) control to remain an irrepressible force – and a thorn in the side of modern Italy.

LEFT: Via Tribunali, in the historic quarter.
RIGHT: elaborate Gothic sculpture on Naples's Duomo.

Orientation

Naples is a fabulous but frenetic city, so take more care than you would elsewhere in Italy. The only way to get a feel for the city is to walk its different quarters and ride the **funiculars** up the Vomero hill. Also try the glossy **metro** line from Piazza Dante to Vomero, even if you don't need to travel by train. Each station is adorned with bold contemporary artworks.

Make easy forays to **Pompeii, Herculaneum** and **the islands** (*see page 325*) but avoid the crime-infested city sub-

Main attractions
CASTEL NUOVO
TEATRO SAN CARLO
QUARTIERI SPAGNOLI
PALAZZO REALE
MUSEO ARCHEOLOGICO NAZIONALE
GESÙ NUOVO
SANTA CHIARA
DUOMO
SAN LORENZO MAGGIORE
CAPPELLA DI SANSEVERO
PALAZZO REALE DI CAPODIMONTE
CHIAIA

urbs – unless you want to play-act being in *Gomorrah*, a brutal Neapolitan version of *The Godfather*.

From **Piazza Garibaldi ❶**, the long **Corso Umberto I** juts down to the southwest to **Piazza Bovio ❷**, and extends to **Piazza Municipio ❸**. The thoroughfare was carved through the narrow, crowded streets in 1888, in an effort to improve air circulation following a cholera epidemic. The rather drab **Università ❹** looms halfway down. From **Piazza del Plebiscito ❺** the city fans out. After its restoration, this is the heart of town, and home to the Palazzo Reale, the Royal Palace.

Directly north, up Via Toledo, also known as Via Roma, is the **Museo Archeologico Nazionale**. East of the museum, in the triangle it forms with Piazza del Plebiscito and Piazza Garibaldi, lies most of Old Naples, with its medieval streets and churches. North, on a hilltop, stands the art gallery of **Capodimonte**. Further south, on a spur of land out in the bay, rises the egg-shaped **Castel dell'Ovo** and, along the waterfront, Via Partenope, where grand hotels overlook the water. The shoreline then curves away west, passing the delightfully restored **Villa Comunale**, with its famous aquarium, to the marina at **Mergellina**, near Virgil's tomb, and chic **Posillipo** beyond. This stretch of seafront, along with elegant **Chiaia**, offers gracious retreats from the city chaos.

Castles, coffee and music

When Charles I of Anjou built the **Castel Nuovo ❻** (Museo Civico; Mon–Sat 9am–7pm; charge) in 1282, he could not have known that seven centuries later it would still serve as the political hub of the city. The City Council meets in the huge **Sala dei Baroni**, where Charles is said to have performed some of his bloodiest executions. The finest architectural element in this imposing fortress is the Triumphal Arch, built from 1454–67 to commemorate Alfonso I's defeat of the French. It is the only Renaissance arch ever to have been built at the entrance to a castle.

A short walk up Via San Carlo brings you swiftly to the **Teatro San Carlo ❼** (www.teatrosancarlo.it), the largest opera house in

Golfo di Napoli

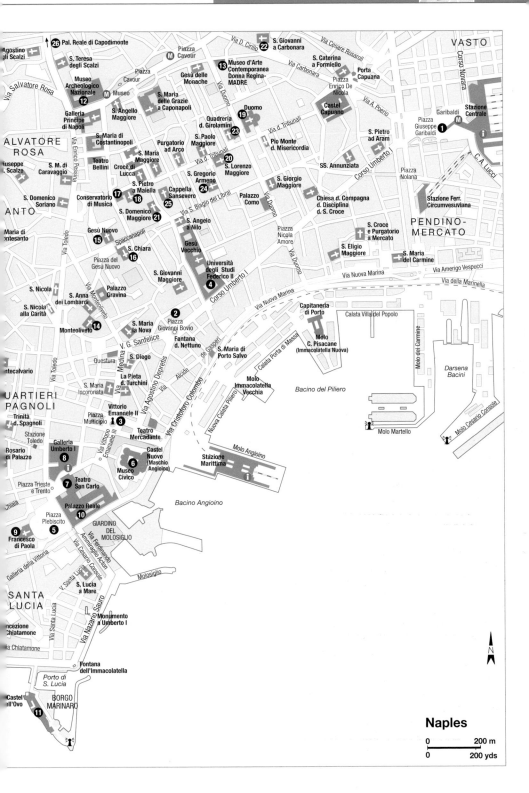

Agostino
li Scalzi

26 Pal. Reale di Capodimonte

S. Teresa
degli Scalzi

Piazza
Cavour

M

Piazza
Cavour

Gesù delle
Monache

13 Museo d'Arte
Contemporanea
Donna Regina-
MADRE

S. Giovanni
a Carbonara

Via D. Cirillo

Via Cesare Rosaroli

S. Caterina
a Formiello

Via Carbonara

Porta
Capuana

VASTO

Corso Novara

Museo
Archeologico
Nazionale **12**

M Museo

S. Maria
delle Grazie
a Caponapoli

Galleria
Principe
di Napoli

S. Angello
Maggiore

S. Maria di
Costantinopoli

ALVATORE
ROSA

iuseppe
. Scalze

S. M. di
Caravaggio

S. Domenico
Soriano

ANTO

Teatro
Bellini

S. Maria
Maggiore

Croce di
Lucca

Conservatorio
di Musica **17**

S. Pietro
a Maiella **18**

S. Domenico
Maggiore **21**

Purgatorio
ad Arco

S. Paolo
Maggiore

Quadreria
d. Girolamini

Duomo

19 Duomo

23

Via d. Tribunali

Pio Monte
d. Misericordia

20 S. Lorenzo
Maggiore

Castel
Capuano

Piazza
Enrico De
Nicola

Via A. Poerio

S. Pietro
ad Aram

SS. Annunziata

Piazza
Giuseppe
Garibaldi

Garibaldi

M

1

Stazione
Centrale

C. A. Lucci

S. Gregorio
Armeno

Cappella
Sansevero **25**

24

S. Giorgio
Maggiore

Via S. Biagio dei Librai

Via Duomo

Chiesa d. Compagna
d. Disciplina
d. S. Croce

Corso Umberto I

Piazza
Nolana

Stazione Ferr.
Circumvesuviana

PENDINO-
MERCATO

Maria di
ntesanto

Gesù Nuovo **15**

Spaccanapoli

S. Chiara **16**

S. Angelo
a Nilo

Palazzo
Como

Piazza
Nicola
Amore

S. Croce
e Purgatorio
a Mercato

S. Maria
del Carmine

Piazza del
Gesù Nuovo

Gesù
Vecchio

S. Giovanni
Maggiore

Università
degli Studi
Federico I **4**

S. Eligio
Maggiore

Via Nuova Marina

Via Amerigo Vespucci

Via della Marinella

S. Nicola

S. Anna
dei Lombardi

S. Nicola
alla Carità

Monteoliveto **14**

Via Monteoliveto

Palazzo
Gravina

2

S. Maria
la Nova

Piazza
Giovanni Bovio

Fantana
d. Nettuno

Corso Umberto I

Via Duomo

Capitaneria
di Porto

Calata Villa del Popolo

Molo del Carmine

Darsena
Bacini

V. G. Sanfelice

Questura

ntecalvario

S. Maria
Incoronata

Via Toledo

Via Medina

S. Diego

La Pieta
d. Turchini

Via Agostino Depretis

Via Alcide

Via Cristoforo Colombo

de Gasperi

Nuova Calata Piliero

S. Maria di
Porto Salvo

Calata Porta di Massa

Molo
Immacolatella
Vecchia

Bacino del Piliero

Molo
C. Pisacane
(Immacolatella Nuova)

Molo Cesario Console

UARTIERI
PAGNOLI

Trinità
d. Spagnoli

Stazione
Toledo

Galleria
Umberto I
8

Via Vittorio
Emanuele III

Piazza
Municipio

Vittorio
Emanuele II **3**

Teatro
Mercadante

Castel
Nuovo
(Maschio
Angioino)

Stazione
Marittima

Molo
Immacolatella
Vecchia

Molo Angioino

Molo Martello

Rosario
di Palazzo

7

Teatro
San Carlo

6

Museo
Civico

Chiaia

9
Francesco
di Paola

Palazzo Reale

10

Piazza
Plebiscito

5

Piazza Trieste
e Trento

GIARDINO
DEL
MOLOSIGLIO

Bacino Angioino

Galleria della Vittoria

SANTA
LUCIA

ncezione
Chiatamone

 a Chiatamone

Via Ferdinando

Via Ammiraglio Acton

Via Cesario Console

S. Lucia
a Mare

Molosiglio

Monumento
a Umberto I

Fontana
dell'Immacolatella

Porto di
S. Lucia

Castel
ll'Ovo

11

BORGO
MARINARO

Naples

0   200 m

0   200 yds

N

Castel Nuovo, built by Charles I in 1282.

BELOW: inside the Archaeological Museum, Naples.

Italy and one of the finest in the world. It is all red velvet and gold trim, with six tiers of boxes rising from the stage. Constructed in 1737, under the direction of Charles III of Bourbon, the theatre retains its perfect acoustics.

Across the street is the **Galleria Umberto I** ❽, erected in 1887 on a neoclassical design similar to that of its older brother in Milan. Its glass ceiling, 56 metres (184ft) high, and its mosaic-covered floor were reconstructed after bomb damage in World War II. Just west, beyond the other side of **Via Toledo**, lies the **Quartieri Spagnoli** (Spanish Quarter), a kasbah where little sunlight penetrates a grid-like maze built to garrison Spanish troops in the 17th century. With its low-slung, windowless houses, washing strewn across alleys, and urchins and hawkers in full flow, this is the picturesque Neapolitan slum of legend.

The **Piazza Plebiscito** around the corner is embraced by the twin arcades of the **Chiesa di San Francesco di Paola** ❾ (1817–32), modelled on the Pantheon in Rome. Considered the heart of a revitalised

Naples, the pedestrianised square is popular with buskers and artists as well as being the setting for art installations and open-air concerts. On the corner stands **Caffe Gambrinus**, the city's sleekest old-world café, a place to try Neapolitan coffee, arguably the best in Italy because of the city's distinctive water.

The sprawling red facade of the **Palazzo Reale** ❿ (Royal Apartments; Thur–Tues 9am–8pm; charge) looms across the street with its eight statues illustrating the eight Neapolitan dynasties. At the foot of its monumental marble staircase stand the original bronze doors from the Castel Nuovo. The cannonball lodged in the left door is a reminder of an early siege. Upstairs are a throne room and a small but lavish theatre. Further rooms stretch off in a seemingly endless series of period furniture and Dresden china.

Another famous castle, the **Castel dell'Ovo** ⓫ (Mon–Sat 9am–6pm, Sun 9am–1pm; free) on the waterfront, is used for hosting exhibitions and cultural events. Its oval shape (hence the name) is the product of its evolution from Roman villa to Norman bulwark to Spanish fortress. Beneath the ramparts, appealing restaurants line the shore; children belly-flop from the causeway, and the speedboats of the Guardia di Finanza (Fraud Squad) lurk just along the quay.

House of history

The **Museo Archeologico Nazionale di Napoli** ⓬ (Wed–Mon 9am–7.30pm; charge) is one of the great museums of the world, housing the most spectacular finds from Pompeii and Herculaneum and fine examples of Greek sculpture. A trip to the museum will take an entire morning. The highlights include the so-called "Secret Cabinet" (Gabinetto Segreto), a collection of erotic images which lift the lid on the racy ancient world. Graphic sex scenes are depicted on Greek vases, Roman terracottas and Etruscan mirrors. In the steam room,

for instance, scenes show nymphs and satyrs disporting themselves, or an over-endowed Priapus simultaneously impaling several victims on his many-pronged member.

The ground floor is devoted to classical sculpture and Egyptian art. In the main entrance hall, a monolithic sarcophagus depicts Prometheus creating man out of clay. Another sarcophagus presents a raucous Bacchanalian celebration. Through a doorway to the right, a pair of statues of Harmodius and Aristogeiton, who killed the tyrant Hipparchus, fairly leap out at you as you enter the room. These are actually Roman copies of originals once installed in the Agora in Athens.

In a further room stands a Roman copy of the famous statue of Doryphorus by Polycleitus (440 BC), considered the "canon of perfection" of manly proportions. This statue, found at Pompeii, is evidence of the refined tastes of early Greek settlers. The Farnese Collection includes a Hercules and the *Farnese Bull* (the largest piece of antique sculpture ever found) from Rome's Baths of Caracalla.

The rich collection of mosaics on the mezzanine floor come from houses unearthed at Pompeii. The freshness and colour of these works after centuries buried in ash are an amazing tribute to the craftsmanship of their ancient makers.

The Nile scenes in Room LX, from a later period, feature ducks, crocodiles, hippopotami and snakes. These mosaics originally framed the *Battle of Issus*, in Room LXI. In this scene, Alexander the Great is presented in his victorious battle against the Persian emperor Darius III in 333 BC. The thicket of spears creates the illusion of an army far larger than that actually shown.

Rooms on the first floor show paintings of Pompeii and a reconstruction of the Villa of the Papyri in Herculaneum, including an extraordinary collection of marble and bronze sculptures.

Through the large Salone dell'Atlante at the top of the stairs is a series of rooms containing wall paintings from various Campanian cities. Especially startling is the 6th-century BC *Sacrifice of Iphigenia*, the Greek equivalent of the biblical sacrifice of Isaac. The deer

The tarantella, a boisterous folk dance, is currently enjoying a revival, with squares in the historic centre of Naples welcoming nightly hordes of talented dancing fans. Accompanied by guitar and tambourines, the dancers weave and twirl around the musicians, often clicking castanets.

BELOW: a professional at work.

Home of the Pizza

Pizza was born in Naples, and genuine Neapolitan pizza is unbeatable. Its secret, apart from the fresh mozzarella – another regional speciality – lies in the baking. It is cooked quickly, at a high temperature, in a dome-shaped, wood-fired brick oven. The classic Neapolitan pizza is the *Margherita*, topped by tomatoes and mozzarella, and supposedly invented in 1889 to welcome Queen Margherita on her visit to Naples. Its rival is the *marinara*, made with tomatoes and oregano. Authentic pizzerias, which are often cramped and crowded, with marble-top tables, include **Di Matteo** (Via Tribunali 94; tel: 081-455 262) and **Da Michele** (Via Sersale 1; tel: 081-553 9204). The Piazza Sannazzaro, at the heart of the Mergellina district, also has a reputation for excellent pizza.

San Lorenzo Maggiore, which was built on top of the ancient Greek high street.

BELOW: majolica-tiled walls in the cloisters of Santa Chiara.

borne by Artemis in the top of the picture replaced Iphigenia at the last minute, just as Isaac was replaced by a ram. Far happier is *The Rustic Concert*, in which Pan and nymphs tune up for a Roman celebration.

Set on Via Settembrini just east, **MADRE ⓭**, the Museo d'Arte Contemporanea (Wed–Mon 10am–9pm, weekends until midnight; www.museomadre.it) is a celebration of contemporary art in all its forms.

Neapolitan churches

The churches of Naples, like the churches of any Italian city, offer glimpses into Italian life. In the south, a visit to a church, a quick confession, a genuflection in front of an altar are still a daily ritual for some people. Because of this, churches open every day (but close 1–4.30pm), so no opening times are given.

The church of **Monteoliveto ⓮**, halfway up Via Roma, contains a wealth of Renaissance monuments hidden away in surprising corners. Far in the back of this aisle-less basilica, begun in 1411, stands a bizarre group

of terracotta figures by the artist Guido Mazzoni. The eight statues, looking almost alive in the dim light that filters into the chapel, represent the *Pietà*, and are said to be portraits of Mazzoni's 15th-century friends. Further back, down a side passage, is the Old Sacristy, containing frescoes by Vasari and wooden stalls inlaid with biblical scenes. Another passage leads to the Piccolomini Chapel, where a relief of a Nativity scene by the Florentine Antonio Rossellino (1475) is a delight to behold.

Unlike in Rome, which is heavily Baroque, no single architectural style predominates in Naples. The Gothic, the Renaissance and the Baroque are all represented. The **Gesù Nuovo ⓯** on **Trinità Maggiore** presents perhaps the most harmonious example of Neapolitan Baroque. The embossed stone facade originally formed the wall of a Renaissance palace. At noon on Saturdays, when weddings take place here, the massive front doors are thrown open to give a splendid view of fully lit Baroque at its best. The coloured marble and bright frescoes seem

to spiral up into the dome. Directly above the main portal, just inside the church, stretches a wide fresco by Francesco Solimena (1725) depicting Heliodorus driven from the temple. The ubiquitous Solimena dominated Neapolitan painting in the first half of the 18th century.

At the other end of the scale, the Provencale Gothic church of **Santa Chiara ⑯** (Mon–Sat 9.30am–5.30pm, Sun 10am–2.30pm) maintains an austere beauty, and houses the medieval tombs of the Angevin kings. This church became the favourite place of worship of the Neapolitan nobility. But the showpiece is the stunning decoration in the cloisters, a testament to the Neapolitans' love of colour and exoticism. Majolica-tiled pathways meander through a half-tamed garden of roses and fruit trees, the same species grown here in Bourbon times. Restoration has revealed medieval frescoes under the arcades and newly unearthed mosaics.

The steep **Via Santa Maria di Costantinopoli** climbs up to the **Conservatorio di Musica ⑰**, founded in 1537, and the oldest *conservatoire* in Europe. It has an important library and museum (tel: 081-564 4411), but it is also enjoyable to wander through its courtyard listening to the music of violins, organs, harps and pianos spilling down from upper storeys. Further along, the Gothic church of **San Pietro a Maiella ⑱** is a masterpiece by the 17th-century Calabrian painter Mattia Preti.

Superstition – a way of life

The Naples **Duomo ⑲** is a magnificent Gothic reliquary from every period of the city's history. In a chapel off the right aisle are the head of San Gennaro, the patron saint of the city, and two phials of his blood (chapel Mon–Sat 8am–12.30pm and 4.30–7pm, Sun 8am–1.30pm and 5–7.30pm). The mysterious powers of the congealed blood are the subject of what Mark Twain called "one of the wretchedest

of all the religious impostures in Italy – the miraculous liquefaction of the blood". The miracle has been taking place every year on the first Saturday in May, 19 September and 16 December since the saint's body was brought to Naples from Pozzuoli, the place of his martyrdom, by Bishop Severus in the time of Constantine. It is said that if the blood fails to liquefy a disaster is in store for the city. The last great eruption of Vesuvius in 1944 and the earthquake northeast of Naples in 1980 occurred in years that the blood did not liquefy.

Another notable church in the historic heart is **San Lorenzo Maggiore ⑳**, where archaeological excavations have revealed the old *Decumano* (main street) running through the cloisters, and the Roman forum built over the Greek agora. Also significant are the Gothic **San Domenico Maggiore ㉑**, the 14th-century **San Giovanni a Carbonara ㉒**, **Girolamini ㉓** and **Santa Patrizia**, with its monastery of **San Gregorio Armeno ㉔**. The adjoining street, **Via San Gregoria Armeno**, set on the main artery of the Roman city,

BELOW: inside Naples's Duomo.

Display of the sweet lemon liqueur known as Limoncello.

is famous for its workshops producing *presepi* (Christmas cribs), an important Neapolitan tradition. This "street of superstitions" also sells bizarre talismans that ward off the "evil eye".

The **Cappella di Sansevero** 🟤 (Mon–Sat 10am–6pm, Sun 10am–1.30pm; charge), a small deconsecrated church near the church of San Domenico Maggiore, should not be missed. It contains a moving and remarkably realistic sculpture known as the *Cristo Velato* (Veiled Christ) carved out of a single piece of marble by Giuseppe Sammartino. The chapel was once the workshop of Prince Raimondo, a well-known 18th-century alchemist who was excommunicated by the Pope for dabbling in the occult. In the crypt are the gruesome results of some of his experiments.

Museums with a view

Two of the greatest museums in Naples stand high on bluffs overlooking the city. The **Museo Nazionale di Capodimonte** occupies the **Palazzo Reale di Capodimonte** 🟤 (Thur–Tues 8.30am–7.30pm; charge). Set in a shady park, this 18th-century Bourbon palace can also be admired for its grand public apartments. The museum contains some of the best paintings in southern Italy. At its heart is the important Farnese collection, which by the late 18th century numbered over 1,700 paintings. Among the high points are Bellini's *Transfiguration*, various works of Titian, Caravaggio's *Flagellation* and Andy Warhol's *Vesuvius* (1985). The Salottina di Porcellano is lined throughout with magnificent Capodimonte porcelain tiles which were made in King Charles III's factory in 1757. These originally adorned the queen's parlour in the royal palace at Portici.

A trip up the Montesanto funicular brings the visitor to the top of the Vomero hill, home of the **Certosa e Museo di San Martino** 🟤 (Thur–Tues 8.30am–7.30pm; charge), located in the well-restored 14th-century Carthusian monastery of the same name. Like so many buildings in Naples, the Certosa has been given a Baroque makeover. Some of the foremost painters of the Neapolitan Baroque are repre-

BELOW:
Palazzo Reale di Capodimonte.

sented here, including Salvator Rosa, Francesco Solimena and the prolific Luca Giordano. Belvederes give access to the best views in town – the wide sweep of the Bay of Naples.

Good views can also be had from the **Castel Sant'Elmo ㉘** (Thur–Tues 8.30am–7.30pm; charge) next door, a 14th-century fortress long used as a prison for political troublemakers. Also on the Vomero, the stately gardens of the **Villa Floridiana ㉙** (daily 9am to 1 hour before sunset; free) house the **Museo Nazionale della Ceramica ㉚** (Tues–Sun 9.30am–12.30pm; charge) home to an extensive collection of porcelain.

Escaping the crowds

When the appeal of the chaotic city centre palls, succumb to the allure of **waterfront strolls** punctuated by leisurely stops for seafood, ice cream or café life. To appreciate the splendour of the bay, walk through the **Villa Comunale gardens ㉛** west towards **Mergellina ㉜**, the departure point for ferries to the islands of Capri and Ischia (*see page 327*). The Villa Comunale itself is a serpentine park containing a small **aquarium** (Tues–Sat 9am–6pm, Sun 10am–6pm in summer, Tues–Sat 9am–5pm, Sun 9am–2pm in winter; charge), where 200 species of fish cavort in murky tanks. Both Mergellina and **Posillipo,** the chic, villa-studded district further west, represent enticing summer escapes, with the neighbouring fishing village of **Marechiaro** particularly appealing to seafood-lovers. Mergellina also makes a delightful early evening stroll along the Via Caracciolo waterfront. From Mergellina, views stretch back over the entire city, with Mount Vesuvius looming in the background haze.

Naples renaissance

Alternatively, head to the hilly **Vomero** residential district, or to elegant **Chiaia**. If you take a funicular, such as the Funicolare di Chaia from Piazza Amedeo, the teeming masses are swiftly left behind. The chic Chiaia quarter exudes a sense of ease and elegance otherwise lacking in Naples. While the smug atmosphere, cutting-edge art galleries and stylish boutiques characterise the lower part, the upper part is more maze-like and evocative. Bustling Piazza dei Martiri is the place for *aperitivi*, while the **PAN ㉝** (Palazzo delle Arti Napoli; Mon and Wed–Sat 9.30–7.30pm, Sun 9.30am–2pm; www.palazzoartinapoli.net) is spearheading Naples's commitment to contemporary art, architecture and photography. Chiaia is at the heart of a Neapolitan resurgence, with stylish B&Bs and boutique hotels. But Neapolitan creativity even goes underground: 11 metro stations have been turned into temples of modern art, with more to come.

In unruly Naples, the joke is that the red traffic light is only kept "to brighten the place up". But this subversive spirit also bubbles over into artistic creativity, summer street theatre and music in city squares. As always, any Neapolitan cultural resurgence will follow its own wayward path. ❏

BELOW: display in the aquarium.

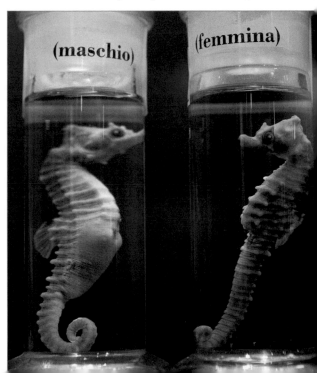
(maschio)   (femmina)

THE CAMPANIA COAST

An endless succession of jewel-like coves
ripples down the Naples Coast,
with Pompeii and Herculaneum just inland

BELOW: fresco
at Villa dei Misteri.

In classical times, Naples was a mere stripling overshadowed by its powerful parent **Cumae** ❶ (Cuma), 30km (19 miles) to the west, the first Greek colony on the Italian mainland and a beacon of Hellenistic culture.

Here Aeneas came to consult the Sybil before his descent into the Underworld. The famous **Antro della Sibilla Cumana** (Cave of the Cumaean Sybil; daily 9am–1 hour before sunset; charge) consists of a trapezoidal *dromos* (corridor), 44 metres (144ft) long, punctuated by six airshafts. At the far end is a rectangular chamber cut with niches where the Sybil apparently sat and uttered her prophecies. The eerie echo of footsteps in the corridor recalls Virgil's description of "a cavern perforated a hundred times, having a hundred mouths with rushing voices carrying the responses of the Sybil". From the cave's mouth it is possible to climb up to the acropolis, whose ruined, lizard-haunted temples offer fine views of the coastline and the sea.

The geologically unstable region between Cumae and Naples is known as the **Campi Flegrei** (Phlegrean Fields). These "fiery fields" were mythologised by Homer as the entrance to Hades, the mythical Greek Underworld, hellishly conjured up in a succession of rumblings and gaseous exhalations. The **Lago di Averno**, a once gloomy lake in the crater of an extinct volcano, is the legendary "dark pool" from which Aeneas began his descent into Hades. No bird was said to be able to fly across this lake and live, due to the poisonous gases.

This theory was cruelly tested at the **Grotta del Cane** on the nearby Lago d'Agnano. Dogs were subjected to the carbon dioxide that issued from the floor of the cave until they expired. "The dog dies in a minute and a half – a chicken instantly," reported Mark Twain. The experiment was repeated nine or 10 times a day for the benefit of tourists.

Volcanic crater

Pozzuoli ❷, a wealthy trading centre in Greek and Roman times but later devastated by wars and malaria, is now famous for its **Solfatara** (daily 8.30am–1 hour before sunset; charge), a volcanic crater releasing jets of sulphurous gases. The Solfatara is thought to have inspired Milton's description of Hell in *Paradise Lost*. Pozzuoli also boasts a well-restored amphitheatre, the third-largest in Italy (daily 9am–3.30pm; charge) and used for summer concerts. Pozzuoli was also the birthplace of fiery actress Sophia Loren. On the waterfront, enclosed in a small park, lies a rectangular structure formerly known as the **Serapeo** (Temple of Serapis), but now thought to have been a market hall.

Baia ❸ derives its name from Baios, Odysseus' navigator. Here Roman society came to swim. The modern town, with its view across the Gulf of Pozzuoli, contains extensive ruins of Roman palaces enclosed in a picturesque **Parco Archeologico** (Tues–Sun 9am–1 hour before sunset; tel: 081-868 7592; charge) on the hillside. At the lowest level of the park is a rectangular *piscina* (bathing pool) and a domed bathhouse, a circular structure identified as the model for the Pantheon in Rome.

Pompeii and Herculaneum

The region's most popular sight is the Roman city of **Pompeii ❹** (Apr–Oct daily 8.30am–7.30pm, Nov–Mar daily 8.30am–5pm, last entry 90 mins before closure, special night openings in summer; tel: 081-857 5348; charge; for information on Pompeii and Herculaneum, tel: 081-857 5347; www2.pompeiisites. org). To reach Pompeii, take the Circumvesuviana line from Naples and get off at the Pompeii-Villa dei Misteri stop.

Pompeii and Herculaneum, buried by the eruption of Mount Vesuvius in AD 79, have solved what the archaeologist Amedeo Maiuri has called "the essential problem in the history of civilisation: the origin and development of the house". Pompeii, earlier ruled by the Greeks, was a Roman playground and commercial centre at the time of its sudden immersion in pumice stone and ash. It was a city of shops, markets and merchant houses, with paved streets, a stadium, two theatres, temples, baths and brothels. Its chance rediscovery in the 16th century, and subsequent years of excavation, have revealed an intimate picture of life in a 1st-century Roman city.

The Pompeian house is thought to have evolved from the relatively simple design of the Etruscan farmhouse. The structure was built around a central courtyard (*atrium*) whose roof sloped inwards on all four sides to a rectangular opening in the centre known as the *compluvium*. Through the *compluvium*, rainwater fell into a corresponding rectangular tank called the *impluvium*. Around the *atrium* itself were the various family quarters, including the bedrooms (*cubicula*), the dining rooms (*triclinia*) and, directly opposite the narrow entranceway (*vestibule*), the living room (*tablinum*).

As the plan developed, a further peristyle courtyard was added, often

Pompeii is drenched in erotic imagery. Frescoes on view here and in Naples's Archaeological Museum depict the illicit loves of Mars and Jupiter, especially the sexual antics of Jupiter, who disguised himself as a human in order to seduce mortals.

Pompeii Revisited

Pompeii is Italy's most contentious major attraction. The site suffers from galloping decay, caused by neglect but exacerbated by the sheer number of visitors. In November 2010, the collapse of the 2,000-year-old House of Gladiators led to calls for the city to be privatised. Institutional apathy, incompetence and lack of funding means that swathes of the site are often closed and only a handful of houses attest to the full glory that was Pompeii. Restoration goes at snail's pace. Nor is there an interpretation centre, which would help channel visitors in a more coherent and sustainable fashion.

On the positive side, the finest frescoes are on display in Naples *(see page 318)*, even if museum cuts mean that certain galleries are only open in rotation. In Pompeii itself, there are attempts to make the site more user-friendly. Parts can be explored by bike (free rental), while families with pushchairs can follow the "Family Pompeii" route. Restoration work is still ongoing, with the *Termopolio*, a Roman snack-bar, the latest unveiling. The *Lupanare*, the main city brothel, was opened in 2006 after lengthy restoration. Pompeii's eye-opening erotic art, including frescoes of a foursome, is showcased on evening tours. *"Lune di Pompeii"* tours are a new way of exploring the ruins, with summer *son et lumière* shows (tel: 081-1930 3885; www.lelunedipompeii.com).

TIP

From Naples, the best way to reach Pompeii and Herculaneum is to take the Circumvesuviana railway (www. vesuviana.it) to either destination. To reach the top of Vesuvius, take the same train to Ercolano Scavi (Herculaneum), then take a bus and walk the final stretch (20 minutes).

containing a fountain. Shops were built into the front of the house; sections of the house were subdivided and let, with separate entranceways, to strangers (for example, the **Villa di Julia Felix**); another storey was added up top, until the Etruscan prototype had metamorphosed into the palatial townhouses typified by the **Casa dei Vettii** and the **Casa del Fauno**.

Wedding whips

A striking feature of the Pompeian house was the colourful and often highly refined frescoes, many of which have been taken to the Museo Archeologico in Naples (*see page 318*). But many are still *in situ*, including at the **Villa dei Misteri**, just outside Porto Ercolano, where a series of 10 scenes depict the sometimes alarming initiation of brides into the Dionysiac mysteries.

The meaning of these paintings, which feature, among other things, the whipping of a young bride, is still far from clear, although it is generally agreed that the woman in the final scene is probably a portrait of the mis-

tress of the house, who may have been a Dionysiac priestess.

The most remarkable thing about Pompeii is the mass of detail, including images of phalluses, carved into paving stones. In Roman times, signs displaying phalluses were considered symbols of good luck, as well as of virility and fertility, and it was believed they would ward off evil spirits. A sign of a phallus outside a bakery might also indicate a plentiful supply of fresh loaves.

Walls are covered with inscriptions, from lists of upcoming plays to the scribbled accounts of shopkeepers, from election notices to billets-doux. "It is a wonder, O Wall," wrote one cynic on the wall of the basilica, "that thou hast not yet crumbled under the weight of so much written nonsense."

Herculaneum and Mount Vesuvius

Herculaneum ❺ (Ercolano) (Apr–Oct daily 8.30am–7.30pm, Nov–Mar daily 8.30am–5pm, last admission 90 minutes before closure; tel: 081-857 5348; charge) was built for the enjoyment of sea breezes and views across the Bay of

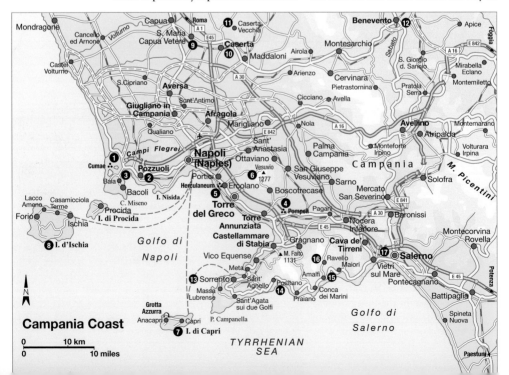

Campania Coast

Naples. Instead of the compact town-houses of Pompeian businessmen, there are sprawling villas of wealthy patricians. There is a free, spontaneous form of architecture, and the houses, freed of the mud in which they were encased for so long, are generally in a better state of preservation than those of Pompeii.

One of the pleasures of Hercula-neum (aside from the fact that it is less crowded than Pompeii) is the carbon-ised pieces of wooden furniture, door mouldings and screens still inside the houses. Fine frescoes, such as *The Rape of Europa* in the **Casa Sannitica**, adorn the walls, and mosaics carpet the floors. Particularly striking are the black-and-white mosaics on the floor of the **Casa dell'Atrio a Mosaico** and the frescoes and statuary in the **Casa dei Cervi** (House of the Stags).The newest dis-covery on view is the **Barca Romana** (Roman Boat), which has been pains-takingly restored. The **Villa dei Papiri**, believed to contain the "lost library" of Latin and Greek literary masterpieces, is closed for long-term restoration, but a number of the papyrus scrolls have gone to Naples Archaeological Museum.

Herculaneum is the best start-ing point for an afternoon ascent of **Mount Vesuvius ❻**, which looms over the modern city of **Ercolano**. Buses leave regularly from the Ercolano Scavi train station and drop passengers at the road, from where there is a 20-minute climb up a well-beaten track.

Just before the fateful eruption of AD 79, trees and olive groves covered Vesuvius up to its very peak. In the 20th century, a constant plume of smoke billowed from a cone inside the crater until 1944, when, dur-ing the volcano's last major erup-tion, the cone was destroyed. Aware that 1 million people are sitting on a time bomb and that a major erup-tion is overdue, the Italian authorities offered to help re-house local families, but the take-up from Neapolitans has been minimal.

Islands of pleasure

Of the three islands just outside the Gulf of Naples, **Capri ❼** is the star. This is Italy's St Tropez, where the mild climate, lush vegetation and sybaritic lifestyle have captivated writers, artists and Roman emperors. Emperor Tiberius retired here in AD 27, reportedly to indulge in the secret orgies which the historians Tacitus and Suetonius claim characterised the closing years of his reign. While on Capri, writes Suetonius, the emperor "devised little nooks of lechery in the woods and glades… and had boys and girls dressed up as Pans and nymphs posted in front of caverns or grottoes; so that the island was now openly and generally called 'Caprineum' because of his goatish antics." The writer Nor-man Douglas, who also lived on Capri, attributed such legends to the idle exaggerations of resentful peasants.

Today's traveller, arriving by ferry or hydrofoil from Naples or Sorrento, can reach the remains of **Tiberius' Villa** (Villa Jovis; daily 9am–1 hour before sunset; charge) by bus from the town of Capri. A boat trip will whisk the

Capri colour and style.

BELOW: the view down to the bay from the Giardini di Augusto, Capri.

The royal palace of Caserta took 22 years to complete. The facade is 249 metres (815ft) long, it has 2,000 windows, and its 1,200 rooms are spread across five floors connected by 34 stairways. Most impressive of all are the 120 hectares (300 acres) of magnificent parkland.

weary to the celebrated cavern of the **Grotta Azzurra** (Blue Grotto), supposedly Tiberius' private bathing pool.

From **Anacapri**, on the far side of the island, a chair lift climbs up **Monte Solaro** (from Piazza Vittoria; charge). Its 360-degree view encompasses the southern Apeninnes, Naples, Vesuvius, Sorrento and Ischia. In Anacapri itself, the church of **San Michele** (daily 9am–7pm, 9.30am–3pm in winter) is worth a visit for its majolica-tiled pavement. In Capri town, stroll through the lush **Giardini di Augusto**, created over a Roman settlement, before taking the winding Via Krupp down to the sea. **Marina Piccola** is a beguiling spot for walks and a seafood lunch by the bay. Limoncello di Capri, the lemon-infused liqueur, enhances any melodramatic view. Contrary to its reputation, Capri's sultry lifestyle and cliffside trails are far more enticing than the celebrity antics and designer shopping.

Ischia ❽ is less enchanting than Capri, but this verdant volcanic outcrop delights in rejuvenating thermal springs, delicious cuisine and

the loveliest garden in southern Italy. Compared with Capri, Ischia is larger, wilder and decidedly less manicured than its chic but more sought-after neighbour. Bustling **Ischia Porto** is close to **Ischia Ponte**, a causeway leading to the **Castello Aragonese** (daily 9am–7pm; charge), a moody castle and monastery built by Alfonso I of Naples in 1450. (After wandering the ruined castle, you might be tempted by the terraces of the decidedly un-monastic hotel café.)

Lacco Ameno, on the north coast, is synonymous with its mud baths, which contain the most radioactive waters in Italy, perfect for a winter break. More appealing are the **Giardini di Poseidon** thermal baths on the south coast, which can be treated as a day spa. Nearby, **Sant'Angelo**, a prettified fishing village, has some of the best beaches on the island. But Ischia's star attraction is the garden of **La Mortella** (Tues–Thur and Sat–Sun 9am–7pm; tel: 081-986 220) created by the English composer William Walton (1902–83) and his late wife, Susana. The Mediterranean and tropical gar-

BELOW: Ischia stands proud.

dens still provide a magnificent setting for chamber music and orchestral performances, including in the open-air Greek Theatre.

Procida, the smallest of the three islands, has good beaches and a thriving fishing industry. Unlike its bigger sisters, it remains refreshingly demure, old-fashioned and immune to mass tourism.

Old Campania

Inland from Naples, at **Santa Maria Capua Vetere** ❾, are the remains of Italy's second-largest amphitheatre after the **Colosseum** (Tues–Sun 9am–until 1 hour before sunset, museum 9am–6pm). This magnificent crumbling structure reveals the subterranean passages where wild beasts once roamed.

Caserta ❿, is often called the Versailles of Naples for its lavish **Reggia** (Royal Palace and gardens; Wed–Mon 8.30am–7.30pm; charge; for evening visits, tel: 0823-329 607, www.nuovipercorsi diluce.it), designed by Luigi Vanvitelli in 1752 for the Bourbon king Charles III. The brick-and-stone colossus doesn't quite achieve the elegant beauty of Versailles, but it is impressive nonetheless, especially the vast gardens. These come into their own on summer *son et lumière* displays that combine Bourbon history with Baroque music as light plays on the fountains in the newly restored royal gardens.

Caserta Vecchia ⓫, set on a hilltop 10km (6 miles) northeast, is an engaging medieval town with a Romanesque cathedral. In the mountains, further east, the former Roman colony of **Benevento** ⓬ suffered from bombing raids in World War II but several Roman sites survived. On the ancient **Via Appia** stands the **Arch of Trajan,** decorated with magnificently bombastic reliefs depicting Trajan's military triumphs. Antiquities are also on display in the **Museo del Sannio** (Tues–Sun 9am–7pm; charge), but the abbey complex, and its delightful cloisters, are just as appealing.

Sorrento

The visitor to **Sorrento** ⓭, whether arriving from the noisy streets of Naples or from the scorched ruins of Pompeii, will find a peaceful retreat and a sedate resort that, unlike much of the south, caters supremely well to tourists. There's not much more to Sorrento than sniffing lemon groves and quaffing Limoncello from cafés with cliffside views – but that is exactly what Sorrento has been doing beautifully for centuries. Charming, slightly faded hotels and gracious service compensate for the tiny beaches. Above all, Sorrento makes a serene base from which to sally forth to Capri and the Amalfi Coast, as well as to make more energy-sapping sorties to Naples and Pompeii.

The dramatic **Amalfi Coast** stretches from **Positano** to **Salerno** and has some of the most spectacular scenery in Italy. The thrilling **Amalfi Drive** doggedly follows each frightening twist of the shoreline, with fabulous views at every turn. Pastel-painted houses cling to the slopes, and gardens descend in tiers to the sea.

Fresh local produce is often for sale along the roadside.

BELOW: local pastime in Sorrento.

Positano and Amalfi

Positano **⑭**, with its cute cottages clustered on a steeply shelving slope, enjoys a mystique at odds with its self-conscious simplicity. Although beloved by the *dolce vita* crowd, picturesque Positano is best appreciated out of season or reached on a summer boat trip from another Amalfi Coast resort.

The precipitous Positano–Amalfi road passes through several tunnels before reaching the **Grotta di Smeraldo**, a cavern bathed in emerald-green light. (The cavern can also be reached on a boat trip from Amalfi.) Through yet more tunnels (watch out for cyclists) lies **Amalfi ⑮**, a major trading centre in Byzantine times but now visited for its cathedral, picturesque alleys and engaging seafront. From the main piazza, adorned by a fountain, a flight of steps ascends to the 11th-century bronze door of Amalfi's **Duomo**. The cathedral is a Romanesque affair complemented by Saracen-influenced cloisters. In the crypt lies the body of St Andrew the Apostle, delivered from Constantinople in 1208. Before leaving, linger over a Limoncello or window-shop for Vietri ceramics and Amalfi handmade paper.

Ravello

The loveliest town on the Amalfi Coast is **Ravello ⑯**, which luxuriates in lush gardens and vertiginous views, the best on the coast. Ravello's **Duomo** is celebrated for its Romanesque bronze doors and fine marble pulpit, held aloft by six roaring lions. The pulpit was presented to the church in 1272 by the Rufolo dynasty, who built the splendid **Villa Rufolo** (daily 9am–8pm, until 6pm in winter; charge) opposite. The villa's romantic gardens and Moorish cloister overlook the sea and are the setting for the Ravello Festval, a highbrow summer music celebration (tel: 089-858 422).

But the most memorable views are from the extensive gardens at the **Villa Cimbrone** (daily 9am–8pm, until 6pm in winter; charge), built at the end of the 19th century by a wealthy Englishman, Ernest William Beckett.

Salerno

It was just south of **Salerno ⑰** that the Allies began their assault on Italy

on 9 September 1943. A belated restoration of the historic centre has been helped by the successful revival of the medieval Fiera Vecchia, a large food and handicrafts fair held in May. The city, strung out along the shore, has a good beach and one of the loveliest cathedrals in southern Italy, which is reached through an atrium incorporating 28 columns from Paestum. Inside, the removal of 18th-century plaster has revealed a number of medieval frescoes.

Paestum and the Cilento

The English novelist George Eliot regarded the **Temple of Neptune** at **Paestum** (daily 9am–1 hour before sunset, last entry 1 hour earlier; charge) as "the finest thing, I verily believe, we have seen in Italy". Her words echo the sentiments of many 19th-century travellers, for whom this Greek city was the final stop on the Grand Tour.

There are few sights so arresting as Paestum's three well-preserved Doric temples standing empty on the grassy plain that surrounds them. The Temple of Neptune, the most majestic of

these, was built in the 5th century BC of a reddish travertine whose warmth, as Eliot wrote, "seems to glow and deepen under one's eyes".

The so-called **basilica** beside the Temple of Neptune dates from the 6th century BC. The third temple, the **Temple of Ceres**, is separated from the other two by the **Roman forum** and **baths**, and a **Greek theatre**. Across the street, in the **museum** (daily 8.45am–7pm; closed 1st and 3rd Mon of the month; charge) are famous mural paintings from the **Tomb of the Diver** (480 BC).

Paestum is the gateway to the **Cilento**, one of the most engaging parks in the south, and where the locals holiday near quiet coves, clean beaches and authentic mountain villages. Celebrated by Homer and Virgil, the dramatic shoreline rivals the Amalfi Coast. Atmospheric **Castellabate** makes a good base for exploring a rugged coastline riddled with caverns and dotted with watchtowers, as at Punta Licosa. Tuck into picnics of mozzarella and tomato in the confidence that both are sourced locally.   ❏

The spectacular coastline near Positano.

BELOW:
Temple of Neptune at Paestum.

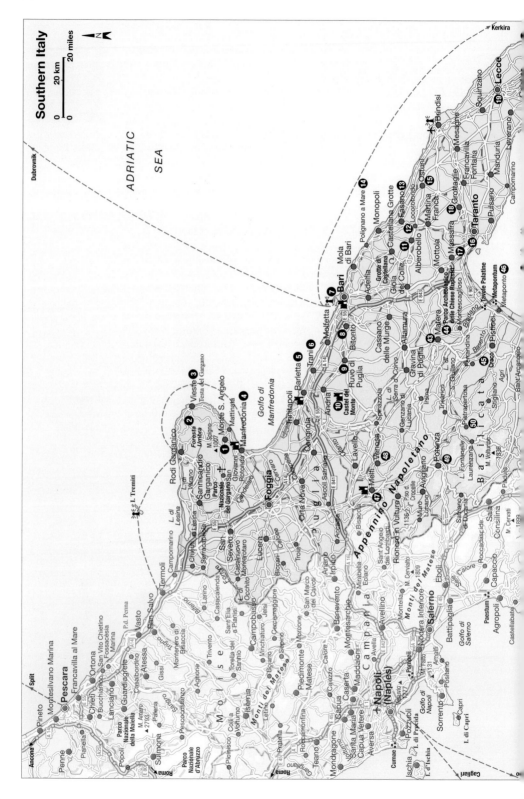

Southern Italy

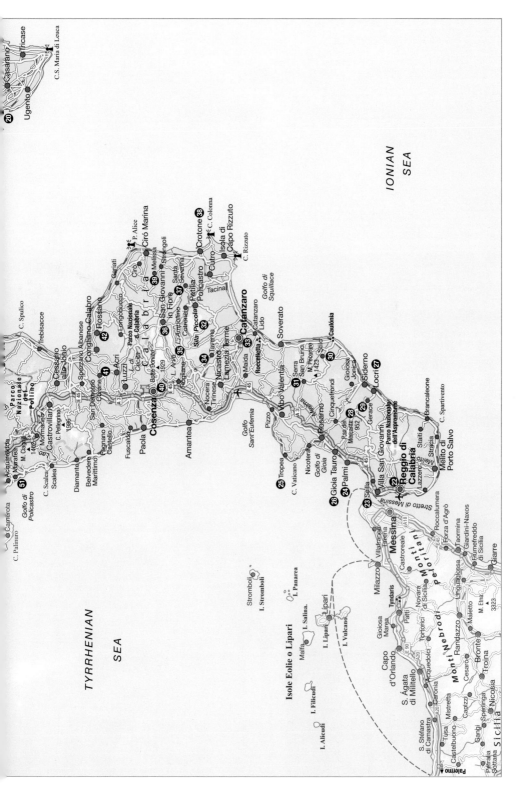

PUGLIA

Forming the heel and spur of Italy's boot, Puglia abounds in glorious churches, castles, fortified farmhouses and sun-drenched beaches

Everyone with a fleet has invaded Puglia, from the Greeks and Romans to the Byzantines, Saracens and Normans. Puglia has been a port of call for Aeneas and Odysseus, as well as for Greek traders and oriental merchants. Most invaders have left a mark, but none more so than Frederick II of Hohenstaufen, Holy Roman Emperor, King of Germany and King of Sicily. Known to his 13th-century contemporaries as *stupor mundi et immutator mirabilis* – wonder of the world and extraordinary innovator – Frederick built most of the castles that define the region. He also founded splendid churches, carrying on the tradition of Puglian Romanesque begun by his Norman predecessors a century before.

If Frederick II is the predominant figure in Puglia's history, then Puglian Romanesque is its architectural legacy. The style, fusing Byzantine, Saracenic and Italian decorative techniques with the French-Norman forms, first appeared in the church of San Nicola at Bari in 1087.

Not that Puglia can be reduced to its exotic architecture. As a fertile land of plenty, Puglia possesses more olive trees than people. Dotted with traditional walled, whitewashed towns, bulging with basilicas, Puglia promises a sun-bleached Mediterranean lifestyle. Dis-

cerning visitors, drawn to the laidback lifestyle, fresh produce and chic farmhouse hotels, have put Puglia firmly on the map.

The Gargano promontory

The landscape of northern Puglia is dominated by endless wheatfields, hence the region's fame as a pasta producer. The only real mountains are clustered on the **Gargano promontory**, a thickly forested peninsula that juts out into the Adriatic to form the "spur" of the boot of Italy. The landscape

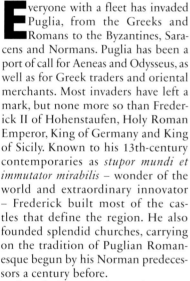

Main attractions
GARGANO PROMONTORY
TRANI
BARI
BITONTO
ALBEROBELLO
LOCOROTONDO
MASSERIE (FORTIFIED FARMHOUSES)
OSTUNI
TARANTO ARCHAEOLOGICAL MUSEUM
LECCE

LEFT: Lecce's ornate cathedral.
RIGHT: verdant orchard.

ranges from a wooded interior to a rocky eastern coast with lagoons and sandy beaches in the north.

The oldest settlement here is **Monte Sant'Angelo ❶**, home to the **Santuario di San Michele** (July–Sept daily 7.30am–7.30pm, Oct–June daily 7.30am–12.30pm and 2.30–5pm; charge). This cave is reputed to be where the Archangel Michael revealed himself to local bishops at the end of the 5th century. The cave is entered through a pair of bronze doors forged in Constantinople in 1076 and adorned with brass rings that were supposed to be knocked loudly to wake the Archangel within.

Monte Sant'Angelo is a good place to buy a picnic lunch to eat in the **Foresta Umbra ❷**, where ancient beech, oak and chestnut trees shade winding trails. From here, you can drive along the coastline to **Vieste ❸**, a bright town on the tip of the promontory containing a castle built by Frederick II. The road continues west along a serpentine coastline studded with beaches and grottoes, passing an impressive rock formation known as

Pizzomuno, referred to by locals as "the top of the world".

Catholics will be drawn to a neighbouring pilgrimage shrine, **San Giovanni Rotondo**, dedicated to Padre Pio (1887–1968). Canonised in 2002, Padre Pio was, according to Pope John Paul II, the personification of simplicity, charity and prayer. Padre Pio made lesser claims: "I am a poor brother who prays." Millions of faithful fans have already visited the friar's beloved monastic church, where the latter-day saint worshipped for half a century. However, Padre Pio's fame prompted the resident friars to commission an immense domed church, designed by Renzo Piano and consecrated in 2004.

Manfredonia ❹ is a port and beach resort with a pretty historic centre including a castle, begun by Manfred (son of Frederick II) in 1256 but extended by the Angevins and Spanish. Near Manfredonia are the beautiful medieval churches of **Santa Maria di Siponto**, with a 5th-century crypt and an altar made from an early Christian sarcophagus, and **San Leonardo**, with

a facade guarded by two stone lions. Siponto, once a thriving medieval port, also has good, though crowded, sandy beaches.

Coastal route

The coastal route to Bari is lined with seaport towns, all doing a brisk trade in vegetables, fruit and wine. The oldest, most important and, today, least attractive of these is **Barletta** ❺, where Manfred established his court in 1259.

Here, at the junction of the corsos Garibaldi and Vittorio Emanuele, stands the intriguing **Colosso**, a 4th-century Byzantine statue thought to represent the Emperor Valentinian I (364–75). Only the head and torso are original; the rest was recast in the 15th century. Behind rises the **Basilica di San Sepolcro**, with a nice Gothic portal and an octagonal cupola reminiscent of Byzantine designs. Barletta's **Duomo** is a confusing edifice built on a Romanesque plan, with five radiating apses in French Gothic style and a Renaissance main portal. By the sea lies Manfred's 13th-century castle, much expanded in later centuries.

A far more picturesque port, 13km (8 miles) south of Barletta, is **Trani** ❻, the cosmopolitan centre of the local wine trade. Its Romanesque cathedral (daily 9am–noon and 3.30–6pm in summer, reduced hours in winter), founded in 1097 but not completed until the middle of the 13th century, is perhaps the most beautiful church in Puglia.

Beneath its richly carved rose window is a smaller window flanked by pillars resting on the backs of elephants. The wonderful bronze doors are the work of the local artist Barisano da Trani, who is also responsible for the celebrated doors on the cathedral at Ravello.

The interior of the church, bright and austere, has the usual three apses and three naves, with triforium arcades above the side-aisles supported, here, by six pairs of columns on either side. Steps descend to the underground church of **Santa Maria della Scala** and the crypt. Even further down is the underground **Ipogeo di San Leucio**, 1.5 metres (5ft) below sea level, containing two primitive but delightful frescoes.

EAT

Hearty Puglian specialities range from sweet pastries to pasta, fresh fish, charcoal-grilled lamb and *fava e cicoria*, a purée of broad beans infused with garlic and wild chicory. When in Bari, be sure to try the local ear-shaped pasta – *orecchiette*.

BELOW:
Castel del Monte, built by Frederick II.

Frederick II

Some people visit Puglia for its architecture, some for its landscape and some for its food, but all go away haunted by memories of a single man: Frederick II of Hohenstaufen.

Holy Roman Emperor and King of Germany and Sicily, Frederick was an enlightened ruler who waged a bitter and ultimately unsuccessful feud with the popes in Rome. He was also an avid sportsman whose brilliant treatise on falconry still ranks among the most accurate descriptions of the subject. His just laws and tolerance of the Islamic beliefs of the Saracens are legendary. Frederick's death in 1250 and the tragic defeat of his illegitimate son, Manfred, at the battle of Benevento in 1266, ushered in a period of economic and spiritual decline that is only now being reversed.

The tower of Fiera del Levante in Bari.

Bewildering Bari

Ancient **Bari ❼**, founded by the Greeks and developed by the Romans as an important trading centre, was destroyed by William the Bad in 1156 and restored by William the Good in 1169. Today it is the largest and most important commercial centre in Puglia. The city is divided into two distinct parts: the kasbah-like Città Vecchia, at the end of Corso Cavour, with its tight tangle of medieval streets and dazzling white houses, and the Città Nuova, the modern city, with wide, grid-like boulevards. The tortuous alleyways of the Moorish-style Old City protected the inhabitants from the wind and from invaders. Although intriguing and generally safe, this maze of alleys can be bewildering, so visitors are advised to keep their wits about them.

The basilica of **San Nicola** was founded in 1087 to house the relics of St Nicholas, patron saint of Russia – stolen from Myra in Asia Minor by 47 sailors from Bari. Most Puglian Romanesque churches were inspired by this seminal basilica, with its austere facade, fortress-like towers, tall

BELOW: festive Bari.

gabled section and lavish portals carved with animals, flowers and biblical scenes. Its facade echoes that of the cathedral at Trani, though is even plainer. The interior is best visited in the early evening, when the dying sun illuminates the three great transverse arches. Beyond the choir screen is the 12th-century *ciborium* (freestanding canopy) over the high altar and, behind it, an 11th-century episcopal throne supported by three grotesque telamones. To the left is a Renaissance altarpiece, *Madonna and Four Saints*, by the Venetian Bartolomeo Vivarini. The crypt contains the precious relics of St Nicholas, visited by pilgrims for centuries.

Bari's Puglian-Romanesque **Duomo**, west of San Nicola, was erected between 1170 and 1178 over the remains of a Byzantine church destroyed by William the Bad during his rampage through the city in 1156. Basilican in plan, the church follows San Nicola in most details of its design, with deep arcades along both flanks and a false wall at the rear that masks the protrusions of the three semicircular apses. A particularly fine window adorns the rear facade.

Nearby, off the Piazza Federico II di Svevia, is the **Castello** (Tues–Sun 9am–1pm and 3–7pm; charge), built in Norman times, refurbished by Frederick II, and enlarged by Isabella of Aragon in the 16th century.

Bari's **Pinacoteca Provinciale** (Tues–Sat 9am–1pm and 4–7pm, Sun 9am–1pm; charge), containing paintings from the 11th century to the present, is in the less appealing part of town, the Città Nuova, along the Lungomare Nazario Sauro. The best painting is undoubtedly Bartolomeo Vivarini's *Annunciation* in Room II. Further rooms contain Giambellino's startling *San Pietro Martire* and works by Neapolitan Baroque painters, including Antonio Vaccaro and the prolific Luca Giordano. Francesco Netti, the Italian Impressionist, a native son of Bari, is also represented,

and there is in addition a collection of contemporary art.

Heading inland

A day-long excursion into Puglia's architectural past begins 18km (11 miles) west of Bari in the olive-oil-producing centre of **Bitonto** ❽. The city cathedral, built between 1175 and 1200, is perhaps the fullest expression of Puglian Romanesque. The beautiful facade boasts a rose window and richly carved main portal, flanked by the familiar lions. The pelican above the doorway is a symbol of Christ – in medieval times, the pelican was thought to peck at its own flesh to feed its young, bleeding as Christ did on the cross for humanity.

The town of **Ruvo di Puglia** ❾, 18km (11 miles) further west, was known as Rubi in Roman times, when it was famous for its ceramics. The 13th-century **Duomo** was widened in the 17th century to provide room for Baroque side-chapels, and, though restorations have shrunk the interior's width back to its original Romanesque proportions, the wide facade retains its Baroque girth, giving the church a somewhat squat appearance. Fortunately, the medieval sculpture on the facade largely remains; the seated figure at the top is thought to represent the ubiquitous Frederick II. Beneath the nearby **Chiesa del Purgatorio** lie some Roman remains. Ruvo's excellent **Museo Archeologico Jatta** (Sun–Wed 8.30am–1.30pm, Thur–Sat until 7.30pm; free) is devoted to Rubian ceramics excavated from nearby necropolises and dating from the 5th to the 3rd century BC.

On a hilltop 30km (19 miles) west of Ruvo stands the **Castel del Monte** ❿ (daily 10.15am–7.45pm in summer, 9.15am–6.45pm in winter; charge), Frederick II's architectural wonder. The eight-sided building has two storeys and eight Gothic towers; curiously enough, the main entrance is adorned with a Roman triumphal arch. Historians disagree as to whether

Frederick II erected the small fortress as a hunting lodge or as a military outpost, but all agree that he married his daughter, Violanta, to the Count of Caserta here in 1249. The castle was later abandoned, becoming a hideout for brigands and political exiles. The eerie emptiness is accentuated by its isolated position on a hilltop perch that's visible for miles around. Much speculation also hinges on the arcane symbolism of the number eight, as the number is an integral part of the castle's architectural design.

Trulli country

Alberobello ⓫, southeast of Bari, is celebrated for its conical (and somewhat comical) peasant dwellings known as *trulli (see panel below)*. Nobody knows the exact origins of these whitewashed houses, but they did allow for easy home-extension through the addition of another unit, and modern building in the area is often based on the *trulli* shape. Many have been turned into B&Bs or bizarre gift shops awash with local liqueurs, fabrics and sculpture. This area has witnessed the

Masseria Torre Maizza, one of many old fortified farmhouses in the area which have been converted into upmarket accommodation.

In 2010 a record 36 beaches in Puglia (including Ostuni, Otranto and Nardo) were awarded the Blue Flag, an accolade only given to the cleanest Italian beaches.

greatest increase in visitors staying in *masserie*, the traditional Puglian farmsteads *(see page 339)*.

South of Alberobello, less touristy **Locorotondo** ⓬ is another place to find *trulli*. This fortified hilltop outpost is a member of the *Borghi più belli d'Italia*, the most beautiful villages in Italy. The circular streets all seem to lead back to the Rococo Palazzo Morelli, generally via shops selling local wines.

The rural route between neighbouring **Fasano** ⓭ and Ostuni is lined with cypresses and *masserie*, working farms offering cheese, olive oil, jam and Locorotondo wine. The flat coast is given over to gnarled olive trees, but becomes more undulating above Fasano, with limestone escarpments, compact walled towns, and hairpin bends shooting down to the coast.

Perched on top of limestone cliffs, **Polignano a Mare** ⓮, just north of Monopoli, is an appealingly scruffy port with a low-key charm and whitewashed medieval centre. Few visitors can resist dining at the foot of the cliffs in the Grotta Palazzese (tel: 080-424 0677). This romantic seafood restaurant occupies a sea-washed grotto that was created as a banqueting hall in the 18th century.

The **Grotte di Castellana** (daily 8.30am–7pm; guided tours on the hour; charge; www.grottedicastellana.it) is another of the region's great attractions. The 20km (12-mile) network of caves contains pools, grottoes and ceilings that drip with stalactites. You can opt for a one- or two-hour trip; the latter takes in the spectacular Grotta Bianca (White Cave).

To the east, beyond the olive groves, is the whitewashed hill town of **Ostuni** ⓯, a kasbah of a place, with its 15th-century cathedral and labyrinthine alleys that are a delight to wander around. As elsewhere in Puglia, the town is both deeply authentic and surprisingly contemporary, typified by Caffe Cavour (tel: 0831-301 709), a cool cave-bar converted from a 12th-century olive mill. The success of the local *masserie* hotels *(see page 339)* means that the designer boutiques are doing as well as the shops selling ceramics, leather sandals, and baskets woven from olive branches.

BELOW RIGHT: *trulli* in Alberobello.

Trulli Extraordinary

With their grey conical roofs, whitewashed walls and mystical graffiti, Puglia's *trulli* are Italy's most curious houses. These twee homes originally served as storehouses or as overnight lodgings for farmers, but a 15th-century tax dodge led to a whole town of *trulli* springing up at Alberobello. The Count of Conversano enjoyed feudal rights over Alberobello, but did not enjoy paying his masters for the privilege. The emperor taxed every home in the count's domain – but not farmers' lodgings. So the crafty count ordered that the only buildings in Alberobello would be *trulli*. The Albererobelesi became people of the *trulli*. There are 1,500 of them, and even a double-topped *trullo*, once home to two brothers who fell in love with the same woman. The girl was promised to the elder, but fell for the younger, and the brothers fought until the only solution was to divide the house.

The *trulli* roofs are painted with primitive symbols: hearts and crosses blending Christian and erotic love; icons to Saturn, Jupiter and Mercury; to the pagan powers of the earth, sun and sky. Designed to be easy to dismantle, these hobbit houses are only too permanent today, and are sought-after shops or quaint holiday homes. Long Travel (www.longtravel.co.uk; tel: +44-01694-722 193) is a UK-based tour operator specialising in *trulli* holidays, including *trulli* with pools and vineyards.

Spartan Taranto

Taranto ⓰, the ancient Taras founded by Spartan navigators in 706 BC, was in the 4th century BC the largest city in *Magna Graecia*, boasting a population of 300,000 and a city wall 15km (9 miles) in circumference. It was, like many towns on this coast, a centre of Pythagorean philosophy and visited by such luminaries as Plato and Aristoxenus (author of the first treatise on music). Today, little remains from the Spartan period; the city was also severely damaged in World War II and is girdled by heavy industry. The en–gaging Old Town, once a Roman citadel, is effectively an island separated from the modern and industrial quarters by canals. Taranto is still worth visiting for its superb archaeological museum.

In the modern town, Taranto's **MARTA (Museo Nazionale d'Archeologia;** daily 8.30am–7.30pm, and until 10.30pm on Sat–Sun in summer) is the second-most important archaeological museum in southern Italy. The newly refurbished collection is rivalled only by its equivalent in Naples for the splendour of its antiquities. Set in a monastery, the displays recall Taras' importance as a centre of *Magna Graecia*. The collection includes Greek and Roman sculpture, Roman floor mosaics and a superb collection of ancient ceramics. The highlights include Doric friezes, Greek funerary monuments, Hellenistic busts, ancient jewellery crafted in Taras, and Roman mosaics depicting griffons.

In Taranto's Old City is the church of **San Domenico Maggiore**, founded by Frederick II in 1223, rebuilt in 1302 by Giovanni Taurisano, but heavily altered in Baroque times. Nearby, on the Via Cariati, is a lively fish market. Here, too, is the **Duomo**, which contains a catacomb-like crypt, Byzantine mosaic floors and antique columns from pagan temples.

A fascinating side-trip (21km/13 miles) can be made from Taranto to the nearby town of **Massafra** ⓱, known for its early Christian cave churches hewn into the sides of a deep ravine that snakes through the centre of the town. The Santuario della Madonna della Scala contains a 12th-century *Madonna and Child* fresco, reached

BELOW: fisherman.

via a Baroque staircase from the town centre. At the bottom of the ravine is the Farmacia del Mago Gregorio – a maze of caves and tunnels once used by monks as a herb store. Enquire about access to the cave churches while in Taranto (tourist office, Corso Umberto I; 121; tel: 099-4532392).

From Massafra by back roads (37km/23 miles), or from Taranto by *superstrada* (22km/14 miles), you can reach **Grottaglie** ⓲, a hilltop town where you can watch Puglian potters make the ceramic pitchers, plates, bowls and cups available across the region. The decorative spaghetti plates produced here are known throughout Italy.

Baroque Lecce

Southern Italians have long known about **Lecce** ⓳ and its glorious profusion of Baroque mansions and churches. But foreign tourism has only recently discovered the city. Unlike many southern cities, Lecce is enjoying something of a renaissance, with renovation matched by renewed confidence and the opening of new cafés and restaurants.

Lecce owes its appearance to the malleable characteristics of the local sandstone, which is easy to carve when it comes out of the ground but hardens with time. The growth of religious orders, particularly the Franciscans, Jesuits and Theatines, in the 17th and 18th centuries led to intensive building which created an architectural uniformity unique in southern Italy. Churches drip with ornate altars and swirling columns. Outside, shadeless streets meander past curving yellow palaces bright with bursts of bougainvillea.

The heart of Lecce is the cobblestoned **Piazza Sant'Oronzo**. At its centre stands a single Roman column which marked the southern terminus of the Appian Way (Via Appia) from Rome. A bronze statue of St Orontius, patron saint of the city, stands on top of the column. The southern half of the square is dominated by excavations of part of a well-preserved **Roman amphitheatre** (Mon–Fri 10am–1pm, weekends 6–9pm; charge) dating from the 2nd century AD. Discovered in the 1930s, it was reopened in the year 2000 as a concert venue. A small museum on

BELOW: the Baroque cathedral at Lecce.

the site displays some fine frescoes and mosaics. The unusual Renaissance pavilion used to be the town hall but now houses the tourist information office.

Lecce's harmonious **Piazza del Duomo**, just off the **Corso Vittorio Emanuele**, is framed by the facades of the **Duomo**, the **Palazzo Vescovile** and the **Seminario**, all built or reworked in the 17th century. The Duomo actually has two facades: the lavish one facing the Corso, with its statue of St Orontius, and the more austere one facing the Palazzo Vescovile. The altars inside the Duomo, carved with flowers, fruit and human figures, are typical of the ornate local style.

The most complete and impressive expression of Leccese Baroque is the **Basilica di Santa Croce** (daily 8am–1pm and 4–7.30pm), built in 1549–1679. Its exuberant facade sports a balcony supported by eight grotesque caryatids. The bright interior has an overall restraint that unifies the different designs of its chapels. A chapel in the left transept contains a series of 12 bas-reliefs showing the life of St Francis of Paola.

Lecce's **Museo Provinciale** (Viale Gallipoli 28; Mon–Sat 9am–1.30pm and 2.30–7.30pm, Sun 9am–1pm; free), just outside the Old City, is built around a spiral ramp reminiscent of the Guggenheim Museum in New York.

Best beaches

The rewards of travelling in Puglia, as in neighbouring Basilicata and Calabria, include the pleasure of ending the day on a beach. Puglia has the longest coastline in Italy, a fact which has made it peculiarly attractive to foreign invaders, from the ancient worshippers of Zeus to the sun-worshipping visitors of today. Lecce is within easy reach of beaches at **Gallipoli** ⍀ on the Ionian Sea and **Otranto** ⍁ on the Adriatic. Otranto has the added attraction of a Romanesque cathedral (daily 8am–noon and 3–7pm in summer, 8am–noon and 3–5pm in winter) with an impressive mosaic floor.

Given the pristine nature of Puglian beaches, you could easily while away your days dreaming of the heroes who washed up in Puglia, from brave Odysseus to brooding Frederick II.   ❏

The Moorish-style Villa Sticchi, built in the late 19th century, is in Santa Cesarea Terme, a seaside resort south of Otranto.

BELOW: the beach at Vieste.

CALABRIA

When Rome was still a village of shepherds, Pythagoras was teaching philosophy here. But today, behind miles of shoreline, Calabria conceals some of the remotest spots in Italy

Calabria is closer in spirit than any other region to the Italy of Byron and Shelley – the land of crumbling ruins that inspired the romantic thoughts of 19th-century travellers. Yet the region still seems torn between honouring its illustrious classical past and being enslaved by its lethargic present. The completion of the motorway from Salerno to Reggio Calabria should have brought dividends to the fledgling tourism industry, along with public pronouncements against the crime syndicates. However, apart from pockets such as Tropea, tourism often feels like an afterthought. Compared with Puglia, there are few distinctive hotels, despite delightful restaurants and romantic scenery beyond the development-ravaged cities. Frustratingly, much of Calabria's heritage also lies buried among the roots of its lovely olive trees.

The rugged landscape is dominated by a backbone of mountains that descend in a series of fantastic foothills to the sea. Not surprisingly, it was from the sea that Calabria's first invaders, the Greeks, came in the 8th century BC, crossing the Straits of Messina from Sicily. The dream of building a bridge across the 3km (2 mile) Straits may finally become reality as work began on the Calabrian side in 2010. If not shelved, *"il ponte"* will become

the world's longest suspension bridge. While supporters see the bridge as a boost to the local economy, both seismologists and environmentalists oppose the project. There are also grave fears that the building contracts will simply be shared out between the Sicilian Mafia and the Calabrian 'Ndrangheta, which still holds sway over the region (*see page 70*).

Spectacular treasure trove

Also from the sea are the **Bronze Warriors** – Calabria's most celebrated

Main attractions
BRONZES OF RIACE
MUSEO DELLA MAGNA GRAECIA
TROPEA PROMONTORY
THE TYRHENNIAN COAST
SCILLA
ALBANIAN VILLAGES
ROSSANO

LEFT: Calabrian folk dancer in Tropea.
RIGHT: sunset at Scilla.

Close-up of one of the Riace warriors, which date from around 450 BC but were only found in 1972.

reminder of those early settlers. Discovered by fishermen off Riace in 1972, these two colossal Greek statues – thought to have been lost overboard from a ship sailing between Calabria and Greece 2,000 years ago – are the star attractions in the **Museo Nazionale della Magna Graecia** in **Reggio di Calabria** ② (closed until late 2011, but currently on display in the seat of the Provincial Government, *see panel below*).

Along the Tyrhennian coast

The coastline just north of Reggio was first described by Homer in Book XII of the *Odyssey*, the earliest navigational guide to the Tyrrhenian Sea. Here lurked the infamous monster Scylla, whose "six heads like nightmares of ferocity, with triple serried rows of fangs and deep gullets of black death" did away with six of Odysseus' best men. **Scilla** ㉓ itself is a charming fishing port whose spirit, dialect and traditions feel more Sicilian than Calabrian. The view over the Straits of Messina at sunset is stunning, but might be marred by views of the con-

troversial suspension bridge. Stroll down to Chianalea and explore the picturesque fishermen's quarters. The houses are built on the water, so each one has two entrances – one facing the sea and the other facing the street. Further north, **Palmi** ㉔ is worth visiting for its **Ethnographic Museum** just outside town (Mon–Fri 8am–2pm and 3–6pm; charge), which has an extensive collection of ceramic masks designed to ward off the evil eye, and collections of agricultural and maritime life.

Rising dramatically from sea level at Reggio is the **Parco Nazionale dell'Aspromonte**, a craggy wilderness, and a tempting area for walking and mountain-biking, despite the presence of clan villages. Its highest point is Montalto at 1,955 metres (6,410ft), dominated by an immense statue of Christ.

Tropea ㉕, suspended from a cliff over one of the many fine beaches that line the shore, is the most picturesque town on the Tyrrhenian Coast, a welcome change from the bleaker Ionian Coast, which is best visited for its archaeological sites. Tropea is

The Riace Bronzes

In 1972 a holidaymaker saw a bronze arm emerge from the Riace Marina. Fate decreed that it appear at exactly the same spot where the locals immersed the reliquary of the Saints Cosma and Damiano to summon rain. For the faithful, there was no doubt that this was the divine intervention of the two miraculous martyrs. The so-called Bronzes of Riace have brought great fame to the Ionian coastal town. After restoration in Florence, and display in Rome, these two Greek bronzes returned "home" to the Museo Nazionale della Magna Graecia in Reggio Calabria and were greeted with the veneration normally attached to saints. Many Calabresi tried to caress the statues and lifted babies to touch them. The atmosphere was similar to that of a southern Italian religious festival.

These glorious, virile 2-metre (7½-ft) warriors are a patriotic reminder for the Calabresi that their remote toe of the Italian boot was once home to some of the Western world's most important cities in a land of philosophers and artists. Created in the 5th century BC, these bronzes were commemorative offerings presented to the winners of races carried out in full armour. The museum is being refurbished until late 2011, but in the meantime the star exhibits, including the bronzes, are on view in the seat of Reggio's Regional Council (Sala Monteleone, Palazzo Campanella, Via Cardinale Portanova).

infinitely more appealing and deservedly the most popular destination in Calabria for discerning visitors. The Tyrrhenian Coast is a place for savouring the laidback Calabrian lifestyle over long, languorous meals. The Old Town boasts a beautiful **Norman cathedral** and, behind the high altar, the *Madonna di Romania*, a portrait supposedly painted by St Luke.

Crossing the toe

Highway SS111 is the loneliest road in Calabria. It twists across the central mountain chain following an ancient trade route connecting **Gioia Tauro** ㉖ on the Tyrrhenian Sea with **Locri** ㉗ on the Ionian Sea. Fierce brigands once ruled this wooded terrain. From the **Passo del Mercante** ㉘, the road's highest and loneliest point, both seas are visible. From here the road descends to the beautiful town of **Gerace** ㉙, situated on a seemingly inaccessible crag. It is best to visit Gerace in the evening on foot, to appreciate the romantic sunset views from the grassy ruins of its castle. Before the 10th century, a miracle-working saint – San Antonio

del Castello – conjured up a spring of pure water in a cave in the cliff that surrounds the castle. Multi-layered Gerace justifies the phrase, "If you know Gerace, you know Calabria." The cathedral, Calabria's largest, was begun in 1045 on top of an older church – now in the crypt. Both cathedral and crypt contain columns from the Greek settlement at Locri. Some parts of this 7th-century BC town, including walls and temples, can still be seen.

The **Cattolica** at **Stilo** ㉚, one of the best-preserved Byzantine churches, is a reminder that in medieval times Calabria's rugged interior was a vibrant religious centre. The tiny 9th-century church, built on a square floor plan with five cylindrical cupolas, clings to the flank of Monte Consolino, just above Stilo, like a miniature castle overlooking its town. Its bright interior is adorned with fragments of frescoes. The four columns supporting the vault are from a pre-Christian temple, but were placed upside down to symbolise the Church's victory over paganism.

Another important religious centre

In the Serra San Bruno monastery, 16 bearded, white-robed monks live according to the vows of silence prescribed by Bruno of Cologne in the 11th century. The monks eat no meat but make excellent cheese which is sold in the town.

BELOW LEFT: the Cattolica at Stilo.
BELOW: medieval rooftops of Gerace.

In antiquity Calabria was celebrated as Enotria, the land of wine. Calabrian wines date back to the Ancient Greeks, when the victorious athletes from the Olympic Games were toasted with Kremissa wine (from Kremisi, between Sibari and Crotone).

further inland is the Carthusian monastery at **Serra San Bruno** , where you can visit the **Museo della Certosa** (Tues–Sun 9am–1pm and 3–6pm; charge).

Where shepherds wander

Of Calabria's four great mountain clusters – the Aspromonte, the Sila Piccola, the Sila Grande and the Sila Greca – the **Sila Piccola** ⓷, in the middle, has most to offer. (The Apromonte, in all its scorched beauty, is a base for the Calabrian Mafia.) Silla revels in its dense pine groves and cool meadows, where shepherd boys still wander with their flocks. The climate up here is refreshing after the dry heat of the coast. The twisting road up to **Catanzaro** ⓷ climbs first to **Taverna** ⓷, the home town of Calabria's foremost painter, Mattia Preti, who made his name in Naples. The church of **San Domenico**, just off the main square, contains the best of Preti's Baroque art, with more in Santa Barbara and San Martino.

A few resorts dot the vast pine groves of the **Sila Grande**, includ-

ing ski resorts and fishing centres, reached by long winding roads, but the overwhelming sense of isolation remains. Nature rules even around **Lago Ampollino** ⓷, an appealing man-made lake and reservoir.

San Giovanni in Fiore ⓷, the biggest town in the Sila, is noted for the black-and-purple costumes of its womenfolk. More compelling is the lovely hilltop town of **Santa Severina** ⓷, famed for its medieval scholastic tradition and castle. Attached to the cathedral is an 8th–9th-century Byzantine baptistery built originally as a *martyrium* (a shrine for the sacred relics of honoured members of the local Christian community) when it stood alone. At the entrance to the town, the Byzantine church of **San Filomena** has a cylindrical dome of Armenian inspiration, and three tiny apses that seem to anticipate Romanesque design.

The coastal town of **Crotone** ⓷, also a gateway to the Sila, was founded by Greeks in 710 BC. Here the mystical mathematician Pythagoras came up with his theorem on right-angled triangles and taught the doctrine of metempsychosis, in which the soul is conceived as a free agent which, as John Donne later imagined, can as easily attach itself to an elephant as to a mouse before briefly inhabiting the head of a man. Other than scholarly associations, the modern town on its crowded promontory has little to offer apart from an **Archaeological Museum** (Tues–Sat 9am–7.30pm; charge) which in 2010 saw the return of the Askos, a Greek bronze Siren which had been illegally sold to the Getty Museum. Find time to try wine since antiquity from the nearby village of **Melissa** ⓷.

Northern Calabria

The Old Town of **Cosenza** ⓸ stands on a hilltop surrounded by the featureless, sprawling modern city. In the heart of the *centro storico* stands a beautiful Gothic cathedral, consecrated in

BELOW: pastureland on the Sila Grande.

the presence of Frederick II in 1222. In the **Tesoro dell'Archivescovado** behind the cathedral is a Byzantine reliquary cross that Frederick II donated to the church at the time of its consecration. The partially ruined **Castello** (daily 8am–8pm; free) at the top of the Old Town has excellent views.

When the travel writer Norman Douglas visited the Albanian village of **San Demetrio Corone ❹** in 1911, he was told by the amazed inhabitants that he was the first Englishman ever to have set foot in the town. Although visitors are no longer a rarity in these parts, be prepared for the curious stares of barbers, policemen, shopkeepers and women in bright Albanian dresses.

The Albanians first fled to Calabria in 1448 to escape persecution by the Arabs. Today they form the largest ethnic minority in the region. They have their own language, literature and dress, and their own Greek Orthodox bishop. As isolated as San Demetrio is in the backhills of the Sila Greca, this was once one of the most important centres of learning in Calabria, the

site of the famous Albanian College where the revolutionary poet Girolamo de Rada taught for many years. Inside the college, the little church of Sant'Adriano contains a Norman font and a wonderful mosaic pavement.

On the Ionian Coast, overlooking the sea, stands lonely **Rossano ❷**, a major centre in the south between the 8th and 11th centuries. It is home to the famous **Codex Purpureus**, a rare 6th-century Greek manuscript adorned with 16 colourful miniatures drawn from the Gospels and the Old Testament. This extraordinary book can be seen in the **Museo Diocesano** (June–mid-Sept daily 9am–1pm and 4.30–8pm, mid-Sept–May Tues–Sat 9.30am–12.30pm and 4–7pm, Sun 10am–noon and 4.30–6.30pm; tel: 0983-525 263; charge) beside the cathedral. At the top of the greystone town, the five-domed Byzantine church of **San Marco** offers views across the valley. Below the Old Town lies the bustling resort of Rossano Scalo, somewhat at odds with the ethos of Calabria, which is dedicated to life in the slow lane. ❏

In the Sila national park, wolves, wild cats and weasels still roam, while the Pollino National park, straddling both Calabria and Basilicata, is the place for hiking, mountain-biking and canoeing.

BELOW: the Codex Purpureus, a 6th-century Greek manuscript in Rossano.

Calabrian Food

You will not be disappointed by the food in Calabria. A true Calabrese breakfast, typical of Reggio and the Ionian Coast up to Crotone, features several round brioches soaked in a glass of iced almond milk. For lunch, you can enjoy the Greek influence which is still present in the local cuisine, in the form of aubergines, olives, swordfish and plenty of sweet-toothed treats such as figs, honey and almonds. Peppers, chillies and ginger are used more liberally than in other regions.

Also popular are *porcini* mushrooms, which grow in the forests of the Sila and the Serre. And in this land of shepherds and their flocks, a variety of succulent cheeses are abundant wherever you go. Try ricotta, Pecorino or Caciocavallo washed down with Calabrian red wine.

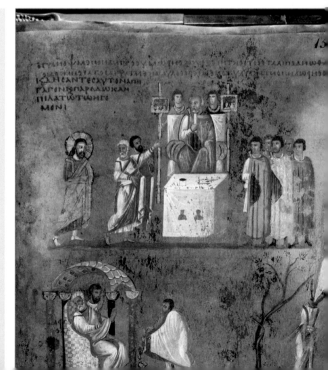

BASILICATA

With its primeval forests, sandy coves, chic cave dwellings, castles and ancient rock-hewn churches, Basilicata is both a timeless biblical land and a beguiling new destination

Even for Italians, Basilicata is off the beaten track and little known, despite being portrayed as biblical Palestine in countless film epics. But the crusader castles, ravishing coast, eclectic archaeological parks, and cool cave-hotels should stir even the most jaded visitors.

Matera and the Sassi

The region's most beguiling city is **Matera** ⓭, a fabulous troglodyte town of prehistoric grottoes, cave tabernacles, abandoned hovels and Renaissance houses – all excavated into the luminous limestone tufa.

The rock-cut cave dwellings – known as the Sassi – date back to Byzantine times. Up until the 1950s the caves were home to peasants who lived alongside their donkeys in dark hovels. Then the Italian government, embarrassed by the poverty, re-housed the entire population.

By the 1980s a number of intrepid Materani started to return, and now the Sassi are the region's main attraction – recognised by Unesco as the finest example of "cave architecture" in the Mediterranean.

A hill splits the Sassi into two areas: Sasso Caveoso and Sasso Barisano. The only way to penetrate this mysterious world is on foot, exploring galleries and

shops to see the inventive use of cave interiors. The caves may look crumbling but many are now cool B&Bs or bars, which have burgeoned ever since Mel Gibson's epic *Passion of the Christ* put Matera on the map *(see margin page 353)*. You can pick up maps from the tourist office (Via de Viti de Marco 9; tel: 0835-331 983) and book tours at the **Museo della Scultura Contemporanea** (**MUSMA**; Tues–Thur, Sat–Sun 10am–2pm, 4–8pm, Fri 10am–3pm, 4–8pm; charge), the refurbished sculpture museum, set in moodily lit caves.

Map on page 332

Main attractions
MATERA
ROCK CHURCHES
CAVE CHURCHES
TAVOLE PALATINE
MELFI
VENOSA
VOLO DELL'ANGELO ZIPWAY
MARATEA
PARCO NAZIONALE DEL POLLINO

LEFT: in the Sassi, many of Matera's homes are hewn out of the rocks. **RIGHT:** the perfect vehicle for the narrow Sassi streets.

Beautiful frescoes can be seen on the walls of Matera's rock churches.

fresco in a rock church, Matera.

Across the canyon from the Caveoso and Barisano are the original cave dwellings, dating back to 6 BC. This Stone Age history is documented in the **Museo Ridola** (Via Ridola 24; Tues–Sun 9am–8pm, Mon 2–8pm).

The great legacy of Byzantine civilisation in Basilicata are the so-called *chiese rupestri*: 9th–15th-century rock-hewn churches with built-in altars, pilasters, domes and frescoes. Over 150 survive, with some 48 in the Sassi themselves. Among the most important and best preserved are Santa Barbara, Santa Maria de Idris, Santa Lucia alle Malve, San Nicola dei Greci and Santa Maria della Valle. They are not easy to find, so go with a guide, who will often have keys to unguarded churches.

Other attractions include the Baroque **Palazzo Lanfranchi** (Piazza Giovanni Pascoli; Tues–Sun 9am–8pm; tel: 0835-256 262), which houses Italian paintings from the 13th–18th centuries.

The Baroque **Chiesa del Purgatorio**, dedicated to the medieval cult of the Holy Souls of Purgatory, features a curvaceous facade and gruesome Halloween-style decorations carved into the main doorway.

At the junction of Via Ridola and Via del Corso is the 17th-century Chiesa di San Francesco, home to painting by the early Renaissance master Bartolomeo Vivarini. The nearby Piazza del Sedile, dominated by the local *conservatoire*, leads into Via Duomo, with its Romanesque cathedral. Dedicated to Matera's patron saint, the Madonna della Bruna, she is depicted in the Byzantine-style fresco above the first altar to the left. Of the rock churches, **Santa Lucia** contains the two most famous medieval frescoes in Matera, the *Madonna del Latte* and *San Michele Arcangelo e San Gregorio*.

More rock churches

In the **Murgia** area, around 14km (9 miles) from Matera, lies the fascinating Unesco-listed **Parco Archeologico delle Chiese Rupestri ㊹** (tel: 0835-336 166), studded with over 100 rock churches (*chiese rupestri*). Many date back to the days when Matera was part of the Byzantine Empire. The most spectacular is the **Cripta**

Cool Caves

Matera is undergoing a style makeover, with intriguing cafés, inns, hotels and galleries opening in the Sassi, the caverns gouged out of the side of a canyon by cavemen 9,000 years ago. **Le Grotte della Civita** (tel: 0835-332 744; www.sassidimatera.com) is the most magical of the new cave-hotels. The owners wanted to maintain the caves' integrity, "without turning the hotel into a peasant theme park" – and succeeded. The beds are raised on metal trusses, echoing the ancient technique for discouraging domestic animals from hopping into bed too. The **Locanda di San Martino** (Via Fiorentini; tel: 0835-256 600) is a romantic honeycomb of a cave-hotel incorporating a deconsecrated church and a cave spa. **Domus del Barisano** (Via Lombardi 16; tel: 0835-335 450) represents a charming B&B in the Sassi area. **Baccanti** (Via Sant'Angelo 58; tel: 0835-333 704) is a creative cave-restaurant serving local pasta and full-bodied Aglianico del Vulture red wine. More bizarre is **19A Buca** (Via Lombardi 3; tel: 0835-333 592), an eclectic restaurant and wine bar that also slots a virtual golf course into an ancient underground cistern. Set on a rocky spur dividing Matera, the **Palazzo Gattini** (Piazza Duomo; tel: 0835-334 358; www.palazzogattini. it) is a luxurious designer retreat overlooking the Sassi. Naturally, the chic new spa is set in a cave complex.

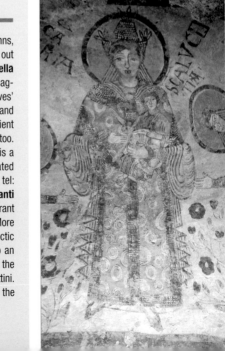

del Peccato Originale, the Crypt of Original Sin. Its bold 9th-century frescoes depict Adam and Eve and God the Creator. (Given the logistics, a guided tour is advisable, booked through MUSMA, *see page 351*.) If travelling between Matera and the Parco Pollino *(see panel page 355)*, stop at **Craco ⑮**, a bewitching ghost town abandoned after a landslide, which is now used as a film set.

Historic sites

It's an easy day trip from Matera to Basilicata's Ionian Coast, which is dotted with ancient ruins. Just north of **Lido di Metaponto ⑯** are the remains of the Greek colony of Metapontum. This is the only ancient Mediterranean colony where archaeologists have completely mapped the urban layout. Even more evocative are the **Tavole Palatine** (daily 9am until 1 hour before sunset; tel: 0835-745 327), the remains of 15 standing columns from the 6th-century BC Doric Temple of Hera.

Like Metaponto, **Policoro** offers little to detain a visitor except a dip in the sea. Excavations are still in progress at the **Parco Archeologico di Policoro** (daily 9am until 1 hour before sunset), where the remains of the 5th-century BC Acropolis of Heraclea are on view. The **Museo della Siritide** (Wed–Mon 9am–8pm, Tues 2–8pm; charge) displays bronzes and statuettes.

Melfi ⑰, between Foggia and Potenza, was once the stronghold of Holy Roman Emperor Frederick Barbarossa's Swabian dynasty, and houses a museum in a **crusader castle** where the First Crusade was launched by Pope Urban II (Tues–Sun 9am–8pm, Mon 2–8pm; charge).

The Melfi area is dominated by the Vulture mountain range, with its extinct volcanic craters filled by two lakes, the Laghi di Monticchio. A cableway between Lago Grande (Big Lake) and Lago Piccolo (Small Lake) with amazing views ascends to Monte Vulture (1,326 metres/4,350ft). Another splendid view is from the heavily restored Norman Abbazia di San Michele, located on the wooded slopes of the Lago Piccolo crater.

Film tourism is increasingly popular in Basilicata, with guided tours around places associated with Mel Gibson's Passion of the Christ *(2004), Francesco Rosi's* Christ Stopped at Eboli *(1979) and Pasolini's* St Matthew *(1964). Both Pasolini and Gibson used Matera's Porta Pistola gate as the entrance to Jerusalem.*

BELOW: the Sassi of Matera.

The castle at Venosa, where you'll find the Archaeological Museum.

Roman Venusia

Less than an hour away from Melfi is **Venosa ㊽**. Originally the prosperous Roman city of Venusia, it has survived thanks to its dominant position. For centuries it was a centre of learning, and was also the birthplace of the Latin poet Horace (65–8 BC). According to legend, he lived in Vico Orazio, where the remains of a Roman structure known as the Casa di Orazio are visible. The castle is home to the **Museo Archeologico** (Wed–Mon 9am–8pm, Tues 2–8pm; charge).

Take the Via Frusci which leads out of the town centre to the fascinating ruins in the **Parco Archeologico di Venosa** (tel: 0972-36095). Centred on the Abbazia della Trinità, the site includes Roman and Palaeo-Christian remains, Jewish and Christian catacombs, thermal baths and a 10,000-seat amphitheatre.

The **Abbazia della Trinità** (May–Sept Wed–Sun 9am–7pm, Tues 2–5pm, Oct–Apr variable; tel: 0972-34211) is one of the most intriguing abbeys in the south, and the largest monastic complex in Basilicata. It is made up of the *chiesa vecchia* (the old Norman church), and the roofless *chiesa nuova*, a later Benedictine foundation. Built of stones recycled from a Roman temple on the site, the abbey is a treasure trove of inscriptions, crusader tombs and frescoes emerging from the small olive grove.

Potenza and the Apennine Dolomites

Built on a spur of rock between two valleys, the historic centre of **Potenza ㊾** looks down on modern suburbs scattered at its feet. The capital of Basilicata has been battered by earthquakes: since the last big tremor in 1980, reconstruction has not exactly been miraculous. The highlight is the **Museo Archeologico Provinciale** (Via Ciccotti; Sun–Mon 9am–1.30pm and Tues–Sat 4pm–7pm), as well as the attractive churches along Via Pretoria.

South of Potenza stretch the **Lucano Apennines**, the Apennine Dolomites. Along the River Basento these bare, pointed peaks have been beaten into bizarre forms by the elements. The

BELOW: houses perched on steep cliffs in Parco Nazionale del Pollino.

best-known attraction is **Pietraper-tosa** ❺⓿ (southeast of Potenza, off the SS407). The lofty village is dominated by a rugged fortress and encircled by anthropomorphic spires. From here, the foolhardy can take the exhilarating **Volo dell'Angelo Zipway** and, strapped into a safety harness, "fly like angels" between Pietrapertosa and Castelmuzzo (tel: 0971-986 020).

The Portofino of the South

Maratea ❺❶ looks down on a cluster of coastal villages strung out along a spectacular, jagged coastline, and also on the **Porto di Maratea** yachting marina. The hillsides are covered with pines, carobs and oak trees sweeping down to the Gulf of Policastro and sightings of ruined watchtowers.

Maratea's unmistakable landmark is a statue of Christ the Redeemer – designed to ward off misfortune. The Redeemer's charms worked during the 1960s when Maratea was dubbed "the Portofino of the South". Its status was underscored by a visitor list featuring Frank Sinatra, Richard Burton and Princess Diana.

Maratea's faded charm is back in fashion. The town's revival was spearheaded by the local bigshot behind the Mediterranean-style Santavenere resort (tel: 09738-76910). It was Pietro Carnivale who wanted to give Maratea "the joys of the Amalfi coastline, without the permanent traffic jam and the vulgar chaos".

The result is laidback southern style without noise, nightclubs or bling. Not that the yachts and beautiful people are absent from Porto di Maratea; they are just not so prevalent. On the shore, the stalactite-encrusted **La Grotta delle Meraviglia** is a rare sea-cave accessible on foot.

Up on the hill, Maratea's **Old Town** is picturesquely distressed, at one with the limestone cliffs and *dolce vita* lifestyle. Lolling along the side of Monte San Biagio, medieval houses and myriad churches bear the cracks of an earthquake which struck in the 1980s. The unpolished Old Town looks down on Santavenere's ritzy resort with insouciance. Any trip to Maratea should end in a romantic inn with a promise to return. ❏

Archaeologists have recently unearthed the remains of a 6th-century BC Hellenistic temple, complete with detailed assembly instructions likened to an IKEA do-it-yourself furniture pack. The site is at Torre Satriano near Potenza, an area once part of Magna Graecia.

BELOW LEFT:
age, Italian-style.

A Walk on the Wild Side

Maratea is sandwiched between two competing national parks. Bordering the Calabrian side is the **Parco Nazionale del Pollino** (www.parcopollino.it) – a great place for walking and wildlife. The enormous park stretches across 200,000 hectares (500,000 acres) of wilderness which host many protected species, including a colony of wolves, black squirrels, golden eagles, vultures, falcons, buzzards and otters. The park's symbol is the rare loricate pine. It has declined since the last Ice Age as the climate has warmed, and is only found here and in the Balkans. There are underground caves with bat colonies and craft workshops demonstrating the art of bagpipe-making. The park is also home to ethnic Albanians who tenaciously preserve their Arbëreshe (Italian-Albanian).

To the north, the sprawling **Parco del Cilento** in Campania stretches from the Tyrrhenian Coast to the foot of the Apennines in Basilicata, and includes the peaks of the Alburni Mountains, a wild mountain chain with caves, large beech forests and stark rocks. An endangered population of wolves and wildcats survive in a few remote corners of the park, as well as over 1,800 species of plants. Instead, closer to Matera, the Unesco-listed **Murgia Park** *(see page 352)* is fascinating, as are the flinty granite outcrops around **Pietrapertosa**. (For information on all Italian parks, visit www.park.it.)

SICILY

The island of Sicily, set in the middle of the Mediterranean and once the centre of the known world, has the finest array of classical and Moorish sites in Italy

"**D**o you really think, Chevalley, that you are the first who has hoped to channel Sicily into the flow of universal history?" The Prince's challenge in *The Leopard* hangs heavily in the torpid atmosphere. Sicily may be Italian, but the islanders are Latin only by adoption. They may look back at *Magna Graecia* or Moorish Sicily but mostly sleepwalk their way through history. Set against Sicilian fatalism is a kaleidoscope of swirling foreignness, the legacy of a land whose heyday was over 700 years ago. It is most visible in the diversity of architectural styles, from Roman and Hellenistic to Arab-Norman and Spanish Baroque. Sicily's great epochs were Greek colonisation (8th–3rd century BC), the Arab invasions (9th–10th century) and Norman domination (11th–12th century).

Sicily was, in Cato's words, "the Republic's granary, the nurse at whose breast the Roman people is fed". But the Romans did not operate a scorched-earth policy against the earlier cultures. Greek language and traditions prevailed despite Latinisation.

Sicily is an enigma, "a paradise disguised as hell, a hell disguised as paradise", according to Sicilian writer Gesualdo Bufalino. "That is probably why the ferry that brings tourists across the Straits of Messina has been nick-named *Charon*, after the boatman who

ferried souls to the Underworld." Goethe too found Sicily intoxicating, from the Classical temples and Etna's eruptions to the volcanic nature of the Sicilians. "To have seen Italy without seeing Sicily is not to have seen Italy at all – for Sicily is the key to everything."

The Ionian coastline

A ferry crosses between Villa San Giovanni in Calabria and **Messina ❶** in half an hour, but in the future there might well be a bridge over the Straits *(see page 345)*. Cradled by the Peloritani

(see page 345)

Main attractions
TAORMINA
MOUNT ETNA
SYRACUSE
NOTO
RAGUSA
VILLA ROMANA DEL CASALE
VALLE DEI TEMPLI
  (VALLEY OF THE TEMPLES)
SELINUNTE
SEGESTA
MONREALE
PALERMO
CEFALÙ
ISOLE EOLIE (AEOLIAN ISLANDS)

LEFT: Arab-Norman cloisters at Monreale.
RIGHT: on Salina, one of the Aeolian Islands.

Sicily

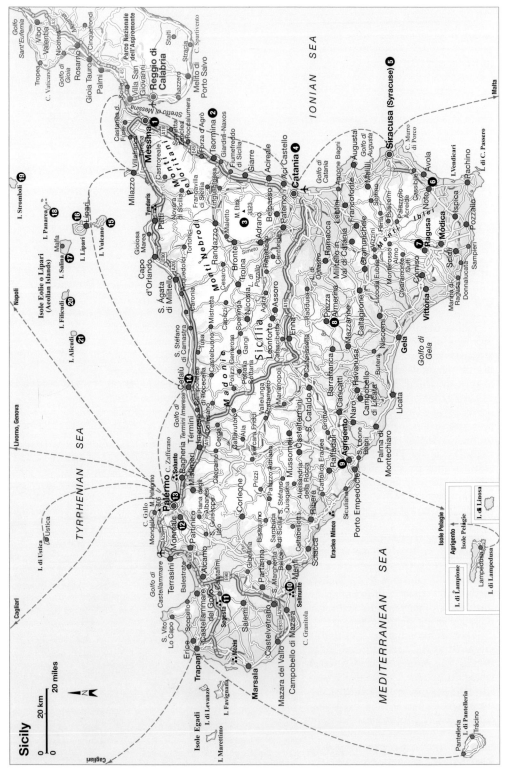

mountains, Messina swiftly reveals itself as a grid-like city with low-rise buildings and wide avenues.

Although founded in the Classical Age by Greek settlers and flourishing between the 15th and 17th centuries, Messina has little to show for its ancient origins. On a fateful morning in 1908, terrifying earthquake jolts, followed by a violent seaquake, shook the city and razed it to the ground. Despite this disaster, several churches survived, including the **Duomo**, as well as the Orion fountain, designed by a pupil of Michelangelo. At midday, the astronomical clock on the cathedral bell tower puts on a bold show, mixing mythological and religious figures with sound effects, such as a crowing cock and lion's roar.

In the shadow of Etna

After 45km (28 miles), the road from Messina winds up to a town that is the essence of Sicily. "It is the greatest work of art and nature!" exclaimed Goethe in *Italian Journey*. **Taormina ❷** is Sicily's most dramatic resort, a stirring place celebrated since classical times. Its beauty is made up of light, colour and sea. It slopes down a cliff "as if", wrote Guy de Maupassant, "it had rolled down there from the peak". Its shoulders are embraced by the looming Mount Etna.

Climb the hill to the **Greek Theatre** (daily 9am–7pm in summer, until 4pm in winter; charge; also open for summer concerts, opera and drama July–Sept, tickets and information from the tourist office; tel: 0942-23243), Taormina's most famous monument. Built in the 3rd century BC, but completely remodelled by the Romans in the 2nd century AD, it illustrates the Greeks' knack of choosing settings where nature enhances art. The jagged coastline of Taormina is dramatic: outcrops of rocks are intercut by narrow creeks, ravines and inlets.

Corso Umberto, which cuts through the old centre, is the place for browsing, grazing and people-watching.

Despite the cosmopolitan crowd and designer nonchalance, the atmosphere somehow remains villagey. You can see this village in its churches or in the grand *palazzi* with their mullioned windows, marble tracery, scrolls and billowing balconies. Taormina is often likened to a Sicilian St Tropez, stylish but slightly unreal. Cynics insist the city is uncontaminated by corruption because even the Mafia likes a crime-free holiday haunt.

Sicily's smokestack

The landscape south of Taormina is dominated by **Mount Etna ❸**, the majestic volcano (3,323 metres/ 10,959ft) with its snow-capped peak. It is one of only a few active volcanoes in the world. Its surface is punctuated by about 200 cones, smaller craters, accumulated layers of lava, gashes and valleys. Etna's history is one of semi-ruinous eruptions, from the one in 396 BC which halted the Carthaginians, to one in 1981, which destroyed part of the cableway. Even a smaller eruption in 1992 required help from the US marines to staunch the lava flow. The

To present-day Sicilians, Etna is still an atavistic god. As Pino Torrisi, a carpenter, says: "You must never speak badly of Etna. She was here 200 million years ago, and we are guests on her slopes; we are nothing against her will."

BELOW: the rich interior of Catania's Duomo.

volcano has been in eruptive mode for over a decade but what happens next, of course, is as unpredictable as ever. Etna can be a damp squib smelling of rotten eggs or prove the most dramatic memory of your stay. To discuss options of getting close to Mount Etna, usually by the northern route via Linguaglossa, book a tour through Taormina or Catania tourist offices. For advice on conditions and hiking routes, visit the Etna Park in Nicolosi (tel: 095-821 111).

Catania 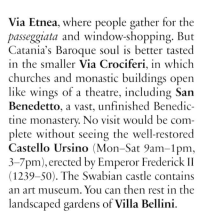, set in a fertile plain at the southern foot of Mount Etna, was an important Greek colony, and still sees itself as more Greek, compared with the Moorish spirit prevalent in Palermo. If Palermo is perceived as being fatalistic, Catania is seen as more entrepreneurial. Destroyed twice by violent earthquakes (in 1169 and 1693), the city was covered in 1669 by lava which even advanced into the sea for about 700 metres (2,300ft).

Catania is the hub of the richest area of Sicily and has a modern feel, with an urban plan characterised by wide avenues and dark lava-stone palaces. Its main axis is the elegant, austere

BELOW: scooters in Syracuse.

Via Etnea, where people gather for the *passeggiata* and window-shopping. But Catania's Baroque soul is better tasted in the smaller **Via Crociferi**, in which churches and monastic buildings open like wings of a theatre, including **San Benedetto**, a vast, unfinished Benedictine monastery. No visit would be complete without seeing the well-restored **Castello Ursino** (Mon–Sat 9am–1pm, 3–7pm), erected by Emperor Frederick II (1239–50). The Swabian castle contains an art museum. You can then rest in the landscaped gardens of **Villa Bellini**.

Town of tyrants

From Catania head for **Syracuse** 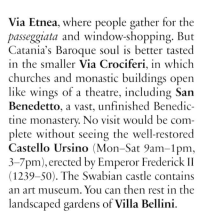 (Siracusa) through landscapes of classical beauty, counterpointed by archaeological remains. Built in 734 BC by a group of Corinthian farmers who settled on the small isle of **Ortigia**, Syracuse became one of the most important centres of the Mediterranean. After a dalliance with democracy, Syracuse flourished under despotism, and Dionysius.

Newly revitalised Syracuse is Sicily's most charming large city, especially in Ortigia, the island at the heart of the Greek city. This quietly cultured backwater is a place for aimless wandering between bold churches, Baroque curlicues and windswept views. The most compelling sight is the **Tempio di Atena** (5th century BC), a Greek temple which later became the **Duomo**.

Leave Ortigia across the **Ponte Nuovo** and head north to **Neapolis** (daily 9am–6pm; charge), the sprawling archaeological park home to the **Teatro Greco**, one of the greatest theatres in the Greek world, which accommodated 15,000 spectators. Here, in summer, a series of high-quality classical performances allow lucky visitors to end up in the very spot where Plato or Archimedes sat for their night on the town. (For details, tel: 06-4807 8400; www.indafondazione.org.)

Nearby lie the **Latomie**, ancient honeycombed quarries which were used as prisons for Athenians sentenced to hard labour. In the **Latomia del Paradiso,** a man-made cave known as Dionysius' Ear has an amazing echo. A whisper amplified by the walls permitted the tyrant Dionysius to eavesdrop on prisoners. If you relish ancient legends, stop at the lively bars by the **Arethusa Fountain** back in Ortigia. According to local lore, the beautiful nymph jumped into the sea in order to escape from the river god Alfeus and was transformed into this spring.

From Syracuse, an excursion through the parched interior visits the theatrically Baroque town of **Noto ❻**. It stands on a ridge of the **Iblei Mountains,** furrowed by a long and straight road which widens out into wonderful inclined squares. Here Spanish Baroque architecture triumphs in churches, palaces and monasteries, all cast in golden-coloured stone. Piazza Municipio encompasses a riot of pilasters, adorned windows, loggias, terraces and bell towers. Another highlight is **Palazzo Villa-Dorata**: a facade incorporating Ionic columns and balconies awash with lions, cherubs, gorgons and monsters.

From Noto, either visit the clean **beaches** to the south, or head west to **Ragusa ❼**, a city divided into two distinct entities, with Ragusa Ibla the star, and undergoing a revival. As a Baroque city recreated on a medieval street plan, an old-world intimacy prevails. Ibla is a place of moods rather than sights, graced by secret shrines, tawny-coloured mansions, filigree balconies and friendly bars. **Piazza Duomo** is lined by palm trees and mansions but the centrepiece is San Giorgio, a masterpiece of Sicilian Baroque.

Sicily's harsh and imposing heart

From the coast, an excursion leads through the bare interior, with its reddish sulphur mines, to Sicily's greatest Roman wonder. Outside the hilltop town of **Piazza Armerina ❽** is the **Villa Romana del Casale** (Mon–Fri 3–8pm, Sat–Sun 9am–8pm; charge), an imperial mansion or grand hunting lodge. The 3rd- and 4th-century villa was classified as a Unesco World Heritage site because "as the mainstay of the rural economy of the Western Roman

Land and property confiscated from the Mafia is increasingly being put to public use. Law-abiding Sicilians are also challenging the Mafia's protection rackets. There is now a map of businesses which refuse to pay protection money, known as the "pizzo".

BELOW: mosaics from the Villa Romana del Casale in Piazza Armerina.

An ideal first glimpse of Agrigento's temples is by night: the crest of temples was designed to be visible from the sea, both as a beacon for sailors and to show that the gods guarded the sacred city from mortal danger.

Empire, the villa symbolises the Roman exploitation of the countryside and is one of the most sumptuous examples of its type". Indeed, the villa's splendid mosaics triumph as "the last pagan achievement in Sicily executed under the old dispensation". The vaulting may be lost and the frescoes faded but the villa's magic lies in the 50 rooms covered in Roman-African mosaics. Their vitality set them apart from models in Tunisia or Antioch. The stylisation of these mosaics is undercut by humour, realism, sensuality and subtlety.

Land of the gods

Luminous **Agrigento ❾**, described by the Greek poet Pindar as "the most beautiful city of mortals", is a magnificent sight linked to a disappointing city. Syracuse may have been the most powerful city in Greek Sicily but Agrigento (Akragas) was the most hedonistic. The origins of Agrigento date from 581 BC. Here, for a fleeting moment, the classical world comes alive. The Valley of the Temples forms a natural amphitheatre, with a string of Doric temples straddling a ridge south of the

city. This is still a valley of wild thyme, fennel, silvery olive groves and almond blossom. Ideally, glimpse it first at night, when the temples glow in the black countryside, radiating a sense of serenity.

The classical city, **Valle dei Templi** (Valley of the Temples; main zone daily 8.30am–7pm; charge) comprises magnificent temples and tombs. The finest are: Tempio di Giove (Olympian Zeus), the largest Doric temple ever known; Tempio di Giunone (Juno/Hera), which commands a view of the valley; and Tempio della Concordia, one of the best-preserved temples in the world.

The splendid temples of **Selinunte ❿** (daily 9am–7pm, until 4pm in winter; charge) can be seen from afar, on a promontory between a river and a plain in the middle of a gulf with no name. Selinunte looks like a puzzle made of stone pieces: divided columns, chipped capitals, and white-and-grey cubes are all heaped together, as if a giant hand had mixed the pieces to make the reassembling of the original image more difficult. However, the stones speak volumes, revealing libraries, warehouses, courthouses, temples – all testifying to a prosperous ancient town in the middle of fertile lands. Amid the stones grows *selinon*, the wild parsley which gave its name to the powerful Greek colony.

Selinunte was destroyed in its attempt to expand at the expense of Segesta: in 409 BC, 16,000 citizens of Selinunte were slain by their Carthaginian rivals. To complete the plunge into the past, go to the rival **Segesta ⓫** (daily 9am–7pm in summer, until 4pm in winter; charge). In spite of the frequent devastations of wars between the Greeks and the Carthaginians, an imposing Doric **temple** has survived. It stands on the side of an arid, windbeaten hill, and is propped up by 36 columns. Further up is the **Theatre** (Teatro), constructed in the 3rd century AD over the top of Mount Barbaro and from which stretches a splendid view

BELOW: the Tempio della Concordia at Agrigento.

over the **Gulf of Castellammare**; during July and August there are open-air performances.

The Conca d'Oro

Enclosed by a chain of mountains, the Conca d'Oro is a valley of citrus groves, fast succumbing to ribbon development. The valley is dominated by **Monreale ⑫**, which was founded in the 11th century around a famous Benedictine abbey. The **cathedral** (daily 8am–6pm; chapel and terraces closed noon–3.30pm) is a masterpiece of 12th-century Arab-Norman architecture. The church owes its fame to the mosaics, made by Byzantine and Venetian artists and craftsmen. The mosaics illustrate biblical scenes, from the Creation to the Apostles, in

a golden splendour which fades away into grey, giving a tone of "sad brightness" summed up by the glance of the huge Pantocrator (Almighty). The **cloisters** (Mon–Sat 9am–7.30pm, Sun 9am–1.30pm) are the most sumptuous Romanesque cloisters in the world. The sophistication of these columns suggests a Provençal influence, while the Moorish mood, evoked by mosaic inlays or arabesque carvings, conjures up the Alhambra.

After admiring the view of the Conca d'Oro from the church's terraces (180 steps), proceed to **Palermo ⑬**, the island capital. Lying at the bottom of a wide bay enclosed by Capo Zafferano and Mount Pellegrino, Goethe described it as "the most beautiful promontory in the world".

At the cloisters in Monreale, 109 groups of capitals were ornately decorated by 12th-century craftsmen.

Palermo

The puppet theatre in Sicily goes back centuries, retelling the story of the battles between Charlemagne's knights (the Paladins) and the Saracen invaders.

BELOW: in the gardens of Villa Giulia.

Discovering Palermo

Sicily's capital is a synthesis of sumptuous Arab-Norman and Baroque splendour interspersed with an intriguing Moorish muddle. It was only with Arab colonisation that Palermo prospered as the most multiracial city in Europe. The city was home to Jewish merchants, Greek craftsmen, Persian artists and Berber slaves. Out of such diversity was born a complex city culture that knows many masters.

Palermo remains an exotic jumble of periods and styles: no map does justice to the city's confusion.

Begin in the **Palazzo dei Normanni** **Ⓐ**, the splendid Norman palace and seat of the Sicilian parliament (also known as the Palazzo Reale). Inside are the **Cappella Palatina** (Mon–Sat 9–noon and 2–5pm, Sun 8.30am–2pm; charge) and the **Sala di Re Ruggero**, featuring glittering chambers enlivened with mosaics. The Cappella's ceiling is unique in a Christian church, a composition of ineffable oriental splendour. The Normans asked Arab craftsmen to portray paradise and they maliciously obliged with naked maidens which the Normans prudishly clothed and crowned with haloes.

From there, follow the **Via Vittorio Emanuele** **Ⓑ** to the **Quattro Canti** **Ⓒ**, a busy crossroads in the centre of the Old Town, adorned by Baroque fountains and statues. Another beautiful 16th-century fountain stands in **Piazza Pretoria** **Ⓓ**, once nicknamed the Piazza Vergogna (Square of Shame), due to the saucy nudes cavorting in its fountain. Near the Vucciria market are elaborately decorated **Oratorio di Santa Zita** and the **Oratorio del Rosario di San Domenico**.

A few more steps lead back to the Arab-Norman age, when Palermo was defined by the geographer Idrisi as the "town which turns the head of those who look at it". Here are two churches: **La Martorana** **Ⓔ**, decorated with Byzantine mosaics, and **San Cataldo** **Ⓕ**, which preserves three red Moorish domes. The nuns of La Martorana are famous for inventing *pasta reale*, the popular marzipan fruit-shaped sweets.

Between Via Maqueda and the Palazzo dei Normanni extends the **Albergheria Quarter**. In spite of the architectural chaos, **Ballarò market** is a triumphant spectacle. Palermo's markets serve up gastro-porn at its most deadly: writhing octopus, slithery eels and bloody swordfish glisten on ice blocks; beyond are cartloads of lemons, barrels of olives, bunches of mint, trays of saccharine pastries and sacks of spices.

Isolated by an oasis of green is the small church of **San Giovanni degli Eremiti** **Ⓖ** (Tues–Sun 9am–7pm), a masterpiece of medieval architecture. Its five Moorish domes recall the 500 mosques that once dotted the town, as described by the traveller Ibn Hawqal in the 10th century. Urban regeneration is bringing new life back to the **Kalsa**, the southeastern quarter, with **Piazza Marina** the liveliest area. A witness to its turbulent history is the splendid 14th-century **Palazzo Chiaramonte** **Ⓗ** (not open to the public), a Catalan Gothic fortress which

became the headquarters of the Inquisition in the 17th century. Nearby in the ancient harbour, the church of **Santa Maria della Catena ❶** is a synthesis of Gothic and Renaissance art. Via Alloro, the hub of the quarter, contains Sicily's most important art gallery in the imposing **Palazzo Abatellis ❻**. The **Galleria Regionale della Sicilia** (Tues–Fri 9am–1pm and 2.30–7pm, Sat–Mon 2.30–7pm; charge) has a collection of medieval paintings.

Stroll in **Villa Giulia ❸**, 18th-century Italianate gardens, before visiting the **Orto Botanico ❶** (Mon–Fri 9am–5pm, Sat–Sun 8.30am–1.30pm; charge), among whose exotic plants and rare trees Goethe loved to rest. Beyond lies the **Foro Italico**, an esplanade leading to the **Cala ❿**, the old port. Although it no longer functions as a port, the Cala remains a picturesque shelter for gaily coloured fishing boats.

The rather characterless commercial city centre embraces **Via Ruggero Settimo** and **Viale della Libertà ❶**, an area redeemed by elegant shops and cafés. Palermo's picturesque side is more visible in such food markets as the **Vucciria** and in the **Castello della Zisa** in the suburbs (Tues–Sun 9am–7pm; charge), built in 1160 by William I, which recalls the time when Palermo was virtually the centre of the known world.

Along the Tyrrhenian Coast

Sitting snugly below a headland, **Cefalù ❶** is Taormina's west coast rival. Taormina has better hotels, nightlife and atmosphere, but Cefalù is more compact, peaceful and family-oriented. Cefalù's fame lies in its medieval charm and great Arab-Norman cathedral. These luminous Byzantine mosaics are among the earliest created by the Normans yet are also praised as the purest extant depiction of Christ. Along with Monreale Cathedral and Palermo's Arab-Norman district, **Cefalù Cathedral** is a candidate for Unesco World Heritage listing.

Aeolian Islands (Isole Eolie)

Situated off the north coast of Sicily, the mythical **Aeolian Islands**, were named after Aeolus, the Greek god of the winds. This is Sicily's most enchanting archipelago, with the best beaches and most exotic experiences. **Vulcano ❶**, the first ferry stop, offers yellow sulphurous baths and volcanic craters. **Lípari ❶**, the largest and most populated island, is the richest historically and, on its pumice beach, offers the only white sand in the archipelago. **Salina ❶**, the highest and greenest island, is topped by two symmetrical volcanoes.

Panarea ❶, the most exclusive summer retreat, is a picturesque anchorage for yachties and celebrities. **Stromboli ❶**, the "black giant", boasts two villages, separated by burning lava flows. Like Etna, it is constantly active, and regular rumblings can be heard. At night you get the best view of the orange lava.

The quietest, most eco-friendly islands are **Filicudi ❷** and **Alicudi ❷**, refuges not only for divers and marine-life enthusiasts but for lovers of peace and solitude. ❑

Palermo's superb archaeological museum has a large collection of classical finds. In the inner courtyard amidst lush vegetation, you can see fine examples of Egyptian and Greek statuary.

BELOW: a freshly caught swordfish in Lípari.

THE LIVING EARTH: ITALY'S VOLCANOES

Bubbling, seething and angry, or silent, solemn and threatening, Italy's volcanoes dictate the way of life of those in their shadow

The area from the island of Sicily north to Campania on the Italian mainland is notoriously unstable geologically. Here, the earth's crust continues to suffer earthquakes, changes in land levels and volcanic activity. From Vesuvius brooding over the Bay of Naples to imperious, seething Etna on Sicily, Italian volcanoes have shaped the way of life of local people for centuries. The destruction and devastation that has followed major eruptions has on the one hand caused trepidation and exodus but, on the other, has offered long-term compensation in the legacy of fertile soil enriched with volcanic extract.

SPREADING THE WORD

The fame of Italy's volcanoes owes much to its classical writers. Virgil and Pliny the Younger both described the might of volcanic activity in the region. Pliny, in particular, left us a detailed account of the eruption of Vesuvius in AD 79 which saw the death of his uncle, Pliny the Elder, and destroyed the towns of Herculaneum and Pompeii. In turn, Vesuvian mud and ash has preserved for us a unique picture of life in Roman times (see page 325).

ABOVE: Vesuvius, although officially "active", has not shown any major activity since 1944. Etna, however, remains a constant threat. in 2007–8 there were intense eruptions on the flanks of the southeastern crater.

LEFT: the seas around the Aeolian Islands can be radioactive and in places be warmed by underwater jets of steam. Sulphurous mud pools are sought out for the treatment of rheumatism.

RIGHT: you can walk to the Silvestri craters on Mount Etna, a typical volcanic landscape.

THE MIGHT AND POWER OF THE GODS

The power of Italy's active volcanoes is a phenomenon which defied explanation in ancient times. The Romans attributed the fiery convulsions to Vulcan, the god of fire and metalworking, whom they believed lived deep beneath the Aeolian island of Vulcano. In addition, the poet Virgil told of the giant Enceladus who, he declared, was interred below Mount Etna, his groanings and rumblings accounting for the earth-shaking, violent eruptions.

Early Christians, too, saw divine activity in volcanic outbursts. In the year 253, the mere production of the veil covering the tomb of the recently martyred St Agatha was said to have staunched the lava flow from Etna that threatened to envelop Catania and its people. Even in relatively modern times, the citizens of Naples have been quick to turn to their patron saint, Januarius (San Gennaro), for help whenever Vesuvius belches smoke.

However, some observers over the centuries have been more pragmatic about the causes of volcanic activity. One anonymous Roman poet suggested that the phenomenon was wind-induced: "It is the winds which arouse all these forces of havoc: the rocks which they have massed thickly together they whirl in eddying storm…"

BELOW: volcano tourism really began in the 19th century when Vesuvius, then Etna *(below)* became part of the traveller's itinerary. Sedan chairs or donkeys were used to convey lazy visitors to the top.

ABOVE: Etna is Europe's largest active volcano and Italy's highest mountain outside the Alps. Though it is prone to eruption, and the area around the main crater is now out of bounds, it is possible to climb – provided common sense and local advice are heeded. Wear warm clothing, even in the height of summer, and strong shoes.

LEFT: sheep graze in the Parco delle Madonie, with Mount Etna looming large in the background.

SARDINIA

Seven thousand prehistoric stone towers, countless beaches and more sheep than people make Sardinia the perfect place to get away from it all

BELOW: in Santa Teresa, Capo Testa.

Sardinia has little in common with the rest of Italy. The Mediterranean's second-largest island offers a restricted diet of art and architecture; rather, its appeal lies in its beaches, rocky coastline, rugged landscape and rural hotels. Much of its 1,600km (1,000-mile) coastline is given over to duney sands and romantic coves nestling in pine and juniper woods. The interior, where sheep outnumber humans, is wild and mountainous, and covered in a knotty carpet of herby, shrubby *macchia*. Even the island's cui-

sine is different from the mainland's. Here, the robust, meat-based cuisine comes in the form of roast lamb and suckling pig, as well as Pecorino cheese made from ewe's milk, *seadas* or cheese pastries served with honey, and *carta da musica* – crisp, wafer-thin bread said to resemble sheets of music.

Most holidaymakers come for stay-put beach holidays. Many base themselves in the purpose-built, ritzy resorts that have put the island on the tourist map, but there are more down-to-earth alternatives. The large distances involved and the paucity of sights make Sardinia less than ideal for a touring holiday. There are, however, some unique attractions, notably the intriguing remnants of the prehistoric nuraghic civilisation: an astonishing 7,000 stone towers, or *nuraghi*, which from a distance look like giant dung heaps, litter the countryside.

Lying within Gallura, the sparsely inhabited northeastern region of Sardinia where pinky, granite rocks tower like castles over swathes of *macchia* and juniper, cork and oak woods, is the **Costa Smeralda ❶**, or Emerald Coast. In the early 1960s, the Aga Khan and associates bought up this impossibly picturesque little piece of coastline – a mere 10km (6 miles) end to end by road – and turned it into a hedonistic bolt-hole, now the flagship of the island's tourism. Development is rigorously controlled. Virtually every hotel and apartment complex comes in regulation "Mediterranean" style, with pan-tiled roofs and pink-and-russet walls.

Even if you can't afford to partake in the jet-set lifestyle, it makes a great spectator sport. Head for **Porto Cervo**, the only resort where Armani and Versace boutiques compete for attention with extravagant yachts, and **Cala di Volpe**, half Moorish castle, half rustic homestead and the most stylish of the hotels. Many of the gorgeous coves are inaccessible, but you can wander through groves to those on the Cappriccioli peninsula. Impressive **Cala Liscia Ruja**, just south, is the area's biggest beach, but **Spiaggia del Principe** is dreamier, as are the twin beaches of overpopular Capriccioli. The resort of **Baia Sardinia**, just north of the Costa Smeralda proper, is equally contrived, but far less pretentious and more affordable.

Much of the rest of the Galluran coastline is being spoilt by overdevelopment. This is true of scruffy **Palau**, the departure point for ferries to **La Maddalena** ➋, part of the Maddalena archipelago. Formerly a NATO military zone, the island now has a restored Arsenal, marina, naval museum, new exhibition centres, as well as good beaches, and a new bridge to **Caprera** ➌, where you can visit the house in which Garibaldi spent his last years. Back on the mainland, **Santa Teresa di Gallura** ➍ is a study in pink, and there are a couple of great sandy beaches at nearby **Capo Testa**, fringed by bizarre rocks the size of houses.

Alghero

Northwestern Sardinia is a more benign, softer region than the northeast, with sandy strands cupped in pine woods. Its big draw is **Alghero** ➎, the resort with the most genuine character and history: in the 14th century, the port was occupied by Catalans, and street names are still written in that language. Alghero's charm lies in its Catalan atmosphere, breezy bastions and sea views. After admiring the Romanesque cloisters in **San Francesco**, succumb to coffee and cake at

an old-world café on Piazza Civica. The best beach is **Spiaggia di Maria Pia**, matched by a boat trip across the bay to the **Grotta di Nettuno** ➏, a cave system at the foot of a towering, tilted cliff. Nearby, the Capo Caccio headland has exhilarating views over the city and is also home to peregrine falcons and griffon vultures.

Un-touristy **Sassari** ➐, a 45-minute drive inland, has enjoyably earthy backstreets between the overblown, neo-Gothic **Piazza d'Italia** and the Baroque-fronted cathedral, and a noted **Archaeology Museum** (Tues–Sat 9am–8pm; charge), which, after Cagliari's, is the best place to immerse yourself in the nuraghic culture.

Sardinia's dramatic interior – with imposing tablelands, pine woods, massive walls and granite amphitheatres – is the historic, cultural and geographic heart of the island. Here, safely sheltered from foreign invaders, a population of shepherds developed a fierce and isolated society. The growth of delightful rural hotels now makes this a much more authentic way of exploring the whole island.

TIP

Alghero is arguably the best place on the island for fresh seafood. Stop at the market in Via Sassari for lobster, sea urchins and squid, or try the local restaurants.

BELOW: Capo Testa, a promontory of huge granite boulders.

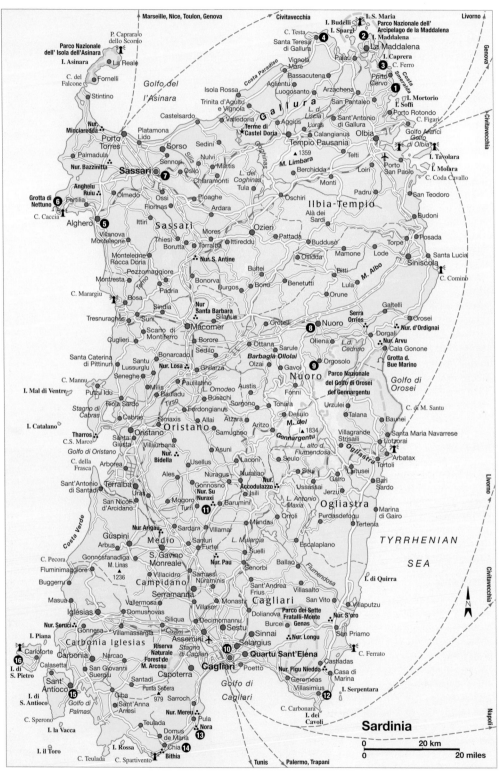

Marseille, Nice, Toulon, Genova   Civitavecchia   Livorno

P. Caprarolo
dello Sconto

Parco Nazionale
dell' Isola dell'Asinara
I. Asinara   La Reale

Parco Nazionale dell'
Arcipelago de la Maddalena

I. Budelli
I. S. Maria
I. Spargi
La Maddalena
I. Maddalena
I. Caprera
C. Ferro
Costa Smeralda
Porto Cervo

C. del
Falcone   Fornelli

Stintino

Golfo del
l'Asinara

Isola Rossa

Trinita d'Agultu
e Vignola

C. Testa
Santa Teresa
di Gallura

Vignola
Mare

Bassacutena

Aglientu

Luogosanto

Arzachena

San Pantaleo

I. Mortorio
I. Soffi
Porto Rotondo
C. Figari

Nur.
Minciaredda

Palmadula

Porto
Torres

Platamona
Lido

Sorso

Castelsardo

Valledoria

Terme di
Castel Doria

Aggius
Luras
Calangianus

Sant'Antonio
di Gallura

Golfo Aranci
Golfo
di Olbia

Olbia

I. Tavolara

Nur. Bazzinitta

Sassari

Sennori

Sedini

Nulvi

Oschiri

Tempio Pausania

Berchidda

Telti

Loiri
Porto
San Paolo

I. Molara
C. Coda Cavallo

Anghelu
Ruiu

Olmedo

Osilo
Martis
L. del
Coghinas
Tula

M. Limbara

Monti

Padru

San Teodoro

Grotta di
Nettuno
Fertilia

Ittiri

Ploaghe
Chiaramonti

Ilbia-Tempio

Budoni

C. Caccia   Alghero

Sassari   Mores

Florinas

Ardara

Alà dei
Sardi

Posada

Villanova
Monteleone

Thiesi
Borutta

Torralba
Ittireddu

Ozieri

Pattada

Buddusò

Mamone
Lode

Torpe

Santa Lucia
Siniscola

C. Comino

Monteleone
Rocca Doria

Pozzomaggiore

Nur. S. Antine

Bonorva

Bultei

Osidda

Bitti

Lula

M. Albo

Montresta

Pádria
Burgos
Bono
Benetutti

Orune

Galtelli

C. Marargiu   Bosa

Sindia

Nur
Santa Barbara
Silanus

L. d.
Cedrino
Orosei
Nur. d'Ordignai
Nur. Arvu
Cala Gonone

Tresnuraghes

Suni

Scano di
Montiferro

Borore

Orotelli

Nuoro

Serra
Orrios

Cuglieri

Macomer

Sedilo

Ottana
Sarule

Oliena

Dorgali

Grotta d.
Bue Marino

Santa Caterina
di Pittinuri

Santu
Lussurgiu

Nur. Losa

Ghilarza

Olzai

Gavoi

Barbagia Ollolai

Orgosolo

Nuoro

Parco Nazionale
del Golfo di Orosei
del Gennargentu

Golfo di
Orosei

Seneghe

Paulilatino

Milis

Bauladu

Tirso

L. Omodeo

Austis

Fonni

Urzulei

C. di M. Santu

C. Mannu

Putzu Idu

Riola Sardo

Ferdongianus

Busachi

Sorgono

Tonara

Desulo

M. del
Gennargentu

Talana

Baunei

I. Mal di Ventre

Stagno di
Cabras

Cabras

Simaxis

Allai

Samugheo

Aritzo

1834

Villagrande
Strisaili

Santa Maria Navarrese
Lotzorai

I. Catalano   Tharros

Oristano

Villaurbana

Asuni

Laconi

L. alto di
Flumendosa

Seulo

Ogliastra

Arbatax
Tortoli

C.S. Marco

Santa
Giusta

Nur.
Bidella

Usellus

Nuragus
Nutaliao

Seui

Lanusei

Golfo di Oristano

Ales

Nur.
Accodulazzo
Isili

Ussassai

Gairo
Jerzu

C. della
Frasca

Arborea

Uras

Mogoro
Turri

Barumini

L. Antonio
Maxia

Bari
Sardo

Sant'Antonio
di Santadi

Terralba

San Nicolò
d'Arcidano

Gonnosno
Nur. Su
Nuraxi

Ortoli

Ogliastra

Marina
di Gairo

Perdasdefogu

Tertenia

Nur Arigau
Sardara
Villamar
Mandas

Escalaplano

TYRRHENIAN

Guspini

Arbus

Medio

Sanluri
Furtei

L. Mulargia

Ballao

SEA

C. Pecora

Gonnosfanadiga

S. Gavino
Monreale

Suelli

Senorbi

Flumendosa

I. di Quirra

Fluminimaggiore

M. Linas
1236

Nur. Pau

Sant'Andrea
Frius

Villasalto

Buggerru

Villacidro

Sant'Antioco

Samassi
Nuraminis

Campidano

Villasor

Monastir

San Vito

Villaputzu

Masua

Serramanna

Dolianova

San Priamo

Iglesias

Domusnovas

Villamassargia

Siliqua

Decimomannu

Burcei

Parco dei Sette
Fratalli-Monte
Genas

Nur. S'oro

Nur. Seruci

Gonnesa

Cixerri

Sestu

Sinnai

Nur. Longu

I. Piana
Carloforte

Assemini

Selargius

C. Ferrato

I. di
S. Pietro

Calasetta

Riserva
Naturale
Forest'de
M. Arcosu

Stagno
di Cagliari

Quartu Sant'Elena

Castiadas

Sant
Antioco

Carbonia Iglesias

Carbonia

Narcao

San Giovanni
Suergiu

Santadi

Cagliari

Poetto

Nur. Figu Niedda

Geremeas

Casa di
Marina

I. di
S. Antioco

Giba

Golfo di
Palmas

Punta Sebera
979
Sant'Anna
Arresi

Sarroch

Villasimius

I. Serpentara

C. Sperone

Teulada

Nur. Mereu

Domus
de Maria

Pula
Nora

Golfo di
Cagliari

C. Carbonara

I. dei
Cavoli

I. la Vacca

Chia

I. il Toro

I. Rossa

Bithia

C. Teulada   C. Spartivento

Tunis   Palermo, Trapani

Sardinia

0   20 km
0   20 miles

N

Nuoro ❸, the area's capital, is only worth visiting for its folk museum, the **Museo della Vita e delle Tradizioni Sarde** (mid-June–Sept daily 9am–8pm, Oct–mid-June 9am–1pm and 3–7pm; charge). Immediately south is the most accessible part of the region, where vineyards and olive groves are intensively cultivated on the hillsides. Down the road lies unwelcoming but fascinating **Orgosolo** ❾, once the Barbagia's "bandit capital", where anti-capitalist murals cover much of the wall space along its high street. The long, lonely drive south on the SS125, which clings unnervingly to mountainsides from Dorgali to Arbatax and beyond, is the island's most exhilarating.

The south

Cagliari ❿, the island's hectic capital, is rewarding if you ignore the traffic-ridden port and climb up into **Castello**, the medieval centre where steep, atmospheric streets lie within 13th-century walls and towers. The cathedral, a hotchpotch of styles, and a Roman amphitheatre are outshone by the **Museo Archeologico Nazionale** (Tues–Sun 9am–8pm; fee), famous for exquisite bronze statuettes and votive boats from the nuraghic culture.

An hour's drive north, skirting the fertile **Campidano** plain, brings you to the island's most impressive *nuraghe*, **Su Nuraxi** ⓫ (daily May–Sept 9am–7pm; winter closes between 4 and 6pm; charge) at Barumini. Dating from the 13th–16th century BC, the colossal fortification is made up of beautifully formed, beehive-shaped rooms; the maze of low stone walls at its base was once a dependent village.

The coastal road east from Cagliari leads to enormous tranches of the finest sand in the island's isolated southeastern corner. However, **Villasimius** ⓬ and the **Costa Rei**, the un-fancy resorts that have grown up around them, are rather characterless, comprising mainly campsites and self-catering complexes.

The gentle, pine-clad coastline southwest from Cagliari, scattered with holiday homes and a few smart hotels, is more interesting. Punic and Roman **Nora** ⓭ (daily 9am–8pm, winter until 5.30pm; charge) is Sardinia's most extensive classical site, with clearly defined houses, as well as a temple, theatre and mosaics. Equally rewarding is the waterside location, on a little peninsula next to a long curve of sand. Many finds from Nora are housed in the **Museo Archeologico** (Tues–Sun 9am–8pm, winter until 5.30pm; charge) in nearby **Pula**.

Just south lies the **Forte Village**, a famous resort which adjoins a good beach, even if the area's best is at **Chia** ⓮, backed by hillock-high dunes. The drive beyond along the **Costa del Sud** passes craggy headlands and azure waters in deep inlets on its way to **Sant'Antíoco** ⓯. Linked to the mainland by an ancient causeway, the island's eponymous town has Christian catacombs under its main church.

Ferries run to **San Pietro** ⓰, known for the bloody *mattanza*, when schools of tuna were slaughtered en masse until overfishing recently led to the curtailment of this barbaric pursuit.   ❏

Traditional folk costume.

BELOW: mask in the Archaeological Museum, Cagliari.

373

TRANSPORT

ACCOMMODATION

EATING OUT

ACTIVITIES

A – Z

LANGUAGE

�Insight Guides TRAVEL TIPS
ITALY

TRANSPORT

GETTING THERE
AND GETTING AROUND

Airports

Rome

Leonardo da Vinci/Fiumicino
Rome's main airport is 35.5 km (22½ miles) southwest of central Rome.
A direct train, the Leonardo Express, runs every 30 minutes (daily 6.36am–11.36pm, from Rome 5.52am–22.52pm) between Fiumicino airport and Termini station in central Rome. Tickets cost €14, or €15 if bought on the platform at Termini (accompanied children aged under 12 travel free). They can be bought in advance online and at the airport from station counters, vending machines and newsstands. Tickets not bought online must be validated (stamped) in machines by the platform before you board the train. The journey takes 31 minutes.
A cheaper and slower local train (FR1 line, around €8) runs roughly every 15 minutes (daily 5.57am–11.27pm, from Rome around 5am–11.30pm) and stops at Trastevere, Tiburtina, Ostiense and several other suburban stations across Rome, connecting with the Rome metro; the journey to Trastevere takes about 40 minutes. Information and bookings are available through www.trenitalia.com. Shuttle bus services and private transfers are also available, notably with Sitbus Shuttle (www.sitbusshuttle.it).
Catching a white taxi with a meter (unofficial taxis can charge extortionate fares and even be dangerous) from the airport can be a good alternative, but check the fare

beforehand. Surcharges are made for luggage, at night and on Sunday, and there is also a special airport supplement, but fares should be in the region of €40.

Roma Ciampino
Rome's second airport is only 12km (7½ miles) southeast of the city centre, and used especially by low-cost airlines such as easyJet and Ryanair. There is no rail link, but several bus services. The efficient Terravision bus shuttle runs to Via Marsala, near Termini station (daily roughly 8am–midnight, from Rome 4.30am–9.20pm; single tickets €4; www.terravision.eu), and the Sit-Bus Shuttle, which works in association with easyJet, operates on the same route, usually 7.15am–10.10pm, from Via Marsala 4.30am–9.30pm, and offers a range of fair deals.
Alternatively, the COTRAL airport bus runs roughly every 30 minutes, 6am–10.40pm, from the airport to Anagnina metro station at the end of Linea A, for just €1.20. From there, it's 30 minutes to Termini and the centre of town. The cost of a taxi between Ciampino and central Rome (including supplements) should be €30, but may be more at night.

Northern Italy

Bergamo (Orio al Serio)
A local airport "discovered" by low-cost airlines, especially Ryanair, which refers to it as "Milan-Bergamo" and has services to it from across Europe. It is 45km (28 miles) east of Milan; a Terravision bus runs to the city (www.terravision.eu), and there are buses to Bergamo train station (10 minutes). The airport is also convenient for exploring the Lakes and Lombardy.

Brescia
Convenient for Lake Garda, Verona, the Dolomites and Trentino-Alto Adige, and used by Ryanair, with flights from London Stansted and Spain, and connections to Sardinia. Ryanair calls this airport "Verona-Brescia", though it is actually 40km (25 miles) from Verona, which can lead to confusion.

Genoa
Useful for Genoa itself and the Ligurian Coast, and served by Ryanair from London Stansted and BA from Gatwick.

Milan
Milano Malpensa, Milan's intercontinental airport, is 40km (25 miles) from the centre of Milan.
The *Malpensa Express* **train** runs from the airport's Terminal 1 to the centre of Milan (Cadorna station, which is on the metro; note that this is different from Stazione Centrale, Milan's main railway station). The train takes about 40 minutes and operates daily 6.45am–9.45am; single fare is €9. A free shuttle bus runs to the airport station from Terminal 2. During 2010–11 suburban rail line S10 will also be extended to Malpensa, providing an alternative rail link.
Alternatively, *Malpensa Shuttle* **buses** ferry passengers between the airport and Stazione Centrale train station. Buses run around the clock (more frequently during the day) and take around 50 minutes; single fare is around €7.50.
A **taxi** to the centre will take 45minutes–1 hour and cost around €75; negotiate a price beforehand.
Milano Linate, Milan's second airport (apart from Bergamo, *see above*), is only 8km (5 miles) from the centre, and has European and Italian

domestic flights, with Air France, Iberia, Alitalia and British Airways and easyJet from the UK. The **ATM bus 73** runs regularly (approximately 6am–midnight) from the airport to Piazza San Babila in the city, and the **Starfly** airport bus runs to Stazione Termini (daily 6am–11.45pm, every 30 minutes). There is also a shuttle bus connection to Malpensa.

Turin
Small but handy for Piedmont, its vineyards, the Italian Alps and the Valle d'Aosta.

Venice
Marco Polo airport is at Tessera on the mainland 8km (5 miles) north of Venice. To reach Venice there are **buses** to Piazzale Roma station (30 minutes), a private **land taxi** (20–25 minutes) or the hourly **Alilaguna waterbus**, which crosses the lagoon to various destinations in Venice, and takes about 75 minutes, depending on your stop. Tickets cost €12–25. The luxury option is a private **water-taxi**, which costs from about €98 for up to four people with luggage. Buses also run to Mestre train station, on the mainland, which is the best place to get trains to areas around Venice.

Venice/Treviso
Treviso, 20km (12½ miles) north of Venice, is used as an alternative Venice airport by low-cost airlines, especially Ryanair, which calls it "Venice-Treviso". It also has rapid access to the Veneto and northeast Italy. **ATVO buses** run between Treviso airport, Mestre station and Piazzale Roma in Venice. Single fare is €5; for information see www.atvo.it.

Verona
Verona airport, 5km (3 miles) west of the city, is convenient for the Lakes or the Veneto. Note there can be confusion between this airport and Brescia.

Central Italy

Ancona
Convenient for the Marche region, parts of Tuscany, Emilia and Umbria, and used by Ryanair and Italian domestic airlines.

Bologna
One of Italy's larger regional airports and well placed for Emilia-Romagna, Rimini or north and east Tuscany. It has flights from a great many European and North African destinations. The **Aerobus-BLQ** shuttle bus runs to the city every 30 minutes (single fare €5), and there are also direct buses to Modena and

Siena. A **taxi** takes 15 minutes, and costs around €15.

Bologna's "alternative" airport at **Forlì**, 60km (38 miles) south, is now mainly used by Italian budget airline Windjet.

Florence
Florence's **Peretola** airport is only 4km (2½ miles) northwest of the city, but is very small, and used by only a few airlines. Far more Tuscany flights use Pisa.

Parma
A smaller alternative to Bologna; Ryanair flies from Stansted, and has connections to Sicily and Sardinia.

Pescara
Abruzzo airport is a good destination for exploring the Adriatic Coast, the Abruzzo and Molise. It has flights from Europe with low-cost airlines.

Pisa
Galileo Galilei is the principal airport for Tuscany and so the most usual entry point for international visitors to Florence. Pisa is served by many airlines, and in summer there are direct Delta flights from New York. The airport has its own **train station**, with a 5-minute shuttle service to Pisa Centrale station in the city, from where there are frequent connections to Florence (about one hour).

Rimini
Naturally handy for the Adriatic, **Federico Fellini airport** is another small one used by Ryanair, Air Berlin and other low-cost operators.

Southern Italy

Bari and Brindisi
Both city airports are useful for exploring Italy's heel – Puglia and Basilicata. Bari is the busiest, with services with British Airways, Ryanair and many Italian domestic flights, while Brindisi is mainly used by Ryanair and Alitalia.

Calabria
Calabria's **Lamezia-Terme** airport was created in the middle of nowhere, between the region's three main cities (Catanzaro, Cosenza and Reggio Calabria).

Naples
The largest airport in the south, Naples is served by major carriers and low-cost operators. Airport **buses** (3S or Alibus) run every 30 minutes to central Naples and Piazza Garibaldi (the main train station); the Alibus also stops at the quays for boat services to Capri and other islands. A **taxi** should cost about €15–25.

Sardinia
Cagliari-Elmas is best for the southern end of the island. More convenient for northern Sardinia are **Olbia,** on the Costa Smeralda, and **Alghero**.

Sicily
Palermo's Punta Raisi airport is 32km (20 miles) west of the city, but there is a frequent train link, which takes about 45 minutes. Some low-cost airlines prefer to use **Trapani** airport, 98km (60 miles) west of Palermo. A **Terravision** bus runs from there to Trapani town and Palermo (www.terravision.eu).

Catania-Fontanarossa, the airport for eastern Sicily, is 7km (4 miles) southwest of Catania and has many Italian domestic and European flights.

By Car

When calculating the cost of driving to Italy, if you intend to travel quickly, allow for the price of motorway tolls in France, Switzerland and Italy (those in Germany are toll-free) as well as accommodation en route and fuel. The busiest road routes into Italy are, from France, the Mont Blanc Tunnel from Chamonix and the Tunnel du Fréjus between Grenoble and Turin, and, from Switzerland, the Grand St-Bernard Tunnel between Sion and Aosta. If you avoid tunnels, be aware that many of the Alpine passes are seasonal, so check on current conditions before setting off.

To take your car into Italy, you will need a valid driving licence (with an Italian translation if it's not a standard EU licence), the vehicle registration document and insurance documents. You must carry a warning triangle and a yellow reflective waistcoat for use in case of breakdown; if you have to pull over by the roadside, you must put on the reflective jacket, and place the warning triangle 100 metres/yards behind the car.

By Rail

Compared with flying, travelling to Italy by rail is naturally slower and, depending on when you go, more expensive. However, it can be a very attractive way to travel, especially if you stop off en route. From the UK, for example, one route to Rome is on a daytime Eurostar to Paris, where you change from Gare du Nord to the Gare de Bercy, from where a Palatino-Artesia sleeper train leaves daily at 6.52pm, arriving in Rome's Stazione Termini the next morning at 10.12pm. The same train also stops in Bologna and Florence, and there are also direct sleeper trains from Paris to Milan and Venice, and a spectacular route across the Alps to Milan from Zurich.

Information and bookings can be obtained through **Rail Europe**, tel: (UK) 08448-484 061, (US) 1-800-622 8600, (Canada) 1-800-361 7245; www.raileurope.com, and all kinds of information can be found on www.seat61.com.

GETTING AROUND

By Air

State-owned Alitalia continues to serve the whole country, but is increasingly challenged by low-cost operators such as Meridiana Fly (www.meridiana.it), Sicily-based Windjet (www.volawindjet.it), and Blu-express (www.blu-express.com), with frequent fare offers.

By Rail

In general the cheapest, fastest and most convenient way to travel around Italy is by train. Most rail lines are operated by **Trenitalia** (www.trenitalia.com). There are several types of train: the figureheads of the network are the *Eurostar Italia* (shown on timetables as ES-AV or ES*) luxury high-speed trains between major cities; next down are the *Eurostar City* trains (ES City) which are slightly slower but also very comfortable, and then the *InterCity* (IC), which are also air-conditioned and comfortable, but stop rather more frequently. Supplements (*supplementi*) are charged for these trains, and it is also obligatory to reserve a seat, although this can be done up to a few minutes before the train departs. On long-distance routes overnight sleeper trains are also available.

More local trains may be called *Regionale*, *Diretto*, *Interregionale* or, rather inappropriately, *Espresso*. They are much slower, since they generally stop at a great many stations. No reservations are necessary.

Some local lines are operated by regional companies, notably **Ferrovie Emilia-Romagna** (FER; www.fer-online.it) around Bologna, **Ferrovie Nord Milano** (www.ferronord.it) from Milan, SAD (www.sad.it) in the Dolomites and **Ferrovie della Sardegna** (www.ferroviesardegna.it) in Sardinia, which in summer runs *Trenino Verde* sightseeing trains on a spectacular line through the centre of the island (which also has Trenitalia lines). All these companies have their own fare systems. In the south and

Train Information

Train information is available from *Uffici Informazioni* at major stations, and all stations have lists of all arrivals (*arrivi*) and departures (*partenze*) from that station.

Information and bookings for all Trenitalia services: tel: **892 021** (from outside Italy, **0039-06-6847 5475**); **www.trenitalia.it**

From outside Italy you can also check **www.raileurope.com**.

Sicily, buses can be a better option because some areas are poorly served by rail. Exceptions to this are the fascinating *Circumetnea* line around Etna and the Naples *Circumvesuviana*, which is the best way of seeing Pompeii, Herculaneum and other classical sites.

Train Tickets

Tickets for nearly all Trenitalia trains can be bought online through www.trenitalia.com (in English) and at stations, which have self-service ticket machines that accept cash and credit cards. If you book online or by phone you will be given or emailed a booking code; when you get on the train, you show this to the ticket collector, who will issue your ticket. If you have a conventional paper ticket from a counter or a machine you must validate it by stamping it in one of the yellow machines on station platforms just before you board the train; otherwise you can be fined.

The Trenitalia website sometimes rejects non-Italian credit and debit cards, so you may still have to go to a station. Some suggestions on how to get around this are on www.seat61.com. Mainline trains can also be booked through Rail Europe, but a booking fee will be added. Substantial discounts are also offered if you book in advance.

Rail Passes

Because of the generally low level of Italian rail fares, and the discounts available, rail passes such as InterRail (for European residents) and Eurail (for the rest of the world) are of limited benefit in Italy. For long-distance Italian trains passholders still have to pay a supplement, and must reserve a seat. See www.raileurope.com.

By Bus

Each province in Italy has its own regional bus company. This can lead to confusion since, particularly in Sicily, rival firms do not provide

information about one another and connections are not always co-ordinated. However, in some areas such as the south, and in mountains, buses are the best method of travel. The journey from Siena to Florence is also faster by bus than by train. **SITA** (www.sitabus.it) is a large company that runs long-distance services and regional services in several parts of Italy. Some other major regional companies are listed below.

Rome

COTRAL, tel: 800-174 471; www.cotralspa.it; covers Lazio.

Milan

Autostradale, tel: 02-7200 1304; www.autostradale.it. Services across Lombardy and the Lakes, and sightseeing tours.

Trentino

Trentino Trasporti, tel: 0461-821 000; www.ttesercizio.it; runs bus services throughout the Trentino area.

Alto Adige

SAD, Bolzano, tel: 840-000 471; www.sad.it. Bus services throughout the Alto Adige (South Tyrol), and rail lines along the Val Venosta, Val Pusteria and to the Brenner Pass.

Florence

Lazzi, Via Mercadante 2, tel: 055-363041, www.lazzi.it. Services throughout Tuscany.

Ferries and Hydrofoils

Frequent car and passenger ferries run between mainland ports and Italy's islands. For **Sardinia**, there are ferries to Cagliari from Civitavecchia, Naples and Palermo, to Olbia from Civitavecchia, Livorno and Genoa, to Porto Torres from Genoa and Civitavecchia, and to smaller ports. There are also regular ferries to Corsica and mainland France. For **Sicily** the fastest route is Caronte Lines, 20-minute shuttle between Villa San Giovanni, near Reggio di Calabria, and Messina, but there are also ferries to Palermo, Catania and Trapani from Genoa, Livorno, Civitavecchia, Naples and Salerno.

The Sicilian Ustica Lines also operates boat connections to the **Aeolian Islands**, **Pantelleria** and other small islands around Sicily, while ferries to **Elba** are operated by Moby Lines from Piombino. Frequent fast hydrofoils and car ferries run from Naples to **Capri**, **Ischia** and other islands in the bay, mainly with Caremar and Aliscafi-SNAV, which also has services to the Aeolian Islands.

Ferries and hydrofoils also operate on the northern **lakes** of Como, Garda, Iseo and Maggiore, and some lake towns are linked by car ferry. Information and timetables are available from tourist offices and, for smaller ferries, at the jetties *(imbarcaderi)*. See www.ferriesonline.com.

By Car

Italian motorways *(autostrade)* are generally fast and uncongested, except in midsummer and on key holidays, such as Easter. Tolls are charged for virtually all *autostrade*; an *autostrade* website (in English, www.autostrade.it/en) allows you to check current tolls for any journey, and provides extensive further information. Tolls can be paid in cash or by credit card, and for convenience you can also buy a Viacard at various outlets, prepaid with *autostrada* credits from €25, €50 or €75. Regular users can register for a Telepass subscription, but this is of little use for visitors. Do not drive through Telepass lanes at toll stations (signed in yellow) if you are not registered.

Dipped headlights must be turned on during the day in poor visibility, and in tunnels. In mountain areas in winter, it is often compulsory to fit snow chains, and they must be carried in the car even when not needed; check on current conditions with the nearest tourist office.

Having a car in Italy is naturally excellent for exploring the countryside, but generally of little use in cities, due to the often impenetrable traffic. For outsiders, city driving is especially to be avoided in Rome and above all Naples, where local drivers customarily do not stop at red lights (this is true, not a stereotype). Also, be aware that in

many Italian towns the old centre *(centro storico)* is closed to all drivers except residents, as a *Zona a Traffico Limitato* (ZTL). A sign with a red circle on white and *traffico limitato* indicates when this is so. If you are staying at a hotel in the historic centre of any town, ask the hotel beforehand what to do with your car.

Parking

Parking space is also at a premium in towns, so again, it is best to leave your car in a hotel car park. Pay attention to street "no parking" signs, as illegally parked vehicles may be towed away. In a city, if you cannot use a hotel car park, find a pay car park, and leave the car for the day; charges are generally reasonable. Never leave valuables inside.

Car Rentals

Hiring a car is relatively expensive in Italy. International agencies such as Avis, Hertz and Europcar have offices at airports and in main towns, and in tourist areas there are local agencies. Nowadays, to get the best rates it's advisable to book ahead through major travel websites or specialists such as www.auto-europe.co.uk. Collision damage waiver is nearly always included in the price, and additional insurance cover is available for an extra cost. The renter must be over 21 and have a valid driver's licence and a credit card, for a deposit.

Speed Limits

Urban areas:
50km/h (31mph)
Roads outside urban areas:
90km/h (55mph)
Dual carriageways:
110km/h (70mph)
Motorways *(autostrade)*:
130km/h (80mph)

Inner-City Travel

Rome

Most visitors rely on public transport, taxis or their feet to access the centre of Rome, as only residents' cars are allowed there. If you drive into Rome for the day, there are large car parks around the central area, the biggest of them **ParkSi** near Villa Borghese, where you can leave a car for the day for around €15. Taxi ranks are plentiful.

The Roman metro covers a limited area but is efficient, and there are several suburban rail lines. There are also night buses and tourist bus routes. Rome also now has cycle routes and a rather unsuccessful "bike-sharing" scheme. Tourist offices have more information; cycling in Rome is daunting during the week, but more enjoyable on Sundays.

Buses

Rome's city buses and metro are run by the transport authority **ATAC**, while buses around Lazio are operated by **COTRAL**. The great hub of the transport system is Stazione Termini. ATAC information and route maps are available from the kiosk in Piazza dei Cinquecento in front of Termini, main metro stations and tourist offices. City bus routes cover every part of the city and run 5.30am–midnight, after which time there are night services. A range of ATAC *Metrebus* tickets is available from metro stations, tobacco shops, newsstands, some bars and tourist offices. All are equally valid for city buses, the metro and rail lines within the city. A single *BIT* ticket (€1) is valid for one bus journey of up to 75 minutes, or one metro or train trip; a *Multibit* ticket (€5) gives five journeys, usable on separate days; a *BIG* ticket (€4) gives unlimited travel for one day; the *BTI* tourist ticket (€11) for three days; and the *Carta Settimanale* (€16) gives unlimited travel for seven days. Monthly and longer-term passes and regional tickets are also available.

Among the most useful city bus routes are the 40 and 64, which connect Termini with Piazza Venezia, the Centro Storico and the Vatican (the 64 stops more often). The city also has small electric buses which cope with the narrow alleys of the historic centre: line 116 passes through or close to Piazza Navona, Campo de' Fiori and St Peter's.

Two open-top double-decker tourist bus routes are run by Trambus Open (www.trambusopen.com). The **110** route covers all the main sites, including the Colosseum, Piazza Navona and St

BELOW: driving in Naples is not for the faint-hearted.

TRANSPORT

ACCOMMODATION

EATING OUT

ACTIVITIES

A – Z

LANGUAGE

Peter's, in a two-hour tour that leaves every 20 minutes from outside Termini daily 8.30am–8.25pm. Tickets (not the same as for city buses) cost around €15 and allow you to get on and off all day. They can be bought online, from the kiosk on Piazza dei Cinquecento, or on board. The **Archeobus** also starts from Termini (daily, 8.30am–4.30pm) and runs out of the city along the Via Appia.

Metro
Rome's metro system (Metropolitana) has two lines, A and B, forming a cross and meeting at Stazione Termini. They run daily 5.30am–11.30pm, and are most useful for getting to areas outside the centre. Suburban rail lines connect with the metro particularly at Termini, Tiburtina, Tuscolana and Ostiense.

Milan
Milan has a highly efficient integrated transport system, operated by the ATM (www.atm-mi.it). The **Metropolitana Milanese** (MM) is the best underground railway in Italy, with three lines (M1, M2, M3), and there's a comprehensive bus and tram network and local rail lines. Tickets valid for all systems are bought from the usual outlets (tabacchi shops, news kiosks, metro stations). A single ticket costs €1 and once stamped is valid for 75 minutes' travel on any system within the urban area. Useful for visitors can be a carnet of 10 tickets (€9.20), which can be shared by several people) or unlimited travel passes for one or two days or a week (€3–€6.70). Separate passes cover travel in "Greater Milan" and Lombardy.

For **taxis**, which are all white, go to one of the many ranks (such as San Babila or Stazione Centrale). Milan also has a bike-sharing scheme, which functions more effectively than the one in Rome (www.bikemi.com).

Roma Pass
If you're in Rome for a few days, the Roma Pass, a three-day tourist card, can be a worthwhile investment. The €25 pass includes unlimited travel on the entire transport network, free entrance to the first two museums or archaeological sites you visit, plus further discounts on entrance to museums, concerts and events. A map and events guide are included. Roma Pass can be bought from the sites themselves, from tourist offices or in advance through www.romapass.it.

Rome: ATAC, tel: 06-57003; www.atac.roma.it; in English, but less user-friendly than the city tourism site, http://en.turismoroma.it.
Taxis: 06-3570, 06-4157 or 06-6645.
Milan: ATM: tel: 800-808181; www.atm-mi.it. Taxis: tel: 02-4040 or 02-8585.
Naples: ANM, tel: 800-639 525.

Linea Circumvesuviana: tel: 800-053 939; www.vesuviana.it.
Linea Cumana-Circumflegrea: tel: 800-053-939. Taxis: use an official rank or call: 081-556 0202 or 081-202 020.
Florence: ATAF, tel: 800-424 500; www.ataf.net. Taxis: use a rank, or call: 055-4390 or 055-4499.

Florence
The main **bus** company is ATAF; and its kiosk in Piazza Stazione has free bus maps. Tickets are sold at the usual outlets (with an ATAF sticker) and at machines by bus stops, and once stamped a single ticket (€1.20) is valid for 90 minutes. One-day tickets (€5), 10-ticket carnets and longer-term passes (3 days, €12) are available. Unusually, single tickets can be bought on board, but they are more expensive.

Most of central Florence is closed to non-resident vehicles as a ZTL, but large car parks are provided on the edge of town (eg Piazza Independenza), linked by public transport. Really, the simplest way of getting around is on foot, but Florence also has a cycle route network, and the tourist office provides information on bike-hire shops. In the centre, you can also get around by horse-drawn carriage or rickshaw, and taxi ranks are easy to find.

Venice
Venice's transport system, coordinated by the **ACTV**, is naturally unique. The city is small enough to be covered on foot, but a good map is essential for exploring the maze of alleys and squares. For longer or faster trips, the main form of transport is the **vaporetto** (water-bus). Route information is available at the ACTV offices on Piazzale Roma, from tel: 041-2424, or on www.actv.it. Tickets can be bought online through the ACTV or the tourist office (www.veniceconnected.com), or from authorised outlets in Venice. A single ticket costs €6.50 and once stamped is valid for 60 minutes, but several other options are available, such as a 24-hour card for €18, or a 3-day travelcard for €33. Children aged under 3 travel free.

The most scenic, but slowest, line is the No. 1 Accelerato, down the Grand Canal. Line 82 provides a faster service on the same route. Vaporetti also run to the Lido and the outer islands of Murano, Burano and Torchello. **Water-taxis** take up to four people and, like regular taxis, display

meters. There are water-taxi "ranks" at main points in the city. Charges are high, and often complicated; two of the main services are Consorzio Motoscafi Venezia, tel: 041-522-2303, www.motoscafivenezia.it, and Venice Link, tel: 041-240 1715, www.venicelink.com, which also offers tours.

The official rate for hiring a **gondola** during the day is around €80 for 40 minutes and another €40 for each 20 minutes thereafter, and after 8pm it's €100, though it is advisable to haggle. A singing gondolier costs extra. A maximum of six people are accepted, and gondolas booked as a group tour may be cheaper. Very much cheaper are traghetto gondolas, which cross the Grand Canal where there are no bridges.

Naples
The hub of Naples's transport is Piazza Garibaldi, by the main train station, where most bus routes originate. Due to the city's chaotic traffic, buses often move very slowly, so it can be easier just to walk. Naples's **metro** lines, the Metropolitana FS (which mostly run above ground), are elderly but naturally faster, and Line 2 is especially useful for getting from Piazza Garibaldi through the centre to Mergellina, for Capri and Ischia ferries. The same Unico Nápoli tickets are used on metro and buses, and the famous funiculars that help get up the city's steep hills; single tickets are €1, or a day pass costs around €3.

Taxis can obviously be as traffic-snarled as buses. Naples taxis have a bad reputation for scams, so use only licensed taxis (with a city crest on the door and a number) from a rank, and check the meter is turned on (at zero) when you get in.

Ferries to the islands in the Bay of Naples leave from Molo Beverello, in the centre, and the more attractive Mergellina. Two enjoyable **local railways** are the Circumvesuviana, which goes from Piazza Garibaldi to Pompeii, Herculaneum and Sorrento, and the Circumflegrea, which runs around the west side of the Bay of Naples.

A CCOMMODATION

WHERE TO STAY

Italy has a wonderful variety of accommodation in all categories, from luxury villa hotels and palatial apartments to small family-run hotels, rustic retreats and simple B&Bs.

Hotels

The once stuffy Italian hotel scene has smartened up its act in recent years with the creation of new concepts from grand guesthouses and fortified farmhouses to hip design hotels, Zen-like spas and urban design dens.

Boutique and Design Hotels

Given Italians' sense of style and aptitude for family-run businesses, it is no surprise the country is now dotted with small hotels that offer a more intimate atmosphere as an alternative to the established big hotels, although in Italy the "boutique hotel" concept is often associated with traditional palazzo opulence (gilt, marble, rich fabrics) rather than contemporary design adventures. Nevertheless, Italy's celebrated modern designers have also leapt into the hotel business, from Ferragamo and Ferretti to Bulgari and Benetton. Ferragamo dominates the Florentine hotel scene, while the Alberta Ferretti fashion dynasty has several designer hotels on the Adriatic Riviera. In Milan, the design capital, the Bulgari is the epitome of cool, and with Turin the city also has some of Italy's most distinctive modern hotels.

Eco-Hotels

Eco-hotels are a new buzzword, presented as an answer to rural depopulation and a creative extension of the *agriturismo* concept *(see page*

*380). In the Abruzzo, the ancient hamlet of Santo Stefano di Sassanio has been restored but not prettified, leaving the smoke-blackened walls as a tribute to those who once eked out a living here, and now attracts summer ramblers and winter skiers. In Tuscany, near Urbino, Locanda della Valle Nuova flaunts its combination of green credentials and modern chic.

Gastro-Hotels

Showcases for celebrity chefs, gastro-hotels commonly contain cookery schools, wine estates and even spas as well as superb restaurants. Two of the best known are L'Albereta, near Lake Iseo, run by chef Gualtiero Marchese, and L'Andana in Tuscany, set up by Alain Ducasse.

Villa Hotels

In the north, lakes Como and Garda are home to some of the country's grandest, most luxurious villa hotels. Villa Feltrinelli, overlooking Lake Garda, was Mussolini's last bolt-hole, but is now the ultimate hideaway. In the Dolomites, chic chalets such as Virgilius resort offer skiing in style, and other romantic, intimate villas are on islands, such as those on Capri, or above Taormina in Sicily.

Spa Hotels

Italian spa hotels used to be synonymous with scary doctors in white coats, but a growing number of ultra-indulgent spas dedicated to serious pampering has appeared across the countryside, and many of Italy's traditional grand hotels have added luxury spas to keep up with international trends, which has obliged even established spas to

soften their old, clinical style. Many of the most sybaritic modern hideaways are in Tuscany, such as those at Fonteverde and Grotta Giusti. For more details, *see pages 286 and 395.*

Spiritual Retreats

Italy abounds in former monasteries that have been transformed into luxurious hotels. However, there are also perfect pads in religious houses that retain their spiritual vocation. In Piedmont, you can stay in the mountains at the Santuario d'Oropa, and many religious foundations have guest houses, with modest but comfortable rooms at low prices, especially in Rome and Venice. The Monastery Stays agency (www. monasterystays.com) handles bookings for over 300 monastery and convent guest houses.

Hotel Groups

The following is a selection of the most noteworthy hotel groups.
Abitare La Storia: Operating under the banner of "Living History", this is an association of independently run hotels, each of which occupies an historic palazzo or villa, often with lovely grounds. Tel: 0322-772 156; www.abitarelastoria.it.
Baglioni Hotels: A group that operates several of the finest luxury hotels in Rome, Milan, Venice and other cities, with great style; www. baglionihotels.com.
Charming Hotels and Resorts: A group of independent luxury hotels spread around Italy, including traditional city grand hotels, beach hotels, ski hotels, spas and even upscale apartments. Tel: 06-977 459; www.charminghr.com.

NH Hotels: In 2007 Jolly Hotels, Italy's largest hotel group, was taken over by the Spanish NH group, which has given its often elderly properties an overdue upgrade. There are NH hotels in nearly every city in Italy; business-oriented, they don't have great character, but offer reliable service and facilities and very good value; tel: (Italy) 848-390 398, (UK) 0870 735 0358; www.nh-hotels.com

Sina Hotels: An Italian group that runs stylish luxurious hotels in Milan, Rome, Florence and several other locations. They can be booked through the central website, www.sinahotels.com.

Starhotels: Another Italian upscale hotel group that specialises in hotels in the centres of cities, with a fresh, contemporary style. Tel: (UK and Italy) 00-800-0022 0011, (US) 1-800-816 6001; www.starhotels.it

THI Collection: Traditional classic hotels in Northern Italy, characterised by high standards of service and an

Only in Italy

Some of Italy's most memorable places to stay are found in converted examples of the country's most bizarre traditional houses, many dating back centuries. Most famous are the *trulli*, the round, conical-roofed, one-room houses around Alberobello in Puglia. Rather like man-made caves, *trulli* are now in considerable demand as rustic accommodation *(see page 340)*. Nearby on the Puglia Coast, many of the region's *masserie fortificate*, massive-walled farmhouses fortified against pirate attacks, have also been turned into chic hotels *(see page 339)*. In Matera, in deepest Basilicata, you can stay in a real cave, in the town's Sassi *(see page 351)* – homes carved out of the local tufa stone, most of them thousands of years old, which Mel Gibson featured in *The Passion of the Christ*. Around the countryside, above all in the south, Sardinia and Sicily, many *agriturismo* farmhouses incorporate stones, walls or whole rooms that date back to the early Middle Ages, or even further. Other "conversions" are a little more modern, such as the Antica Stazione Ficuzza on Sicily, a former train station built to serve the Bourbon kings' hunting estates, which is now a tiny hotel and jazz venue.

ABOVE: Regina Hotel Baglioni in Rome.

air of old-fashioned luxury. Tel: (Italy) 011-515 1911; www.thi.it.

UNA Hotels: Milan-based group with several hotels in the city and others throughout Italy. Mainly business-oriented, they're fairly functional, but have very good facilities and frequent good-value offers. Tel: (Italy) 800-606 162; www.unahotels.it.

B&Bs and Guesthouses

Italy was slow to get onto the B&B bandwagon, but legal changes have led to a boom in Bed & Breakfasts, especially in certain regions such as Venice, Bologna and Rome, and particularly for budget travellers. The quality of accommodation is variable, but places are generally clean, simple and welcoming. In many sought-after cities, chic guesthouses have replaced the peeling *pensione*, a category that no longer exists, officially at least. The model is, curiously enough, the English guesthouse, but the Italian version is keener on eclecticism than cosiness.

Many websites advertise B&Bs around Italy, and take bookings: among the most useful are www.bbitalia.it (general), or www.b-b.rm.it (Rome) and www.domueposada.it (Sardinia).

Agriturismo

Parallel to the growth in town B&Bs has been the expansion in possibilities for staying on farms, or *agriturismo*. This began in the 1980s, in part in response to the needs of small farmers to diversify their income, and in part to the desire of

city dwellers, Italian and foreign, to get back in touch with small-scale production and rural life, and especially locally produced traditional foods. *Agriturismo* now covers a very diverse range, embracing everything from real traditional farms to adventurous organic cooperatives and luxury accommodation on grand wine estates. Many offer classes in cookery and other rural traditions. Tuscany and Umbria are the two areas where *agriturismo* developed first, especially around Florence, Siena, San Gimignano and Chianti, but there are now others all over the country, and notably in Sicily and Sardinia.

Regional and local tourist offices have lists of *agriturismo* properties in their area. For information on farmhouse stays throughout Italy, good sources are www.agriturismo.it, www.agriturismo.net or www.agriturismo.com.

Villa Holidays

Private villas with their own pool usually cost a premium in Italy, and tend to be booked up very quickly. Some so-called "villas" are actually apartment complexes, so check exactly what you're getting.

Tuscany tends to be the most expensive region, but Umbria is catching up in price and quality; there are also magnificent Palladian villas available for rent in the Veneto. In the south, except for some chic sites in Sardinia, Capri and the Amalfi Coast, prices tend to be lower.

Prices and Seasons

Nearly all Italian hotels have a low and high season for prices (and often a "mid season" as well), with great variations between them. Around the coast and in the big tourist sites such as Florence peak season is Easter and July–August; in business cities like Milan it's during trade fairs and fashion weeks; in winter resorts it's naturally late December–February. Chose your time to travel carefully, and you can cut costs by as much as half.

Note also that Italians only go to beach destinations around summer, and so most beach hotels around Rimini, the Amalfi Coast or in Sicily and Sardinia close up tight between November and March. However, in order to extend their income more hotels are now experimenting with catering to off-season visitors, particularly in the mountains, where many smaller ski hotels now open in summer.

ROME

Rome has an impressive range of accommodation, particularly at the top end of the scale. However, high demand means that prices are high, and good hotels need to be booked well in advance. *See page 136* for Rome's designer hotels.

Grand Hotels

Aldrovandi Villa Borghese
Via Ulisse Aldrovandi 15
Tel: 06-322 3993
www.aldrovandi.com
This 18th-century palace overlooks the Villa Borghese gardens, and its suites are among the most expensive in the city. Decor is sumptuous rather than stylish – a mood that is reflected in the facilities and service. The many amenities include an outdoor swimming pool – exceptional for Rome. €€€€
Hotel Hassler Roma
Piazza Trinità dei Monti 6
Tel: 06-699 340
www.hotelhassler.com
At the top of the Spanish Steps, this classic hotel has long enjoyed the status of one of the best in Rome (and the world). Staff take care of every detail for their guests, rooms are palatial, and the famous roof-garden restaurant has fabulous views. €€€€
Hotel De Russie
Via del Babuino 9
Tel: 06-328 881
www.hotelderussie.it
A favoured 19th-century haunt of the Russian imperial family, later frequented by Picasso and Jean Cocteau, this very grand hotel in Rome's most fashionable shopping area (the Tridente) has been returned to its luxurious best as part of the Rocco Forte group. Its gardens are a tranquil oasis in the heart of town, and subtly decorated rooms feature state-

of-the-art technology. A lavish spa and superb restaurant – Le Jardin de Russie – add to its celebrity appeal. €€€€
Parco dei Principi Grand Hotel and Spa
Via G. Frescobaldi 5
Tel: 06-854 421
www.parcodeiprincipi.com
Beautifully located in ample grounds on the edge of Villa Borghese gardens, this luxurious modern hotel prides itself on its range of facilities and attention to detail. Amenities include a lovely garden pool, panoramic suites, a comprehensively equipped spa and fine restaurants. €€€€
Regina Hotel Baglioni
Via Veneto 72
Tel: 06-421 111
www.baglionihotels.com
Recently renovated with chic modern touches to add to its period elegance, the 62-room Regina has brought a touch of class back to the Via Veneto, which had lost some of its sparkle. €€€€
Rome Cavalieri
Via A. Cadlolo 101
Tel: 06-35091
www.romecavalieri.com
A giant hotel in extensive grounds near the Vatican that has recently been taken to an extra level of luxury as part of the Waldorf Astoria group. Sumptuous facilities including two magnificent swimming pools, a fabulous spa, several restaurants and rooms in palatial Roman style. €€€€
St Regis Grand Hotel
Via Vittorio E. Orlando 3
Tel: 06-47091
www.starwoodhotels.com
Between Termini station and the Via Veneto area, this dignified hotel occupies a patrician palace, with oriental rugs, chandeliers and antiques. It has been

beautifully restored, but retaining its traditional style. Personal butler service available. €€€€

Boutique Hotels

Casa Howard
Via Capo La Case 18 (off Spanish Steps)
Tel: 06-6992 4555
www.casahoward.com
Tucked away in a secluded palazzo is a delightful "home-from-home" created by style gurus Massimiliano Leonardi and Jennifer Howard Forneris. Modelled on an English guesthouse, its design is far more eclectic. Instead of a concierge, "house-genie" Cristy oversees the guest-house, from the Turkish *hammam* (steam bath) to the "honesty fridge" and five themed bedrooms. There is also now a second Casa Howard in Rome, at Via Sistina 149 (same phone and website), with idiosyncratically chic rooms designed by Tommaso Ziffer, and another house in Florence. €€€
Hotel Capo d'Africa
Via Capo d'Africa 54
Tel: 06-772 801
www.hotelcapodafrica.com
One of a glut of recent boutique hotels in Rome: the palm-tree-lined entrance bodes well, an impressive collection of contemporary art is on show and the 64 rooms are refreshingly stylish and comfortable – one suite has its own private terrace. Views are delightful, and the Colosseum is only a five-minute walk away. €€€
Hotel Celio
Via Santissimi Quattro 35/C
Tel: 06-7049 5333
www.hotelcelio.com
This 20-room boutique hotel is just a stone's throw from both the Colosseum and the Forum and

occupies a charming palazzo that has been sensitively restored, including its fine mosaics. The atmosphere is intimate, and it has many fans. €€€
Hotel San Francesco
Via Jacopo de' Settesoli 7
Tel: 06-5830 0051
www.hotelsanfrancesco.net
In Trastevere, overlooking medieval cloisters, this former seminary is now a stylish hotel with a roof garden, great breakfasts, stylish sitting room and cosy bedrooms, and unusually low prices. €€
La Residenza "A"
Via Vittorio Veneto 183
Tel: 06-486 700
www.hotelviaveneto.com
On the first floor of a *palazzo* in the swanky but dull Via Veneto, this very chic little hotel has seven carefully-styled rooms with contemporary art on the walls and superior facilities. Service is excellent, and spa treatments are available. €€€

Mid-Range

Caesar House Residenze Romane
Via Cavour 310
Tel: 06-6792674
www.caesarhouse.com

PRICE CATEGORIES

Price categories are for a double room in mid-seaon without breakfast:
€ = up to €100
€€ = €100–160
€€€ = €160–300
€€€€ = more than €300

This peaceful, traditionally styled family-run hotel (just five minutes from the Colosseum) offers highly personalised service, including babysitting, bike hire or guided tours. €€€

Hotel Centrale
Via Laurina 34
Tel: 06-8740 30890
www.hotelcentraleroma.it
Near Piazza del Popolo, this veteran hotel was comprehensively renovated in 2007, and its 21 simple but comfortable rooms now have good modern facilities including WiFi. Accessible rates make it one of Rome's best-value hotels. €€

Hotel Columbia
Via del Viminale 15
Tel: 06-488 3509
www.hotelcolumbia.com
This charming hotel is centrally located near to the Via Nazionale, and has large, elegantly furnished rooms with good modern facilities. There is also a roof garden for breakfast. €€–€€€

Hotel dei Consoli Vaticano
Via Varrone 2/D
Tel: 06-6889 2972
www.hoteldeiconsoli.com
Occupying a 19th-century building restored in

traditional style (but with modern facilities and electronics), this hotel has a fine view of St Peter's cupola from its spectacular rooftop terrace and many of the 28 bedrooms. €€–€€€

Hotel Gregoriana
Via Gregoriana 18
Tel: 06-679 4269
www.hotelgregoriana.it
Close to the Spanish Steps, this former 17th-century monastery is now a tranquil modern hotel, recently renovated in a style that mixes Art Deco and contemporary design. There is no restaurant, but an attractive breakfast room. €€

Hotel Mozart
Via dei Greci 23/B
Tel: 06-3600 1915
www.hotelmozart.com
Warm, elegant atmosphere in the heart of the fashionable Tridente area, close to ancient history and modern shopping and just a few steps from Piazza di Spagna. The owners also have ample suites nearby in the Vivaldi Luxury Rooms, and self-contained apartments (bookable through the hotel

website). €€€

Hotel Santa Maria
Vicolo del Piede 2
Tel: 06-589 4626
www.htlsantamaria.com
This small jewel of a hotel in tranquil Trastevere takes its name from the nearby church of Santa Maria. A former 17th-century cloister, it has been sympathetically renovated and offers high standards of comfort, as well as a courtyard garden that is an oasis of calm. €€

Hotel Teatro di Pompeo
Largo del Pallaro 8
Tel: 06-6830 0170
www.hotelteatrodipompeo.it
Just off picturesque Campo de' Fiori, this popular family-run hotel stands on the site of Pompey's Theatre, dating from 55 BC. The walls of the breakfast room were hewn from the theatre's tufa stone, and bedrooms are a cosy blend of cream decor and terracotta-flagged floors. €€–€€€

Other Options

aRoma
Via Palestro 49
Tel: 34-0284 7643
www.aromabb.it
In the centre of Rome, not

far from Termini station, this is a popular B&B in a quiet palazzo with vaulted ceilings. The owners also have apartments for short-term rentals. €–€€

The Beehive
Via Marghera 8
Tel: 06-4470 4553
www.the-beehive.com
A chic but incredibly cheap option near Termini station run by an American couple with a dorm room, apartments and guest rooms decorated in a colourful contemporary style. It has a welcoming garden, its own café and knowledgeable staff. €

Casa Trevi
Via in Arcione 98
Tel: 335-6205768
www.casatrevi.it
Though close to the Trevi fountain in central Rome, this cluster of modern apartments (sleeping 2–5) are peaceful, minimalist but warm, and overlook a courtyard with olive trees and oranges. The same owners also have the Casa in Trastevere (Vicolo della Penitenza 19), another charming self-contained apartment (sleeping 2–6), which is close to the Trastevere bar and restaurant scene, but

MILAN

Since the city is Italy's foremost business centre, Milan's hotels are in biggest demand during the working months of the year, when they need to be booked well ahead. During the main trade fairs it can be almost impossible to find a room, leaving no alternative but to stay outside the city. Conversely, they can be quite easy to find at weekends or in July–August.

Grand Hotels

Carlton Hotel Baglioni
Via Senato 5
Tel: 02-77077
www.baglionihotels.com
In the heart of Milan,

overlooking ultra-chic Via della Spiga, this luxurious hotel offers the ultimate in elegance and refinement. Rooms are furnished with exquisite silk brocade, antiques and marbled bathrooms. The "Baretto al Baglioni" restaurant is renowned, and the Caffè Baglioni an ever-fashionable meeting-point. €€€€

Four Seasons Hotel Milano
Via Gesù 6/8
Tel: 02-77088
www.fourseasons.com
One of Milan's most exclusive hotels, in a much-altered former convent, with attentive but unobtrusive service. The setting is delightful, with the former

monastic cells converted into supremely luxurious bedrooms around garden courtyards, and the restaurants and spa are of a style to match. Popular for its proximity to the Quadrilatero shopping district. €€€€

Hotel Principe di Savoia
Piazza della Repubblica 17
Tel: 02-62301
www.hotelprincipedisavoia.com
This Milanese institution revels in old-fashioned luxury, with a self-consciously grand interior. Its more than 400 rooms include the most splendid presidential suite in the city, favoured by celebrities, models and heads of state, and with its own private

pool. As well as such glitzy touches, this classic luxury hotel offers superb service and excellent facilities, including a rooftop fitness centre and pool with glorious views over the city. €€€€

Park Hyatt Milan
Via Tommaso Grossi 1
Tel: 02-8821 1234
www.milan.park.hyatt.com

ACCOMMODATION ♦ 383

TRANSPORT

ACCOMMODATION

EATING OUT

ACTIVITIES

A - Z

LANGUAGE

ABOVE: Principe di Savoia.

Cool understatement has been combined with opulence at this giant modern luxury hotel: bedrooms feature travertine-clad walls, Venetian stucco and lovely touches such as hand-blown Venetian-glass light sconces. A stone's throw from La Scala, the Duomo and a Prada shop. €€€€

Boutique and B&Bs

Antica Locanda Leonardo
Corso Magenta 78
Tel: 02-4801 4197
www.leoloc.com
Small but quite luxurious family-run hotel with 20 individual rooms in traditionally plush style, several with lovely garden views. It's close to the church of Santa Maria delle Grazie and Leonardo's Cenacolo. €€–€€€
Antica Locanda dei Mercanti
Via San Tomaso 6
Tel: 02-805 4080
www.locanda.it
The name may suggest an "Old Inn", but inside this 18th-century building the 14 rooms – the best with their own terraces – have been imaginatively designed with subtle but comfortable modern styling and excellent facilities. There are well-stocked bookshelves, service is exceptional, and breakfast (which can be served in bed) is included. €€€

Ariston Hotel
Largo Carrobbio 2
Tel: 02-7200 0556
www.aristonhotel.com
In a rather noisy, traffic-filled area, this ecologically minded hotel is an experiment in healthy living and an asthma-sufferer's dream: rooms come equipped with atomisers and ionisers as well as other extras, and the breakfast bar uses organic produce. Competitive rates make it exceptional value. €€
Bulgari Hotel Milano
Via Privata Fratelli Gabba 7/B
Tel: 02-805 8051
www.bulgarihotels.com
A monument to contemporary Milanese chic, a short stroll from the style capital's most famous fashion street, Via Montenapoleone, the Bulgari was purpose-built with exquisite attention to every detail. Elegant minimalism and the use of fine materials reign throughout: the restaurant, gardens and spa are all stunning. Naturally a fashion-crowd favourite. €€€€
Foresteria Monforte
Piazza Tricolore 2
Tel: 3402-370 272
www.foresteriamonforte.it
Billed as a boutique B&B, this chic spot reflects the location, near San Babila in Milan's shopping district. There are just three rooms, all airy, contemporary and studded with design detail. €€–€€€
The Gray Milano
Via San Raffaele 6
Tel: 02-720 8951
www.hotelthegray.com
In the heart of Milan, close to the Duomo, the Scala and Galleria Vittorio Emanuele, this design hotel has become one of the city's most fashionable. The 21 rooms are all individually styled, and there is a suitably sleek restaurant. €€€€
Hotel Gran Duca di York
Via Moneta 1
Tel: 02-874 863
www.ducadiyork.com
Close to the Duomo and the main shopping area, this popular 33-room hotel is

housed in a an 18th-century former palazzo that has been stylishly renovated. Service is attentive and professional. €€€
Hotel Spadari al Duomo
Via Spadari 11
Tel: 02-7200 2371
www.spadarihotel.com
Exclusive little jewel of a hotel around the corner from the Duomo and La Scala, this "art hotel" was developed around a private collection of contemporary art and designer furniture, creating 40 individually stylish rooms. Service is professional and friendly, and breakfast is included. €€€
Tara Verde
Via Delleani 22
Tel: 02-3653 4959
www.taraverde.it
This very colourful yet very tasteful B&B near the Fiera district (metro De Angeli) is an exotic retreat, with a charming garden. Just three lovely rooms, with lower prices for stays of over two nights. €€

Mid-Range and Budget

Antica Locanda Solferino
Via Castelfidardo 2
Tel: 02-657 0129
www.anticalocandasolferino.it
Traditional furniture and a gracious atmosphere create a charming ambience in this 11-room hotel in the elegant Brera quarter. In tune with the low-key mood, breakfast is served in your room. Book well in advance. €€€
Hotel Vittoria
Via Pietro Calvi 32
Tel: 02-545 6520
www.hotelvittoriamilano.it
This pleasant, family-run traditional hotel is about 10 minutes' walk from the cathedral. The 40 bedrooms have been recently renovated, with air-con, noise insulation and modern electronics, although some are a little small. The cosy breakfast room overlooks a nice garden where breakfast is served in fine weather. €€

Hotel Aspromonte
Piazza Aspromonte 12–14
Tel: 02-236 1119
www.hotelaspromonte.it
The 19 rooms at the Aspromonte have plenty of the comforts of a mid-range hotel – good bathrooms, WiFi, air-con – but ultra-low rates make it an amazing bargain. It's well connected by metro, and needs to be booked well ahead. €
Hotel Michelangelo
Via Scarlatti 33
Tel: 02-67551
www.milanhotel.it
Close to the Central Station, this is an archetypal business hotel – with 300 rooms in a multi-storey block – but has good facilities, and is good value. €€
NH President
Largo Augusto 10 (corner of Piazza Luigi di Savoia)
Tel: 02-77461
www.nh-hotels.com
Extensively renovated like other former Jolly Hotels since its acquisition by the NH group; functional, but centrally located and with good modern facilities at very accessible rates. There are 10 more NH hotels around Milan. €€
UNA Hotel Century
Via Fabio Filzi 25B
Tel: 02-675041
www.unahotels.it
One of a chain of business-oriented hotels found around Italy (and with six more hotels in Milan), this modern tower-block hotel close to Stazione Centrale nevertheless offers a friendly atmosphere, space and a sense of privacy. The 144 suites are functional but very spacious, and exceptional value. Other amenities include a small fitness centre and a good restaurant and café. €€

PRICE CATEGORIES

Price categories are for a double room in mid-seaon without breakfast:
€ = up to €100
€€ = €100–160
€€€ = €160–300
€€€€ = more than €300

LOMBARDY AND THE LAKES

Many of the best hotels in Lombardy, Piedmont and the Veneto occupy lakeside sites, with glorious views and a steep price. Lake Como has some of the grandest resort hotels, especially around Bellagio; Lake Garda is a little less exclusive and intimate, and is excellent for water-sports.

Bergamo

Hotel Excelsior San Marco
Piazza della Repubblica 6
Tel: 035-366 111
www.hotelsanmarco.com
A large, modern but traditionally styled hotel in the centre of town, with fine service, an attractive restaurant and a roof garden. €€

Brescia–Franciacorta

Al Rocol
Via Provinciale 79, Ome, Brescia,
Tel: 030-685 2542
www.alrocol.com
In the heart of the Franciacorta wine country between Brescia and Lake Iseo, this is a foodie escape on the lovely farm and wine estate of the Castellini family. There are 15 cosy bedrooms; guests can take cookery courses, visit other vineyards, explore the countryside or just enjoy the superb meals made with the estate's own produce. €

Il Santellone Resort
Via del Santellone 116
Tel: 030-241 0126
www.santelloneresort.it
This splendid resort occupies an 11th-century abbey close to the Franciacorta wine country on the outskirts of Brescia. It is connected with Vita E Spa, the most seductive spa in the area, and joint packages are avaiable. The design of the bedrooms and public spaces, in off-whites and earth tones, complements the spare grandeur of the abbey walls. €€€

Lake Como

Grand Hotel Tremezzo
Via Regina 8, Bellagio
Tel: 0344-42491
www.grandhoteltremezzo.com
Overlooking the western shore of Lake Como, this giant Art Nouveau-style villa-hotel has fine lake views on one side and an Alpine panorama on the other. Popular as a congress centre, it has three fine restaurants, a floating swimming pool on the lake and a sumptuous spa. €€€€

Grand Hotel Villa Serbelloni
Via Roma 1, Bellagio
Tel: 031-950 216
www.villaserbelloni.it
Another of Como's historic palace-hotels, in a fabulous patrician villa. The views, grounds, facilities (including two pools, tennis courts and spa) and service are all impeccable; the Michelin-starred terrace restaurant overlooks the palm-filled grounds and the lake. €€€€

Hotel du Lac
Piazza Mazzini 32, Bellagio
Tel: 031-950 320
www.bellagiohoteldulac.com
A more economical option on Como, centrally located in Bellagio town overlooking the boat landing, this warm family-run hotel has many return guests. There's a pleasant roof garden, and the terrace restaurant has lovely panoramic views. €€–€€€

Lake Garda

Grand Hotel Terme di Sirmione
Viale Marconi 7, Sirmione
Tel: 030-916 261
www.termedisirmione.com
An elegant hotel that's part of the giant Terme di Sirmione spa complex, with all kinds of pampering treatments and excellent pools and sports facilities. The Terme also contains two other more moderately priced hotels. €€€–€€€€

Hotel Gardesana
Piazza Calderini 20, Torri del Benaco
Tel: 045-722 5411
www.hotel-gardesana.com
This delightful medieval harbour-master's house overlooking Lake Garda has been converted into a welcoming, cosy small hotel. Bedrooms on the third floor are the quietest, and have lovely views over the lake. Wonderful value for money. €

Hotel du Lac et du Parc
Viale Rovereto 44, Riva del Garda
Tel: 0464-566 600
www.hoteldulac-riva.it
This part-old, part-modern hotel in Riva del Garda enjoys a lakeside location where motor boats are banned. As well as the hotel, there are holiday chalets in the spacious grounds, restaurants, a piano bar, tennis, a sailing and windsurfing school and a fitness centre. Prices can be surprisingly reasonable. €€€–€€€€

Palazzo Arzaga
Via Arzaga 1, Calvagese della Riviera, Brescia
Tel: 030-680 600
www.palazzoarzaga.com
A few kilometres west of the lake, this palace-resort occupies a former country estate, with finely restored palazzo, and combines its own golf course with a luxury spa escape – typically a his-and-hers option. Rooms range from country casual to frescoed splendour; pools, restaurants and other facilities are equally impressive. €€€–€€€€

Villa Feltrinelli
Via Rimembranza 38–40, Gargnano
Tel: 0365-798 000
www.villafeltrinelli.com
Built for the Feltrinelli publishing family, the villa that was Mussolini's last bolt-hole in Italy is now Lake Garda's most opulent (and expensive) hotel – the ultimate hideaway and the height of decadence, from fabulous frescoes to Frette sheets. Guests can take a lake cruise on La

Contessa before dinner prepared by your personal chef. €€€€

Lake Iseo

L'Albereta
Via Vittorio Emanuele II 23, Erbusco
Tel: 030-776 0550
www.albereta.it
A destination for gastronomes who want to splurge, as its restaurant is the domain of one of Italy's most celebrated chefs, Gualtiero Marchesi. The hotel occupies a compact rural estate, consisting of farmhouses and a tower-house, and inside there are delightful rooms and a pampering spa. €€€€

Relais I Due Roccoli
Via S. Bonomelli, Colline di Iseo
Tel: 030-982 2977
www.idueroccoli.com
Perched above Lake Iseo, this elegant country hotel enjoys a romantic setting in the hills. The restaurant has views over the lake and there's a courtyard for summer dining; it's excellent value. €€

Val Camonica

Agriturismo Belotti
Via Cesare Battisti 11,
Villa Dalegno di Temù, Ponte di Legno
Tel: 0364 91850/333 527 7159
www.agriturismobelotti.it.
This genuine B&B-inn is in a hamlet in the Val Camonica, above Iseo. Bedrooms are basic, but the hospitality is warm and cooking delicious, using farm-produced cheese, meat, jams and yoghurts. Tuck into gnocchi with Alpine herbs after a mountain walk. €

TURIN

Most of Turin's hotels cater largely to a business clientele, but the city is trying to broaden its appeal, especially since low-cost airlines and a good deal of investment have made it a city-break destination.

Art Hotel Boston
Via Massena 70
Tel: 011-500 359
www.hotelbostontorino.it
A hip boutique hotel designed with a sense of originality. Common areas and many of the 87 bedrooms are hung with contemporary art, and the Fibonacci Bar has style to match. €€–€€€

Grand Hotel Sitea
Via Carlo Alberto 35
Tel: 011-517 0171
www.thi-hotels.com
One of the city's most traditional "grand hotels",

with sumptuous furnishings and marble fittings. Located in the heart of the city, but the ambience is both relaxing and luxurious. €€€

Hotel Victoria Torino
Via Nino Costa 4
Tel: 011-561 1909
www.hotelvictoria-torino.com
This centrally located hotel has few rivals for atmosphere and service at mid-range prices. The public areas are full of antiques and objets d'art, and each of the 106 spacious bedrooms is individually decorated. In summer, breakfast is served in the garden under the gazebo, and there's also a spa and gorgeous indoor swimming pool. €€–€€€

Le Meridien Turin Art+Tech
Via Nizza 230

Tel: 011-664 2000
www.lemeridienturin.com
Architect Renzo Piano created this spectacular minimalist hotel, and the high-tech vision is clear in the vertiginous lifts, glass-roofed, cavernous central hall, and the ultra-sleek rooms. The same group also has Le Meridien Lingotto, where the former Fiat car plant has been given an entirely original Piano makeover, with the rooftop racing track now serving as a jogging track with fabulous views. €€€

NH Ambasciatori
Corso Vittorio Emanuele II 104
Tel: 011-57521
www.jollyhotels.it
A large business hotel typical of the NH chain, with, as usual, no great charm but reliably good facilities

and service and great-value rates. €–€€

Starhotel Majestic
Corso Vittorio Emanuele II 54
Tel: 011-539 153
www.starhotels.it
One of an imaginatively run chain, this hotel has modern facilities for business or leisure guests, and a convenient location, opposite Porta Nuova station. Rates are reasonable, and there are frequent online offers. €€

PIEDMONT AND VALLE D'AOSTA

Piedmont (Piemonte) has appeal for wine-lovers and nature-lovers exploring its national parks, and in winter for skiiers who flock to the fabulous ski resorts.

Alba

I Castelli
Corso Torino 14
Tel: 0173-361 978
www.hotel-icastelli.com
Modern business-oriented hotel built in the 1990s in the heart of town, with spacious, well-equipped rooms. There's a pleasant restaurant and other facilities. €–€€

Hotel Villa San Carlo
Corso Divisioni Alpine, Cortemilia
Tel: 0173-81546
www.hotelsancarlo.it
Run by a down-to-earth chef and sommelier, this remains a simple, family-run hotel in the heart the truffle country south of Alba. Embark on foodie forays; do a short wine and cookery course; or simply enjoy the tajarin pasta in white truffles. €–€€

Allessandria Province

La Traversina
Cascina La Traversina, Stazzano
Tel: 0143-61377
www.latraversina.com
Run by the irrepressible Rosanna, this eccentric *agriturismo* in wine country south of Alessandria overflows with warmth, flowers, food and pets. Delicious home-made food is matched by quirky style. €

Aosta

Albergo Milleluci
Località Porossan Roppoz 15
Tel: 0165-235 278
www.hotelmilleluci.com
An impressive mountain inn with 31 rooms with panoramic views over the city, a breakfast room in traditional Val d'Aosta style and, a great plus, a gorgeous swimming pool. €€–€€€

Hotel Europe
Piazza Narbonne 8
Tel: 0165-236 363
www.hoteleuropeaosta.it

In the historic centre of Aosta, this traditional hotel has an atmosphere of cosy elegance and tranquility. Staff are obliging, and it's an exceptional bargain. €

Asti

Hotel-Ristorante Reale
Piazza V. Alfieri 5
Tel: 0141-530 240
www.hotelristorantereale.it
This lovely palazzo in the heart of the Old Town has been a hotel since 1793, and is renowned above all for its restaurant and wine collection, both showcases for local produce. Rooms are simple but tasteful. €€

Biella

Santuario di Oropa
Biella Oropa
Tel: 015-2555 1200
www.santuariodioropa.it
This lodging house forms part of a sanctuary dedicated to the Virgin of Oropa, high up in the mountains just north of Biella. It has 300 perhaps

surprisingly comfortable guest rooms, in a wonderful setting for meditation, walks, or even wine-tasting and gourmet trails. €

Bra

Albergo dell'Agenzia
Via Fossano 21, Pollenzo
(7km/4 miles southeast of Bra)
Tel: 0172-458 600
www.albergoagenzia.it
A luxury hotel in part of what

PRICE CATEGORIES

Price categories are for a double room in mid-seaon without breakfast:
€ = up to €100
€€ = €100–160
€€€ = €160–300
€€€€ = more than €300

was once the neo-Gothic country residence of King Carlo Alberto. It's now also part of the "University of Gastronomic Sciences", and its restaurant is a showcase for the philosophy of Slow Food. The 47 rooms are spacious and elegant, and the gardens contain an attractive pool. €€€

Cogne

Hotel Miramonti
Viale Cavagnet 31
Tel: 0165-74030
www.miramonticogne.com
This friendly, family-run "hôtel de charme" is an ideal base for exploring Gran Paradiso National Park. It's furnished with antiques and antiquarian books, with blazing fires in winter, and the wood-panelled Cœur de Bois restaurant is noted for its local specialities and mouth-watering desserts. There's also a pool and beauty centre, and it's exceptional value.
€–€€

Canelli

Agriturismo La Casa in Collina
Località Sant'Antonio 30
(2km/1¼ miles west of Canelli)
Tel: 0141-822 827
www.casaincollina.com
This lovely house sits on a hill overlooking vineyards and enjoys stunning views of the snowy Alpine peaks in the distance. There are six spacious, comfortable rooms furnished with period pieces and antiques, and views from the breakfast room are breathtaking. Very good value. €–€€

Sestriere

Hotel Cristallo
Via Pinerolo 5
Tel: 0122-750 707
www.newlinehotels.com
A popular modern hotel in the middle of the Sestriere ski resort, close to the slopes and the mountain paths for summer walking, and with everything needed for relaxing after skiing.
€€–€€€

LIGURIA AND THE ITALIAN RIVIERA

Genoa has a shortage of individual hotels, but there is a huge range of accommodation on the Ligurian Coast. Note that many beach hotels close in winter.

Genoa

Hotel Bristol Palace
Via XX Settembre 35
Tel: 010-592 541
www.hotelbristolpalace.it
Traditionally Genoa's grandest hotel, the Bristol Palace is on the city's most elegant shopping street, close to Old Genoa. The modest entrance belies its history and though rooms vary in attractiveness, some have special features, such as marble bathrooms.
€€€–€€€€
NH Marina
Molo Ponte Calvi 5
Tel: 010-25391
www.nh-hotels.com
This purpose-built hotel created on a pontoon in Genoa harbour in 2000 has nautical-style fittings to match the setting. As the only hotel in Porto Antico marina, it enjoys sweeping views of the Old Port, and like other NH hotels it has reliable modern equipment and is very good value. The chain also has another more conventional Genoa hotel, the NH Plaza. €€
Locanda di Palazzo Cicala
Piazza San Lorenzo 16

Tel: 010-251 8824
www.palazzocicala.it
Facing the cathedral, this perfectly located 16th-century palace has been turned into a boutique hotel that is a subtle showcase of contemporary design, with rooms that subtly integrate the latest electronics. The hotel has equally charming period apartments nearby, also at mid-range rates. €€

Alassio

Hotel Beau Rivage
Lungomare Roma 82
Tel: 0182-640 585
www.hotelbeaurivage.it
This late 19th-century villa is run with laidback charm by its friendly owners, and its restaurant provides excellent fresh Ligurian dishes and fine local wines. Some rooms feature frescoed ceilings; others have terraces. €–€€

Bordighera

Grand Hotel del Mare
Via Portico della Punta 34, Capo Migliarese
Tel: 0184-262 201
www.grandhoteldelmare.it
An exclusive traditional palace hotel overlooking the sea, popular for its peace, comfort and beautiful rooms, and which now adds an indulgent spa to its traditional luxuries. €€€–€€€€

Hotel Parigi
Lungomare Argentina 16–18
Tel: 0184-261 405
www.hotelparigi.com
Centrally located with panoramic views over the beach and sea, this hotel has recently been renovated and has a fresher, more contemporary style than many Riviera hotels. Rooms are spacious, rates are moderate, and there is also a wellness centre. Special facilities are provided for cyclists. €€–€€€

Camogli

Hotel Cenobio dei Dogi
Via Cuneo 34
Tel: 0185-7241
www.cenobio.com
Overlooking the sea and surrounded by a lovely park, this hotel offers beautiful rooms, a good restaurant, saltwater pool, solarium and private beach. €€€

Portofino

Hotel Eden
Via Dritto 20
Tel: 0185-269 091
www.hoteledenportofino.com
Occupying a 1920s Ligurian villa, this pretty hotel makes a lovely family-run mid-range alternative to the Splendido (below). There are only 12 rooms, and the atmosphere and gardens are delightful.
€€–€€€

Hotel Splendido
Salita Baratta 16
Tel: 0185-267 801
www.hotelsplendido.com
One of the grandest hotels on the Ligurian Riviera is set above an exclusive little port, and all kinds of facilities are available within its hillside grounds, with exquisite views of the Portofino headland. Every comfort is provided, including a private speedboat; prices are very, very high. €€€€

Rapallo

Excelsior Palace Hotel
Via San Michele di Pagana 8
Tel: 0185-230 666
www.thi.it
A beautifully appointed luxury hotel overlooking the Gulf of Tigullio and Portofino. It combines a rich history with every modern amenity, including pools and a health spa. €€€€
Hotel Europa
Via Milite Ignoto 2
Tel: 0185-669 521
www.hoteleuropa-rapallo.com

This Art-Nouveau hotel was restored to its former glory a few years ago, and now houses a fine Ligurian restaurant to go with its comfortable, spacious rooms. Staff are very helpful. €€–€€€

Santa Margherita Ligure

Imperiale Palace Hotel
Via Pagana 19
Tel: 0185-288 991
www.imperialepalacehotel.com
Occupying an 1880s mansion, this grand hotel is in the neighbouring, but less

chic, resort to Portofino. Its appeal lies in the ornate decor, antique furnishings, spacious rooms and excellent service, and there's also a private beach. €€€€

San Remo

Royal Hotel Sanremo
Corso Imperatrice 80
Tel: 0184-5391
www.royalhotelsanremo.com
This luxury hotel is the choice of high-rollers at the casino and Italian stars during the San Remo Song Contest each February.

Giant rooms overlook sea or hills, and extensive facilities include a spa, swimming pool, tennis courts, giant gardens and a choice of restaurants. €€€€

Sestri Levante

Grand Hotel dei Castelli
Via Penisola di Levante 26
Tel: 0185-487 020
www.hoteldeicastelli.com
The Grand is centred around a 16th-century tower, amid a large park, which retains some of its stone fireplaces and other original features. Rooms and suites are

decorated in harmoniously traditional styles, and facilities include a lift down to the private beach. €€€

Ventimiglia

La Riserva di Castel d'Appio
Castel d'Appio 71
Tel: 0184-229 533
www.lariserva.it
Set 5km (3 miles) outside Ventimiglia, this charming, moderately sized hotel has fabulous views of the Riviera dei Fiori and the Costa Azzurra from most of its rooms. €€–€€€

VENICE

There is almost no off-season in Venice, so many hotels are full all year round. Unfortunately, this means that some hoteliers do not try hard to keep guests happy. Room prices can be up to 30 percent higher than on the mainland. The basic rules are: book early, check what view a room has and ask what the price differential is between "good" rooms and "bad" rooms (which often means those with canal views, or poky back rooms with little natural light.) Even in Venice's famous grand hotels, there can be big differences between "star" and standard rooms.

Grand Hotels

Hotel Cipriani
Isola della Giudecca 10
Tel: 041-520 7744
www.hotelcipriani.com
The most glamorous of Venetian hotels. Lavish rooms are furnished with Fortuny fabrics, and amenities include one of Venice's few hotel swimming pools, gardens, tennis courts, a yacht harbour, water-launches to whisk guests to San Marco, and the "Casanova Wellness Centre" spa. On the down side, service can be frosty. €€€€
Hotel Danieli
Riva degli Schiavoni 4196, Castello

Tel: 041-522 6480
www.danielihotelvenice.com
In a pre-eminent position on the waterfront, the Danieli is rich in memories of eminent guests: George Sand, Dickens, Balzac, Wagner. The splendid Gothic foyer is an attraction in itself, and the older rooms are very plush, although the modern extension is devoid of charm. Unless you are a celebrity, a regular or a big tipper, service can be supercilious. €€€€
Hotel Gritti Palace
Campo Santa Maria del Giglio 2467, San Marco
Tel: 041-794 611
http://gritti.hotelinvenice.com
The 15th-century Gritti, decorated with Murano-glass chandeliers and 16th-century damask furnishings, is perhaps the most legendary Venetian hotel and has a price tag to match. Renowned for its formal luxury, fabulous setting on the Grand Canal and discreet, attentive service, it has hosted many famous names. Refined cuisine is served on the canalside terrace. €€€€
Hotel Monaco and Grand Canal
Calle Vallaresso 1332, San Marco
Tel: 041-520 0211
www.hotelmonaco.it
Owned by the Benetton group, this stately hotel

occupies a prime spot opposite Santa Maria della Salute church, where the Grand Canal flows into the lagoon. It has been revamped with a contemporary twist: a glass-roofed lobby now forms part of the Ridotto, a private casino that was once the haunt of Casanova. €€€€
Luna Hotel Baglioni
Calle Larga dell'Ascensione 1243, San Marco
Tel: 041-528 9840
www.baglionihotels.com
The Luna is the oldest hotel in Venice, first founded in 1118 as a lodge for pilgrims travelling to Jerusalem. Countless refurbishments mean that it does not look its age, and as part of the Baglioni group it now has all modern extras to go with its traditional luxuries. The decor is a riot of Murano glass, marble, gleaming woodwork and swagged curtains. €€€€
Metropole Hotel
Riva degli Schiavoni 4149, Castello
Tel: 041-520 5044
www.hotelmetropole.com
This sumptuous 16th-century patrician residence is decorated in lavish Venetian style and dotted with well-chosen antiques, and has a more intimate feel than some of the grand hotels. There are beautiful views over courtyards and

the lagoon, and the MET restaurant has all of two Michelin stars. €€€€

Boutique Hotels

DD724
Dorsoduro 724
Tel: 041-277 0262
www.thecharminghouse.com
This intimate design hotel, named after its postcode, is a softly lit urban retreat, with attention to every detail in the blending of chic modern style and the Venetian setting; expect geometric lines, and muted earth colours. Attached to it there are now stunning suites (i-Qs) and apartments (DD694). €€€–€€€€

PRICE CATEGORIES

Price categories are for a double room in mid-seaon without breakfast:
€ = up to €100
€€ = €100–160
€€€ = €160–300
€€€€ = more than €300

ABOVE: enjoy views of Venice from your pool.

Hilton Molino Stucky
Giudecca 810
Tel: 041-272 3311
www.molinostuckyhilton.com
A recent addition to Venice's upscale hotels, this giant former flour mill was transformed into a luxurious Hilton in 2007. It includes over 500 rooms (with 50 suites) and Venice's largest conference centre; the decor is a little lighter than Venetian traditional, and there are five restaurants and bars, a rooftop pool and a luxurious spa. €€€–€€€€

Locanda Orseolo
Corte Zorzi 1083, San Marco
30124 Venice
Tel: 041-520 4827
www.locandaorseolo.com
A charming, friendly, family-run guesthouse in a carefully restored Venetian house with exceptionally helpful staff close to San Marco. Cosy Venetian-style rooms overlook the canal or courtyard. €€–€€€

Venissa
Fondamenta Santa Caterina, Isola di Mazzorbo
Tel: 041-527 2281
www.venissa.it
Run by the Bisol Prosecco dynasty, this chic island guesthouse occupies the former buildings of a wine estate on Mazzorbo island, off Burano. There's also a gourmet restaurant, which revels in creative cuisine (gastro menu €60). Take *vaporetto* 41/42 from Fondamenta Nuove to Burano, then cross the footbridge to Mazzorbo. €€–€€€

Mid-Range

Hotel Bucintoro
Riva San Biagio 2135, Castello
Tel: 041-528 9909
www.hotelbucintoro.com
Spectacular views over the Riva degli Schiavoni, the Basin of San Marco and San Giorgio Maggiore are a special plus at this plush little family-run hotel on the waterfront, with just 20 comfortable rooms and suites, and could justify the often lofty prices. Service is attentive. €€€€

Hotel Flora
Calle dei Bergamaschi 2283/A, San Marco
Tel: 041-520 5844
www.hotelflora.it
This friendly 43-room hotel is in a quiet alley off a shopping street just five minutes' walk from San Marco. Art Nouveau-style touches, such as the staircase, are particularly appealing; bedrooms vary enormously, but the best have lovely views, and all have good modern facilities. There's a secluded garden-bar that's a great setting for breakfast. €€–€€€

Hotel Giorgione
SS Apostoli 4587
Tel: 041-522 5810
www.hotelgiorgione.com
Situated near the Ca'd'Oro, San Marco and the Rialto, this traditional hotel has an interior that's a tribute to Venetian style, with lots of chandeliers and Murano glass. Superior rooms are considerably bigger than standard ones; the restaurant, Osteria Giorgione, is very good. €€–€€€

Hotel La Fenice et des Artistes
Campiello della Fenice 1936, San Marco
Tel: 041-523 2333
www.fenicehotels.com
This individual hotel is very close to La Fenice opera, and has traditionally been popular with singers and musicians. Rooms are traditionally styled but each one is different, the restaurant is elegant, and very variable rates make this one of Venice's unusual bargains. €€–€€€

Hotel Saturnia and International
Calle Larga XXII Marzo 2398, San Marco
Tel: 041-520 8377
www.hotelsaturnia.it
A distinctive hotel in a 13th-century palace close to a busy shopping street by Piazza San Marco. The hotel has a medieval air, which, depending on taste, comes across either as romantic or austere. Rooms are intimate and comfortable. €€€

Pensione Accademia Villa Maravege
Fondamenta Bollani 1058, Dorsoduro
Tel: 041-521 0188
www.pensioneaccademia.it
In the Dorsoduro district within easy walking distance of the Accademia, this remodelled Gothic palace has an intimate charm, with delightful gardens front and back, and its 27 traditional rooms and suites are plushly comfortable. Reserve months in advance. €€€

San Cassiano Ca' Favretto
Calle della Rosa, Santa Croce 2232
Tel: 041-524 1768
www.sancassiano.it
On the Grand Canal, this converted 14th-century palazzo was once the residence of 19th-century painter Giacomo Favretto, and retains the romantic style of an upper-class Venetian home. About half the rooms have canalside views, but they vary a lot in size and attractions; the stairs are steep and there's no lift. But, the hotel has its own jetty, so you can arrive in style in a gondola. €€€–€€€€

Hotels on the Lido

Grand Hotel Excelsior
Lungomare Marconi 41
Tel: 041-526 0201
www.hotelexcelsiorvenezia.com
This huge five-star beach hotel is the grandest on the Lido, its impressive facade reminiscent of a Moorish castle. Attractions include numerous sports facilities and a free launch service into Venice. Open Apr–Oct only. €€€€

Hotel des Bains
Lungomare Marconi 17
Tel: 041-526 5921
http://desbains.hotelinvenice.com
This prestigious four-star hotel is remembered for its role in Thomas Mann's *Death in Venice* and still finds favour with stars who flock to the September Venice Film Festival. Atmospheric and characterful, it has a private beach. Open Apr–Oct only. €€€–€€€€

Other Options

Given the high cost of Venetian hotels, apartments, particularly for a family or small group, can be an attractive good-value option.

Monastery Stays
www.monasterystays.com
Several religious orders in Venice have hostels with simple, comfortable rooms, many with private bathrooms, that are open to guests of all kinds. Some incorporate Gothic cloisters and gardens. The same website also books monastery hostels in other parts of Italy, including Florence and Rome. €–€€

Venetian Apartments
271 Regent Street, London W1B 2ES
Tel: 020-3178 4180
www.venice-rentals.com
London-based Venetian Apartments has a wide selection of individual apartments on offer. €€–€€€

THE VENETO

At the top end of the market, the Veneto has a good selection of Palladian villa hotels, and is also home to several of Italy's most prestigious ski resorts.

Asolo and area

Hotel Villa Abbazia
Via IV Novembre, Follina
Tel: 0438-971 277
www.hotelabbazia.it
An elegant hotel in a tranquil village in the midst of Prosecco wine country, equally convenient for visiting Palladian villas and Venice. This welcoming patrician villa has frothy, boudoir-style bedrooms, a cosy, family-run feel and a noted gourmet restaurant (try the radicchio risotto). €€€
Hotel Villa Cipriani
Via Canova 298, Asolo
Tel: 0423-523 411
www.villaciprianiasolo.com
This luxurious ochre-washed Palladian villa was once the home of Robert Browning. Set in the low Veneto hills, the romantic Cipriani has a welcoming, lived-in feel, and its pastel-coloured bedrooms overlook manicured grounds. €€€€

Bassano del Grappa

Bonotto Hotel Belvedere
Piazzale Giardino 14

Tel: 0424-529845
www.bonotto.it
Some rooms in the centrally located Belvedere are nicely old-fashioned, while others are more modern, with a bit less character. Service is charming, and the hotel has a noted restaurant. €€–€€€

Padua (Padova)

If Venice is fully booked or too pricey, consider making Padua your base, as it has much to offer, and Venice is only a short train ride away.
Hotel Majestic Toscanelli
Via dell'Arco 2
Tel: 049-663 244
www.toscanelli.com
This cosy traditional hotel lies in the heart of the old quarter, close to Piazza delle Erbe. Some of the 32 rooms are lovely, if rather small. There is no restaurant, but the hotel is handy for exploring historic Padua, including the local osterie and boutiques. €€–€€€

Treviso

19 Borgo Cavour – Design Bed and Breakfast
19 Borgo Cavour
Tel: 0422-419 145
www.designbedandbreakfast.it
Make sorties to Venice (20 minutes away by train) from

this charmingly arty B&B in a 17th-century house in historic Treviso, with a walled garden. Owner Marta also advises on trendy bars and plans unusual cultural and foodie trails, including tours of Palladian villas. €€

Verona

Hotel Giulietta e Romeo
Vicolo Tre Marchetti 3
Tel: 045-800 3554
www.giuliettaeromeo.com
In the historic centre, close to the Roman Arena, this is a popular, good-value hotel. The 50 comfortable rooms are decorated in good taste and have spacious bathrooms; there's no restaurant, but plenty of good options in the surrounding streets. €€–€€€
Hotel Victoria
Via Adua 8
Tel: 045-590 566
www.hotelvictoria.it
In the heart of the old quarter of Verona, this historic 12th-century palazzo has been creatively yet sensitively converted. The bedrooms are inviting, combining traditional style and modern fittings, and the reception rooms have original Roman and medieval features. The staff are helpful. €€€

Vicenza

Hotel Giardini
Viale Giuriolo 10
Tel: 0444-326 458
www.hotelgiardini.com
This recently renovated albergo is well located in the centre of Vicenza. It's modern, comfortable and offers good value for money, and the owners are especially helpful and keen to please. €€
Hotel Villa Michelangelo
Via Sacco 35, Arcugnano, near Vicenza
Tel: 0444-550 300
www.hotelvillamichelangelo.com
In a beautiful location in Arcugnano, 7km (4½ miles) south of Vicenza, this huge and handsome 18th-century villa surveys the vine-clad slopes from its eyrie on a hill, and is now a luxurious retreat. La Loggia restaurant serves refined local cuisine, and there's a gorgeous swimming pool in the gardens. €€€

FRIULI-VENEZIA GIULIA

Trieste

Grand Hotel Duchi d'Aosta
Piazza Unità d'Italia 2
Tel: 040-760 0011
www.duchi.eu
This luxurious hotel, first

opened in Habsburg times in 1873, has an imposing location in the centre of Old Trieste. It's dignified and a little old-fashioned, with a magnificent spa and swimming pool (the "Thermarium"), and rooms are large and well appointed. €€€–€€€€
NH Trieste
Corso Cavour 7
Tel: 040-760 0055
www.nh-hotels.com
This modern business-oriented hotel has all the usual reliable comforts of the NH chain, with efficient,

helpful service. The downside can be the anonymous, functional decor, but on the plus side are the excellent-value rates. €–€€

Udine

Astoria Hotel Italia
Piazza XX Settembre 24
Tel: 0432-505 091
www.hotelastoria.udine.it
In the historic centre of Udine, this peaceful spot combines excellent modern comforts with a little more character than most

business hotels, and the stylish restaurant serves delicious local cuisine. The same owners also have a slightly simpler, more economical hotel nearby, the Hotel Friuli (same website). Both offer superior value. €€–€€€

PRICE CATEGORIES

Price categories are for a double room in mid-season without breakfast:
€ = up to €100
€€ = €100–160
€€€ = €160–300
€€€€ = more than €300

TRANSPORT · ACCOMMODATION · EATING OUT · ACTIVITIES · A – Z · LANGUAGE

TRENTINO-ALTO ADIGE (SOUTH TYROL)

Trentino is best known for its ski stations in the Dolomites, such as Madonna di Campiglio. The atmosphere of this bilingual province is Germanic rather than Italian, and accommodation ranges from quaint flower-bedecked Tyrolean chalets to family-run inns and grand castles.

Cavalese

Hotel La Stua
Piazza Dante
Tel: 0462-340 235
www.hotellastua.com
A one-of-a-kind hotel in the Dolomite resort of Cavalese, popular both for winter skiing and summer rambling. It calls itself a "motorbike hotel" and it has special facilities for bikers touring the mountain valleys; non-bikers can stay too, and the wood-panelled rooms are cosy and exceptional value. Staff are very friendly, and there's a restaurant with hearty local cuisine, and even a spa. €

Cognola

Hotel Relais Villa Madruzzo
Via Ponte Alto 26, Cognola
Tel: 0461-986 220
www.villamadruzzo.it
This grand hilltop villa is set in lovely grounds just east of Trento and is more appealing than most hotels in the town itself, 3km (1½miles) away. The villa's elegant interior is matched

by attentive service and good traditional cuisine, with dishes featuring the local mushrooms. A good base for exploring Trento and the Dolomites. €€

Lana

Vigilius Mountain Resort
Vigiljoch Mountain, Lana, Val Venosta
Tel: 0473-556 600
www.vigilius.it
A style hotel in the mountains, designed as a chic chalet, Virgilius is a Zen-like lodge tuned in to its Alpine ambience, as soothing as it is functional and eco-friendly. The resort suits keen hikers, skiers and spa-lovers, and the restaurant serves cuisine that combines local ingredients with a fresh, modern approach. €€€€

Levico Terme

Grand Hotel Imperial
Via Silva Domini 1
Tel: 0461-706 104
www.imperialhotel.it
This grand, sensitively restored Habsburg villa in the traditional spa town of Levico Terme, east of Trento, is a lasting reminder of what this area must have been like under Austrian rule. The atmosphere is formal, but the impressive facilities include indoor and outdoor pools and tennis courts as well as all sorts of spa treatments. €€–€€€

Madonna di Campiglio

Biohotel Hermitage
Via Castellatto Inferiore
Tel: 0465-441 558
www.chalethermitage.com
Created with personal flair by the Maffei family, using fine natural materials throughout, this serene and welcoming hotel is one of the most fashionable places in this stylish ski resort. For summer (when prices are very accessible), there are spectacular hiking, biking and rafting possibilities in the mountains. €€–€€€
Hotel Diana
Via Cima Tosa 52
Tel: 0465-441 011
www.hoteldiana.net
This giant Alpine chalet is extremely popular during the skiing season. Bedrooms are in good taste, and facilities include a sauna, steam room and solarium. As in many other mountain resorts, guests must stay on a half-board at peak times, and many other times of the year. €€–€€€

Merano

Castel Rundegg
Schennastrasse 2
Merano
Tel: 0473-234 100
www.rundegg.com
This fairytale Tyrolean castle in landscaped grounds close to Merano is now a health and beauty farm. Some rooms have Gothic vaulting, beams and panelling; it's

atmospheric, though the style may seem contrived for some tastes. The upmarket restaurant can cope with special diets as well as Mediterranean and Germanic cuisine. Facilities include an indoor pool, and there are naturally all kinds of spa treatments. €€€
Villa Tivoli
Via Verdi 72
Tel: 0473-446 282
www.villativoli.it
Peacefully located within its own gardens, this small Art Nouveau hotel is an oasis of tranquillity, and deservedly attracts high acclaim. Rooms are understatedly pretty, the "rock lagoon" swimming pool is beautiful, and in summer meals are served on a terrace with panoramic view. €€€

Trento

Albergo Accademia
Vicolo Colico 4–6
Tel: 0461-233 600
www.accademiahotel.it
In a medieval building in the historic heart of Trento, this family-run hotel has considerable character, given by such details as wooden shutters, geranium-filled window boxes, vaulted ceilings, but bedrooms have been fully modernised. The restaurant serves good local dishes and wines, and service is obliging. €€–€€€
Hotel Buonconsiglio
Via Romagnosi 16–18
Tel: 0461-272 888
www.hotelbuonconsiglio.it
The renovation of this centrally located hotel hasn't conserved much of its traditional character, but its comfortable, well equipped, professionally run and excellent value. €–€€

BELOW: views to die for from the Vigilius Mountain Resort.

EMILIA-ROMAGNA

There's a particularly good choice of bed and breakfast accommodation in Bologna, which compares favourably with 2/3-star hotels in terms of price, atmosphere and location, but early booking is essential.

Bologna

Art Hotel Commercianti
Via De' Pignattari 11
Tel: 051-745 7511
www.art-hotel-commercianti.it
In a side street close to San Petronio, this frescoed medieval palace is home to a seductive city-centre "art hotel" combining Renaissance-style plush with modern extras. Well-restored public rooms lead to romantic bedrooms under the eaves, many of which have lovely views over the rooftops; free use of bicycles. €€–€€€

Art Hotel Orologio
Via IV Novembre 10
Tel: 051-745 7411
www.art-hotel-orologio.it
In the heart of the historic centre, and under the same ownership as the Commercianti, this former palazzo offers every comfort and excellent service.
€€–€€€

Beatrice
Via dell'Indipendenza 56
Tel: 051-246 016
www.bb-beatrice.com
Set on the main city boulevard, linking the historic centre with the station, this lofty apartment has three guest rooms, all with bathroom, and views over the rooftops from the terrace. The owners are charming, and it's well located for restaurants and sightseeing. €–€€

Break 28
Via G. Marconi 28
Tel: 333-331 3560
www.break28.it
An apartment on the top floor of a Rationalist tower with two B&B rooms and minimalist designer interior to match. The location is central, between the historic centre and the station. €–€€

Ca' Fosca Due Torri
Via Caprarie 7
Tel: 051-261 221
www.cafoscaduetorri.com
Set in the shadow of Bologna's medieval "two towers", this central two-room B&B boasts a gracious Art Nouveau-inspired interior, with breakfast served in the Art Deco winter garden. €€

Porta Saragozza
Viale Carlo Pepoli 26
Tel: 051-644 7437
http://web.tiscali.it/portasaragozza
Set in a quiet residential zone just outside the city walls, this is a charming bed and breakfast retreat; the reception rooms are studded with antiques; the two bedrooms have a shared (but spacious and modern) bathroom. €

Royal Hotel Carlton
Via Montebello 8
Tel: 051-249 361
www.monrifhotels.it
This giant modern hotel lacks any historical features but is very comfortable and close to the centre of Bologna. The professional ambience, excellent range of services and first-rate modern fittings make it a popular choice for business travellers and tourists alike.
€€€–€€€€

Ferrara

Hotel Duchessa Isabella
Via Palestro 70
Tel: 0532-202 121
www.duchessaisabella.it
This small 15th-century palazzo is the finest hotel in Ferrara, with authentic features such as inlaid ceilings and Baroque woodwork, and extravagantly ornate bedrooms full of antiques. Facilities on offer include bicycles and a horse-drawn carriage, and in summer breakfast is served in a lovely garden. €€€

Hotel Ripagrande
Via Ripagrande 21
Tel: 0532-765 250
www.ferrarahotelripagrande.com
This Renaissance palace in the heart of historic Ferrara, close to the former Jewish ghetto, has been thoroughly renovated to incorporate modern fittings, but without losing its traditional character, and the restaurant is particularly attractive. The only jarring note can be the big differences in size and quality between bedrooms, but it's good value. €€–€€€

Parma

Hotel Stendhal
Via Bodoni 3
Tel: 0521-208 057
www.hotelstendhal.it
The long-running Stendhal rejects blandness in favour of character throughout. In an 18th-century palace in the heart of town, it combines comfort and decent prices, and La Pilotta restaurant serves classic local cuisine. €€

MOH Villa Ducale
Via Moletolo 53/A
Tel: 0521-272 727
www.myonehotel.it
This veteran hotel, the original building of which was an aristocratic villa, has lately been comprehensively transformed by the My One Hotel group, which brings a stylish modern approach to Italian mid-range hotels. Facilities and service are excellent. Online rates are a great bargain. €€

Ravenna

Best Western Hotel Bisanzio
Via Salara 30
Tel: 0544-217 111
www.bisanziohotel.com
This modern, comfortable hotel lies close to the city's Byzantine monument of San Vitale. It offers marble-clad interiors, spacious rooms, good breakfasts and a pleasant garden, and since affiliating to Best Western facilities have been extensively modernised.
€€–€€€

Palazzo Manzoni
Via Ponte della Vecchia 23, San Zaccaria
Tel: 0544-554 634
www.palazzomanzoni.it
Not far behind the Adriatic coast in San Zaccaria, 15km (9 miles) south of Ravenna but a world apart, this working farm and *agriturismo* around a 15th-century mansion has seven cosy bedrooms, all with bathrooms, and superb meals featuring the estate's own wines and produce. Cookery, sailing and other courses are available. Expect rural charm, period furnishings – and bicycles. €€

Rimini and Riviera Romagnola

Carducci 76
Viale Carducci 76, Cattolica
Tel: 0541-954 677
www.carducci76.it
This curvy Art Deco villa on the coast south of Rimini is owned by the Ferretti fashion family, like Montegridolfo *(see below)*, and is the best known of the Adriatic Riviera's design hotels. Rooms are all minimalist chic, and the Vicolo Santa Lucia restaurant is very mellow. €€€–€€€€

Castello di Montegridolfo
Via Roma 38, Montegridolfo, Rimini
Tel: 0541-855 350
www.montegridolfo.com
A medieval hill village 37km (23 miles) south of Rimini, complete with drawbridge,

PRICE CATEGORIES

Price categories are for a double room in mid-seaon without breakfast:
€ = up to €100
€€ = €100–160
€€€ = €160–300
€€€€ = more than €300

TRANSPORT
ACCOMMODATION
EATING OUT
ACTIVITIES
A – Z
LANGUAGE

gatehouse and church, provides the setting for this seductive resort created by fashion designer Alberta Ferretti. Apart from the main boutique hotel itself, Palazzo Viviani, there are apartments and studios in other parts of the village, as well as fine restaurants and a lovely pool. **€€€–€€€€**

duoMo Hotel
Via Giordano Bruno 28, Rimini
Tel: 0541-24215/6
www.duomohotel.com
The concept of this much-hyped Ron Arad-designed style hotel comes complete with red lacquer doors, a bronze bar, resident DJs, bright colours throughout and many more one-off

features, all devised by one of the world's most innovative designers. It's one of the hippest spots in the Rimini summer scene, and an equally chic beach club is an integral part of the hotel. **€€€**
Hotel Il Villino
Via Ruggeri 48, Santarcangelo di Romagna

Tel: 0541-685 959
www.hotelilvillino.it
A delightful inn in a 17th-century residence in a medieval village just inland from Rimini. The tone is set by the deft mix of antiques and individual modern fittings, and there's a luscious garden full of fragrant plants. **€€**

FLORENCE

Florence has lots of good accommodation but prices are high, and rooms need to be booked well in advance. Instead of staying in the city centre, which gets very hot in summer, many head for the cooler hill villages above the city, such as Fiesole, 8km (5 miles) outside town.

Grand Hotels

Four Seasons Hotel Firenze
Borgo Pinti 99
Tel: 055-26261
www.fourseasons.com/florence/
Two Renaissance *palazzi* – the Gherardesca and the Conventino – have been converted by the Four Seasons group to become a new contender for the title of Florence's top hotel. Rooms are magnificently opulent, and special features include the gardens, dotted with follies, and the separate area of Il Conventino, a "hotel within a hotel". **€€€€**
Grand Hotel Baglioni
Piazza dell'Unità Italiana 6
Tel: 055-23580
www.hotelbaglioni.it
Open since 1903 (and entirely separate from the Baglioni hotel group), this classic hotel retains its air of discreet elegance while providing luxurious and extremely comfortable rooms that have kept up with modern needs. The Terrazza restaurant has superb views. **€€–€€€**
Grand Hotel Villa Medici
Via Il Prato 42
Tel: 055-277 171
www.villamedicihotel.com

With its huge bedrooms – some Florentine-ornate, others much more contemporary – roof-garden restaurant and garden swimming pool, this 18th-century villa-hotel offers every kind of comfort, and is in a good location near the station. **€€€–€€€€**
Hotel Savoy
Piazza della Repubblica 7
Tel: 055-27351
www.hotelsavoy.it
On one of the city's grandest squares, the Savoy is a Florentine institution that is now owned by the Rocco Forte group, which has beautifully restored and modernised it while respecting its traditional look and appeal. It remains an Italian classic in style and service, with rooms decorated in Venetian style and sumptuous restaurants. **€€€€**
Relais Santa Croce
Via Ghibellina 87
Tel: 055-234 2230
www.relaisantacroce.com
Recently restored by the stylish Baglioni group, this is an intimate palazzo for dangerous liaisons, with expansively opulent rooms that are matched by a noted restaurant, Guelfi e Ghibellini. Plus, dining packages are available with Enoteca Pinchiorri next door, the city's most sought-after restaurant. **€€€€**

Boutique Hotels

Hotel Lungarno
Borgo San Jacopo 14
Tel: 055-27261
www.lungarnohotels.com

The Lungarno hotels are a delectable group of boutique hotels and apartments clustered along the Arno, owned by the Ferragamo fashion dynasty. Each of the hotels has its own character. The **Hotel Lungarno** itself, overlooking the river, is a stylish take on a classic hotel, including a suite with canopied bed in a medieval tower. **Hotel Gallery Art** is a contemporary space with a global-fusion cuisine restaurant, and **Hotel Continentale** is hipper still, with a stunning rooftop "Sky Lounge". Suites, apartments and a villa in the hills complete the group, which has a common website and booking system. **€€€–€€€€**
Hotel Regency
Piazza Massimo d'Azeglio 3
Tel: 055-245 247
www.regency-hotel.com
This 19th-century villa is perfect for those seeking tranquillity, 5-star luxury and an intimately romantic feel. The 35 rooms are all surprisingly spacious and all different, and some have their own terraces; plus the hotel has a lovely garden, beautiful furniture, a gourmet restaurant and impeccable service. **€€€–€€€€**
JK Place
Piazza Santa Maria Novella 7
Tel: 055-264 5181
www.jkplace.com
This coolly elegant boutique hotel is the embodiment of chic, styled to blend contemporary with tradition.

Despite its understated luxury, it aims for a "home from home" style, assuming one's home has the requisite glamour, of course. Fittings are naturally state-of-the-art. **€€€€**
Palazzo dal Borgo
Via della Scala 6
Tel: 055-216 237
www.arshotels.com
Every bedroom is different in this gorgeous 15th-century palazzo: some have original frescoes, and some overlook an inner courtyard or the cloisters of Santa Maria Novella. The rooms on the lower floor have more character but the top floor has the views. The same Ars Hotels group has three more similar hotels in Florence. **€–€€**

Mid-Range

Best Western Hotel Rivoli
Via della Scala 33
Tel: 055-278 686
www.hotelrivoli.it
Conveniently close to Santa Maria Novella, this former Franciscan friary is now a comfortable family-owned hotel, with rooms overlooking gardens in the former cloisters, and a quality restaurant next door. Staff are very obliging. **€€**

Hotel Annalena
Via Romana 34
Tel: 055-222 402
www.annalenahotel.it
On the south side of the Arno not far from the Ponte Vecchio, this charming traditional hotel offers a lovely Florentine experience at a very reasonable price. The frescoed entrance leads to tasteful antique-furnished bedrooms. €–€€

Hotel Tornabuoni Beacci
Via de' Tornabuoni 3
Tel: 055-212 645
www.tornabuonihotels.com
This atmospheric hotel occupies the upper floors of a Renaissance palazzo on the most elegant shopping street in Florence. Each of its plushly styled rooms is different, and there's a very relaxing bar in a roof garden for watching the sunsets. €€–€€€

Plaza Hotel Lucchesi
Lungarno della Zecca Vecchia 38
Tel: 055-26236
www.plazalucchesi.it
This tranquil, charmingly old-fashioned hotel beside the Arno boasts superb views of Santa Croce on one side and San Miniato on the other: it's like living in a Renaissance time capsule. For all the hotel's old-world style, facilities have been well modernised, and there's an enjoyable restaurant and friendly service. €€

Florentine Hills

Pensione Bencistà
Via Benedetto da Maiano 4, Fiesole
Tel: 055-59163
www.bencista.com
Situated between Fiesole and San Domenico, this 15th-century villa is

decorated with low-key rustic good taste and attracts a loyal clientele with its peaceful grounds, pleasant summer terrace and typically Tuscan cuisine. Rooms are available on a B&B, half-board or full-board basis. Closed from mid-November to mid-March. €€

Villa La Massa
Via della Massa 24, Candeli
Tel: 055-62611
www.villalamassa.com
Some 7km (4 miles) east of Florence, this cluster of beautifully converted 17th-century mansions and gardens radiates refined luxury. There's a choice of three fine restaurants, one beside a river, and a pool, a spa and other facilities. Should you ever wish to leave, there's a free shuttle into the city. Closed mid-

November–mid-March. €€€€

Villa Le Rondini
Via Bolognese Vecchia 224, Trespiano
Tel: 055-400 081
www.villalerondini.it
Set in the hills 4km (2½ miles) from Florence, this villa has been modernised out of all recognition yet retains a great deal of character, and is surrounded by lovely grounds. The 30 bedrooms and suites are simple and comfortable, and the restaurant is excellent, serving produce from the owners' farm. What really sets the villa apart, though, are the superb views over the city, especially when enjoyed from the delightful pool amid olive groves. A shuttle service is provided to Florence. €€€

TUSCANY

Arezzo

Castello di Gargonza
Gargonza, Monte San Savino
Tel: 0575-847 021
www.gargonza.it
This meticulously restored medieval hamlet lies in the Tuscan hills between Arezzo and Siena. Rooms and apartments, all different, are spread across several houses around the village, and incorporate modern comforts while retaining their traditional character. The excellent restaurant serves Tuscan dishes, and there is a swimming pool in the grounds. €€–€€€

Hotel Patio
Via Cavour 23
Tel: 0575-401 962
www.hotelpatio.it
Innovative, special hotel in an old palazzo in the historic heart of Arezzo, carefully restored with colourful decor inspired by the work of travel writer and novelist Bruce Chatwin. The atmosphere is unique, and service very personal. €€–€€€

Grosseto and the Maremma

L'Andana
Tenuta La Badiola, Castiglione della Pescaia
Tel: 0564-944 800
www.andana.it
The former estate of Grand Duke Leopold II of Tuscany has been transformed into a refined hotel and spa by one of France's most celebrated chefs, Alain Ducasse, who also has his own vineyards here. The height of luxury. €€€€

Antica Fattoria La Parrina
Km 146 Via Aurelia, Albinia
Tel: 0564-862 626
www.parrina.it
A very impressive *agriturismo* among vineyards, olive groves and orchards on the Maremma plains. It has retained the traditional decor of a country estate, but also offers very comfortable rooms and apartments, as well as garden terraces, a pool, a farm shop and bicycles. €€€

Hotel Torre Di Cala Piccola
Strada Panoramica, Monte

Argentario, 8km/5 miles from Porto Santo Stefano
Tel: 0564-825 111
www.torredicalapiccola.com
A charming cliff-top hotel, built around a 17th-century Spanish lookout tower on the Monte Argentario peninsula. Rooms and apartments sit above a private beach, and have superb views. Open March–October. €€€

Lucca

Albergo San Martino
Via della Dogana 9
Tel: 0583-469 181
www.albergosanmartino.it
A warm, welcoming hotel with just 10 rooms in a quiet location, within the city walls a short walk from the Duomo. The staff are very helpful and provide a wide range of information to help guests enjoy the city. €–€€

Hotel Villa La Principessa
Via Nuova per Pisa 1616, Massa Pisana
Tel: 0583-370 963
www.hotelprincipessalucca.it
This rambling villa opulently decorated in stately 18th-

century style stands within its own ample park 4.5 km (3 miles) from Lucca. Bedrooms are dotted with antiques, public rooms are hung with works of art, and the traditional restaurant is similarly charming. €€–€€€

Hotel Villa Rinascimento
Via del Cimitero, Santa Maria del Guidice
Tel: 0583-378 292
www.villarinascimento.it
This beautifully restored

PRICE CATEGORIES

Price categories are for a double room in mid-seaon without breakfast:
€ = up to €100
€€ = €100–160
€€€ = €160–300
€€€€ = more than €300

17th-century villa lies on the road to Pisa, 9km (5 miles) southwest of Lucca, and has panoramic views over the surrounding hills. Interiors are simple yet lovely, some rooms are distinctly baronial, and the grounds contain a pool and olive groves. Open mid-January to end February. €€

Vallicorte
Compignano, Massarosa
Tel: (UK) +44 (0) 20 7680 1377
www.vallicorte.com
A very attractive British-owned B&B in a beautifully restored Tuscan farmhouse between Pisa and Lucca, with four spacious bedrooms and a garden swimming pool. Cookery courses are a speciality, led by local chef Gianluca Pardini. €€

Pisa

Hotel Ariston
Via Cardinale Maffi 42
Tel: 050-561 834
www.hotelariston.pisa.it
Literally in the shadow of the Leaning Tower, this upretentious hotel has been recently renovated to a high standard, and low rates make it a great bargain. €-€€

Hotel Locanda La Lanterna
Via Santa Maria 113
Tel: 050-830 305
www.locandalalanterna.com
Pleasant and friendly no-frills bed and breakfast hotel, close to the Leaning Tower, and very good value for money. €

Hotel Relais dell'Orologio
Via della Faggiola 12–14
Tel: 050-830 361
www.hotelrelaisorologio.com
Conveniently located between the Campo dei Miracoli and Piazza dei Cavalieri, this gracious 14th-century manor house has been transformed into an ornate, smartly elegant boutique hotel. With a romantic courtyard garden, it's ideal for a luxurious treat. €€€-€€€€

Royal Victoria Hotel
Lungarno Pacinotti 12
Tel: 050-940 111

www.royalvictoria.it
The most characterful hotel in the city opened in 1837, and played host to Dickens and many other Grand Tourists. Its atmosphere is unchanging, fittings are a bit elderly and some rooms are noisy, but nevertheless those overlooking the Arno are always in great demand. €€

San Gimignano and Chianti Country

Belvedere di San Leonino
Località San Leonino, Castellina in Chianti
Tel: 0577-740 887
www.hotelsanleonino.com
Imposing 15th-century country villa surrounded by olive trees and vineyards, with oak-beamed rooms, an airy, rustic-style restaurant and a pool In the garden. €€

Hotel La Cisterna
Piazza della Cisterna 23, San Gimignano
Tel: 0577-940 328
www.hotelcisterna.it
A medieval palazzo in the centre of San Gimignano, with a much-admired restaurant. One of the most atmospheric and popular hotels in town. €-€€

Hotel Pescille
Località Pescille, San Gimignano
Tel: 0577-940 186
www.pescille.it
This large manor house 3km (2 miles) southwest of San Gimignano has, like most villas, lovely Tuscan-style rooms, and the best have balconies for taking in the superb views. In the gardens there's a fine pool, and tennis courts. €€€

Tenuta di Ricavo
Loc. Ricavo 4, Castellina in Chianti
Tel: 0577-740 221
www.ricavo.com
A highly rated hotel occupying a series of rustic houses in a medieval hamlet, east of San Gimignano and 5km (3 miles) from Castellina. It's exquisitely peaceful, and the Pecora Nera restaurant has outstanding Tuscan cuisine. Open Easter–October only. €€€-€€€€

L'Ultimo Mulino
Loc. La Ripresa di Vistarenni, Gaiole in Chianti
Tel: 0577-738 520
www.ultimomulino.it
A snugly atmospheric hotel created in a 15th-century mill, with ample comforts to go with the exposed beams and old brick walls. There's a fine pool, and it's ideally placed for exploring Chianti. €€-€€€

Villa Miranda
Radda in Chianti
Tel: 055-787 4647
www.villamiranda.it
An appealing Chiantishire villa, run by the same family since the 1840s, and surrounded by their own vineyards. The owners also have a second house nearby, the Relais Santa Cristina, with slightly more luxurious apartments and double rooms (and slightly higher prices) and an especially large pool. €-€€

Villa San Paolo
Strada per Certaldo, San Gimignano
Tel: 0577-955 100
www.villasanpaolo.it
This delightful Tuscan villa is on a hillside 4 km (2½ miles) from San Gimignano, and its terraced grounds contain a pool and tennis courts. The bedrooms are very light and charming, and service is helpfully friendly. €€-€€€€

Siena

Accommodation can be scarce in Siena in summer, particularly around the time of the Palio race in July and August.

Certosa di Maggiano
Strada di Certosa 82/86
Tel: 0577-288 180
www.certosadimaggiano.com
This 14th-century Carthusian monastery is one of the oldest in Tuscany. Since the 1970s it has been a luxury hotel, adorned with antiques and with a prestigious restaurant, a fine spa, a library and a pool beside the lovely cloisters. €€€€

Hotel Garden
Via Custoza 2

Tel: 0577-567 111
www.garden-hotels.it
This 18th-century patrician villa is now a comfortable traditional hotel with formal Italian gardens and a pool. The hosts are welcoming, and La Limonaia restaurant is one of the prettiest in Siena. €€€

Palazzo Ravizza
Pian dei Mantellini 34
Tel: 0577-280 462
www.palazzoravizza.it
This atmospheric, romantic family-run villa is five minutes' walk from the historic centre of Siena, and yet feels like a country retreat. It has its own English bookshop; the breakfast room overlooks the garden, and there is a fine restaurant. Half-board encouraged in summer. €€-€€€

Villa Scacciapensieri
Strada di Scacciapensieri 10
Tel: 0577-41441
www.villascacciapensieri.it
This delightful late 18th-century villa is set on a hill 3.5km (2 miles) from Siena, and from many rooms and the classically landscaped gardens there are sweeping views over the city. Rooms vary quite a lot, but are all pretty, and there's a good-sized pool. €€-€€€€

South of Siena

Agriturismo Le Case
Castiglione d'Orcia
Tel: 0577-888 983
www.agriturismolecase.com
A delightful hilltop farmhouse overlooking the Val d'Orcia, in ideal hiking country close to Castiglione d'Orcia and the spa centres of Bagni San Filippo and Bagno Vignoni. This rural B&B is run by an English-speaking Italian couple and has 5 double rooms, each with its own bathroom, that are a wonderful bargain. €

Hotel Il Borghetto
Via Borgo Buio 7, Montepulciano
Tel: 0578-757 535
www.ilborghetto.it
A 16th-century palazzo in the heart of the Old Town of Montepulciano that has

been converted into an unassuming hotel. Rooms are small, but comfortable and full of character. Be sure to request one with views over the valley. €€

Hotel Il Giglio
Via Saloni 5, Montalcino
Tel: 0577-848 167
www.gigliohotel.com
An archetypically Tuscan, compact family-run hotel above the town walls of Montalcino, with just 12 rooms that all offer fabulous views over the lush Val d'Orcia, and equally classic Tuscan cuisine in the fine restaurant. €€

Hotel Relais Il Chiostro di Pienza
Corso Il Rossellino 26, Pienza
Tel: 0578-748 400
www.relaisilchiostrodipienza.com
A small hotel with a touch of luxurious style in a beautifully converted medieval convent, with exquisite cloister, in the heart of Pienza. The atmosphere is very welcoming; service, and the restaurant, are immaculate. €€–€€€

Locanda dell'Amorosa
Località L'Amorosa, Sinalunga
Tel: 0577-677 211
www.amorosa.it
Sinalunga is not the most attractive of Tuscan towns, but it matters little to guests at the Locanda. This lovely collection of medieval buildings is famed for its gastronomic excellence, but the romance of the rooms, courtyards and gardens (with pool) means that the bedrooms and suites are as sought after as the restaurant tables. €€€

I Savelli
Località Gallina, Castiglione d'Orcia
Tel: 0577-880 266
www.isavelli.it
An oasis of peace in the middle of the unspoilt Val d'Orcia landscape, this venerable farmhouse contains four spacious, sensitively renovated rural apartments, with kitchens, and has an outdoor pool. €€

Spa Hotels

In the last few years several new-style spa hotels and

health retreats have appeared in Tuscany to complement the region's very traditional spas, located especially around the Val d'Orcia and Bagno Vignoni, south of Siena.

Adler Thermae Toscana
San Quirico d'Orcia
Tel: 0577-889 001
www.adler-thermae.com
Set in rolling hills, this is a romantic, perfectly groomed destination spa, with inclusive t'ai chi, yoga and Pilates. It is also one of the most child-friendly resorts, with clubs and pools to entertain kids while parents indulge in serious pampering. €€€

Bagni di Pisa
Largo Shelley 18, San Giuliano Terme
Tel: 050-88501
www.bagnidipisa.com.
Between Pisa and Lucca, this atmospheric 18th-century spa and hotel is a romantic retreat (with private *hammam*). After the treatments of your choice, enjoy views of the Leaning Tower while tucking into

superb steak, pasta with truffles and Antinori wines. €€–€

Fonteverde Natural Spa Resort
Località Terme, San Casciano dei Bagni
Tel: 0578-57241
www.fonteverdespa.com.
Tuscany's most beguiling destination spa, Fonteverde is a favoured hideaway for Italian celebrities, with a seductive combination of laidback luxury and a gorgeous natural setting. The spa is equally strong in traditional and oriental treatments. €€€€

Grotta Giusti Spa Resort
Via Grotta Giusti Monsummano Terme
Tel: 0572-90771
www.grottagiustispa.com
Not far from Montecatini Golf Course, this historic spa resort appeals to couples keen to combine a few rounds with innovative spa treatments. Spread around an elegant villa, the resort offers steam treatments in a natural cavern, the *grotta*. €€€–€€€€

UMBRIA AND THE MARCHES

Assisi

Hotel Subasio
Via Frate Elia 2
Tel: 075-812 206
www.hotelsubasioassisi.com
Assisi's most famous hotel, next door to the Basilica, a privilege enjoyed over the years by the likes of Charlie Chaplin and Elizabeth Taylor. Rooms are quite simply decorated, but many have fine views and terraces. €€

Hotel Umbra
Vicolo degli Archi 6 (off Piazza del Comune)
Tel: 075-812 240
www.hotelumbra.it
A charming 13th-century palazzo, atmospherically located in the heart of Assisi. The 25 rooms are comfortable, but small and low-key, and the restaurant is excellent, with service on the garden terrace in summer. €€

Gubbio

Hotel Bosone Palace
Via XX Settembre 22
Tel: 075-922 0688
www.jpmoser.com/bosonepalace.html
Dante was once a guest in the aristocratic palace, which is now a rather grand hotel with rates that are still far lower than those current in more expensive parts of Italy. The 25 rooms are comfortable, but not all of the same standard: those overlooking the valley are the best. €–€€

Park Hotel ai Cappuccini
Via Tifernate
Tel: 075-9234
www.parkhotelaicappuccini.it
Set at the foot of the Gubbio hills, this austere 17th-century convent has been transformed into a striking luxury hotel. Modern comforts include a gourmet

restaurant, indoor pool (which opens onto a terrace in summer), and spa, as well as an impressive range of modern art. €€€

Perugia

Hotel Brufani Palace
Piazza Italia 12
Tel: 075-573 2541
www.brufanipalace.com
Recently renovated by the stylish Sina hotel group, this grand 19th-century hotel is furnished with antiques, and has a spectacular indoor pool incorporating part of an Etruscan ruin. From the restaurant terrace – where truffles are a speciality – there are lovely views across the valley. €€–€€€

Hotel Fortuna
Via Bonazzi 19
Tel: 075-572 2845
www.hotelfortunaperugia.com

This comfortable mid-range hotel has kept up with modern demands to go with its medieval dining room and cosy bedrooms, some with small terraces. The garage is a big plus point for drivers. €€

PRICE CATEGORIES

Price categories are for a double room in mid-seaon without breakfast:
€ = up to €100
€€ = €100–160
€€€ = €160–300
€€€€ = more than €300

Hotel Priori
Via dei Priori
Tel: 075-572 3378
www.hotelpriori.it
This attractive, very affordable hotel is conveniently
located in the centre of the
town, and some of its rooms
have eye-catching views.
The views are also excellent
from the huge terrace,
where breakfast is served
whenever weather allows. A
great bargain. €

Le Tre Vaselle
Via Garibaldi 48, Torgiano, Perugia
Tel: 075-988 0447
www.3vaselle.it
Umbria's foremost luxury
hotel, this historic manor
house in the village of
Torgiano is owned by the
Lungarotti wine estate.
Rooms are sumptuous, the
restaurant is one of the
region's best, and other
modern additions include
two pools and a spa. €€€

Spello

Hotel Palazzo Bocci
Via Cavour 17
Tel: 0742-301 021
www.palazzobocci.com
A stately hotel with frescoed
interiors, a stone-arched
dining room and a lovely
garden with breakfast
terrace and a tiny pool.
Rooms are not quite as
spectacular, but the best are

impressively spacious.
€€–€€€

Spoleto

Il Castello di Poreta
Località Poreta (just off the SS3
Flaminia)
Tel: 0743-274 134
www.castellodiporeta.it
An enchanting castle in
Poreta, a short drive northeast of Spoleto, rescued from
ruin by a local foundation
and now used to produce
fine olive oil, saffron and
other local specialities, which
also contains an *agriturismo*
with a fine restaurant and
two spacious, rather rustic-
chic B&B rooms. €–€€

Hotel Gattapone
Via del Ponte 6
Tel: 0743-223 447
www.hotelgattapone.it
A romantic hotel, oozing
charm and atmosphere, with
chic 1960s styling, a
curvaceous bar and picture
windows overlooking the
Ponte delle Torri. A popular
choice, so book early.
€€–€€€

Todi

Agriturismo La Ghirlanda
Località Saragano, Gualdo Cattaneo
Tel: 0742-98731
www.laghirlanda.it
The former hunting lodge of
a Todi landowner, among

vineyards and olive groves,
this villa has been turned
into a distinctly plush *agriturismo* establishment, with
luxury-standard suites and
rooms, cosy sitting rooms, a
bar, a pool overlooking the
Martani hills and lovely
terrace restaurant for sampling the estate's wines and
other specialities. €€–€€€

Urbino

Hotel Bonconte
Via delle Mura 28
Tel: 0722-2463
www.viphotels.it
This delightful villa-hotel is
within the famous walled
town, near the Ducal Palace.
Rooms and interiors are
traditionally styled and comfortable, and the restaurant
has a solid local reputation.
The local VIP hotels group
also has several more good-
value hotels in Urbino and
Pesaro. €€

Locanda della Valle Nuova
La Cappella 14, 61033 Sagrata di
Fermignano
Tel/fax: 0722-330 303
www.vallenuova.it
In gentle hills surrounded by
ancient oaks and within sight
of Urbino, this large farm
produces fine organic meat,
vegetables and wine, and
schools horses. An
unexpectedly modern
conversion has given it the

feel of a chic modern hotel,
with three rooms and two
apartments. Breads, pastas
and jams are home-made;
heating is solar or from wood
stoves, and outside there is a
lovely pool. €€

Valle Umbra

Il Chiostro di Bevagna
Corso Matteotti 107, Bevagna
Tel: 0742-361 987
www.ilchiostrodibevagna.com
A warm welcome and a good
night's sleep are guaranteed
at this serene hotel in a
converted Dominican
convent near the lovely main
square of little Bevagna, a
medieval village west of
Foligno. The owners make
everyone feel at home, and
it's an excellent base for
exploring the area. €

Hotel Villa Pambuffetti
Viale della Vittoria 20, Montefalco
Tel: 0742-379 417
www.villapambuffetti.com
In shady grounds of oak,
cedar and cypress trees, this
grand 19th-century villa just
outside Montefalco is a
peaceful and luxurious
refuge. Breakfast is served in
the courtyard in summer, and
the restaurant extends onto
the terrace on warm even-
ings. There's a garden pool,
and cookery courses on
Umbrian cuisine are a
speciality. €€–€€€

ABRUZZO AND MOLISE

Bomba

Isola Verde
Via G. Carboni 1, Lago di Bomba
Tel: 0872-860 475
This family holiday centre on
Lago di Bomba, a mountain
lake south of Pescara, contains cottages with 4–5
beds, a youth hostel and a
campsite. There's a big
swimming pool with water
slide, and fishing, mountain-
bike rides and boat trips.
€–€€

Chieti

Castello di Semivicoli
Via San Nicola 24, Cascanditella

Tel: 0871-890 045
www.castellodisemivicoli.it
The Masciarelli family, producers of some of the
Abruzzo's finest wines, have
renovated this imposing
castle in the tiny village of
Cascanditella as a stylish
rural retreat of 14 rooms and
suites, without damaging the
castello's authentic character. Vineyard tours are
naturally a speciality. €€€

Loreto Aprutino

Castello Chiola
Via degli Aquino 12
Tel: 085-829 0690
www.castellochiolahotel.com

This magnificent medieval
castle in the centre of an
ancient town inland from
Pescara has been sensitively
converted and, anywhere but
Abruzzo, would be far pricier.
Rooms are luxurious, and
other highlights include the
restaurant in the medieval
cellars and a stunning pool
overlooking much of the
Abruzzo. €€–€€€

Paganica

Villa Dragonetti
Via Oberdan 4, Paganica, 7km/4
miles from L'Aquila
Tel: 0862-680 222
www.villadragonetti.it

This hotel on the borders of
the Gran Sasso National
Park occupies a 16th-
century villa with elegant
bedrooms, a large park
with a pool, a traditional
Italian garden and a fine
restaurant focusing on local
produce. €€

Pescara

Hotel Esplanade
Piazza 1 Maggio 46
Tel: 085-292 141
www.esplanade.net
A smart hotel overlooking the beach, with spacious if rather characterless rooms that have recently been modernised. This is a reliable mid-range option that's good value for money. €€

Sporting Hotel Villa Maria
Contrada da Pretaro, Francavilla al Mare
Tel: 085-450 051
www.sportingvilllamaria.it
Among pine and olive groves outside Pescara, this former monastery is now an attractive spa hotel, with a good pool and range of treatments, that's also conveniently located for the Adriatic beaches. €€€

Santo Stefano di Sassanio

Sextantio Albergo Diffuso
Santo Stefano di Sassanio
Tel: 0862-899 112
www.sextantio.it
The restoration and revitalisation of the semi-abandoned hamlet of Santo Stefano has been a model for rural tourism and sustainable development (see page 307). There are six wonderfully atmospheric rooms in the Renaissance Palazzo delle Logge, and others in houses around the village. A memorable place. €€€

NAPLES

Best Western Hotel Paradiso
Via Catullo 11
Tel: 081-247 5111
www.hotelparadisonapoli.it
A reliable hotel in Posillipo, on a hilltop above the noise and pollution of the city. Its best asset is the panoramic view of the bay and Vesuvius from the terrace restaurant; rooms are less exciting, but good value. €€

Caravaggio Hotel
Piazza Sisto Riario Sforza 157
Tel: 081-211 0066
www.caravaggiohotel.it
In a 17th-century building near the Duomo and within walking distance of the city's most famous sights, this modernised traditional hotel has well-appointed rooms. €€–€€€

Grand Hotel Parker's
Corso Vittorio Emanuele 135
Tel: 081-761 2474
www.grandhotelparkers.com
Established in 1870, this august traditional hotel has long been considered one of Naples's finest. The best rooms have wonderful views of the bay, and there are superb restaurants and a rooftop champagne bar. €€€–€€€€

Grand Hotel Santa Lucia
Via Partenope 46
Tel: 081-764 0666
www.santalucia.it
One of a row of grand seafront hotels, in a prime position opposite the Castel dell'Ovo, which manages to be refined without being stuffy. Rooms are spacious, several have great views, and some have hot tubs. €€€

Hotel Chiaja
Via Chiaia, 216 (1st floor)
Tel: 081-415 555
www.hotelchiaia.it
A boutique-style hotel with ornately comfortable rooms in a building full of history close to Piazza Plebiscito, that is popular with musicians and artists performing at the nearby Teatro San Carlo. Staff are very helpful. €€

Parteno B&B
Lungomare Partenope 1
Tel: 081-245 2095
www.parteno.it
Homely and perfectly positioned B&B on the first floor of a palazzo next to the Villa Comunale, and with sea views from one room. €€–€€€

CAMPANIA COAST AND ISLANDS

Amalfi

Grand Hotel Convento di Amalfi
Via Annunziatella 46
Tel: 089-871 877
www.nh-hotels.com
A former monastery on the Amalfi cliffs, with delightful gardens and an Arab-Norman cloister to add to its panoramic views. It has been acquired by the NH chain, but renovation has been carried out with more style than is usual in the group's business hotels. €€€–€€€€

Hotel Luna Convento
Via Pantaleone Comite 33
Tel: 089-871 002
www.lunahotel.it
Ibsen penned much of *The Doll's House* in this converted 13th-century monastery. In summer, breakfast is served in the Byzantine cloister, and rooms and the pool area enjoy wonderful views. €€€–€€€€

Capri

Capri Palace Hotel and Spa
Via Capodimonte 2B, Anacapri
Tel: 081-978 0111
www.capripalace.com
Impeccable service and 85 tastefully luxurious rooms – four with their own swimming pools – are features of this ultra-opulent clifftop retreat. Capri's choice for the rich and famous, or a serious splurge. Closed November–March. €€€€

Villa Brunella
Via Tragara 24
Tel: 081-837 0122
www.villabrunella.it
A modestly sized, quiet hotel with a lovely flower-filled terrace and pool, comfortable family atmosphere and traditionally smart, airy rooms. The restaurant has unforgettable views over the sea and the island. €€€

Villa Sarah
Via Tiberio 3/A
Tel: 081-837 7817
www.villasarah.it
A relaxing hotel that's good value by Capri standards, in a tranquil setting, a 10-minute walk from the Piazzetta. The 20 rooms have balconies facing onto well-tended grounds, and breakfast is served on a pleasant garden terrace. €€–€€€

Ischia

L'Albergo della Regina Isabella
Piazza Santa Restituta 1, Lacco Ameno
Tel: 081-994 322
www.reginaisabella.it
Rooms at this big modern resort hotel range from tasteful, country-house chic to contemporary opulence, with plunge pools or Jacuzzis on the balconies of the best suites. Friendly staff and a superb restaurant complement a somewhat clinical spa. €€€€

Albergo Il Monastero
Castello Aragonese, Ischia Ponte
Tel: 081-992 435
www.castelloaragonese.it
Fairytale hotel in the former convent of the Castello Aragonese, at the top of soaring cliffs on a rocky islet off Ischia. The former nuns' cells have been tastefully decorated, and have incredible views, which can also be enjoyed from a lovely communal terrace. €€

Positano

Hotel Palazzo Murat
Via dei Mulini 23
Tel: 089-875 177
www.palazzomurat.it
A charming 18th-century Baroque palazzo, with bright, relatively understated traditional rooms. Recitals, concerts and exhibitions are sometimes held here, and there's the obligatory lovely garden terrace, but no pool. €€€–€€€€

Hotel Poseidon
Via Pasitea 148
Tel: 089-811 111
www.hotelposeidonpositano.it
This newly refurbished villa hotel is more charming than ever. Rooms are partly decorated with antiques, and it has Positano's first real hotel spa dotted with antiques. The pool terrace has the requisite stunning view, and a complimentary speedboat is available to whisk you to secluded coves. Closed Nov–Mar. €€€

Le Sirenuse
Via Colombo 30
Tel: 089-875 066
www.sirenuse.it
A luxury hotel in a patrician villa in Positano town, with wonderful views from the terrace, pool area and most bedrooms and delicious Campanian cuisine in the atmospheric restaurant. All kinds of facilities are on call. €€€€

Villa Franca
Via Pasitea 318
Tel: 089-875 655
www.villafrancahotel.it
First-rate, very likeable family-run hotel with pastel-pretty, comfortable rooms, most with windows and balconies looking out over the sea, and a terrace pool at the top of the hotel. €€€

Sorrento

Grand Hotel Ambasciatori
Via Califano 18
Tel: 081-878 2025
www.ambasciatorisorrento.com
One of Sorrento's most prestigious traditional hotels, with rooms of different sizes that have no great character but provide all the necessary comforts. Service is correct, and the gardens, bars and restaurants are very pretty. €€€

Grand Hotel Excelsior Vittoria
Piazza Tasso 34
Tel: 081-877 7111
www.exvitt.it
The most refined of Sorrento's grand cliff-top hotels, set among citrus trees. Most rooms have marble bathrooms and a balcony overlooking the sea or the grounds. The pool and spa are especially gorgeous, and there's a private lift down to the sea. €€€–€€€€

Hotel Rivage
Via Capo 11
Tel: 081-878 1873
www.hotelrivage.com
A great mid-range hotel on the western edge of Sorrento. Most rooms have small terraces facing the water, and while there's no pool, there is a nicely relaxing terrace. €€

PUGLIA

Puglia offers some unique accommodation options, from the delightful *trulli* (see page 340) to a *masseria pugliese*, a fortified manor house (see page 339).

Alberobello

This village is famed for its *trulli*, quaint conical stone houses.

Hotel dei Trulli
Via Cadore 32
Tel: 080-432 3555
www.hoteldeitrulli.it
Furnishings here are simple to the point of austerity, but that is all part of the fun. However, if the novelty of living in a cone does start to wear off, the pleasant grounds with swimming pool may compensate, and the hotel can suggest all sorts of visits in the surrounding area. €€–€€€

Trullidea
Via Monte San Gabriele 1
Tel: 080-432 3860
www.trullidea.com
Trullidea is made up of 25 *trulli*, dating from the 15th century, all in the centre of Alberobello. Some *trulli* are self-contained apartments, but there is a restaurant, and B&B and half-board are available. Guests can also rent bikes. €€

Cisternino/Ostuni

Il Frantoio
(5km/3 miles from Ostuni)
Tel: 0831-330 276
www.masseriailfrantoio.it
A more low-key conversion of a *masseria*, this B&B nestles in the Itria Valley, not far from medieval Ostuni, and close to the sea. Rooms are traditionally furnished and unfussily comfortable, and superb Puglian country cooking is also on offer. €€€

Savelletri di Fasano

Borgo Egnazia
Contrada Masciola
Tel: 080-225 500
www.borgoegnazia.com
A demonstration of Puglia's newly chic status, this swish spa and golf resort is in contemporary style but inspired by traditional, creamy Apulian architecture. Choose from large rooms or villas with pools and private gardens. €€€€

Masseria San Domenico
Strada Litoranea 379 (54km/33 miles from Brindisi)
Tel: 080-482 7769
www.imasseria.com
Luxurious *masseria fortificata* with ancient origins, designed as both a fortress and a farm, that is now a very comfortable rural retreat with a well-equipped spa, two swimming pools, a gym, a golf course and its own private beach. €€€€

Masseria Torre Coccaro
Contrada da Coccaro 8
Tel: 080-482 9310
www.masseriatorrecoccaro.com
This *masseria* is now a luxurious, chic yet curiously authentic Puglian country hotel. Outside, there are formal gardens, orchards, olive groves, a lake-style pool and a private beach club; inside, a subterranean Aveda spa competes with a hotel chapel, a bar in a tower, atmospheric grotto-like bathrooms, and rooms occupying vaulted towers or old hay-lofts. €€€€

CALABRIA AND BASILICATA

Cosenza

Grand Hotel San Michele
Località Bosco 8–9. Cetraro
(16km/10 miles northwest of
Cetraro)
Tel: 0982-91012
www.sanmichele.it
This hotel occupies a
magnificent setting, at the
top of a sheer cliff dropping
down to the sea on
Calabria's west coast.
There's a varied choice of
rooms or apartments, and
other facilities include golf,
tennis, a delightful pool and
a lift down to the beach. €€

Hotel Excelsior
Piazza Matteotti 14
Tel: 0984-74383
www.htlexcelsior.it
A simple but reliably decent
hotel on Cosenza's main
piazza, opened in the 1900s
and renovated in 2008
without too many innovations
in its unchanging traditional
style. €€

Maratea

Argonauti Resort
Lido di Macchia, Marina di Pisticci
Tel: 080-769 633

www.argonauti.com
This very large modern
holiday complex on the
Ionian Coast contains a
hotel, apartments and villas
of different sizes, around a
yacht marina, an enormous
swimming pool and lots of
other leisure facilities. €

**La Locanda delle Donne
Monache**
Via Carlo Mazzei 4
Tel: 0973-876 139
www.locandamonache.com
This very comfortable hotel
has been converted from a
300-year old convent.
Rooms face onto a pool
terrace and garden, and the
decor blends chic modern
design with the historic
setting. An impressive
range of activities can be
tried out in the surrounding
countryside. €€€

Santavenere Hotel
Via Conte Stefano Rivetti 1,
Fiumicello di Maratea
Tel: 0973-876 910
www.hotelsantavenere.it
In the '60s, the Santavenere
was a signature hotel in
southern Italy for the *dolce
vita*, as the leather-bound
guest book testifies. It still

has a lot of style, with a cliff-
top bar and restaurant, spas
and its own dock for yachts.
€€€€

Matera

Matera's cave hotels have
become very fashionable –
see also page 352.

Locanda di San Martino
Via di San Fiorentini 71
Tel: 0835-256 600
www.locandadisanmartino.it
To sample caveman chic,
try this special place that
incorporates a
deconsecrated church and
cosy rooms in cave
dwellings, all connected by
cunicoli, secret passages in
the rocks. There's also a
spa using hot springs, and
the hotel is in the heart of
the Sassi district. €–€€

Sassi Hotel
Via San Giovanni Vecchio 89
Tel: 0835-331 009
www.hotelsassi.it
This likeable cave hotel has
been enjoying great
success thanks to the new
attention drawn to Matera
and its cave houses as a
result of their use as a

location for Mel Gibson's
movie, *The Passion of the
Christ*. Expect a labyrinth of
Stone Age walls, carved
facades, niches and
curious-shaped courtyards,
and friendly, easygoing
service. €

Reggio di Calabria

Grand Hotel Excelsior
Via Vittorio Veneto 66
Tel: 0965-812 211
www.montesanohotels.it
Reggio's traditional leading
hotel, facing the Museo
Nazionale, the Excelsior
has recently been
modernised to incorporate
new facilities, but without
any major changes to its
opulent, heavily carpeted
decor. €€€

SICILY

Aeolian Islands

Capofaro Malvasia Resort
Via Faro 3, Isola di Salina
Tel: 090-984 4330
www.capofaro.it
This 20-room hotel feels like
the essence of the Mediterranean in its "barefoot luxury"

BELOW: Capofaro Malvasia Resort.

simplicity, with whitewashed
interiors, a stylish bar and
restaurant, a dazzling pool
and surrounded by Malvasia
vineyards. €€€–€€€€

Hotel Raya
Via San Pietro, Isola di Panarea
Tel: 090-983 013
www.hotelraya.it

A cult hotel, at once
contemporary and timeless,
on the most chic island in
the Aeolians, but still
laidback and charming.
White-walled rooms are
divided between three
houses by the beach, which
share the hip Raya Bistro
restaurant. €€€–€€€€

Agrigento

Hotel Villa Athena
Via Passeggiata Archeologica 33
Tel: 0922-596 288
www.hotelvillaathena.it
A stylish 18th-century villa
hotel very close to the
Temples, with a fine view of
the Temple of Concord.
Rooms are comfortable and
modern (though with the
usual Italian traditional
styling), and the terrace
restaurant is excellent. €€€

Cefalù

This is the chief rival as a
resort to Taormina, but
without so much luxury, so
prices are a little lower.

PRICE CATEGORIES

Price categories are for a
double room without
breakfast:
€ = under €100
€€ = €100–150
€€€ = €150–200
€€€€ = more than €200

ABOVE: view over the bay from Villa Ducale, Taormina.

Hotel Baia del Capitano
Località Mazzaforno
Tel: 0921-420 003
www.baiadelcapitano.it
Whitewashed walls and mellow colours mark the Mediterranean-chic style of this modern hotel in an olive grove 5km (3 miles) east of Cefalù. The hotel pool and garden restaurant invite you to linger, but it's also a short walk from the beach. €€–€€€

Hotel Kalura
Via V. Cavallaro 13, Località Caldura
Tel: 0921-421 354
www.hotel-kalura.com
Above the sea 2km (1¼ miles) out of town, this unfussy beach hotel has light, spacious rooms, all with balconies. There's a nice pool in the grounds, and access to a private beach. Good for families, with an emphasis on sports facilities. €€–€€€

Erice

Just outside Trapani, this lovely old village makes an excellent base for exploring the west of the island.

Baglio Santa Croce
Località Valderice
Tel: 0923-891 111
www.bagliosantacroce.it
Just outside the village of Erice on the flanks of Monte Erice, this 17th-century farmhouse with beamed ceilings and brick floors is the loveliest place to stay in this area, and also has a pool and great views towards Trapani. The same owners also have another

hotel nearby, the Hotel Ericevalle, with a slightly more modern look (same website). €€

Hotel Elimo
Via V. Emanuele 75
Tel: 0923-869 377
www.hotelelimo.it
This welcoming, cosy hotel, with touches of "boutique" individuality in the decor, has been converted from a 17th-century palazzo in the middle of Erice. Some rooms have panoramic views. €€–€€€

Ficuzza

Antica Stazione di Ficuzza
Via Vecchia Stazione, Ficuzza
Tel: 091-846 0000
www.anticastazione.it
In a village south of Palermo, this is a former railway station that once served the Bourbon kings' hunting estates. Now, it's a small rural hotel, restaurant and music venue run by an enthusiastic Sicilian jazz fan. Bedrooms, tucked under the station roof, are quiet, but with skylights rather than windows. €€

Palermo

Grand Hotel et des Palmes
Via Roma 398
Tel: 091-602 8111
www.hotel-despalmes.it
This old-fashioned, centrally located grand hotel has Art Nouveau-style public rooms and a chequered history that includes a Mafia convention on the premises, and Wagner completing

Parsifal here in 1885. The modernised rooms vary a lot in quality and size. €€€

Principe di Villafranca
Via G. Turrisi Colonna 4
Tel: 091-611 8523
www.principedivillafranca.it
This centrally located hotel has been given a makeover, with understated but very well-equipped rooms and suites and an attractive bar and restaurant. Reliable quality has made it very popular. €€€

Syracuse

Hotel Roma
Via Roma 66
Tel: 0931-465 626
www.hotelromasiracusa.it
This attractive hotel is in the heart of the lovely peninsula-island of Ortygia, the oldest part of Syracuse. Recently totally renovated, it still retains its palazzo style and has plenty of period features, and a quality restaurant. €–€€

Zaiera Resort
Contrada Zaiera, Solarino
Tel: 0931-461 046
www.zaieraresort.com
In the hills 15km/9 miles from Syracuse, this modern country resort hotel has a fine view of Mount Etna. The 41 rooms have bright contemporary styling, and there's a spa, good sports facilities and a beautiful pool. €€–€€€

Taormina

Sicily's most prestigious resort is renowned for

its luxurious villa hotels, so prices are higher than elsewhere in Sicily.

Villa Ducale
Via Leonardo da Vinci 60
Tel: 0942-28153
www.villaducale.com
This villa hotel with 17 rooms has a delightful atmosphere, with a style that mixes traditional opulence and a modern lightness of touch. The cosy mood is enhanced by a small library, and there's a romantic breakfast terrace and views of Etna from some rooms. €€€

Villa Fiorita
Via Pirandello 39
Tel: 0942-24122
www.villafioritahotel.com
An atmospheric villa above the town, with lovely garden terraces – with a swimming pool – and grand reception rooms. The bedrooms are decorated with restrained good taste, and some have balconies or even terraces. €€€

Villa Sant'Andrea
Via Nazionale 137, Taormina Mare
Tel: 0942-23125
www.hotelvillasantandrea.com
One of the largest villa hotels, the Sant'Andrea enjoys an exquisite location, overlooking the sea on the bay of Mazzarò just north of Taormina. Elegant rooms are part-decorated with antiques, the gardens are restaurant are beautiful, and an indulgent spa has recently been added to its facilities. €€€€

Vittoria

Relais Parco Cavalonga
Donnafugata, near Vittoria
Tel: 0932-619 605
www.parcocavalonga.it
This original rural retreat contains both a stylish contemporary hotel and country cottages, set around a large park near Donnafugata Castle, 10km/6 miles from the sea, but also close to Baroque Ragusa and the Nero d'Avola wine route. The estate also contains a spa and a stunning pool. €€–€€€

SARDINIA

Most beach hotels in Sardinia close from around November to late March.

Alghero

Hotel El Faro
Porto Conte
Tel: 079-942 010
www.hotelvillalastronas.com
Next to a medieval tower on the lovely bay of Porte Conte, surrounded by fine beaches and just west from Alghero, this modern 88-room hotel has a light, unfussy feel, and ample facilities including two pools and a spa. €€€

Villa Las Tronas Hotel and Spa
Lungomare Valencia 1
Tel: 079-981 818
www.hotelvillalastronas.com
This renowned hotel, in a villa first built for Italy's royal family, stands in splendid isolation on a rocky headland. Rooms have a suitably regal air, with plenty of rich fabrics, and the best have terraces with splendid views. Facilities include a sumptuous spa, and a pool above the rocks. €€€€

Arbatax

Hotel Il Vecchio Mulino
Via Parigi
Tel: 0782-664 041

www.hotelilvecchiomulino.it
Perfect for a relaxing break, this mellow 24-room hotel in an old mill has warm, stylish interiors filled with interesting artwork. The hospitality is especially warm, and the breakfasts, with home-made cakes and breads, exceptional. Open all year. €–€€

Arzachena

Lu Pastruccialeddu
PO Box 39, Arzachena
Tel: 0789-81777
www.pastruccialeddu.com
In a hilltop farm inland from the Costa Smeralda, this delightful *agriturismo* B&B looks like it was carved out of the rocks, but has lovely, comfortable rooms and a garden pool, and the owners are ultra-hospitable. €–€€

Cagliari

Hotel Miramare
Via Roma 59
Tel: 070-664 021
www.hotelmiramarecagliari.it
In a 19th-century palazzo on one of the city's main shopping streets, this imaginative hotel has quirky style in abundance. The 20 rooms and suites, each one different, blend chic modern features with the historic

BELOW: ultimate luxury at the Hotel Cala di Volpe.

structure, and the breakfast bar, with a great view of the port, is full of plants, books and huge platters of fruit. €€–€€€

Sa Domu Cheta
Via Portoscalas 30
Tel: 070-655 002
www.sadomucheta.it
A friendly, family-run little hotel in the centre of town, with just five high-ceilinged rooms combining character and modern features, including air-con. Book well ahead. €–€€

Cala Gonone

Hotel Costa Dorada
Lungomare Palmasera 45
Tel: 0784-93332
www.hotelcostadorada.it
With a delightful location on the bay of Cala Gonone, this good-value family beach hotel has everything needed for a relaxing stay, including its own boat for exploring the spectacular beauty spots along the coast.
€€–€€€

Costa Smeralda

Hotel Cala di Volpe
Cala di Volpe, Porto Cervo
Tel: 0789-976 111
www.starwoodhotels.com
One of the summits of luxury on the glitziest part of the Costa Smeralda, a complex of villas inspired by traditional Mediterranean architecture, with a raft of facilities including private yacht moorings, and a very stylish clientele. €€€€

Hotel Nibaru
Cala di Volpe, Porto Cervo
Tel: 0789-96038
www.nibaru.it
A more moderate option, still in a beautiful location, this 50-room beach hotel has a pool poised above the sea, a pleasant bars and restaurant, and rooms with terraces opening onto flower-filled gardens. €€€

Olbia

Hotel Panorama
Via Mazzini 7

Tel: 0789-26656
www.hotelpanoramaolbia.it
This recently opened hotel lives up to its name with spectacular views from many of its rooms and its rooftop terrace, ideal lounging while peering out over Olbia. The decor is much more conventional by comparison, but it's well equipped, and has an attractive spa. €€

Sant'Antíoco

Hotel Luci del Faro
Località Mangiabarche, Calasetta
Tel: 0781-810 089
www.hotellucidelfaro.com
This modern hotel complex sits in remote countryside on the west coast of Sant'Antíoco, with fine views of the nearby lighthouse. Service is excellent, and there's an inviting pool and enjoyable restaurant.
€€–€€€

Villasimius

Cala Caterina
Via Largo Maggiore
Tel: 070-797 410
www.mobygest.it
A beautiful boutique-style beach hotel in an elegantly converted villa, a short walk away from a gorgeous beach through equally lovely gardens. Rooms are decorated with colourfully arty touches, and the pool is heavenly. €€€

TRANSPORT
ACCOMMODATION
EATING OUT
ACTIVITIES
A – Z
LANGUAGE

EATING **O**UT

RECOMMENDED RESTAURANTS, CAFES AND BARS

What to Eat

Italian **breakfast** *(colazione)* is usually a light affair, consisting of a *cappuccino* and *brioche* (pastry), biscuits or crispbreads, or simply a *caffè* (black, strong *espresso*).

Lunch *(pranzo)* has traditionally been the main meal of the day, but this is gradually changing as Italy comes more into line with international trends, particularly in the north and in industrial cities. However, when Italians have the time to indulge in a long lunch, this might begin with an *antipasto* (hors d'oeuvre), followed by a *primo* (pasta, rice or soup), then a *secondo* (meat or fish, with a vegetable *contorno* or just a salad), and then *dolci* or dessert. Italians usually drink an *espresso* after lunch and sometimes a liqueur, such as *grappa, amaro* or *sambuca*. Traditionally, **dinner** *(cena)* is similar to lunch, but lighter. However, where it has become more normal to eat less at lunchtime, dinner is the main meal of the day.

Every region in Italy has its own typical dishes: Piedmont specialises in pheasant, hare, truffles and *zabaglione* (a hot dessert made with whipped egg yolks, sugar and Marsala wine). Lombardy is known for *risotto alla Milanese* (saffron and onions), minestrone, veal and *panettone* (a sweet, Christmas bread made with sultanas and candied fruits). Trentino-Alto Adige is the place for dumplings and thick, hearty soups to keep out the cold; Umbria is best for roast pork and black truffles, and Tuscany is good for wild boar, chestnuts, steak and game. Naples is the home of Mozzarella cheese and pizza and is good for seafood, and Sicily the place to enjoy delectable sweets; Sardinia has a whole range of strong cheeses and fish and seafood dishes of its own, especially featuring lobster.

Italy still claims the best ice cream in the world, as well as the Sicilian speciality *granita* (crushed ice with fruit juice or coffee).

Where to Eat

Italian restaurants go by a wide variety of names, which can be confusing – what is the difference, for example, between a *ristorante* and an *osteria*? Although *osteria* means an inn, it can refer to a chic restaurant in a gentrified rustic style. Generally, a *trattoria* suggests a relatively casual style of restaurant for everyday dining. If you don't want a multi-course meal, you could have just a single dish in a bar, a *tavola calda* or *rosticceria* (grill), but in any restaurant you can also forgo the *antipasto* and take just a *primo* and *secondo* instead.

Restaurant Listings

It is hard to generalise about prices since so much depends on the choice of dishes – even noted chefs may offer a cheaper set menu alongside the main menu. The price ranges should therefore only be used as general guidelines.

R E S T A U R A N T   L I S T I N G S

ROME

Agata e Romeo
Via Carlo Alberto 45
Tel: 06-446 6115
www.agataeromeo.it
This little temple to gastronomy has had a Michelin star for several years. Traditional and modern Roman and southern Italian cuisine are

seamlessly blended, and the wine list is among Rome's best. Vegetarians are well catered for. Reservations essential; closed Sat, Sun and Aug. **€€€€**
Agustarello
Via Giovanni Branca 98
Tel: 06-574 6585

Traditional, long-established *trattoria* specialising in real *cucina romana* based on offal. The owners use every part of the animal, and create delicious offerings such as *coda alla vaccinara* (oxtail with tomatoes, pinenuts, raisins and bitter chocolate). Popular with

locals, so reservations are recommended. Closed Sun and mid-Aug–early Sept. **€€**
Bio Restaurant
Via Otranto 53
Tel: 06-4543 4943
As its name suggests, this restaurant highlights organic and natural produce, and you can eat

very well in these calming, earth-toned surroundings. Closed Sun. €–€€

Cantina Cantarini
Piazza Sallustio 12
Tel: 06-485528
Informal, bustling taverna in the workaday Sallustiano district serving simple but very good dishes. From Thursday to Saturday evening only fish features on the menu. At other times the menu is meat-based Roman and *marchigiana* (from the Marche region). Closed Sun and two weeks in Aug. €€

Checchino dal 1887
Via di Monte Testaccio 30
Tel: 06-574 3816
www.checchino-dal-1887.com
The place for an authentic old-time family atmosphere, plus Roman cuisine of the offal variety – hardly surprising since this area, Testaccio, is the historic home of Rome's slaughterhouses and meat-processing industry. Not one for vegetarians. Reserve. Closed Sun, Mon, Aug and Christmas. €€€

Il Convivio Troiani
Vicolo dei Soldati 31
Tel: 06-686 9432
www.ilconviviotroiani.com
Run by three brothers, Il Convivio is one of the city's foremost temples to food and culinary innovation. Equal emphasis is placed on vegetables, fish and meat, always combined with the unexpected. Closed Mon lunch and Sun. €€€€

Cul de Sac
Piazza Pasquino 73
Tel: 06-6880 1094
One of the best-stocked *enoteche* (wine bars) in Rome, which also has traditional and Middle Eastern-influenced snacks, hearty soups and salads on the menu. No bookings are taken and it gets packed, so be prepared to queue. €–€€

Da Benito e Gilberto
Via del Falco 19
Tel: 06-686 7769
www.dabenitoegilberto.com
Tucked away in the Borgo area between St Peter's and the Castel Sant'Angelo, this intimate, family-run

restaurant is a great favourite with locals. Its speciality is superb fresh fish and seafood. Reservations essential. Dinner only. Closed Sun and Mon. €€€

Da Giggetto al Portico d'Ottavia
Via del Portico d'Ottavia 21A
Tel: 06-686 1105
www.giggettoalporticodottavia.it
Long a feature of the ghetto area, this is one of the most traditional of Rome's Jewish restaurants, specialising in *carciofi alla giudea* (fried artichokes), fish soups and courgette flowers in batter. The atmosphere is friendly and bustling, and the location – next to the 1st-century Portico d'Ottavia – spectacular. €€

Da Michele
Via dell'Umiltà 31
Tel: 349-252 5347
Formerly at the renowned Zi Fenizia pizzeria in the ghetto, owners Michele and Cinzia have relocated to this equally compact spot towards the Trevi fountain, where they continue to produce an amazing range of kosher pizzas (so no mixing of meat with cheese) that are among Rome's best. Only a few tables, so many people buy slices to eat in the street. Closed Fri pm and Sat. €

Dar Poeta
Vicolo del Bologna 45
Tel: 06-588 0516
www.darpoeta.com
In Trastevere, this is hailed by many as Rome's best pizzeria, with a great selection of thin Roman-style pizzas matched by rich desserts. Be prepared to queue, as bookings are not taken. €

Ditirambo
Piazza della Cancelleria 75
Tel: 06-687 1626
www.ristoranteditirambo.it
Numerous vegetarian options such as ricotta flan with raw artichokes and pomegranate vinaigrette are an unusual feature of the varied menu at this pleasant traditional restaurant in the *centro storico*. The wine list is extensive too. €€

Le Fate
Viale Trastevere 130
Tel: 06-580 0971
www.lefaterestaurant.it
This reliable and relaxed little Trastevere restaurant focuses on light, regional dishes, including salami from Lazio served with Mozzarella, or filling pasta dishes and home-made desserts. The friendly owners also have a B&B and apartments for rent nearby. €€

Il Gonfalone
Via del Gonfalone 7
Tel: 06-6880 1269
www.il-gonfalone.com
This smallish space provides a restrained gourmet experience, with lovely outdoor seating on a quiet street, superb bread and cuisine based on Roman and Neopolitan cooking with a modern twist. Closed Mon. €€€

Matricianella
Via del Leone 3–4
Tel: 06-683 2100
www.matricianella.it
For the traditional, family-run *trattoria* experience, look no further than this popular restaurant near Via del Corso. The kitchen serves up classic, no-frills Roman fare, and service is friendly. Reserve. €€

Obikà
Via dei Prefetti 26 (corner of Piazza Firenze)
Tel: 06-683 2630
www.obika.it
Rome's original "Mozzarella bar", although they serve plenty of light, fresh larger courses too, all prepared with the best ingredients. Now a chain with another branch on Campo de' Fiori and others around the world; the setting is minimalist-hip, but welcoming, and its lunch menus are great value. €–€€

Il Pagliaccio
Via dei Banchi Vecchi 129A
Tel: 06-6880 9595
www.ristoranteilpagliaccio.com
Chef Anthony Genovese's smart little restaurant has a shortish but inventive menu incorporating international influences, and with an

emphasis on beautiful presentation and quality ingredients, while French pastry chef Marion Lichtle provides delectable desserts. Reserve. Closed Sun and Mon, and dinner only July–mid-Sept. €€€€

La Pergola
Rome Cavalieri Hotel
Via A. Cadlolo 101
Tel: 06-35091
www.romecavalieri.com/lapergola
This sophisticated rooftop restaurant at the grand Rome Cavalieri hotel is renowned as one of Italy's finest, and under head chef Heinz Beck has attained all of three Michelin stars. The views are spectacular, the interior sumptuous and the menu a gourmet dream, if naturally of a price to match. Dinner only; reservations essential. Closed Sun, Mon and part of Jan and Aug. €€€€

Piperno
Via Monte de' Cenci 9
Tel: 06-6880 6629
www.ristorantepiperno.com
Traditional yet discreetly upmarket *trattoria* on a little piazza in the heart of the ghetto district. The menu features classic Roman dishes such as veal and offal. Closed Sun dinner, Mon, part of Aug and Christmas. €€€–€€€€

Roscioli
Via dei Giubbonari 21
Tel: 06-687 5287
www.salumeriaroscioli.com
This deli-cum-restaurant has long had rave reviews for the quality of its authentic produce and its inventive food combinations. Try their signature dish, *tonnarelli* with grouper, pistachios and fennel seeds. €€–€€€€

Il Sanpietrino
Piazza Costaguti 15
Tel: 06-688 06471
www.ilsanpietrino.it

Located in the former stables of an 18th-century palazzo, Oscar di Mauro's acclaimed restaurant offers a mixture of ghetto food and other Roman dishes, served with award-winning wines from his family vineyard. Reserve. Dinner only. Closed Sun. €€€

Il Simposio
Piazza Cavour 16
Tel: 06-320 3575
This Art Nouveau-style restaurant adjoins the Bacchanalian paradise of the same owners' Costantini

enoteca (wine bar). The cellars hold over 4,000 bottles of wine to match the delicious, creative food. Reserve. Closed Sun and Aug. €€€–€€€€

Sora Lella
Via Ponte Quattro Capi 16
Tel: 06-686 1601
www.soralella.com
This celebrated Roman trattoria is in a palazzo on the magical Isola Tiberina, the "Tiber Island" next to Trastevere, and has long been renowned as one of the places to find traditional

cooking and home-made pasta, even though it now has a notably fashionable air. Reserve. Closed Sun and Aug. €€€

Taverna Angelica
Piazza Amerigo Capponi 6
Tel: 06-687 4514
www.tavernangelica.it
A warm and welcoming establishment, ideal for a romantic candlelit dinner, in the labyrinth of lanes of the Borgo area north of St Peter's. A constantly changing menu reflects the seasons, with an emphasis

on seafood. Reserved. Dinner only except Sun. €€–€€€

Trimani Wine Bar
Via Cernaia 37B
Tel: 06-446 9630
This very popular enoteca is the place to enjoy a glass or two chosen from the huge selection of wines on the lists of Trimani, one of Rome's leading wine merchants, along with tasty snacks such as torte salate (savoury tarts). There's also a fine daily specials menu. Closed Sun and Aug. €–€€

ROME'S ENVIRONS

Frascati, of wine fame, is one of the best known of the hill towns just outside the city where Romans traditionally go in summer to escape the heat, and is the place to eat porchetta (suckling pig). Nemi has a strawberry festival, where the red fruit is served in white wine. Castel Gandolfo is the place to try guanciale (similar to bacon), smoked with olive, oak and laurel wood and served with red pepper.

Frascati

Cacciani
Via A. Diaz 13
Tel: 06-940 1991
www.cacciani.it
In the centre of Frascati, with views over the hills from the terrace, Cacciani has refined local dishes and fish specialities, and, of course, Frascati wine. Closed Mon, 2 weeks in Jan and 2 weeks in Aug. €€€

Ostia

Allo Sbarco di Enea
Vicolo dei Romagnoli 675, Ostia Antica
Tel: 06-565 0034
A perennially popular restaurant by the water in Rome's seaside port of Ostia, with excellent gamberoni and other seafood to go with the setting. Closed Mon and Feb. €€€

Palestrina

Hotel Stella
Piazzale della Liberazione 3
Tel: 06-953 8172
www.hotelstella.it
Homely and unpretentious, the restaurant at this long-established hotel has a high reputation for its regional cuisine, prepared with care and attention to detail. €€

Tarquinia

Ristorante Arcadia
Via Mazzini 6
Tel: 0766-855 501
The young owners offer a warm welcome in this very pleasant, quite smart restaurant, very near Tarquinia's Etruscan Museum. Fish is the speciality. Closed Mon (except July–Aug) and Jan. €€–€€€

Tivoli

Ristorante Vesta
Piazza della Mole 19
Tel: 0774-333 786
A fresh, original restaurant with a contemporary take on Italian cuisine; specialities include lots of fish, and home-made variations on the beloved tiramisù dessert. Dinner only except Sun; closed Wed. €€–€€€

Civitavecchia

Trattoria L'Angoletto
Via P. Guglielmotti 2
Tel: 0766-32825
Good, traditional seafood, soups and home-made pasta, and a warm welcome in an attractive setting near the promenade. Closed Mon and Christmas. €€

Nemi

La Taverna
Via Nemorense 13
Tel: 06-936 8135
This inn is rustic and charming and serves traditional food, including satisfying, properly prepared Roman pizzas. Reserve. Closed Wed and Jan. €€

MILAN

For additional chic Milan restaurants, see page 215.

Al Mercante
Piazza di Mercanti 17
Tel: 02-805 2198
www.ristorante-milano-centro.it
A friendly restaurant on the lovely Piazza di Mercanti, specialising in local cuisine, with a rich selection of antipasti. In summer, the historic loggia is a very pleasant place to eat.

Reserve. Closed Sun, Aug and 1–7 Jan. €€€

Alla Cucina delle Langhe
Corso Como 6
Tel: 02-655 4279
www.trattoriaallelanghe.com
This exclusive traditional Piedmontese restaurant offers such typical specialities as tartufo bianco (white truffle) and delicious polenta dishes, in a snugly elegant setting.

Reservations recommended. Closed Sun and Aug. €€€

Armani/Nobu
Via Pisoni 1
Tel: 02-6231 2645
www.armaninobu.it
Innovative cuisine in the very Milanese-chic setting of the Emporio Armani store; there's a sushi bar, and the restaurant's fusion-food menu blends flavours from Japan, Latin America

and Europe. Reserve. Closed Sun and Mon lunch, Aug and Christmas. €€€–€€€€

Bice
Via Borgospesso 12
Tel: 02-7600 2572
www.bicemilano.it
A Milanese institution of the best kind: a reliable top-class restaurant serving exquisite classic Italian dishes, including some

EATING OUT ♦ 405

TRANSPORT

ACCOMMODATION

EATING OUT

ACTIVITIES

A – Z

LANGUAGE

Tuscan specialities, and with friendly, attentive service. During the fashion weeks or other big events in town, Bice is nearly always full. Reserve. Closed Sun dinner, and Aug. €€€–€€€€

Bistrot Duomo
La Rinascente, 7th floor, Via San Raffaele 2, 7th floor
Tel: 02-877 120
This modern restaurant is on the top floor of La Rinascente, Milan's swanky department store, and can be enjoyed as much for its view of the Duomo as for its reliable food. Milanese specialities predominate but classic Italian cuisine is also on offer. Closed Sun and 3 weeks in Aug. €€€

Boeucc
Piazza Belgioioso 2
Tel: 02-7602 0224
www.boeucc.com
This temple of old-school gastronomy is a Milanese institution. The atmosphere is formal; classic Italian cuisine is leavened with Milanese dishes, and there is a cool portico for summer dining. Dress smartly, and reserve. Closed Sat and Sun lunch, Aug and Christmas/New Year. €€€€

El Brellin
Vicolo del Lavandai
Alzaia Naviglio Grande
Tel: 02-5810 1351
www.brellin.com
This romantic corner of old

Milan, incorporating a former washhouse beside a canal, has a suitably traditional menu, celebrating Milanese cuisine in all its forms, including several variations on risotto. Closed Sun dinner. €€

Cracco
Via Victor Hugo 4
Tel: 02-876 774
www.ristorantecracco.it
With two Michelin stars, this bastion of gourmet cuisine is under the guidance of one of Italy's finest young chefs, Carlo Cracco. It's very stylish, expensive and outstanding. Reservations essential. Closed Sun and lunch Sat, Mon, and Christmas/New Year. €€€€

Demetria Café
Viale Bligny 3
Tel: 02-8738 8200
www.ristorantecracco.it
A stylish modern combination of enoteca (wine bar) and casual café-restaurant, with olives, cheeses, cold cuts, polenta, spelt soup, lasagne and ravioli all on the menu. Closed Sat dinner and Sun. €

Il Luogo di Aimo e Nadia
Via Montecuccoli 6
Tel: 02-416 886
www.aimoenadia.com
Acclaimed as one of the top places to eat in Italy, with a Michelin star, Aimo Moroni's restaurant differs from other top Milanese restaurants

with its light dining room, decorated with modern art, and fresh, less formal approach. Some Tuscan influence characterises the deceptively simple but superbly executed dishes. Reservations essential. Closed Sat lunch, Sun, Aug and Christmas. €€€€

Sadler
Via Ascanio Sforza 77
Tel: 02-5810 4451
www.sadler.it
The opulent domain of one of Italy's most esteemed chefs, Claudio Sadler, is smartly modern, providing a luxuriously stylish backdrop to his very refined creative cuisine, including many uses of white truffles (in season). Service is impeccable; reservations essential. Dinner only, closed Sun and part of Jan and Aug. €€€€

Sadler Chic'n Quick
Via Ascanio Sforza 77
Tel: 02-8950 3222
www.sadler.it
The name sums up the concept of Sadler's "modern trattoria", offering dishes that are naturally simpler than those in the main restaurant, but still innovative, and at much more accessible prices. The daily set menu is a wonderful bargain. Closed Sun, Mon lunch, and part of Jan and Aug. €€–€€€

Savini
Galleria Vittorio Emanuele 11
Tel: 02-7200 3433
www.savinimilano.it
Formal decor, professionalism and classic Italian cuisine can be expected from a restaurant that has been perfecting its formula since 1867, in the spectacular setting of the Galleria Vittorio Emanuele. However, the effect can be marred by supercilious service and a chilly atmosphere. Reserve. Closed Sun, Sat lunch, Aug and first week of Jan. €€€–€€€€

Torre di Pisa
Via Fiori Chiari 21
Tel: 02-874 877
www.trattoriatorredipisa.it
On the liveliest street in the elegant Brera district, this intimate, appealing Tuscan trattoria has exceptional cuisine based on seasonal produce. Arrive early to allow time for a drink in one of Brera's numerous nearby bars. Closed Sat lunch. €€€

Trattoria Aurora
Via Savona 23
Tel: 02-8940 4978
In the Navigli district, this atmospheric, very popular restaurant specialises in Piedmontese cuisine, and has tables in a delightful garden terrace in summer. Closed Sun dinner. €€–€€€

LOMBARDY AND THE LAKES

Da Vittorio
Via Cantalupa 17
Tel: 035-681 024
www.davittorio.com
One of Italy's top restaurants, in the "gastrohotel" of the hugely talented Cerea brothers. Their cooking, based on local cuisine, is superb, service is impeccable, and the setting is delightful. Closed Wed and Aug. €€€€

Lio Pellegrini
Via San Tomaso 47
Tel: 035-247 813
www.liopellegrini.it

In an elegantly modernised former sacristy, chef Lio Pellegrini presents a partly Tuscan-inspired menu, with tables in an exquisite garden in summer. Reservations essential. Closed Mon and Tues lunch. €€€€

Taverna Colleoni dell'Angelo
Piazza Vecchia 7, Città Alta
Tel: 035-232 596
www.colleonidellangelo.com
Lombard specialities are served in a 14th-century palace, which has been used as a restaurant since 1740. The atmosphere is

calm and relaxing, and service excellent. Closed Mon. €€€

Trattoria del Teatro
Piazza Mascheroni 3, Città Alta
Tel: 035-238 862
This old-fashioned restaurant serves simple but delicious traditional food, including many dishes that make excellent use of the local favourite polenta, in a cosy atmosphere. Closed Mon. €–€€

Cremona

Martinelli
Via degli Oscasali 3

Tel: 0372-30350
An elegant restaurant in a venerable palazzo that's a timeless local favourite, specialising in traditional cuisine and fish dishes. Booking in advance is recommended. Closed Sun, Wed dinner and Aug. €€€

PRICE CATEGORIES
The price of a three-course meal for one (not including wine):
€ = under €25
€€ = €25–50
€€€ = €50–80
€€€€ = more than €80

Lake Garda

Vecchia Lugana
Piazzale Vecchia Lugana 1,
Sirmione
Tel: 030-919 012
www.vecchialugana.com
Centred on a venerable inn
– much extended – dating
from around 1500 near the
Sirmione peninsula, this
very refined *trattoria* on the
lake has been a favourite
of Maria Callas and
numerous Italian literary
figures. The award-winning
cuisine features delectable
flavours, in a gorgeous

setting. Closed early Jan–
mid-Feb; Nov open only Fri
dinner, Sat and Sun.
€€€–€€€€
Villa Fiordaliso
Corso Zanardelli 150, Gardone
Riviera
Tel: 0365-20158
www.villafiordaliso.it
The luxurious lakeside villa
where Mussolini entertained
his mistress Claretta Petacci
is now one of Italy's most
opulent "gastrohotels". The
beautiful restaurant is a
showcase for creative
cuisine, with subtle
combinations of ingredients

exquisitely presented. A
great place for a special
occasion. Closed Mon and
Tues lunch, and Nov–mid-
Feb. €€€€

Mantua (Mantova)

**Il Cigno Trattoria dei
Martini**
Piazza Carlo d'Arco 1
Tel: 0376-327 101
Set on a lovely piazza in the
heart of Mantua, in a fine
old building with lofty
shuttered windows, Cigno
offers delicious regional
food and excellent service.

Reserve. Closed Sun, Mon
and Aug. €€€

Pavia

Il Cigno
Via Massacra Pasquale 2
Tel: 0382-301 093
Well-presented modern
cuisine as well as traditional
local standards are served
in this small, intimately
atmospheric restaurant in
the historic town of Pavia,
with attentive, courteous
service. Reserve. Closed
Mon, Aug and early Jan.
€€–€€€

PIEDMONT

Piedmontese cuisine is
considered one of the best
in Italy, and worthy of a
gastronomic pilgrimage in
itself. The region produces
several of Italy's best wines,
such as Barolo and
Barbaresco, and the Langhe
area south of Asti and Alba
is renowned for its
treasured white truffles and
other gastronomic delights.

Alba and the Langhe

**Hotel-Ristorante Villa San
Carlo**
Corso Divisioni Alpine, Cortemilia
Tel: 0173-81546
www.hotelsancarlo.it
Carlo Zarri, chef, sommelier
and cookery book author,
concocts superb
Piedmontese fare in his
family's modest hotel (see
page 385) and restaurant in
Alba's truffle country.
Depending on the season,
expect creamy risotto,
dishes with local hazelnuts,
cheeses or Barolo wine, or
tajarin pasta in white
truffles. Short wine and
cookery courses are offered
too. €€–€€€
Locanda del Pilone
Località Madonna di Como 34
(5km/3 miles southeast of Alba)
Tel: 0173-366 616
www.locandadelpilone.com
Overlooking hills and
vineyards, this elegant
Michelin-starred restaurant

specialises in local cuisine
– in autumn the *crema al
parmigiano e tartufo bianco
d'Alba* (parmesan and white
truffle soup) is sublime.
There are also six
bedrooms, for gourmet
stopovers. Reservations
essential. Closed Tues and
Wed lunch, Christmas–mid-
Jan and late July–Aug. €€€€

Asti

L'Angolo del Beato
Vicolo Cavallieri 2
Tel: 0141-531 668
www.angolodelbeato.it
Entering the discreet
doorway of this small,
family-run restaurant feels
like going into someone's
home, but inside the decor
is stylish, and the
seasonally based regional
cuisine highly sophisticated.
Rabbit often features in
winter months, presented in
many surprising ways.
Closed Sun, Christmas/New
Year and 3 weeks in Aug.
€€€

Barolo

Locanda nel Borgo Antico
Via Boschetti 4
Tel: 0173-56355
www.locandanelborgo.com
Highly acclaimed restaurant
in a former country
nobleman's house
surrounded by vineyards
outside Barolo. Chef

Massimo Camia's forte is
creative Piedmontese
cuisine, and the menu
varies according to the
season. The wine selection,
local, Italian and
international, is spectacular.
€€€€

Rivoli

Combal.Zero
Piazza Mafalda di Savoia
Tel: 011-956 5225
This strikingly modern
restaurant in the Castello di
Rivoli (home of the Museo
d'Arte Contemporaneo) is
the place to find
adventurous gourmet
cuisine created by chef
Davide Scabin, a culinary
experimenter in the style of
Ferran Adrià or Heston
Blumenthal. In season the
local truffles, especially, turn
up in all kinds of original
combinations. Reservations
essential. Closed Sun, Mon.
€€€€

Turin

Al Garamond
Via Giuseppe Pomba 14
Tel: 011-812 2781
www.algaramond.it
This elegant restaurant in
the heart of the city offers
creative modern cuisine in a
mellow setting. Antipasti are
a speciality, and set menus
are excellent value. This is
one of Turin's most popular

restaurants, so always
reserve. Closed Sat lunch
and Sun. €€€
Caffè Torino
Piazza San Carlo 204
Tel: 011-545 118
A historic café with gilded
mirrors, frescoed ceiling and
twinkling chandeliers where
little has changed since it
opened in 1903. Expensive,
but great for a cocktail or
maybe a vermouth – a
Torinese invention. €€
La Pista del Lingotto
Via Nizza 270
Lingotto
Tel: 011-631 3523
www.pista.eu
Taking its name from the
rooftop car test track on top
of the former Fiat car plant
at Lingotto centre (as seen
in the *Italian Job*), now
transformed by architect
Renzo Piano into a stunning
design hotel (Le Méridien
Lingotto), this smart terrace
restaurant beside the track
has spectacular views of the
city and the snow-peaked
Alps in the distance.
Excellent menus mix
traditional Piedmontese
dishes with original
delicacies, and there's a
well-chosen wine list.
Reserve. Closed Sun, lunch
Sat, and 1 week in Jan and
3 weeks in Aug. €€€
Ristorante del Cambio
Piazza Carignano 2
Tel: 011-546 690
This grand local institution,

first opened in 1757, is one of the most impressive-looking restaurants in Italy, with elaborate Baroque decor. Staff are formally correct, and the specialities include superb ravioli and a spectacular seafood *fritto misto* (which must be pre-ordered). Reservation essential. Closed Sun and Aug. €€€€

Sotto La Mole
Via Montebello 9
Tel: 011-817 9398
www.sottolamole.eu
Opposite the Museo Nazionale del Cinema,

overlooked by the Mole Antonelliana, this comfortable, brick-vaulted little restaurant is very popular, with Piedmontese classical and innovative dishes to tantalise the taste buds. Reserve. Closed Mon. €€

Spada Reale
Via Principe Amedeo 53
Tel: 011-817 1363
This modern *trattoria* and restaurant is especially popular with young professionals, both for its eclectic mix of Tuscan and Piedmontese cuisine and

for its lack of stuffiness. Reservations recommended. Closed Sun and Aug. €€-€€€

Tre Galline
Via Bellezia 37
Tel: 011-436 6553
www.3galline.it
Tre Galline is a typical old-fashioned *piola* or Piedmontese inn, which has recently been refurbished. The atmosphere is warm and friendly, and as well as hearty Piedmontese specialities there are lighter salads, pastas, soups and cheeses. Reservation

recommended. Closed Sun, Mon lunch and Aug. €€

Le Vitel Etonné
Via San Francesco da Paola 4
Tel: 011-812 4621
www.leviteletonne.com
Very close to Piazza Castello, this very buzzing modern *vineria*-cum-restaurant is equally good for a glass of fine wine and nibbles, a light lunch or a full dinner. The menu changes daily but, true to its name, always features *vitello tonnato* (veal in tuna sauce). Closed dinner Wed and Sun. €€-€€€

VALLE D'AOSTA

The chilly Alpine Valle d'Aosta is noted for its salami, terrines and cured meats, as well as its fondues, made from *fontina*, arguably the best cow's milk available. You may also be offered a *caffe valdostano nella grolla*, coffee laced with wine and grappa, which is set alight.

Aosta

Sapori di Aosta
Classhotel Aosta, Corso Ivrea 146
Tel: 0165-41845
www.classhotel.com
In a rather bland modern hotel just outside Aosta, this restaurant nevertheless has

a strong reputation for its "tastes of Aosta" – especially good cheeses. Closed Mon dinner and Tues. €€

Vecchio Ristoro
Via Tourneuve 4
Tel: 0165-33238
www.ristorantevecchioristoro.it
This former watermill is now home to one of the area's best restaurants, with superb seasonal cuisine and Alpine specialities such as *bollito misto* (beef broth), as well as attentive, welcoming service. Reserve. Closed Sun and Mon lunch, June and early Nov. €€€-€€€€

Breuil-Cervinia

Les Neiges d'Antan
Frazzione Cret Perrères 10
Tel: 0166-948 775
www.lesneigesdantan.it
On a mountainside 4.5km (2 miles) southwest of Breuil-Cervinia, this quiet inn comes into its own in the skiing season, when tables are in great demand. Typical Valdostana cuisine predominates, from soufflés to trout and *fonduta* (fondue), and there's a superior wine list. Reservation essential. Open 6 Dec–Apr and July–mid-Sept. €€€

Gignod

Locanda La Clusaz
Località La Clusaz
Tel: 0165-56075
www.laclusaz.it
Located 9km (6 miles) north of Aosta off the road towards the Great St Bernard tunnel, this delightful inn (with 14 bedrooms) offers local specialities such as grain soups, polenta and warming dishes of chestnuts and bacon, prepared with great skill and flair. Closed Tues and lunch Wed, and from mid-May–mid-June and early Nov–early Dec. €€€

GENOA AND LIGURIA

Ligurians are said to have one of the world's healthiest diets. Curiously, they do not eat nearly as much fish as one might expect from a coastal region, and typical foods include basil-scented *pesto* sauce – Liguria's signature dish – superb olive oil, salt-cod stew, excellent artichokes, and exceptional salads and vegetables.

Bordighera

Maresol
Lungomare Argentina
Tel: 0184-262 293

Look out over the seafront while choosing from delicious fish and seafood dishes such as the *linguine allo scoglio* ("reef pasta", with mixed seafood) or cuttlefish in pesto, all washed down with excellent local wines. €€

Genoa

Antica Osteria del Bai
Via Quarto 12, Quarto dei Mille
Tel: 010-387 478
www.osteriadelbai.it
This illustrious restaurant inside a fortress overlooking the sea is where Garibaldi

dined in 1860, but this is not its only claim to fame. Under chef Gianni Malagoli it continues to maintain very high standards, with Genoese classics and especially good seafood, whether in pasta sauces or elaborate Adriatic fish dishes. Reserve. Closed Mon. €€€€

La Bitta nella Pergola
Via Casaregis 52r
Tel: 010-588 543
This acclaimed, elegant Michelin-starred restaurant specialises in fresh seafood and offers regionally based cooking in a comfortable

maritime atmosphere. Reserve. Closed Mon, dinner Sun, all day Sun in July, and Aug. €€€€

Le Cantine Squarciafico
Piazza Invrea 3r
Tel: 010-247 0823
www.squarciafico.it
Between the Old Town and the port, this atmospheric

PRICE CATEGORIES

The price of a three-course meal for one (not including wine):
€ = under €25
€€ = €25–50
€€€ = €50–80
€€€€ = more than €80

wine bar and restaurant occupies the restored cellars of a lovely 16th-century palazzo. Wines from every region of Italy are on offer, accompanied by predominantly Ligurian dishes. Open daily, closed early Jan and part of July–Aug. €€

Gran Gotto
Viale Brigata Bisagno 69r
Tel: 010-564 344
www.mangiareinliguria.it/grangotto
Near Stazione Brignole, this is a classic and elegant spot dedicated to regional cooking and seafood. Try the seafood pasta, the hot seafood *antipasto* or the *trenette al pesto*, Genoa's signature dish. Reserve. Closed Sun and lunch Sat. €€€€

Panson dal 1790
Piazza delle Erbe 5r
Tel: 010-294 903
This lovely restaurant is in a slightly dilapidated but safe square close to Via XX Settembre, and is very popular with local families. Genoese classics such as *pansoti al sugo di noci* (pasta with walnuts) and *pesto alla genovese* (pasta with basil sauce) are menu highlights. Closed Sun and 2 weeks in Aug. €€–€€€

Lerici

La Calata
Via Mazzini 4
Tel: 0187-967 143
www.lacalata.it
This long-running restaurant on the harbour is known for its seafood prepared with top-quality fresh ingredients. In summer you can dine on the terrace, with fabulous views over the Gulf. Closed Tues and Dec. €€€

Portofino

This is a chic destination, so expect even the simplest restaurant to charge above-average prices. (*See Where to Stay, page 386*, for details on dining in hotels here.)

Da u'Batti
Vico Nuovo 17
Tel: 0185-269 379
An intimate restaurant with a very pretty terrace on a small piazza. As well as a bounty of good seafood, there are wonderfully indulgent fresh desserts. Closed Mon and Dec–mid-Jan. €€€

Il Pitosforo
Molo Umberto I, 9
Tel: 0185-269 020

Numerous VIPs and the international yachting fraternity meet on this celebrated terrace to compare boats and bank balances. Ligurian specialities and international dishes feature on the menu. Reserve. Closed Sun and Jan–Feb. €€€€

Riomaggiore

La Grotta
Via Cristoforo Colombo 247
Tel: 0187-920 187
In the southernmost of the Cinque Terre coastal villages, this little place remains as authentic and simple as its medieval vaulted interior, providing great-value earthy and healthy Ligurian home cooking. €

San Remo

This destination is popular during the February San Remo Song Contest and in summer.

Il Bagatto
Corso G. Matteotti 145
Tel: 0184-531 925
Old-fashioned, formal service and fine meat- and fish-based Ligurian dishes,

in a lovely setting in the old palazzo Borea d'Olmo. The wine list is also impressive. Reserve. Closed Sun. €€€

Paolo e Barbara
Via Roma 47
Tel: 0184-531 653
www.paolobarbara.it
Over more than 20 years Paolo and Barbara Masieri have won many awards for their very refined cooking, using only the most carefully sourced local ingredients. The restaurant is quite small, so reservations are essential. Closed Wed and Thur; mid-June–mid-Sept open dinner only; July open Fri–Sun only; and closed entirely 2 weeks Dec, 1 week Jan. €€€–€€€€

Vernazza

Gambero Rosso
Piazza Marconi 7
Tel: 0187-812 265
www.ristorantegamberorosso.net
Vernazza is the most popular of the scenic Cinque Terre coastal villages, and Gambero Rosso, a sophisticated little *osteria* by the port, tends to be full at lunchtime but quiet in the evening. Closed Mon (except Aug) and mid-Dec–Feb. €€€

VENICE

Restaurants are listed here according to the area (*sestriere*) in which they are located. A feature of Venice is the large number of cheap and cheerful *bacari* (singular: *bacaro*), traditional wine bars that also serve simple, good snacks, rather like tapas, called *cicchetti*. Most close early (usually by 9.30pm) and they often keep odd hours. Many *bacari* are hidden away in the warren of alleys around the Rialto and the San Polo district.

Cannaregio

Algiubagió
Fondamenta Nuova,
Cannaregio 5039
Tel: 041-523 6084

www.algiubagio.net
By the Murano and Burano *vaporetto* stops on the Fondamenta Nuova, with an ever-fascinating view of the lagoon and San Michele cemetery island from its bustling terrace, this attractive modern restaurant has a broader menu than is common in Venice, including plenty of light dishes and vegetarian options. Exceptional value for Venice. €€

Alla Vedova (Ca' d'Oro)
Ramo Ca'd'Oro, Cannaregio 3912
Tel: 041-528 5324
This old-world, basic *bacaro* near the Ca' d'Oro ferry stop (Ca' d'Oro being its proper name, although locals call it Alla Vedova) has no-nonsense pasta and

other dishes and Venetian bar snacks, and equally straightforward wines. Closed Thur and lunch Sun, and Aug. €

Vini da Gigio
Fondamenta San Felice,
Cannaregio 3628/A
Tel: 041-528 5140
www.vinidagigio.com
An attractive modern variation on the traditional Venetian *bacaro* in a canalside setting, with inventive meat- and fish-based dishes and especially good pasta options. Reserve. Closed Mon, Tues and part of Jan and Aug. €€

Castello

L'Aciugheta
Campo San Filippo e Giacomo,

Castello 4357
Tel: 041-522 4292
Excellent, good value *bacaro* (wine bar) with fine Friuli wines that also has a proper menu featuring a range of dishes from Adriatic fish to truffles and oysters. €–€€

Al Covo
Campiello della Pescaria,
Castello 3968
Tel: 041-522 3812
www.ristorantealcovo.com
Close to the Arsenale ferry stop, this enthusiastically run restaurant serves fresh local fish, wild duck (in season), wonderful desserts and other seasonal dishes with a quality, "slow food" philosophy, and has a great wine list. Lunch is

excellent value. Closed Wed, Thur and Jan and 2 weeks and Aug. **€€€–€€€€**

Dorsoduro

Ai Gondolieri
Fondamente de l'Ospedaleto, Dorsoduro 366
Tel: 041-528 6396
Close to the Guggenheim museum, this popular restaurant serves up exceptional risottos in a sedate traditional setting. In contrast to most traditional Venetian dishes, it highlights meat dishes more than fish. Reserve. Closed Tues. **€€€**

Antica Trattoria La Furatola
Calle Lunga San Barnaba 2869/A, Dorsoduro
Tel: 041-520 8594
An unpretentious little place where locals outnumber tourists and the traditional fish dishes such as tuna *carpaccio* have a high reputation. Service is charmingly welcoming. Closed Mon lunch, Jan and Aug. **€€€**

Cantinone Già Schiavi
Fondamenta San Trovaso 992, Dorsoduro
Tel: 041-523 0034
This canal-side wine bar is extremely popular with locals. It's especially atmospheric at cocktail hour from 7–8pm; do as the Venetians do and enjoy *cichetti*, typical bar snacks, with a glass of wine. Closed Sun. **€–€€**

Taverna San Trovaso
Fondamenta Priuli, Dorsoduro 1016
Tel: 041-520 3703
www.tavernasantrovaso.it
This cheap and unfussily comfortable traditional inn serves very enjoyable food in a lovely spot by the canal, near the gondola repair yard. Closed Mon. **€€**

San Marco

Acqua Pazza
Campo Sant'Angelo, San Marco
Tel: 041-277 0688
www.veniceacquapazza.com
This stylish Neapolitan pizzeria on one of Venice's most fashionable squares is

the place to find huge pizzas and other southern dishes, served with complimentary Limoncello. **€€**

Al Graspo de Ua
Calle dei Bombaseri, San Marco 5094/A
Tel: 041-241 3326
www.algraspodeua.it
Near the Rialto Bridge, this centuries-old restaurant has kept up with modern trends with considerable style, and is a delight for those seeking both a distinctive ambience and traditional Venetian fare. Closed Mon and part Jan. **€€€–€€€€**

Al Volto
Calle Cavalli 4081, San Marco
Tel: 041-522 8945
www.alvoltoenoteca.it
This is Venice's oldest *enoteca* or wine bar, where you can choose between thousands of different wines, accompanied by delicious meals prepared with a light touch. Extremely popular. Closed Thur. **€–€€**

Antico Martini
Campo Teatro Fenice 2007, San Marco
Tel: 041-522 4121
www.anticomartini.com
Next to the Fenice opera house, with a neat terrace on the square, the venerable Martini has served many artistic figures, from Igor Stravinsky to countless actors and opera stars. The menu features international dishes as well as refined Venetian classics. Reserve. **€€€**

Caffè Quadri
Procuratie Vecchie, Piazza San Marco 121
Tel: 041-522 2105
www.quadrivenice.com
One of the grand cafés of Piazza San Marco, opened in 1775, the Quadri is awash with Murano glass and sumptuous furnishings, and equally full of history, having welcomed Byron, Wagner, Balzac and many others. Many visitors just go for a coffee, but its cuisine is also of a high standard, if predictably expensive. Reservations essential. Closed Mon Nov–Mar. **€€€€**

Harry's Bar
Calle Vallaresso, San Marco 1323
Tel: 041-528 5777
www.harrysbarvenezia.com
A symbol of gastronomic Venice. Although prices are high, standards are also impressive, and if you don't go for a full meal you can of course just have one of its renowned cocktails instead. Once a writers' haunt, it's now patronised mainly by very wealthy Venetians, expatriates and tourists; to eat, expect good home-made pastas at exorbitant prices. Reserve. **€€€€**

Vino Vino
Calle delle Veste, San Marco
Tel: 041-241 7688
An informal wine bar near the Fenice opera house area where you can rub shoulders with gondoliers over tasty tapas, from sweet-and-sour sardines to salt cod and polenta. Good food, but gruff service. **€**

San Polo

Vini Da Pinto
Campo delle Beccarie, San Polo 367
Tel: 041-522 4599
This bustling, slightly rough-and-ready *bacaro* in the market area of the Rialto district is a good place to begin a wine crawl and great for authentic Venetian *cicchetti* snacks – the seafood varieties are particularly tasty. Closed Mon. **€**

Osteria Da Fiore
Calle del Scaleter, San Polo 2002
Tel: 041-721 308
www.dafiore.net
Small and chic, this Michelin-starred gourmet restaurant near Campo San Polo is considered by many to be the city's best. Chef Mara Martin's cooking is both sophisticated and generous, the atmosphere comfortably relaxing. Reserve. Closed Sun and Mon. **€€€€**

Trattoria alla Madonna
Calle della Madonna, San Polo 594
Tel: 041-522 3824
www.ristoranteallamadonna.com
Thoroughly traditional, with years of accumulated

pictures around the walls, this fish and seafood restaurant near the Rialto is always full, thanks to its good-value food (by Venetian standards). Service, though, can be a little brusque. Reservations advised. Closed Wed, Jan and part of Aug. **€€€**

Santa Croce

Trattoria Antica Bessetta
Salizada de Cà' Zusto, Santa Croce 1395
Tel: 041-721 687
This authentic family-run *trattoria*, one of the city's oldest, is a bit off the beaten track near San Giacomo dell'Orio, and has great seafood risotto and other local dishes, remains good value despite recent price rises. Closed Tues and Wed lunch. **€€–€€€**

Vecio Fritolin
Calle della Regina 2262, Santa Croce
Tel: 041-522 2881
www.veciofritolin.it
Irina Freguia's cosy but quirky fish restaurant near the Rialto Bridge is the place to go for a seafood extravaganza at a reasonable price – but is also fine for a more modest pasta lunch. Closed lunch Mon and Tues. **€€–€€€€**

The Lagoon Islands

Trattoria Da Romano
Via B. Galuppi 221, Burano
Tel: 041-730 030
www.venissa.it
An ever-popular traditional standby on the colourful island of Burano, not far from the waterfront, visited by many artists over the years, with an easygoing welcome and tasty, straightforward cuisine. Closed Tues and Dec. **€€**

PRICE CATEGORIES
The price of a three-course meal for one (not including wine):
€ = under €25
€€ = €25–50
€€€ = €50–80
€€€€ = more than €80

Venissa
Fondamenta Santa Caterina,
Isola di Mazzorbo
Tel: 041-527 2281
www.venissa.it
On Venice's only wine

estate, on Mazzorbo, a
small island off Burano,
creative cuisine is de
rigueur, using local produce
from the lagoon and the
Veneto (radicchio, cheeses,

meats and salamis) as
well as the owner's own
wines. The dining room and
terrace are chic and
spacious, and there's also a
hotel (see page 388). To get

to the estate, take
vaporetto 41/42 from
Fondamenta Nuove to
Burano, then cross the
footbridge to Mazzorbo.
€€€–€€€€

THE VENETO

Padua (Padova)

Dotto di Campagna
Via Randaccio 4 (Ponte di Brenta)
Tel: 049-625 469
This rustic restaurant is
6km (4 miles) northeast of
Padua but is worth the trip
for its authentic Veneto
cuisine. Try the gnocchi,
roast meats, pasta e fagioli
(pasta and beans) and
baccalà (salt cod). Reserve.
Closed Sun dinner, Mon and
Aug. €€–€€€

Treviso

Ristorante da Gigetto
Via A. de Gasperi 5, Miane, Follina
Tel: 0438-960 020
www.ristorantedagigetto.it
In a lovely hamlet just
north of Treviso, a
convenient springboard
into Prosecco country, this
charmingly run restaurant
provides a fine introduction
to Venetian dishes, using
exceptional seasonal
ingredients. The plush

traditional decor is made
unstuffy by the warmth of
the welcome. €€€

Verona

Expect above-average
prices in this chic, perenially
popular city. Many
restaurants here are first-
class acts, matching
unusual cuisine with
atmospheric settings and
lovely Veneto wines such as
Bardolino.
12 Apostoli
Corticella San Marco 3
Tel: 045-596 999
www.12apostoli.it
Just off Piazza delle Erbe,
this atmospheric family-run
restaurant is known for the
timeless standards of its
Veronese and classic Italian
cuisine, and a magnificent
wine selection. Reserve.
Closed Sun dinner, and
Mon. €€€
Bottega Del Vino
Via Scudo di Francia 3
Tel: 045-800 4535
www.venissa.it

In the historic heart of
Verona, just off Piazza delle
Erbe, this traditional inn
(osteria) was a haunt of
Futurist painters such as
Boccioni. It is still
frequented by an artistic
set, as well as by those who
simply appreciate Veronese
and classic Italian cooking.
Closed Tues except July and
Aug. €€–€€€
Locanda di Castelvecchio
Corso Castelvecchio 21/A
Tel: 045-803 0097
www.ristorantecastelvecchio.com
One of the city's most historic
restaurants, in a beautiful
corner of the old town and
still with the ambience of a
traditional osteria. Service is
courteous, and the Veronese
cuisine exquisite. Closed
Tues and Wed lunch. €€
Il Desco
Via Dietro San Sebastiano 7
Tel: 045-595 358
www.ildesco.com
In a distinguished old
palazzo, this is one of Italy's
finest restaurants, where
Verona-born chef Elia Rizzo

combines rare and
expensive ingredients with
more traditional basics to
create foodie heaven. The
main restaurant is hugely
expensive, but Rizzo also
has a nearby trattoria with
fine cooking at more
accessible prices (Trattoria I
Masenini, Via Roma 34; tel:
045-806 5169; www.
imasenini.com; €€–€€€).
Reservations essential; Il
Desco closed Sun, Mon
(July–Aug and Dec only) and
2 weeks June, 2 weeks
Dec–Jan. €€€€

Vicenza

**Antico Ristorante agli
Schioppi**
Contrà piazza del Castello 26
Tel: 0444-543 701
In Vicenza's historic centre,
this rustic yet elegant
restaurant in a palazzo
presents enjoyable Veneto
cuisine, and has an attractive
outside terrace for people-
watching in summer. Closed
Sun, lunch Mon. €€–€€€

FRIULI-VENEZIA GIULIA

Trieste

Al Bagatto
Via Cadorna 7
Tel: 040-301 771
www.albagatto.it
A snug but gracious little
restaurant in the centre of the
city, serving up flavoursome
seafood and the best fresh
fish, with dishes such as
creamed salt cod or sea bass
tartare. Very popular, so
reserve your table. Closed
Sun. €–€€
Antica Trattoria Suban
Via Comici 2
Tel: 040-54368
www.suban.it

Run by the same family
since 1865, this massive
old inn is a symbol of
Trieste. It nevertheless
remains friendly and simple
in style, with cosy dining
rooms and a lovely terrace
for summer dining, and
serves local cuisine that
typifies Trieste's blend of
Italy and Central Europe.
Reserve. Closed Tues and
part of Jan and Aug. €€€
Trattoria Al Faro
Scala Sforzi 2
Tel: 040-410 092
www.trattoriaalfaro.it
A 10-minute drive out of
Trieste on the road north

towards Udine, this
restaurant is at the foot of the
Vittoria lighthouse, facing the
Gulf of Trieste. From the
beautiful terrace there are
fabulous views, to go with
excellent seafood dishes and
wines. Closed Mon. €€€

Udine

Alla Vedova
Via Tavagnacco 9
Tel: 0432-470 291
A very old and traditional
Friulian restaurant, with
outdoor tables in summer,
and hefty traditional cooking
and fine risottos. Reserve.

Closed Sun dinner and Mon,
and 3 weeks Aug. €€
Là di Moret
Best Western Hotel Là di Moret,
Viale Tricesimo 276
Tel: 0432-545 096
Inside the Là di Moret Hotel,
this restaurant has survived
under the direction of the
Marini family through several
makeovers and changes in
style in the hotel. Locals
regard is as one of the best
places to find traditional
Friulian cooking, but its chefs
are also open to other
influences. Closed Sun
dinner and Mon lunch, and 2
weeks in July–Aug. €€–€€€

TRENTINO-ALTO ADIGE

These Alpine regions offer mountain food with an Italian or Austrian twist. Wholesome dishes prevail, from hearty pork and beef sausages to polenta and pulse-filled soups. In the Alto Adige, food is distinctly Germanic – smoked meats, sauerkraut, red-cabbage goulash, dumplings, gnocchi and apple strudel are all popular.

Bolzano (Bozen)

Laurin
Parkhotel Laurin, Via Laurin 4
Tel: 0471-311 000
www.laurin.it
A high-ceilinged, airy restaurant in one of the area's smartest hotels, where chef Luca Verdolini presents innovative cuisine based in both Mediterranean and Alpine traditions. Plus there's a very good wine list, and an attractive bar. Closed Sun lunch. €€€–€€€€

Pinzolo

Mezzosoldo
Via Nazionale 196, Spiazzo Rendena, near Pinzolo
Tel: 0465-801 067
www.mezzosoldo.it
This cosy mountain inn is in the Val Rendena area south of Pinzolo, not too far from the ski resort of Madonna di Campiglio. The reason for making the journey is simple: great home-cooking. The Lorenzi family pick many of their ingredients, including herbs and mushrooms, themselves. The inn also has simple, good-value bedrooms. Closed part of May and Oct. €€–€€€

Trento

Lo Scrigno del Duomo
Piazza del Duomo 29
Tel: 0461-220 030
www.scrignodelduomo.com
Combining traditional and

contemporary elegance, this restaurant opened in 1999 after restoration work revealed many of the original features, including a Roman wall, in the medieval palazzo it occupies. With a Michelin star, it is a showcase for fine local cuisine, while the *enoteca* has an excellent choice of wines. Reserve. Closed Mon. €€€–€€€€

Osteria a Le Due Spade
Via Don A. Rizzi 11
(corner Via Verdi)
Tel: 0461-234 343
www.leduespade.com
Said to have opened its doors to receive delegates to the Council of Trent in 1545, this historic, atmospheric *osteria* is a temple to the rich flavours of Trentino gastronomy. A real treat. Reservations essential. €€€€

Ristorante al Vò
Vicolo del Vò 11
Tel: 0461-198 5374

www.ristorantealvo.it
All of Trento's typical inns have their history, but Al Vò takes the trophy: dating back to 1345, it is the oldest establishment in town. It has been regularly renovated, and on the menu in the spacious dining room are meats and salamis and rustic cheeses, lake fish, vegetarian options and especially good polenta dishes. €–€€

Ristorante Chiesa
Parco San Marco 64
Tel: 0461-238 766
www.ristorantechiesa.it
Occupying one floor of a 17th-century cloistered palace, this smart restaurant nevertheless has a bright contemporary style, with multicoloured furnishings and quirky decor. The service is great, and the food is both refined and innovative. Closed Sun. €€€

EMILIA-ROMAGNA

The gastronomic capital of Italy, Bologna also has its fair share of traditional taverns serving simple hearty cuisine. The city is famous for pasta of every description, and for velvety sauces, salami and cold meats. Each town in the region has its specialities, from Parmesan and Parma ham in Parma to *aceto balsamico* in Modena. Emilian wines include Trebbiano, Cabernet Sauvignon and Lambrusco.

Bologna

Buca San Petronio
Via de' Musei 4
Tel: 051-224 589
Excellent-value restaurant in a palazzo in Bologna's old centre, with traditional Bolognese cooking and fresh pasta, and an outdoor terrace for the summer. Closed Wed dinner and Aug. €–€€

Caffè dei Commercianti
Strada Maggiore 23/C
Tel: 051-266 539
A bar, *pasticceria* and ice-cream parlour that's an established breakfast spot and watering hole for the intelligentsia of Bologna, with a bill of fare that runs from fabulous fresh-fruit ices to the best Martini in town. €

Cantina Bentivoglio
Via Mascarella 4B
Tel: 051-265 416
www.cantinabentivoglio.it
Typical of Bologna, this popular *enoteca*-restaurant combines a time-worn setting – in the cellars of a palazzo – with a laidback style, and attracts a young crowd. The Emilian specialities are great, and there's regular live jazz and other music. Open evenings only. €€

Da Bertino
Via delle Lame 55
Tel: 051-522 230

www.ristorantedabertino.it
A lively and friendly Emilian *trattoria*, with irresistible versions of local classics like *tagliatelle alla bolognese* and *scaloppa ai funghi*. Closed Sun and Mon dinner Sept–May, Sat evening and Sun June–Aug. €€

Osteria de' Poeti
Via de' Poeti 1
Tel: 051-236 166
www.osteriadepoeti.com
This long-established cellar restaurant and wine bar could be mistaken for a tourist trap, but is very popular with locals, attracted by the live music, fine wines and well-prepared local cuisine at good-value prices. Opt for the "quiet room" if the music fails to appeal. Closed Mon and Sun dinner. €€

Pappagallo
Piazza della Mercanzia 3C
Tel: 051-232 807
www.alpappagallo.it

This restaurant is very popular not only for its location, near the two towers, but also for its Bolognese specialities, including perfect pasta and refined fish dishes. Closed Sun and part of Aug. €€–€€€

La Pernice e La Gallina
Via dell'Abbadia 4
Tel: 051-269 922
Highly acclaimed, sleekly modern restaurant in the centre of Bologna, where traditional and innovative cuisine are skilfully blended with a touch of fantasy to produce gourmet delights. Closed Sun, and part of Aug. €€€

PRICE CATEGORIES

The price of a three-course meal for one (not including wine):
€ = under €25
€€ = €25–50
€€€ = €50–80
€€€€ = more than €80

Le Stanze Café
Via Borgo di San Pietro 1
Tel: 051-228 767
www.lestanzecafe.com
In a 16th-century former chapel, with frescoed walls, this spectacular bar is a place where the smart set go to be seen. To eat, there are pricey but refined snacks. Closed Sat lunch. €€

Ferrara

Trattoria La Romantica
Via Ripagrande 36
Tel: 0532-765 975
www.trattorialaromantica.com
In the heart of medieval Ferrara, this well-established restaurant serves classic Italian cuisine including a few Jewish *Ferrarese* dishes, and its traditional decor is as romantically quaint as the name suggests. Closed Sun dinner and Mon lunch, and part of July–Aug. €€

Modena

Oreste
Piazza Roma 31
Tel: 059-243 324
This traditional restaurant

has a pleasant "retro" atmosphere, and fine meat specialities and own-made pasta. Closed Sun dinner and Wed, 2 weeks July and Christmas/New Year. €€
Ristorante Fini
Rua dei Frati Minori 54
Tel: 059-205 1530
A Modenese classic, this smart yet still nicely homely restaurant presents near-definitive versions of local dishes such as tortellini *in brodo di cappone* (cooked in chicken broth) and cured meats, and making fine use of the town's famous balsamic vinegars. Reserve. Closed Mon and Tues, 2 weeks in Aug and Christmas/New Year. €€€–€€€€

Parma

The home of Parma ham and Parmesan cheese is a centre of gastronomic excellence. It is pretty difficult to eat out badly in town, but prices often reflect this.
Il Cortile
Borgo Paglia 3
Tel: 0521-285 779
www.trattoriailcortile.com

This very likeable and welcoming traditional restaurant, with bare timbers and impressive arches in the dining room, celebrates stuffed pasta such as *tortelli*, as well as mushroom and truffle dishes. €–€€
Le Sorelle Picchi
Via Farini 27
Tel: 0521-233 528
This brisk, centrally located, no-nonsense trattoria is also a *salumeria* (charcuterie delicatessen), and so the thing to try is the region's fabulous salamis, renowned as the most subtly flavoured in Italy. €–€€

Ravenna

Antica Trattoria Al Gallo 1909
Via Maggiore 87
Tel: 0544-213 775
This elegant Art Nouveau restaurant has been run by the same family for almost a century. The regional menu changes according to the seasons, and includes good vegetarian options. Closed Sun dinner, Mon, Tues, Easter and Christmas/New Year. €€–€€€

San Marino

Righi-La Taverna
Piazza della Libertà 10
Tel: 0549-991 196
Near San Marino's Palazzo del Governo, Righi has two separate spaces: a smart, formal first-floor restaurant with a Michelin star and an expensive gourmet menu, and a more casual *taverna* downstairs, with more accessible but still imaginative food. Closed Wed in winter, and first 2 weeks Jan. €€–€€€€

Soragna

Locanda del Lupo
Via Garibaldi 64
Tel: 0524-597 100
www.locandadellupo.com
This atmospheric inn in a small town northwest of Parma has been beautifully restored, to provide a fitting backdrop to its sophisticated versions of Emilian country cuisine and fine wines. Afterwards, if you don't feel like driving back to Parma, you can stay the night in one of the Locanda's baronial bedrooms. €€€

FLORENCE

Alle Murate
Via del Proconsolo 16r
Tel: 055-240 618
www.allemurate.it
Intimate modern restaurant in an unmistakably Florentine setting – combining Renaissance frescoes, cave-like chambers and contemporary design – which is very fashionable with young locals. The excellent cuisine takes in creative Tuscan and international dishes. Reserve. Dinner only; closed Mon and last three weeks of Dec – check dates in advance. €€€–€€€€
La Baraonda
Via Ghibellina 67r
Tel: 055-234 1171
Located in the historic Santa Croce quarter, this

very pleasant *trattoria* is convivial and atmospheric. Earthy Tuscan cuisine and good fish dishes are on offer, plus excellent hand-made pasta. Reservations essential as it's very popular. Closed Sun, Mon lunch and 3 weeks Aug. €€€
Benedicta
Via Benedetta 12r
Tel: 055-264 5429
www.ristorantebenedicta.it
In a surprisingly bright, stylishly modern dining room, this innovative restaurant presents enjoyable, subtle variations on Italian classics and Tuscan specialities. Unpretentious, and very good value. Dinner only, closed Sun. €€
Cibrèo-Cibreino
Via del Verrocchio 8r (restaurant)

Via dei Macci 122r *(trattoria)*
Tel: 055-234 1100
This universally respected Tuscan restaurant operates a double-pricing system. Those unfamiliar with the place often book in the main restaurant, with delicious, formally presented food at lofty prices; those in the know eat virtually the same things in the adjoining more modest *trattoria* for a fraction of the price. Reserve. Closed Sun, Mon, Aug and Christmas/New Year. €€ *(trattoria)*; €€€€ (restaurant)
Enoteca Pinchiorri
Via Ghibellina 87
Tel: 055-242 777
www.enotecapinchiorri.it
One of Florence and Italy's most prestigious restaurants, in a 17th-

century palace, with a delightful courtyard for dining in the open air. One of the guiding lights is French, so the ultra-refined cuisine incorporates French as well as Italian influences. Opulent, very expensive, and (some find) snooty, but an experience. Reservations essential. Closed Sun, Mon, Tues and Wed lunch, Aug and late Dec–early Jan. €€€€
La Loggia del Piazzale Michelangelo
Piazzale Michelangelo 1
Tel: 055-234 2832
www.ristorantelaloggia.it
Outside central Florence, part-way up a hill on a grand square presided over by a copy of Michelangelo's *David*, La Loggia's garden terrace has a bewitching

EATING OUT ◆ 413

TRANSPORT
ACCOMMODATION
EATING OUT
ACTIVITIES
A – Z
LANGUAGE

view down over the bowl of Florence. On the menu are Tuscan delicacies and international dishes. Closed Mon. €€€

Ristorante del Fagioli
Corso Tintori 47r
Tel: 055-244 285
Utterly traditional Florentine

cuisine is on offer in this typical family-run *trattoria*, with fresh fish the highlight on Fridays. Friendly, relaxed, very good value and popular, so reservation is advisable. Closed Sat, Sun and Aug. €€

Trattoria Omero
Via Pian de' Giullari 11r, Località

Arcetri
(5km/3 miles from Florence)
Tel: 055-220 053
www.ristoranteomero.it
On a hill south of the city, this gentrified rustic *trattoria* has tables outside in summer from which to take in the splendid view,

which is matched by the rich Tuscan cuisine, prepared with excellent ingredients. Tasty standards include ravioli stuffed with ricotta and herbs, and great grilled meats. Reserve. Closed Tues and Aug. €€€

TUSCANY

Arezzo

Antica Osteria l'Agania
Via Mazzini 10
Tel: 0575-295 381
www.agania.com
Very pleasant, family-style restaurant specialising in good, simple local cuisine, served in generous portions, and excellent value. Closed Mon. €–€€

Castelnuovo di Garfagnana

Osteria Vecchio Mulino
Via Vittorio Emanuele 12
Tel: 0583-62192
www.vecchiomulino.info
In the heart of the Garfagnana area north of Lucca, this stunning little restaurant and traditional food store embodies all that's best about Italy's "Slow Food" movement. Andrea Bertucci assembles (rather than cooks) the finest local produce, especially salamis, hams, mushrooms and fabulous local cheeses. It can also be explored on a local food trail with www.sapori-e-saperi.com. €

Colle di Val d'Elsa

Ristorante Il Cardinale
Via Piemonte 10
Tel: 0577-923 453
www.ristoranteilcardinale.com
The Relais della Rovere began life in the 11th century as an abbey, but was promoted to a cardinal's residence 400 years later. The smartly gentrified Cardinale restaurant and *enoteca* occupies the estate's former wine cellars, and its Tuscan menu is matched by

the excellent local wines. Closed 15 Jan–Feb. €€–€€€

Cortona

Il Falconiere
Località San Martino a Bocena
(4km/2½ miles north of Cortona)
Tel: 0575-612 679
www.ilfalconiere.it
In a lovely setting in the hills, this elegant hotel makes you feel as though time stands still, and the imaginative and delectable cuisine, gracious summer terrace and pampering service all perfectly complement the experience. Reservations essential. Closed Mon and Tues lunch (except Mar–Oct). €€€€

Gaiole in Chianti

Badia a Coltibuono
5km/3 miles outside Gaiole
Tel: 0577-749 031
www.coltibuono.com
In Chianti country, outside the wine-producing village of Gaiole, this estate was founded by Vallombrosan monks c.1000. It's now a "wine resort", with rather luxurious B&B rooms and apartments, wine courses, vineyard tours and a charming country-style restaurant that makes excellent use of local produce. Slightly twee, so perhaps not to everybody's taste. Closed Mon Nov–April, and from mid-Jan–mid-Mar. €€€

Lucca

La Buca di Sant'Antonio
Via della Cervia 3
Tel: 0583-55881

www.bucadisantantonio.it
Open since 1782, with two centuries of old pans and other mementoes cluttered around the walls and ceiling, this traditional *osteria* (inn) remains one of the best places in town to sample Lucca's own specialities like *zuppa di farro* (spelt or faro-wheat soup) and other rustic dishes. Closed Sun dinner, Mon, early Jan and 2 weeks July. €€

Da Giulio
Via delle Conce 47
Tel: 0583-55948
A classic neighbourhood *trattoria* with functional decor, warm service and good plain food, especially the minestrone and bean soups, stout meat dishes and, in season, game. Closed Sun (except third Sunday in month) and Aug. €

Montalcino

Osteria di Porta al Cassero
Via della Libertà 9
Tel: 0577-846 116
This popular *trattoria* is run by ex-barber Piero and his family, who make sure everyone is well served with great energy. It has tables in a courtyard as well as in a traditional dining room, and good own-made pasta and local standards. Closed Wed. €

Taverna Il Grappolo Blu
Via Scale di Moglio (off Via Mazzini)
Tel: 0577-847 150
This intimate, well-run inn is the best in quaint, medieval Montalcino. The atmosphere is rustic but the cuisine is above average,

and service is friendly but correct. Typical dishes include filling soups, rabbit dishes and pasta with *funghi porcini* (ceps), and there's an excellent wine list. Closed Fri. €–€€

Montepulciano

Caffè Poliziano
Via Voltaia del Corso 27–9
Tel: 0578-758 615
www.caffepoliziano.it
Open since 1868 and lovingly restored in the 1990s, this magnificent café/bar is an unmissable local institution. Walk in off the street and you enter a gloriously ornate Art Nouveau café; carry on through the long room and you emerge onto a terrace that looks out over the Tuscan countryside from an apparently immense height. Open all day for breakfast, snacks, coffee and drinks, the Poliziano also serves a good-value lunch menu, and hosts a variety of cultural events. €€

La Grotta
Località San Biagio
Tel: 0578-757 479
In the 1990s David Mazzuoli and his sister converted this 15th-century post house next to San Biagio chapel into a restaurant. The atmosphere is discreet and stylish, and the menu features lots of

PRICE CATEGORIES

The price of a three-course meal for one (not including wine):
€ = under €25
€€ = €25–50
€€€ = €50–80
€€€€ = more than €80

local dishes; there's also, of course, a fine collection of Montepulciano's own *Vino Nobile*. Closed Wed. €€€

Pienza

Il Prato
Viale Santa Caterina
Tel: 0578-749 924
Opened by local chef and restaurateur Riccardo Valenti in a converted hay loft, Il Prato offers country food in a smart ambience. Valenti is fastidious about selecting the freshest high-quality ingredients, so the house speciality, *pasta al tartufo*, comes with different truffles according to the season. The terrace dining area offers great views of the valley. Closed Tues. €€

Trattoria Latte di Luna
Via San Carlo 2–4
Tel: 0578-748 606
This family *trattoria* is run by the sweet and smiling Roberto Bartolucci, and takes its name from the dancing light cast by the moonstone found in the valleys around Pienza. Find a table on the terrace next to the piazza, and be sure to try the excellent home-made *semi-freddo* ice cream. Closed Tues. €€

Pisa

Antica Trattoria Il Campano
Via Cavalca 19
Tel: 050-580 585
www.ilcampano.com
In a quiet spot by the marketplace, this charming restaurant dating back to medieval times has excellent seafood, and also Tuscan specialities featuring *cinghiale* (wild boar). In summer its terrace is a particularly pleasant spot to eat outside, and the wine list is impressive. Closed Wed and lunch Thur. €–€€

San Gimignano

Dorandò
Vicolo dell'Oro 2
Tel: 0577-941 862
www.ristorantedorando.it
An intimate little restaurant off the Piazza Duomo. Marcello Bisogni and chef Duccio Ferri spent a lot of time researching Etruscan, Roman and medieval cuisine before opening, and their enthusiasm and dedication to the authenticity of their menu is humbling. Closed Mon Nov–Easter and Dec–Jan. €€

L'Eco Divino
Relais La Collegiata, Località Strada 27
Tel: 0577-943 201
www.lacollegiata.it
"The Divine Echo" occupies the former chapel in this spectacular palazzo hotel, amid idyllic gardens. It is

worth eating here just to marvel at the service: waiters whisper in cabals, forming strategies to bring a dish to your table, and the four-stage wine service is a piece of performance art. Fortunately the food lives up to the setting and preliminaries. €€€–€€€€

Siena

Ristorante Guido
Vicolo Pier Pettinaio 7
Tel: 0577-280 042
www.ristoranteguido.com
In a 15th-century building with beautiful brick arches curving across the dining room, this elegant restaurant has the gentrified-rustic style that Tuscans have perfected. Service is courteous, and the regional specialities include Etruscan-style *pici* (Tuscan spaghetti) and superior Florentine steak. Closed Wed and Jan. €€–€€€

Tullio Ai Tre Cristi
Vicolo Provenzano 1/7
Tel: 0577-280 608
Managed for 40 years by the same family, this very traditional *trattoria's* specialities include bean soups, fish and Tuscan pasta dishes such as *pappardelle alla lepre*, with wild hare. The walls are suitably adorned with the crests of the different

contrade (districts) that race in the Siena Palio. Closed Tues. €€–€€€

Sinalunga

Le Coccole dell'Amorosa
Locanda dell'Amorosa
Località l'Amorosa
Tel: 0577-677211
www.amorosa.it
This fine restaurant is part of an enchanting hotel created in a stunning complex of medieval buildings on an estate just outside the village of Sinalunga. Occupying the giant former stables, the restaurant has varied food that mixes the traditional and the new, and there's no better place to eat a *bistecca chianina* (farmed locally). Reserve. Closed to non-hotel guests Mon and lunch Tues. €€€€

Locanda La Bandita
Via Bandita 72, Bettole
Tel: 0577-624 649
www.locandalabandita.it
The family-run La Bandita occupies an 18th-century farmhouse in the countryside near Bettolle, a village east of Sinalunga. The restaurant is very relaxing; menu highlights include home-made pasta, subtle *antipasti* and Tuscan-inspired desserts featuring plenty of cinnamon and cream. Reserve. Closed Tues and Feb. €€–€€€

UMBRIA AND THE MARCHE

What Umbria does best on the food front is unpretentious home cooking: specialities include pork, cured meats, *carpaccio* of *funghi porcini* and warm, nourishing soups. And not forgetting the most prized local ingredient of all, the black truffle (*tartufo nero*), which is added to anything, from scrambled eggs upwards.

Ancona

Il Passetto
Piazza IV Novembre 1
Tel: 071-33214
An elegant spot on the waterfront, with lovely sea views from the terrace, good service and traditional seafood-based cuisine. Reservation recommended. Closed Sun dinner, Mon and part of Aug. €€€

Assisi

San Francesco
Via San Francesco 52
Tel: 075-812 329
www.ristorantesanfrancesco.com
In front of the Basilica of San Francesco, this is where you'll

find the finest Umbrian dishes, served beside a medieval fireplace and with delightful views. Specialities include *carpaccio* of *funghi porcini*, lentil-based dishes, wild herbs and lamb, ricotta from Norcia and wines from Montefalco. Closed Wed and first two weeks of July. €€–€€€

Foligno

Villa Roncalli
Via Roma 25
Tel: 0742-391 091
Umbrian specialities

naturally feature strongly on the menu in this lovely old Patrician villa, which is mainly a restaurant but also has some rooms. Dine in the garden in summer, with splendid panoramic views. Reserve. Closed Mon and 5–30 Aug. €€–€€€

Orvieto

La Grotta
Via Lucca Signorelli 5
Tel: 0763-341 348
Just off the Piazza Del Duomo, this long-running restaurant is homely and

TRANSPORT

ACCOMMODATION

EATING OUT

ACTIVITIES

A – Z

LANGUAGE

unassuming, but owners the Titocchia family take great care over their food, making use of the best local produce, and especially fine meats. Friendly, generous, and one of the region's gourmet bargains. Closed Tues. €–€€

I Sette Consoli
Piazza Sant'Angelo 1A
Tel: 0763-343 911
www.isetteconsoli.it
Refined, excellent interpretations of local cuisine are on offer at this traditional favourite, a few steps from Orvieto's Duomo. Depending on the seasons the menu might include *crostini* with ricotta, stuffed rabbit, salt cod marinated in apple vinegar, and bean

soup with fennel. Reserve. Closed Wed and Sun dinner Nov–Mar. €€–€€€

Perugia

Il Falchetto
Via Bartolo 20
Tel: 075-573 1775
www.ilfalchetto.it
Serves authentic, unpretentious local cuisine using the best ingredients, including plenty of game (in season) and black truffles. Closed Mon and part of Jan/Feb. €–€€

Spello

Il Molino
Piazza Matteotti 6/7
Tel: 0742-651 305

Housed in a converted 14th-century mill, this charming restaurant has plenty of Umbrian character, and its cooking makes great use of local specialities such as *funghi porcini*, black truffles, herbs and, in winter, game. Closed Tues and 7–22 Jan. €€

Spoleto

Il Tartufo
Piazza Garibaldi 24
Tel: 0743-40236
www.ristoranteiltartufo.it
Renovated in the last few years, the Tartufo is one of Spoleto's most esteemed restaurants, and serves traditional cuisine in a

quiet, dignified setting. Typical dishes include *baccalà* and asparagus, rich soups, pork dishes and pear soufflé, and truffles feature in many ways. Reserve. Closed Sun dinner, Mon, 10 Feb–10 Mar. €€–€€€

Todi

Ristorante Umbria
Via San Bonaventura 13
Tel: 075-894 2737
In a *c.*1400 building in the *centro storico*, the Umbria nevertheless has a terrace with fine views over the surrounding hills. The local dishes are rich and satisfying. Closed Tues and Christmas–9 Jan. €€

ABRUZZO AND MOLISE

Mutton, lamb and kid are the most important meats in the rugged Abruzzo, with lamb generally roasted or grilled. Adriatic fish is also in abundance, as is salami from the mountains and garden produce from the hinterland. Peppers, potatoes, figs and grapes also figure largely. Molise produces good pasta, served with chilli or tomato sauce.

Campobasso

Vecchia Trattoria da Tonino
Corso Vittorio Emanuele 8
Tel: 0874-415 200
This lovely old *trattoria* in the heart of Campobasso has a welcoming atmosphere, but also enjoys a grand reputation for chef Mario Lombardi's inventive modern variations on local dishes and fine wines. Reserve. Closed Sun, Mon and lunch Sat and July. €€–€€€

Chieti

Ristorante Venturini
Via Cesare de Lollis 10
Tel: 0871-330 663
A long-established local standby in a former convent,

with a pleasant terrace and *abruzzese* specialities including roast game and fish dishes. Closed Tues and part of July. €€–€€€

Guardiagrele

La Grotta dei Raselli
Località Comino, Via Raselli
Tel: 0871-808 292
www.lagrottadeiraselli.it
Young chef Franco Spadaccini was actually born in England, but returned to Italy to inspire the kitchens of this fine modern restaurant, a surprising gourmet discovery in a village south of Chieti. Closed Wed. €€–€€€

Paganica

Villa Dragonetti
Via Oberdan 4, Paganica, 7km/4 miles from L'Aquila
Tel: 0862-680 222
www.villadragonetti.it
Paulo Bazattelli restored this beautiful villa in the 1990s, and it's now an elegant hotel, with 17th-century frescoes decorating the dining room. The locally based cuisine is suitably sophisticated, and for a place of such style, this is

a ridiculously economical place to dine. €€

Pescara

Osteria La Lumaca
Via delle Caserme 51
Tel: 085-451 0880
www.osterialalumaca.com
In Pescara's Old Town, La Lumaca combines the qualities of a traditional inn with modern touches, and provides fine Abruzzese food, particularly hams, salamis, meaty main courses and regional cheeses. An excellent wine list too. Closed Tues. €–€€

Loreto Aprutino

Il Celliere
Castello Chiola, Via degli Aquino 12
Tel: 085-829 0690
www.castellochiolahotel.com
Dine on regional and other Mediterranean dishes at Il Celliere, in the vaulted cellars or grand courtyard of the Castello Chiola hotel *(see page 396)*. After dinner take a stroll onto the terrace to admire the Abruzzo hills. €€

Rocca Calascio

Rifugio della Rocca
Località Rocca Calascio

Tel: 338-805 9430
www.rifugiodellarocca.it
A family-run *trattoria* in the highest village in the Appenines, restored and reoccupied in the last few years after having been abandoned for decades. To eat there's hearty mountain food – local cheeses, salami, grilled vegetables, wild boar ragù, the local *chitarra* pasta – and rooms if you wish to stay over. €

Teramo

Duomo
Via Stazio 9
Tel: 0861-241 774
www.ristoranteduomo.com
Close to Teramo's Duomo, this is where locals go to find fine-quality regional cuisine, including unusual options such as *scrippelle 'mbusse*, a kind of light crêpe with cinnamon and cheese. Reserve. Closed Mon, Sun dinner and 2 weeks Jan. €€

PRICE CATEGORIES

The price of a three-course meal for one (not including wine):
€ = under €25
€€ = €25–50
€€€ = €50–80
€€€€ = more than €80

NAPLES

Naples lays claim to being the original home of the pizza – against the counter-claims of Rome – and its *pizzerie* are the main culinary institutions. The Neapolitan pizza base is quite thin (though thicker than the very thin and crispy *pizza romana*) and the range of toppings, set by tradition, is generally fairly limited. In restaurants, seafood figures heavily on Neapolitan menus.

Antica Pizzeria da Michele
Via Cesare Sersale 1–3
Tel: 081-553 9204
www.damichele.net
One of Naples's original, definitive pizzerias, run by a family that began pizza-making in 1870 and has since been copied around the world. In line with strict tradition, there are very few options: essentially, classic pizza Margherita and fishy pizza marinara. No frills, and very noisy. Closed Sun and Aug. €

La Cantina di Triunfo
Riviera di Chiaia 64
Tel: 081-668 101
A wine bar that also serves up excellent traditional Neapolitan dishes, with a shortish menu that varies according to the days of the week and whatever are the

best ingredients in the market that day. Dinner only. Closed Sun and Aug. €–€€

La Cantinella
Via Cuma 42, Lungomare Santa Lucia
Tel: 081-764 8684
www.lacantinella.it
On the seafront, this is an elegant, modish seafood-centred restaurant, with internationally influenced variations on Neapolitan favourites, using particularly intricate, sybaritic sauces. Reserve. Closed Sun June–Sept, and part Aug. €€€€

La Chiacchierata
Piazetta Matilde Serao 37
Tel: 081-411 465
A tiny family-run *trattoria*, La Chiacchierata – "the chatterbox" – is one of the best places to have a meal in the historic centre. Neapolitan specialities are naturally the staples, such as tender *polpette* (octopus) and hearty bean-based soups. Reserve. Lunch only except Fri. Closed Sun and Aug. €€€

Ciro a Santa Brigida
Via Santa Brigida 71–4
Tel: 081-552 4072
In the old heart of Naples, open since 1932, this is a monument of unchanging Neapolitan restaurant tradition, and one of the

best places in town to sample such favourites as deep-fried meat and seafood, octopus and rigatoni with meatballs. Closed Sun (except Dec) and 7–25 Aug. €–€€

Di Matteo
Via dei Tribunali 94
Tel: 081-455 262
Another excellent place to find authentic rustic wood-fired pizzas, a short walk from the Duomo. Closed Sun and Aug. €

Da Tonino
Via Santa Teresa a Chiaia 47
Tel: 081-421 533
A relic of the traditional *osteria*, where Neapolitans came to drink out of the barrel and have a bite of whatever was on the fire; today it still serves up wonderfully satisfying local classics. Lunch only Mon–Thur, also dinner Fri, Sat; closed Sun and Aug. €–€€

Don Salvatore a Mergellina
Via Mergellina 4A
Tel: 081-681 817
www.donsalvatore.it
This airy and lively restaurant is very popular – both for its food and its location, by the Mergellina waterfront near the boat quays for Capri and Ischia, with big windows giving

lovely views. Specialities include a buffet of antipasti and delicious fresh fish. Closed Wed. €€–€€€

Giuseppone a Mare
Via Ferdinando Russo 13, Posillipo
Tel: 081-575 6002
Established for some two centuries, this restaurant on the seafront in Posillipo has a giant menu including all the local specialities and, of course, great seafood. Closed Mon and dinner Sun, and 2 weeks Aug. €€€

Ristorante la Fazenda
Via Marechiaro 58/A
Tel: 081-575 7420
La Fazenda overlooks the Gulf of Naples and Capri, with an outside terrace in summer, and serves fine grilled seafood and other typically Mediterranean dishes. Closed Sun dinner, Mon lunch and part Aug. €€

Sbrescia Antonio
Rampe di Sant'Antonio a Posillipo 109
Tel: 081-669 140
On a steep street climbing the hills above the city, with another of Naples's fabulous views of the Gulf, this classic restaurant offers finely seasoned fresh seafood, pasta, pizza and other favourites. Reserve. Closed Mon and part Aug. €€–€€€

CAMPANIA COAST AND ISLANDS

Amalfi

Da Gemma
Via Fra' Gerardo Sasso 9
Tel: 089-871 345
www.trattoriadagemma.com
Next to the Duomo, with a delightful terrace to provide the necessary Amalfi view, this stylish *trattoria* offers sophisticated versions of traditional cooking, especially seafood. Reservations recommended. Closed Wed and Jan. €€€

Capri

Canzone del Mare
Via Marina Piccola 93

Tel: 081-837 0104
www.lacanzonedelmare.com
In the former home of English singer Gracie Fields, this resort hotel was a jet-set destination in its heyday, and remains a little reminiscent of the 1960s. The location of the terrace restaurant remains as stunning as ever, beside a swimming pool surrounded by gardens with views of the Faraglioni, and the food is of good quality, if expensive. Open lunch only Easter–Oct, plus dinner in Aug. €€€€

La Capannina
Via le Botteghe 12/14

Tel: 081-837 0732
www.capannina-capri.com
This chic restaurant in Capri town serves classic, traditional seafood, as well as regional and international cuisine. One of Capri's ever-fashionable eating spots; reservations recommended. Closed Wed (except June–Sept) and Nov–Mar. €€€–€€€€

Le Grottelle
Via Arco Naturale 13
Tel: 081-837 5719
Diners get a unique view of Capri's *Arco Naturale* or natural arch, overlooking the Gulf of Salerno, from this rustic-style restaurant

and pizzeria, housed in a natural grotto. Regular dishes include home-reared rabbit and barbecued fish. Closed Thur except July–Aug, and late Oct–mid-Mar. €€€–€€€€

La Pigna
Via la Palazzo 30
Tel: 081-837 0280
The perfect place for a romantic dinner, especially on the terrace, with its view over the Gulf of Napes. The Neapolitan cuisine is prepared with flair, and served with professional courtesy. Closed Mon and Feb. €€–€€€

Ischia

Il Melograno
Via Giovanni Mazzella 110, Forio
d'Ischia
Tel: 081-998 450
www.ilmelogranoischia.it
In Forio on the west side of
the island, Il Melograno is
noted as much for its fine,
Michelin-starred cuisine as
its picturesque setting among
olive groves. Creative fish
dishes are the speciality.
Reserve. Closed Jan–Mar,
and Mon Oct–Jan. €€€€
**Trattoria da Peppina di
Renato**
Via Montecorvo 42, Località Forio
Tel: 081-998 312
Furnished with old barrels,
this enticing *trattoria* offers
local cuisine, such as *pasta
mischiata* (pasta with
beans, lentils or chickpeas)
and home-made *crostate*
(tarts) and cakes. Reserve.
Dinner only. Closed Wed,
except June–Sept, and
Nov–Mar. €€–€€€

Paestum

Ristorante Nettuno
Via Nettuno 2,
Zona Archeologica

Tel: 0828-811 028
www.ristorantenettuno.com
Next to the ruined temples
of Paestum, this pretty
restaurant provides a
charming place to relax
after a visit, with a garden
terrace and fine classic
Italian cooking. Reserve.
Lunch only, except Fri and
Sat July and Aug; closed
part Nov. €€–€€€

Positano

La Buca di Bacco
Via Rampa Teglia 4
Tel: 089-875 699
www.bucadibacco.it
In a beautiful location on
Positano's precipitous
hillside, this hotel
restaurant has a huge
terrace from which to
admire the dazzling colours
of the sea while enjoying the
classic seafood fare. Closed
Nov–Mar. €€€–€€€€
Chez Black
Via del Brigantino 19/21
Tel: 089-875 036
www.chezblack.it
Long established as a prime
celebrity meeting point
above the beach of Spiaggia
Grande, this smart

restaurant-pizzeria and
terrace highlights on fish
and seafood, with a
celebrated mixed *frittura di
mare*. The wine list is
celebrated too. Closed early
Jan–early Feb. €€€

Salerno

Al Cenacolo
Piazza Alfano 1, 4/6
Tel: 089-238 818
The most reliable option in
Salerno, with no surprises
but good fish dishes, fresh
pasta, tasty desserts and a
decent wine range. Closed
Sun dinner, Mon, part Aug
and Christmas/New Year.
€€€

Sorrento

Don Alfonso 1890
Corso Sant'Agata 11, Sant'Agata
sui due Golfi
(9 km/5½ miles from Sorrento)
Tel: 081-878 0026
www.donalfonso.com
In a spectacular location on
the mountain road between
Sorrento and Positano, this
shrine to gastronomy is one
of the best restaurants in
southern Italy. The Iaccarino

family's seasonal menus
are exquisitely executed,
and served in gracious
surroundings. Reservation
essential. Closed Mon and
Tues lunch June–Sept.
€€€€
La Fenice
Via degli Aranci 11
Tel: 081-878 1652
www.ristorante-la-fenice.com
A brightly pretty restaurant
and pizzeria with a nice
welcoming atmosphere, not
far from the seafront.
Seafood and delicious
antipasti are the
specialities, on a menu that
has something for all
budgets. Closed Mon except
Aug. €€–€€€

BELOW: pizza alfresco.

PUGLIA

The heel of Italy has a rich
agricultural heritage. Herbs
play a major role in local
cooking, and olives, olive oil,
almonds, aubergines, figs
and watermelons are
highlights of many dishes.
The most common form of
pasta here is *orecchiette*
("little ears"), with a variety
of delicious sauces.

Alberobello

Il Poeta Contadino
Via Indipendenza 21
Tel: 080-432 1917
www.ilpoetacontadini.it
In an old stable refurnished
in conventionally ornate
style, this upscale
restaurant serves award-
winning fine Italian cuisine.
Don't miss the basil ice-
cream dessert, and check
out the top-drawer wine list,

kept in a cellar in an ancient
well. Closed Mon and 3
weeks Jan. €€

Bari

Ai 2 Ghiottoni
Via Putignani 11
Tel: 080-523 2240
www.ai2ghiottoni.it
An outpost of contemporary
chic in out-of-the-way
Puglia, with creative
variations on Puglian dishes
using the best local
ingredients, and a superb
wine list. There is also a
similarly stylish 2 Ghiottoni
pizzeria for more casual
dining, at Via Amendola 197
(tel: 080-546 7134; €–€€).
Closed Sun. €€–€€€
Murat
Palace Hotel, Via Lombardi 13
Tel: 080-521 6551
www.palacehotelbari.it

The pink and plush Murat
restaurant in Bari's
premier hotel, the Palace,
offers an interesting choice
of regional dishes, fine
cheeses and moderately
priced set menus. Another
draw is the panoramic
view. Closed Aug. €€€

Barletta

Il Brigantino
Litoranea di Levante
Tel: 0883-349 227
You can't miss this giant
terrace restaurant above
the beach in Barletta's lido,
offering, naturally, a mainly
fish and seafood menu.
Hugely popular, serving
thousands of contented
diners each summer.
There's also a smaller
indoor dining room. Closed
Jan. €€€

Brindisi

La Lanterna
Via G. Tarantini 14
Tel: 0831-564 026
Near Brindisi's cathedral, La
Lanterna is housed in a
15th-century palazzo and
specialises in inventive twists
on regional cuisine, with lots
of original recipes. Closed
Sun, Sat lunch and Aug. €€

Lecce

Ristorante Picton
Via Idomeneo 14

PRICE CATEGORIES

The price of a three-course
meal for one (not including
wine):
€ = under €25
€€ = €25–50
€€€ = €50–80
€€€€ = more than €80

Tel: 0832-332 383
www.ristorantepicton.com
In a Baroque palazzo,
Lecce's smartest restaurant
focuses on local cuisine
with an emphasis on
inventive, light, seasonal
dishes. Closed Mon, part
June and Nov. €€–€€€

Manfredonia

Coppola Rossa
Via dei Celestini 13
Tel: 0884-582 522
www.coppolarossa.com

Bright and friendly,
Coppola Rossa is a relaxed
trattoria offering first-rate
local fish and seafood
dishes and juicy home-
made desserts. Closed
Mon, Sun dinner and
Christmas/New Year. €–€€

Taranto

Ristorante Ponte Vecchio
Piazza Fontana 61
Tel: 099-470 6374
A stylish seafood and fish
restaurant with a lovely

harbourside terrace and
imaginative cooking;
lobster and clams are
particular specialities.
Closed Tues. €€

Trani

Il Melograno
Via Bovio 187
Tel: 0883-486 966
www.ilmelograno.it
A welcoming, family-run
restaurant in the centre of
picturesque Trani. Fish is
the speciality, but local

pasta and meat dishes with
fine seasonal produce also
feature. Closed Wed and
Jan. €€–€€€
Palazzo Giardino Broquier
Via Beltrani 17
Tel: 0883-506 842
In the heart of the Old Town,
this acclaimed restaurant
has a stylish setting in a
former palazzo, with tables
inside or in a very pretty
garden. The food has
luxurious touches to match.
Reserve. Closed Mon, dinner
Sun and Nov. €€–€€€

CALABRIA AND BASILICATA

Cosenza

Da Giocondo
Via Piave 53
Tel: 0984-29810
Reliable and comfortable
family restaurant in the Old
Town; don't miss the pickled
mushrooms, the local
cheeses (from the Sila), the
maccheroni in kid sauce,
and delicious local honey-
based desserts. Closed Sun
dinner and Aug. €€

Maratea

Santavenere Hotel
Via Conte Stefano Rivetti 1,
Fiumicello di Maratea
Tel: 0973-876 910
www.hotelsantavenere.it

From seafood to pasta, chef
Vincenzo Pinto makes sure
everything here is prepared
to the highest standard at
this long-established but still
stylish cliff-top hotel. Not
cheap, but very enjoyable,
and good value. €€€

Matera

Il Casino del Diavolo
Via la Martella
Tel: 0835-261 986
Matera's speciality is bread
made from durum wheat
baked in wood-fired ovens –
several of which you will find
around town. In this family-
run *trattoria*-pizzeria you
can find a choice of peasant
dishes made with durum

bread, and to follow try the
mantecato di panna –
forest fruit and chilled
cream. €€
Le Botteghe
Piazza San Pietro Barisano 22
Tel: 0835-344 072
www.lebotteghemt.it
Earthy regional dishes such
as roast meat, excellent
cheese and home-made
orchiette pasta, served in
the evocative atmosphere of
one of Matera's Sassi cave
houses, dug into the rock. €

Reggio di Calabria

Baylik
Vico Leone 3
Tel: 0965-48624
www.baylik.it

The freshest of fresh fish,
simply cooked, is the star
attraction at this
celebrated restaurant,
close to Reggio harbour.
It's possible to dine untill
midnight on the catch of
the day, and the swordfish
with pumpkin flowers is
fabulous. Closed Thur and
part Aug. €€–€€€
**Hotel Residence il
Gabbiano**
Via Punta Alice, Cirò Marina
Tel: 0962-31338
www.gabbiano-hotel.it
This modest family beach
hotel outside Reggio has a
large restaurant that's plain
to look at but serves up
good-quality pasta, fish and
seafood. €

SICILY

Sicily's historic influences
are perpetuated in its food;
the Arab legacy has given
Sicilians a sweet and spicy
cuisine, while Spanish rule
brought a more refined style
of cooking. Typical dishes
include *pasta con le sarde*
(pasta with sardines), *pasta
alla norma* (with
aubergines), fish couscous,
stuffed aubergines, deep-
fried rice balls and chickpea
fritters.

Catania

La Siciliana
Viale Marco Polo 52/A

Tel: 095-376 400
www.lasiciliana.it
A classic, elegant
restaurant, run by a family
with a long tradition in
cooking; specialities include
pasta alla norma and rice
with cuttlefish. Reserve.
Closed Sun dinner and Mon.
€€€
Osteria I Tre Bicchieri
Via San Giuseppe al Duomo 31
Tel: 095-715 3540
One of Sicily's best
restaurants, in the centre of
Catania. There is an
enoteca wine bar, and the
vaulted dining room serves
excellent creative and

traditional dishes. Fish and
seafood feature strongly, but
carnivores will also be
happy. Dinner only. Closed
Aug. €€€–€€€€

Palermo

Charleston le Terrazze
Viale Regina Elena, Mondello
(11km/7 miles from Palermo)
Tel: 091-450 171
On the pier at Palermo's
favourite beach lido of
Mondello, this stylish
restaurant and its Art
Nouveau-fantasy dining
room attract a fashion-
conscious local clientele in

summer. The menu is strong
on fish and seafood,
especially swordfish. Closed
Wed in Nov–Mar, and early
Jan–early Feb. €€€
Santandrea
Piazza Sant'Andrea 4
Tel: 091-334 999
Just beside Palermo's
Vuccira market, this well-
regarded restaurant has
first choice of the freshest
produce, which is
imaginatively presented.
Specialities include
spaghetti with fresh
sardines, and ultra-rich dark
chocolate mousse. Closed 3
weeks Aug. €€–€€€

Syracuse

Archimede
Via Gemmellaro 8
Tel: 0931-69701
An ever-enjoyable traditional *trattoria* and pizzeria in the lovely quarter of Ortygia. Tasty fish dishes are rivalled by mouth-watering, mostly vegetarian antipasti, and there's a

pretty courtyard. It's a good idea to reserve a table. Closed Sun. **€€**

Taormina

Al Duomo
Vico Ebrei 11
Tel: 0942-625 656
www.ristorantealduomo.it
Pretty and comfortable restaurant in the centre of

Old Taormina, with a special menu of Sicilian specialities. Reserve ahead as it's very popular. Closed Mon, Jan and Nov. **€€**

La Giara
Vico la Floresta 1
Tel: 0942-23360
www.lagiara-taormina.com
With its all-white decor, white linen and white stone floor, La Giara's

dining room and candlelit terrace can appear like an elegant vision looking down from the heights over Taormina. The delicate cuisine is equally stylish, and there's a chic lounge bar. Reservations essential. Dinner only. Closed Mon (except Aug) and Nov–Mar open Fri, Sat only. **€€€–€€€€**

SARDINIA

A little world of its own, Sardinia is remarkably self-sufficient in food as in other things, and many restaurant menus on the island feature only local dishes. Excellent fish and seafood are naturally highlights around the coast, and spit-roasted meats inland; Sardinian pasta variations include *culingiones*, small ravioli-like parcels, while the island produces a wonderful range of honeys and very strong cheeses, especially from sheep and goat's milk. Sardinia also produces a remarkably high-quality variety of wines, both red and white.

Alghero

Ristorante Borgo Antico
Via Zaccaria, off Piazza della Misericordia
Tel: 079-982 649
Charmingly friendly and unfussy, this family-run restaurant in the centre of Old Alghero has all the traditional features – plain tiled floors, wooden furniture – as a backdrop to cooking, especially of fish and seafood, that's worthy of a much grander setting. In true Sard style everything is local, from the giant langoustines to the fine wines. Closed Sun. **€€**

Ristorante La Lepanto
Via Carlo Alberto 135
Tel: 079-979 116
The most consistent and the most reliable of the many restaurants near Alghero's seafront. The dining room, effectively an enclosed

terrace, is comfortable and air-conditioned, and service very courteous; lobster is the foremost speciality, served several different ways, and this and other fish, seafood and meat dishes are prepared with a fine eye to quality and traditional care. Closed Mon. **€€**

Bosa

Hotel Ristorante Sa Pischedda
Via Roma 8
Tel: 0785-373 065
www.hotelsapischedda.it
This lovely hotel above the charming old river harbour of Bosa, south of Alghero, has a delightful terrace restaurant. Menu highlights include the fragrant *alisanza* pasta with scorpion fish and basil, lobster and scrumptious desserts, and the wine range is equally well cared for. **€€–€€€**

Cabras

Sa Funta
Via Garibaldi 25
Tel: 0783-290 685
On a good day much of Cabras village fills this atmospheric restaurant, just inland from the superb beaches of the Sinis peninsula. The helpful owner guides newcomers through the menu, which is strong on distinctive Sardinian specialities such as smoked fish, roast cheeses and *sebadas*, sweet pastries. Ingredients, especially the local vegetables, are

outstanding. Closed Sun. **€–€€**

Cagliari

Antica Hostaria
Via Cavour 60
Tel: 070-665 870
www.anticahostaria.it
One of Cagliari's historic eating places, open since the 1850s, continues to present excellent Sardinian traditional cooking in its beautifully decorated, unchanging dining room. Seafood pasta dishes are exceptional. Reserve. Closed Sun and Aug. **€€€**

Ristorante Lisboa
Via Tuveri 2
Tel: 070-43707
Seasonal local produce is put together in innovative combinations at this smart modern restaurant, with an equally contemporary near-minimalist look. If you want a still lighter meal, there are great cakes and *tramezzini* sandwiches. **€–€€**

Costa Smeralda

I Frati Rossi
Località Pantogia, Porto Cervo
Tel: 0789-94365
www.fratirossi.com
It's not always necessary to blow the budget to find something special in Porto Cervo. On a hilltop south of the main town, with stunning views of the islands offshore, the "Red Friars" is a rustic gourmet heaven, presenting Sardinian classics – especially fish and seafood – with Ligurian and Tuscan influences. **€€€**

Muravera

L'Escargot
Costarei Muravera
Tel: 070-991 6111
A wonderful beachfront location and big covered terrace make this modest restaurant, in a village on the Costa Rei north of Villasimius, a special place. Not surprisingly snails feature on the menu, alongside more tasty seafood classics like pasta with mussels, prawns, clams or squid. Closed Nov–Mar. **€**

Oliena

Su Gologone
Località Su Gologone
Tel: 0784-287 512
www.sugologone.it
A remarkably luxurious, seductive retreat on a beautiful old farm in the rugged hills inland from Cala Gonone, with stylishly rustic bedrooms, Su Gologone also delivers an exquisite take on Sardinian country cuisine in its restaurant. The array of antipasti is fabulous, and other highlights include the freshest Cagliata cheese, rare local pasta variations and succulent roast lamb, pork and goat. **€€€**

PRICE CATEGORIES

The price of a three-course meal for one (not including wine):
€ = under €25
€€ = €25–50
€€€ = €50–80
€€€€ = more than €80

A CTIVITIES

THE ARTS, NIGHTLIFE, FESTIVALS, FOOD AND CULTURE, OUTDOOR ACTIVITIES AND SHOPPING

THE ARTS

Italy has such a long recorded history that the biggest problem facing the traveller interested in culture is how to choose between the nation's countless attractions.

Opera and Classical Music

Classical music- and opera-lovers will feel very much at home in Italy. Opera is not at all a minority taste here, as it is in so many other countries, and magnificent concerts can be enjoyed all year round.

Rome

The city's most important music venue is the **Auditorium Parco della Musica** (www.auditorium.com). Designed by Genoan architect Renzo Piano and inaugurated only in 2002, it incorporates its own set of Roman ruins, three indoor halls and an outdoor amphitheatre, and hosts concerts that range from classical to electronica.

Opera, ballets and concerts are also held at the **Teatro dell'Opera**, Piazza Beniamino Gigli 7, www.operaroma.it, which relocates to the Baths of Carcalla in high summer. Concerts are also held in various churches, smaller auditoriums and outdoor venues during the summer-long festival called **Estate Romana**.

Florence

The most important musical event in Florence is the international music and arts festival, **Maggio Musicale Fiorentino** (www.maggiofiorentino.com), which takes place in May and June at the Teatro Comunale, the principal opera house and concert hall. Open-air concerts are held in the **Boboli Gardens** and in the cloisters of the **Badia Fiesolana** on July and August evenings. Another younger, but important, summer festival is **Estate Fiesolana**, which runs from June until August. This event fills the ancient Roman theatre in Fiesole and several churches in Florence with opera, concerts, theatre, ballet and films (www.estatefiesolana.it).

Milan

Milan's hallowed **Teatro alla Scala** has undergone complete renovation in recent years. Upcoming programme details and tickets sales are available through the theatre website (www.teatroallascala.org). Reservations open two months before the date of the performances, and tickets often sell out on the first day. Any tickets unsold one month before the performance are available at the La Scala box office; for information call 02-7200 3744. Expect to be on hold for some time.

Turin

In Turin, classical music is at its peak from late August until the end of September, when **Settembre Musica** takes over the city. This international music festival, which Turin shares with Milan, features the cream of national and international performers (www.mitosettembremusica.it).

Venice

Venice's renowned **La Fenice** opera house (www.teatrolafenice.it) has fully recovered from the fire that devastated it in 1996, and now hosts an extensive programme of opera, ballet and more eclectic concerts.

Verona

Verona's annual open-air opera season at the Roman arena, the **Arena di Verona**, runs from June to August . For bookings, see www.arena.it. The programme sticks to great operatic classics like Madama Butterfly, Turandot or Aida, and the marvellous open-air acoustics always make for a memorable occasion.

Naples

Naples is blessed with the largest opera house in Italy – **San Carlo** – a place with fine acoustics that draws performers and audiences throughout the year. The main opera, ballet and concert season runs from January to mid-July (www.teatrosancarlo.it). At the **Teatro delle Palme** (www.teatrodellepalme.it), a classical music season runs from January to April. Pick up a free copy of Qui Napoli from the tourist office to find out what's on when in the city.

Palermo

Opera is also performed here in at grandiose setting. Palermo's **Teatro Massimo** (www.teatromassimo.it) opera house has been finely restored after languishing in a state of abandonment for decades. Ask the tourist office for a copy of its Agenda magazine, an up-to-date listing of events throughout the city (in English and Italian) or visit www.palermotourism.com.

Theatres

If your Italian is fluent enough for you to be able to enjoy a play, check the listings sections of local newspapers for information on performances.

In **Rome**, the principal theatres are: **Teatro Sistina**, Via Sistina 129, tel: 06-420 0711, www.ilsistina.com; **Teatro Valle**, Via del Teatro Valle 21, tel: 06-6880 3794, www.teatrovalle.it; and **Teatro Argentina**, Largo Argentina 52, tel: 06-684 0001, www.teatrodiroma.net. Two theatre companies put on plays in English: the **Miracle Players**, www.miracleplayers.org, summer only; and the **English Theatre of Rome**, www.rometheatre.com.

In **Milan**, the hub of the theatre scene is the **Piccolo Teatro**, Via Rovello 2, and its offshoots **Teatro Studio**, Via Rivoli 6, and the **Teatro Strehler** on Largo Greppi (bookings for all theatres: 848-800-304; www.piccoloteatro.org).

In **Florence**, you can take in productions in Italian at **Teatro Comunale** (www.maggiofiorentino.org), **Teatro della Pergola**, (www.teatrodellapergola.com) or **Teatro Verdi** (www.teatroverdionline.it). All these theatres also host concerts.

In **Naples**, the **Teatro Stabile de Napoli** company (www.teatrostabilenapoli.it) appears in several theatres, notably the **Mercadante,** the smaller and modern **San Ferdinando** and **Ridotto**, and the lovely, ornate 19th-century **Bellini**.

NIGHTLIFE

In recent years, **Milan** and **Florence** have been the main centres of hip Italian nightlife: Milan for its rock and dance scene and Florence for its clubs. In the south, **Naples** and **Catania** have some of the liveliest nightlife. In **Palermo**, nightlife was, until recently fairly non-existent, concentrated only around the summer lido of Mondello, but since 2000 the historic centre of Palermo has been coming to life again, especially around Lo Spasimo cultural centre, a converted former church and cloister where concerts, exhibitions and other events draw visitors of all ages.

In **Rome**, jazz and blues have long had a following, but nowadays Latin and Brazilian dance music, techno, rap and other contemporary styles are far more popular in dance bars and clubs. The main hub of the contemporary Roman nightlife scene – or at least the one that is most accessible to visitors – is Testaccio. Trastevere, the old heart of Rome at night in the 1980s, is still quite lively, although mainly for bars and restaurants.

Venice is much less of a city for nightlife. Although there are piano bars, the casino and the odd folk club, most people prefer sitting in cafés and walking through the beautiful, labyrinthine streets here. In summer those desperate to go clubbing tend to drive at breakneck speed to the **Lido di Jesolo** coastal resort, a world away from sleepy Venice in atmosphere. The other major centre of summer nightlife on the Adriatic is **Rimini**, where some of Italy's most style-conscious beach clubs open only from May to September.

In **Turin** the best nightlife from a visitor's point of view lies in the seductive 19th-century cafés. The most famous are **Baratti E Milano** in Piazza Castello and **Caffè Torino** on Piazza San Carlo.

Below is a list of current hotspots. Trust advice on the ground, as the scene in each city is always changing. Be aware that by law at many Italian clubs you are obliged to take out a membership *(tessera)* in order to enter. The fee is usually pretty nominal (and many places now wave people through without it), but this can add a little to the cost of a first-time visit.

Rome

To find out what's on in Rome, check the weekly *Roma C'e*, a useful listings magazine that comes out every Wednesday with a section in English, and has an Italian-only website (www.romace.it). One thing to note – many Rome nightspots close for several weeks in summer, when DJs and audiences decamp to beach clubs, some nearby at Ostia Lido.

Nightspots

Campo de' Fiori
On summer nights, this lovely, rambling square and its surrounding medieval streets become a lively and popular rendezvous point. An all-time classic on the square is the **Vineria**, at no. 15, but any other bar will do just as well to indulge in some memorable people-watching.

The Pantheon
Just east of Piazza Navona is the Pantheon district, which is extremely lively and beautifully illuminated at night. Apart from the sheer romance of this locality, the fine *gelaterie* (ice-cream parlours), especially the **Cremeria Monteforte** at Via della Rotonda 22, are another great draw.

Piazza Navona
This elegant Renaissance square becomes a good place for a night-time amble. Try the legendary *tartufo* ice from **I Tre Scalini** at no. 28.

Trastevere
On the left bank of the Tiber, Trastevere is an intimate and atmospheric part of town, even if parts of it are now quite touristy. Its alleyways and tiny squares are lined with family-run inns and restaurants, and convivial bars. **Freni e Frizioni** (Via del Politeama 4–6) is hip and ever-popular, and has food as well as a bar.

Testaccio
Rome's former slaughterhouse district, and above all its leafy and winding thoroughfare, Via di Monte Testaccio, is dotted with nightclubs and bars.

Music Clubs, Cabaret & Cinema

Alibi
Via di Monte Testaccio 44
Tel: 06-574 3448
Rome's longest-running gay venue, with various events and theme nights, many popular with non-gays. Open Thur–Sun.

Alien
Via Velletri 13–19
Tel: 06-841 2212
One of Rome's biggest dance clubs, with amazing lighting and special effects.

Big Mama
Vicolo San Francesco a Ripa 18
Tel: 06-581 2551
Bastion of Rome's jazz and blues scene, this cosy Trastevere club offers live music most nights by Italian and international acts. Closed Mon.

Black Out Rock Club
Via Saturnia 18
Tel: 06-7049 6791
Suitably dark, no-frills club that's the place for indie, punk and rock music, with some performances by British and US bands and a crowd dressed in black.

Caffè Latino
Via di Monte Testaccio 96
Tel: 06-5728 8556
Live Latin American music on most nights for an audience who know their dance steps. Later, DJs also play funk and acid jazz, and on some nights there are film screenings and cabaret.

Casa del Jazz
Viale di Porta Ardeatina 55
Tel: 06-704 731
This subsidised concert space, founded with the help of Rome's former mayor jazz aficionado Walter Veltroni, attracts big jazz names, and also has a stylish café and restaurant.

Jackie O'
Via Boncompagni 11
Tel: 06-4288 5457
This very glamorous club with

Roman Bars and Cafés

Many Romans prefer going on café-crawls to hitting the latest club. Here are some of the more popular.

Antico Caffè della Pace
Via della Pace 3/7
Classic ivy-swathed café that also serves good *aperitivi* and *digestivi*.

Bar Navona
Piazza Navona 67
Familiar Roman spot on one of Rome's loveliest squares.

Bar San Calisto
Piazza San Calisto 4
Gritty and rough-hewn, but no less classic. It serves cheap coffee, beer,

alcohol and ice cream.

L'Oasi della Birra
Piazza Testaccio 41
The place for beer – over 500 varieties – and grappa in the fun Testaccio district.

Rosati
Piazza del Popolo 4/5
A historic café, *pasticceria* and restaurant that affords great views over the elegant Piazza del Popolo.

Tazza D'Oro
Via degli Orfani 84
Bustling bar and coffee roastery that sells the city's best coffee. No seating.

restaurant and piano bar has been famous since the *dolce vita* era, but you still may have to queue. It pays to don your finest gear, and emulate the Roman style of *bella figura*.

Joia
Via Galvani 20
Tel: 06-574 0802
This stylish Testaccio club boasts a dance area with cosy banquette seating, an intimate restaurant and a large terrace for alfresco dancing in the summer months.

Nuovo Olimpia
Via in Lucina 16g
Tel: 06-686 1068
On a side street off Via del Corso, this cinema always has at least one screen showing a film in "VO" (original version), rather than dubbed into Italian. Wednesday is the day to catch a film in Rome as prices are reduced.

Supperclub
Via de' Nari 14
Tel: 06-6880 7207
Exclusive haunt of Rome's well-heeled crowd, who come for the DJs and first-class cocktails, this bar-club-restaurant also hosts themed club events. The door policy is tight; closed Wed.

Milan

Given the eclectic nature of Milanese nightlife, it is tricky to categorise places – sometimes the same place performs several functions. Nightlife of the hot, youthful variety is centred on the Navigli district, the canal quarter. You should just be able to turn up in the evening and see what is on offer. However, to plan ahead, check what's on in the *ViviMilano* insert in Wednesday's *Corriere della Sera* or visit www.hellomilano.it. More refined bars and low-key clubs can be found in the Brera area.

Alcatraz
Via Valtellina 25

Tel: 02-6901 6352
One of the trendy mega clubs, with two dance floors, three bars, two performance areas and a pub.

Bar Daila Café
Via San Vicenzo 15
Tel: 02-5811 2288
This friendly jazz café has live music on some evenings (usually Thursday and Friday), and a nicely relaxed atmosphere the rest of the time.

Bar Jamaica
Via Brera 32
Tel: 02-876 723
This bar in the Brera has no special gimmicks and doesn't look anything special, but it is a piece of Milanese history – a traditional meeting place for artists, intellectuals and celebs. Despite its fame, it's a calm place for drinking cocktails or sampling Italian regional dishes. Open all day.

Blue Note
Via Borsieri 37
Tel: 899-700 022
A franchisee of the legendary New York jazz club, featuring some of the biggest names around. Also a restaurant and bar, and its Sunday brunch is increasingly popular. Open daily.

Blueshouse
Via Sant'Uguzzone 26
Tel: 02-3956 0756
Live music on most nights, with tribute bands honouring legendary names such as Led Zeppelin and the Rolling Stones. At other times bands play blues, rock and even folk.

El Brellin
Vicolo dei Lavandai,
Via Alzaia Naviglio Grande 14
Tel: 02-5810 1351
In a quaint old former washhouse in the Navigli area, a relic of Old Milan, this atmospheric restaurant also has a popular and equally attractive bar-café.

Café L'Atlantique
Viale Umbria 42
Tel: 199-111 111

Sleek and stylish and one of the city's top nightspots, this dance club and restaurant offers mostly hip-hop and house music in luxurious surroundings. Dress accordingly.

Café Teatro Nobel
Via Asciano Sforza 81
Tel: 02-8951 1746
Multi-purpose space hosting shows, jazz and cabaret, as well as a bar, in the lively Navigli canal quarter.

Gasoline Club
Via Bonnet 11/A
Tel: 334-7577 441
Near Corso Como, this is one of Milan's most happening dance clubs, gay-friendly and popular with models on Friday nights. Adventurous theme nights keep the party going.

Gattopardo Café
Via Piero delle Francesca 47
Tel: 02-3453 7699
Giant, plush disco in a former church, with the bar in the position of the altar, dancing in the nave amongst marble columns and evocative lighting. R&B, mainstream, house music. A fashion-conscious crowd, and demanding door policy.

Hollywood Rythmoteque
Corso Como 15
Tel: 02-6559 8996
Another of Milan's most fashionable nightspots, with a high-energy crowd studded with celebs and sports stars; be prepared to queue. Especially popular with the glitterati on Sundays.

Lime Light
Via Castelbarco 11–13
Tel: 02-5831 0682
A big, mainstream, unpretentious disco, popular with students – Wednesday is "university evening". Open Wed–Sun.

Pitbull Café
Corso Como 11
Tel. 02-2900 2343
A more mature but still stylish locale on fashionable Corso Como, with chic white interior and soft lighting. Music ranges from soft rock to disco, and there's a very well-stocked bar with renowned cocktails.

Plastic
Viale Umbria 120
Tel: 02-733 996
One of Milan's favourite venues, open for years but still popular, attracting models and a big gay crowd. House and electro music usually reigns, and Sunday is one of the wildest, most glam nights.

Rolling Stone
Corso XXII Marzo 32
Tel: 02-733 172
With three floors and a big space for live music, Rolling Stone is Milan's temple of rock during the week, and

hosts high-energy DJ sessions after the acts at weekends.

La Salumeria della Musica
Via Pasinetti 4
Tel: 02-5680 7350
Cabaret and live music are on the menu in this former factory, transformed into a buzzing club. As in a real *salumeria*, hams and sausages dangle over the bar. Closed Sun.

Le Scimmie
Via Asciano Sforza 49
Tel: 02-8940 2874
A well-established jazz, blues and cabaret club in the Navigli area, which also has a restaurant with Italian or French cuisine.

Shocking Club
Via Bastioni di Porta Nuova 12
Tel: 02-6291 0156
Another smart and louche Milan club, favoured by models and showbiz types, with '70s-kitsch decor. Wednesday is "shocking" night.

Sio Café
Via Piero e Alberto Pirelli 6
Tel: 02-6611 8087
A venue in the up-and-coming Bicocca area, with a summer garden, a bright restaurant open all day, and a fresh, un-snooty approach, with live music and varied DJ nights through the week. Closed Mon.

Florence

Classic Cafés

Caffè Giacosa a Palazzo Strozzi
Piazza degli Strozzi
This is a low-key meeting place, popular for evening *aperitivi*.

Caffè Gilli
Piazza della Repubblica 39r
Tel: 055-213 896
This historic café, an institution on the piazza, is also an excellent patisserie. Stand at the bar, where prices are far lower than at tables.

Caffè Rivoire
Piazza della Signoria 4r
Tel: 055-214 412
Open since 1872, and still one of the best places to be seen in Florence, with an especially large terrace. Closed Mon.

Vivoli
Via Isola delle Stinche 7
Tel: 055-292 334
Universally acknowledged as the city's best *gelateria* (ice-cream parlour), so expect big queues in summer. Closed Mon.

Fashionable Bars

Most trendy bars lie in the more bohemian Oltrarno, on the south side of the river. At night, lively quarters include the vaguely alternative Santo Spirito area and the bohemian-chic Santa Croce. However, good Florentine bars and clubs are dotted throughout the city, and even in the Tuscan countryside.

Dolce Vita
Piazza del Carmine 6
Tel: 055-284 595
This glamorous spot is the place to go for cocktails, live music and general hanging out. Open daily.

Rose's
Via del Parione 26r
Tel: 055-287 090
This was Florence's first sushi bar, but doubles as a more traditional café during the day. Good for cocktails and long drinks.

Salamanca
Via Ghibellina 80r
Tel: 055-234 5452
A Spanish restaurant and tapas bar, open until 2am, that also presents live music, including flamenco and Latin dance bands, and hot salsa, merengue and other Latin styles from DJs.

Clubs

Check times carefully; places only start to fill up very late, after young Florentines have had their fill of hanging out in *pizzerie* and *gelaterie*.

Escopazzo
Lungarno Colombo, Bellariva
Tel: 055-676 912
This eclectic Latin club has regular themed nights, from Cuban to Caribbean music. After midnight, however, you are more likely to be dancing to mainstream sounds.

Maramao
Via de Macci 79r
Tel: 055-244 341
Sample the *dolce vita* at this intimate club, one of the most fashionable in town for the last few years, attracting a well-dressed crowd. Closed Mon and May–Sept.

Meccanò
Parco delle Cascine
Viale degli Olmi 1
Tel: 055-331 371
In Cascine park, Meccanò is the best-known and biggest club in Florence, with a restaurant and large garden, and appeals to a wide age group. There are '80s nights on Saturdays, floor shows at other times, and it continues to draw visiting VIPs and Florentine poseurs. Open Tues–Sat in summer, Thur–Sat in winter.

Space Electronic
Via Palazzuolo 37
Tel: 055-293 082
A big, no-nonsense disco club that is a favourite with a younger crowd.

Universale
Via Pisana 77r
Tel: 055-221 122
This former cinema has been transformed into a huge venue, where you can eat, drink, dance and watch shows and concerts. A very versatile club. Closed Mon, Tues and June–Sept.

Naples

Neapolitan nightlife is concentrated in the chaotic historic centre, stretching towards the sea, and the Pozzuoli district by the port. The old Borgo Marinaro area is now popular with all ages, although the bars and *trattorie* are just the same as they were 30 years ago.

Classic Cafés, Wine Bars and Live Music

Aret' A' Palm
Piazza Santa Maria La Nova
Tel: 339-848 6949
Called "Behind the Palms" in Neapolitan dialect, this wine bar and inn (*osteria*) is in a palazzo run by the Austrian-Neapolitan Alan Wurtzburger. Unpretentious, it has an excellent wine list and good bar snacks at very reasonable prices, and the live music includes performances every Wednesday by the musician-owner himself.

Gran Caffè Gambrinus
Via Chiaia 1–2, Piazza Plebiscito
Tel: 081-417 582
This is the city's most famous bar, an elegant place adorned with gilt-and-plaster reliefs. The terrace is a good spot for watching the world go by, sipping *aperitivi* or downing a sweet coffee. Open from early morning until 10 or 11pm.

KsFà Live Club
Via V. Bellini 8
Tel: 081-544 5919
The emphasis at this imaginative venue is on live music of all kinds – jazz, world music, contemporary – but it also hosts exhibitions and other events, and DJ sessions late night, so there's always something interesting going on.

Otto Jazz Club
Piazzetta Cariati 23
Tel: 081-551 3765
A prestigious, mellow venue that often hosts major international names as well as Italian jazz musicians.

Slovenly R 'n' R Bar
Vico San Geronimo 24 (next to Via Benedetto Croce)
Tel: 081-552 6108
Lively rock bar in a cave-like cellar that often hosts international indie bands that are just breaking through.

Vinarium

Vico Cappella Vecchia 7
Tel: 081-764 4114
This centrally located classic wine bar is popular with smart 30-something professionals, but has a relaxing feel in spite of the relatively formal surroundings. A quick stroll away, Via Carlo Poerio is bursting with bars, pubs and wine bars.

Vineria del Centro

Via Palladino 8
This atmospheric wine bar was once a student haunt, but now attracts a wider cross-section. The atmosphere is defined as "intellectual yet homely", a mood enhanced by low lighting and wood-and-marble fixtures and fittings. Closed Mon.

Clubs

The following are among the most stylish or fashionable places for dancing in Naples, but the city is not known for cutting-edge clubs and avant-garde music. Most places tend to play a similar mix of classics from the 1970s and '80s to rap, house or the current chart hits, and are closed on Monday.

Chez Moi

Via del Parco Margherita 13
Tel: 081-407 526
In the upmarket Chiaia area, this chic dance bar caters for a stylish, well-heeled crowd, with a fussy door policy.

Chiatamon Sax Café

Via Chiatamone 16/18
Tel: 081-764 404
An informal but fashionable bar overlooking the seafront of Via Caracciolo, with live music during the week and dancing courtesy of DJs on most weekends, and very popular with young Neapolitans.

Dug Out

Via Mergellina 6
Tel: 081-660 023
This buzzing club is hewn out of soft tufa rock, a cavern in a courtyard, echoing its name. Check on the week's theme nights before going.

Kiss-Kiss

Via Sgambati 47
Tel: 081-546 6566
In the Vomero district, this big two-floor club has a restaurant and attracts a young, studenty clientele.

La Mela

Via dei Mille 40B, Chiaia
Tel: 081-410 270
A smart, trendy place catering to a very style-conscious crowd, so dress to match if you hope to get in. The music is typically unadventurous.

Velvet Club

Via Cisterna dell'Olio 11
Tel: 339-670 0234

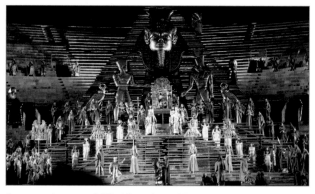

ABOVE: a performance of *Aida* at Verona's amphitheatre.

A series of dark, sweaty spaces that keep throbbing until 6am. Different sounds range from pop to techno, hip-hop, rock and more.

Virgilio Sports Club

Via Tito Lucrezio Caro 6
Tel: 081-575 5261
The name is a bit misleading, even if there is a sports club here too, since this is now a music bar for 20- and 30-somethings. However, in true Neapolitan style, different sets of people have their favourite nights, with Thursday a typical night for *per bene* (well-bred) over-30s. There are sea views from the terrace.

FESTIVALS

The festive year embraces religious and traditional celebrations, such as historical re-enactments, as well as arts festivals, food and wine festivals. These are the highlights of Italy's festive calendar, but there are many more local events.

January–April

Carnevale (Carnival), the period of festivities preceding Lent (usually February) is celebrated in unrivalled style in Venice. Elsewhere, expect excellent carnivals in Viareggio on the Tuscan Coast, and in Acireale and Sciacca in Sicily.

Easter involves major celebrations in Italy, especially in Sicily. The most dramatic and passion-filled festivals are the Mysteries (*I Misteri*) at Trapani, the Easter Devils at Prizzi and the Albanian festivities outside Palermo. The *Scoppio del Carro* (Explosion of the Carriage) takes place in Florence on Easter Sunday. A mechanical dove swoops through the cathedral and ignites a golden carriage filled with

fireworks, symbolising the Resurrection (www.firenzeturismo.it).

May/June

The *Sagra del Pesce* (Fish Festival) takes place in May in Camogli, near Portofino, and is a communal affair, with fish cooked in a 5-metre (16ft) wide saucepan.

Calcio in Costume is a Renaissance-costumed "historical football" event, when an early form of football is played, held in Florence on 19, 24 and 28 June (www.firenzeturismo.it).

The **Florence Opera Festival** is a June/July celebration in Florence and San Galgano Abbey (www.festivalopera.it)

The **Festival dei Due Mondi** is a highbrow arts festival from June to July in Spoleto in Umbria, celebrating theatre and music (www.festivaldispoleto.it).

Torre del Lago is a summer opera festival in honour of local boy Puccini (www.puccinifestival.it).

The **Venice Biennale** is a major modern art fair held in Venice every June–October in odd-numbered years, with exhibits and events in the Biennale pavilions, gardens, and old Arsenale (www.labiennale.org).

July/August

The **Arena di Verona** is a major summer opera festival held in Verona's Roman amphitheatre (www.arena.it).

Bolzano Danza is a July dance festival in Bolzano, in the South Tyrol (www.bolzanodanza.it).

The Cattolica Clam Festival is held in Cattolica on the Adriatic Riviera in July, and celebrates *vongole* (clams), a staple in these parts (www.emiliaromagnaturismo.it).

The **Estate Musicale Chigiana** is a July/August festival of classical music in Siena (www.chigiana.it).

The **Festival Terme Caracalla** is an opera festival held in the ruined Baths of Caracalla in Rome each July and August (www.operaroma.it).

The *Festa del Redentore* is held in Venice on the third Saturday of July, and celebrates the city's deliverance from the Plague in 1567 with fireworks and a procession on the lagoon (www.comunevenezia.it).

Il Palio di Siena, the city's celebrated horse race, takes place annually on 2 July and 16 August (www.ilpalio.org).

Musica Riva is a July classical music/dance festival at Riva, Lake Garda (www.musicarivadelgarda.com).

Rimini beach festivals are staged in July and include fireworks, cookery courses and partying on the beach (www.riviera.rimini.it and www.riminiturismo. it).

Sferisterio Opera Festival is an August event in Macerata, in the Marche (www.sferisterio.it).

The *Palio dei Normanni* is a medieval re-enactment of the conquest of Sicily, staged in August in Piazza Armerina in Sicily (www. feditgiochistorici.it).

The **Badiamusica** festival in Alta Badia in the South Tyrol (www.altabadia. org) and the **Sounds of the Dolomites** in neighbouring Trentino (www.isuonidelledolomiti.it) are summer music festivals, with performances often staged in wonderful mountain scenery.

September/October
The **Stresa Festival** is a September celebration of classical music at Stresa and locations around Lake Maggiore (www.stresafestival.eu).

Marostica Live Chess takes place in even years in Marostica near Vicenza and features human chessmen in medieval costumes (www.marosticascacchi.it).

The Italian Formula one Grand Prix is held at Monza every September (www.monzanet.it).

The **Chianciano Biennale** is a celebration of contemporary art, staged in Chianciano in Tuscany in September in uneven years (www. museodarte.org).

The **Centomiglia Regatta** is staged on Lake Garda every September (www.centomiglia.it).

The *Giostra del Saracino* is a medieval jousting match inspired by the Crusades, and staged on the last Sunday in August and the first Sunday in September in Arezzo in Tuscany.

The **Venice International Film Festival** is held at the Lido in Venice in September and is second only to Cannes in status (www.labiennale.org).

The **Salone del Gusto**, a celebration of traditional food, produce and drinks sponsored by the Slow Food movement, is held in October on alternate years in Turin (www.salonedelgusto.com).

November/December
All Saints' Day, 1 November, is a major holiday throughout Italy.

7 December celebrates Milan's patron saint, Sant'Ambrogio, and is also the start of the opera season at La Scala.

December in Italy means traditional **Christmas fairs**, with the best in Rome, Trento, Bressanone (Alto Adige/South Tyrol) and Naples. In Naples it is linked to a crib *(presepi)* festival.

FOOD AND CULTURE TOURS

Themed Tours and Guides

The Association of British Tour Operators to Italy (www.loveitaly.co.uk) is a good place to start when planning holidays to Italy and booking unusual themed itineraries, ranging from art trails to adventures, including foodie, wine and walking trails.

Sapori + Saperi (tel: +44-(0)7768-474 610; www.sapori-e-saperi.com) specialise in food-centred tours in the Lucca and Garfagnana area of northern Tuscany, culinary adventures to meet local wine and food producers and get a taste of their lives, far from Chiantishire stereotypes.

Tuscany Pass (tel: Italy 050-991 3928; www.tuscanypass.com) is a Pisa-based operation that provides an events calendar and some of the best day trips in Tuscany. Choose from day-long cookery courses to Vespa trips to the wine-growing Chianti; arty Florentine walking tours; designer shopping excursions; or even quad-biking around Lucca.

Link (tel: Italy 055-218 191; www. linkfirenze.it) is a Florence-based guide service that covers personalised thematic tours, ranging from art-centred walking tours to nature rambles and gastro-tours of markets and Chianti wine estates.

Wine and Cookery Courses

Italy abounds in foodie courses but these are three of the best, which remain small, authentic, professional, and memorable.

Camilla in Cucina (tel: 055-461 381; smaccari@iol.it; also via Link, *see below left*). Tour the Florence food markets with chef-guide Silvia Maccari before cooking up a storm at her home. The experience includes tasting cheese, balsamic vinegar and olive oil as well as learning about the cultural and historical traditions that are so tightly intertwined with Italian food.

Carlo Zarri (tel: 0173-81546; www. hotelsancarlo.it) is a celebrated chef and sommelier yet remains a down-to-earth Piedmontese host. Stay in his family-run hotel near Alba's truffle and Barolo country, not far from Turin, while doing a short course with Carlo, who has also written a book (in English) on Piedmontese cookery.

Cucina Giuseppina (tel: 0571-650 242, www.cucinagiuseppina.com) is a warm yet authentic cookery school in medieval Certaldo, not far from San Gimignano. The chef, helped by her wine-specialist son, guides you through regional recipes. The school also offers wine-appreciation and truffle-hunting experiences.

OUTDOOR ACTIVITIES

National and Regional Parks

Italy has some stunningly beautiful national parks. The regions of Abruzzo, Piedmont, Trentino and Alto Adige are just a few of the many areas that should be able to supply information on parks in their territory. A useful website for information on all nature parks and reserves in Italy is www.parks.it.

The Dolomites
The Dolomites, which run across the Veneto, Trentino and Alto Adige (South Tyrol) regions, have some of the most spectacular natural landscapes in Italy, and can be explored on skis or along marked hiking trails (*see below*). For information see the useful tourist-board websites: for Trentino, www.visittrentino.it, and for the Alto Adige/South Tyrol, www.suedtirol.info.

Etna, Sicily
An intriguing and well-organised park, centred on the active volcano of Mount Etna. Many excursions explore this strange area, which encompasses fertile areas from ancient eruptions and the volcanic moonscapes of the most recent lava flows. The Catania tourist office (tel: 095-093 7024; http://turismoprovincia.ct.

Hiking in the Alps

If you want to go hiking in the mountains, get a good-quality walking map, showing all the established paths and the more than 80 overnight areas with shelters. For less experienced walkers, and anyone trying Alpine hiking for a first time, it will always be better to go with a guide and/or a specialist outdoor travel company *(see opposite)* rather than planning an independent trip; high mountain weather can change at any time, and even experienced walkers not familiar with the terrain can easily get lost. Paths are marked with numerous red signs and distinctive small flags. Most stages in the main trails call for 5 to 7 hours of hiking time, at an average of around 1,000 metres (3,300ft) in altitude.

At the overnight rest areas (*rifugi*, or refuges) there are shelters with double-decker bunks, essential services and a kitchen. While many are in idyllic but fairly isolated spots, others are near hamlets or resorts, where it is possible to buy food, phone home, rest for a day, visit rural museums, chat with the local inhabitants and, last but not least, eat a good meal at an inn.

An itinerary can last a month, a week or a day. Local tourist offices provide lists of recommended guides. From the Maritime Alps in the west to Lake Maggiore, on a route stretching for 650km (400 miles) that spans five provinces, the hiker crosses many splendid parks, such as the Gran Paradiso, the Orsiera-Rocciavrè, the Alta Val Pesio and the Argentera. All national park areas are open to the public between July and September.

it) provides free maps, brochures and information on trips available to the top or around the base, and the park authority's website (www.parcoetna.it) gives further details (in Italian). Alternatively, contact the guides of Gruppo Guide Alpine Etna Sud, Via Etnea 49, Nicolosi, tel: 095-791 4755; www.etnaguide.com. Access to the mountain is restricted in periods of volcanic activity.

Parco Naturale dello Sciliar

This park is in the Alto Adige (South Tyrol) region and overlooks the vast plateaux of the Swiss Alps, with jagged rock faces, steep peaks and impressive ledges. Wildlife includes chamois, marmots and golden eagles. The park was established by the authorities of Bolzano (Bozen) – contact the tourist office there on 0471-307 000; www.bolzano-bozen.it.

Parco Nazionale del Gran Paradiso

Home of the last Alpine ibex in Italy, this Alpine park is the oldest in the country and covers 720 sq km (278 sq miles). Spreading over parts of Valle d'Aosta and Piedmont, it has plenty of refuges and trekking facilities. For details contact the tourist boards of **Piedmont**, tel: 00-800-111 33300; www.piemonteitalia. eu, and **Valle d'Aosta**, tel: 0165- 33352; www.regione.vda.it/turismo.

Parco Nazionale dell'Abruzzo

This park extends from the southern section of the Apennines and includes limestone and a Dolomitic landscape. King of the beasts here is the brown bear – some of the last in Italy live in remote splendour in one of the highest sections of the Apennines. Other wildlife include the Apennine wolf, the white-backed woodpecker and Orsini's viper, which is less poisonous than the majority of Italian vipers. For information, tel: 0863- 91131; www.parcoabruzzo.it.

Parco Nazionale dello Stelvio

Italy's biggest park, at 1,350 sq km (520 sq miles), is close to the Swiss border and rich in forests and animal life. The mountains are beautiful, and there are plenty of hotels nearby (open all year). For information tel: 0342-911 448 (Lombardy) or 0463- 746 121 (Trentino), or visit www. stelviopark.it.

Parco Regionale della Maremma

This wonderful Tuscan park is a mixture of meadows, pine forests, sandy shores and swampland along the Tuscan Coast. Wildlife includes wild boar, porcupines, peregrine falcons and the pond tortoise. There are countless trails and opportunities for riding. However, it is advisable to check on itineraries and facilities with the park authority before arriving, via tel: 0564-393 211; www.parco-maremma.it.

Riserva Miramare and the Karst

The *carso* or karst limestone plateau above Trieste is in the eastern part of Friuli-Venezia Giulia region, sandwiched between the Slovenian border and the Adriatic. Austere and riddled with caves, the karst landscape forms a bridge between the Mediterranean and Alpine worlds – with coastal Mediterranean vegetation and Alpine plants, and sheer cliffs on the Adriatic Coast. History buffs can spot medieval castles and World War I trenches. On the Gulf of Trieste, the Riserva Miramare (Miramare Marine Park) contains castles and cliff-top walks as well as the marine reserve itself, which has good scuba-diving locations. For general information visit www.turismo.fvg.it, and for the reserve, www.riservamarinamiramare.it.

Climbing

Some of the best climbing in Italy is in the Dolomites. Climbs near Lake Garda take you through different climatic zones, from Mediterranean- style vineyards to Alpine meadows and botanical reserves, glaciated lakes and weird geological formations.

Walking, Hiking and Cycling

Hiking and Cycling Routes

The Alps to Rome The Via Francigena is a pilgrimage route that runs from Canterbury, England, to Rome, passing through lovely scenery in Italy, particularly in Emilia-Romagna and Tuscany (www.viafrancigena.com).
Friuli-Venezia Giulia The "Rilke Path", beloved by the poet Rainer Maria Rilke, runs through the Duino Cliffs nature reserve north of Trieste, and commands views stretching as far as the Alpine foothills, Grado lagoon and the Istrian Coast. For information see www.triesteturismo.net.
Alto Adige (South Tyrol) From San Cassiano in the Alta Badia Dolomites (www.altabadia.org) you can access Alpine walks and mountain inns via the Piz Sorega cable car.
Trentino Dolomites The Dolomites have it all, from testing high mountain trails and Giro d'Italia cycle climbs to easy lakeside strolls. The area has a network of hiker-friendly and cyclist- friendly routes and hotels (www. dolomitiwalkinghotel.it). The Peace Path, in southern Trentino, hugs the former frontline from the Great War and is an intriguing trail, running from Austro- Hungarian military fortifications to Roman ruins and vineyards (www. visittrentino.it).
Liguria On the **Riviera**, the San Remo Cycle Trail, the first on the Italian coast, currently runs for 24km (15 miles), but should extend to 74km (46 miles) by 2015 (www.area24spa.it). It also

suits walkers and roller-bladers. Bicycles can be hired in towns en route. Above in the nearby **Monti Liguri** mountains there are also fine high-altitude hiking and mountain-biking trails, "between eagles and whales" through the peaks that soar up above the sea (www. altaviadeimontiliguri.it). Further south near **Lerici**, the "Poets' Trail", in the footsteps of Byron and Shelley, runs from Porto Venere to Lerici, overlooking coastal cliffs and islands (www.winetrekking.it/ilsentierodeipoeti), while in the **Cinque Terre**, the celebrated Blue Trail *(Sentiero Azzuro)* clings to the coast for 13km (8 miles) from Riomaggiore to Monterosso (www. parconazionale5terre.it).

Emilia-Romagna The region has a network of well-planned trails between "cities of art" (Ferrara, Modena, Ravenna) and urban trails in these cycle-friendly cities (www. cycle-r.it).

Tuscany Make the most of walks that combine hills, history and cosy inns by booking through a specialist, such as Headwater (www.headwater.com), which offers a variety of Tuscan trails, with luggage transported to the next inn while you're walking.

Umbria A particularly lovely series of dreamy trails have been marked out around Todi, combining rolling hills and Roman routes with a mystical atmosphere. Information is available from Todi tourist office, tel: 075-894 5416.

The South For many hikes in the south, including Sicily, Sardinia and the Amalfi Coast, it's sensible to go through a specialist operator. The Bourbon Cycle Route *(Ciclovia dei Borboni)* is a long-distance route linking Bari and Naples via Matera in Basilicata (www.viaggareinpuglia.it). Puglia suits cyclists of all abilities, with quiet country roads and varied off-road cycling. Based in Monopoli, Puglia in Bici (www.pugliainbici.com) will deliver bikes and route maps to your hotel.

Specialist UK Tour Operators

In Italy, whether you aim to travel by yourself or in a group, booking through an outdoor travel specialist often ensures a better deal, together with the use of tried and tested routes, not subject to the vagaries of regional maps or "lost in translation" itineraries.

Collett's Mountain Holidays, tel: +44-(0)1763-289 660; www.colletts.co.uk.
Inntravel, tel: +44-(0)1653-617 001; www.inntravel.co.uk.

Headwater, tel: +44-(0)1606-720 199; www.headwater.com.
Hedonistic Hiking, tel: +44-(0)845-680 1948; www.hedonistichiking.com.au.

SPORT

Spectator Sports

Football (Soccer)

The national sport in Italy is football. Almost every city and village has a team, and the major teams that play in *Serie A* (Italy's First Division) attract a passionate following and massive media attention. The traditional leading teams from major cities such as Juventus of Turin, AC Milan and Internazionale (usually just called Inter) from Milan or Roma and Lazio in Rome have fan bases across the country, but other teams such as Nápoli, Fiorentina (Florence) or Verona have equally dedicated if more local fans.

The football season for all divisions normally runs from September to May. If you want to see a game, check newspaper listings. It can be difficult to get tickets for some matches (especially those with other major European teams in the Champions' League), but surprisingly easy to get into Italian league matches, particularly those featuring "lesser" teams. Prices vary according to the importance of the team, the game, and the location of the seat you want. For some years Italian football has had a worsening problem of hooliganism. Passions are most intense at local derbies (Roma–Lazio, Milan–Inter), which, though, are also the games with most atmosphere. To avoid problems, get a seat on the side of the pitch, not at either end.

A peculiarity of Italian football is that even big teams do not have their own stadia but share one owned by the city. Hence in Rome both Roma and Lazio play at the Stadio Olimpico, on alternate weekends (except when they play each other). To get to the stadium, take metro line A to Flaminio, then tram 225 to Piazza Mancini, or metro line A to Ottaviano, then bus 32 to the stadium. In Milan both AC Milan and Inter play at the vast Stadio San Siro, which has a museum and offers guided tours (metro line 1 to Lotto; details from Milan tourist office, *see page 435*, or www.sansiro.net).

Buying Tickets

In any city tickets for football matches can usually bought at kiosks around

Motor Racing

Formula One motor racing has an intense following in Italy, centred above all around Ferrari, a national icon that, after a few years in the doldrums after the first retirement of the all-conquering Michael Schumacher, has lately revived its fortunes with Fernando Alonso and Felipe Massa. There are always big crowds at the circuit in Monza, where the Italian Grand Prix is held in September, and the home of Ferrari in Maranello, near Modena, has a glittering museum and art gallery that is a place of pilgrimage for all fans and petrolheads (Via Dino Ferrari, Maranello; tel: 0536-949 713; www.ferrari.com).

the ground (and sometimes in city centres), and at lottery *(lotto)* outlets. The bigger clubs also have stores around their home cities and sometimes elsewhere that sell tickets for their own games. Every major club also now has a website that sells tickets in advance online, and tickets for various clubs are also handled by several booking sites such as www.ticketone.it or www. bestticket.it. Ticket prices generally begin around €10–15 and for the top teams may go up as high as €80 for the best seats, although for other clubs they're rarely over €25. An excellent source of information in English on all aspects of Italian football is www.football-italia.com.

Other Sports

Almost every other sport is enjoyed in Italy, including basketball, golf, water polo, horseracing, rugby union, rowing and sailing. In addition, you can ski in the Alps, Dolomites and the Apennines. To get tickets for sports events, check booking websites *(see above)*, or consult local tourist offices.

May is an important month for sport in Italy. The Giro d'Italia cycle race is a major event on the cycling circuit, and there is also the Italian Open tennis tournament, held at the Foro Italico in Rome. Equestrian sports followers also enjoy their major competition of the year in May, held in Rome's Villa Borghese gardens.

Golf

Golf is increasingly popular in Italy, with good clubs in Piedmont, Lombardy and the Veneto, especially around the northern lakes, as well as in Sicily and Sardinia. Framed by white Alpine peaks, the courses of the lakes area are as hilly or gentle as you wish. One of the world's finest golf resorts is the luxurious Palazzo Arzaga (www.palazzoarzaga.com) on Lake Garda, near Verona.

Sicily's Il Picciolo (www.ilpicciologolf.com) provides the opportunity to play on the flanks of Mount Etna, while in southern Sicily, the Rocco Forte Collection's lavish Verdura Golf and Spa resort (www.verduraresort.com) boasts two championship courses and a 9-hole, designed by Kyle Phillips. Sardinia's Costa Smeralda has one of Europe's most beautiful courses at Pevero (www.golfclubpevero.it), sculpted out of granite and the island's *macchia* scrub.

Horse-Riding

Equestrian Escapes, tel: +44-(0)1829-781 123, www.equestrian-escapes.com, offers tailor-made riding holidays on the Tuscan–Umbrian border.
Horse-Riding in Italy, tel: (Italy) 346-338 2224, www.horseridinginitaly.co.uk, provides riding holidays around Norcia and the Sibillini park in Umbria.
Riding in Rimini. Explore Rimini and its hinterland on horseback, including sea views and un-taxing rides in the surrounding countryside with the **Circolo Ippico Riminese**, tel: 0541-758 515; www.circoloippicoriminese.it.

Watersports

Sailing is the supreme sport on the northern Italian lakes, especially on Lake Garda, Italy's unofficial wind-surfing capital, and one of the best places in Italy for watersports. One of

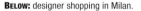

BELOW: designer shopping in Milan.

Winter Sports

Italy has superb scenery, reliable snowmaking systems, well-groomed runs, challenging *off-piste* runs – and some of the world's best mountain food and wine. Also on offer are snow-shoeing, ice-skating, husky rides and tobogganning. Two of the best UK-based ski and mountain tour operators offering trips to Italy are **Crystal** (tel: +44-(0)871-231 5659; www.crystalski.co.uk) and **Inghams** (tel: +44-(0)20-8780 6680; www.inghams.co.uk). Below is a selection of the main ski areas, but upcoming areas and hidden secrets include Abruzzo (www.abruzzoturismo.it) for skiing near the Mediterranean, and, near Trieste, Friuli-Venezia Giulia (www.turismo.fvg.it).

Courmayeur in the Aosta Valley is a charming village cradled by Mont Blanc, Europe's highest mountain. Close by, Italian La Thuile links with the French resort La Rosière. The Monterosa ski area covers 180km (112 miles) of pistes, including Cervinia. Off-piste opportunities are great there, especially at Alagna (www.monterosa.com), which has gained cult status for powder hounds. The *Via Lattea* or "Milky Way" (www.vialattea.it) is a string of Alpine ski resorts above Turin, which straddles the Italian–French border and were primary locations for the Winter

Garda's several yacht clubs is Fraglia Vela in Desenzano (www.fragliavela.it), and the windsurfing is best at Torbole, near Riva del Garda (www.visittrentino.it). Lake Maggiore and Lake Iseo offer jet-skiing and kayaking, and there are also windsurfing and kayaking centres on Lake Como.

Olympics in 2006. Sauze d'Oulx charms with its tangle of cobbled streets and buzzing bars, while snow-sure Sestriere was the Alps' first purpose-built resort, designed by Agnelli, the Fiat magnate. This is also the Milky Way's smartest resort, with the most challenging skiing, a galaxy of good restaurants and glorious scenery.

Few other areas match the Dolomites for jaw-dropping scenery. In Trentino, Madonna di Campiglio in the Brenta Dolomites is chic and popular with affluent Italians (www.visittrentino.it). Cortina d'Ampezzo, surrounded by dramatic pink-tinged peaks, is a famed jet-set resort, with stunning scenery, long runs and superb mountain restaurants (www.dolomiti.org).

Some 45 resorts and 460 lifts in the area are covered by Dolomiti Superski lift pass (www.dolomitisuperski.com). Many are in the German-speaking area of Alto Adige/South Tyrol (www.suedtirol.info). All benefit from state-of-the art snowmaking and superb grooming. One of the most popular resorts is Selva Val Gardena, which is well positioned for access to the 23km (14-mile) Sella Ronda circuit, ideally suited to intermediates, passing through magical scenery.

SHOPPING

Shopping is an Italian passion, not just because the natives are natural consumers, in love with the latest designs, but also because it's often viewed here as an art, involving the search for the beautifully crafted object, the right coffee cups, or the right garment in the right shade and fabric. In addition, since most Italians also attach great importance to finding the right foodstuffs, you are likely to find good quality just about everywhere, even in the simplest street market.

Shopping Areas

Rome

The best district for fashion shopping is the **Tridente** at the bottom of the Spanish Steps, the heart of Rome's design world, with the elegant **Via Condotti** lined with the most exclusive fashion names (Gucci, Ferragamo, Prada, Armani, Bulgari).

Other fashionable streets run parallel to Via Condotti, such as **Via Borgognona** (with Dolce & Gabbana and Hogan), **Via delle Carrozze** or **Via Frattina** (for ceramics, lingerie and costume jewellery), **Via Vittoria** (with a Laura Biagiotti store) and **Via della Croce**. In **Largo Goldoni**, off Via Condotti, is the Palazzo Fendi, the brand's extravagantly opulent headquarters and megastore. Most of these streets are closed to traffic.

For antiques, go window-shopping along **Via del Babuino** (which also has a huge Emporio Armani and other fashion shops), along **Via Margutta**, or **Via dei Coronari** in the *centro storico*, with even more antiques in the streets leading to Piazza Navona. Another fine shopping section is along the Via del Corso between Piazza del Popolo and Largo Chigi, where **Via del Tritone** begins.

Less expensive and more popular shopping streets include **Via Nazionale**, near the railway station, which is good for everyday clothes shops, and **Via Cola di Rienzo**, a busy shopping thoroughfare in the Prati district.

"The other face of fashion" is represented by the open markets, such as the one in Via Sannio, which sells new and second-hand clothes, and, of course, the famous flea market at Porta Portese, open only on Sunday, from sunrise–2pm, where you can find almost everything. Via del Governo Vecchio, near Piazza Navona, is the place for inexpensive jewellery and vintage clothing bargains.

Milan

Milan is home to the major fashion houses and is a consumer paradise during the twice-yearly showing of the new collections. This city, more than Rome, is Italy's principal centre for international fashion.

For those with expensive tastes, the most chic shopping streets are: **Via Montenapoleone, Via della Spiga** and **Via Sant' Andrea**, an area known as the *Quadrilatero* or "Golden Triangle" within walking distance of the Duomo and La Scala. These elegant streets are home to such fashion icons as Krizia, Giò Moretti, Trussardi, Kenzo, Sanlorenzo and Ferragamo, as well as Versace, Gucci, Ermenegildo Zegna, Comme des Garçons, Valentino, Dolce & Gabbana, Hermès, Chanel, Moschino, Prada, Ferre and Fendi. **Spazio Armani**, Giorgio Armani's spectacular "multi-concept store", with every one of the group's brands and a Nobu restaurant, is nearby on Via Manzoni, no. 31.

The **Brera district** is also a smart and discreet shopping location, with a good selection of clothing and antiques. Pick up a shopping guide from the Milan tourist office.

Even the Milanese are not indifferent to questions of cost, and their solution is to use **factory outlets**, which sell the products of major labels at often massive discounts. They tend to be outside the centre, or outside the city entirely, and so can be hard to get to without a car. Two that are a taxi ride from central Milan and stock a wide range of fashion labels are RJ Outlet, Via Zumbini 31, tel: 02-8915 9068; and Outlet 2000, Via Marghera 24, tel: 02-481 5768.

Florence

The whole centre of Florence could be considered a huge marketplace, crowded as it is with tourists and well-dressed locals. Handicrafts are fast disappearing, leaving the place to smart clothing shops. The most fashionable streets are still **Via dei Calzaiuoli**, **Via Roma** and **Via de' Tornabuoni**, home to the famous Ferragamo fashion house – visit its shoe museum in Palazzo Spini-Feroni – as well as **Via della Vigna Nuova** and **Via degli Strozzi** for the likes of Neuber, Principe and Diavolo Rosa.

Ponte Vecchio is famous the world over for gold and silver jewellery and antique shops, but prices can be extortionate and quality variable. In gold or jewellery, you will find better prices and ranges in Arezzo, or in Verona in the Veneto.

The area near the church of **Santa Croce** is full of top-quality leather goods, while for other handicrafts check out the city's two markets, sprawling **San Lorenzo** and covered **Mercato Nuovo**, near Piazza della Signoria.

The **Oltrarno area**, south of the Ponte Vecchio bridge, is home to what remains of Florence's renowned craft industries, from picture restorers to makers of marbled paper. Ask for a list from the tourist office (*see page 434*).

Just 27km (17 miles) away, at **The Mall**, Via Europa 8, Leccio Reggello; tel: 55-865 7775; www.outlet-firenze.com, you can snap up designer labels at up to 80 percent off the original price. Call for details of shuttle bus pick-ups from hotels in Florence or take the train to Rignano sull'Arno and taxi to Leccio.

Venice

The most exclusive shopping area in Venice is the **Via XXII Marzo** and the streets around **St Mark's Square**. Try

Shopping in the Ghetto

Rome's artistic community has fallen for the ghetto's quiet charm, transforming a shady side street, Via della Reginella, into an artistic quarter. While Piazza Navona and Campo de' Fiori have turned themselves over to Irish theme pubs and your-name-on-a-grain-of-rice artists, the ghetto is holding on to its old traditions.

Il Museo del Louvre: Via della Reginella 26/28. Giuseppe Casetti's antiquarian bookshop and gallery set the trend for the new arts community in the ghetto.

Roberto Arzu: Via della Reginella 4. Arzu's sculptures take their inspiration from Ancient Rome and Renaissance masterpieces.

Salvatore Savoca: Via della Reginella 25. Savoca's iconic oils on canvas are created in the upstairs studio and exhibited in the gallery below, together with work by other artists. Much loved by high stylists.

Tonino Carcione: Via della Reginella 13. If you are looking for period restored furniture, this workshop offers a great selection.

the Rialto Bridge and San Polo for local shopping. A market is held on the **Lido** on Tuesday morning.

Bargains in this city are rare, but shoes, clothes, gifts and fur coats are local specialities. However, few tourists leave without a supply of at least one kind of Venetian craftwork, such as hand-blown Murano glassware, or colourful carnival masks. The full range of Italian designer goods are on sale in Venice, but prices tend to be higher than on the mainland.

Naples

Naples is the capital of Italian fakes, so look out for cheap copies of designer goods on the streets or in markets. However, the city also has its own designer shops and crafts, such as Christmas cribs and their accompanying tiny figurines (a local art form) and Capodimonte porcelain.

The best shopping area is around **Piazza Amedeo** to **Piazza Trieste e Trento**. **Via dei Mille** and **Via Filangieri** are home to numerous famous-name designer shops. Mariella, one of Italy's most famous and expensive menswear outlets, is located nearby, in **Via Riviera di Chiaia**. A less expensive street is **Via Roma**, quite near to San Carlo opera house.

A–Z

A HANDY SUMMARY OF PRACTICAL INFORMATION, ARRANGED ALPHABETICALLY

A dmission Charges

The price of admission for an adult to major museums such as the Capitolini in Rome or the Uffizi in Florence, and major monuments such as the Colosseum or the ruins of Pompeii, is generally around €11–15, while for smaller museums it's usually around €5–10. Admission is free (or in a few cases only discounted) to all public museums and monuments for European Union citizens aged under 18 or over 65. Private museums such as the Venice Guggenheim have their own charges (also around €8–12) and discounts for older and younger visitors, as do the Vatican Museums, which are free to under-6s and to everyone on the last Sunday of each month. Nearly all the major museums now have websites that allow you to book tickets online. This is highly advisable for big attractions such as the Uffizi, especially in peak seasons, as demand is high and booking online allows you to miss some of the queues.

The Roma Pass (www.romapass.it), MilanoCard (www.milanocard.it) and Venicecard (www.hellovenezia.com)

provide unlimited (or in Rome, discounted) entry to public and some private museums in their respective cities, together with unlimited use of public transport and some other benefits, for a set period of time. Depending on how you organise your sightseeing, they can be a real bargain, especially in Milan, where the card costs just €10 for 72 hours; Roma Pass costs €25 for 3 days, while the Venicecard is more expensive, at €73 for an adult 3-day card (the minimum period), so if you are only going to make a few visits it will not be worth having. In towns and cities with more than one attraction there are often joint-ticket systems where admission to one also lets you into another (or gives a discount), which also saves you money.

Admission to churches and religious buildings is usually free, but some charge an entry fee (generally €5–12, with reductions for children) to cover maintenance costs. In addition, the number of visitors allowed per day to see some major sights in churches (such as Giotto's Scrovegni chapel in Padua) is limited

for conservation reasons, so you need to book a visit. This can often be done online, as well as through local tourist offices. Also, you need to carry some change when visiting churches, to feed the coin-in-slot machines that illuminate frescoes and other details.

B udgeting for Your Trip

The cost of travelling in Italy varies enormously depending on where you go and how you travel. Florence, Venice, the northern lakes, much of Tuscany, Capri, and beach areas like Rimini in high summer are notoriously expensive places, but in less prominent areas and cities – rural Emilia-Romagna, the Marche, Sicily, Sardinia, even parts of non-touristy Milan – prices can be lower by as much as half. Hotel prices also vary enormously by season. In general, though, prices overall, even in the countryside, tend to be a bit higher north of Rome than south of it and in the islands.

If you order a drink or a meal at an outside table you will always pay more than inside, and more if you have a

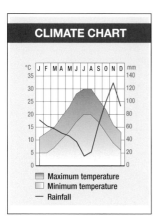

CLIMATE CHART

°C | J F M A M J J A S O N D | mm
35 | | 140
30 | | 120
25 | | 100
20 | | 80
15 | | 60
10 | | 40
5 | | 20
0 | | 0

▓ Maximum temperature
▢ Minimum temperature
— Rainfall

coffee at any table than standing at the bar Italian-style. The amount added on for *terrazza* service varies, so the price of sitting on the most celebrated terraces of Rome, Florence or Venice is astronomical. Hence people take their time. Beer is peculiarly expensive in Italy, especially at outside tables, often at around €4–6 for a smallish glass, and so is drunk relatively little; wine bought by the glass is similarly expensive, often around €5, except in traditional basic wine bars (*enoteche* or in Venice *bacari*), so in many cases you might as well order a bottle or a carafe. To eat, in most cities – even well-touristed ones – you can find unfussy restaurants that provide *tavola calda* lunch menus for around €15–20, while a generous pizza costs around €7–8. An enjoyable three-course meal with wine in mid-range restaurants can be found in Venice or Florence for around €40, in less fashionable places for closer to €30. Gourmet restaurants will cost from around €60–70 per person and upwards, although again in less trodden spots you can often find remarkable food for much less.

Hotel rooms, especially attractive ones, are expensive in Rome, Florence, Venice and some other areas, and it's hard to find a pleasant double room in a hotel for much under €80 a night. Comfortable mid-range rooms cost around €150, while these cities and some other areas – the northern lakes, rural Tuscany – conversely have a great deal of luxury accommodation for an indulgent splurge, with rooms for €400 and upwards. Hence travellers to the main cities seek out more economical options, such as monastery stays, apartment rentals,

B&Bs or bland but good-value business hotels like those of the NH chain. In less expensive parts of Italy, there are plenty of decent rooms to choose from for around €100, and even some luxury hotels are a little cheaper. B&B rooms on farms (*agriturismi*) are economical in most areas, often around €60, but there are also luxurious variations.

For long-distance travel, train fares are very reasonable (*see p.376*). A daytime taxi journey within the centre of most cities should cost around €10. In most cities and towns a single transport ticket costs €1, but most have systems that allow you to buy multiple tickets, saving time and money. In Rome, Milan and Venice the tourist cards (*see above*, Admission Charges) include unlimited transport for a set time, and the Venicecard is available as a transport-only card, which can be useful if you take a lot of waterbuses.

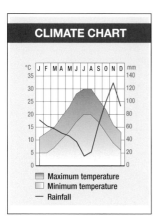hildren

Italy is a very child-friendly country and very few restaurants ever object to admitting them, even very grand ones (although they will be expected to behave and sit at table properly). Few restaurants have special children's menus, but then Italian cuisine is full of things kids like – pasta, pizza, ice cream. Accompanied small children (generally under 5, or more traditionally under 1 metre (3ft) tall) travel free on most public transport. Admission is also free to most public museums and monuments for EU citizens aged under 18, and there is usually a reduced price for non-EU under-18s.

Many hotels have family rooms, or offer the option of an additional bed in the parents' room. Hotel bedsitting services, however, are fairly scarce except in more expensive hotels. An exception are the family-oriented holiday hotels (often called a *centro de vacanze* rather than a hotel) around the Italian coasts, lakes and islands, usually open in summer only, which have play areas, kids' pools and many other facilities.

Climate

Italy experiences marked regional variations, from the more temperate north to the typically Mediterranean south, Sicily and Sardinia. Summers tend to be hot and dry along mainland coastal areas, with mild winters, but the mountains are cool in summer and snowy in winter, especially in the

Alps and Apennines. Cities in the north can get considerable snow, and winters can be freezing across the foggy plains of Lombardy and Emilia-Romagna, or in river cities such as Florence and Verona, while Ancona and the eastern Apennines are subject to blizzards. South of Florence the climate becomes more Mediterranean. Italy's east coast is not as wet as the west coast, but is usually colder in winter. As for temperature, there is considerable variation between north and south, especially in winter. In January, Milan might be a snowy –2°C (28°F), with Turin a freezing –12°C (10°F), and Palermo a cloudy but mild 17°C (63°F). Winter lows can reach –14°C (7°F) in the Po Valley, or –5°C (23°F) in Florence, while summer highs of 46°C (115°F) have been recorded in Catania (Sicily) and Alghero (Sardinia).

What to Wear
Unless you are visiting mountain areas, the moderate climate makes heavy clothing unnecessary in summer. A light jacket should be adequate for summer evenings. In winter (November–March), the climate can be cold and wet throughout Italy, so pack warm clothes and waterproofs.

Crime and Security

Violent crime, particularly involving foreigners, is in general relatively rare in Italy. The main problem for tourists is petty crime – pickpocketing, bag-snatching and theft from cars, of which, naturally, there is a greater risk in some cities than others; it is more of a problem in Rome, for example, than in Florence or Venice. All travellers should have travel insurance, covering loss or theft of all their possessions. The likelihood of street theft can also be reduced with a few basic, sensible precautions. Always lock your car and never leave luggage, cameras or other valuables inside. While walking around, always keep a shoulder bag closed, hold it at your front, not at the back, and keep a hand on the bag; when sitting at a table, especially outside, put your bag on your lap or the table in front of you, never on the ground or on the back of a chair. Only use ATMs in main streets, and during the day. Be extra-careful in big train stations, and avoid walking alone at night in deserted alleys of the historic centres of towns such as Bari, Genoa or Palermo, and stay where there are people. Special care is needed in Naples, where women especially should be wary of bag theft at all times, and if in doubt only visit the historic centre in a group. In small towns and rural areas, theft of any kind is very unlikely.

If you are the victim of a crime, or lose anything, it is essential to make a report at the nearest police station and get documentation to support an insurance claim. Italy has several police forces, the responsibilities of which are complex, but you can report a crime at any station of the national police (*Polizia*) or the semi-military *Carabinieri*. To phone for the police, dial **113** for the *Polizia* or **112** for the *Carabinieri*.

Customs Regulations

Residents of EU countries can carry any amount of goods into and out of Italy without extra duty so long as they are for their personal use. Examples of amounts normally accepted to fit this criteria are 10 litres of spirits or strong liqueurs, 90 litres of wine, 3,200 cigarettes and 110 litres of beer.

For non-EU residents, duty-free allowances include: 200 cigarettes, 50 cigars or 250 grams tobacco, 1 litre of spirits and gifts worth up to €175. Any amount of currency exceeding €10,000 or equivalent must be declared on entry, and when leaving Italy.

Value-Added Tax (sales tax, currently 20 percent) can be reclaimed by non-EU residents when they leave Italy on single items costing more than €180. They must be bought in a shop with a "Euro Tax Free" sticker in the window; when buying the item, tell the shop staff that you want to do this and they should give you a "Tax Free Shopping Cheque" with your receipt, together with a form with instructions on how to claim the refund. When you leave Italy, take all these papers to a customs desk and get them stamped. This can take time, so get to the airport early.

Disabled Travellers

Italy's older cities are not easily navigable for disabled travellers: cobblestones, narrow pavements and cramped lifts make getting around tricky. The Rome-based organisation CO.IN offers information (currently in Italian only) on disabled facilities in restaurants, shops and stations; tel: 800-271 027; www.coinsociale.it. In Rome, Roma Per Tutti is a useful information service for disabled travellers, again in Italian, although

Emergency Numbers

General Emergency Assistance and police: 113 (24-hour service)
Caribinieri **(Police):** 112
Fire Brigade: 115
Medical emergencies, ambulance: 118
Breakdown service: 803 116

some staff may speak English; tel: 06-5717 7094; www.romapertutti.it.

Transport in Italy's larger cities is becoming more accessible, with increasing numbers of wheelchair-friendly buses and trams. For train travel check the Trenitalia website www.trenitalia.com; the wheelchair symbol denotes accessible trains, and there is a special helpline, tel: 199-303 060.

Accessible Italy is a non-profit body that organises accommodation and tours for people with disabilities; tel: (Italy) 378-941 111; www.accessibleitaly.com.

Electricity

220 volts, with the standard European two-round-pin plugs. You will need adaptors to operate British three-pin equipment, and with older North American 110-volt flat-pin appliances, you may need a transformer as well as a plug adaptor.

Embassies and Consulates

The following consulates and embassies are all based in Rome, but can put you in touch with other consulates. Dial the Rome code, even if calling from within Rome.
Australia: tel: 06-852 721
Canada: tel: 06-854 441 (24-hour emergencies 613-996 8885)
France: tel: 06-686 011
Germany: tel: 06-492 131
Ireland: tel: 06-697 9121
New Zealand: tel: 06-853 7501
UK: tel: 06-4220 0001
US: tel: 06-46741

Etiquette

Italians are known for their sense of style, and if you stay or dine anywhere expensive, or try to get into any of the sleeker city clubs and bars, you will feel distinctly out of place (or be turned away) if you are unable to dress up at least a little. Elsewhere, dress can be much more casual. However, when sightseeing, both men and women are advised to cover their shoulders and avoid wearing shorts (or short skirts),

as some churches, especially in Rome and Venice, bar visitors who are deemed unsuitably dressed.

Gay and Lesbian Travellers

Gay life in Italy is becoming more mainstream, helped by increasing numbers of club nights and festivals such as Rome's summer-long Gay Village. Attitudes are generally more tolerant in the north: Bologna is regarded as Italy's gay capital, and Milan, Turin and Rome all have a lively gay scene. The Bologna-based Arcigay network provides all kinds of information in Italian (tel: 051-095 7241; www.arcigay.it), while range of information in English is on www.gayfriendlyitaly.com.

Health and Medical Care

EU citizens should obtain a European Health Insurance Card (EHIC) before leaving home to be able to get emergency treatment from the Italian state health service. Some medicines may have to be paid for. However, this will not entitle you to repatriation in the event of serious illness, so you may wish to have private travel health insurance as well. Citizens of non-EU countries must pay for medical assistance and medicines, and so should always have full travel health insurance against all eventualities. Most hospitals have a 24-hour emergency department (*Pronto Soccorso*), but a stay in an Italian hospital can be a grim experience, particularly in the south.

For minor complaints, seek out a *farmacia* (signs have a green cross). Normal opening hours are 9am–1pm and 4–7.30 or 8pm, Monday to Friday, and on Saturday mornings. Outside these hours there is always at least one *farmacia* on duty in each town, and its address will be posted in the windows of all pharmacies in the area.

Internet

Upscale hotels and a growing number of mid-range ones now offer WiFi connections, usually for no extra charge. All Italian cities now have a few internet cafés, usually near tourist sites or main train stations, but in smaller towns they are much harder to find.

Lost Property

Ask about lost items at the local lost property office (*ufficio oggetti smarriti*), usually in the town hall.

Items lost on public transport are generally directed to the transport authority's own lost property office. In Rome, items found on the city's buses, trams and metros are sent to Via Bettoni 1; tel: 06-581 6040.

M edia

The Italian press is concentrated in Milan and Rome. The biggest papers are La Repubblica and Il Corriere della Sera, which publish regional editions. However, La Gazzetta dello Sport, the pink sports paper, is probably the one you will notice most.

Most major cities have weekly listings magazines: Roma C'e, with a section in English at the back, is a guide to everything going on in Rome and is available from newsstands every Wednesday. La Repubblica also publishes Trovaroma, a what's-on section, every Thursday, and Wednesday's Corriere della Sera has a listings supplement, ViviMilano.

Television stations include RAI (the national network with three channels), the Vatican network, plus privately owned national channels (the largest all owned by Prime Minister Berlusconi), and over 450 local stations. Many European channels, CNN and other international channels can be seen in hotels.

Money

The currency in Italy is the euro (€), which is available in 500, 200, 100, 50, 20, 10 and 5 euro notes, and 2 euro, 1 euro, 50 cent, 20 cent, 10 cent, 5 cent, 2 cent and 1 cent coins. There are 100 cents to one euro.

Italy is a society that prefers cash to credit cards, except for large purchases, or, for instance, hotel bills. In modest restaurants and smaller shops, it is still usual to pay in cash. Check beforehand if there is any doubt, or at least have sufficient euro cash with you, just in case.

Banks are generally open 8.30am–1.30pm and for 1 hour or 90 minutes in the afternoon (usually 2.45–4.15pm), Monday to Friday only, so bear this in mind before each weekend. Travellers' cheques can still be useful in Italy, as they can be replaced if stolen or lost. Unfortunately, however, most banks are notoriously inefficient at changing cash or cheques, and currency conversion can turn into a tedious saga, so many travellers just use ATMs (cashpoints) wherever

Area Codes

When dialling numbers inside or outside your area in Italy, the main number must always be preceded by the area code, including the zero. Area codes of some main cities are:

Bologna	051
Florence	055
Genoa	010
Milan	02
Naples	081
Palermo	091
Pisa	050
Rome	06
Turin	011
Venice	041

To call abroad from Italy, dial 00, followed by:

Australia	61
Canada	1
Irish Republic	353
New Zealand	64
South Africa	27
UK	44
US	1

Then dial the number, omitting the initial "0" if there is one.

possible. There are also private bureaux de change in tourist cities, at airports and main railway stations, with more flexible hours. Avoid changing money in hotels, where commission will be high.

Cash Machines and Credit Cards

Given the long queues for money-changing in Italy, it is simplest to get cash from ATM machines, which are widely available. Most Bancomats (cash machines) accept all major international credit and debit cards. In cities, many restaurants, hotels and larger stores will take major cards, and they can also be used to book train and museum tickets online, but in small shops and rural areas, as mentioned, you may be able to pay only in cash.

O pening Hours

Smaller shops are usually open roughly 9am–1pm and 4pm–7.30 or 8pm, Monday to Saturday, although some work only a half-day on Saturdays, either morning or afternoon. Some traditional shops also close on Monday mornings. In cities, the only shops generally open on Sundays are big stores, supermarkets and malls, which also do not close for lunch during the week. In tourist areas many shops of

all kinds also open on Sundays, especially during peak seasons. A special regime applies to pharmacies (see above, Health).

Offices traditionally work from around 8.30am–12.30 or 1pm and 3–6pm, Monday to Friday, although in major cities many now take a shorter lunch break. For bank hours, see above, Money. Nearly all museums close on one day each week, usually Monday, although some close on Tuesday.

P ostal Services

Local post offices open 8am–1.30pm Mon–Fri only, but cities generally have a main post office that is open throughout the day, untill about 7–8pm. Post offices provide a wide range of services such as raccomandata (registered post) and parcel post. Stamps (francobolli) can be bought at all tobacco shops (tabacchi) and in many bars.

Public Holidays

January New Year's Day (1)
Epiphany (6)
March/April Easter Day, Easter Monday
April Liberation Day (25)
May Labour Day (1)
August Assumption of the Virgin Mary (15)
November All Saints' Day (1)
December Immaculate Conception (8), Christmas Day (25), St Stephen's Day (26)

In addition to these national holidays, almost all cities have a holiday to celebrate their own patron saint, for example St Mark, 25 April (Venice); St John the Baptist, 24 June (Turin, Genoa and Florence); SS Peter and Paul, 29 June (Rome); St Rosalia, 15 July (Palermo); St Gennaro, 19 September (Naples); St Petronius, 4 October (Bologna); St Ambrose, 7 December (Milan).

R eligion

Roman Catholic Mass is celebrated every day and several times on Sundays in Italian. Some non-Catholic churches hold services in English; in Rome, you can find services in English at the Church of England All Saints, Via del Babuino 153B and at the Scottish Presbyterian St Andrew's, Via XX Settembre 7. The Jewish Synagogue is at Lungotevere Cenci 9. The city's mosque is in Via della Moschea. Ask at the local tourist office about places of worship in the area.

Top Three Tourist Destinations – Rome, Florence and Venice

Rome

APT **Rome** (main office): Via Leopardo 24; **tourist information phoneline**, daily 9am–9pm, tel: 06 06 08; http://en.turismoroma.it.

There are 10 tourist information points around the capital, most of them open daily 9.30am–7pm: at **Via Giovanni Giolitti** (outside Termini station, daily 8am–8.30pm); **Piazza Pia** (in front of Castel Sant'Angelo); **Via Minghetti** (near Fontana di Trevi); **Piazza delle Cinque Lune** (off Piazza Navona); **Via dell'Olmata** (by Santa Maria Maggiore); **Via Nazionale** (near Palazzo dello Esposizioni); **Piazza Sonnino** (in Trastevere); **Fiumicino** and **Ciampino** airports (both daily 9am–6.30pm); and **Ostia Lido**.

The privately run tourist office **Enjoy Rome**, located near the railway station, is staffed by helpful English-speakers and provides a wide range of useful services, including guided tours round the city; Via Marghera 8A; tel: 06-445 1843; www.enjoyrome.com.

Florence

APT **Florence** (main office): Via Manzoni 16; tel: 055-23320; www.firenzeturismo.it.

There are also information points run by the province or the city at **Via Cavour 1r** (tel: 055-290 832; just north of the Duomo; Mar–Oct Mon–Sat 8.30am–6.30pm, Sun 8.30am–1.30pm; Nov–Feb Mon–Sat 8.30am–6.30pm); **Piazza Stazione 4** (by the railway station; Mon–Sat 8.30am–7pm, Sun 8.30am–2pm); **Borgo Santa Croce 29r** (same hours); and at **Peretola airport** (daily 7.30am–11.30pm).

Venice

APT **Venice** (main office): Castello 5050, on Fondamenta San Lorenzo; information phoneline tel: 041-529 8711; www.turismovenezia.it.

The main tourist office for the public is at **Piazza San Marco 71** (same phone; daily 9am–3.30pm, with extended hours in summer); there are other offices at **Stazione Santa Lucia** train station (daily 8am–6.30pm); **Piazzale Roma** (daily 9.30am–4.30pm); and **Marco Polo airport** (daily 9.30am–7pm), as well as in other parts of the province. The tourist office also runs the **Venice Pavilion**, a bookshop and information centre dedicated to everything about Venice, at the Ex-Giardini Reale (on the waterfront, just west from San Marco); daily 10am–6pm.

Hello Venezia, tel: 041-2424; www.hellovenezia.com, is a separate information service set up by the Venice transport authority ACTV, with full details of the transport system and other information. It also handles sales of the Venicecard, which gives discounts on travel, museums and other attractions.

Smoking

Since 2005 smoking has been banned in all indoor public places in Italy, including all bars and restaurants except those that have a separate smoking room fairly tightly isolated from the rest of the establishment. However, the law has many loopholes, and the general impression is that while it is quite well enforced in the north it is often ignored in the centre and the south.

Students

In the UK, the Italian Cultural Institute provides advice on courses in Italy, particularly language-based; tel: 020-7235 1461; www.icilondon.esteri.it. In the US, try the American Institute for Foreign Study; tel: 866-906 2437; www.aifs.org; and Study Abroad Italy, www.saiprograms.com.

To study in an Italian university, you will need to get your certificates translated and validated by the Italian consulate in your own country before making your application at the *ufficio stranieri* (foreign department) of the university of your choice in Italy; www.study-in-italy.it offers useful advice.

Telephones

Public telephones are plentiful, particularly in cities. Most accept phonecards (*carte telefoniche* or *schede telefoniche)*, available from tobacco shops, bars or post offices; few telephones accept coins. Post offices and many bars also have pay phones where you can make a call and then pay afterwards.

The cheapest time for long-distance calls is between 10pm and 8am Monday to Saturday, and all day Sunday.

For directory enquiries dial 12. For international enquiries call 176, and for the international operator and to make a reverse-charge (collect) call, dial 170.

Italy has an extremely high ownership of mobile (cell) phones, and in all cities and towns it's possible to buy or rent one on a cheap, short-term pay-as-you-go deal. The main mobile networks in Italy are TIM, Vodafone and Wind, which have shops in every part of the country. Non-Italian mobiles will all work in Italy provided they have at least a tri- or quad-band system and have their roaming facility enabled, but always check with your home service provider on current charges before using a foreign mobile here. Many phone companies offer "bundles" of international calls for a set fee, which helps to limit costs.

Time Zone

Italy follows Central European Time (GMT plus 1 hour, EST plus 6 hours: add one hour in summer).

Tipping

Italians generally tip very little or not at all. In restaurants, bills often include a cover and bread charge (*coperto* e *pane*) of around €5 per head, plus a 10 percent service charge (*servizio*), plus the extra charge if you sit outside, so there is no obligation to leave anything more. Some people (especially foreigners) leave a little extra as an acknowledgement if service has been particularly good. In taxis, it's common to add on around 5–10 percent for good service, but many people just round the fare up to the nearest euro. In Venice, water-taxi men expect fat tips because they are so used to dealing with wealthy foreigners. In hotels, an especially helpful concierge could be tipped around €10–15, a chambermaid €2–5.

Tourist Information

Regions and Provinces

Administratively, Italy is divided into regions (*regioni*) such as Tuscany and Sicily, then into provinces (*provincie*). Every provincial capital has an **Azienda Provinciale per il Turismo** (APT), with subsidiary offices in many smaller towns, especially in popular tourist areas. As well as all kinds of helpful information, APT offices should provide free local maps.

Tourist offices in main towns are listed below; many districts also have their own websites.

Italian State Tourist Board

The Italian State Tourist Board, ENIT (Ente Nazionale per il Turismo), provides general tourist information.

In the UK, ENIT, 1 Princes Street, London W1B 2AY; tel: 020-7408 1254; www.enit.it.

In the US, ENIT, Suite 1565, 630 Fifth Avenue, New York, NY 10111; tel: 212-245 5618; www.italiantourism. com. There are also offices in Chicago, Los Angeles and, in Canada, Toronto.

Main Tourist Offices
Lombardy-Piedmont-Liguria
Bergamo: Bergamo Turismo, Piazzale Marconi (zone Stazione); tel: 035-210 204; http://turismo.provincia.bergamo.it.
Cinque Terre (La Spezia): tel: 0187-187 8687; www.turismoprovincia.laspezia. it. More information is on www. cinqueterre.it.
Genoa: tel: 010-557 22874; www. turismo.comune.genova.it. Information offices in Via Garibaldi and at the airport.
Lake Como (Lago di Como): Piazza Cavour 17, Como; tel: 031-330 0128; www.lakecomo.org.
Lake Garda (Lago di Garda): Corso Repubblica 8, Gardone Riviera; tel; 030-374 8736; www.lagodigarda.it. Also offices in Desenzano, Riva del Garda, Sirmione and other lake towns.
Lake Maggiore (Lago Maggiore): Corso Italia 18, Stresa; tel: 0323-30416; www.lagomaggiore.it.
Liguria: Via Roma 11/3, Genoa; tel: 010-530 821; www.turismoinliguria.it.
Lombardy: Via Pola 12/14, Milan; tel: 02-6765 6259; www.turismo.regione. lombardia.it.
Milan: Piazza Duomo 19/A; tel: 02-7740 4343; www.turismo.milano.it.
Piedmont: tel: (international toll-free number) 00-800-111-33300; www. piemonteitalia.eu.
Turin: Piazza Castello 161; tel: 011-535 181; www.turismotorino.org. Also at the main train station and the airport.
Valle d'Aosta: Viale Federico Chabod, Aosta; tel: 0165-33352; www.regione. vda.it/turismo.

Veneto-Trentino-Emilia-Romagna
Alto Adige–South Tyrol: Piazza Parocchia/Pfarrplatz 11, Bolzano/ Bozen; tel: 0471-999 999; www. suedtirol.info.
Bologna: Piazza Maggiore 1e, Palazzo del Podestà; tel: 051-239 660; http:// iat.comune.bologna.it. Also at the airport.
Bolzano (Bozen): Piazza Walther 8, Alto Adige; tel: 0471-307 000;

www.bolzano-bozen.it.
Emilia-Romagna: www. emiliaromagnaturismo.it.
Friuli-Venezia Giulia: Piazza Manin 10, Codroipo, Udine; tel: 0432-815 111; www.turismofvg.it; also local offices.
Padua: Riviera dei Mugnai 8; tel: 049-876 7911; www.turismopadova.it.
Parma: Via Melloni 1A; tel: 0521-218 889; http://turismo.parma.it.
Rimini: Piazzale Fellini 3; tel: 0541-704 587; www.riminiturismo.it.
Trentino: Via Romagnosi 11, Trento; tel: 0461-219 300; www.trentino.to; APT Trento, Via Manci 2; tel: 0461-216 000; www.apt.trento.it.
Veneto region: Palazzo Sceriman, Cannaregio 161, Venice; tel: 041-279 2644; www.veneto.to.
Verona: Via degli Alpini 9; tel: 045-806 8680; www.tourism.verona.it.
Vicenza: Via Fermi 134; tel: 0444-994 770; www.vicenzae.org; also Piazza Matteotti 12; tel: 0444-320 854.

Tuscany-Umbria-Marche
Arezzo: Emiciclo Giovanni Paolo II; tel: 0575-182 2770; www.arezzoturismo.it.
Assisi: Piazza del Comune 12; tel: 075-813 680.
Elba: Viale Elba 4, Portoferraio; tel: 0565-914 671; www.aptelba.it.
Lucca: Piazza Guidiccioni 2; tel: 0583-91991; www.luccatourist.it.
Marche–Ancona: Via della Loggia 50, Ancona; tel: 071-358 991/800 222 111; www.le-marche.com.
Orvieto: tel: 0763-393 453; www. orvietoturismo.it. Information office Piazza Duomo 20.
Perugia: Piazza Matteotti 18; tel: 075-573 6458; http://turismo.comune. perugia.it.
Pisa: Piazza Arcivescovado 8; tel: 334-641 9408; www.pisaunicaterra.it.
San Gimignano: Piazza Duomo 1; tel: 0577-940 008; www.sangimignano.com.
Siena: APT Siena, Piazza del Campo 56; tel: 0577-280 551; www.terresiena.it.
Tuscany: www.turismo.intoscana.it.
Umbria: www.umbria-turismo.it.
Urbino: Borgo Mercatale, Rampa di Francesco di Giorgio; tel: 0722-2631; www.urbinoculturaturismo.it.

Abruzzo-Molise
Abruzzo: Corso Vittorio Emanuele II 301, Pescara; tel: 085-448 2301; www.abruzzoturismo.it.
Molise: Piazza della Vittoria 14, Campobasso; tel: 0874-415 662; www.discovermolise.com.

Naples to Calabria
Calabria: Via San Nicola 8, Catanzaro; tel: 0961-792 723; www. turiscalabria.it.
Campania: Via Terracina 230,

Naples; tel: 081-230 1659; www.incampania.com.
Capri: Piazza Umberto I; tel: 081-837 0686; www.capritourism.com. Also at Marina Grande and Anacapri.
Naples: Via Santa Lucia 107; tel: 081-240 0914; www.inaples.it. Also at Via San Carlo 9 and Piazza del Gesù.
Puglia: Piazza Moro 33A, Bari; tel: 080-990 9341; www.viaggiareinpuglia.it.
Sorrento: Via Luigi De Maio 35; tel: 081-807 4033; www.sorrentotourism.com.

Sicily
Catania: Via Etnea 63/65; tel: 095-401 4070; http://turismo.provincia.ct.it.
Palermo: Piazza Castelnuovo 34; tel: 091-605 8351; www.palermotourism.com.
Sicily region: Via Notarbartolo 9, Palermo; tel: 091-707 8100; www. regione.sicilia.it/turismo.
Taormina: Piazza S. Caterina; tel: 0942-23243; www.gate2taormina.com.

Sardinia
Cagliari: Piazza Matteotti; tel: 070-669 255; http://visit-cagliari.it.
Sardinia region: Viale Trieste 105, Cagliari, tel: 070-606 7226; www. sardegnaturismo.it.

V isas and Passports

EU citizens can enter Italy with only a national identity card, but those without them, such as UK and Irish citizens, must have full passports. Visitors from Australia, Canada, Japan, New Zealand, the United States and several other countries must have full passports but do not require visas for stays of no more than three months. All travellers to Italy are theoretically still supposed to register with the local police within three days of arrival. This will be taken care of by your hotel; if you are not staying in a hotel, supposedly you should contact the local police station, but virtually no one does.

Travelling with Pets

Pets must be vaccinated against rabies, and you should obtain an official document stating that your animal is healthy no more than one month before you arrive in Italy.

W eights and Measures

The metric system is used for all weights and measures. For a quick conversion: 2.5cm is approximately 1 inch, 1 metre about a yard, 100g is just under 4oz and 1kg is 2lbs 2oz. Distance is quoted in kilometres. One kilometre equals 0.62 of a mile, so 100km is 62 miles.

LANGUAGE

UNDERSTANDING THE LANGUAGE

Basic Communication

Yes/No *Sì/No*
Thank you *Grazie*
Many thanks *Grazie mille/tante grazie/molte grazie*
You're welcome *Prego*
All right/OK/that's fine *Va bene*
Please *Per favore/Per cortesia*
Excuse me (to get attention) *Scusi* (singular), *Scusate* (plural)
Excuse me (to get through a crowd) *Permesso*
Excuse me (to attract attention, eg of a waiter) *Senta!*
Excuse me (sorry) *Mi scusi* (singular), *Scusatemi* (plural)
Wait a minute! (informal) *Aspetta!* (formal) *Aspetti!*
Could you help me? (formal) *Potrebbe aiutarmi?*
Certainly *Ma certo*
Can I help you? (formal) *Posso aiutarla?*
Can you help me? (formal) *Può aiutarmi, per cortesia?*
I'm sorry *Mi dispiace*
I don't understand *Non capisco*
Do you speak English/French/ German? *Parla inglese/francese/ tedesco?*
Could you speak more slowly, please? *Può parlare più lentamente, per favore?*
slowly/quietly *piano*
here/there *qui/là*
What? *Cosa?*
When/why/where? *Quando/perchè/ dove?*
Where is the lavatory? *Dov'è il bagno?*

Greetings

Hello (good day) *Buon giorno*
Hello/hi/goodbye (familiar) *Ciao*

Emergencies

Help! *Aiuto!*
I've had an accident *Ho avuto un incidente*
Call a doctor *Per favore, chiami un medico*
Call an ambulance/the police/ the fire brigade *Chiami un'ambulanza/la Polizia/i Carabinieri/i pompieri*
Where is the nearest hospital? *Dov'è l'ospedale più vicino?*
I want to report a theft *Voglio denunciare un furto*

Good afternoon/evening *Buona sera*
Goodnight *Buona notte*
Goodbye *Arrivederci*
Pleased to meet you (formal) *Piacere di conoscerla*
I am English/American/Canadian *Sono inglese/americano/canadese*
Do you speak English? *Parla inglese?*
How are you? (formal) *Come sta* *come stai?* (informal)
Fine thanks *Bene, grazie*
See you soon *A presto*
Take care (formal) *Stia bene*, (informal) *Stammi bene*

In the Hotel

Do you have a room free? *Avete camere libere?*
I have a reservation *Ho fatto una prenotazione*
I'd like... *Vorrei...*
a single/double room (with double bed) *una camera singola/doppia (con letto matrimoniale)*
a room with twin beds *una camera a due letti*

a room with a bath/shower *una camera con bagno/doccia*
for one night *per una notte*
for two nights *per due notti*
Could you show me another room? *Potrebbe mostrarmi un'altra camera?*
How much is it? *Quanto costa?*
on the first floor *al primo piano*
Is breakfast included? *È compresa la prima colazione?*
half/full board *mezza pensione/pensione completa*
It's expensive *È caro*
Do you have a room with a balcony/view of the sea? *C'è una camera con balcone/con vista sul mare?*
Can I see the room? *Posso vedere la camera?*
I'll take it *La prendo*
big/small *grande/piccola*
What time is breakfast? *A che ora è la prima colazione?*
Please give me a call at... *Mi può chiamare alle...*
Come in! *Avanti!*
Can I have the bill, please? *Posso avere il conto, per favore?*
dining room *la sala da pranzo*
key *la chiave*
lift *l'ascensore*
towel *l'asciugamano*

Eating Out

Bar Snacks and Drinks

I'd like... *Vorrei...*
coffee *un caffè* (espresso: small, strong and black)
un cappuccino (with hot, frothy milk)
un caffè latte (milky coffee)
un caffè lungo (weak)
uno corretto (laced with alcohol – usually brandy or grappa)
tea *un tè*
herbal tea *una tisana*

TRANSPORT

ACCOMMODATION

EATING OUT

ACTIVITIES

A – Z

LANGUAGE

hot chocolate *una cioccolata calda*
orange/lemon juice (bottled) *un succo d'arancia/di limone*
fresh orange/lemon juice *una spremuta di arancia/di limone*
orangeade *un'aranciata*
water (mineral) *acqua (minerale)*
fizzy/still mineral water *acqua minerale gasata/naturale*
with/without ice *con/senza ghiaccio*
red/white wine *vino rosso/bianco*
beer (draught) *una birra (alla spina)*
milk *latte*
a (half) litre *un (mezzo) litro*
bottle *una bottiglia*
ice cream *un gelato*
sandwich *un tramezzino*
Anything else? *Desidera qualcos'altro?*
Cheers *Salute*

In a Restaurant

I'd like to book a table *Vorrei riservare un tavolo*
Have you got a table for... *Avete un tavolo per...*
I have a reservation *Ho fatto una prenotazione*
lunch/supper *il pranzo/la cena*
I'm a vegetarian *Sono vegetariano/a*
Is there a vegetarian dish? *C'è un piatto vegetariano?*
The menu, please? *Ci dà il menu, per favore?*
wine list *la lista dei vini*
What would you like? *Che cosa prende?*
What would you recommend? *Che cosa ci raccomanda?*
What would you like to drink? *Che cosa desidera da bere?*
a carafe of red/white wine *una caraffa di vino rosso/bianco*
fixed-price menu *il menu a prezzo fisso*
the dish of the day *il piatto del giorno*
VAT (sales tax) *IVA*
cover charge *il coperto/pane e coperto*
That's enough; no more, thanks

Basta (così)
The bill, please *Il conto per favore*
Is service included? *Il servizio è incluso?*
Where is the toilet? *Dov'è il bagno?*

Menu Decoder

Antipasti (Hors d'oeuvres)

caponata **mixed aubergine, olives and tomatoes**
insalata caprese **tomato and Mozzarella salad**
insalata di mare **seafood salad**
insalata mista/verde **mixed/green salad**
melanzane alla parmigiana **fried or baked aubergine** (with Parmesan cheese and tomato)
mortadella/salame **salami**
pancetta **bacon**
peperonata **vegetable stew** (made with peppers, onions, tomatoes and sometimes aubergines)

Primi (First Courses)

Typical first courses include soup, risotto, gnocchi or varieties of pasta in a wide range of sauces. Risotto and gnocchi are more common in the north.
il brodetto **fish soup**
il brodo **consommé**
gli gnocchi **potato dumplings**
la minestra **soup**
pasta e fagioli **pasta and bean soup**
il prosciutto (cotto/crudo) **ham**
i tartufi **truffles**
la zuppa **soup**

Secondi (Main Courses)

Main courses are typically fish-, seafood- or meat-based, with accompaniments *(contorni)* that vary greatly from region to region.

La Carne (Meat)

arrosto **roast meat**
ai ferri **grilled**
al forno **baked**

al girarrosto **spit-roasted**
alla griglia **grilled**
stufato **braised, stewed**
ben cotto **well done** (steak, etc.)
al puntino **medium** (steak, etc.)
al sangue **rare** (steak, etc.)
l'agnello **lamb**
la bistecca **steak**
il capriolo/cervo **venison**
il cinghiale **wild boar**
il coniglio **rabbit**
il controfiletto **sirloin steak**
le cotolette **cutlets**
il fagiano **pheasant**
il fegato **liver**
il filetto **fillet**
il maiale **pork**
il manzo **beef**
l'ossobuco **shin of veal**
il pollo **chicken**
le polpette **meatballs**
la salsiccia **sausage**
il saltimbocca (alla romana) **veal escalopes with ham**
le scaloppine **escalopes**
lo stufato **stew**
il sugo **sauce**
il tacchino **turkey**
la trippa **tripe**
il vitello **veal**

Frutti di Mare (Seafood)

surgelati **frozen**
alla griglia **grilled**
fritto **fried**
ripieno **stuffed**
al vapore **steamed**
le acciughe **anchovies**
l'aragosta **lobster**
il baccalà **dried salted cod**
il branzino **sea bass**
i calamari **squid**
i crostacei **shellfish**
le cozze **mussels**
il fritto misto **mixed fried fish**
i gamberi **prawns**
i gamberetti **shrimps**
il granchio **crab**
il merluzzo **cod**
le ostriche **oysters**
il pesce **fish**
il pesce spada **swordfish**
il polipo **octopus**
il risotto di mare **seafood risotto**
le sarde **sardines**
la sogliola **sole**
la trota **trout**
il tonno **tuna**
le vongole **clams**

I Legumi/La Verdura (Vegetables)

gli asparagi **asparagus**
le carote **carrots**
la cipolla **onion**
i fagioli **beans**
i fagiolini **French (green) beans**
il finocchio **fennel**
i funghi **mushrooms**

Pronunciation and Grammar Tips

Italian-speakers claim that pronunciation is easy – you pronounce it as it is written – but there are a few rules to bear in mind: *c* before *e* or *i* is pronounced "ch", eg *ciao, mi dispiace, la coincidenza*. *Ch* before *i* or *e* is pronounced as "k", eg *la chiesa*. Likewise, *sci* or *sce* are pronounced as in "sheep" or "shed" respectively. *Gn* in Italian is rather like the sound in "onion", while *gl* is softened to resemble the sound in "bullion".

Nouns are either masculine (*il*, plural *i*) or feminine (*la*, plural *le*). Plurals of nouns are most often formed by changing an *o* to an *i* and an *a* to an *e*, eg *il panino, i panini*; *la chiesa, le chiese*.

Words are generally stressed on the penultimate syllable unless an accent indicates otherwise.

Italian has formal and informal words for "You". In the singular, *Tu* is informal while *Lei* is more polite. It is best to use the formal form unless invited to do otherwise.

Days and Dates

morning/afternoon/evening *la mattina, il pomeriggio, la sera*
yesterday/today/tomorrow *ieri/ oggi/domani*
the day after tomorrow *dopodomani*
now/early/late *adesso/presto/ ritardo*
Monday *lunedì*
Tuesday *martedì*
Wednesday *mercoledì*
Thursday *giovedì*
Friday *venerdì*
Saturday *sabato*
Sunday *domenica*

l'insalata mista **mixed salad**
l'insalata verde **green salad**
la melanzana **aubergine**
le patate **potatoes**
le patatine fritte **chips/French fries**
i peperoni **peppers**
i pomodori **tomatoes**
il radicchio **red, bitter lettuce**
i ravanelli **radishes**
la rughetta **rocket**
gli spinaci **spinach**
la verdura **green vegetables**
gli zucchini **courgettes**

I Dolci (Desserts)

al carrello **(desserts) from the trolley**
un semifreddo **semi-frozen dessert**
la cassata **Sicilian ice cream with candied peel**
le frittelle **fritters**
un gelato (di lampone/limone) **(raspberry/lemon) ice cream**
una granita **water ice**
una macedonia di frutta **fruit salad**
il tartufo (nero) **(chocolate) ice cream dessert**
il tiramisù **cold, creamy cheese and coffee dessert**
la torta **cake/tart**
lo zabaglione **sweet dessert made with eggs and Marsala wine**
la zuppa inglese **trifle**

La Frutta (Fruit)

le albicocche **apricots**
le arance **oranges**
le banane **bananas**
il cocomero **watermelon**
le ciliegie **cherries**
i fichi **figs**
le fragole **strawberries**
i lamponi **raspberries**
la mela **apple**
il melone **melon**
la pesca **peach**
la pera **pear**
il pompelmo **grapefruit**
l'uva **grapes**

Basic Foods

l'aceto **vinegar**
l'aglio **garlic**
il burro **butter**
il formaggio **cheese**
la frittata **omelette**
i grissini **bread sticks**
l'olio **oil**
la marmellata **jam**
il pane **bread**
il pane integrale **wholemeal bread**
il parmigiano **Parmesan cheese**
il pepe **pepper**
il riso **rice**
il sale **salt**
la senape **mustard**
le uova **eggs**
lo zucchero **sugar**

Sightseeing

Si può visitare...? *Can one visit...?*
Suonare il campanello **ring the bell**
aperto/a **open**
chiuso/a **closed**
chiuso per la festa/ferie/restauro **closed for the festival/holidays/ restoration**
Is it possible to see the church? *È possibile visitare la chiesa?*

At the Shops

What time do you open/close? *A che ora apre/chiude?*
Closed for the holidays *Chiuso per ferie*
Pull/push *Tirare/spingere*
Entrance/exit *Entrata/uscita*
Can I help you? *Posso aiutarla?*
What would you like? *Che cosa desidera?*
I'm just looking *Stò soltanto guardando*
How much is it? *Quant'è, per favore?*
How much is this? *Quanto viene?*
Do you take credit cards? *Accettate carte di credito?*
this one/that one *questo/quello*
Have you got...? *Avete...?*
We haven't got (any)... *Non (ne) abbiamo...*
Can I try it on? *Posso provare?*
the size (for clothes) *la taglia*
What size do you take? *Qual'è la sua taglia?*
the size (for shoes) *il numero*
Is there/do you have...? *C'è...?*
Yes, of course *Sì, certo*
That's too expensive *È troppo caro*
cheap *economico*
It's too small/big *È troppo piccolo/grande*
I (don't) like it *(Non) mi piace*
I'll take/leave it *Lo prendo/lascio*
Anything else? *Altro?*
Give me some of those *Mi dia alcuni di quelli lì*

a (half) kilo *un (mezzo) chilo*
100/200 grams *un etto/due etti*
more/less *più/meno*
with/without *con/senza*
a little *un pochino*
That's enough/No more *Basta così*

Types of Shop

antique dealer *l'antiquario*
bakery/cake shop *la panetteria/ pasticceria*
bank *la banca*
bookshop *la libreria*
boutique *il negozio di moda*
bureau de change *il cambio*
butcher *la macelleria*
chemist *la farmacia*
delicatessen *la salumeria*
department store *il grande magazzino*
fishmonger *la pescheria*
florist *il fioraio*
food shop *l'alimentari*
greengrocer *il fruttivendolo*
grocer *l'alimentari*
hairdresser *il parrucchiere*
ice-cream parlour *la gelateria*
jeweller *il gioielliere*
post office *l'ufficio postale*
shoe shop *il negozio di scarpe*
supermarket *il supermercato*

Health

Is there a chemist nearby? *C'è una farmacia qui vicino?*
Which chemist is open at night? *Quale farmacia fa il turno di notte?*
I don't feel well *Non mi sento bene*
I feel ill *Sto male/Mi sento male*
Where does it hurt? *Dov'è Le fa male?*
It hurts here *Ho dolore qui*
I have a headache *Ho mal di testa*
I have a sore throat *Ho mal di gola*
I have stomach ache *Ho mal di pancia*
antiseptic cream *la crema antisettica*
sunburn *scottatura da sole*
sunburn cream *la crema antisolare*
insect repellent *l'insettifugo*
mosquitoes *le zanzare*

Numbers

1	*uno*	16	*sedici*
2	*due*	17	*diciassette*
3	*tre*	18	*diciotto*
4	*quattro*	19	*diciannove*
5	*cinque*	20	*venti*
6	*sei*	30	*trenta*
7	*sette*	40	*quaranta*
8	*otto*	50	*cinquanta*
9	*nove*	60	*sessanta*
10	*dieci*	70	*settanta*
11	*undici*	80	*ottanta*
12	*dodici*	90	*novanta*
13	*tredici*	100	*cento*
14	*quattordici*	200	*duecento*
15	*quindici*	1,000	*mille*

FURTHER READING

General

Bitter Almonds, by Mary Taylor Simeti and Maria Grammatico. Poignant memoir of a much-fêted Sicilian chef and former nun, and a collection of her recipes.

La Bella Figura – A Field Guide to the Italian Mind, by Beppe Severgnini. A wry look at the Italian psyche.

Cosa Nostra: A History of the Sicilian Mafia, by John Dickie. A comprehensive history.

The Dark Heart of Italy, by Tobias Jones. A provocative portrait of Italy highlighting the interplay between politics, society and crime.

Go Slow Italy, by Alastair Sawday. A delightful look at special places to stay (including rustic inns and farm-stays) as well as Slow Travel and Slow Food.

Gomorrah, by Roberto Saviano. Terrifying, immensely brave insight into the world of organised crime in Naples.

Italian Neighbours, by Tim Parks. Engaging, often surprising insights into Italian life by a British writer long resident in Verona. Also very worth finding by the same author are *A Season with Verona* (on football), and *An Italian Education*.

The Italians, by Luigi Barzini. Originally published in the sixties, this is still worthwhile reading for the frankness of Barzini's portrait of his fellow countrymen.

The Last Supper, by Rachel Cusk. Impressions of a summer in Tuscany and Naples.

Mafia Women, by Clare Longrigg. A courageous investigation into the changing role of women in Cosa Nostra.

The Prince, by Niccolò Machiavelli. The new Penguin translation by Tim Parks is the liveliest version in years of Machiavelli's classic treatise on power in the Renaissance.

Slow Food: The Case for Taste, by Carlo Petrini. A book that powerfully challenges our attitude to eating and shopping.

Special Places to Stay Italy. edited by Florence Oldfield (pub. Alastair Sawday). Self-catering accommodation and city apartments as well as big country houses, with a welcome green orientation.

Venice for Pleasure, by J.G. Links. A guide to the city – not practical, but beautifully written by a man who is passionate about his subject.

Art and Architecture

The Architecture of the Italian Renaissance, by Peter Murray. The classic guide to art and architecture of the Renaissance period.

Brunelleschi's Dome: The Story of the Great Cathedral in Florence, by Ross King. This book celebrates one of the greatest architectural feats ever accomplished, and its creator.

Fellini on Fellini, by Federico Fellini. Essays, letters and interviews charting the film director's life and work.

Italian Architecture from Michelangelo to Borromini, by Andrew Hopkins. A comprehensive guide tracing the background to the artistic patrimony of Florence and other Italian cities.

The Italian Painters of the Renaissance, by Bernard Berenson.

Send Us Your Thoughts

We do our best to ensure our books are as up-to-date as possible. However, some details (such as telephone numbers and opening times) are liable to change, and we are ultimately reliant on our readers to put us in the picture.

We welcome your feedback, especially your experience of using the book "on the road". Maybe we recommended a hotel that you liked (or another that you didn't), or you came across a great bar or new attraction we missed.

We will acknowledge all contributions, and we'll offer an Insight Guide to the best letters received.

Please write to us at:
Insight Guides
PO Box 7910
London SE1 1WE
Or email us at:
insight@apaguide.co.uk

Hard to find, this remains a good guide to many great figures in Italian art, including Caravaggio and Giotto.

The Stones of Florence and Venice Observed, by Mary McCarthy. A travel companion and an accessible introduction to art history.

Culture and History

The Civilisation of the Renaissance in Italy, by Jacob Burckhardt. Published in 1860, this book effectively defined the concept of "Italian Renaissance", and remains enormously illuminating.

Florence: The Biography of a City, by Christopher Hibbert. Weaves together the history and culture of Florence, with excellent photographs and illustrations; equally fascinating are the same author's *The Rise and Fall of the House of Medici* and *Rome: The Biography of a City*.

A History of Sicily, by M.I. Finley and Dennis Mack Smith. The best overall Sicilian history.

The Merchant of Prato, by Iris Origo. An intimate and accessible account of the life of a 14th-century Italian merchant, pieced together from a huge cache of letters and documents unearthed in 1870.

Mussolini, by Dennis Mack Smith. Penetrating biography that illustrates clearly the viciousness and incompetence of Italy's dictator.

The Oxford Illustrated History of Italy, by George Holmes. An extensive, but still concise, insight into the whole of Italy's colourful past.

Renaissance Florence on Five Florins a Day, by Charles FitzRoy. Witty, very entertaining tour through Florence in its golden age written in the style of a contemporary guidebook.

The Twelve Caesars, by Suetonius. All the scandals and misdemeanours of the founders of the Roman Empire, by one of history's greatest gossips.

The Venetian Ghetto, by Roberta Curiel. A history of the city's Jewish community.

Venice: Pure City, by Peter Ackroyd. Grand history, anecdotes and endlessly surprising details from an always original writer.

TRANSPORT · ACCOMMODATION · EATING OUT · ACTIVITIES · A – Z · LANGUAGE

ART AND PHOTO CREDITS

INDEX

Main references are in bold type

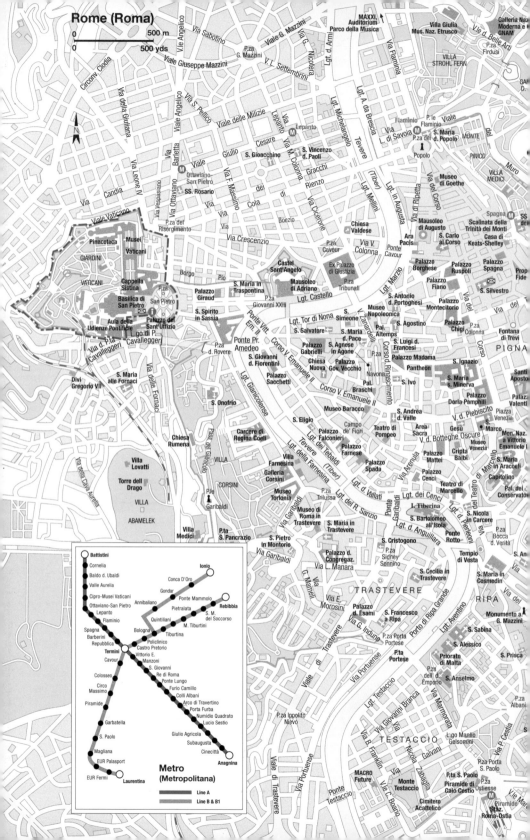